W9-DGI-357

THE SHAPING OF AMERICAN DIPLOMACY

**THE SHAPING
OF AMERICAN
DIPLOMACY**

Volume I

1750 -1914

SECOND EDITION

Edited with commentary by
William Appleman Williams
Oregon State University

Rand McNally & Company   CHICAGO

RAND McNALLY SERIES IN AMERICAN HISTORY

Fred Harvey Harrington, CONSULTING EDITOR

Third Printing, 1972

for Bea, Warren, and Claire

PREFACE TO THE SECOND EDITION

This new edition does not represent a change in the original objective: the purpose remains that of providing the student with a selection of readings and documents to help him use the teacher's guidance to develop his own understanding of American foreign relations. It is designed to be employed either as a supplement to a conventional textbook, or as a base around which the teacher can develop his own thematic and interpretative lectures.

The contents have been revised on the basis of suggestions offered by various teachers and students who used the original volumes, new research and analyses by other historians, and my own continuing efforts to understand various episodes and patterns of development.

I am grateful to those who found the first edition useful, and hope they will consider this revision equally helpful.

W.A.W.

Corvallis, Oregon
August, 1969

CONTENTS, VOLUME I

INTRODUCTION

America's sustained and extensive involvement in world affairs since World War II, which has included two wars and several smaller military interventions, as well as a great expansion of its economic and political influence, has had a paradoxical effect on the nation's thinking about the history of its foreign relations. On the one hand, Americans have become routinely aware of their country as a major power operating on the basis of having interests and responsibilities in every part of the world. And, along with their leaders, large numbers of citizens are directly or indirectly engaged in such overseas operations, and in discussions and debates about the policies most appropriate to such a global position and the related activities.

On the other hand, the character and intensity of many recent experiences, such as the Korean War, the Cuban missile crisis, and the war in Vietnam, have reinforced a traditional feeling and belief that the United States was never seriously engaged in world affairs until after the Spanish-American War—or even until American entrance into World War I. Perhaps the most revealing manifestation of that outlook is provided by the way that critics of contemporary policies and actions have been accused of seeking to return to an earlier policy of isolationism.

Whatever the outcome of the present disagreement over policy, the confrontation serves as a useful introduction to a study of American foreign relations. First, it underscores the point that there have always been differences about the most desirable and effective course of action. Second, it dramatizes the truth that the United States is now more directly and widely involved in foreign affairs than it was in the past. And that, in turn, suggests a third consideration: America's present position as a superpower is not the result of a sudden change, but is the product of a long process that began with the American Revolution.

The conflict, agitation, and war that established the United States as an independent nation between 1763 and 1784 created a world power. The men who carried through those actions understood that point very clearly. Americans had not been isolationist even while they were citizens of the major colony in the British Empire, and they did not become isolationist afterwards. From 1689 to 1763, for example, they participated in five wars; and, counting the Revolutionary War, engaged in five more such conflicts, and carried on a running battle with the Indians, during a similar period after 1763.

Hence it is neither accurate nor useful to define the primary issues connected with American foreign relations in terms of the pseudo-question of deciding when the nation stopped being isolationist. Instead, the challenge is to understand the causes and the nature of the nation's changing involvement with other nations, the character of such interaction, and the consequences down through time to the present. This volume contains two kinds of material chosen to help illuminate and answer those kinds of questions. One is the work of various historians who have attempted to probe and resolve those problems. The other items are documents, policy statements, explanations, and analyses offered by the protagonists involved in making American foreign policy since 1763. Taken together, they are designed to assist the reader in developing his own understanding of the shaping of American diplomacy.

The selections in this collection do not provide a complete history of American foreign relations. No single book can tell the entire story. They are offered to provide two things: one, an awareness and a feeling for the differences and conflicts among Americans concerning foreign policy; and, second, a sense of the continuity in outlook and action that, despite the disagreements, have carried the United States from being a colony in 1763 to its present position as a major imperial power.

It is often helpful, when beginning to study foreign policy, to look carefully at each of the different aspects of a nation's relationships with the rest of the world. The trade it carries on with other countries, and the foreign loans and investments it makes, often seem undramatic and secondary. Even if they attract some initial attention, they are usually forgotten by many citizens. But such economic activities are very significant in determining policy because they grow out of the way that various individuals and groups think they can solve their problems, achieve their objectives, and fulfill their ideals and responsibilities. Once undertaken, such economic ventures play a central part in defining American interests, and thus do much to determine whether or not an action by another country is viewed as friendly or unfriendly. They also help shape the attitudes of other nations toward the United States.

In the beginning, therefore, political and military questions are often defined by economic activity. If the Founding Fathers had not considered foreign markets important, for example, the interruption of American shipping by the Barbary Pirates would not have led to war. In a similar way, the urge to acquire more wealth and opportunity in the form of land played a vital part in the two-century long conflict with the Indians, the struggle with the Spanish over Florida, the clash with Mexico over Texas and California, and even contributed to the antagonism toward the British that culminated in the War of 1812.

The relationship between economic activity and foreign policy has continued throughout the 20th century. As the economy became ever more industrialized and interdependent, moreover, American leaders increasingly *thought about economic needs and opportunities in terms of the entire system as well as from the point of view of one or another special interest. In the case of raw materials (such as oil or bauxite), for example, the result was that the nationalization of such resources by a foreign country came to be viewed as a danger to the entire American economy as well as a blow at one or more giant corporations. In a similar way, great stress came to be placed on the need for markets by officials who were not personally involved in any business operations.*

Once the economic tension has been generated, and a confrontation has occurred, however, political and military considerations become more immediately important. The questions of how to maneuver for allies, or to avoid bringing other nations into the conflict, and of how to use the force available in the most effective manner, take precedence. But decisions on those issues in turn affect existing and future overseas economic interests, and how they can be handled, and in such fashion the solution to one problem often—even usually—creates another set of difficulties and opportunities.

Such a review of the way that economic, political, and military factors interact in the making of foreign policy decisions should make it apparent that the vital consideration involves the way that individuals and groups decide what is important to them. Or, to phrase it differently, the crucial elements are the way men list their priorities, and the way they explain the inter-relationships between those factors. These are the intellectual and emotional elements in the shaping of foreign policy, but the terminology should not be taken to mean either that men make foreign policy in the abstract, or that they do so as irrational beings.

The mind works on the reality it encounters, and that includes the existing structure of the economy, religious and secular beliefs about the nature of the world, and the psychological forces that modern man perceives as being especially real. And the kind of antagonisms or attachments that influence economic and military analyses are often generated—or modified—by earlier experiences with the countries in question.

Thus some men believe that a moral responsibility to spread freedom to other peoples, or the necessity to extend it (or preserve it) everywhere in order to maintain it at home, are the most important factors in deciding foreign policy. Such individuals often discount the economic, political, or military requirements and consequences of their proposals, and insist upon pursuing a course of action that undermines their avowed objective. It is easy to dismiss such men on the grounds they are irrational, but that is not often true.

Their priorities and logic are different because they understand and explain the world in a different manner, but they can usually provide an analysis of the relationship between their priorities. Americans of the late 19th century who emphasized the moral necessity of extending freedom to other countries often argued that such action would improve economic conditions and increase the security of the nation. For that matter, many Americans have always insisted that the expansion of freedom elsewhere was necessary for the free and proper functioning of the economy at home.

In the narrowest sense, studying the past helps us comprehend the ideas, attitudes, and actions that have carried us as a people to our present position, and provides us with a better understanding of the momentum that influences our contemporary choices. In the broader sense, the study of history enables us to watch other men make foreign policy, and that allows us to review and evaluate the consequences of acting on various outlooks and beliefs. That in turn can assist us in formulating—and changing—our own. The purpose of this volume is to facilitate that never-ending process.

RADICALS

AND

EMPIRE

BUILDERS

CHAPTER 1

The Diplomacy of Revolution

and Independence

T*he American Revolution provides an excellent introduction to the foreign affairs of the United States, offering a particularly good example of the close relationship between domestic and foreign policy. At the outset there was a struggle within the thirteen colonies between those who wished to compromise with Great Britain and those who sought independence. Once independence had been declared, the revolutionary leaders differed over the best means for achieving and maintaining it. And, in addition, the policies and conflicts of foreign nations sometimes helped and at other times hindered these American efforts to establish and secure the new United States.*

In the first article that follows, Professor Curtis P. Nettels discusses the mercantile system established by Great Britain in the century prior to the American Revolution. This combination of policy, regulations, and economic investments was designed to promote England's development and transform it into a strong nation, and to create a profitable and growing colonial political economy. In a very real sense, it succeeded only too well: England did become a major power between 1660 and 1760, but in the process the colonies became powerful enough to challenge Britain's increasingly tight controls. That conflict became ever more intense after the English and the Americans combined forces to defeat the French between 1754 and 1763, and as both groups in the British Empire sought to exploit that victory for their own specific and separate purposes.

At first the colonists intended only to force Great Britain to relax its controls. All the while, however, the colonists were growing in self-consciousness and self-confidence. As Professor Max Savelle shows in the second article, they felt they were becoming as important to England as England was to them. Indeed, they insisted that their militiamen had done more to drive the French from North America than had the British regulars. Americans were in no mood for new restrictions on their commerce and their political liberties. They were outraged by such measures as the proclamation of 1763, which seemed to close off the great western lands to speculator, planter, and frontiersman alike. And they also disliked the way the English began to form alliances with the Indians as soon as the French had been defeated.

Most conservative colonial leaders, reluctant to leave the British Empire, continued to seek compromise and adjustment, but some of them came to advocate a rupture of the imperial tie. One of these was George Washington, probably the wealthiest colonist of all, yet deeply in debt like the rest of the Virginia planters. If the planters were to lighten their debts to the London merchants who handled their tobacco, they would have to diversify their farming, deal in western lands, establish control of their own money supply, and in other ways evade the British regulations. So Washington believed. He and a few other conservatives, especially among the planters of the South, privately worked for a break with England long before they openly declared themselves for independence. These men thought of building an empire, not of instigating a social revolution. They sought independence in order to escape from British authority and take unchecked advantage of the many opportunities in America.

Still other colonists were becoming complete revolutionaries. These radicals sought not only national independence but also a democratic reorganization of American society, which in turn would give them greater individual freedom. They saw in the disputes with Britain a chance to break the connection between English power and colonial conservatism. Then, they thought, the workers, artisans, and small landowners would rally to a democratic program and write new state constitutions allowing them to manage their own affairs. In his insightful study, Professor Jesse Lemisch discusses the way that merchant seamen came to oppose the British—and those colonists who supported or acquiesced in the policies of the empire.

Outstanding among the radicals was Samuel Adams of Boston, sometimes called the "propagandist of the American Revolution." Document 1 gives a good overview of his philosophy. Adams was quite sure that all the restrictions on money, land, and the vote were the work of an unholy alliance between colonial aristocrats and the British crown. He hoped, by provoking a war with Great Britain, to give himself and other radicals like Patrick Henry of Virginia a chance to handle the conservatives in America without any interference from London. At every opportunity he aroused his fellow Americans with his speeches and pamphlets, and he organized them for revolutionary action in the Committees of Correspondence and the Sons of Liberty.

The more moderate conservatives, who had yet to accept the idea of a *break with the mother country, were inclined at first to applaud the Adams-led radicals, whose agitation reinforced the conservative demand for repeal of the mercantilist rules. "A little rioting is a good thing," commented one conservative. But they soon changed their opinion when they realized that the radicals were out to overthrow the established order and challenge the rights of property. To avoid the danger of a social revolution at home, the moderate conservatives became more willing to compromise with the imperial government abroad.*

But the British government did little to help these unwarlike conservatives. Occasionally it gave in to them, but each time it soon imposed new regulations and restrictions. Thus frustrated, the moderate conservatives increasingly accepted Washington's leadership and joined the movement for independence, though not the movement for remaking society. In independence they saw a chance to make "the world our oyster," that is, to trade and manufacture as they wished. John Adams, the conservative cousin of Sam Adams, was an early exponent of this policy, as outlined in Document 2. Here, in a letter to James Warren, Adams tells how difficult it was to get other conservatives to risk a radical victory at home in order to win the opportunities of independence. Adams was willing to take this risk, but he worked hard to prevent the radicals from winning control of the new government.

The promise and possibilities of freedom of action ultimately attracted many moderates to the revolutionary cause. One of the best presentations of the middle-of-the-road argument for independence is Tom Paine's pamphlet Common Sense, *portions of which comprise Document 3. Even the persuasiveness of Tom Paine failed to convince all the colonists of the value of a war for independence, however, and many of them left for England or Canada. Others stayed home but refused to fight for independence. For a time these Loyalists, or Tories, suffered loss of prestige, and some of them were imprisoned or otherwise treated harshly by the Patriots.*

During the years of the Revolutionary War and the establishment of a new government, the coalition of radicals and conservatives was held together by the common need to achieve and to maintain independence. For both groups the main problem was national survival. Hence radicals like Sam Adams did not oppose as vigorously as they might have done the successful attempts by the conservatives to overthrow the government under the Articles of Confederation and replace it with the Constitution of 1787.

Documents 4 and 5 illustrate the most important side of America's wartime diplomacy: economic and military assistance from France against Great Britain. The Continental Congress sought aid from almost every country in Europe, even sending an agent as far as Russia. It arranged loans in Holland but got the most help from France. Both the French and the Americans hoped to get assistance from Spain, but the Spanish hesitated to abet a war for independence which might serve as an example for their own colonies in the New World. The Spanish also feared that an independent United States would soon conquer their possessions to the south and west, in Florida and Louisiana. As the price of aid to the Americans, Spain demanded territorial guarantees and concessions which were unacceptable to radicals and con-

servatives alike. For these reasons the ambitious treaty plans of the Continental Congress fell short of realization.

Once victorious in the war against Great Britain (Document 6), Americans began to debate the wisdom of continuing the "perpetual" alliance with France. They also differed in their attitudes toward the French Revolution, which began in 1789, the year of Washington's first inauguration as president. The followers of Thomas Jefferson, who represented the landed interest and the old colonial radicalism, and who later organized the Republican party, viewed the French Revolution with more sympathy. The Federalists, more narrowly conservative and commercial, denounced the revolutionaries of France. When France and England went to war again, the Federalists strove to maintain good relations with England, since they hoped to reestablish their prerevolutionary routes of commerce.

With the rise of Napoleon Bonaparte and the threat of his conquering Europe, even Jefferson lost some of his enthusiasm for the French. He was aware that the war between France and England held real dangers for the United States. Though not in sympathy with commerce as a way of life, he nevertheless realized that trade was essential to the agricultural sector of the economy, as well as to traders, and at the same time understood that the country was exposed to possible attack from the sea. In Document 7 he sets forth his arguments for standing firm against encroachments by any foreign power—including France as well as Britain—on America's right to freedom of the seas. While he does not mention it here, Jefferson also feared that Napoleon might block American territorial expansion to the south and west.

Federalists like Alexander Hamilton were even more eager to evade the obligations of the French alliance. President Washington indicated that the United States was not bound to aid France when he issued his Proclamation of Neutrality in 1793 (Document 8). He did not abrogate the alliance (that was done later), but he used neutrality as a technique for avoiding war at a time of domestic weakness. By staying out of the European war Americans benefited in three respects. They escaped the great danger of having to fight again before recovering fully from the struggle for independence. They gained the profits of shipping and trade with both belligerents. And regardless of the final outcome of the war, they stood to win increased national security as a result of the distractions of both the victor and the defeated. As Washington sought to make clear in his Farewell Address (Document 9), Americans should not handicap their national development by "excessive partiality for one foreign nation" or by "excessive dislike of another." He warned against permanent alliances, such as the one with France, not against temporary and limited pacts for times of great emergency.

Finally, in 1800, France and the United States agreed to terminate the treaty of 1778. In his instructions to the American agents in Paris (Document 10), President John Adams followed Washington's advice and stressed the importance of avoiding long-term obligations. He also reflected the Federalist concern for good Anglo-American relations when he cautioned that the new arrangement with France must not violate any commercial agreements already in effect with England. Jefferson, though by no means accepting all Federalist ideas or policies, did agree as to the need for keeping the

United States out of the Napoleonic Wars, and he went along with the cancellation of the old treaty with France. In his first inaugural address (Document 11), Jefferson emphasized his view that neutrality would offer America the best chance to gain strength and exploit the great opportunities at hand. It was Jefferson who used the phrase "no entangling alliances," which often has been attributed mistakenly to Washington. Jefferson's interest in a policy of landed expansion, rather than the promotion of overseas commerce, is suggested by his reference to the need for an army and his failure to mention the navy.

In the last article, Professor Albert K. Weinberg unravels the long-standing confusion over neutrality and isolation. The Founding Fathers sought time to gain strength, which they hoped to use eventually in whatever manner they saw fit. They did not want isolation: they wanted freedom of action. Neutrality was a policy designed to provide such freedom, not a technique for retreating from the world.

BRITISH MERCANTILISM AND
THE ECONOMIC DEVELOPMENT
OF THE THIRTEEN COLONIES[1]   *Curtis P. Nettels*

Mercantilism is defined for this discussion as a policy of government that expressed in the economic sphere the spirit of nationalism that animated the growth of the national state in early modern times. The policy aimed to gain for the nation a high degree of security or self-sufficiency, especially as regards food supply, raw materials needed for essential industries, and the sinews of war. This end was to be achieved in large measure by means of an effective control over the external activities and resources upon which the nation was dependent. In turn, that urge impelled the mercantilists to prefer colonial dependencies to independent foreign countries in seeking sources of supply. If the state could not free itself completely from trade with foreign nations, it sought to control that trade in its own interest as much as possible. To realize such objectives, mercantilism embraced three subordinate related policies. The Corn Laws fostered the nation's agriculture and aimed to realize the ideal of self-sufficiency as regards food supply. State aids to manufacturing industries, such as the protective tariff, sought to provide essential finished goods, including the sinews of war. The Navigation Acts were intended to assure that foreign trade would be carried on in such a way as to yield the maximum advantage to the state concerned.

Since the mercantilist states of Europe lacked the resources for complete self-sufficiency, they could not free themselves from dependence on foreign supplies. Economic growth therefore increased the importance of external trade, and the preference for colonies over foreign countries intensified the struggle for dependent possessions. The importance in mer-

[1] *The Journal of Economic History*, XII, No. 2 (Spring, 1952), 105–14. Reprinted with permission.

cantilism of a favorable balance of trade and of a large supply of the precious metals is a familiar theme. We need only to remind ourselves that the mercantilists considered it the duty of government to obtain and to retain for the nation both a favorable trade balance and an adequate stock of gold and silver. To this end the state should help to build up a national merchant marine and should foster domestic manufacturing industries. The chief means of procuring raw materials, a favorable trade balance, and an ample supply of the precious metals was that of exporting high-priced manufactured goods and shipping services.

Despite its emphasis on government action, mercantilism was not socialism. In England, the system invoked the initiative and enterprise of private citizens. It encouraged the merchants, shippers, and manufacturers by conferring benefits upon them and by identifying their private interests with the highest needs of the state. So close was this identification that one may properly regard the theory of mercantilism as a rationalization of the special interests of dominant groups of the time. The mercantilist policy was an expression of an accord between landowners and merchant-capitalists in alliance with the Crown.

* * *

... The thirteen colonies experienced a phenomenal development during the 150 years in which they were subject to the regulating policies of English mercantilism. ...

To what extent did English mercantilism contribute to this "real wealth"—this "exchangeable value of the annual produce of ... lands and labor?" Lands and labor. Two of the most fundamental factors in the growth of the thirteen colonies were the character of the people and the nature of the land and resources to which they applied their labor. The connecting link between the two that gave the thirteen colonies their unique character was the system of small individual holdings that came into being, usually at the start of settlement. It provided a strong incentive to labor and was therefore a major factor in their development. Crèvecoeur spoke of "that restless industry which is the principal characteristic of these colonies," and observed: "Here the rewards of ... [the farmer's] industry follow with equal steps the progress of his labor; his labor is founded on the basis of nature, self-interest, can it want a stronger allurement ... ? As farmers they will be careful and anxious to get as much as they can, because what they get is their own."

Although the land system of the thirteen colonies has not usually been considered an element of mercantilism, yet it was not divorced from it. Why did the English Government grant to its colonies a benefit that was not commonly bestowed on settlers by the other colonizing powers? Small holdings inspired the colonists to work; their labor expanded production; and increased production enlarged English commerce. The resulting trade was more susceptible to control by the state than a comparable trade with foreign countries would have been. For this reason, the colonial land system may be regarded as an expression of mercantilist policy. Viewed in this light, mercantilism contributed directly to the growth of the settlements.

Such also was the effect of the policy of England with reference to the peopling of its part of America. The government opened the doors to immigrants of many nationalities and creeds. Its liberality in this respect was unique. It harmonized with the mercantilist doctrine. The Crown admitted dissenters and foreigners in order to expand colonial production and trade. Such immigrants were, to a large extent, industrious, progressive, and energetic. Their productivity was stimulated by the climate of freedom in which they lived—a climate that was made possible in good measure by the indulgence of the government. The resulting growth of English trade served the needs of the state as they were viewed by the mercantilists.

We shall next consider the effects of specific mercantilist laws and government actions on the economic development of the thirteen colonies. It appears at once that such laws and actions did not create or sustain any important industry or trade in Colonial America. The major economic pursuits of the colonies grew out of, and were shaped by, the nature of the resources of the land, the needs of the settlers, and the general state of world trade in the seventeenth century. No important colonial activity owed its birth or existence to English law. The statutes and policies of mercantilism, with an exception or two, sought to control, to regulate, to restrain, to stimulate, or to protect. In the great majority of instances it was not the role of the government to initiate, to originate, to create.... Ordinarily, the government did not subject a colonial activity to regulation by law until it had proved itself to be profitable. In Virginia, for instance, the government did not initiate the tobacco industry or attempt to stimulate its early development. Rather, the Crown sought to discourage it. After it had taken root under the influence of general economic conditions, the government stepped in to regulate it. The major Navigation Act was passed in response to the success of the Dutch in world commerce. The English Government did not legislate against certain industries in the colonies until they had grown of their own accord to the extent that they menaced their English counterparts. The currency policy which England applied to its colonies was worked out not in a vacuum but in answer to practices in which the colonists were engaging.

The effects of mercantilist laws naturally depended upon their enforcement. Since they almost invariably sought to prevent something that the colonists had found to be profitable, the task of enforcement was difficult. It required the exercise of force and vigilance.

In a general way, the government attained a reasonable success in its efforts to enforce the policies that bore directly on the southern mainland colonies, whereas the principal acts which were designed for the Middle Colonies and New England could not be made effective.

The program for the plantation area embraced several policies. The Navigation Act of 1661 excluded from its trade all foreign merchants and foreign vessels. By the terms of the Staple Act of 1663 the planters must buy most of their manufactured goods from England. Slaves must be bought from English slave traders. The area must depend upon English sources for capital and credit, and the planters could not avail themselves of legal devices in order to ease their burdens of debt.

The government made a strenuous effort to enforce these policies. The decisive action centered in the three Dutch wars between 1652 and 1675. The defeat of the Dutch drove them from the southern trade and enabled the English merchants to hold it as in a vise. After 1665, the development of the plantation colonies proceeded in conformity with the tenets of mercantilism. The effect was to retard that development, since the planters were subjected to a virtual English monopoly and were denied the benefits of competitive bidding for their crops and the privilege of buying foreign goods and shipping services in the cheapest market.

Certain conditions of the period 1675 to 1775 favored the English mercantilists in their efforts to enforce the southern policy. The geography of the Chesapeake country made it easy to exclude foreign vessels, since the English navy had to control only the narrow entrance to the bay in order to keep foreign vessels from reaching the plantations. That the tobacco ships had to move slowly along the rivers made concealment impossible for interlopers. Secondly, there was the factor of debt. Once a planter had become indebted to an English merchant, he was obliged to market his crops through his creditor in order to obtain new supplies. Hence he lost the advantage of competitive bidding for his export produce. And finally, the four wars with France, 1689–1763, served to rivet the plantation area to Britain, as mercantilism intended. The British navy provided convoys for the tobacco ships, and the expenditures of the Crown in America for military purposes provided the planters with additional buying power for English goods, thereby increasing their dependence on British merchants, vessels, and supplies.

By reason of the acts of government, the economic development of the southern colonies exhibited after 1665 about as clear an example of effective political control of economic activity as one can find. The trade of the southern colonies was centered in Britain. They were obliged to employ British shipping, to depend on British merchants, and to look only to British sources for capital and credit. They were not permitted to interfere with the British slave trade. British investments enjoyed a sheltered market in that the Crown excluded the foreign investor from the area and prohibited the colonists from taking any legal steps that would impair the claims of British creditors. The resulting dependence of the plantation country gave it a strongly British character, retarded its development, fostered discontent, and goaded the planters to resistance and revolt.

The initial enforcement of the Navigation Acts in the 1660's reduced the profits of the tobacco planters and forced them to cut the costs of production. Slavery was the answer. Appropriately at this time the English Government undertook to furnish its colonies with an ample supply of slaves. The planters were obliged to buy them on credit—a main factor in reducing them to a state of commercial bondage. The English Government forbade the planters to curtail the nefarious traffic. American slavery was thus one of the outstanding legacies of English mercantilism. That resolute foe of English mercantilist policy, George Washington, subscribed to the following resolve in 1774: "We take this opportunity of declaring our most earnest wishes to see an entire stop forever put to such a wicked, cruel, and unnatural trade."

In another sense the Navigation Act of 1661 had a discernible effect on American development. It stimulated the shipbuilding and shipping industries in New England and the Middle Colonies. It did not, however, create those industries. But the English Government drove the Dutch from the trade of English America before English shipping could meet the full needs of the colonies. The Navigation Act gave to English colonial shipbuilders and shipowners the same privileges that were given to English shipbuilders and shipowners. Undoubtedly this favored treatment spurred on the shipping industries of New England. Shipbuilding flourished there, since the colonial builders were permitted to sell their product to English merchants, and New England shipowners could employ their American-built vessels in the trade of the whole empire. New England benefited directly from the expulsion of the Dutch from the trade of English America. After New England's shipbuilding industry had become fully established (and had proved itself more efficient than its English rival) the British Government refused to heed the pleas of British shipowners who wished to subject it to crippling restraints.

* * *

The policies that affected the Middle Colonies and New England differed materially in character and effect from the policies that were applied to the South. The northern area received the privilege of exporting its chief surplus products—fish, meats, cereals, livestock, lumber—directly to foreign markets. As already noted, the northern maritime industries flourished under the benefits conferred upon them by the Navigation Acts. Freedom to export the staples of the area in company with vigorous shipbuilding and shipping industries induced the northerners to engage in a varied foreign trade. This outcome, however, was in part a result of certain restrictive measures of the English Government. It prohibited the importation into England of American meats and cereals, thereby forcing the colonists to seek foreign markets for their surplus.

The resulting trade of the northern area—with southern Europe, the Wine Islands, Africa, and the foreign West Indies—did not prove satisfactory to the English mercantilists. It built up in the colonies a mercantile interest that threatened to compete successfully with English traders and shipowners. It carried with it the danger that the northerners might nullify those features of the Navigation Acts which aimed to center most of the trade of English America in England. Nor did their reliance on foreign trade prove to be entirely satisfactory to the colonists. In time of war, their vessels were exposed to the depredations of the French. The English navy could not protect the diverse northern trades with convoys, as it protected the simpler, more concentrated commerce of the plantation area. The wartime disruption of the northern trade deprived the area of the foreign money and products that in peacetime its merchants carried to England for the purpose of buying English goods for the colonial market. The resulting decline of the exportation of English merchandise was then deplored by the English mercantilists. Unable to procure finished goods in England, the northerners were driven to manufacture for themselves. Thence arose what the mercantilists regarded as a fatal danger—the prospect that the colonies would manufacture for themselves, decrease their purchases in England, and produce a surplus of finished goods that would compete with English wares in the markets of the world.

To avoid this danger, the English mercantilists devised their major experiment in state planning of the early eighteenth century. They undertook to foster the production of naval stores in the Middle Colonies and New England. Such products would be sent directly to England as a means of paying for English goods. They would divert the colonists from domestic manufacturing and free them from their dependence on diverse foreign trades. They would transform the commerce of the northern area in such a way that it would resemble that of the plantation area—a simple, direct exchange of American raw products for English finished goods.

The naval-stores program was constructive in intent. The government sought to shape the development of the northern area, thereby solving a serious problem. But the policy failed. It did not stimulate the production of naval stores in the northern area sufficiently to provide it with adequate payments for English goods, or to divert the northerners from their foreign trades, or to halt the trend toward home manufacturing.

This failure led the mercantilists to embrace a purely negative policy. As the trade of the northern area with the foreign West Indies increased, the English Government undertook to stop it altogether. Such was its intent in imposing upon the colonies the Molasses Act of 1733. But that effort did not succeed. Again, a mercantilist policy failed to bear its expected fruit.

The early policies of mercantilism had a marked effect on the growth of the northern area. But the result turned out to be unpleasing to the English authorities. Their endeavors to give a new direction to the development of the area failed completely after 1700. A problem had arisen for which English mercantilism never found a solution.

The main element in this problem was the trend in the northern area toward domestic manufacturing. Since that trend menaced all the essentials of mercantilism, the English Government did its best to thwart it. Thus there was no more important ingredient in English policy than the determined effort to retard or prevent the growth in America of industries that would produce the sort of goods that England could export at the greatest profit. Such, chiefly, were cloth, ironware, hats, and leather goods. The effectiveness of the laws and orders against colonial manufacturing is a subject of dispute. It is difficult to prove why something did not happen. If the colonies were slow in developing manufacturing industries, was it the result of English policy or of other factors? The writer believes that English policies had a strong retarding influence. The barriers erected were extensive and formidable. British statutes restrained the American woolen, iron, and hat industries. The colonies could not impose protective tariffs on imports from England. They could not operate mints, create manufacturing corporations, or establish commercial banks—institutions that are essential to the progress of manufacturing.

It was easier to enforce a policy against American fabricating industries than a policy that aimed to regulate maritime trade. A vessel could slip in and out of the northern ports. A manufacturing plant and its operations could not be concealed, unless, as in later times, it was engaged in mountain moonshining. The exposure of factories to the gaze of officials undoubtedly deterred investors from building them in defiance of the law.

New industries in an economically backward country commonly needed the positive encouragement and protection of government. It was the rule of mercantilism that handicaps to home manufacturing should be overcome by tariffs, bounties, and other forms of state aid. Such stimuli were denied to the colonies while they were subject to English mercantilism. Not only was the imperial government hostile; equally important, the colonial governments were not allowed to extend assistance to American promoters who wished to establish industries on the basis of efficient, large-scale operations.

An important aspect of the influence of state policy is its effect on the attitude of the people who are subjected to its benefits and restraints. The colonists as a whole were not seriously antagonized by the British imperium prior to 1763. Its most detrimental policy—that of the Molasses Act—was not enforced. In time of war (which meant thirty-five years of the period from 1689 to 1763) the military expenditures of the Crown in America helped to solve the most crucial problem of the colonies by supplying them with funds with which they could pay their debts and buy needed supplies in England. The shipbuilders and shipowners of the northern area shared in the national monopoly of imperial trade. Underlying all policy and legislation was the extremely liberal action of the English Government in making land available to settlers on easy terms and of admitting into the colonies immigrants of diverse nationalities and varied religious faiths.

After 1763 the story is different. The colonies no longer received the sort of easy money that they had obtained from military expenditures during the wars. Instead, they were called upon to support through British taxes the defense establishment that was to be maintained in America after the war. Britain now abandoned its old liberal practice regarding land and immigration and replaced it with restrictive measures suggestive of the colonial policies of France and Spain. The Crown proceeeded to enforce with vigor all the restraints it had previously imposed on colonial enterprise. Most of the features of the imperial rule that had placated the colonists were to be done away with. Not only were the old restraints to be more strictly enforced; they were to be accompanied by a host of new ones. The policies of Britain after 1763 merely intensified the central difficulty of the trade of the colonies. How might they find the means of paying for the manufactured goods that they must buy from England? If they could not get adequate returns, they would have to manufacture for themselves.

In its total effect, British policy as it affected the colonies after 1763 was restrictive, injurious, negative. It offered no solutions of problems. In the meantime, the colonists, having lived so long under the rule of mercantilism, had become imbued with mercantilist ideas. If the British imperium would not allow them to grow and expand, if it would not provide a solution of the central problem of the American economy, the colonists would have to take to themselves the right and the power to guide their economic development. They would find it necessary to create a new authority that would foster American shipping and commerce, make possible the continued growth of settlement, and above all stimulate the growth of domestic manufacturing industries. Thus another result of English mercantilism was the American Revolution and the creation thereafter of a new mercantilist state on this side of the Atlantic.

THE APPEARANCE
OF AN AMERICAN ATTITUDE
TOWARD EXTERNAL AFFAIRS,
1750–1775[1]

Max Savelle

In the *Pennsylvania Gazette* of January 15, 1751, appears the following jingle, which was copied from the English *Westminster Journal* of October 8, 1750:

> While Britain complains of *Neutrality* broke,
>   De Puysieux collogues like a subtle Iago,
> And tells us his King will *restore* at a stroke,
>   St. Lucia, St. Vincent, Domin'ca, Tobago.
>
> But while they *croud People*, and *fortify Bays*,
>   The Talks at *Barbados* unless they will wink-a,
> Must see the *French settling*, whate'er Puysieux says,
>   St. Vincent, St. Lucia, Tabago, Domin'ca.
>
> Shall Britons believe, when *both Parties* are heard,
>   Our *Creole* all *Sland'rers*, their *Neighbours* all inn'cent?
> Or claim, with a *Lye*, giv'n to each *Frenchman's Beard*,
>   Domin'ca, Tobago, St. Lucia, St. Vincent?
>
> To settle this Point send out *forty good Sail*,
>   With Warren or Hawke to inspect each *Minutia*;
> They'll teach us *to whom shall belong*, without fail,
>   Tobago, Domin'ca, St. Vincent, St. Lucia.

This political doggerel refers to the dispute then going on between France and England over the so-called "neutral Islands" of the West Indies. The fact that the verses were copied in an American newspaper is fairly revealing; for it throws light upon an American interest in international affairs that was both wide and deep.

* * *

Certainly as long as the French and their Indian allies, both great and terrible enemies, stood athwart the westward march to empire, the British-

---

[1] *The American Historical Review*, LII, No. 4 (July, 1947), 655–66. Reprinted with permission.

Americans were bound to watch closely every move of the great European imperial rivals. This had to be, since the very survival of the British colonies might well depend upon the fickle behavior of the scales in the European balance of power. Moreover, there were weightier reasons for an interest in European international affairs close at hand. Frenchmen had been fighting Englishmen for the wilderness ever since the beginnings of English and French colonization; and that conflict had its roots and its reasons for being here in America and would probably have had to be fought out even had France and England never raised a hand against each other. But they had, and the local American conflict was part of the larger imperial competition around the world. The Americans knew it; and they also knew that their own fate might well hang upon the outcome of this first world war. Their interest in the Anglo-French conflict, therefore, sprang from involvements in it that were vital to them.

But the Americans were not deeply interested in this struggle of the titans merely because they were tied to one of them. The fact that they were the offspring of England gave them a psychological and emotional tie of loyalty that probably would have kept alive in them an interest in England and all things English, even had there been no Anglo-French conflict. Yet the two things went together; the need for protection combined with patriotic attachment in the mid-eighteenth century to produce a burst of British-American patriotism that has seldom, if ever, been equaled.

The colonial newspapers of the 1750's were full of it; it found expression both in patriotic and anti-French news and articles copied from English newspapers and in diatribes composed by Americans. At the same time, the official attitude, represented by such men as Governors James Glen of South Carolina, Robert Dinwiddie of Virginia, Horatio Sharpe of Maryland, and William Shirley of Massachusetts, was one of patriotic alarm....

Needless to say, the official alarm of the governors was shared by the imperialists in all the colonies, but particularly in those which had frontiers in the areas claimed by both French and English. Such imperialists, for example, were Dr. William Clarke of Boston and William Livingston of New York.... The British colonies, [Clarke] said, were doubling in population every twenty years, and would in the future consume enormous quantities of British manufactures; but he warned that this great market and source of material strength would be lost to Britain if France were allowed to seize the British colonies....

This thoroughly mercantilistic argument was echoed by William Livingston, who elaborated it into an American version of the theory of the balance of power as dependent upon colonial commerce. For Livingston saw the colonies as an inexhaustible magazine of national wealth, "and if suffered to fall into the hands of the French, such will be the accession to their [France's] already extended commerce and marine strength, that Great Britain must not only lose her former lustre, but, dreadful even in thought! cease to be any longer an independent power."...

The attitude of many American officials and imperialists was thus distinctly mercantilist in nature. Needless to say, these imperialists were none too scrupulous about the validity of their claims to the lands beyond the

13

Allegheny watershed, and they were all for the "offensive defensive" to beat the French to them.[2]

There were some American imperialists, on the other hand, who, like Thomas Lee of Virginia, were more interested in land than they were in commerce. Lee, as is well known, was the moving spirit in the Ohio Company, and extremely active in trying to arouse support in other colonies for his belief that Britain owned America all the way to the Pacific and his own frank purpose "to extend the British empire"[3] by defeating the French on the Ohio.

The alarm and the aggressiveness of the imperialists were not shared by the colonial assemblies, however. Several of the assemblies, if not all, were distinctly cool, to say the least, toward the official and journalistic patriotic fervor. The Maryland assembly refused to grant any money to aid Virginia until after Washington's defeat at Fort Necessity, and the Pennsylvania assembly, even as late as January, 1755, remarked to their governor that the French activities in the west seemed to have been exaggerated; the territory involved, they said, lay in Virginia anyway: why should Pennsylvania concern itself? The New York assembly, which might have been expected to be interested in westward expansion, stated flatly that the building of a fort by the French at French Creek "may, but does not by any Evidence or Information, appear to us to be an Invasion, of any of his Majesty's Colonies, nor does the Government of *Virginia*, seem to look upon it as such," since Dinwiddie's letter appealing for aid says only that "the Plan of Operation

---

[2] Author's note.—The word "mercantilist" is used here to indicate the political philosophy that dominated the minds of most European statesmen in the middle of the eighteenth century. This was a body of ideas that varied from statesman to statesman and from country to country, but it held, in general, that the power of a state rests ultimately upon the extent and the profitableness of its commerce. Colonies, in such a polity, were regarded as being areas of the national market, to be monopolized, as far as possible, by the mother country; as sources of raw materials to be exploited as exclusively as possible by the mother country; and as having a commerce of their own that was to be encouraged only so long as it redounded, in the long run, to the profit of the mother country and to be discouraged in every point where it seemed to be in rivalry with the commerce of the mother country or where it appeared to cause a net loss to the merchants of the mother country. For example, as Professor C. W. Alvord has shown in his *Mississippi Valley in British Politics* (2 vols., Cleveland, 1917), the British mercantilists were divided over the policy Britain should follow with regard to the Mississippi Valley, because they could not agree whether settlement of the valley or reservation of the area for the fur trade with the Indians would be more profitable for British commerce as a whole. Mercantilism was the sort of thinking that led General Thomas Gage to oppose settlement of the valley because he thought the colonists there would not send their products to the English market: "I [think it would] be for our interest to keep the Settlers within reach of the Sea-Coast as long as we can; and to cramp their Trade as far as it can be done prudentially. Cities flourish and increase by extensive Trade, artisans and Mechanicks of all Sort's are drawn thither, who teach all sorts of handicraft work before unknown in the Country, and they soon come to make for themselves what they used to import. I have seen this Increase, and I assure your Lordship that Foundations are laid in Philadelphia that must create Jealousy in an Englishman." Thomas Gage, *The Correspondence of General Thomas Gage,* ed. by Clarence E. Carter, 2 vols. (New Haven, 1933), II, 616.

In the realm of international relations it was this same mercantilist philosophy which led the duc de Choiseul to write, in 1758, that "The King [of France] believes, Monsieur, that it is possessions in America that will in the future form the balance of power in Europe, and that, if the English invade that [the Spanish] part of the world, as it appears they have the intention of doing, it will result therefrom that England will usurp the commerce of the nations, and that she alone will remain rich in Europe." AE. Cor. Pol. Naples, 78: 44–54; quoted in Max Savelle, "The American Balance of Power and European Diplomacy," in R. B. Morris, ed., *The Era of the American Revolution* (New York, 1939), pp. 160–61.

[3] Author's note.—Quoted in Kenneth P. Bailey, *The Ohio Company of Virginia* (Glendale, 1939), p. 39. See also *Minutes of the Provincial Council of Pennsylvania,* V, 422, *et passim*. It should be remembered that the Anglo-French competition in North America was part of a world-wide conflict of mercantilist empires, and that the rival penetrations of the Ohio Valley were only one scene in the North American theater which must be studied along with the concurrent disputes over Acadia and the Neutral Islands. Title to the upper Ohio was certainly not clear, either to the French or to the British, although the French seem to have had a little the best of the argument. In Acadia, on the other hand, the positions were reversed, and the British claims were probably more justified than the French.

is no more, than to take Possession of the Lands in his Majesty's Name, and built Forts agreeable to his Command." Even the Virginia house of burgesses, of all the colonial assemblies the one most directly interested in the French movements, attached to the bill appropriating £20,000 for the support of measures to be taken to defend the Virginia frontier a rider requiring that £2,500 be paid to Peyton Randolph as agent representing the house of burgesses in London! . . .

Aside from the religious scruples of the Quakers in Pennsylvania, it seems evident that the coolness of the colonial assemblies toward the Anglo-French conflict . . . is to be explained largely in terms of their struggle for political autonomy and against prerogative, whether royal or proprietary.

When we observe the popular reactions to the Anglo-French conflict, however, it becomes crystal clear that most articulate Americans were ardent British patriots. Dr. William Douglass of Boston probably expressed the thought of many of his fellow citizens when he wrote, late in the 1740's, that

The French are the common Nusance and Disturbers of Europe, and will in a short time become the same in *America*, if not mutilated at Home, and in *America* fenced off from us by Ditches and Walls, that is, by great Rivers and impracticable Mountains. . . . In order to preserve a Ballance in *Europe*, they ought to be curtail'd or dismembered there, which will effectually at the same Time prevent their too great Growth in America.

The hatred of France and all things French was complemented by love of Britain, and celebrated in patriotic speeches that have a familiar ring, even today. . . .

* * *

The patriotism to which these men appealed was very real. Nor was it confined to politicians and preachers, for it permeated every form of expression. As might be expected, it is often to be encountered in the budding native poetry. For example, John Maylem of Newport prayed for power to avenge the monstrous perfidy of the French in his poem "Gallic Perfidy":

> Amazing Perfidy! . . .
> 　　Ye Powers of Fury lend
> Some mighty Phrensy to enrage my Brest
> With solemn Song, beyond all Nature's Strain! . . .
> O Chief in War! of all (young) Albion's Force,
> Invest me only with sufficient Power;
> I (yet a Boy) will play the Man, and chase
> The wily Savage from his secret Haunts:
> Not Alpine Mounts shall thwart my rapid Course;
> I'll scale the Craggs, then, with impetuous Speed,
> Rush down the Steep, and scow'r along the Vale;
> Then on the Sea-Shore halt; and last, explore
> The green Meanders of eternal Wood.

And young Francis Hopkinson, budding poet of the Philadelphia salon, celebrated the fall of Louisbourg in 1758 in lines that are both patriotic and aristocratic:

At length 'tis done! The glorious conflict's done!
And *British* valour has the conquest won!
Success our arms, our heroes, *Honor* crowns,
And Louisbourg an *English* monarch owns....

Give your loose canvas to the breezes free
Ye floating thund'rers, bulwarks of the sea!
Haste bear the joyful tidings to your king,
And with the voice of war declare 'tis Victory you bring.
Let the wild *Croud* that catch the breath of fame,
In mad *Huzzas* their ruder joys proclaim;
Let their loud thanks to Heav'n in flames ascend,
Whilst mingling shouts the azure concave rend.
But let the *Few*, whom *Reason* makes more wise,
In tears of *Gratitude* uplift their eyes;
Oh may their breasts dilate with *sober* joy,
Let Pray'r their hearts, their tongues let *Praise* employ!
To bless our *God* with me let all unite;
He guides the conqu'ring sword, *he* governs in the fight.

"If ever there was a national war," wrote Benjamin Franklin in 1760, "this [the Seven Years' War] is truly such a one; a war in which the interest of the whole [Anglo-American] nation is directly and fundamentally concerned."

* * *

The wave of British-American patriotism that swept through the colonies between 1754 and 1760 may have expressed the feelings of the majority of the Americans. At the same time, even in the midst of war, the colonial assemblies continued to be jealous of their rights and privileges, and to eye with a certain amount of distrust the moves of the British government and of the British commanders in America. As soon as the war was over, American distrust of British motives, coupled with the colonial dislike of the patronizing airs of their English cousins, broke out into the open, and the Americans began to ask, "Who won the war, anyway?" ...

... This growing self-assurance was unquestionably one of the psychological factors that emboldened the Americans to resist the Grenville program of reorganization after the Seven Years' War was over. As the American resistance grew, and the debate waxed warm, Daniel Dulany brought the "who-won-the-war" question right out into the open and stated it in the following explicit terms:

It is presumed that it was a notable service done by *New England*, when the militia of that colony reduced *Cape-Breton*, since it enabled the *British ministers* to make a peace less disadvantageous and inglorious than they otherwise must have been constrained to submit to, in the humble state to which they were then reduced.... [Furthermore, it is clear] that the general exertion of *the colonies in North America*, during the last war [1756–1763], not only facilitated, but was indispensably requisite to the success of those operations by which so many glorious conquests were achieved....

An *American*, without justly incurring the imputation of ingratitude, may doubt, whether some other motive, besides pure generosity, did not prompt the *British Nation* to engage in the defense of the colonies. He may be induced to think that the measures taken for the protection of the plantations, were not only connnected with the interests, but [were] even necessary to the defense of *Great-Britain* herself, because he may have reason to imagine that Great-Britain, could not long subsist as an independent kingdom after the loss of her colonies.

This sort of thinking betrays a new mood—or rather the maturation of an old one—among the Americans. Not only were they the decisive factor in the winning of the war for Great Britain, according to Dulany; they were absolutely necessary to Britain's continued survival: and Britain had better have a care to treat them with respect.

As the debate blew hot and cold between 1765 and 1775, but generally hotter, the orientation of the Americans toward the continuing Anglo-French rivalry slowly shifted. It is true that the newspapers contained brief notices of French actions, the movements of the French fleet, and the like, and spoke of the French people as "our" enemies; but such news items were relatively rare. Space was now filled up with the "Virginia Resolves," the "Massachusetts Resolves," Dickinson's *Letters of a Pennsylvania Farmer*, and other discussions of the relationships of the colonies with the empire. The interest of the Americans was now obviously directed toward American relations with Great Britain rather than with other parts of the world. As is well known, the Americans were now struggling to find a definition of their place in the British Empire that would be conformable both to their ideas of their own importance in the empire and to their drive for economic and political autonomy.

* * *

As for the Anglo-French conflict, there was little thought about it in America between 1764 and 1774. As the tension with Britain approached the breaking point, however, the Americans began to re-discuss the old Anglo-French balance of power and they easily discovered the possibility of exploiting it for their own advantage. Franklin observed from London in 1769 and 1770 that all Europe was watching the dispute of Britain with her colonies and that sympathy was generally on the side of the colonies. At the same time, he said, "the malignant Pleasure, which other Powers take in British Divisions, may convince us on both sides of the Necessity of our uniting." But the interest of Europe in the dispute, and particularly the interest of France, was soon recognized by the Americans as a possible trump in their own hand, rather than as a reason for compromising their difficulties with Britain.

It was John Adams who probably saw most clearly the potential value of the Anglo-French rivalry to the American cause; and although his first motion in the Continental Congress to send ambassadors abroad failed, he continued to argue for exploiting the Anglo-French enmity for the benefit of the embattled colonists. . . .

So far had the weather vane of the American attitude shifted, between 1750 and 1775. The ancient enemy, France, for the description of whom in 1755 no language was powerful enough, no epithet scurrilous enough, was now become the prospective ally, to be courted for her aid; circumspectly and cautiously courted, to be sure, almost as a male black widow spider might court his deadly bride, but courted nonetheless. And for what?

To bring to realization the maturing sovereignty of the Anglo-American states. To give fruition to the drive for autonomy that had been in them for a century. It is of interest to observe that the basic concept of international

17

affairs, for those who thought seriously on the subject, was still the concept of a mercantilistic balance of power—a balance in which the American colonies were thought to be the decisive makeweight. But the most significant fact that emerges from all the discussion, perhaps, is that the American people, divided though they were, were moving steadily and surely toward a national self-consciousness, though always, be it said, demanding only to be the first-born in a closely knit British family of autonomous states. The orientation of the slowly self-conscious American people toward the outside world was moving, in the years between 1750 and 1775, toward a demand for acceptance as a new member, or as a group of new members, albeit young and unproven, of the Atlantic community of nations.

JACK TAR IN THE STREETS: MERCHANT SEAMEN IN THE POLITICS OF REVOLUTIONARY AMERICA[1]

Jesse Lemisch

Here comes Jack Tar, his bowed legs bracing him as if the very Broadway beneath his feet might begin to pitch and roll. In his dress he is, in the words of a superior, "very nasty and negligent," his black stockings ragged, his long, baggy trousers tarred to make them waterproof. Bred in "that very shambles of language," the merchant marine, he is foul-mouthed, his talk alien and suspect. He is Jolly Jack, a bull in a china shop, always, in his words, "for a Short Life and a Merry one," and, in the concurring words of his superiors, "concerned only for the present . . . incapable of thinking of, or inattentive to, future welfare," "like froward Childeren not knowing how to judge for themselves."

Clothes don't make the man, nor does language; surely we can do better than these stereotypes. Few have tried. Maritime history, as it has been written, has had as little to do with the common seaman as business history has had to do with the laborer. In that *mischianza* of mystique and elitism, "seaman" has meant Sir Francis Drake, not Jack Tar; the focus has been on trade, exploration, the great navigators, but rarely on the men who sailed the ships. . . .

The merchant marine was a place full of forces beyond the seaman's control: death and disease, storms, and fluctuations in employment. Indeed, the lack of "old salts" in . . . [the] merchant marine might reflect a sombre irony: was the average seaman young because mobility rapidly brought him to another trade or because seamen died young? A man in jail, said Dr. Johnson, was at least safe from drowning, and he had more room, better food, and better company. The Quaker John Woolman was one of the few sensitive enough to see that if the "poor bewildered sailors" drank and

[1] *William and Mary Quarterly,* Third Series, XXV, No. 3 (July, 1968), 371–95. Reprinted with permission. Also see "Listening to the 'Inarticulate': William Widger's Dream and the Loyalties of American Revolutionary Seamen in British Prisons," *Journal of Social History,* September, 1969.

cursed, the fault lay not so much in themselves as in the harsh environment and the greed of employers. . . .

The presence of such men, fugitives and floaters, powerless in a tough environment, makes *wanderlust* appear an ironic parody of the motives which made at least some men go to sea. Catch the seaman when he is not pandering to your romanticism, said former seaman Frederick Law Olmsted a century later, and he will tell you that he hates the sight of blue water, he hates his ship, his officers, and his messmates—and he despises himself. Melville's Ishmael went to sea when he felt grim, hostile, and suicidal: "It is a way I have of driving off the spleen." No matter what we make of Ishmael, we cannot possibly make him into one of Morison's "adventure-seeking boys." Others, perhaps, but not Ishmael. The feelings of eighteenth-century Americans toward seafaring and seamen, and what evidence we have of the reasons men had for going to sea indicate that there were many like Ishmael in the colonial period, too, who left the land in flight and fear, outcasts, men with little hope of success ashore. These were the dissenters from the American mood. Their goals differed from their fellows ashore; these were the rebels, the men who stayed on to become old salts.

Admiralty law treated seamen in a special way, as "wards." Carl Ubbelohde says that seamen favored the colonial Vice Admiralty Courts as "particular tribunals in case of trouble," and Charles M. Andrews and Richard B. Morris agreed that these courts were "guardians of the rights of the seamen." The benefits of being classified as a "ward" are dubious, but, regardless of the quality of treatment which admiralty law accorded to seamen, it certainly does not follow that, all in all, the colonial seaman was well treated by the law. Indeed, if we broaden our scope to include colonial law generally, we find an extraordinarily harsh collection of laws, all justifying Olmsted's later claim that American seamen "are more wretched, and are governed more by threats of force than any other civilized laborers of the world." There are laws providing for the whipping of disobedient seamen and in one case for their punishment as "seditious"; laws prohibiting seamen in port from leaving their vessels after sundown and from travelling on land without certificates of discharge from their last job; laws empowering "every free white person" to catch runaway seamen. We find other laws, less harsh, some seeming to protect the seaman: laws against extending credit to seamen and against arresting them for debt, and against entertaining them in taverns for more than one hour per day; laws against selling them liquor and prohibiting them from playing with cards or dice; laws waiving imprisonment for seamen convicted of cursing; laws requiring masters to give discharge certificates to their seamen and laws prohibiting hiring without such certificates. Finally, there are laws which clearly do help the seaman: laws requiring masters to provide "good and sufficient diet and accommodation" and providing for redress if the master refused; laws providing punishment for masters who "immoderately beat, wound, or maim" their seamen; laws providing that seamen's contracts be written.

These harsh or at best paternalistic laws add up to a structure whose purpose is to assure a ready supply of cheap, docile labor. Obedience, both at sea and ashore, is the keystone. . . .

Thus if we think of Jack Tar as jolly, childlike, irresponsible, and in many ways surprisingly like the Negro stereotype, it is because he was treated so much like a child, a servant, and a slave. What the employer saw as the necessities of an authoritarian profession were written into law and culture: the society that wanted Jack dependent made him that way and then concluded that that was the way he really was.

Constantly plagued by short complements, the Royal Navy attempted to solve its manning problems in America, as in England, by impressment. Neil Stout has recently attributed these shortages to "death, illness, crime, and desertion" which were in turn caused largely by rum and by the deliberate enticements of American merchants. Rum and inveiglement certainly took a high toll, but to focus on these two causes of shortages is unfairly to shift the blame for impressment onto its victims. The navy itself caused shortages. Impressment, said Thomas Hutchinson, caused desertion, rather than the other way around. Jack Tar had good reasons for avoiding the navy. It would, a young Virginian was warned, "cut him and staple him and use him like a Negro, or rather, like a dog"; James Otis grieved at the loss of the "flower" of Massachusett's youth "by ten thousands" to a service which treated them little better than "hewers of wood and drawers of water." Discipline was harsh and sometimes irrational, and punishments were cruel. Water poured into sailors' beds, they went mad, and died of fevers and scurvy. Sickness, Benjamin Franklin noted, was more common in the navy than in the merchant service and more frequently fatal. In a fruitless attempt to prevent desertion, wages were withheld and men shunted about from ship to ship without being paid. But the accumulation of even three or four years' back wages could not keep a man from running. And why should it have? Privateering paid better in wartime, and wages were higher in the merchant service; even laborers ashore were better paid. Thus . . . [the] claim that the navy was "forced" to press is only as accurate as the claim that the South was forced to enslave Negroes. Those whose sympathies lie with the thousands of victims of this barbaric practice—rather than with naval administrators—will see that the navy pressed because to be in the navy was in some sense to be a slave, and for this we must blame the slave owners rather than the slaves.

Impressment angered and frightened the seamen, but it pervaded and disrupted all society, giving other classes and groups cause to share a common grievance with the press-gang's more direct victims: just about everyone had a relative at sea. Whole cities were crippled. A night-time operation in New York in 1757 took in eight hundred men, the equivalent of more than one-quarter of the city's adult male population. Impressment and the attendant shortage of men may have been a critical factor in the stagnancy of "the once cherished now depressed, once flourishing now sinking Town of Boston." . . .

From the very beginning the history of impressment in America is a tale of venality, deceit, and vindictiveness. Captains kept deserters and dead men on ships' books, pocketing their provision allowances. In 1706 a captain pressed men and literally sold them to short-handed vessels; his midshipman learned the business so well that after his dismissal he became a veritable entrepreneur of impressment, setting up shop in a private sloop. Another commander waited until New York's governor was away to break a no-press agreement and when the governor returned he seriously considered firing on the Queen's ship. In Boston in 1702 the lieutenant-governor *did* fire, responding to merchants' complaints. "Fire and be damn'd," shouted the impressing captain as the shots whistled through his sails. The merchants had complained that the press was illegal under 1697 instructions which required captains and commanders to apply to colonial governors for permission to press. These instructions, a response to complaints of "irregular proceedings of the captains of some of our ships of war in the impressing of seamen," had clearly not put an end to irregularities. In 1708 a Parliament fearful of the disruptive effect of impressment on trade forbade the practice in America. In the sixty-seven years until the repeal in 1775 of this "Act for the Encouragement of the Trade to America" there was great disagreement as to its meaning and indeed as to its very existence. Did the Sixth of Anne, as the act was called, merely prohibit the navy from impressing and leave governors free to do so? At least one governor, feeling "pinioned" under the law, continued impressing while calling it "borrowing." Was the act simply a wartime measure, which expired with the return of peace in 1713? Regardless of the dispute, impressment continued, routine in its regularity, but often spectacular in its effects.

Boston was especially hard-hit by impressment in the 1740's, with frequent incidents throughout the decade and major explosions in 1745 and 1747. Again and again the town meeting and the House of Representatives protested, drumming away at the same themes: impressment was harmful to maritime commerce and to the economic life of the city in general and illegal if not properly authorized. In all this the seaman himself becomes all but invisible. The attitude towards him in the protests is at best neutral and often sharply antagonistic. In 1747 the House of Representatives condemned the violent response of hundreds of seamen to a large-scale press as "a tumultuous riotous assembling of armed Seamen, Servants, Negroes, and others ... tending to the Destruction of all Government and Order." While acknowledging that the people had reason to protest, the House chose to level *its* protest against "the most audacious Insult" to the governor, Council, and House. And the town meeting, that stronghold of democracy, offered its support to those who took "orderly" steps while expressing its "Abhorence of such Illegal Criminal Proceedings" as those undertaken by the seamen "and other persons of mean and Vile Condition."

Protests such as these reflect at the same time both unity and division in colonial society. All kinds of Americans—both merchants and seamen—opposed impressment, but the town meeting and the House spoke for the merchant, not the seaman. They opposed impressment not for its effect on the seaman but for its effect on commerce. Thus their protests express antagonism to British policy at the same time that they express class division. These two themes continue and develop in American opposition to impressment in the three decades between the Knowles Riots of 1747 and the Declaration of Independence. . . . And in 1769 lawyer John Adams used the

21

threat of displaying the statute book containing the Sixth of Anne to frighten a special court of Admiralty into declaring the killing of an impressing lieutenant justifiable homicide in necessary self-defense.

There were two kinds of impressment incidents: those in which there was immediate self-defense against impressment, usually at sea, and those in which crowds ashore, consisting in large part of seamen, demonstrated generalized opposition to impressment. This is what the first kind of incident sounded like: a volley of musketry and the air full of langrage, grapeshot, round shot, hammered shot, double-headed shot, even rocks. "Come into the boat and be damned, you Sorry Son of a Whore or else Ile breake your head, and hold your tongue." Small arms, swords and cutlasses, blunderbusses, clubs and pistols, axes, harpoons, fishgigs, twelve-pounders, six-pounders, half-pounders. "You are a parsill of Raskills." Fired five shots to bring to a snow from North Carolina, pressed four. "You have no right to impress me . . . If you step over that line . . . by the eternal God of Heaven, you are a dead man." "Aye, my lad, I have seen many a brave fellow before now."

Here is hostility and bloodshed, a tradition of antagonism. From the beginning, impressment's most direct victims—the seamen—were its most active opponents. . . .

. . . Seamen did not go peacefully. Their violence was purposeful, and sometimes they were articulate. "I know who you are," said one, as reported by John Adams and supported by Thomas Hutchinson. "You are the lieutenant of a man-of-war, come with a press-gang to deprive me of my liberty. You have no right to impress me. I have retreated from you as far as I can. I can go no farther. I and my companions are determined to stand upon our defence. Stand off." (It was difficult for Englishmen to fail to see impressment in such terms—even a sailor *doing* the pressing could feel shame over "fighting with honest sailors, to deprive them of their liberty.")

Ashore, seamen and others demonstrated their opposition to impressment with the only weapon which the unrepresentative politics of the day offered them—riot. In Boston several thousand people responded to a nighttime impressment sweep of the harbor and docks with three days of rioting beginning in the early hours of November 17, 1747. Thomas Hutchinson reported that "the lower class were beyond measure enraged." Negroes, servants, and hundreds of seamen seized a naval lieutenant, assaulted a sheriff and put his deputy in the stocks, surrounded the governor's house, and stormed the Town House where the General Court was sitting. The rioters demanded the seizure of the impressing officers, the release of the men they had pressed, and execution of a death sentence which had been levied against a member of an earlier press-gang who had been convicted of murder. When the governor fled to Castle William—some called it "abdication"—Commodore Knowles threatened to put down what he called "arrant rebellion" by bombarding the town. The governor, who, for his part, thought the rioting a secret plot of the upper class, was happily surprised when the town meeting expressed its "Abhorence" of the seamen's riot.

After the French and Indian War press riots increased in frequency. Armed mobs of whites and Negroes repeatedly manhandled captains, officers, and crews, threatened their lives, and held them hostage for the men they pressed. Mobs fired at pressing vessels and tried to board them; they threatened to burn one, and they regularly dragged ships' boats to the center of town for ceremonial bonfires. . . .

Long before 1765 Americans had developed beliefs about impressment, and they had expressed those beliefs in words and deeds. Impressment was bad for trade and it was illegal. As such, it was, in the words of the Massachusetts House in 1720, "a great Breach on the Rights of His Majesties Subjects." In 1747 it was a violation of "the common Liberty of the Subject," and in 1754 "inconsistent with Civil Liberty, and the Natural Rights of Mankind." Some felt in 1757 that it was even "abhorrent to the English Constitution." In fact, the claim that impressment was unconstitutional was wrong. (Even *Magna Charta* was no protection. *Nullus liber homo capiatur* did not apply to seamen.) Instead impressment indicated to Benjamin Franklin "that the constitution is yet imperfect, since in so general a case it doth not secure liberty, but destroys it." "If impressing seamen is of right by common law in Britain," he also remarked, "slavery is then of right by common law there; there being no slavery worse than that sailors are subjected to."

For Franklin, impressment was a symptom of injustice built into the British Constitution. In *Common Sense* Tom Paine saw in impressment a reason for rejecting monarchy. In the Declaration of Independence Thomas Jefferson included impressment among the "Oppressions" of George III; later he likened the practice to the capture of Africans for slavery. Both "reduced [the victim] to . . . bondage by force, in flagrant violation of his own consent, and of his natural right in his own person."

Despite all this, and all that went before, we have thought little of impressment as an element in explaining the conduct of the common man in the American Revolution. Contemporaries knew better. John Adams felt that a tactical mistake by Thomas Hutchinson on the question of impressment in 1769 would have "accelerated the revolution. . . . It would have spread a wider flame than Otis's ever did, or could have done." Ten years later American seamen were being impressed by *American* officers. The United States Navy had no better solution for "public Necessities" than had the Royal Navy. Joseph Reed, President of Pennsylvania, complained to Congress of "Oppressions" and in so doing offered testimony to the role of *British* impressment in bringing on revolution. "We cannot help observing how similar this Conduct is to that of the British Officers during our Subjection to Great Britain and are persuaded it will have the same unhappy effects viz., an estrangement of the Affections of the People from the Authority under which they act which by an easy Progression will proceed to open Opposition to the immediate Actors and Bloodshed." Impressment had played a role in the estrangement of the American people from the British government. It had produced "Odium" against the navy, and even six-year-olds had not been too young to have learned to detest it. The anger of thousands of victims did not vanish. Almost four decades after the Declaration of Independence an orator could still arouse his audience by tapping a folk-memory of impressment by the same "haughty, cruel, and gasconading nation" which was once again trying to enslave free Americans.

23

The seamen's conduct in the 1760's and 1770's makes more sense in the light of previous and continued impressment. What may have seemed irrational violence can now be seen as purposeful and radical. The pattern of rioting as political expression, established as a response to impressment, was now adapted and broadened as a response to the Stamp Act. In New York General Gage described the "insurrection" of October 31, 1765, and following as "composed of great numbers of Sailors." The seamen, he said, were "the only People who may be properly Stiled Mob," and estimates indicate that between a fifth and a fourth of New York's rioters were seamen. The disturbances began among the seamen—especially former privateersmen—on October 31. On November 1 they had marched, led primarily by their former captains; later they rioted, led by no one but themselves. Why? Because they had been duped by merchants, or, if not by merchants, then certainly by lawyers. So British officials believed—aroused by these men who meant to use them, the seamen themselves had nothing more than plunder on their minds. In fact, at that point in New York's rioting when the leaders lost control, the seamen, who were then in the center of town, in an area rich for plunder, chose instead to march in an orderly and disciplined way clear across town to do violence to the home and possessions of an English major whose provocative conduct had made him the obvious political enemy. Thus the "rioting" was actually very discriminating.

Seamen and nonseamen alike joined to oppose the Stamp Act for many reasons, but the seamen had two special grievances: impressment and the effect of England's new attitude toward colonial trade. To those discharged by the navy at the end of the war and others thrown out of work by the death of privateering were added perhaps twenty thousand more seamen and fishermen who were thought to be the direct victims of the post-1763 trade regulations. This problem came to the fore in the weeks following November 1, 1765, when the Stamp Act went into effect. The strategy of opposition chosen by the colonial leadership was to cease all activities which required the use of stamps. Thus maritime trade came to a halt in the cities. Some said that this was a cowardly strategy. If the Americans opposed the Stamp Act, let them go on with business as usual, refusing outright to use the stamps. The leaders' strategy was especially harmful to the seamen, and the latter took the more radical position—otherwise the ships would not sail. And this time the seamen's radicalism triumphed over both colonial leadership and British officials. Within little more than a month the act had been largely nullified. Customs officers were allowing ships to sail without stamps, offering as the reason the fear that the seamen, "who are the people that are most dangerous on these occasions, as their whole dependance for a subsistence is upon Trade," would certainly "commit some terrible Mischief." Philadelphia's customs officers feared that the seamen would soon "compel" them to let ships pass without stamps. Customs officers at New York yielded when they heard that the seamen were about to have a meeting. . . .

Many of these animosities flared in the Boston Massacre. What John Adams described as "a motley rabble of saucy boys, negroes and molattoes, Irish teagues and out landish jack tarrs," including twenty or thirty of the latter, armed with clubs and sticks, did battle with the soldiers. Their leader was Crispus Attucks, a mulatto seaman; he was shot to death in front of the Customs House. One of the seamen's reasons for being there has been too little explored. The Massacre grew out of a fight between workers and off-duty soldiers at a ropewalk two days before. That fight, in turn, grew out of the long-standing practice in the British army of allowing off-duty soldiers to take civilian employment. They did so, in Boston and elsewhere, often at wages which undercut those offered to Americans—including un-employed seamen who sought work ashore—by as much as 50 per cent. In hard times this led to intense competition for work, and the Boston Massacre was in part a product of this competition. Less well known is the Battle of Golden Hill, which arose from similar causes and took place in New York six weeks before. In January 1770 a gang of seamen went from house to house and from dock to dock, using clubs to drive away the soldiers em-ployed there and threatening anyone who might rehire them. In the days of rioting which followed and which came to be called the Battle of Golden Hill, the only fatality was a seaman, although many other seamen were wounded in the attempt to take vengeance for the killing. The antipathy between soldiers and seamen was so great, said John Adams, "that they fight as naturally when they meet, as the elephant and Rhinoceros." ...

Impressment meant the loss of freedom, both personal and economic, and, sometimes, the loss of life itself. The seaman who defended himself against impressment felt that he was fighting to defend his "liberty," and he justified his resistance on grounds of "right." It is in the concern for liberty and right that the seaman rises from vindictiveness to a somewhat more com-plex awareness that certain values larger than himself exist and that he is the victim not only of cruelty and hardship but also, in the light of those values, of injustice. The riots ashore, whether they be against impressment, the Stamp Act, or competition for work express that same sense of injustice. And here, thousands of men took positive and effective steps to demonstrate their opposition to both acts and policies.

... When Jack Tar went to sea in the American Revolution, he fought, as he had for many years before, quite literally, to protect his life, liberty, and property. ...

THE HISTORICAL MEANING

OF THE AMERICAN DOCTRINE

OF ISOLATION[1]   *Albert K. Weinberg*

The classic definition of American isolation is that it is not a theory but a predicament. In all seriousness, isolation is not a theory of American foreign policy. Isolation is a theory about a theory of American foreign policy. Because this interpretation is a poor theory, misrepresentative even if taken only semi-literally, it has placed the discussion of American foreign policy

[1] *American Political Science Review*, XXXIV, No. 3 (June, 1940), 539–47. Reprinted with permission.

in a sad predicament of obfuscation, not without its influence upon national decisions.

. . . Perhaps the only reference to isolation in the classic statements of American foreign policy is in Seward's assertion that a course based upon Washington's counsel seems one of isolation if "superficially viewed." Isolation as a superficial description of American policy was the coinage, not of advocates of reserve, but of opponents seeking to discredit them by exaggeration. About the middle of the nineteenth century, interventionists, desirous that "Young America" help actively Europe's revolutionary liberalism, called upon those less rash than themselves for an abandonment of "isolation," and thus for the first time identified it not merely with a geographical situation but with a theory of foreign relations. The further history of the term exhibits the increasing use by anti-isolationists of this conscious or unconscious strategy, the repeated denunciation of it not only by adherents of moderate reserve but by "irreconcilables" as well, and, finally and only rather recently, the bravado or thoughtlessness of an extremist minority in accepting a label that misrepresented even them. If, together with the other spectators, diplomatic historians came to use the word, it was only because they were well aware that mere scholars can change no social habit.

The concept of isolation is useful only in so far as it indicates the misunderstanding of an ideology, serves as a point of departure for investigation, and contains in its connotation certain suggestive half-truths. The history of American foreign policy, while abundant in economic and social collaboration, does exhibit what Secretary Forsyth called a "national reserve," a deliberate and more or less regular abstention from certain political relationships usually considered instrumental to either interest or duty. The scope of this reserve can as easily be underestimated as overestimated; in its fully developed form, it comprises no less than eight distinct policies, prohibitions of broad types of international action. . . . Amazingly broad and persistent in its influence, a principle existed that was used to discriminate between injurious international relationships and those innocuous, to convey the common attribute of all that are injurious, and to define generally America's desirable relation to the world. This principle is the counterpart in reality of the mythical doctrine of isolation; but, unlike isolation, it makes sense; indeed this American folk product is an important, and certainly in some measure wise, contribution to the ideology of nationalism.

So far from isolation is the so-called isolationist's ideal that its inmost essence is something desired by all peoples. The ideal is the non-juridical counterpart of sovereignty and, as regards its parentage, a blood-brother of sovereignty. A nation's insistence upon sole authorship of its legal acts derives from the natural desire of every people for maximum self-determination, which is identified with the probability of attaining maximum interest and dignity. Unfortunately, however, sovereignty does not ensure freedom from alien interference except in a Christian world or a world where but one nation is sovereign. Limitations of freedom of action arise in the first place from the hostile or competitive impacts of other nations. Accordingly, there ensures a paradox: for the very sake of maximum self-determination—or for independence itself, as in America's alliance with France—nations have traditionally entered into agreements of mutual aid that limit self-determination by imposing reciprocal obligations and consequently interconnections of experience.

But there are conditions under which the dominative phase of this ambivalent system may appear more evil than its liberative phase may seem good. While long before American independence such conditions had prompted notable reserve, the determinants of the new life in the West were peculiar in a fashion that disposed Americans, and incipiently even those of colonial times, to a scarcely precedented transvaluation of values that had been generally predominant in Western international relations. A geographical detachment, a virgin continent, and cultural-institutional divergencies were reflected in political thinking in a sense of relative security, in the conviction of having interests different from Europe's, and in a political theory that made of freedom almost the key to all good. Influenced by such factors, Americans expressed their view of the alliance-system in the virtually novel application to it of a certain pejorative term, the most common and significant in the history of American isolationism: "entangling" or "entanglement." An entanglement, in international life as in the love life, is not a mere association but a relationship so intimate that two destinies become intertwined —and by implication not for better but for worse.

The conception of alliances as entanglements appeared as early as 1775 in the nationalistic and wary thought of John Adams, who, though yielding later to necessity, was apprehensive that an alliance with France would destroy our "real" independence in both domestic and foreign affairs. But the most influential warning against such relationships in terms of entanglement was in the Farewell Address, which posed the rhetorical question: "Why, by interweaving our destiny with that of any part of Europe, entangle our peace and prosperity in the toils of European ambition, rivalship, interest, humor, or caprice?" Because "Europe has a set of primary interests which to us have none or a very remote relation," that is, interests rooted in aggressiveness or imperilment and foreign to a nation of "detached and distant situation," permanent alliance committed America to "frequent controversies, the causes of which are essentially foreign to our concerns." At the same time, such alliances injured what was primary in our concern, the interest of true independence. In the youth of the nation, peace alone would permit uninterrupted progression to "that degree of strength and consistency which is necessary to give it, humanly speaking, the command of its own fortunes." This self-determination included not only the ability to choose peace or war according to interest, but also freedom from foreign influence and interference—values heightened by the traumatic experiences of the French alliance and by the danger of a tightening of that alliance.

* * *

... What is really envisaged in non-entanglement is freedom of action in so far as it is preserved through the avoidance of certain relationships with others. However, though all treaties are restrictive, by no means are all regarded as sources of entanglement. The reason is that the true criterion of entanglement is the seriousness of the limitation of freedom from the view-

27

point of what is considered vital. While this criterion permits of many commitments, it at the same time forbids certain actions that do not rest upon any commitment. International action frequently entails moral obligations or compulsive external consequences by virtue of which, to quote an early isolationist, "without any formal compact, a nation may find itself as completely entangled...as by a solemn treaty stipulation." In sum, nonentanglement is the absence of voluntarily incurred relationships, formal or informal, which remove the substantial control of the nation's action, or even of its experience, from its own choice by placing it in the will, influence, or career of other nations.

* * *

From the viewpoint of isolationism as an ideology, the policies of reserve are the successively emerging and developing embodiments of non-entanglement, an ideal that is incarnated only in its aversions:

1. *Entangling alliances with none.* Leaving Washington in the position of semi-isolationist, a progressive caution interdicted successively American as well as European permanent alliances, temporary alliances, informal alliances, implicit alliances, and, though not until 1920, a type of engagement that Wilson considered "disentangling" because it was made with all nations in behalf of world peace. The pervasive objection to all commitments to the use of force was that "every alliance is...entangling which places our peace on the discretion or movements of any other government."

2. *Non-intervention.* Exceeding greatly the prohibitions of international law, this policy forbids not merely participation in foreign conflicts, but any trespass upon the external or internal sovereignty of others that is not warranted by defense of serious national rights. Intrusive force was regarded as a boomerang that endangered America's own sovereignty or chosen way of life in either or both of two ways: the provocation of counter-intervention, especially feared in our early history, or the plunging of the nation into a swift and uncontrollable current of foreign life that carries it away from the moorings of all its values.

3. *Non-interference and non-participation in European politics.* While the principle of non-intervention is merely intensified, a novel element is the prohibition of even peaceful and neutral action in matters pertaining wholly or primarily to the politics of Europe or to their ramifications in other areas. Connected in its origin with the rise of the Spanish-American republics, the policy centered in an ideal of hemispheric self-determination: in return for our abnegation in relation to the Old World, Europe was to refrain from participation as well as intervention in American affairs, and thus leave unimpaired not only this nation's security but also its freedom of action in its own hemisphere.

4. *Avoidance of joint action.* Such action, which, as distinguished from coincident or concerted action, has an aspect of unity, is forbidden both in relations with other powers and in the exercise of administrative obligations. Examples are commonly subscribed interposition or intervention,

international maintenance of the Monroe Doctrine, and *condominia* over backward regions or an isthmian canal. All partnership, even that which is *ad hoc* or lacking in formal obligation, is considered entangling because it involves moral obligations, a pooling of interests, and responsibility for the partner's acts.

5. *No entangling commitments.* The principle of freedom of action in unknown contingencies, first associated with the no-alliance rule, became a criterion applied to all commitments and prohibited those which impaired future self-determination too greatly or which lay in spheres where circumstances are especially variable. In its procedural phase, the policy led earlier American statesmen to shrink from indissoluble, long-term, multipartite, and not quite essential treaties. In its substantive phase, largely still extant, the principle was manifested in reluctance to bind the future in issues with such changing contexts as expansion, arbitration, and the commitment to support or oppose other powers in any way.

6. *Non-limitation of "essential" rights of sovereignty.* Jurisdictional control and self-defense, while rights claimed by all sovereignty, have had in American interpretation a scope reflecting, not conventional jurisprudence or prudence, but an extreme reluctance to fetter action upon more or less important interests. American reserve towards self-limitation in joint or collective interest, however lessened in recent times, has been manifested in unwillingness to permit any alien determination of what domestic questions and self-defense (or the Monroe Doctrine) are; in exclusions of immigration and tariff policies from the range of international agreement; and in disapproval of the League commitments to suspend resort to war and to limit national control over armament and the trade in arms.

7. *Independence of any political "super-authority."* The blind commitment to accept the authority of any political body, whether the League of Nations, its alleged adjunct, the World Court, or even a temporary congress, is regarded as not only empowering others to do us evil but as surrendering our very sovereignty. Though particular repugnance is aroused by formal obligation to accept a majority decision, the concept of external domination is so broad as to include mere recommendation, regarded as a source of moral obligation, and, indeed, on the logic of nationalist emotion, even membership in a "super-authority" without any authority.

8. *Insulation against entanglement.* This policy, which accounts for the most articulate isolationism of today, is distinctive in that it interdicts, not a definite entanglement, but all action or lack of action creating a serious danger that temptation or necessity will lead to any entanglement. Transgression of this principle of due caution is like sin—something to be recognized in the particular even though one does not know what it is in general. At one time, conformity to the principle dictated chiefly the avoidance in various ways—the Monroe Doctrine, continental expansion, and anti-expansionism in relation to Europe and Asia—of magnetic proximity to areas of world politics. Today the principal concern is an isolation from war (the phrase of President Roosevelt) that consists chiefly in avoiding incident-producing economic relationships with distant belligerents.

America's *Index Actionum Prohibitarum* ends at a point that leaves, believe it or not, at least as much outside as within. Permissible because lacking in commitment or meddlesomeness is all single-handed action, from interposition to war, in behalf of national rights, and, when in accord with comity, in behalf of world interest; moreover, even intervention in behalf of world interest is allowable when there is a coincident national equity. Nor is entanglement seen in free international collaboration such as consultation and coincident action. Those commitments are permissible that do not involve vital political interests demanding flexibility: for example, commitments in respect to economic and humanitarian issues, renunciation of aggression, and consultation. Further, aside from the fact that virtually all of the policies have been subject to exceptions in emergency, more can be tolerated by *America's Index* than appears on its face or on the record. Fundamentally, nothing is entangling or disentangling but thinking makes it so. . . .

SAMUEL ADAMS ON REVOLUTION

AND INDEPENDENCE   *Document 1*

Letter to the editor of the Boston Gazette, *January 21, 1771.*
. . . The people in general seldom complain, without some good reason. The inhabitants of this continent are not to be dup'd "by an artful use of the words *liberty* and *slavery*, in an application to their passions," as Philanthrop [a conservative colonist] would have us think they are; like the miserable Italians, who are cheated with the names *"Excommunication, Bulls, Crusades,"* etc. They can distinguish between *"realities* and *sounds"*; and by a proper use "of that reason which Heaven has given them", they can judge, as well as their betters, when there is danger of *slavery:* They have as high a regard for George the III. as others have, & yet can suppose it possible they may be made slaves, without *"enslaving* themselves by their own *folly* and *madness";* . . . The *true patriot* therefore, will enquire into the causes of the *fears* and *jealousies* of his countrymen; and if he finds they are not *groundless*, he will be far from endeavoring to allay or stifle them: On the contrary . . . he will by all proper means in his power *foment* and *cherish* them: He will, as far as he is able, keep the attention of his fellow citizens awake to their grievances; and not suffer them to be at rest, till the causes of their complaints are removed. . . .
Mankind have entered into political societies, rather for the sake of restoring *equality;* the want of which, in the state of nature, rendered existence uncomfortable and even dangerous. I am not of levelling principles; But I am apt to think, that constitution of civil government which admits equality in the most extensive degree, consistent with the true design of government, is the best. . . . A subordination, which is so far from conducing "to the welfare and happiness of the whole," that it necessarily involves the idea of that

worst of all evils of this life, a tyranny ... disgraces the human nature, and sinks it to that of the most despicable brute....

JOHN ADAMS TO JAMES WARREN,
APRIL 22, 1776   *Document 2*

... After all, my friend, I do not at all wonder that so much reluctance has been shewn to the measure of independency. All great changes are irksome to the human mind, especially those which are attended with great dangers and uncertain effects....

We may please ourselves with the prospect of free and popular governments, but there is great danger that these governments will not make us happy. God grant they may! But I fear that in every Assembly members will obtain an influence by noise, not sense; by meanness, not greatness; by ignorance, not learning; by contracted hearts, not large souls. I fear, too, that it will be impossible to convince and persuade people to establish wise regulations.

There is one thing, my dear sir, that must be attempted and sacredly observed, or we are all undone. There must be decency and respect and veneration introduced for persons in authority, of every rank, or we are undone. In a popular government this is the only way of supporting order, and in our circumstances, as our people have been so long without any government at all, it is more necessary than in any other....

"COMMON SENSE," BY THOMAS PAINE,
PUBLISHED ON JANUARY 10, 1776   *Document 3*

... As to government matters, 'tis not in the power of Britain to do this continent justice; the business of it will soon be too weighty and intricate to be managed with any tolerable degree of convenience, by a power so distant from us, and so very ignorant of us; for if they cannot conquer us, they cannot govern us. To be always running three or four thousand miles with a tale or a petition, waiting four or five months for an answer, which, when obtained, requires five or six more to explain it, will in a few years be looked upon as folly and childishness. There was a time when it was proper, and there is a proper time for it to cease....

A government of our own is our natural right; and when a man seriously reflects on the precariousness of human affairs, he will become convinced that it is infinitely wiser and safer to form a constitution of our own in a cool deliberate manner, while we have it in our power, than to trust such an interesting event to time and chance....

I am not induced by motives of pride, party or resentment to espouse the doctrine of separation and independence; I am clearly, positively, and conscientiously persuaded that it is the true interest of this Continent to be so; that everything short of *that* is mere patchwork, that it can afford no lasting felicity....

I have heard it asserted by some that, as America has flourished under her former connection with Great Britain, the same connection is necessary towards her future happiness, and will always have the same effect. Nothing can be more fallacious than this kind of argument... for I answer roundly that America would have flourished as much, and probably more, had no European power taken any notice of her. The commerce by which she hath enriched herself are the necessities of life, and will always have a market while eating is the custom of Europe....

I challenge the warmest advocate of reconciliation to show a single advantage that this continent can reap by being connected with Great Britain. I repeat the challenge; not a single advantage is derived. Our corn will fetch its price in any market in Europe, and our imported goods must be paid for, buy them where we will.

As Europe is our market for trade, we ought to form no partial connection with any part of it. It is the true interest of America to steer clear of European contentions, which she never can do, while, by her dependence on Britain, she is made the makeweight in the scale of British politics.

Europe is too thickly planted with kingdoms to be long at peace, and whenever a war breaks out between England and any foreign power, the trade of America goes to ruin, *because of her connection with Britain....*

Wherefore, instead of gazing at each other with suspicious or doubtful curiosity, let each of us hold out to his neighbor the hearty hand of friendship.... Let the names of Whig and Tory be extinct; and let none other be heard among us, than those of *a good citizen; an open and resolute friend; and a virtuous supporter of the RIGHTS of MANKIND and of the FREE AND INDEPENDENT STATES OF AMERICA.*

FRENCH REASONS FOR AN ALLIANCE
WITH THE AMERICAN COLONIES   *Document 4*

Memorandum of the French Foreign Ministry, 13 January 1788.

The quarrel which exists between England and the Colonies of North America is as important to France as to Great Britain, and its issue will have equal influence on the reputation and power of those two Crowns. It is, therefore, essential that France should decide upon and fix the policy it is advisable she should adopt in such a conjuncture....

There exist two courses only,—that of abandoning the Colonies, and that of supporting them.

If we abandon them, England will take advantage of it by making a reconciliation, and in that case she will either preserve her supremacy wholly or partially, or she will gain an ally. Now it is known that she is disposed to sacrifice that supremacy and to propose simply a sort of family compact, that is to say, a league against the House of Bourbon.

The result of this will be that the Americans will become our perpetual enemies, and we must expect to see them turn all their efforts against our possessions, and against those of Spain. . . .

Thus the coalition of the English and the Americans will draw after it our expulsion, and probably that of the Spaniards, from the whole of America; it will limit our shipping and our commerce to the European seas only, and even this trade will be at the mercy of English insolence and greed. . . .

Such will be the effects of the independence of the United States of America, if it is established without our concurrence.

It follows from this that the glory, the dignity and the essential interest of France demand that she should stretch out her hand to those States, and that their independence should be her work.

The advantages which will result are innumerable; we shall humiliate our natural enemy, a perfidious enemy who never knows how to respect either treaties or the right of nations; we shall divert to our profit one of the principal sources of her opulence; we shall shake her power, and reduce her to her real value; we shall extend our commerce, our shipping, our fisheries; we shall ensure the possession of our islands, and finally, we shall re-establish our reputation, and shall resume amongst the Powers of Europe the place which belongs to us. There would be no end if we wished to detail all these points; it is sufficient to indicate them in order to make their importance felt.

In presupposing that the independence of the Americans is to be the work of France, it is necessary to examine what line of conduct it is desirable for us to observe in order to attain that end; there is but one,—to assist the Colonies.

But in order to determine the sort of assistance to be given, it is essential not to deviate from the two following truths: 1st, that whatever sort of assistance we give the Americans, it will be equivalent to a declaration of war against Great Britain: 2nd, that when war is inevitable, it is better to be beforehand with one's enemy than to be anticipated by him.

Starting with these two principles, it appears that France cannot be too quick in making with the Americans a treaty of which recognized independence will be the basis, and that she should take her measures for acting before England can anticipate her. . . .

In all that has just been said, the co-operation of Spain has been presupposed.

But in the event of that Power not adopting the principles and plan of France, or of her judging the moment of putting it into execution not yet arrived . . . France must undertake the war for the maintenance of American independence, even if that war should be in other respects disadvantageous. . . .

Thus France must espouse the American cause, and use for that purpose all her power, even if Spain should refuse to join her. . . .

TREATY OF ALLIANCE BETWEEN
FRANCE AND THE UNITED STATES   *Document 5*[1]

Ratified by the Continental Congress on May 4, 1778.

... *Article 1.* If War should break out between France and Great Britain, during the continuance of the present War between the United States and England, his Majesty and the said United States, shall make it a common cause, and aid each other mutually with their good Offices, their Counsels, and their forces, according to the exigence of Conjunctures as becomes good & faithful Allies.

Article 2. The essential and direct End of the present defensive alliance is to maintain effectually the liberty, Sovereignty, and independence absolute and unlimited of the said United States, as well in Matters of Government as of commerce . . . .

Article 5. If the United States should think fit to attempt the Reduction of the British Power remaining in the Northern Parts of America [Canada], or the Island of Bermudas, those Countries or Islands in case of Success, shall be confederated with or dependent upon the said United States.

Article 6. The Most Christian King renounces for ever the possession of the Islands of Bermudas as well as of any part of the continent of North America which before the Treaty of Paris in 1763, or in virtue of that Treaty, were acknowledged to belong to the Crown of Great Britain, or to the United States heretofore called British Colonies, or which are at this Time or have lately been under the Power of The King and Crown of Great Britain . . . .

Article 8. Neither of the two Parties shall conclude either Truce or Peace with Great Britain, without the formal consent of the other first obtain'd: and they mutually engage not to lay down their arms, until the Independence of the United States shall have been formally or tacitly assured by the Treaty or Treaties that shall terminate the War. . . .

Article 11. The two Parties guarantee mutually from the present time and forever, against all other powers, to wit, the United States to his most Christian Majesty the present Possessions of the Crown of France in America as well as those which it may acquire by the future Treaty of peace: and his most Christian Majesty guarantees on his part to the United States, their liberty, Sovereignty, and Independence absolute, and unlimited, as well in Matters of Government as commerce and also their Possessions, and the additions or conquests that their Confederation may obtain during the war. . . .

---

[1] *Spelling has been modernized.*

TREATY OF PEACE BETWEEN
THE UNITED STATES AND GREAT BRITAIN,
SEPTEMBER 3, 1783   *Document 6*

Article 1. His Britannic Majesty acknowledges the said United States, viz. New-Hampshire Massachusetts Bay, Rhode-Island, and Providence Plantations, Connecticut, New York, New Jersey, Pennsylvania, Delaware, Maryland, Virginia, North Carolina, South Carolina, & Georgia, to be free sovereign & Independent States; that he treats with them as such, and for himself his Heirs & Successors, relinquishes all Claims to the Government Propriety & Territorial Rights of the same & every Part thereof. . . .

Article 3. It is agreed that the people of the United States shall continue to enjoy unmolested the Right to take Fish of every kind on the Grand Bank and on all the other Banks of New-foundland, also in the Gulph of St. Lawrence, and at all other Places in the Sea where the Inhabitants of both Countries used at any time heretofore to fish. And also that the Inhabitants of the United States shall have Liberty to take Fish of every Kind on such Part of the Coast of New-foundland as British Fishermen shall use, (but not to dry or cure the same on that Island) And also on the Coasts Bays & Creeks of all other of His Britannic Majesty's Dominions in America, and that the American Fishermen shall have Liberty to dry and cure Fish in any of the unsettled Bays Harbours and Creeks of Nova Scotia, Magdalen Islands, and Labrador, so long as the same shall remain unsettled but so soon as the same or either of them shall be settled, it shall not be lawful for the said Fishermen to dry or cure Fish at such Settlements, without a previous Agreement for that purpose with the Inhabitants, Proprietors or Possessors of the Ground.

Article 4. It is agreed that Creditors on either Side shall meet with no lawful Impediment to the Recovery of the full Value in Sterling Money of all bona fide Debts heretofore contracted.

Article 5. It is agreed that the Congress shall earnestly recommend it to the Legislatures of the respective States to provide for the Restitution of all Estates, Rights and Properties which have been confiscated belonging to real British Subjects; and also of the Estates Rights and Properties of Persons resident in Districts in the Possession of his Majesty's Arms, and who have not borne Arms against the said United States. And that Persons of any other Description shall have free Liberty to go to any Part or Parts of any of the thirteen United States and therein to remain twelve Months unmolested in their Endeavours to obtain the Restitution of such of their Estates Rights & Properties as may have been confiscated, And that Congress shall also earnestly recommend to the several States, a Reconsideration and Revision of all Acts or laws regarding the Premises, so as to render the said Laws or Acts perfectly consistent, not only with Justice and Equity, but with that Spirit of Conciliation which, on the Return of the Blessings of Peace should universally prevail. And that Congress shall also earnestly recommend to the several States, that the Estates, Rights and Properties of such last mentioned Persons shall be restored to them, they refunding to any Persons who may be now in Possession, the Bona fide Price (where any has been given) which such Persons may have paid on purchasing any of the said Lands, Rights or Properties, since the Confiscation.

And it is agreed that all Persons who have any Interest in confiscated Lands, either by Debts, Marriage Settlements, or otherwise, shall meet with no lawful Impediment in the Prosecution of their just Rights.

Article 6. That there shall be no future Confiscations made nor any Prosecutions commenc'd against any Person or Persons for or by Reason of the Part, which he or they may have taken in the present War, and that no Person shall on that Account suffer any future Loss or Damage, either in his Person Liberty or Property; and that those who may be in Confinement on such Charges at the Time of the Ratification of the Treaty in America shall be immediately set at Liberty, and the Prosecutions so commenced be discontinued.

Article 7. There shall be a firm and perpetual Peace between his Britannic Majesty and said States and between the Subjects of the one, and the Citizens of the other, wherefore all Hostilities both by Sea and Land shall from henceforth cease: All Prisoners on both Sides shall be set at Liberty, and his Britannic Majesty shall with all convenient speed, and without causing any Destruction, or carrying away any Negroes or other Property of the American Inhabitants, withdraw all his Armies, Garrisons & Fleets from the said United States, and from every Port, Place and Harbour within the same; leaving in all Fortifications the American Artillery that may be therein: And shall also Order & cause all Archives, Records, Deeds & Papers belonging to any of the said States, or their Citizens, which in the Course of the War may have fallen into the Hands of his Officers, to be forthwith restored and deliver'd to the proper States and Persons to whom they belong.

Article 8. The Navigation of the River Mississippi, from its source to the Ocean shall for ever remain free and open to the Subjects of Great Britain and the Citizens of the United States. . . .

JEFFERSON REPORTS ON

AMERICAN COMMERCE, DECEMBER, 1793   *Document 7*

. . . Our navigation involves still higher considerations. As a branch of industry, it is valuable, but as a resource of defence, essential.

Its value, as a branch of industry, is enhanced by the dependence of so many other branches on it. In times of general peace, it multiplies competitors for employment in transportation, and so keeps that at its proper level; and in times of war, that is to say, when those nations who may be our principal carriers, shall be at war with each other, if we have not within ourselves the means of transportation, our produce must be exported in belligerent vessels, at the increased expense of war-freight and insurance, and the articles which will not bear that, must perish on our hands.

But it is as a resource of defence, that our navigation will admit neither neglect nor forbearance. The position and circumstances of the United States leave them nothing to fear on their land-board, and nothing to desire beyond their present rights. But on their sea-board, they are open to injury, and they have there, too, a commerce, which must be protected. This can only be done by possessing a respectable body of citizen-seamen, and of artists and establishments in readiness for ship-building. . . .

It is not to the moderation and justice of others we are to trust for fair and equal access to market with our productions, or for our due share in the transportation of them; but to our own means of independence, and the firm will to use them. . . .

WASHINGTON'S PROCLAMATION
OF NEUTRALITY, APRIL 22, 1793   *Document 8*

Whereas it appears that a state of war exists between Austria, Prussia, Sardinia, Great Britain, and the United Netherlands on the one part and France on the other, and the duty and interest of the United States require that they should with sincerity and good faith adopt and pursue a conduct friendly and impartial toward the belligerent powers:

I have therefore thought fit by these presents to declare the disposition of the United States to observe the conduct aforesaid toward those powers respectively, and to exhort and warn the citizens of the United States carefully to avoid all acts and proceeding whatsoever which may in any manner tend to contravene such disposition.

And I do hereby also make known that whosoever of the citizens of the United States shall render himself liable to punishment or forfeiture under the law of nations by committing, aiding, or abetting hostilities against any of the said powers, or by carrying to any of them those articles which are deemed contraband by the modern usage of nations [shall be punished by law] . . . .

WASHINGTON'S FAREWELL ADDRESS,
SEPTEMBER 17, 1796   *Document 9*

. . . Observe good faith and justice toward all nations. Cultivate peace and harmony with all. Religion and morality enjoin this conduct. And can it be that good policy does not equally enjoin it? . . .

In the execution of such a plan nothing is more essential than that permanent, inveterate antipathies against particular nations and passionate attachments for others should be excluded, and that in place of them just and amicable feelings toward all should be cultivated. The nation which indulges toward another an habitual hatred or an habitual fondness is in some degree a slave. It is a slave to its animosity or to its affection, either of which is sufficient to lead it astray from its duty and its interest. Antipathy in one nation against another disposes each more readily to offer insult and injury, to lay hold of slight causes of umbrage, and to be haughty and intractable when accidental or trifling occasions of dispute occur.

Hence frequent collisions, obstinate, envenomed, and bloody contests. The nation prompted by ill will and resentment sometimes impels to war the government contrary to the best calculations of policy. The government sometimes participates in the national propensity, and adopts through passion what reason would reject. At other times it makes the animosity of the nation subservient to projects of hostility, instigated by pride, ambition, and other sinister and pernicious motives. The peace often, sometimes perhaps the liberty, of nations has been the victim.

So, likewise, a passionate attachment of one nation for another produces a variety of evils. Sympathy for the favorite nation, facilitating the illusion of an imaginary common interest in cases where no real common interest exists, and infusing into one the enmities of the other, betrays the former into a participation in the quarrels and wars of the latter without adequate inducement or justification. It leads also to concessions to the favorite nation of privileges denied to others, which is apt doubly to injure the nation making the concessions by unnecessarily parting with what ought to have been retained, and by exciting jealousy, ill will, and a disposition to retaliate in the parties from whom equal privileges are withheld. . . .

Excessive partiality for one foreign nation and excessive dislike of another cause those whom they actuate to see danger only on one side, and serve to veil and even second the arts of influence on the other. Real patriots who may resist the intrigues of the favorite are liable to become suspected and odious, while its tools and dupes usurp the applause and confidence of the people to surrender their interests.

The great rule of conduct for us in regard to foreign nations is, in extending our commercial relations to have with them as little *political* connection as possible. So far as we have already formed engagements let them be fulfilled with perfect good faith. Here let us stop.

Europe has a set of primary interests which to us have none or a very remote relation. Hence she must be engaged in frequent controversies, the causes of which are essentially foreign to our concerns. Hence, therefore, it must be unwise in us to implicate ourselves by artificial ties in the ordinary vicissitudes of her politics or the ordinary combinations and collisions of her friendships or enmities.

Our detached and distant situation invites and enables us to pursue a different course. If we remain one people, under an efficient government, the period is not far off when we may defy material injury from external annoyance; when we may take such an attitude as will cause the neutrality we may at any time resolve upon to be scrupulously respected; when belligerent nations, under the impossibility of making acquisitions upon us, will not lightly hazard the giving us provocation; when we may choose peace or war, as our interest, guided by justice, shall counsel.

Why forego the advantages of so peculiar a situation? Why quit our own to stand upon foreign ground? Why, by interweaving our destiny with that of any part of Europe, entangle our peace and prosperity in the toils of European ambition, rivalship, interest, humor, of caprice?

It is our true policy to steer clear of permanent alliances with any portion of the foreign world, so far, I mean, as we are now at liberty to do it. . . .

Taking care always to keep ourselves by suitable establishments on a respectable defensive posture, we may safely trust to temporary alliances for extraordinary emergencies. . . .

There can be no greater error than to expect or calculate upon real favors from nation to nation. It is an illusion which experience must cure, which a just pride ought to discard. . . .

PRESIDENT ADAMS INSTRUCTS THE AMERICAN COMMISSION TO FRANCE, OCTOBER, 1799

Document 10

. . . The following points are to be considered as ultimated:

1. That an article be inserted for establishing a board, with suitable powers, to hear and determine the claims of our citizens, for the causes herein before expressed, and binding France to pay or secure payment of the sums which shall be awarded.

2. That the treaties and consular convention, declared to be no longer obligatory by act of Congress, be not in whole or in part revived by the new treaty; but that all the engagements, to which the United States are to become parties, be specified in the new treaty.

3. That no guaranty of the whole or any part of the dominions of France be stipulated, nor any engagement made, in the nature of an alliance.[1]

4. That no aid or loan be promised in any form whatever.

5. That no engagement be made inconsistent with the obligations of any prior treaty; and, as it may respect our treaty with Great Britain, the instruction herein marked XXI[2] is to be particularly observed. . . .

---

[1] The Treaty of Alliance with France of May 4, 1778 (Document 5 above) was abrogated by the Convention of Peace, Commerce and Navigation signed by France and the United States on September 30, 1800.—Editor.

[2] By the Treaty of 1794 with Great Britain, the United States had given way before British demands for unlimited rights of search and seizure. Instruction XXI reminds the commissioners of that fact.—Editor.

JEFFERSON'S FIRST INAUGURAL ADDRESS,
MARCH 4, 1801   *Document 11*

... We are all Republicans, we are all Federalists. If there be any among us who would wish to dissolve this Union or to change its republican form, let them stand undisturbed as monuments of the saftey with which error of opinion may be tolerated where reason is left free to combat it....

Let us, then, with courage and confidence pursue our own Federal and Republican principles, our attachment to union and representative government. Kindly separated by nature and a wide ocean from the exterminating havoc of one quarter of the globe; too high-minded to endure the degradations of the others; possessing a chosen country, with room enough for our descendants to the thousandth and thousandth generation; entertaining a due sense of our equal right to the use of our own faculties, to the acquisitions of our own industry, to honor and confidence from our fellow-citizens, resulting not from birth, but from our actions and their sense of them; enlightened by a benign religion, professed, indeed, and practiced in various forms, yet all of them inculcating honesty, truth, temperance, gratitude, and the love of man ... with all these blessings, what more is necessary to make us a happy and a prosperous people? ...

About to enter, fellow-citizens, on the exercise of duties which comprehend everything dear and valuable to you, it is proper you should understand what I deem the essential principles of our Government.... I will compress them within the narrowest compass they will bear.... Equal and exact justice to all men, of whatever state or persuasion, religious or political; peace, commerce, and honest friendship with all nations, entangling alliances with none ... a jealous care of the right of election by the people— a mild and safe corrective of abuses which are lopped by the sword of revolution where peaceable remedies are unprovided ... a well-disciplined militia, our best reliance in peace and for the first moments of war ... the supremacy of the civil over the military authority....

THE

COUNTING HOUSE

VERSUS

THE FARM

CHAPTER 2

The First Great Debate

*J*efferson *and Hamilton (and most of their followers) agreed on the necessity of keeping out of European wars, and to this extent both the Jeffersonians and the Federalists adhered to what nowadays would be called a "bipartisan" foreign policy. But they disagreed on the question of what was to be done once the United States had achieved the necessary minimum of national security. Thus the newly developing political parties struggled for the control of foreign as well as domestic policy.*

These parties arose as a result of a division between landed and commercial interests, and as a result of philosophical differences grounded in their respective life styles. The Jeffersonians—or Republicans (ancestors of the modern Democrats)—depended primarily upon the planter aristocrats for leadership and upon the small farmers for votes. As successors to the revolutionary radicals, the Jeffersonians also attracted many of the day laborers, artisans, and small shopkeepers in the growing towns and cities. As early advocates of territorial expansion, they also won over some of the more important urban businessmen who profited from transactions in land or the products of the soil.

In the first years after the Revolution, however, the Federalists—friends of England, of foreign trade, and of a strong central government—succeeded in framing the Constitution and getting it adopted, and at first they dominated the new government. The men of the agricultural interests, preoccupied with their farms and with local and state affairs, were late in organizing a party. In the 1790's they formed in opposition to Hamilton's economic program—a national bank, a large national debt, an excise tax (falling on farmers), and the Federalist policy of appeasing England, as symbolized by Jay's Treaty. For many years, until Jefferson's election to the Presidency in 1800, they could not control foreign policy but they could exercise some influence on important issues.

Professor Samuel Flagg Bemis tells the story of an early veto in his selection on the negotiations between Spain and the United States over the Mississippi region in the 1780's. John Jay, a pro-British spokesman for the business and professional population, seemed willing to sacrifice the West for the benefit of the East, but was prevented from doing so by the power of the landed interest in the Congress. Document 1, consisting of excerpts from the Articles of Confederation, reveals the concern of the landed interest for expansion, especially in the provision for admitting Canada to the United States. The lack of a strong department of foreign affairs also reveals the indifference of these men to early militant overseas activity, and their confidence that the state governments could deal effectively with the issues of land and trade.

In Document 2, an exchange of letters between George Washington and John Jay, the conservative fear of radical control of local governments is very clearly shown. But while these two leaders were fellow conservatives who shared a desire to overthrow the Articles of Confederation, Jay, as a representative of the commercial community, did not quite see eye to eye with Washington, a planter. Thus when these two men and their sympathizers sat down to the job of organizing a new government and spelling out its powers and prerogatives in a written document which became the Constitution, they immediately began to disagree. Professor R. Earl McClendon explains how this conflict between landed and commercial conservatives was compromised by the provision requiring a two-thirds majority in the Senate for the ratification of treaties. Each interest group was given a veto over any extreme proposal advanced by the other.

After reading McClendon's article it is wise to turn to Document 3, selections from the debates over this issue, to see how directly and frankly it was discussed. There, too, one can see the South's early concern over the slave trade. Perhaps the commercial interests sought to offset this two-thirds rule by strengthening the powers of the president. In any event, Hamilton was a vigorous proponent of centering great authority in the chief executive, as can be seen in the selections from the Federalist *Papers (Document 4). The powers of the president (Document 5) became very important in later generations when the president began to sign executive agreements, over which Congress had little control, and to handle foreign affairs through executive agents, whose appointment did not have to be approved by the Senate.*

A boom in exports followed the adoption of the Constitution, but it is difficult to say whether the Constitution was directly responsible. Some recovery from the postwar depression was already under way when the conservatives prevailed in their efforts to destroy the Articles of Confederation. Their victory no doubt gave them a psychological lift, which may have unfrozen more money, credit, and ideas for making profits than did the provisions of the Constitution itself. Whatever the cause, G. G. Huebner outlines the growth of this export trade in the third reading selection.

By the uses they made of the powers granted to the national government, the Federalists soon began to irritate the Jeffersonians. They especially outraged them by the treaty they negotiated with Great Britain in 1794. Frontiersmen disliked the treaty, in particular the idea of giving the British more commercial rights on the Mississippi; they were already having enough trouble with Englishmen who were making friends with the Indians and poaching furs on territory claimed by the westerners. Also, as farmers, they were afraid their westward expansion would be limited by a coalition between the Spanish in New Orleans and the English in Canada.

Not all Federalists approved the treaty either. Some shippers disliked the limits set by the British definition of freedom of the seas even more than they valued the indirect protection they gained from the Royal Navy when they conformed to the English laws. Conservative planters who had followed Washington into the Federalist camp were also upset. Jay's Treaty held them accountable for their old debts to London merchants without exacting any compensation for slaves who had been freed by the British during the Revolutionary War. Vehement protests were made against the treaty, as shown in Frank Monaghan's story of "The Damnation of Mr. Jay." In perspective, the reaction to Jay's Treaty can be interpreted as the turning point in the rise of an organized opposition to Federalist foreign policy.

Professor Charles A. Beard reviews the philosophy which led Jefferson to favor territorial expansion and outlines the main features of early action along this line in his sketch of "Jeffersonian Foreign Policy." Jefferson found an opportunity in Napoleon's difficulties. Earlier he had gone along with the Federalists on the neutrality issue, partly because he feared that one of the belligerents would establish itself in a strong position at the mouth of the Mississippi if America supported the other side. Here was a double danger: New Orleans under a strong power would be a barrier against future expansion, and also it might serve as a base for outright attack on the United States. Jefferson also had domestic political considerations behind his interest in the area. By getting full control of the Mississippi he could satisfy an insistent demand of his western followers, who wanted the river opened up as a cheap thoroughfare for their agricultural surpluses going to eastern and overseas markets. Thus for many years to come he could expect votes for his party from the settlers who moved into the new land.

For these reasons Jefferson was interested in buying the Spanish claims to the trans-Mississippi West long before Napoleon secretly acquired the property from Spain. His concern can be seen in his letter to Robert Livingston of April 18, 1802 (Document 6). He was already in the market when Napoleon offered the land for sale. Some Federalists fought his purchase of the Louisiana Territory. They used constitutional arguments against it, but their real objection was that it would increase the political influence of the West and decrease the force behind a foreign policy favorable to commerce. Document 7 provides a sample of the congressional debate over the question. On the other hand, there were some Federalists who realized that the development of such a huge area would give them plenty of opportunities to trade, invest, and speculate. Along with Jefferson, these men glimpsed the great significance of the bargain, a subject which is developed by Professor Frederick Jackson Turner in the seventh reading selection. Jefferson had moved to penetrate and control the area even before the deal with France was completed (Document 8).

But the foreign policy problems of the United States were not solved by this real estate transaction. Napoleon sold the land the better to war on Britain, and these two contestants grew less and less mindful of the rights of neutrals the longer they fought one another. Both sides clamped down on foreign shipping and trade with the other (Document 9). Having spent over 15 million dollars to avoid one possible source of war, Jefferson had little inclination to find other grounds for war in these violations of America's maritime rights, a war which would have been waged primarily for the commercial interests. Jefferson was willing, though not eager, to undertake small-scale battles for the traders—he sent a squadron to harass the Barbary pirates—but he did not relish a big war in their behalf. And even when dealing with the pirates he preferred to spend money rather than lives. In the case of British and French actions against American shipping, he was willing to risk an economic depression at home rather than use force in his efforts to induce the European belligerents to honor the rights of neutrals.

Jefferson's idea, which had been used effectively before the Revolution, was predicated upon the importance of American shipping and exports: cut off all commerce with the belligerents and thus force Britain and France to respect America's right to trade with all nations (Documents 10 and 11). The policy demanded a kind of patience that the President's agricultural followers—as well as Federalist traders and shippers—did not have. The planters and freehold farmers needed markets for their surplus production. Jefferson managed to resist their rising criticism until he left office in 1809, but the growing demand from the agricultural businessmen for markets and land rapidly created intense pressure for commercial and territorial expansion, which incoming President James Madison understood, and with which he broadly agreed. Under his leadership, the great majority of Americans united behind a program—and an ideology—of imperial expansion.

CONGRESS AND THE WESTERN LANDS[1]

Samuel Flagg Bemis

... Gardoqui presented himself at New York, where he found Congress in session, in July, 1785. He bought a commission empowering him, as *encargado de negocios* plenipotentiary, to treat with a properly authorized person for a settlement of commercial intercourse and boundaries between the two countries, and in regard to other points "conducive to the enjoyment of

---

[1] Selected from *Pinckney's Treaty: A Study of America's Advantage from Europe's Distress, 1783–1800*, 2d ed. (Baltimore: Johns Hopkins Press, 1941), pp. 78–102. Reprinted with permission.

these important and beneficial objects." This full power did not permit him to yield the navigation of the Mississippi. Congress received him ceremoniously. It commissioned John Jay, Secretary for Foreign Affairs, to treat with him on the subjects covered by his full powers. Jay was specifically enjoined in any treaty to stipulate the right of the United States "to their territorial bounds and the free navigation of the Mississippi, from the source to the ocean as established in the treaties with Great Britain," and not to conclude anything until he had previously communicated it to Congress and received the approbation of that body. . . .

From the first the Spanish envoy was impressed with the difficulty of securing the consent of Congress to any exclusion from the Mississippi. If the matter rested with Jay alone, he believed that a settlement between Spain and the United States would be easy. Gardoqui's expense accounts have numerous items for entertainment of the Jays as well as influential members of Congress. Mrs. Jay he cultivated from the first. Within a few months after he arrived at New York he felt at home in Jay's house. Jay asked him for a license to import from Spain a Spanish stallion. Gardoqui promptly responded with the gift outright of a splendid animal sent by Carlos III himself, and Jay secured permission from Congress to accept the gift. But the majority of the state delegations in Congress were then set against conceding the Mississippi, and Gardoqui soon realized that back of Jay's genial friendship there stood a wall of public opinion which the secretary dared not openly oppose. That opinion supported the new West. . . .

The negotiators . . . agreed, after several confidential conferences, on heads for a proposed treaty covering points other than the still unsettled issues of the Mississippi Question and the boundary. These included a treaty of commerce and alliance for thirty years, in which Spain accepted commercial reciprocity between the United States and the peninsular domains of the Kingdom as well as the Canary Islands, the merchants of each party to be given the treatment of nationals within the domains of the other in matters of duties. It included reciprocal permission to introduce all the *bona fide* manufactures and products of either party (except tobacco) into the (stipulated) domain of the other, with tariffs to be based on principle of reciprocity according to a scale to be worked out in a separate convention. Each party was to guarantee the other's territory in America as it should be determined by the treaty, against attack by a third party. . . . Finally Spain agreed to mediate between the United States and Great Britain for the recovery of the American posts on the northern frontier, and "will see that they get justice, by force of arms if otherwise it cannot be promptly secured."

Such were the contingent articles to which Jay agreed, and which Gardoqui recommended to his court for acceptance provided the United States would relinquish specifically its claims to the navigation of the Mississippi, and make some compromise in regard to the Florida boundary. It was a notable proposal for an entangling alliance. The article of mutual guaranty specifically stated that neither party, in case of an attack on their dominions in America by a third power, should make peace until the territory of the other, attacked and invaded, should be restored. Spain still denied the one great object for which the West pleaded, while these initialed articles bound the United States to fight for the restoration of any portion of the far-flung colonial domains of the Spanish Empire in North and South America, and set up at the same time a self-denying ordinance against any future expansion at the expense of contiguous Spanish territory. This obviously was the chief value of the arrangement to Spain. The commercial articles were carefully designed to offer powerful inducements to the commerce of the eastern states, and when made public the articles further would have displayed to the country at large a possible means of expelling British garrisons from the northern posts.

Let us now see how the Continental Congress received these articles insofar as they were revealed to it. . . .

The opportune time to present the subject came in May, 1786, when Congress had finally reached a quorum and assembled in full. On the 23rd of that month Gardoqui, with little hope that it would have much effect on Congress, drew up a note to Jay, summarizing the case for Spain. Jay was asked to inform Congress that "the King will not permit any nation to navigate between the two banks belonging to His Majesty, from the extent of his conquests made by his royal arms over the English in East and West Florida, according to the dominion formerly held by the English and the jurisdiction exercised by the commandant of Pensacola, on which it depended, *as well as the countries to the East of the Mississippi, of which formal possession was taken by Captain Don Baltazar de Villers,* commandant of the post at Arkansas, for his Majesty on the 22nd of November, 1780." Having laid down this condition, Gardoqui elaborated the advantages which the United States had already enjoyed because of the "good and generous disposition" of the King; fruitful intercession with the Barbary States, and forbearance to request till now the payment of the principal of the debts contracted by the United States both in Spain and her colonies during the Revolution, not to mention interest thereon. By not yielding the navigation of the river, the United States would run the risk of losing the trade with Spain, the only commerce which brought to America a cash balance. That trade depended on the good will of the Spanish King, whose subjects stood in no necessity of getting their fish, grain, flour and rice from America, nor anything else; a royal regulation could easily exclude them without loss to Spain, particularly when that nation had no appreciable market in the United States. In consideration that nothing be said of the difficulties of navigation and boundaries, and without alluding to the details of his arrangement with Jay, the Spanish agent stated that he believed that His Majesty would consent to guarantee to the United States their rights and dominions as they should be left by the treaty, and he further promised to pray the King "that the satisfaction of the debts due from the United States to Spain may be with such relaxation as may be convenient to them."

If there was little hope that Congress would yield on the point of the Mississippi and repeal the instructions which limited the American negotiator, Jay had already conceived a means of circumventing those limitations. In the spring of 1786 he explained to James Monroe, then a Virginia delegate in Congress, the status of the negotiation, without mentioning the feature of the proposed alliance. He emphasized the unyielding Spanish position on the Mississippi Question. He suggested that the United States, without giving up principle, might *forbear* to use the river within exclusively Spanish limits during the term of the treaty—twenty-five or thirty years. Monroe listened without comment as Jay explained that such a proposal would probably not be acceptable to Congress if presented. He therefore wished Congress to appoint a committee to control him in the negotiation, in lieu of his former instructions. Monroe ended the conversation by significantly reminding Jay that Virginia had specifically instructed her delegates in such a way as to make impossible any such maneuver.

Jay made the same proposal to Congress May 29, 1786, following the receipt of Gardoqui's memoir of the 23rd.

The communication from the Secretary for Foreign Affairs immediately precipitated the most serious issue that agitated the Continental Congress during its five years of peace-time history. A debate followed, behind closed doors, which united the southern states as a block in resistance to the equally undivided position of the seven states from north of Mason and Dixon's line. Could seven states—a bare majority of the thirteen—repeal diplomatic instructions when a vote of nine was necessary to ratify any treaty? The seven northern states, in favor of accepting the Spanish offer, declared yes. The five southern members of the Confederation (Delaware being absent) denied it. Previously warned by Jay's imprudent approach to Monroe, they were horrified at the idea of bartering away the navigation of their great river for commercial privileges for the benefit of the eastern states which were already jealous of the rising population of the West and apprehensive of a shift of the future center of political gravity away from New England and New York.[2] . . .

The southern states held their vast appanages of land on the western waters. They were inhabited by rapidly increasing thousands of settlers who were impelled by the atmosphere of frontier conditions to seek redress of grievances through direct action and to be impatient of control from remote seats of authority. To states with such constituencies the Jay proposal appeared rank political heresy. This strong sectional minority, more than enough to block any two-thirds vote, rallied feverishly to the defense of the Mississippi. . . .

The Mississippi Question monopolized the attention of Congress throughout the whole summer of 1786 and finally ended with a strictly sectional vote of seven to five in favor of repealing Jay's original instructions. The five minority delegations maintained that this was unconstitutional and let it

[2] Author's note.—Rufus King, delegate from Massachusetts, wrote to Jonathan Jackson, a former delegate from that state, a long letter, September 3, 1786, arguing in favor of the proposed treaty: "If, therefore, our disputes with Spain are not settled, we shall be obliged wholly *to give up* the Western Settlers or join *them* in an issue of Force with the Catholic King: the latter we are in no condition to think of, the former would be impolitic for many reasons, and cannot with safety be *now* admitted, although very few men who have examined the subject will refuse their assent to the opinion that every citizen of the Atlantic States, who emigrates to the westward by the Allegheny is a total loss to our Confederacy.

"Nature has separated the two countries by a vast and extensive chain of mountains, interest and convenience will keep them separate, and the feeble policy of our disjointed Government will not be able to unite them. For this reason I have ever been opposed to encouragements of western emigrants." *Massachusetts Historical Society Proceedings,* November, 1915 (italics added).

be understood by both Jay and Gardoqui and by Congress that they would never ratify any treaty signed under the instructions thus amended without the concurring vote of nine states. The staunch attitude of the southern states saved the Mississippi but at the expense of a serious constitutional issue. The movement for the Philadelphia Convention was already under way and the question whether a bare majority of states could sanction a treaty cast an ominous shadow over the approaching deliberations for a more perfect union. The southern states, alarmed by the determination of their western constituents and the depreciating effect which such a treaty as that proposed by Jay would have on their backlands, began to suspect the movement for a new constitution as simply another means by which the eastern anti-Mississippi men meant to lift Jay's instructions. Monroe even smelled a plot of Jay's supporters to force the issue with the South in order to split the Union into two confederacies.

THE ORIGIN OF THE TWO-THIRDS RULE
IN SENATE ACTION
UPON TREATIES[1]   *R. Earl McClendon*

That portion of the Constitution of the United States which relates to treaty making is found in Article II, section 2, clause 2, and, as is well known, reads as follows: "He [the President] shall have Power, by and with the Advice and Consent of the Senate, to make Treaties, provided two-thirds of the Senators present concur...." Few provisions of the Constitution have been criticized more than that which requires the affirmative vote of two-thirds of the members present to give the advice and consent of the Senate to the ratification on the part of the United States of treaties which previously have been negotiated....

In their attacks the critics of the two-thirds rule have taken the occasion to point out that its insertion in the Constitution was largely the result of the precedent which had been established for the approval of treaties, the generally prevailing fear of executive power, and the mutually existing suspicions and jealousies among the individual states. Unquestionably, this general theory is sound. Nevertheless, as has been largely overlooked, the delegates to the Federal Convention acted also from definitely practical considerations when they drew up the treaty-making clause. This paper is an attempt to show that any purely theoretical reasons which may have influenced the adoption of the two-thirds rule were supported by at least two specific aims: the retention of the right to navigate the Mississippi River and the protection of the Newfoundland fisheries.

...Long before the close of the American Revolution the colonists had evinced considerable interest in retaining for themselves after the war was over, their fishing privileges in Newfoundland waters and the right of navi-

---

[1] *The American Historical Review*, XXXVI, No. 4 (July, 1931), 768–72. Reprinted with permission.

gating the Mississippi. The Continental Congress in 1779 . . . had included these two conditions among the terms upon which it would consent to make peace. Although the colonists later receded from this extreme stand, the treaty which made them politically independent of Great Britain did permit the navigation of the Mississippi and gave them the liberty of fishing off the Banks of Newfoundland together with numerous in-shore fishing privileges.

These rights thus obtained, however, were none too secure. That was particularly true with regard to the Mississippi, for Spain at once denied to the United States the right to navigate that important stream. Even though the United States never accepted Spain's contention, Congress in 1786 . . . upon a vote of seven Northern states against five Southern, agreed to permit John Jay, the Secretary for Foreign Affairs, to draw up an agreement whereby American rights to the Mississippi should be relinquished for a period of twenty-five years. This arrangement was not concluded; yet when the Federal Convention met the following year the fact that seven states had indicated their willingness to forego for even a comparatively short period the right of navigating the Mississippi was still fresh in the minds of the Southern delegates. They naturally were more interested in this question, while the Northern members were concerned with that of the fisheries. Each section feared that its own particular interest in these two cases might be sacrificed by the treaty method if a mere majority of the senators should be allowed to approve treaties.

The Convention had been in session almost three months when its attention was turned to the question of treaty making. Technically, the clause originated in the Committee of Detail which made its report on August 6. That part embodying the two-thirds rule, however, was not suggested until September 4, when the Committee of Eleven recommended that the President, with the advice and consent of the Senate, should have power to make treaties, but that no treaty should be made "without the consent of two thirds of the Members present."

Three days later James Madison moved to amend this part of the report by excepting treaties of peace from the two-thirds requirement. Elbridge Gerry, of Massachusetts, objected. It was his opinion that in the case of peace treaties a greater rather than a smaller proportion of votes was necessary. He gave his reasons as follows:

In Treaties of peace the dearest interests will be at stake, as the fisheries, territories &c. In treaties of peace also there is more danger to the extremities of the Continent, of being sacrificed, than on any other occasions.

Madison's amendment was accepted; yet just prior to adjournment for the day Hugh Williamson and Richard Spaight, delegates from North Carolina, moved that at least no peace treaty which affected territorial rights should be made except upon a two-thirds vote of the Senate. Rufus King, of Massachusetts, moved to extend this latter motion to include "all present rights of the U. States." No action was taken on these two amendments. On the following day, however, King was successful in having rescinded the original amendment excepting treaties of peace from the two-thirds vote of the Senate. Gouverneur Morris, although opposing King's motion at the time, voiced the opinion of the majority of the delegates when he spoke of the "Fisheries" and the "Mississippi" as the "two great objects of the Union." After deciding not to exclude peace treaties from the operation of the two-thirds requirement the Convention accepted the treaty-making clause in the exact form as reported by the Committee of Eleven. The Committee on Style later recommended the phraseology in which it is still embodied in the Constitution.

These few brief references to the proceedings in the Convention show to a considerable degree the concern felt for the Mississippi and the fisheries in connection with treaty making. Some events transpiring between the time when the meeting at Philadelphia was concluded and that when the Constitution was ratified, however, furnished further, and probably more conclusive, evidence upon the effect which these questions had upon the two-thirds rule....

The opposition to the Constitution in North Carolina, South Carolina, and Virginia was due in part to the alleged fear that the new government would give up the right to navigate the Mississippi. Writing to Madison in October, 1787, relative to this current opinion, George Washington said in part:

If the subject of the navigation of the Mississippi could have remained as silent, and glided as gently down the stream of time for a while, as the waters do that are contained within the banks, it would, I confess, have comported more with my ideas of sound policy, than any decision that can be come to at this day.

Addressing Henry Knox in March of the following year, Washington stated that in the southern part of Virginia opponents of the Constitution were spreading the belief that the new government "will, without scruple or delay, barter away their rights to navigation of the Mississippi." A resident of the "Western Country" wrote to Thomas Jefferson in August, 1788, that if Kentucky assumed its independence it probably would not ask for admission into the Union, for, as he stated, its inhabitants were

... opposed to the new Constitution apprehending much inconvenience & danger from the Judicial System & fearing that the Powers vested in the General Government may enable [it] to carry into effect the proposed Treaty with Spain relative to the Navigation of the Mississippi.

This general feeling was carried over into the ratifying conventions in the three states mentioned. There the opponents of the proposed new government argued, curiously enough, that under this system, with the representatives of the Southern states absent from the Senate, the senators from five Northern states could give the Senate's approval to a treaty giving up the Mississippi. This rather illogical argument was answered by statements to the effect that it could not be expected that a sufficient number of Southern senators would be absent to permit the Northern members to take this action, when such a momentous question was up for consideration. In other words, one of the main arguments made by those in favor of the Constitution—including several who had helped to frame it—was the assertion that under the system of government being proposed it would be practically impossible by the treaty method to barter away the rights to the Mississippi River. Hugh Williamson, who has been mentioned as a delegate to the Federal Convention from North Carolina, in a letter written to Madison on June 22, 1788, made the positive assertion that the two-thirds rule was inserted in the Constitution to prevent a majority of the Senate from giving up the Mississippi. His letter, in part, was as follows:

Your Recollection must certainly enable you to say that there is a Proviso in the new System which was inserted for the express purpose of preventing a majority of the Senate or of the States which is considered as the same thing from giving up the Mississippi. It is provided that two thirds of the Members present in the senate shall be required to concur in making Treaties and if the southern states attend to their Duty, this will imply 2/3. of the States in the Union together with the President, a security rather better than the present. . . .

No doubt the question of the Mississippi was a more vital one in 1787 than that of the fisheries; but to a large extent the one balanced the other. Although arguing against the Constitution at the time, William Grayson brought out this point before the Virginia convention on June 13, 1788, when he said:

It is well known that the Newfoundland fisheries and the Mississippi are balances for one another; that the possession of one tends to the preservation of the other. This accounts for the eastern policy [during the period of the American Revolution]. They thought that, if the Mississippi was given up, the Southern States would give up the right of the fishery, on which their very existence depends. . . .

And, finally, George Mason, a member of the Constitutional Convention, emphasized the connection between the two and their collective effect upon the adoption of the two-thirds rule when addressing the Virginia convention on June 21. Although feeling that under the proposed Constitution the Southern states would not be fully protected in such matters as commerce, navigation, and territories, he said:

The Newfoundland fisheries will require that kind of security which we are now in want of. The Eastern States therefore agreed, at length, that treaties should require the consent of two thirds of the members present in the Senate.

REASONS FOR THE EARLY GROWTH
OF AMERICAN EXPORT TRADE[1]
G. G. Huebner

There were several reasons for the sudden change from the commercial depression of the years immediately following 1785 to the animated export trade which arose after 1789.

The adoption of the Federal Constitution in 1789 was an event of the highest commercial significance; it meant that the loose confederation was

---

[1] Selected from *History of Domestic and Foreign Commerce of the United States* (Washington: Carnegie Institution, 1922), pp. 15–19. Reprinted with permission.

replaced by a real Federal Government. American ministers abroad had repeatedly found that foreign nations were "sensible of the weakness and inefficiency of the American Confederacy" and therefore refused to enter into commercial treaties or even to treat American merchants and ship-owners with the fairness accorded to those of other countries. John Jay, the American agent to England in 1785, referred to the situation as follows:

This being the state of things, you may depend upon it, the commerce of America will have no relief at present nor, in my opinion, ever, until the United States shall have generally passed navigation acts. If these measures are not adopted, we shall be derided, and the more we suffer, the more will our calamities be laughed at.

* * *

By giving to the Federal Government the exclusive control over the "commerce with foreign nations, and among the several States, and with the Indian tribes," the Constitution laid the basis for removing the great political and governmental obstacles to prosperity in the foreign trade. Articles of commerce could thereafter move freely from one State to another and reach the ports of export without hindrance. The diverse system of import duties and navigation charges and regulations imposed by the individual States was replaced by a uniform national policy. The first Congress which met under the new form of government enacted a tariff and navigation act designed to promote foreign trade and ocean navigation. For the encouragement and promotion of the American deep-sea carrying trade, the act of July 1789 granted a 10 percent discount from the duties on all goods imported in American vessels, and the same law reduced the duties on tea imported from India and China in American vessels as compared with the duties on tea imported from Europe or in foreign vessels, so as to build up the direct trade between the United States and the Orient. Though slightly changed from time to time, this act extending aid to Oriental commerce and protection to the American merchant marine was in force throughout the entire quarter century from 1789 to 1815, and ... its effects upon the foreign trade and the American merchant fleet were highly beneficial. In 1804 Congress further extended the policy of shipping protection by levying a "light money" tonnage duty of 50 cents per ton on foreign vessels.

After the adoption of the Federal Constitution, moreover, foreign nations could no longer scorn requests for commercial treaties and trade arrangements. The trade with Great Britain had since 1783 been carried on according to the Orders in Council authorized by the Parliamentary act of April 1783, no commercial treaty being concluded until November 1794. . . . In 1795 the Federal Government negotiated with Spain a treaty which granted the right of free navigation of the Mississippi River to the people of the United States. A treaty of commerce and navigation was concluded with France in September 1800, as were also a secret treaty concerning Louisiana in October 1800 and the Louisiana cession treaty, which in April 1803 finally solved the problem of the free navigation of the Mississippi River. A commercial treaty was concluded with Prussia in July 1799; and in 1795, 1796, and 1805, after much negotiation and some naval warfare, treaties of commerce, peace, and amity were entered into with Tripoli and Algiers, the piratical African Barbary States.

The adoption of the Constitution, which enabled Congress to promote American trade and navigation by legislation, was followed by the gradual acquisition of a navy to protect the merchant and ship-owner against foreign enemies. The few armed vessels which were the property of the United States Government at the end of the Revolutionary War had been sold by order of Congress. The depredations on American commerce by the Barbary pirates, which had been made during the period of the Confederation, greatly increased after 1793, when Portugal, under a truce with the regency of Algiers, withdrew the squadron of warships which had occupied the Straits of Gibraltar. The attacks on American merchant ships, which had practically no men-of-war to protect them, became so serious that Congress authorized the construction of a small fleet. The unusually violent attacks of the Barbary pirates in 1801 caused the United States to deal swift and vigorous punishment. By 1805 the American naval forces had compelled all of the Barbary powers to agree to cease their depredations on American merchant vessels.

The building of a war fleet was also hastened by the hostile attitude of France and Great Britain, whose naval vessels at various times during the European wars seized American merchant ships on the pretext that they violated the then indefinite and flexible laws of neutrality. During 1799 and 1800 several American warships were used effectively in a brief naval war with France. The prompt and vigorous measures of the newly established government in defense of its commercial rights soon compelled France to seek peace, and at the same time instilled in other foreign nations an increased respect for the American flag....

The adoption of the Constitution and the inauguration of the policy of aid and protection by the Federal Government were accompanied by other economic influences which were responsible for much of the immediate growth in foreign commerce. Foremost among these were the extended European wars, which began in 1793, shortly after the outbreak of the French Revolution, and were not finally concluded until 1814. At first these wars concerned chiefly Great Britain and France, but gradually nearly all the nations of the Old World were drawn into the controversy. What was all but commercial death to the European merchant and ship-owner meant profit to the American, for the wars cut off the usual channels of European trade so effectively that to obtain many of their customary imports the warring nations were obliged to turn to the United States, a neutral power. When the European wars were at their height American shipping was prosperous; when in 1802 and 1803 there was a brief period of peace, it suffered an immediate decline; when the wars were renewed, prosperity returned for a time, until after 1807, when Napoleon Bonaparte, refusing to recognize that there were any neutrals, inflicted his "continental policy" upon the commercial world, and England enforced her Orders in Council with men-of-war. Under the burdensome restrictions imposed by the commercial policies of France and Great Britain, American vessels and American trade suffered almost as severely as those of European neutral countries. When neutrality was denied exports carried in American ships, the highly profitable business of the ship-owners, merchants, and ship-builders of the United States was interrupted.

The European wars were accompanied by European crop failures and insufficient food. Although the most rapid increase in the foreign trade after 1790 was in the reexportation to Europe of foreign products which American merchants and vessels gathered from the West Indies, South America, the Orient, and other parts of the world, there was also an increase in the shipments of domestic foodstuffs to Europe, where crop failures occurred at various times and where the effects of shortage were largely enhanced by the necessity of feeding immense armies of soldiers.

Partly as a result of the European wars and the abnormal demand for American foodstuffs abroad, there was an increase in the output of agricultural products in the United States. During the first decade after 1790 the growth in agriculture was chiefly east of the Alleghenies and the surplus was readily exported. The effect of the heavy export trade upon food prices is illustrated by the prices of flour at Philadelphia, which was then a typical market. The average price from 1785 to 1793 was $5.41 per barrel, while the average price from 1793 to 1807 (excluding the years 1802 and 1803, when Europe was at peace) was $9.12 per barrel, a difference of $3.71. It is noteworthy that during the years 1820 to 1828, after the trade and industry of Europe had returned to its ordinary channels, the average price dropped back to $5.46. After 1800, when the foreign trade received numerous setbacks, westward emigration revived, the volume of foodstuffs produced in the country west of the Alleghenies also increased rapidly, and great quantities of flour, grain, and provisions were sent down the Mississippi River to be exported to Europe from New Orleans. After 1803 the exports from the Michigan territory exceeded those from such States as New Hampshire, Vermont, and Delaware; and in 1807, when the export trade moving down the Mississippi River from the Middle West was at its height, the value of the shipments to foreign markets from New Orleans aggregated $4,321,000.

The banking and credit situation was greatly improved after 1790. In the past the absence of adequate credit in the countries of continental Europe had tended to limit the import trade largely to England, where credit relations had long been established. By restricting the imports from the markets of continental Europe, the insufficiency of credit had also had an unwholesome effect upon American exports to those markets. Inadequate banking facilities had, moreover, exerted an unfavorable influence upon investments in agriculture, shipping, and other industries. When the Constitution was adopted, the only banks in the United States were the Bank of North America, the Bank of New York, and the Bank of Massachusetts. In February 1791, however, Congress created the Bank of the United States. The charter of this institution expired in March 1811, but before its termination many State banks were established. From a total of 3 State banks in 1791, with a capital of $2,000,000, the number grew to 88 in January 1811, and the capital to $42,610,000; and in January 1815 there were 208 State banks, with an aggregate capital of $82,259,000.

THE DAMNATION OF MR. JAY[1] *Frank Monaghan*

The Democratic societies had howled when they learned of Jay's nomination as envoy to Great Britain. They well remembered that he and King had assisted notably in ousting Genêt. Their opposition to his appointment was futile. When the Senate ratified it "the whole Union began to ring with their vociferations." As he sailed from New York the Philadelphia Democratic Society, which Cobbett declared was "never last in the pursuit of mischief," fired a parting volley of invective. The partisans of France wanted a war, not a peace, with George III and "his satanic imp, William Pitt."

Nor were the Democratic societies and the newspapers idle during Jay's absence in London. Every scrap of news that could be picked up concerning his conduct at the British Court was made the object of sarcasm or twisted into a prognostication of his concluding a dishonorable treaty. Even the formality of his presentation to the Queen sent them into fits of indignation. When James Monroe was kissed by the president of the National Convention they celebrated. When Jay kissed the hand of the Queen of England they declared he was "prostrating at the feet of Majesty the sovereignty of a great people," for which he deserved to have "his lips blistered to the bone." . . .

Early in June, 1794, the Republicans of Philadelphia provided a vivid demonstration of what the reception of any treaty with England would be. They made an effigy of Jay and stuffed it with powder. In its right hand was placed an iron rod; in the left, a copy of Swift's detested speech on British depredations. Suspended from the neck by a cord was a copy of John Adams' *Defence of the Constitutions.* The figure was placed on the platform of the pillory while a crowd hooted and jeered. After several hours of exposure they took it down, solemnly guillotined it and set the clothes afire. An explosion scattered the remnants and ended the ceremony. After this, said Cobbett, "the drunkards went home, snorted themselves sober and returned to their employments." In New York an effigy of Jay bearing the inscription "No man e'er reached the heights of vice at first" was disposed of in the same fashion while the crowds danced the "Carmagnole." These activities of the Republicans led Washington to remark dryly to Gouverneur Morris that "The affairs of this country *cannot go amiss.* There are *so many watchful guardians of them,* and such *infallible guides,* that one is at no loss for a director at every turn."

* * *

Washington's exact opinion of the treaty is difficult to ascertain, but it is certain he was far from enthusiastic about it. Hamilton, who knew the provisions of the treaty long before it reached the Senate, is said to have dubbed it "an execrable one" on the part of "an old woman." Since this alleged remark passed through three Francophiles—Talleyrand to Volney

[1] Selected from *John Jay,* pp. 388–90, 399–400. Copyright 1935, reprinted with permission of the publishers, The Bobbs-Merrill Company, Inc.

to Jefferson—it is impossible to know what Hamilton did say. He was determined that it be ratified, but with a suspension of Article XII which related to the trading restrictions. He was bound to support it. It was a treaty of the Federalists, concluded by an envoy of their choosing, whose instructions had been drawn by them. Although he probably would not have admitted it, he had been partly responsible for Jay's lack of success in London.

Debate in the Senate was bitter. For eight days the discussion was general; then the Federalists submitted a form of ratification which called for the suspension of that part of Article XII enumerating the articles American ships could not carry to or from the British West Indies. Senator Aaron Burr moved to postpone ratification and to begin new negotiations, but was voted down. Senator Henry Tazewell moved that the President be advised not to sign the treaty and advanced seven reasons. But this, with other hostile motions, was defeated. On June twenty-fourth, in a strictly party vote, the treaty was approved by twenty to ten, just the requisite number for ratification. Two days later the Senate imposed upon its members a prohibition against publication of any parts of the treaty and adjourned. Hamilton justly lamented that this injunction would give "scope to misrepresentation and misapprehension." . . .

When it was learned that Washington had signed the treaty the Republican press broke forth in a fresh fury. Again there came the roll of drums, marching mobs, torchlight processions by night, speeches, banquets, food, whisky and fraternal huggings. Forth came the dung carts once more, more effigies of Jay, more hangings, more burnings of the treaty. One editor announced the ratification to his readers with a coarse parody on the birth of Jesus. The treaty was the child, "the long-expected embassorial, diplomatic, farcicomical savior of fifteen states." The mother was named Chief Justice, who had been "overshadowed by the prolific spirit of Gracious Majesty at the Court of St. James." In Boston the walls surrounding the house of a prominent Federalist were chalked in large letters: "Damn John Jay! Damn every one that won't damn John Jay!! Damn every one that won't put lights in his windows and sit up all night damning John Jay!!!" The author of *An Emetic for Aristocrats* presented the temptation of Jay by the Devil in Biblical style: "One John, surnamed Jay, journeyed into a far country, even unto Great Britain. 2. And the word of Satan came unto him saying, Make thou a covenant with this people, whereby they may be enabled to bring the *Americans* into bondage, as heretofore: 3. And John answered unto Satan, of a truth . . . let me find grace in thy sight, that I may secretly betray my country and the place of my nativity. . . ."

On September eleventh riots broke out in Boston. The windows of those who favored the treaty were broken by shots. Effigies of Jay were hauled about; one was a watermelon shell cut out to resemble a man's face, the whole decorated with scurrilous labels. They marched up to Governor Adams' house where the staunch old Whig smiled a benediction from the window. When the Federalists appealed to him to restore order he characterized the riot as "a mere watermelon frolic." The mob stoned the home of the author of the *Federal Orrery*, whose barbed wit had long been gall to the Republicans. . . .

The wrath of the Republicans was boundless. Without neglecting "that damned arch-traitor, John Jay," they heaped abuse on Washington as the man who "had completed the destruction of American freedom." The *Aurora* declared that the President had thundered contempt upon the people "with as much arrogance as if he sat upon the throne of Indostan." Since he has abandoned the people let the people no longer regard him as a saint. Indeed, "A Calm Observer," said to have been John Beckley, Clerk of the House, was already preparing a series of newspaper articles to prove that the President was a thief. Another writer declared that to be an opposer of the President would soon be a passport to popular esteem. In Virginia "A speedy Death to General Washington" was toasted; in New York the Thanksgiving Proclamation of Governor Jay was denounced because it ventured to include the preservation "of the valuable life and usefulness of the President of the United States" as one of the subjects worthy of a prayer of thanks. . . .

JEFFERSONIAN FOREIGN POLICY[1]   *Charles A. Beard*

America's first great expansionist, Thomas Jefferson, founder of the Democratic party, under whose auspices the first step in expansion—the Louisiana purchase—took place, had a broad and, on the whole, consistent conception of American civilization, its potentialities, and its interests. He believed that a democratic republic could be securely founded only upon agriculture, accompanied by a wide distribution of land among the cultivators in contrast to the concentration of estates which formed the basis of aristocracies in Europe. With him this was a reasoned conviction derived from experience and the study of history. "Cultivators of the earth," he said, "are the most valuable citizens. They are the most vigorous, the most independent, the most virtuous, and are tied to their country, and wedded to its liberty and interests, by the most lasting bonds." He also believed that the democratic principle of mild government dependent upon the intelligence of the masses would be secure "as long as we remain virtuous; and I think we shall be so, as long as agriculture is our principal object, which will be the case while there remain vacant lands in any part of America. When we get piled up upon one another in large cities, as in Europe, we shall become corrupt as in Europe, and go to eating one another as they do there." The implications of this are clear.

Jefferson founded his party, and through the years built it up, on the assumption that there was a fundamental relation between agriculture and national stability and progress. According to its requirements he shaped his policy. In his political campaigning he bid, as he said, for the support of

[1] Selected from *The Idea of National Interest: An Analytical Study in American Foreign Policy* (New York: MacMillan, 1934; rev. ed. Chicago: Quadrangle Books, 1966), pp. 52–57. Copyright © 1934 by Charles A. Beard. Copyright renewed 1962 by William Beard and Mrs. Miriam B. Vagts.

"farmers whose interests are entirely agricultural," and declared his opposition to government by commercial and financial affiliations. Farmers, he
insisted "are the true representatives of the great American interest, and
are alone to be relied on for expressing the proper American sentiments."
Traders, investors, and manufacturers, he thought, were not attached to the
soil by bonds of interest and affection but were mobile and connected
with similar groups in foreign countries; for this reason they were often
prepared to sacrifice the country to their particular advantage—momentary
gain. On such grounds he bitterly attacked his opponents, the Federalists,
whose seats of power were in the cities, for their "British sympathies,"
their willingness to truck and huckster with Great Britain in the hope of
enlarging their commercial opportunities. Agriculture, ran his formula, is
the fundamental American interest, a guarantee of the perpetuity of American institutions, the source of patriotic devotion to the land and its
government.

Agriculture, moreover, gave the nation a high degree of self-sufficiency
and independence and made it possible for its government to avoid the
intrigues, entanglements, and collisions common to European powers.
Jefferson did not want the American people to depend on "the casualties
and caprice of customers" for their security and chief sources of livelihood.
Trade, he was convinced, was accompanied by chicanery ruinous to morals;
while agriculture was the nursery of independence in spirit and virtue in life.
He thought, as we have seen, that the country would remain virtuous as long
as agriculture predominated, "while there remain vacant lands in any part of
America." This philosophy of politics is, of course, as old as Aristotle, but
it is also as new as Spengler who finds in capitalism the cancer of interna-
tionalism and in agriculture the source of patriotism and the heroic virtues
of the warrior.

With agriculture as the economic sheet anchor, Jefferson naturally
advocated territorial expansion to provide new lands for farmers. As early
as 1801 he wrote to Monroe: "However our present interests may restrain
us within our own limits, it is impossible not to look forward to distant
time, when our rapid multiplication will expand itself beyond these limits,
and cover the whole northern if not the southern continent." Later he
endorsed the idea of annexing Florida, without a war if possible, by means
of colonization and absorption. Still later, with some inconsistency, he
approved a project for taking Cuba, on the ground that it would give us
control over the Gulf of Mexico, the Isthmus, and neighboring countries.
But here he stopped in his over-seas expansion. "Cuba," he said, "can be
defended by us without a navy, and this develops the principle which ought
to limit our views. Nothing should ever be accepted which would require
a navy to defend it." A navy, he held, divorced men from the soil, developed
a bureaucracy which interfered with politics, incurred unprofitable expenditures, and was affiliated with the commercial interest and its party representation. Expansion to obtain land for farmers—continental expansion which
could be defended by a militia-army—such was the Jeffersonian conception
of national interest in territorial extension. The Louisiana purchase was his
first great demonstration of this policy.

Although many Federalists were willing to approve the Louisiana cession on the ground that it opened the Mississippi River to commerce, the weight of opinion in Federalist circles was against the form in which annexation was authorized. Their spokesman in Congress, Griswold, insisted that the treaty was unconstitutional and impolitic. It was unconstitutional because it provided for the incorporation of foreign soil and people with the United States and for the admission of new states into the Union by act of Congress. It was impolitic "because we could not govern so vast a wilderness and a people so unlike our own in language, manners, and religion."

Later this contention was even more strongly emphasized. When the proposal to admit Louisiana as a state came up in Congress, opposition from the commercial sections of the seaboard was placed frankly on the ground that by such action the political power of the commercial regions in the Federal Government would be diminished, that they would be overborne by a majority from the agrarian states, and that the balance of the original partnership of states would be destroyed. "Do you suppose," asked Josiah Quincy in the House of Representatives, "the people of the Northern and Atlantic states will or ought to look with patience and see Representatives and Senators from the Red River and Missouri pouring themselves upon this and the other floor, managing the concerns of a sea-board fifteen hundred miles at least from their residence, and having a preponderancy in councils into which constitutionally they never could have been admitted?" Quincy's answer was that it would be better to dissolve the Union than to have the commercial states submerged in an agrarian flood. Thus the agrarian interest became associated with the national outlook, and the commercial interest became particularistic in policy. . . .

THE SIGNIFICANCE OF THE
LOUISIANA PURCHASE[1]   *Frederick Jackson Turner*

. . . Livingston, Monroe, and Marbois signed the treaty by which France ceded Louisiana to the United States . . . on May 2 [1803], but the document was antedated to April 30. This event in the history of the United States, "worthy to rank with the Declaration of Independence and the formation of the Constitution," was the resultant of three long-continued forces in American history—the advance of the pioneers toward the West, the diplomatic struggle between France, Spain, England, and the United States for the possession of the Mississippi Valley, and the rivalry of these powers over the disintegrating empire which Spain had reared in the New World. When we consider the magnitude and sweep of the advance of American settlement, it is easy to believe that whatever nations might temporarily

[1] *Review of Reviews*, XXVII, No. 160 (May, 1903), 578–84. Reprinted with permission.

secure the Mississippi River, in the long run the vast interior would be under the Government of the American people. Nevertheless, this cannot be affirmed with any certainty, and several times within the period from the adoption of the Constitution to the purchase of Louisiana the Mississippi Valley narrowly escaped being the theater of conflict between the powers of Europe. Into such a conflict, the United States would have been drawn as the ally of one or other of these powers, and thus European interests would have dominated the fortunes of the New World.

In view of the fact that at the beginning of the Union the West was more interested in opening the Mississippi River as a means of exit for its crops than in the newly made federal government, it cannot safely be said that any strong European power which might have taken possession of the Mississippi Valley could not have held it, provided that it treated the Western settlers with liberality. The contest for Louisiana was in reality a contest for the whole Mississippi Valley and for ascendency in the Western Hemisphere.

* * *

Western settlements after the Revolution.

... At the close of the Revolution, the United States had thrust a wedge of settlement along the Ohio and its tributaries between two great Indian confederacies on the north and on the south, each of which was dominated by rival European nations, anxious to check the advance of the United States. She found herself thus threatened on each flank at a time when her own loose confederation seemed about to break asunder. She was unable to chastise the Indians, to protect the Western settlers, or to secure our claims to the navigation of the Mississippi. Such a situation was intolerable to the "men of the Western Waters." Without the freedom of that river, their corn and tobacco must rot in the fields. The great stream of American settlement that poured into Kentucky, Tennessee, and Ohio in the closing years of the Confederation grew turbulent as it found its industrial life dammed up by the Spanish closure of the Mississippi. Under the temptation of this situation, at the close of the Confederation, England supported the Indians in their resistance to the advance of the Americans across the Ohio, and planned to promote the independence of the American settlements beyond the Alleghanies, with a view of making them her dependent allies. At the same time, she laid plans for the recovery of Florida. In the Southwest, Spain developed a similar policy. She strengthened her hold upon the Indians, intrigued with the leading settlers of Kentucky and Tennessee with the view to inducing those communities to transfer their allegiance from the United States to Spain, and as a means of pressure, she refused the navigation of the river. The Western settlers themselves were strongly inclined to believe that their democratic agricultural society had a destiny separate from the merchants and planters on the other side of the Alleghanies.

England's attitude toward Spain.

Although the establishment of the new government checked these intrigues, the French Revolution, which broke out contemporaneously with

Washington's Presidency raised an even more serious danger. One of its more important results was to end the family compact which had bound Spain and France for so many years. In 1790, England and Spain were about to go to war over the question of the seizure of some English vessels by Spain in Nootka Sound. Obviously, such a war would give to England an opportunity to supersede Spain in the control of the Mississippi, to win the support of the Western settlers by the offer of free navigation, and to organize a revolt of Spanish America. This would break the Spanish monopoly and open that immense region to her commerce. . . .

Preparations were actually made by Pitt to seize New Orleans, and an expedition from that city into Mexico was also considered. Thomas Jefferson, who had recently been appointed Secretary of State, saw clearly the danger to the future of the United States. Alarmed by the prospect of England's possession of Canada, Louisiana, and Florida, he wrote: "Embraced from the St. Croix to the St. Marys on one side by their possessions, on the other by their fleet, we need not hestitate to say that they would soon find means to unite to them all the territory covered by the ramifications of the Mississippi." He therefore instructed our representative to point out to Spain that her best policy would be to cede Florida to us and to yield the navigation of the Mississippi, on the condition that we should guarantee her territory west of that river. Washington's cabinet was not ready to advise him to prevent England's expected expedition by arms, but their deliberations showed a keen realization of the importance to us of the possession of New Orleans. Fortunately, the question was not brought to a crisis, because France declined to recognize the family compact, and in her isolation, Spain was obliged to make terms of peace.

French designs on Louisiana and Florida.

By the close of 1792, France, influenced by Miranda, had determined to enrich herself at the expense of the Spanish empire in America and to win back her own American provinces. . . .

Fortunately for the future of the Mississippi Valley, the Reign of Terror compelled France to look to her safety at home and to leave these vast designs of revolutionizing Spanish America to one side. . . . It is hardly too much to say, however, that but for the cold neutrality of Washington, the West, under the banners of France, might have been hurried into a crusade against Spanish America that would have changed the whole current of the history of the United States.

France schemes to get Spanish territory.

The year 1795 marked a turning-point in the history of the struggle for the Mississippi. Jay's treaty put an end to England's influence over the Indians north of the Ohio, and freed the northern flank of the United States from the pressure of a foreign power. At the same time, Spain, realizing her weakness in the Southwest, and apprehending that Jay's treaty might mean a joint attack by England and the United States, yielded our boundaries and free navigation.

This relinquishment of Spanish claims to the eastern bank of the Mississippi was a serious menace to the plans of France. She had vainly demanded Louisiana for herself in the treaty of Basle, which closed her war with Spain in 1795. After Jay's treaty was ratified, she realized that there was but slight hope of winning the United States to the French alliance, and it became her policy to dominate the foreign affairs of Spain and to acquire large sections of American territory. In 1796, therefore, France instructed her minister to Spain to ask the relinquishment of Louisiana and the Floridas to France, as a means of protecting the rest of Spanish America. "We alone," wrote the Directors, "can trace with strong hands the bounds for the power of the United States and the limits for their territory."

* * *

Anglo-American plot against New Orleans.

In fact, the apprehensions felt by Spain and France in this respect were not without foundation. Already plans were being laid by Senator Blount, of Tennessee, to rally the frontier for a descent of the Mississippi River and the capture of New Orleans for Great Britain, with the hope of assistance by a naval force from that country. The plot was discovered, and Blount was expelled from his seat in the Senate; but this enterprise furnished the Spaniards with sufficient excuses for delaying the relinquishment of the promised posts, until at last, in 1798, Godoy, the prime minister, gave an order for their evacuation. . . .

* * *

Proposed alliance of the United States and England against France.

But England and America were now thoroughly aroused to the menace that the growing military greatness of France imposed, and under the Federal party, a closer connection was being established between the two powers. The revelations of the "X.Y.Z. correspondence," showing the insulting demands of the French Government, brought about such a heated condition of the public mind that in 1798 Congress authorized the capture of French vessels, and during 1798 and 1799 actual hostilities existed upon the sea. The aged Washington was made commander-in-chief of the army, and Hamilton was second in command.

Apprehending that the increasing influence of France over Spain after the fall of Godoy might result in transferring the colonial possessions of Spain to the strong French nation, William Pitt, who then guided England's policy, again took up the question of extending British influence in Spanish America. At the beginning of 1798, Miranda, keen of scent for every opportunity to advance the cause of Spanish American revolution, came to him with renewed proposals for English intervention. For the assistance of the revolting Spanish colonies, England was asked to furnish an army and a fleet; of the United States was to be requested the cooperation of five thousand backwoodsmen, familiar with new countries, and officered by veterans of the American Revolution. By February of 1798, Pitt had determined that unless Spain seemed likely to be able to save herself from a revolution and from the resultant domination of France, England would propose some such combined operation with the United States to free Spanish America. Miranda's proposition was transmitted by our minister, Mr. King, to Hamilton, who gave his approval to the undertaking, but preferred that the principal part should fall to the United States, and that we should furnish the whole land force. "In this case," he said, "the command would very naturally fall upon me."

The restless genius of Alexander Hamilton saw in the proposed expedition the chance to become the Washington of Spanish America, and to bring about a renewed intimacy between the United States and England. ... Fortunately, perhaps, for the future of the United States, the Presidential chair was again occupied by a man of cool judgment. John Adams declined to take part in this undertaking, and by a new commission to France, in 1800, he procured a termination of the hostilities between us and that country.

Napoleon gets back Louisiana from Spain.

There now appeared upon the scene the tremendous figure of Napoleon. Napoleon's mind worked with such momentum, his action was so decisive, that the acquisition of Louisiana, upon which he determined, moved rapidly forward. . . .

Jefferson looks to an English alliance.

Rumors of the transfer of Louisiana reached the United States in the early summer of 1801, but the Government did not at once take alarm. When, however, toward the close of the year, President Jefferson received an official copy of the treaty from our minister in England, and at the same time was informed by our representative at Paris that France denied that a cession had been made, he became concerned, and in the spring of 1802 he wrote to Livingston, our minister to France, that "the day that France takes possession of New Orleans fixes the sentence which is to restrain her forever within her low-water mark. It seals the union of two nations who in conjunction can maintain exclusive possession of the ocean. From that moment, we must marry ourselves to the British fleet and nation." It was his policy, however, to wait until the next war between France and England should give to the United States an opportunity to make common cause with England in order to secure our demands. What was desired by Jefferson was the cession of New Orleans, or at least West Florida, as a means of insuring free transit down the Mississippi. In the rest of the territory beyond the Mississippi, he had less immediate interest. Had Napoleon been able promptly to throw a large army of trained veterans into New Orleans, it is more than doubtful whether Jefferson would have resisted this occupation. . . .

Napoleon's dreams of colonial empire.

But France was not able to occupy New Orleans at once. Her armies in San Domingo were swept away by war and pestilence, and the expedition that had been intended to sail for New Orleans at the end of September, 1802, was unable to depart. What the intentions of France were with respect to Louisiana are shown in the instructions which were drawn for the general who was to command the forces of occupation. . . . In short, these instructions lead clearly to the conviction that France was determined to take up the policy of Spain, with a view of securing the controlling power on both sides of the Mississippi. It was not simply Louisiana that Napoleon desired to rule, but the interior of the United States, and all the approaches to the Gulf of Mexico,—a great colonial empire that should replace the Spanish power, which at that very time was falling under his control.

Jefferson sends Monroe to purchase New Orleans.

The closure of the Mississippi by the Spanish intendant at this time stirred the West to its depths, and gave the Federalists their opportunity to demand war with France and Spain. Although Jefferson made earnest efforts to allay the military spirit, he found it necessary to take some decisive action, and he therefore sent Monroe on a special mission to secure our interests. Monroe's instructions of March 2, 1803, contained three alternatives. He was to try to purchase New Orleans and the Floridas, and, if necessary, he might guarantee to France her territory beyond the Mississippi. If, however, France declined to cede New Orleans, an effort was to be made to secure space enough for a large commercial town on the Mississippi as little remote from the mouth of the river as might be, together with provision for the complete right of deposit. It would appear from these instructions that Jefferson would have been willing to accept merely the right of navigation rather than make the Louisiana Purchase an immediate cause of war. . . . Only in case France compelled hostilities by closing the Mississippi was he ready at the present juncture to ask an alliance with England.

Napoleon gives up one empire on the chance of winning another.

In the meantime, Napoleon had determined to reopen the war with England, and while Monroe was still upon the ocean, he unfolded to his ministers, Talleyrand and Marbois, his inclination to relinquish Louisiana. To have held it against the advance of the American settlement would have been a task likely to meet the fate that Napoleon's Continental system met when he tried to dam up the great current of European commerce. The belief that combined action by England and the United States would make it impossible for him to occupy New Orleans was an essential factor in the case. The war already determined upon with England would, he believed, result in the loss of Louisiana. On the other hand, by cementing the friendship of the United States by the sale of the province, he would deprive England of a probable ally and enrich his treasury with funds for his approaching operations. The vision of a great colonial empire in America gave place in his mind to new European projects. After all, his genius was suited rather to land power than to sea power, and colonial empire rests upon a great navy. Whatever the considerations by which he was swayed, there can be no doubt that it was due to the impetuous determination of this Titan of the revolutionary era that Louisiana and the preponderance in the Western Hemisphere passed to the United States without a struggle.

* * *

Results of the Purchase—constitutional and political.

The effects of the Louisiana Purchase upon America were profound. Politically, it resulted in strengthening the loose interpretation of the Constitution. Thomas Jefferson was the author of the Kentucky Resolutions, which affirmed the most stringent doctrine on the subject of State rights and strict construction. Even at this time, Jefferson believed that the treaty of annexation was constitutionally unwarranted. He believed that to carry out the terms of the treaty would be to "make blank paper of the Constitution by construction," and desired a constitutional amendment to validate his action: but to delay was to put the whole acquisition to hazard. His friends among the strictest of the State rights sect argued that the acquisition and incorporation of the territory was constitutional. Practical statesman that he was, he withdrew his doctrinaire ideas in the presence of the splendid opportunities which this acquisition furnished for promoting peace in North America and furnishing the broad foundation of a great democracy. . . . This broad interpretation of the treaty-making power by the strict constructionist and State rights party itself paved the way for an imperial expansion of the United States. Not only that—it laid the foundations for a readjustment of sectional power within the Union.

The treaty provided that the inhabitants of Louisiana should be incorporated into the Union and admitted as soon as possible, according to the principles of the federal Constitution, to the enjoyment of all the rights of citizens of the United States. Louisiana was not to be permanently governed as a colonial dependency by a partnership of sovereign States, but the partnership itself was to be enlarged by the action of the President and twenty-six members of the Senate. New England leaders set up the doctrine that the assent of each individual State was needed to admit a new partner. Against an arrangement which would ultimately swamp New England by the votes of representatives from the West and the South, they made vehement protest, and some even began to consider secession. The importance of the issue thus raised as to whether the new acquisition was to be ruled as an imperial possession or to be absorbed into the Union and thereby overturn the old balance of sections and destroy the safeguards of State sovereignty can hardly be overestimated. The question arose in still another form. By the terms of the treaty, special privileges were extended to vessels of France and Spain in the port of New Orleans. But the Constitution of the United States required that all duties should be uniform throughout the United States. The answer of Jefferson's supporters to the charge that a preference had been given to the ports of one State over those of another was that Louisiana was "territory purchased by the United States in their federate capacity, and may be disposed of by them at pleasure. It is in the nature of a colony whose commerce may be regulated without any reference to the Constitution." The significance of this argument has been illustrated within the last few years by the discussion of the relation of our new Spanish-American possessions to the United States. When the whole sweep of American history and the present tendencies of our life are taken into view, it would be possible to argue that the doctrines of the Louisiana Purchase were farther-reaching in their effect upon the Constitution than even the measures of Alexander Hamilton or the decisions of John Marshall.

* * *

In other ways, the Louisiana Purchase profoundly affected American politics. The area of the Louisiana Purchase furnished the issues which resulted in our Civil War. Merely to name the important steps in the history of the slavery conflict is to show the truth of this assertion. The Missouri Compromise, the Kansas and Nebraska Act, and the civil war in Kansas were the prelude to the Civil War. It was in truth a struggle between the rival institutions and political ideals of the North and the South for the domination of the vast terriory beyond the Mississippi. Rival civilizations projected themselves across the river and struggled for ascendency in a region where nature herself had decreed unity of institutions.

Predominance of the United States in the Western Hemisphere.

The international effects of the Louisiana Purchase were even more significant than its political effect. From it dates the end of the struggle for the possession of the Mississippi Valley and the beginning of the transfer of the ascendency in both Americas to the United States. . . . France, England, and Spain, removed from the strategic points on our border, were prevented from occupying the controlling position in determining the destiny of the American provinces which so soon revolted from the empire of Spain. The Monroe Doctrine would not have been possible except for the Louisiana Purchase. It was the logical outcome of that acquisition. Having taken her decisive stride across the Mississippi, the United States enlarged the horizon of her views and marched steadily forward to the possession of the Pacific Ocean. From this event dates the rise of the United States into the position of a world power.

* * *

THE ARTICLES OF CONFEDERATION

PERTAINING TO FOREIGN AFFAIRS   *Document 1*

Article II. Each state retains its sovereignty, freedom and independence, and every Power, Jurisdiction and right, which is not by this confederation expressly delegated to the United States, in Congress assembled.

Article III. The said states hereby severally enter into a firm league of friendship with each other, for their common defence, the security of their Liberties, and their mutual and general welfare, binding themselves to assist each other, against all force offered to, or attacks made upon them, or any of them, on account of religion, sovereignty, trade, or any other pretence whatever. . . .

Article VI. No state without the Consent of the united states in congress assembled, shall send any embassy to, or receive any embassy from, or enter into any conference, agreement, or alliance or treaty with any King, prince or state. . . . No two or more states shall enter into any treaty, confederation or alliance whatever between them, without the consent of the united states in congress assembled. . . . No state shall lay any imposts or duties, which may interfere with any stipulations in treaties, entered into by the united states in congress assembled. . . . No vessels of war shall be kept up in time of peace by any state, except such number only, as shall be deemed necessary by the united states in congress assembled, for the defence of such state, or its trade . . . but every state shall always keep up a well regulated and disciplined militia. . . . No state shall engage in any war without the consent of the united states in congress assembled, unless such state be actually invaded by enemies, or shall have received certain advice of a resolution being formed by some nation of Indians to invade such state, and the danger is so imminent as not to admit of a delay . . . nor shall any state grant commissions to any ships or vessels of war, not letters of marque or reprisal, except it be after a declaration of war by the united states in congress assembled . . . unless such state be infested by pirates. . . .

Article IX. The united states in congress assembled, shall have the sole and exclusive right and power of determining on peace and war. . . .

Article XI. Canada acceding to this confederation, and joining in the measures of the united states, shall be admitted into, and entitled to all the advantages of this union: but no other colony shall be admitted into the same, unless such admission be agreed to by nine states. . . .

CORRESPONDENCE BETWEEN

JOHN JAY AND

GEORGE WASHINGTON   *Document 2*

Jay to Washington, June 27, 1786:
    . . . Our affairs seem to lead to some crisis, some revolution—something that I cannot foresee or conjecture. I am uneasy and apprehensive; more so than during the war. Then we had a fixed object. . . . The case is now altered; we are going and doing wrong, and therefore I look forward to evils and calamities, but without being able to guess at the instrument, nature, or measure of them. . . .
    There doubtless is much reason to think and to say that we are woefully and, in many instances, wickedly misled. . . . Representative bodies will ever be faithful copies of their originals, and generally exhibit a checkered assemblage of virtue and vice, of abilities and weakness.
    The mass of men are neither wise nor good, and the virtue like the other resources of a country, can only be drawn to a point and exerted by strong circumstances ably managed or a strong government ably administered. . . .
    What I most fear is, that the better kind of people, by which I mean the people who are orderly and industrious, who are content with their situa-

tions and not uneasy in their circumstances, will be led by the insecurity of property, the loss of confidence in their rulers, and the want of public faith and rectitude, to consider the charms of liberty as imaginary and delusive. . . .

Washington to Jay, August 1, 1786:
. . . Your sentiments, that our affairs are drawing rapidly to a crisis, accord with my own. What the event will be, is also beyond the reach of my foresight. We have errors to correct. We have probably had too good an opinion of human nature in forming our Confederation. Experience has taught us, that men will not adopt and carry into execution measures the best calculated for their own good, without the intervention of a coercive power. I do not conceive we can exist long as a nation without having lodged somewhere a power, which will pervade the whole Union in as energetic a manner as the authority of the State governments extends over the several States. . . .

DEBATES IN THE FEDERAL
CONVENTION,
PHILADELPHIA, 1787   *Document 3*

Debates on the slave trade and Navigation Acts, August 22.
Mr. SHERMAN [Conn.] . . . disapproved of the slave trade; yet as the States were now possessed of the right to import slaves, as the public good did not require it to be taken from them, and as it was expedient to have as few objections as possible to the proposed scheme of government, he thought it best to leave the matter as we find it. He observed that the abolition of slavery seemed to be going on in the United States, and that the good sense of the several States would probably by degrees compleat it. . . .
Col. MASON [Va.]. This infernal traffic originated in the avarice of British merchants. The British Government constantly checked the attempts of Virginia to put a stop to it. The present question concerns not the importing States alone but the whole Union. The evil of having slaves was experienced during the late war. Had slaves been treated as they might have been by the enemy, they would have proved dangerous instruments in their hands. But their folly dealt by the slaves, as it did by the tories. . . . Slavery discourages arts and manufactures. The poor despise labor when performed by slaves. They prevent the immigration of whites, who really enrich and strengthen a country. They produce the most pernicious effect on manners. Every master of slaves is born a petty tyrant. They bring the judgment of Heaven on a country. As nations cannot be rewarded or punished in the next world, they must be in this. By an inevitable chain of causes and effects, Providence punishes national sins, by national calamities. He lamented that some of our eastern brethren had from a lust of gain embarked in this nefarious traffic. . . . He held it essential in every point of view that the General Government should have power to prevent the increase of slavery.

Mr. ELLSWORTH [Conn.]. As he had never owned a slave [he] could not judge of the effects of slavery on character: he said, however, that if it was to be considered in a moral light we ought to go farther and free those already in the country. As slaves also multiply so fast in Virginia and Maryland that it is cheaper to raise than import them, whilst in the sickly rice swamps foreign supplies are necessary; if we go no farther than is urged, we shall be unjust towards South Carolina and Georgia. Let us not intermeddle. As population increases, poor laborers will be so plenty as to render slaves useless. Slavery in time will not be a speck in our country. . . .

General PINCKNEY [So. Car.] declared it to be his firm opinion that if himself and all his colleagues were to sign the Constitution and use their personal influence, it would be of no avail towards obtaining the assent of their constituents. South Carolina and Georgia cannot do without slaves. As to Virginia, she will gain by stopping the importations. Her slaves will rise in value, and she has more than she wants. It would be unequal to require South Carolina and Georgia to confederate on such unequal terms. . . .

Mr. GOUVERNEUR MORRIS [Penna.] wished the whole subject to be committed, including the clauses relating to taxes on exports and to a navigation act. These things may form a bargain among the northern and southern states. . . .

August 29: . . . Mr. PINCKNEY [So. Car.] moved to postpone the Report in favor of the following proposition—"That no act of the Legislature for the purpose of regulating the commerce of the United States with foreign powers, or among the several States, shall be passed without the assent of two thirds of the members of each House." He remarked that there were five distinct commercial interests. (1) The fisheries and West India trade, which belonged to the New England States. (2) The interest of New York lay in a free trade. (3) Wheat and flour the staples of the two middle States (N. J. and Penn.). (4) Tobacco the staple of Maryland and Virginia, and partly of North Carolina. (5) Rice and indigo, the staples of South Carolina and Georgia. These different interests would be a source of oppressive regulations if no check to a bare majority should be provided. States pursue their interests with less scruple than individuals. The power of regulating commerce was a pure concession on the part of the southern States. . . .

Mr. SHERMAN [Conn.], alluding to Mr. Pinckney's enumeration of particular interests as requiring a security against abuse of the power, observed that the diversity was of itself a security, adding that to require more than a majority to decide a question was always embarrassing. . . .

Mr. PINCKNEY [So. Car.] replied that his enumeration meant the five minute interests. It still left the two great divisions of northern and southern interests.

Mr. GOUVERNEUR MORRIS [Penna.] opposed the object of the motion as highly injurious. Preferences to American ships will multiply them, till they can carry the southern produce cheaper than it is now carried. A navy was essential to security, particularly of the southern States, and can only be had by a Navigation Act encouraging American bottoms and seamen. . . . Shipping, he said, was the worst and most precarious kind of property, and stood in need of public patronage.

Mr. WILLIAMSON [No. Car.] was in favor of making two-thirds instead of a majority requisite, as more satisfactory to the southern people. No useful measure he believed had been lost in Congress for want of nine votes. . . .

Mr. RANDOLPH [Va.] said that there were features so odious in the Constitution as it now stands, that he doubted whether he should be able to agree to it. A rejection of the motion would compleat the deformity of the system. . . .

On the question to postpone in order to take up Mr. Pinckney's motion, N.H. no. Mass. no. Conn. no. N.J. no. Pa. no. Del. no. Md. ay. Va. ay. N.C. ay. S.C. no. Geo. ay.

EXCERPTS FROM "THE FEDERALIST PAPERS"
PERTAINING TO FOREIGN AFFAIRS   *Document 4*

No. 3 [John Jay] . . . Among the many objects to which a wise and free people find it necessary to direct their attention, that of providing for their *safety* seems to be the first. The *safety* of the people doubtless has relation to a great variety of circumstances and considerations, and consequently affords great latitude to those who wish to define it precisely and comprehensively.

At present I mean only to consider it as it respects security for the preservation of peace and tranquillity, as well as against dangers from *foreign arms and influence*, as from dangers of the *like kind* arising from domestic causes. As the former of these comes first in order, it is proper that it should be the first discussed. . . .

The *just* causes of war, for the most part, arise either from violations of treaties or from direct violence. America has already formed treaties with no less than six foreign nations, and all of them, except Prussia, are maritime, and therefore able to annoy and injure us. . . .

It is of high importance to the peace of America that she observe the laws of nations towards all these powers, and to me it appears evident that this will be more perfectly and punctually done by one national government than it could be either by thirteen separate States or by three or four distinct confederacies.

Because when once an efficient national goverment is established, the best men in the country will not only consent to serve, but also will generally be appointed to manage it. . . .

No. 11 [Alexander Hamilton]. The importance of the Union, in a commercial light, is one of those points about which there is least room to entertain a difference of opinion, and which has, in fact, commanded the most general assent of men who have any acquaintance with the subject. This applies as well to our intercourse with foreign countries as with each other.

There are appearances to authorize a supposition that the adventurous spirit, which distinguishes the commercial character of America, has already excited uneasy sensations in several of the maritime powers of Europe. They seem to be apprehensive of our too great interference in that carrying trade, which is the support of their navigation and the foundation of their naval strength.... Impressions of this kind will naturally indicate the policy of fostering divisions among us, and of depriving us, as far as possible, of an ACTIVE COMMERCE in our own bottoms. This would answer the three-fold purpose of preventing our interference in their navigation, of monopolizing the profits of our trade, and of clipping the wings by which we might soar to a dangerous greatness....

If we continue united, we may counteract a policy so unfriendly to our prosperity in a variety of ways. By prohibitory regulations, extending, at the same time, throughout the States, we may oblige foreign countries to bid against each other, for the privileges of our markets....

Under a vigorous national government, the natural strength and resources of the country, directed to a common interest, would baffle all the combinations of European jealousy to restrain our growth. This situation would even take away the motive to such combinations, by inducing an impracticability of success. An active commerce, an extensive navigation, and a flourishing marine would then be the offspring of moral and physical necessity. We might defy the little arts of the little politicians to control or vary the irresistable and unchangeable course of nature....

No. 64 [John Jay] ... The power of making treaties is an important one, especially as it relates to war, peace, and commerce; and it should not be delegated but in such a mode, and with such precautions, as will afford the highest security that it will be exercised by men the best qualified for the purpose, and in the manner most conducive to the public good. The convention appears to have been attentive to both these points; they have directed the President to be chosen by select bodies of electors, to be deputed by the people for that express purpose; and thy have committed the appointment of senators to the State legislatures....

It seldom happens in the negotiation of treaties, of whatever nature, but that perfect *secrecy* and immediate *despatch* are sometimes requisite. There are cases where the most useful intelligence may be obtained, if the persons possessing it can be relieved from apprehensions of discovery. Those apprehensions will operate on those persons whether they are actuated by mercenary or friendly motives; and there doubtless are many of both descriptions, who would rely on the secrecy of the President, but who would not confide in that of the Senate, and still less in that of a large popular Assembly. The convention have done well, therefore, in so disposing of the power of making treaties, that although the President must, in forming them, act by the advice and consent of the Senate, yet he will be able to manage the business of intelligence in such a manner as prudence may suggest....

No. 70 [Alexander Hamilton]. There is an idea, which is not without its advocates, that a vigorous Executive is inconsistent with the genius of republican government. The enlightened well-wishers to this species of government must at least hope that the supposition is destitute of foundation; since

71

they can never admit its truth, without at the same time admitting the condemnation of their own principles. Energy in the Executive is a leading character in the definition of good government. It is essential to the protection of the community against foreign attacks; it is not less essential to the steady administration of the laws; to the protection of property against those irregular and high-handed combinations which sometimes interrupt the ordinary course of justice; to the security of liberty against the enterprises and assaults of ambition, of faction, and of anarchy. . . .

The ingredients which constitute energy in the Executive are, first, unity; secondly, duration; thirdly, an adequate provision for its support; fourthly, competent powers. . . .

PROVISIONS OF THE CONSTITUTION
PERTAINING TO FOREIGN AFFAIRS   *Document 5*

ARTICLE I

Section 7. All Bills for raising Revenue shall originate in the House of Representatives; but the Senate may propose or concur with Amendments as on other Bills.

* * *

Section 8. The Congress shall have Power To lay and collect Taxes, Duties, Imposts and Excises, to pay the Debts and provide for the common Defence and general Welfare of the United States; but all Duties, Imposts and Excises shall be uniform throughout the United States . . .

To regulate Commerce with foreign Nations, and among the several States, and with the Indian Tribes . . .

To coin Money, regulate the Value thereof, and of foreign Coin, and fix the Standard of Weights and Measures . . .

To define and punish Piracies and Felonies committed on the high Seas, and Offences against the Law of Nations;

To declare War, grant Letters of Marque and Reprisal, and make Rules concerning Captures on Land and Water;

To raise and support Armies, but no Appropriation of Money to that Use shall be for a longer Term than two Years;

To provide and maintain a Navy;

To make Rules for the Government and Regulation of the land and naval Forces;

To provide for calling forth the Militia to execute the Laws of the Union, suppress Insurrections and repel Invasions;

To provide for organizing, arming, and disciplining, the Militia, and for governing such Part of them as may be employed in the Service of the United States, reserving to the States respectively, the Appointment of the Officers, and the Authority of training the Militia according to the discipline prescribed by Congress . . .

Section 9. The Migration or Importation of such Persons as any of the States now existing shall think proper to admit, shall not be prohibited by the Congress prior to the Year one thousand eight hundred and eight, but a Tax or duty may be imposed on such Importation, not exceeding ten dollars for each Person. . . .

No Tax or Duty shall be laid on Articles exported from any State.

No Preference shall be given by any Regulation of Commerce or Revenue to the Ports of one State over those of another; nor shall Vessels bound to, or from, one State, be obliged to enter, clear, or pay Duties in another. . . .

Section 10. No State shall enter into any Treaty, Alliance, or Confederation; grant Letters of Marque and Reprisal; coin Money; emit Bills of Credit; make any Thing but gold and silver Coin a Tender in Payment of Debts; pass any Bill of Attainder, ex post facto Law, or Law impairing the Obligation of Contracts, or grant any Title of Nobility.

No State shall, without the Consent of the Congress, lay any Imposts or Duties on Imports or Exports, except what may be absolutely necessary for executing it's inspection Laws: and the net Produce of all Duties and Imposts, laid by any State on Imports or Exports, shall be for the Use of the Treasury of the United States; and all such Laws shall be subject to the Revision and Controul of the Congress.

No State shall, without the Consent of Congress, lay any Duty of Tonnage, keep Troops, or Ships of War in time of Peace, enter into any Agreement or Compact with another State, or with a foreign Power, or engage in War, unless actually invaded, or in such imminent Danger as will not admit of delay.

ARTICLE II

Section 1. The executive Power shall be vested in a President of the United States of America.

Section 2. The President shall be Commander in Chief of the Army and Navy of the United States, and of the Militia of the several States, when called into the actual Service of the United States . . . .

He shall have Power, by and with the Advice and Consent of the Senate, to make Treaties, provided two thirds of the Senators present concur; and he shall nominate, and by and with the Advice and Consent of the Senate, shall appoint Ambassadors, other public Ministers and Consuls, Judges of the supreme Court, and all other Officers of the United States, whose Appointments are not herein otherwise provided for, and which shall be established by Law; but the Congress may by Law vest the Appointment of such inferior Officers, as they think proper, in the President alone, in the Courts of Law, or in the Heads of Departments.

* * *

ARTICLE III

Section 3. Treason against the United States, shall consist only in levying War against them, or in adhering to their Enemies, giving them Aid and Comfort. No Person shall be convicted of Treason unless on the Testimony of two Witnesses to the same overt Act, or on Confession in open Court.

The Congress shall have Power to declare the Punishment of Treason, but no Attainder of Treason shall work Corruption of Blood, or Forfeiture except during the Life of the Person attainted.

ARTICLE IV

Section 3. The Congress shall have Power to dispose of and make all needful Rules and Regulations respecting the Territory or other Property belonging to the United States; and nothing in this Constitution shall be so construed as to Prejudice any Claims of the United States, or of any particular State.

Section 4. The United States shall guarantee to every State in this Union a Republican Form of Government, and shall protect each of them against Invasion; and on Application of the Legislature, or of the Executive (when the Legislature cannot be convened) against domestic Violence....

ARTICLE VI

All Debts contracted and Engagements entered into, before the Adoption of this Constitution, shall be as valid against the United States under this Constitution, as under the Confederation.

This Constitution, and the Laws of the United States which shall be made in Pursuance thereof; and all Treaties made, or which shall be made, under the Authority of the United States, shall be the supreme Law of the Land; and the Judges in every State shall be bound thereby, any Thing in the Constitution or Laws of any State to the Contrary notwithstanding....

JEFFERSON ON THE IMPORTANCE
OF NEW ORLEANS
Document 6

Letter to Robert R. Livingston, April 18, 1802.

... The cession of Louisiana and the Floridas by Spain to France, works most sorely on the United States.... Of all nations of any consideration, France is the one which, hitherto, has offered the fewest points on which we could have any conflict of right, and the most points of a communion of interests.... There is on the globe one single spot, the possessor of which is our natural and habitual enemy. It is New Orleans, through which the produce of three-eighths of our territory must pass to market, and from its fertility it will ere long yield more than half of our whole produce, and contain more than half of our inhabitants. France, placing herself in that door, assumes to us the attitude of defiance. Spain might have retained it quietly for years. Her pacific dispositions, her feeble state, would induce her to increase our facilities there, so that her possession of the place would hardly be felt by us.... Not so can it ever be in the hands of France: the impetuosity of her temper, the energy and restlessness of her character ... render it impossible that France and the United States can continue long friends, when they meet in so irritable a position. . . . The day that France takes possession of New Orleans . . . we must marry ourselves to the British fleet and nation. . . .

If France considers Louisiana, however, as indispensable for her views, she might be willing to look about for arrangements which might reconcile it to our interests. If anything could do this, it would be the ceding to us the island of New Orleans and the Floridas. . . .

SENATE DEBATE ON THE PURCHASE
OF LOUISIANA, NOVEMBER, 1803   *Document 7*

TIMOTHY PICKERING [Mass.]. . . . It is declared in the third article, that "the inhabitants of the ceded territory shall be incorporated in the Union of the United States." But neither the President and the Senate, nor the President and Congress, are competent to such an act of incorporation. He believed that our Administration admitted that this incorporation could not be effected without an amendment of the Constitution; and he conceived that this necessary amendment could not be made in the ordinary mode by the concurrence of two-thirds of both Houses of Congress, and the ratification by the Legislatures of three-fourths of the several States. He believed the assent of each individual State to be necessary for the admission of a foreign country as an associate in the Union: in like manner as in a commercial house, the consent of each member would be necessary to admit a new partner into the company. . . .

There was another serious objection to this treaty. It purported to contain a cession of Louisiana to the United States. . . . France acquired a right to demand an actual cession of the territory, provided she fulfilled all the conditions on which Spain promised to cede. But we know Spain declares that those conditions have not been fully performed; and, by her remonstrances, warns the United States not to touch Louisiana. . . .

Mr. P. said, that whatever way he turned his eyes, war was in prospect, as the final result of our pacific measures—measures deemed so wise as to have been ascribed to divine inspiration! He wished they might merit that high character; but feared, in the end, they would bear the stamp of indiscretion, perhaps of folly. . . .

JOHN BRECKENRIDGE [Kentucky]. Permit me to examine some of the principal reasons which are deemed so powerful by the gentlemen as to induce them to vote for the destruction of this treaty. Unfortunately for the gentlemen, no two of them can agree on the same set of objections; and what is still more unfortunate, I believe there is no two of them concure in any one objection. . . . An honorable gentleman from Delaware (Mr. White) considers the price to be enormous. An honorable gentleman from Connecticut . . . says he has no objection whatever to the price; it is, he supposes, not too much. An honorable gentleman from Massachusetts (Mr. Pickering) says that France acquired no title from Spain, and therefore our title is bad.... The gentleman from Massachusetts (Mr. Pickering) contends that the United States cannot under the Constitution acquire foreign territory....

As to the enormity of price, I would ask that gentleman, would his mode of acquiring it through fifty thousand men have cost nothing? Is he so confident of this as to be able to pronounce positively that the price is enormous? Does he make no calculation on the hazard attending this conflict? Is he sure the God of battles was enlisted on his side? Were France and Spain, under the auspices of Bonaparte, contemptible adversaries? Good as the cause was, and great as my confidence is in the courage of my countrymen, sure I am, that I shall never regret, as the gentleman seems to do, that the experiment was not made.... To acquire an empire of perhaps half the extent of the one we possessed, from the most powerful and warlike nation on earth, without bloodshed ... through the peaceful forms of negotiation, and in despite too of the opposition of a considerable portion of the community, is an achievement of which the archives of the predecessors, at least, of those now in office, cannot furnish a parallel.

The same gentleman has told us, that this acquisition will, from its extent, soon prove destructive to the Confederacy.

This ... is an old and hackneyed doctrine; that a Republic ought not to be too extensive. But the gentleman has assumed two facts, and then reasoned from them. First, that the extent is too great; and secondly, that the country will be soon populated.... Is the Goddess of Liberty restrained by water courses? Is she governed by geographical limits? Is her dominion on this continent confined to the east side of the Mississippi? So far from believing in the doctrine that a Republic ought to be confined within narrow limits, I believe, on the contrary, that the more extensive its dominion the more safe and more durable it will be. In proportion to the number of hands you intrust the precious blessings of a free government to, in the same proportion do you multiply the chances for their preservation....

PRESIDENT JEFFERSON'S CONFIDENTIAL MESSAGE TO THE CONGRESS ON WESTWARD EXPANSION, JANUARY 18, 1803

Document 8

The Indian tribes residing within the limits of the United States, have, for a considerable time, been growing more and more uneasy at the constant diminution of the territory they occupy, although effected by their own voluntary sales: and the policy has long been gaining strength with them, of refusing absolutely all further sale, on any conditions....

In order peaceably to counteract this policy of theirs, and to provide an extension of territory which the rapid increase of our numbers will call for, two measures are deemed expedient. First: to encourage them to abandon hunting.... Secondly: to multiply trading houses among them, and place within their reach those things which will contribute more to their domestic comfort, than the possession of extensive, but uncultivated wilds.... In leading them to agriculture, to manufactures, and civilization ... I trust and believe we are acting for their greatest good. [Jefferson then goes on to emphasize that all this should be done through government-controlled trading houses. This will drive private operators out of business, thus raising the need to do something for them.]

While the extension of the public commerce among the Indian tribes, may deprive of that source of profit such of our citizens as are engaged in it, it might be worthy the attention of Congress, in their care of individual as well as of the general interest, to point, in another direction, the enterprise of these citizens, as profitably for themselves, and more usefully for the public. The river Missouri, and the Indians inhabiting it, are not as well known as is rendered desirable by their connexion with the Mississippi, and consequently with us. It is, however, understood, that the country on that [Missouri] river is inhabited by numerous tribes, who furnish great supplies of furs and peltry to the trade of another nation [i.e., Great Britain], carried on in a high latitude, through an infinite number of portages and lakes, shut up by ice through a long season. The commerce on that line [i.e., across Canada] could bear no competition with that of the Missouri, traversing a moderate climate, offering, according to the best accounts, a continued navigation from its source, and possibly with a single portage, from the Western Ocean ... [to the Atlantic Ocean]. An intelligent officer, with ten or twelve chosen men, fit for the enterprise, and willing to undertake it, taken from our posts, where they may be spared without inconvenience, might explore the whole line, even to the Western Ocean, have conferences with the natives on the subject of commercial intercourse [etc.].... Their pay would be going on, whether here or there. While other civilized nations have encountered great expense to enlarge the boundaries of knowledge by undertaking voyages of discovery, and for other literary purposes, in various parts and directions, our nation seems to owe to the same object, as well as to its own interest, to explore this, the only line of easy communication across the continent, and so directly traversing our own part of it. The interests of commerce place the principal object within the constitutional powers and care of Congress, and that it should incidentally advance the geographic knowledge of our own continent, cannot be but an additional gratification. The nation claiming the territory [i.e., Spain or France], regarding this as a literary pursuit, which [it] is [in] the habit of permitting within its dominions, would not be disposed to view it with jealousy....

FRENCH AND BRITISH RESTRICTIONS
ON NEUTRAL COMMERCE   *Document 9*

The Berlin Decree of November 21, 1806.
    We have resolved to enforce against England the usages which she has consecrated in her maritime code....

Article I. The British islands are declared in a state of blockade.

Article II. All Commerce and correspondence with the British islands are prohibited....

Article IV. All magazines, merchandise, or property whatsoever belonging to a subject of England, shall be declared lawful prize.

Article V. The trade in English merchandise is forbidden. All merchandise belonging to England, or coming from its manufactories and colonies, is declared a lawful prize....

The British Orders in Council of November 11, 1807.

Whereas certain orders, establishing an unprecedented system of warfare against this Kingdom, and aimed especially at the destruction of its commerce and resources, were ... issued by the Government of France....

His Majesty is therefore pleased, by and with the advice of his Privy Council, to order, and it is hereby ordered, that all the ports and places of France and her allies, or of any other country at war with His Majesty, and all other ports or places in Europe, from which, although not at war with His Majesty, the British flag is excluded, and all ports or places in the colonies belonging to His Majesty's enemies, shall, from henceforth, be subject to the same restrictions in point of trade and navigation, with the exceptions herein after mentioned, as if the same were actually blockaded by His Majesty's naval forces, in the most strict and rigorous manner: And it is hereby further ordered and declared, that all trade in articles, which are of the produce or manufacture of the said countries or colonies, shall be deemed and considered to be unlawful; and that every vessel trading from or to the said countries or colonies, together with all goods and merchandise on board, and all articles of the produce or manufacture of the said countries or colonies, shall be captured and condemned as prize to the captors....

THE EMBARGO ACT
OF DECEMBER 22, 1807

Document 10

Be it enacted, That an embargo be, and hereby is laid on all ships and vessels in the ports and places within the limits or jurisdiction of the United States, cleared or not cleared, bound to any foreign port or place; and that no clearance be furnished to any ship or vessel bound to such foreign port or place, except vessels under the immediate direction of the President of the United States: and that the President be authorized to give such instructions to the officers of the revenue, and of the navy and revenue cutters of the United States, as shall appear best adapted for carrying the same into full effect: *Provided,* that nothing herein contained shall be construed to prevent the departure of any foreign ship or vessel, either in ballast, or with the goods, wares and merchandise on board of such foreign ship or vessel, when notified of this act.

Section 2. And be it further enacted, That during the continuance of this act, no registered, or sea letter vessel, having on board goods, wares, and merchandise, shall be allowed to depart from one port of the United States to any other within the same, unless the master, owner, consignee or factor of such vessel shall first give bond, with one or more sureties to the collector of the district from which she is bound to depart, in a sum of double the value of the vessel and cargo, that the said goods, wares, or merchandise shall be relanded in some port of the United States, dangers of the seas excepted. . . . All armed vessels possessing public commissions from any foreign power, are not to be considered as liable to the embargo laid by this act.

THE NON-INTERCOURSE ACT
OF MARCH 1, 1809   *Document 11*

Be it enacted, That from and after the passing of this act, the entrance of the harbors and waters of the United States and of the territories thereof, be, and the same is hereby interdicted to all public ships and vessels belonging to Great Britain or France, excepting vessels only which may be forced in by distress, or which are charged with despatches or business from the government to which they belong, and also packets having no cargo nor merchandise on board. . . .

Section 3. That from and after the twentieth day of May next, the entrance of the harbors and waters of the United States and the territories thereof be, and the same is hereby interdicted to all ships or vessels sailing under the flag of Great Britain or France, or owned in whole or in part by any citizen or subject of either. . . .

Section 4. That from and after the twentieth day of May next, it shall not be lawful to import into the United States or the territories thereof, any goods, wares or merchandise whatever, from any port or place situated in Great Britain or Ireland, or in any of the colonies or dependencies of Great Britain, nor from any port or place situated in France, or in any of her colonies or dependencies, nor from any port or place in the actual possession of either Great Britain or France. . . .

Section 11. That the President of the United States, be and he hereby is authorized, in case either France or Great Britain shall so revoke or modify her edicts, as that they shall cease to violate the neutral commerce of the United States, to declare the same by proclamation; after which the trade of the United States . . . may be renewed with the nation so doing. . . .

Section 19. That this act shall continue and be in force until the end of the next session of Congress, and no longer. . . .

A WAR FOR TRADE
AND LAND, AND A
MANIFESTO OF EMPIRE

CHAPTER 3

The Rising Thrust for Empire

*F*rom *the beginning of their conflict with Great Britain, Americans defined independence in terms of freedom, trade, and land. As Professor Savelle pointed out in Chapter 1, moreover, those three elements were seen as interrelated parts of an integrated philosophy that involved a conception of empire. Americans considered economic expansion necessary for their general welfare, as well as for their individual profit. Freedom thus became entwined with expansion in two ways: expansion was an expression of American freedom; and, because Americans viewed themselves as being freer than European societies, expansion enlarged the area of true liberty.*

This outlook provided the basis of American thinking about national security, and at the same time generated a growing sense of mission to extend freedom wherever possible. In the early years, two factors inhibited positive action on such an expansionist philosophy. One was the need to avoid action that threatened the consolidation of the new nation. The other involved the differences among Americans over the issue of what freedom meant and how it was to be implemented at home, and over the question of whether commerce or agriculture should have priority.

From the outset, however, it was apparent that a surplus-producing agriculture was intimately related to commerce. The freehold farmers, as well as the planters (and other large agricultural businessmen), had to reach foreign markets, and the money earned by their exports provided capital for other economic development. This interrelationship and its meaning for foreign policy were recognized in the 1780s, as was made clear by the comments of Thomas Jefferson and others (Document 1). But James Madison was the key figure in formulating a general theory about the connection between expansion and freedom. He inverted the classical argument that freedom was causally related to a small society, arguing instead that it required a large system (Document 2). That theory, which integrated the commitment to freedom with the sense of the necessity of economic expansion, was at once an argument that affected other leaders, like Jefferson and James Monroe (Document 3), and a formal statement of a general attitude that was increasingly accepted by a growing number of Americans (Document 4).

As outlined in the first article, all such factors produced an imperial outlook that culminated in the War of 1812 and the Monroe Doctrine. In one sense, true enough, the War of 1812 appears as a negative rather than as a positive action—as a response to British policies that disrupted American trade and limited American freedoms. The crucial factor, however, was the way Americans viewed foreign markets as essential to their welfare. The nature of this trade and the way it affected American thinking are explored by Professors John H. Coatsworth and George Rogers Taylor, and are revealed in Document 4. In addition, significant numbers of Americans viewed the confrontation with Great Britain as an opportunity to acquire Florida from Spain, as well as to expand northward into Canada, while destroying the connection between the British and the Indians.

Two groups of Americans opposed the war. Some southerners like John Randolph decried the movement of men like Madison away from pure agrarianism into a coalition with erstwhile Federalists such as John Quincy Adams. And the diehard Federalists who convened the Hartford Convention against the war (Document 5) were as outraged by Adams as they were by Madison. At first glance, such criticisms seemed warranted by the course of the war. Not only did the United States fail to take Canada and to force Great Britain to change its maritime policies, but it suffered the humiliation of having the British enter Washington and set fire to the Capitol, the White House, and many other buildings.

In less obvious ways, however, the war produced results that strengthened the expansionist outlook. The British recognized that they could not defeat the United States without a major national effort, and that led to the Rush-Bagot agreement concerning armaments on the Great Lakes (Document 6). Even more significantly, the United States emerged from the war as the strongest power in the western hemisphere. John Quincy Adams and Andrew Jackson exploited their awareness of that truth in dealing with Spain as its strength began to ebb ever more rapidly: acquiring the Floridas by military action, and winning a corridor across the continent to the Pacific coast in the negotiations that culminated in the Trans-Continental Treaty of 1819.

Spain's loss of control over many of its New World colonies offered Americans a similar opportunity to expand trade with those emerging nations. How successfully they did this, and the implications of their commerce for foreign policy, is the theme of the article by Charles Lyon

Chandler. To a man like John Quincy Adams, who thought in terms of national development, this growing trade with Latin America was a positive objective to complement his negative aim of keeping other powers from using the wars in South America as an excuse to strengthen their existing claims in the hemisphere or advance new ones.

Along with their interest in land and commerce, Americans like Henry Clay of Kentucky were very enthusiastic about spreading the republican form of government throughout the world. The early revolutionary leaders had appealed to the world for sympathy; these later Americans called on the people of other nations to overthrow their kings. The more rambunctious of them even demanded that the United States intervene abroad to guarantee the success of such attempts. Feeling that the revolutions in Latin America had created profitable markets, these aggressive salesmen of the American way of life wanted the government in Washington to promote revolutions in other parts of the world. Clay's speech on the Latin American revolutions is a good example of this attitude (Document 7).

Congressman Clay was unhappy with the meager support he received from Secretary of State Adams. Adams realized that attempts to determine the affairs of other nations could lead the United States into many difficulties, and might even involve the country in wars from which it would gain little and lose much. He made his most telling answer to Clay in a Fourth of July address in 1821. While declaring that America was "the well-wisher to the freedom and independence of all," he recalled Washington's warning about excessive partiality for one nation and excessive dislike for another. He did not favor grandiose plans to liberate all the people who lived under monarchies and other forms of government. America might become "the dictatress of the world" but "would no longer be the ruler of her own spirit" if she undertook to manage the planet. America should "go not abroad in search of monsters to destroy," Adams concluded.

Adams was quick to act, however, to prevent European powers from restoring Spain's control in South America or strengthening their own position and claims there. The British Foreign Secretary, George Canning, was also disturbed by indications that France and Russia might throw their weight behind the Spanish government, and he suggested that the United States join with England in a declaration designed to forestall such an event. Adams was not anxious to limit America's chances to expand by tying the nation's policy to that of the British, as can be seen in Document 8. But he accepted eagerly the chance to take a strong stand on his own, knowing that the Royal Navy would back him up.

This situation also gave Adams an opportunity to improve his own political position with the expansionists in the West and to counter the criticisms he received from men like Henry Clay. Professor Dexter Perkins tells the story of how these developments led to the Monroe Doctrine. Adams won out over Clay's demands for more direct intervention in behalf of the South American revolutionaries, but Clay's somewhat reckless enthusiasm was reflected in President James Monroe's remarks (Document 9) about the revolt then going on in Greece. These comments are as much a part of the Monroe Doctrine as those sections of the President's message *which deal with foreign colonization in the Western Hemisphere. Adams was content with the more restrained policy of taking an option on North America and keeping Europe from extending its power in the rest of the hemisphere (Document 10).*

So were most other Americans, at least for a time. In that context, there were two principal factors that inhibited further American expansion: internal differences over the priorities to be assigned to particular expansionist projects, and the opposition offered by the Indians and the Mexicans. The Mexicans were the first to be shoved aside as the consensus on an empire for freedom and prosperity produced the emotional outburst that came to be known as Manifest Destiny.

THE AGE OF MERCANTILISM:

AN INTERPRETATION OF THE AMERICAN

POLITICAL ECONOMY TO 1828[1]   *William Appleman Williams*

... Revolutionary leaders were confident of their ability "not only to take territory by the sword, but to hold and govern it under a colonial status." Long before the break with England, for example, Benjamin Franklin was a leader of those who entertained a "burning interest in westward expansion." At the threshold of the revolution he visualized an American Empire including Canada, the Spanish Floridas, the West Indies, and perhaps even Ireland. George Washington, John Adams, John Livingston, and Thomas Lee were among those who shared such conceptions of an American Empire. By the end of the war, such men as Silas Deane looked forward to the time when "Great Britain, America and Russia united will command not barely Europe, but the whole world united." And in 1789, after remarking that "it is well known that empire has been travelling from east to west," Congregational minister and geographer Jedidiah Morse concluded that "probably her last and broadest seat will be America ... the largest empire that ever existed."

While the vigor, even cockiness, of such statements may be explained by the consciousness of having whipped the champion, the underlying emphasis on expansion and empire was an integral part of the general outlook of mercantilism, a conception of the world shared by most of the revolutionary generation. Though they revolted against British mercantilism, there is considerable evidence to suggest that early American leaders did not, as so often is assumed, rebel against the idea and practice of mercantilism itself. In stressing the role of natural-rights philosophy in the thinking of the leaders of the revolution, the traditional view of the American Revolution has slighted this key point.

An acceptance of natural law is not incompatible with mercantilism, as

[1] Selected from *William and Mary Quarterly*, XV, No. 4 (October, 1958), 419–37. Reprinted with permission.

is indicated by John Locke's vigorous espousal of both systems. Much of the talk in America about natural rights, moreover, concerned what Thomas Paine called the "natural right" to one's own empire. And though they were willing to use Adam Smith's polemic in behalf of laissez faire as a weapon against British mercantilism (and against their domestic opponents), most Americans adhered firmly in their own practice to the principle that the state had to intervene in economic affairs. America's romance with Smith's laissez faire came later and was of relatively short duration. Hence it would appear that a better understanding of early American history depends in considerable measure upon a grasp of the nature and practice of American mercantilism as it developed between 1763 and 1825.

Traditionally thought of as little more than a narrow and selfish point of view held by the trading interest, mercantilism was in fact a broad definition and explanation of the world shared by most of Western Europe in the seventeenth and eighteenth centuries. In this sense it was the basic outlook of those who labored to build a dynamic balanced economy of agriculture and business organized on a capitalistic basis within a nationalistic framework. Depending upon their specific function and power at any given stage in the process, mercantilists argued among themselves over the best means to achieve and maintain such a system—and differed in their estimates of whether or not it had been established—but they agreed on the objective and upon the need to use the state as a tool.

Whether agrarian or urban, therefore, mercantilists were essentially nationalists who strove for self-sufficiency through increased domestic production and a favorable balance (and terms) of trade. Their emphasis on production and the control of export markets and sources of raw materials, rather than on consumption and economic interdependence, led them to fear surpluses as a sign of crisis and failure. . . . In this respect, furthermore, mercantilism was reinforced—albeit in a backhanded and even unintentional way—by the broad ethical outlook of Puritanism (which frowned on luxury), even though mercantilism itself was a secular and almost amoral system. Likewise, the concept of a chosen people, so strong in Puritanism, also strengthened the secular and economic nationalism of mercantilism. Thus mercantilists constantly labored to build a tightly organized and protected national market and to increase their share of the world market. The key points in their program were integration at home and expansion abroad.

In the exuberant confidence of their victory over Britain, Americans tended to assume that each new state could survive and thrive as a mercantile empire unto itself. That attitude was not too surprising, for each of the new states appeared to enjoy the raw materials, labor supply, and trading facilities for a balanced economy. That estimate of the situation was supported and reinforced by the conviction, itself part of traditional theory, that a state could remain democratic in political and social life only if it were small and integrated, and by the experiences of the colonies in dealing with Great Britain's imperial policy after 1763. Yet the political outlook and faith contradicted certain basic tenets of mercantilism, which Americans also entertained, or assumed.

The first attempt to reconcile the conflict produced the Articles of Confederation. That instrument of government stressed the independence of the states as self-contained units of mercantilism and democratic republicanism, yet also established a central government for the purposes of war and, as in the case of Canada, future expansion. But specific postwar developments, such as the serious recession, the expansionist conflicts between the states, and the difficulties in dealing with other countries in economic affairs, combined to disillusion many Americans with their experiment in particularistic mercantilism.

Broadly speaking, the resulting movement toward a stronger central government grew out of internal and international economic difficulties analyzed and explained with the ideas of mercantilism. . . .

A letter from James Madison to Thomas Jefferson in the spring of 1786 not only indicates that the agrarian as well as the urban interests favored [such consolidation], but dramatizes the fundamental mercantilism of the entire movement. "A continuance of the present anarchy of our commerce," Madison explained, "will be a continuance of the unfavorable balance on it, which by draining us of our metals . . . [will bring our ruin]. In fact, most of our political evils may be traced up to our commercial ones, and most of our moral may to our political."

Against this background, the Constitution appears as an instrument of centralized national government framed in the classic manner by men thinking within the framework of mercantilism and blessed with the physical and human resources for a balanced economy. It provided the foundation for a national system of economics and politics and organized American strength for the struggle with other mercantile empires and for the conquest of less powerful peoples. The latter considerations were essential, for the Founding Fathers resolved the contradiction between the stress on expansion in mercantilism and the emphasis on a small state in existing democratic political theory by developing a theory of their own which held that democratic republicanism could be sustained by just such expansion. James Madison, often called the Father of the Constitution, provided the most striking formulation of this proposition, but Thomas Jefferson, John Adams, and other early leaders either shared or adopted it in one form or another within a reasonably short time.

Taking his cue from David Hume, the Englishman who attacked Montesquieu's argument that democracy was a system that could work only in small states, Madison asserted that a large state offered a much better foundation for republicanism. Institutional checks and balances could help, and were therefore necessary, but they were not enough in and of themselves. "Extend the sphere," he argued, "and you take in a greater variety of parties and interests; you make it less probable that a majority of the whole will have a common motive to invade the rights of other citizens; or if such a common motive exists, it will be more difficult for all who feel it to discover their own strength, and to act in unison with each other. . . ."

While it is possible to conclude from Madison's remarks that he had in mind a static conception of such a large state, three considerations would appear to weaken that reading of his thesis. First, Madison used the verb "extend" in its active, unlimited sense. Second, he was stating a general theory, not making an argument in behalf of a given territorial settlement. And third, he advocated and vigorously supported the continued expansion of the United States. It seems more probable, therefore, that Madison was proposing, *as a guide to policy and action in his own time*, the same kind of an argument that Frederick Jackson Turner formulated a century later, when he advanced his frontier thesis which explained America's democracy and prosperity as the result of such expansion.

* * *

Madison's original statement of the expansionist thesis was important for two reasons. First, it provided the theoretical basis for an American mercantilism combining commercial and territorial expansion with political democracy. Second, by thus re-emphasizing the idea of empire, and proposing expansion as the key to national welfare, Madison opened the way for a discussion of the basic questions facing American mercantilism. Those issues concerned domestic economic affairs, the kind of expansion that was necessary and desirable, and the means to accomplish such gains while the nation was young and weak.

Washington's Farewell Address formulated a bipartisan answer to the problem of basic strategy. The solution was to build a commercial empire (which included markets for agricultural surpluses) by avoiding political involvement in the European system, meanwhile retaining complete freedom of action to secure and develop a continental empire in the Western Hemisphere. Washington's proposition was classically simple: play from the strength provided by America's basic economic wealth and geographic location in order to survive immediate weakness and emerge as *the* world power. "If we remain one people, under an efficient government," he promised, "the period is not far off when we may defy material injury from external annoyance . . . when we may choose peace or war, as our interest, guided by justice, shall counsel." Sharing that objective, and quite in agreement with the strategy, Thomas Jefferson summed it all up a bit later in one famous axiom: "entangling alliances with none." And with the enunciation of the Monroe Doctrine, freedom of action became the avowed and central bipartisan theme of American foreign policy.

As a condition of that persuasive agreement, however, several serious conflicts had to be resolved. Perhaps they can be discussed most clearly by defining and considering them within the framework of the gradual defeat and amalgamation of the pro-British and pro-French minorities by a growing consensus in favor of an American mercantilism. Such an approach has the additional value of making it possible to organize the analysis around familiar personalities as symbols of certain ideas, functional groups, and special interests. Let it be posited, therefore, that the following men are key figures in the evolution of an American mercantilism: Timothy Pickering, John Adams, and John Quincy Adams of Massachusetts; Alexander Hamilton of New York; and James Madison, Thomas Jefferson, and John Taylor of Virginia.

In many respects, at any rate, Pickering and Taylor represented the nether fringes of American mercantilism. Pickering trod the trail from reluctant revolutionary to threatening secessionist in the name of a domestic merchant aristocracy functioning as a quasi-independent contractual member of the British Empire. His ideal was a central government charged with the responsibility (and armed with the power and authority) to establish and sustain a politically and socially stratified society and to provide the economic assistance (especially funded credit) that was necessary for the rationalized operations of overseas correspondents of British mercantilism and for domestic speculative ventures. Though Pickering and his supporters fit the traditional stereotype of mercantilists, they were in fact and function no more than the agents of British mercantilism. They were very successful agents, to be sure, but they did not view or define America in terms of its own mercantilism. Rather did they visualize it as a self-governing commonwealth of the British Empire. Hence it was only very late and with great reluctance, if at all, that they supported the measures necessary for a mercantilist state in America.

At the other extreme, John Taylor developed his program as a variation on a theme first stated by the French physiocrats. He emphasized the primacy of agriculture as narrowly as Pickering stressed the virtue and necessity of the merchant-trader-speculator. Taylor's tirades against funded debts and bank stock, and his soliloquies in praise of the noble farmer, seem alike in their total opposition to the principles of mercantilism. But in other respects his ideas were not so untainted by mercantilism as his rhetoric indicated. As with most other planters, for example, his theory of labor coincided at all essential points with the view held by British mercantilists. So, too, did his conception of the role of western lands in the economy of the seaboard "mother country."

With respect to foreign trade, moreover, Taylor was trapped by the weakness of the physiocrats in that area of economics. Ostensibly free traders, the physiocrats did not favor the navy essential to such a program. Taylor and other American imbibers of the physiocratic elixir awoke to discover that their vision did not correspond to reality. Taylor himself was not very adaptive, and ended his career in attacks on Jefferson and other agrarians who did develop an American mercantilism. But Taylor's position does dramatize the dilemma faced by the agrarians. The contradiction between theory and actuality confronted them with a rather apparent choice: either they could content themselves with slow economic stagnation or they could build an American maritime system, accept dependence upon a foreign naval power, or support an American industry. In that choice lies a key aspect of the rise of a mature American mercantilism; for it developed most consciously and was ultimately practiced most rigorously by the southern agrarians who are often assumed to have been most rabidly antimercantilist. If nothing else, the weakness of their ideal program drove them into mercantilism.

* * *

... Madison ... emerges as the central figure in the development of an American mercantilism. While there are many illustrations, perhaps his resolutions of January 1794 provide the most illuminating evidence. . . . [Professor] Charles points the way: "The program with which Madison began the first strategic moves against the Federalists was not one which could be called anti-Federalist, particularist, or States' rights." His plan was to combine landed expansion to the west with support for domestic manufacturing and an independent American commercial policy. Considered at the practical political level, it represented a bid to the growing numbers of dissident Federalists who opposed a one-way relationship with Britain. Some of those men eyed a bull market for domestic manufactures. Others thought of an expansionist foreign policy with the established states cast in the role of "mother country." Madison saw such groups as allies for the anti-Federalists, as well as the building blocks of an American mercantilism.

Madison's conception of an American mercantilism was possibly too comprehensive as well as too premature politically to be adopted by Congress in 1794, though it was extensively debated before being sidetracked by Hamilton and Smith. But it did serve as a keen analysis and program for the growing consensus among anti-Federalists. That drive toward economic independence manifested itself in the Non-Intercourse Bill introduced in the summer of 1794, a move which was defeated only by the vote of Vice-President John Adams. Equally significant is the fact that it was backed by congressmen from Pennsylvania and Delaware as well as by those from southern states. Madison's mercantilism picked up new allies very rapidly, and two subsequent events served as catalysts in the process. Considered in the order of their importance, they were Jay's Treaty and the last stage in the defection of John Adams from High Federalism.

Following so closely upon the narrow defeat of the Non-Intercourse Bill, Jay's Treaty added injury to frustration. The great majority of Americans reacted bitterly and vigorously. Already weakened by deep fissures, the Federalist party cracked open under the ensuing attack. It cost them key leaders in such states as New Hampshire and Pennsylvania and alienated unknown numbers of voters south of the Potomac. As one who had cast the deciding vote against the Non-Intercourse Bill only with great reluctance, John Adams provided temporary leadership for such Federalist dissidents.

Adams strengthened his position even more by refusing to go quietly along to war with France at the bidding of the High Federalists. The differences between Hamilton and Adams were numerous, but perhaps none is so important to an appreciation of the maturing American mercantilism as the contrast between Hamilton's passion for a large army and Adams' emphasis on an American navy. Hamilton's military policy was that of the British nabob in North America, while that of Adams represented American mercantilism. Against that background, and in the context of his deciding vote on the Non-Intercourse Bill of 1794, it is possible to appreciate the full impact of Jay's Treaty on Adams. He made peace with France and forced Pickering out of the cabinet.

Little wonder, then, that Jefferson was willing to give way in favor of Adams. But thanks to Madison, who had been organizing a party as well as projecting a theory and a program, Jefferson became president. Once in power, Jefferson and his supporters were prodded by necessity and spurred by their own visions of empire toward the full development of an American mercantilism. There are several explanations for this phenomenon. Among the most important, one might list the following: the foreign-trade dilemma inherent in physiocratic theory (which was intensified by the wars stemming from the French Revolution); the creative leadership provided by such men as Madison and Albert Gallatin (who made his own *Report on Manufactures* in 1810); the political necessities and expediences of unifying and sustaining a national party; and the maturing thought of Jefferson himself. But wherever one chooses to place the emphasis, the fact remains that the Jeffersonians in action were far more mercantilistic than the Federalists had been —even in theory and rhetoric.

* * *

The Louisiana Purchase opened the way to apply the tenets of American mercantilism to the entire hemisphere. It also encouraged an explicit American formulation of the expansionist philosophy of history that was implicit in mercantilism. Americans began to call openly and militantly for further expansion whenever and wherever they encountered domestic or foreign difficulties. Indians and Spaniards had to be pushed out of the way or destroyed. Interference with exports had to be stopped, by war if necessary. Canada offered the solution to other domestic economic problems, and should be taken forthwith.

After 1807, when economic troubles appeared at home, that expansionist outlook and program focused on Great Britain as the chief offender against the American Empire. Growing out of an alliance of business and agrarian interests which favored war to relieve immediate difficulties and forestall future crises, the War of 1812 was a classic mercantilist conflict for trade and colonies. The Jeffersonians' earlier economic and maritime warfare, which almost secured the immediate objectives, and which had appeared capable of clearing the way for a general advance, was just as mercantilistic in nature. Though in many ways it failed to attain its avowed objectives, the War of 1812 was in no sense a strategic defeat for American mercantilism. If only in turning Americans to the west and the south, it focused the general spirit of expansion in a new and powerful manner. Perhaps even more significant, the stalemate strengthened the idea of an American System as opposed to the rest of the world. It was in the wake of the War of 1812, after all, that the vapors of Manifest Destiny gathered themselves for an explosion westward to the Pacific.

John Quincy Adams formulated his own concept of Manifest Destiny as early as 1796, when he assured President Washington that the American system would "infallibly triumph over the European system...." Fifteen years later he defined America as "a nation, coextensive with the North American Continent, destined by God and nature to be the most populous and most powerful people ever combined under one social compact." He pushed overseas economic expansion just as vigorously. Even his harshest critics, the High Federalists of New England who wanted to reenter the British Empire in some form or another, recognized his mercantilism. They called him one of the species of "amphibious politicians, who live on both land and water...."

Both before and after he served as Secretary of State under President James Monroe, Adams devoted his energies to building such an American Empire. His rational program for a dynamic balanced economy at home was too demanding for his countrymen. They grew ever more enamored of a philosophy that assured them that expansion was the way to ease their dilemmas and realize their dreams. Hence they paid little heed to his proposals for domestic development or to his warning that America should go "not abroad in search of monsters to destroy." But to the extent that Adams wanted an empire big enough to sustain such a balanced economy, and to the degree that he partook of the expansionist elixir, he won support and influence. And, indeed, his very presence in the cabinet of Monroe was a symbol of the maturity of American mercantilism. Having broken with the old pro-British party to vote for the Louisiana Purchase and the measures of economic warfare against Europe, Adams became the leader of those business interests which supported territorial as well as commercial expansion.

In timing, authorship, and content, the Monroe Doctrine was the classic statement of mature American mercantilism. Seizing the opportunity presented by the decay of the Spanish Empire, Monroe and Adams moved quickly, decisively, and independently to give substance to Henry Clay's fervent exhortation to "become real and true Americans and place ourselves at the head of the American System." Adams caught the tone and meaning of the doctrine in his famous remark that it was time for America to stop bobbing along as a cock-boat in the wake of the British Empire. Acting in that spirit, he spurned Secretary George Canning's not-so-subtle suggestion that America join England in a joint guarantee of Latin American independence and a pledge against their own expansion in the region. Canning claimed high honors for having brought in the New World to redress the balance of the Old, but one would like to think that Adams enjoyed a hearty chuckle over such ability to put a rhetorical gloss on a policy defeat. For what Canning had done was to block the old empires only to be confronted by the challenge of a mature American mercantilism.

In the negative sense, the Monroe Doctrine was designed to check further European colonization in the Western Hemisphere. But Americans were quite aware of the positive implications of the strategy: it left the United States as the most powerful nation on the scene. America's ultimate territorial and commercial expansion in the New World would be limited only by its energies and its preferences—just as Washington had argued. The negative side of the Monroe Doctrine is the least significant feature about it: the crucial point is that it was, in the minds of its authors, in its language, and in its reception by Americans, the manifesto of an American Empire.

* * *

AMERICAN TRADE WITH EUROPEAN
COLONIES IN THE CARIBBEAN AND
SOUTH AMERICA, 1790–1812[1] *John H. Coatsworth*

In the first decade of American independence, the principal European powers restricted or excluded American trade with their possessions to suit the needs and interests of their own commercial classes. The twenty years of war among these powers which began in 1793 caused the abandonment of commercial monopolies as the belligerents were forced to resort to neutral shipping and to authorize the importation of neutral goods on a wide scale. While the war thus produced an enormous expansion of trade with the West Indies and opened up promising new markets, especially in Spain's continental colonies, American commerce became extremely sensitive to every shift in the course of events. The exhilarating wartime dreams of American commercial supremacy in the region which lingered on long after the war masked the reality of this dependence on external events just as the relative increase in American exports obscured the real poverty of the region's markets.

Precarious as it was, this branch of American foreign trade took nearly one third of all the exports of the United States between 1790 and 1814. The fortunes of a number of important producer groups and regions, of several major seaboard towns, and of a large part of the American merchant class depended on trade with the West Indies and Spanish America. It does not seem strange therefore that economic historians have recently emphasized the importance of the export sector in determining the pace and pattern of early economic growth. Douglass C. North argues that the home market was "too small and scattered" to generate significant expansion alone. Not until "external events" gave rise to rapidly expanding foreign markets did American domestic growth get underway. North identified the years 1793–1807 as the first period of rapid domestic growth. In these years, "the main sources of expansion" in the economy were the wartime re-export and carrying trades.

* * *

The end of the international conflict which arose during the War for American Independence produced a prolonged attempt by the chief colonial powers of Europe, Britain, France, and Spain, to restore the colonial commercial and navigation systems which had been disrupted by the hostilities. Although efforts by the United States to use its economic power to force liberalization of restrictive trade policies ended in failure, colonial needs for certain U.S. products forced both Britain and France to permit a limited intercourse with their West Indian colonies. While the value of U.S. exports

[1] Selected from *William and Mary Quarterly*, XXIV, No. 2 (April, 1967), 243–60. Reprinted with permission.

to the West Indies remained small throughout this period, the low volume of total U.S. foreign trade made its relative importance to the export sector of the American economy very great.

Trade with the French West Indies was least restricted in the decade after independence. Following an initial attempt to restore the Decree of 1767, France in 1784 and 1785 opened five new West Indian ports (including St. Domingue) to U.S. shipping, and abandoned its prohibition on imports of flour and certain other foodstuffs. Due in part to this relaxation, U.S. trade with the French colonies grew more rapidly than trade with the islands of Great Britain or Spain. In the 1780's and early 1790's, St. Domingue ranked as "the world's leading producer of sugar and coffee," and supplied U.S. importers with "practically their entire stock of sugar and molasses." . . .

Great Britain took somewhat smaller steps toward liberalization in 1784, but the stringent regulations adopted in 1786 and 1787 to combat smuggling may have stopped more trade than the earlier measure allowed. Export estimates at the end of the decade indicate a shift in American trade away from the British islands to the French as well as the Dutch colonies in the Caribbean. Despite this shift, the British West Indies remained an important market for certain U.S. exports in this period. The islands were heavily dependent upon the United States for staple foods and lumber products. . . . These U.S. products had to be admitted. The British West Indies were second only to the French islands as importers of flour, taking 18.6 per cent of total U.S. flour exports in 1790. Although the islands were supplied adequately with fish, beef, and pork from other areas within the empire, and British regulations prohibited imports of these American products, the British islands took more corn and corn meal than the French. According to the official estimates, the French West Indies accounted for 16.2 per cent of total U.S. exports in 1790, while the British took 10.2 per cent.

Although Spain reopened Havana and Trinidad to U.S. shipping in 1785, it did so under conditions so restrictive as to keep legal intercourse at a minimum. U.S. exports to the Spanish West Indies constituted less than 1 per cent of total U.S. exports between 1790 and 1793. In the last of these years, on the eve of the war in Europe, U.S. exports to the Spanish colonies were officially valued at a mere $159,426. . . .

Taken together, the exports of the United States to the West Indian colonies of the European powers constituted an extremely important factor in U.S. foreign trade during the first decade after independence. Official estimates for the 1780's do not exist, but it is known that U.S. exports experienced a moderate general recovery from the depression levels of 1785–88 beginning in 1789. In 1790, 31.4 per cent of all U.S. exports were sent to the West Indies.

Several important producer groups and regions were heavily dependent on the West Indies trade. Export statistics after 1789 indicate how extensive this dependence was. Table One illustrates the significance of the West Indies market for producers of the most important commodities exported to the islands in 1790. Over half the flour, fish, beef, pork, lumber, and livestock exports of the United States found their way to the West Indies in 1790.

TABLE 1

PERCENTAGE OF TOTAL EXPORTS OF SEVEN ITEMS
EXPORTED TO THE WEST INDIES IN 1790

Item	Per Cent
Flour	52.0
Corn	32.8
Fish (dried and pickled)	73.5
Beef	81.1
Pork	97.9
Lumber and wood products	64.4
Livestock	95.3

The official estimates, together with other evidence, indicate that grain farmers in the Chesapeake and eastern Pennsylvania regions, the flour milling industry which became concentrated in the Baltimore and Philadelphia areas, the New England fisheries, livestock producers, and meat processors in Connecticut, Massachusetts, North Carolina, and New York, and lumber interests in Virginia, North Carolina, and the Connecticut River valley were chief among them. Table Two lists the states which exported the largest amounts of five of these principal items in the West Indian trade. Since the official estimates do not list the destination of each of the state's exports by country, these figures indicate only the percentage of total exports, not of

TABLE 2

PERCENTAGE OF TOTAL EXPORTS OF FIVE ITEMS BY STATES, 1791

Item	State	Per Cent
Flour	Pennsylvania	38.9
	Maryland	24.4
	New York	14.3
	Virginia	12.2
Beef	Massachusetts	48.8
	Connecticut	28.5
	New York	10.4
Pork	Connecticut	20.5
	New York	18.5
	North Carolina	15.4
	Pennsylvania	12.9
	Massachusetts	11.9
Fish	Massachusetts	77.6
	Rhode Island	12.5
Corn	Pennsylvania	26.7
	Virginia	22.5
	New York	15.8
	North Carolina	12.4
	Maryland	11.8

exports to the West Indies alone, of each commodity, but since a high percentage of each of these items did in fact go to the West Indies, the figures in Table Two give a good indication of the geographic distribution of export producers tied to the West Indian market.

In nearly every state, from North Carolina to New England, important producer groups were heavily involved in trade with the West Indies.

With the outbreak of war among the European colonial powers in 1793, there began a period of rapid expansion of United States trade with the West Indies. New opportunities for trade opened on the southern continents as the war progressively undermined the Spanish and Portuguese monopolies on trade with their American colonies. The commerce of the United States rapidly gained a freedom which neither the exertions of diplomacy nor the enabling clauses of the new Constitution had been able to secure. But as the European powers opened their colonial ports to a freer trade with the United States, they vied with one another in imposing restrictions on neutral trade with their enemies. Periods of expansion in domestic exports and enormous growth in the re-export trade alternated with commercial depressions precipitated by European peace and the United States embargo.

U.S. exports to the French West Indies exceeded those to the British and Spanish islands during the early years of the war, from 1793 to 1798. . . . In each of the years 1794 through 1797, the French colonies took between 39 per cent and 44 per cent of all U.S. exports to the Caribbean and South America. This amounted to between 10 per cent and 15 per cent of total U.S. exports to all countries. In 1799, U.S. exports to the French West Indies fell below the value of exports to the colonies of Britain and Spain for the first time. In that year they dropped to just 10 per cent of U.S. exports to the region, or 3.5 per cent of total exports to all countries. After this decline, U.S. exports to the French West Indies did not again rise to the high levels achieved in 1796 and 1797, when they exceeded $8 million in value each year. Exports to the French islands did recover to a value in excess of $7 million in 1801 and again, after the Peace of Amiens, in 1805. The U.S. embargo put an end to the 1805–07 revival of trade with the West Indies. While trade with the British and Spanish colonies experienced a partial recovery in the years 1809–11, exports to the French islands dropped below $1 million and stayed there until long after the War of 1812.

U.S. exports to the British West Indies rose slowly during the first two years of the war, but jumped from $2.6 million in 1795 to $5.4 million in 1796. French seizures of U.S. vessels trading with the British islands in retaliation against the Jay-Grenville Treaty caused U.S. exports to drop 61.4 per cent in 1797, down to the pre-war level of $2.1 million. Thereafter, exports to the British islands showed rapid increases in 1798, 1799, and 1801. . . . At the apex of the 1798–1801 upswing, when exports to the British islands exceeded those to the colonies of any other power, the islands took 35.1 per cent of U.S. exports to the region and fully 10.1 per cent of U.S. exports to all countries.

* * *

U.S. exports to Spanish America experienced sharper fluctuations in value than those to the British and French islands. From 1793 to 1799, exports to the Spanish colonies rose steadily in value from less than $1 million to a high of $8.9 million, and from less than 10 per cent of U.S. exports to the region in 1794 to more than 35 per cent in 1800. . . .

During the Peace of Amiens, U.S. exports to the Spanish possessions fell precipitously from $8.4 million in 1801 to less than $1 million in 1803. Without the pretext of the wartime emergency, Spain's colonial officialdom bowed to the court's decree restoring a complete monopoly over the colonial trade. The effectiveness of the restoration is indicated by the fact that while U.S. exports to Spanish America exceeded in value those to the colonies of Britain and France in 1800, they were worth much less than exports to these other areas in the period 1802–04. While Spanish America took 30.5 per cent of U.S. exports to the region in 1801, the Spanish colonies' share dropped to 6.6 per cent in 1803.

In the period following the Peace of Amiens, from 1805 to the War of 1812, U.S. exports to Spanish America again exceeded in value those to the colonies of the other powers. In 1805 and 1806, the Spanish colonies took 31.7 per cent and 38.8 per cent of U.S. exports to the region. From 1807 through the War of 1812, the Spanish colonies never took less than 40 per cent of the exports to the Caribbean and South America. In each of the years after 1805, more than 10 per cent of all U.S. exports to all countries went to Spain's American colonies. At its highest point, in 1807, the level of U.S. exports to Spanish America exceeded $12 million. During the embargo, U.S. exports to the Spanish colonies dropped from this high point to $4.1 million in 1808, a fall of some 66.2 per cent. By 1809, however, exports were back above the $6 million level and reached a peak of $7.5 million in 1811.

* * *

The growing importance of U.S. trade with the continental colonies of Spain is indicated by the number of U.S. vessels which called at ports in the La Plata River basin during the war. Figures compiled from contemporary newspaper accounts show that while only 10 U.S. ships were known to have stopped there in 1799, at least 42 stopped in 1806 and 1807, while no less than 30 U.S. vessels put in at Montevideo and Buenos Aires alone in 1810. Similar sources indicate that 47 ships from Baltimore alone docked at Vera Cruz, Mexico in 1806 and 1807.

To United States merchants, trade with Spain's continental colonies was of even greater importance than these figures show. Buenos Aires and Chile supplied specie for the developing China trade, U.S. ships carried beef and hides from Buenos Aires to Havana, Peru imported Asian goods carried in U.S. vessels, and American shipping transported great quantities of colonial products from both Atlantic and Pacific ports to the Mediterranean.

* * *

In every year from 1803 to 1812, domestic exports accounted for more than 89 per cent of all U.S. exports to the British West Indies. These figures reflect the degree of British naval supremacy which allowed British merchants to maintain commercial contact with the colonies without resorting to neutral carriers on a large scale. It is likely that the carrying trade to the British islands was somewhat larger before 1803, because British naval superiority was not so clearly established in the early years of the war.... By 1805 the British felt more secure at sea than earlier, and much more anxious to secure taxable incomes for British shipping interests. The result was the Order in Council prohibiting neutral ships from trading with the British West Indies and the relative stabilization of U.S. exports to the British islands during the 1805–07 period of generally rising U.S. exports to the region.

A more complex pattern is revealed in the statistics for U.S. exports to the French and Spanish colonies. In the case of the French West Indies, domestic exports accounted for less than half the total in years when total exports were highest, 1805–07, and more than half in poor years, 1803, 1808–14. A similar pattern was true for exports to Spanish America. The percentage of domestic exports in the total shipped to the Spanish colonies declined in each year of the 1804–07 upswing, from 64.2 per cent at the low point in 1803, to 20.1 per cent at the apex in 1807.

The embargo cut domestic exports to the Spanish colonies somewhat more severely than foreign re-exports. A similar, though less pronounced, effect was true for exports to the French and British islands. The percentage of domestic exports in the total to Spanish America dropped to 15.1 per cent in 1808.

For the years following the embargo, when exports to Spanish America were once again rising, domestic exports recovered far more rapidly than exports of foreign goods. Domestic exports rose from the embargo level of $.6 million in 1808 to $3.3 million in 1809, an increase of 431.2 per cent. Meanwhile, Spain's shift into alliance with Great Britain removed most of the risks incurred by Spanish shipping in trade with the Spanish colonies. Spanish fleets quickly returned to colonial waters along with the British who at once became a competing carrier, especially of manufactured goods, throughout Spanish America. Foreign re-exports from the United States to the Spanish colonies therefore fell 5.9 per cent *below* the embargo level in 1809. During 1810 and 1811, domestic exports constituted 46.9 per cent and 47.6 per cent of total U.S. exports to Spanish America, higher than in any year of the previous upswing save 1804, when U.S. exports to Spanish America, higher than in any year of the previous upswing save 1804, when U.S. exports had not yet fully recovered from the Peace of Amiens.

... In 1811, the peak year of the second upswing, domestic exports to Spanish America stood 46 per cent higher than during the peak year of the first upswing (1807). Thus, for domestic producers, trade with Spanish America increased in importance in the years 1809–1811, despite the fact that over-all exports to the Spanish colonies in the second period were much lower. During the earlier upswing, in fact, U.S. domestic exports to the British and even the French islands ran higher than domestic exports to Spanish America even while *total* exports to the Spanish colonies during the same period were worth much more than those to either the British or the French colonies.

* * *

Considerable evidence suggests that the most important factors limiting the growth of domestic exports, especially after 1803, occurred not on the supply side, but in the nature of the demand for American goods in the region. Some of these factors involved policy decisions by the belligerent powers and conditions created by the war itself. Civil strife and finally British occupation destroyed the French West Indian market for American domestic exports. The British Orders in Council of 1805 and the restrictive American legislation which followed the embargo provide a part of the explanation for the decline in domestic exports to the British West Indies after 1804.

To these external events must be added the role of other factors, of greater long-run importance, which involved the relative capacity of the colonial markets to absorb increasing quantities of American goods. Slavery and other features of the region's plantation economies limited the growth of demand for many American imports, not only in the British islands, but in the Spanish West Indies and Brazil as well. While demand for American foodstuffs remained strong in the postwar period, it grew very slowly, reflecting the slow pace of internal development in these areas. Unlike the plantation colonies, Spain's continental colonies were largely self-sufficient in foodstuffs. Once they recovered from the ravages of the independence wars after 1820, Mexico, Buenos Aires, Uruguay, and Chile quickly developed exportable surpluses of many of the same commodities the United States was anxious to sell them. Rapid growth and the rise of important industrial sectors might have increased the demand for American imports in the continental colonies. Slow growth in predominantly agrarian societies held little promise.

The quick collapse of mercantilist restrictions on trade with European colonies in South America and the Caribbean appears to have produced an initial and rapid rise in demand for U.S. domestic exports in the region. After ten years of war, however, factors both external and internal to the region's markets were operating to reduce or prevent additional shifts in demand. While the euphoria which surrounded the carrying trade disappeared quickly in the years between the embargo and the War of 1812, it was not until the postwar period that American merchants and producers confronted the slow growth of regional markets directly. Some Americans in the postwar era favored high tariffs and early recognition of Spanish American independence movements as a means of insuring a more rapid growth in U.S. trade with the region. The success of British commercial competition gave impetus to these demands. . . .

AGRARIAN DISCONTENT IN THE
MISSISSIPPI VALLEY
PRECEDING THE WAR OF 1812[1]   *George Rogers Taylor*

Agrarian discontent has so often played an important part in our history that
it is surprising that its importance in the Mississippi Valley preceding the
War of 1812 has not been recognized. Western agriculture suffered, as this
paper will show, a severe economic depression in the years just before the
war, and this depression was an important factor in determining the support
which the frontier gave first to the Embargo and Non-intercourse acts and
finally to war. To understand western discontent, something of the situation
in earlier years must be known. The examination of western economic conditions may well begin, therefore, with the period of prosperity which preceded the hard times of 1808–12.

In the first decade of the nineteenth century, the hunting and trapping
frontier receded to the west and north, and, over wide areas, the valleys of
the Ohio and lower Mississippi became definitely a farming country. For
several years following the Louisiana Purchase this new agricultural West
experienced a pronounced boom. The usual optimism and exaggerated an-
ticipations of wealth which we have since learned to expect in such periods
were abundantly present. The depression which accompanied the Peace of
Amiens had been largely attributed by western farmers to Spanish interference with the Mississippi trade at New Orleans. When, therefore, news
reached the West that the United States had purchased Louisiana, the frontiersmen believed that serious obstacles to western prosperity were a thing
of the past. . . .

From the vantage point of over one hundred years after the event, the
fact is clear enough that the western agriculturist of 1805 was, despite elimination of Spanish interference on the Mississippi, abundant harvests, increased immigration, and high prices for western products, much more
sanguine in his expectations of prosperity than fundamental conditions justified. Even without the embargo and non-intercourse of 1808 and 1809, it
cannot be doubted that the bubble of 1805 would soon have burst. . . .

Most serious was the problem of transportation. The physical obstacles
to getting western products to market in the days before the steamboat and
the railroad were even greater than is generally realized. . . . So great were
the drawbacks to land transportation from western Pennsylvania, to say
nothing of the vast region farther west, that the wagons which brought the
needed imports from Philadelphia to Pittsburgh customarily returned empty.
Such frontier staples as hemp, flour, bacon, and even whiskey simply could
not stand the cost of carriage over the mountain roads.

---

[1] *The Journal of Political Economy*, XXXIX, No. 4 (August 1931), 471–505. Reprinted by permission
of The University of Chicago Press.

In consequence, Ohio Valley produce had to be sent a thousand miles or more down the Ohio-Mississippi river system to Natchez or New Orleans. This trip usually took about a month, and was beset with perils and hardships from beginning to end. . . .

The same difficulties of transportation which hindered western producers from getting their surplus to market made the bringing in of their imports very costly. Though self-sufficing to a considerable extent, the frontier was dependent upon the eastern states and foreign countries for a great variety of products, including most manufactured goods. . . .

Except to ports on the lower Mississippi, such as Natchez and New Orleans, importations up-river remained relatively small until the advent of the steamboat. Forcing a barge up the Mississippi was a peculiarly difficult task. Not only was the current strong and treacherous, but the river bottom was often too soft for poling and the banks unsuited for towing. Every device then known for forcing a craft through water was attempted. Oars, sails, setting poles, treadmills operated by horses, "bush-whacking," and the cordelle, all were tried, and still the journey remained so slow, arduous, and uncertain that the passage from New Orleans to Louisville took three months and freight charges were from three to five times as high as down-river rates.

* * *

Slow and unreliable communication of market information also added to frontier difficulties. This was due in part to the obstacles to travel emphasized above and in part also to the undeveloped trade organization of the frontier community. For news of market conditions the western merchant or farmer depended upon prices current either printed in the newspapers or communicated privately by letter. By 1810 the good-weather time for post riders from Philadelphia to Lexington was still at least two weeks. From New Orleans letters could, under favorable conditions, be delivered in Kentucky in twenty-five days. . . .

This handicap was made all the more serious by the presence of eastern speculators. The editor of the *Kentucky Gazette* complained that because of the slowness of the mail:

A speculator . . . can hasten [from Philadelphia or New Orleans] . . . purchase our production on his own terms, and lay the whole western country under contribution . . . before we can have any information as to the change in price of produce in the markets of those places . . . fortunes have often been made in this way . . . when the loss of a battle, the death of a Bonaparte, or the fall of a minister of state, may change the course of business, and improve or depress markets.

The undeveloped financial organization of the West can hardly be more than mentioned here as still another of those factors which contributed to the fundamental economic difficulties of the frontiersman. A scarcity of money often existed for the payment of taxes or to meet the ordinary needs of trade. Barter, everywhere common for small payments, was almost the only mode of exchange in the remote settlements. Public officers' receipts and land warrants were commonly issued by the frontier states; and, although helping somewhat to make up for the scarcity of other media, they were often unsatisfactory because subject to depreciation.

Banking facilities developed beginning with the establishment of the Kentucky Insurance Company in 1802. But, for most of the West, banks were just getting well started by 1812. . . .

Probably more serious than the imperfect financial machinery was the scarcity of capital. The settlers did not bring much capital with them, nor had the country been settled long enough to develop its own surplus. As yet little eastern capital flowed westward except as Atlantic merchants gave long credits to their frontier customers. The complaint of scarcity of money so frequently found in western newspapers no doubt often arose in reality from a scarcity of capital. . . .

Finally, as a new, extensive, and sparsely settled region, the frontier suffered, as we should expect, from an imperfectly developed business and marketing organization. . . .

But especially in the disposal of his exportable surplus did the frontier agriculturist suffer from lack of adequate marketing machinery. In order to get his produce to market, the farmer had often to assume the risk of carrying his own produce to New Orleans and there disposing of it as best he could. In the words of a contributor to the Frankfort *Palladium* the producer became "a navigator, and a trader." . . .

No one of the drawbacks described above nor all of them together were necessarily fatal to western hopes, for, though difficulties are great and costs high, if prices are still higher, prosperity may yet be obtained. Still these difficulties surely tended to make the West of this period a sort of marginal area in relation to world markets. When world prices ruled high, Monongahela and Kentucky flour could be disposed of in competition with that from Virginia and Maryland. Likewise, when cotton and tobacco brought good prices, the Kentucky and Tennessee product could be sold along with that of the Atlantic states and still yield a profit to distant western farmers. But when markets were dull and prices falling, western producers not only saw the fading of their roseate hopes but often enough found themselves in desperate straits to secure necessary imported commodities or to meet obligations for land bought on credit when hopes ran high with prices.

Free navigation of the Mississippi, unprecedented immigration, and unusually high prices had brought a great wave of optimism to the West following 1803, despite the underlying difficulties just considered. The peak year proved to be 1805, but times were relatively good in 1806 and 1807 except for those parts of the West which were adversely affected by glutted markets and lower prices for west-country provisions. Acute depression did not come until 1808. . . .

Two main remedies for the situation received increasingly enthusiastic support from the frontiersmen in the period of falling prices and hard times, which began for parts of the West as early as 1806, became general by 1808, and continued down to the War of 1812 with but partial and temporary relief in 1809–10. One was the development of manufactures; the other was forcing the European powers to repeal their restrictions on our foreign commerce. . . .

Our attention . . . is centered primarily upon western attempts to mend their failing fortunes through supporting commercial coercion and war. An understanding of the course of frontier opinion in respect to these measures involves, first, a realization of the degree of support which the West gave to the Embargo Act of December, 1807, and, second, an appreciation of the importance of economic motives in prompting the West to support a measure accompanied, as this one was, by widespread depression. An examination of the situation reveals that in his policy of commercial coercion President Jefferson received no more faithful support than that which came from western congressmen. . . .

On the whole, the citizens of the western states were just as enthusiastic for commercial restrictions as their representatives in Congress. . . .

It cannot be denied that traditional attitudes and party loyalty played some part in determining western support for the embargo. To some extent the westerner was playing the role of a good Democrat and supporting his president. In part he was acting as a good patriot and a high-spirited frontiersman who resented insults to the national honor either by France or England. The traditional friendship of Democrats for France doubtless made the westerner quick to resent untoward acts by Britain and slow to see evil in the French aggressions. But these explanations are, at most, not the whole story, for an examination of western opinion clearly indicates that the support which was given the embargo on the frontier had in it a considerable element of economic self-interest.

The western farmer was quite willing to admit his lack of interest in the carrying trade. Even impressment of seamen, though to be deplored, did not seem to him very important. But he did want adequate markets and good prices for his produce, and these he believed impossible so long as Great Britain restricted the West Indian market, forbade direct trade with the Continent, and placed exceedingly burdensome duties upon American imports into Great Britain. In the eyes of the western farmer, the depression of 1808 was primarily the result of the belligerents' decrees and orders in council, not of the embargo which he regarded as a highly desirable act, designed as a measure of retaliation to force the abandonment by foreign nations of their destructive interference with the marketing of our surplus products. "Who now blames the embargo?" demanded a Cincinnati editor. "Who considers it a matter of French interest or procurement? Who does not allow it to be a *saving measure?* . . . The embargo was produced by the foreign belligerent powers. They made it wise, just and necessary. They made its continuance necessary."

In Congress western representatives made no effort to conceal their economic interest in the embargo. Said Senator Pope of Kentucky, in stating the very core of the argument in defense of this measure:

What, Mr. President, is our situation? . . . The dispute between us and the belligerents is not about the carrying trade, but whether we shall be permitted to carry our surplus produce to foreign markets? The privilege of carrying our cotton to market, is one in which, not only the growers themselves are interested, but one which concerns every part of the nation.

. . . By the Non-Intercourse Act, which superseded the Embargo Act in the spring of 1809, direct trade with England and France and their colonies was prohibited. Although there was nothing now to stop an indirect trade with England, the British orders in council still kept American produce from reaching the Continent. On the whole the West did not like the change, and their representatives were right in predicting that such partial opening of trade would glut markets with our products and bring prices still lower. Poindexter denounced England's attempt to monopolize world trade and "tax the product of our farms when exported to foreign markets." He even advocated war against her if necessary, and did not hesitate to recommend to his constituents that cotton be shipped immediately to England via a neutral port so as to get a fair price before markets were glutted.

The course of events during the summer of 1809 was well calculated still further to inflame western hatred for Great Britain and convince the frontier farmers that their surplus could never be exported at a profit until England was somehow forced to permit free trade upon the seas. . . .

The winter of 1809–10 found hard times on frontier farms and western sentiment more bitter than ever against the British as the chief cause of the farmers' troubles. The attempt at commercial coercion had failed, but Congress was not yet ready to declare war. Beginning May 1, 1810, commerce was freed from the restrictive measures of our own government. On the whole, conditions seemed on the mend in the following summer, and western farmers were busy harvesting crops which they hoped might be floated down the river to good markets in 1811. Some thought they perceived a promise of better times, while others saw no assurance of prosperity until foreign restrictions should be withdrawn.

But, instead of improving, conditions actually grew seriously worse during the next two years. . . .

Increased bitterness toward Great Britain and a renewed determination to force her to repeal her commercial restrictions accompanied the depression of 1811–12. But frontiersmen showed no desire to repeat the attempt at commercial coercion; past failures had shaken their faith in pacific measures. The new attitude is epitomized in the following toast offered at a Fourth of July celebration held at Frankfort in 1811: "Embargoes, non-intercourse, and negotiations, are but illy calculated to secure our rights. . . . Let us now try old Roman policy, and maintain them with the sword." . . .

So much has been made of the youthful enthusiasm of the War Hawks, of their national feeling and keen resentment of foreign insults, that it may possibly appear to some that these western leaders were great hypocrites who talked of national honor but acted secretly from economic motives. By way of extenuation it may be suggested that national honor and national interest seldom fail to coincide. Furthermore, the western leaders made no secret of their "interests" even though they did have much to say of "honor." Clay demanded vigorous measures against England, declaring that through failure to fight we lost both commerce and character. "If pecuniary considerations alone are to govern," he said, "there is sufficient motive for the war." Three months later, when writing to the editor of the *Kentucky Gazette* assuring him that war would yet be declared, Clay did not hesitate to state in a letter which was probably intended for publication: "In the event of war, I am inclined to think that article [hemp] will command a better price than it now does."

Confusion has sometimes arisen from the failure to realize that commercial privileges were as essential to those who produced goods for foreign exportation as for the merchants who gained by performing the middleman service.... But one has only to read the words of the southern and western advocates of war to find that their position was clear and straightforward enough. Said Felix Grundy:

It is not the carrying trade, properly so called, about which this nation and Great Britain are at present contending. Were this the only question now under consideration, I should feel great unwillingness ... to involve the nation in war, for the assertion of a right, in the enjoyment of which the community at large are not more deeply concerned. The true question in controversy, is of a very different character; it involves the interest of the whole nation. It is the right of exporting the productions of our own soil and industry to foreign markets.

... As noted at the outset, factors other than those emphasized in this study undoubtedly played a part in bringing on the war. The expansionist sentiment, which Professor Julius W. Pratt has emphasized, was surely present. English incitement to Indian depredations and Spanish interference with American trade through Florida should be noted, as should also the fact that the frontiersmen sought every possible pretext to seize the coveted Indian lands. Restrictions on the carrying trade, even impressment of seamen, may have had some effect in influencing western opinion. No doubt the traditional hostility of the Republican party toward England played a part. Many veterans of the Revolutionary War had settled upon western lands, and time had not failed to magnify the glory of their achievements or to add to the aggressive ardor of their patriotism.

But important as these factors may have been, the attitude of the western settler can hardly be evaluated without an understanding of his economic position. He was, after all, typically an ambitious farmer who moved to the Mississippi Valley in order to make a better living. In the boom times following the Louisiana Purchase he had regarded the western frontier as a veritable promised land. Moreover, the fertile river valleys rewarded his toil with luxuriant harvests. But somehow prosperity eluded him. When, in spite of tremendous difficulties, he brought his produce to market, prices were often so low as to make his venture a failure.

We know now that the farmers' troubles were, in no small degree, fundamentally matters of transportation, of communication, and of imperfect marketing and financial organization. But is it unexpected that in their disappointment (and not unlike their descendants of today who still are inclined to magnify political factors) they put the blame for their economic ills upon foreign restriction of their markets and supported the Embargo and Non-Intercourse acts as weapons to coerce the European belligerents to give them what they regarded as their rights? And when peaceful methods failed and prices fell to even lower levels, is it surprising that the hopeful settlers of earlier years became the War Hawks of 1812?

UNITED STATES COMMERCE WITH
LATIN AMERICA AT THE PROMULGATION
OF THE MONROE DOCTRINE[1]   *Charles Lyon Chandler*

The political aspects of the Monroe Doctrine have been discussed at length by writers both at home and abroad, but as yet no attempt seems to have been made to trace the economic conditions leading up to this all-important pronouncement. With the modern tendency to find the roots of government policies in economic necessities, it surely cannot come amiss to observe the commercial relations of the United States with Hispanic America in the forty years preceding President Monroe's famous Declaration to the United States Congress, December 2, 1823. .

At that time approximately a fifth of the exports of the United States went to Hispanic America, and from Hispanic America came almost an equal proportion of her imports. Moreover, these proportions had been increasing, as will be seen from the following table, the years in all cases ending September 30:

	1821	1822	1823
Percentage of total U.S. exports to Hispanic America	15.0	16.2	18.8
Percentage of total U.S. imports from Hispanic America	17.7	16.8	22.0

... Throughout the wars of Napoleon and for long afterward United States vessels took an active part in bringing European goods to South America and in taking Hispanic-American raw products to Europe. Furthermore, since 1798, the United States had traded direct with Montevideo, with Buenos Aires since 1799, with Rio de Janeiro since 1800, with numerous ports on the Spanish Main at least since 1797, and with Peru since 1792....

By 1821 the efforts of exporters in the United States to "capture the South American market" were becoming systematic. T. and S. Wagner, 29 North Front Street, Philadelphia (a firm founded in 1774 and still in existence), advertise seven barrels of "American segars suitable for the South American Market," in the *American Daily Advertiser* of Philadelphia for July 27, 1821. Nine times in January 1823, Moody, Wyman and Co., of Philadelphia, advertise "2000 pair Men's fine copper nailed shoes, suitable for the South American market, with an extensive assortment of Philadelphia manufactured shoes and boots of every description." A year later "Joseph F. Boardman and Co., Nos. 20 and 21 Green's Wharf, Boston, have for sale 2500 pairs men's fine calf skin shoes, suitable for the Nachitoches or Spanish Main. They will be sold very low for cash or approved credit."

---

[1] *The Quarterly Journal of Economics*, XXXVIII, No. 3 (May, 1924), 466–86. Reprinted by permission of Harvard University Press. Copyright 1924 by the President and Fellows of Harvard College.

Exports of furniture to South America had begun in 1801, when the *Superior* from Providence, Rhode Island, arrived in Buenos Aires, on April 18, with twelve cases of household furniture. Twenty-one years later, Joseph B. Barry, of 134 South 2d Street, Philadelphia, advertised an "elegant stock of furniture—both for use and ornament, a considerable part of which has been calculated for the Spanish or South American market, such as Wardrobes, Libraries, Dining Tables, etc., being all made portable to pack in small compass to save freight." Furniture from the United States seemed to continue popular in Buenos Aires, for the *George and Mary* of Providence, on her arrival June 20, 1810, proved a veritable *Mayflower* with her 108 cases of furniture, fifty-seven dozen wooden chairs, and fifteen wooden settees, while the *Fame* arrived direct from Baltimore with furniture, and the *Valentine* from New York City, August 14, 1810, brought 1,040 chairs.

. . . Stephen Girard had shipped twenty cases of colored cotton goods on the *Voltaire*, which arrived at Buenos Aires from Philadelphia on March 17, 1810, and "eighty thousand yards of brown cotton 3–4 cloths, worth about $10,000 were bought up in Boston for the South American market." Two other commodities for South American export are mentioned for the first time by the *Columbian Centinel* early in 1823: packages of assorted glassware . . . and drugs, medicines and medicine chests fully stocked were advertised in the Spanish language. . . .

* * *

. . . Advertisements in the United States newspapers indicate the importance not only of our exports to Hispanic America, but also of our imports thence. On January 12, 1801, twenty-two years before Monroe's Declaration, the Philadelphia *Gazette* contains the advertisements of four different Hispanic-American products: Buenos Aires Hides, First Quality Caracas Cocoa, Cumana Cotton, and Santo Domingo Coffee; while a study of such advertisements in the Philadelphia and New York newspapers for the year immediately preceding the promulgation of the Monroe Doctrine shows that scarcely a day went by without some product from "America south of the United States" being called to the attention of the public. Coffee from Rio de Janeiro is advertised by four different firms in Philadelphia—John Strawbridge, John H. Linn, J. Percival, and J. Beylard, Jr.— while a number of other firms were engaged in importing this article. . . .

But coffee was not the only beverage that the United States was importing from her southern neighbors. In this same year 1822, "Caraccas cocoa" was advertised in Philadelphia by John H. Linn and Henry Simpson, and in New York by Henry Ogden at the corner of Whitehall and Stone Streets. It had been imported for some time previously into the United States and had been manufactured into chocolate by the Walter Baker Company at Milton, Massachusetts, who advertised it in the newspapers. One of the earliest specific instances of its importation is by way of the ship *Young Eagle*, from La Guaira, which arrived at New York City on December 28, 1801. . . .

Other raw materials were being imported for manufacture in the United States. The Philadelphia *Gazette* for January 12, 1801, contains an advertisement of Buenos Aires hides—the first one the writer has been able to discover in a United States newspaper, although a shipment of hides from Montevideo was received at New York on December 2, 1799. . . . By 1822 two firms in Philadelphia were advertising hides from Buenos Aires, and two from Montevideo. By this time wool from what is now the Argentine Republic had been differentiated into Buenos Aires and Cordoba. . . . Although guanaco, alpaca, llama, and vicuña wool were exhibited at the Philosophical Hall in Philadelphia on June 9, 1812, no one seems to have advertised South American wool for sale in the Philadelphia newspapers of that year, and thereafter the war with England seems to have prevented imports of South American wool until about 1816. With the exception of those years, the United States was importing from the River Plate many kinds of skins and wools, as well as ox horns, for which there appeared to be a continuous demand. . . .

But the War of 1812 was not the only deterrent to the trade of the United States with Hispanic America. Difficult as it was to escape the British blockade or the impressment of United States seamen, to say nothing of the capture of vessels by the British naval forces, other wars during this period added to the burden. In the case of Buenos Aires and Montevideo, so far as can be ascertained, the first steps taken toward separation from the mother country seem not to have appreciably affected their foreign commerce, except in arousing both in England and the United States undue hopes of an increased purchasing power. The United States trade with the River Plate countries therefore continued fairly steady during this period. . . . To be sure, as has been the case in the foreign trade of all countries, there were fat and lean years. At the end of March, 1821, "Produce of every description, except jerked beef, was extremely scarce and high both at Buenos Aires and Montevideo. Vessels generally in both places will be obliged to depart without cargoes." While a year later, "The markets of the La Plata had become glutted with almost every article of importation, particularly with liquors." . . . The scarcity of native products for trade and the glutting of the market with foreign goods seem not so much a consequence of war as the result of an overestimate in Europe and in the United States of the purchasing power of these young republics. A similar overestimate, with equally disastrous consequences, had taken place before the movement for independence, in 1808. . . .

The chief interference with trade between the United States and the West Indies during the years immediately preceding the Monroe declaration was the widespread piracy throughout those waters. Vessels were attacked even in Havana harbor. Every trade route in the "American Mediterranean" was infested with many varieties of buccaneers and pirates, who seemed to regard United States merchant vessels as their especial prey, probably because of the amount of specie carried. . . . President Monroe sent a special message to Congress, asking appropriations of what were at that time large sums of money to suppress this piracy; and it is noteworthy that the success of these efforts is discussed at greater length in his famous Message of 1823. Not only were the appropriations made, but practically the entire navy of the United States was sent out against the pirates. This fact, when compared with the expedition to the Barbary Coast twenty years before, indicates the seriousness of the offense, as do the almost daily accounts of piratical outrages in the newspapers of the time. In Monroe's famous message to Congress of December 2, 1823, far more space is given to the question of piracy and the methods taken by the United States Government to suppress it than to the famous Doctrine itself.

For the most part these pirates seem to have operated in the West Indies, and not to have interfered so much with United States vessels bound for more distant points, unless such vessels happened to pass through West Indian waters. As has been already stated, trade with the West Coast of South America had begun early; but the distance and uncertainties of rounding the Horn prevented much of the speculative shipping, and the Boston trade to California for hides began only in 1822, continuing on a rather small scale for the next few years. So far as can be ascertained, not more than ten United States merchant vessels visited the West Coast of South America in 1822, while there were at least seventy-six at the various Brazilian ports, fifty-five in those of the River Plate, and twenty at La Guaira. . . .

. . . It was the whaling vessels that chiefly rounded the Horn. In the course of the debate in the United States House of Representatives on December 18, 1822, on the bill authorizing the occupation by the United States of the mouth of the Columbia River, Mr. Baylies of Massachusetts, who was one of the committee that reported the bill, spoke at some length, maintaining that the mouth of the Columbia River should be occupied because "if there is one branch of the mercantile industry of the country more important than another it is the whale fishery. . . . Its capital is created by labor; it is dragged up from the bottom of the ocean. . . . It has now become a business of national importance." Baylies continued with the statement that thirty-six of the sixty-five vessels employed in the whale fishery from the port of New Bedford were employed in fishing for spermaceti whales in the Pacific Ocean, and added that all the Nantucket ships except one were there also.

It will be remembered that as early as 1774 United States whalers had begun to cruise along the coast of Brazil. Baylies's next statement was to the effect that since the end of the War of 1812 the greater number of the whaling ships of New Bedford had been employed on the coast of Patagonia and the adjacent waters in fishing for right whales; but oil of that description having fallen in price within the last two years, many vessels had been taken from that fishery, and had been dispatched to the Pacific to fish for spermaceti whales, as the oil made from them had fully sustained its prices. Baylies added that most of the oil which had been obtained from the Pacific was spermaceti oil, although a small amount of black whale oil had been taken on the coast of Chili in the bays and harbors. . . .

In view of the development of the lumber export business from the Pacific Coast of the United States to the west coast of South America during the last twenty years, a quotation from another letter written by Collector Hawes to Congressman Baylies may be of interest as showing the beginnings of an important inter-Pacific trade.

Since my last I have learned, from a very intelligent shipmaster who recently arrived from Valparaiso, that a vessel loaded with spars from Columbia River had arrived there, and found a good market. I am led to believe with him that the lumber trade from the settlement at the mouth of that river to Peru and Chili must be made profitable, as there is not any wood in either of those places proper for spars. I have known spars carried from the Island of New Zealand to those places, which paid a very great freight.

That the importance of the South American trade was recognized by a number of prominent senators to whom Monroe's famous message was addressed, and that this trade was considered important, may be seen from remarks made in the course of the debate in the United States Senate on February 11, 1824, on a bill proposed by Senator James De Wolf, of Rhode Island, allowing a drawback on the exportation of cordage manufactured from foreign hemp. Senator Samuel Smith, of Maryland, in a speech urging the passage of this measure, stated that, if the duty were not refunded on such exportation, our merchants and manufacturers would be seriously hindered from competing in foreign markets. He continued:

It is no more than a fair principle to grant it. It will give employment to a large portion of our shipping. It will assist in making up our assorted cargoes for the South American States. We were the first to acknowledge their independence, and to recognize them as nations. And shall we now shut ourselves out from the enjoyment of their trade? ... The trade to South America is a very important one....

In another speech in favor of the bill Senator Lloyd of Maryland remarked that he "thought that the opportunity of the South American markets would be very advantageous to the home growers of hemp."

From the foregoing it will be gathered that the trade of the United States of America with Hispanic America in 1823 was important as regards both exports and imports; that it had been developing for at least twenty-five years; and that it occupied the attention of many people in the Atlantic Coast ports. What direct influence it exercised on the minds of Monroe and his Secretary of State, John Quincy Adams, in their famous declaration, it is not easy to say; but it seems hard to believe that it was wholly without bearing on that noteworthy statement of our foreign policy.

THE MONROE DOCTRINE[1]   *Dexter Perkins*

The famous message of December 2, 1823, with the possible exception of the Farewell Address the most significant of all American state papers, contains two widely separated passages which have come to be known as the Monroe Doctrine. In discussing American relations with Russia, the President laid down the principle that "the American continents, by the free and independent condition which they have assumed and maintain, are henceforth not to be considered as subject for future colonization by any Euro-

---

[1] Selected from *Hands Off: A History of the Monroe Doctrine*, pp. 28–34, 41–43, 45, 50. Copyright 1941 by Dexter Perkins; reprinted by permission of Little, Brown & Co.

pean power." This phrase occurs early in the document. In its closing paragraphs, on the other hand, Monroe turned to the subject of the Spanish colonies. In language no less significant than that just quoted, he declared that the political system of the allied powers, that is, of the Holy Alliance, was different from that of America. "We owe it, therefore, to candor, and to the amicable relations existing between the United States and those powers," he went on, "to declare that we should consider any attempt on their part to extend their political system to any portion of this hemisphere as dangerous to our peace and safety. With the existing colonies and dependencies of any European power we have not interfered and shall not interfere. But with the governments who have declared their independence and maintained it, and whose independence we have, on great consideration and just principles, acknowledged, we could not view any interposition for the purpose of oppressing them, or controlling in any other manner their destiny, by any European power in any other light than as the manifestation of an unfriendly disposition towards the United States." . . .

That part of the message which was directed against Russia appears to have been the work of John Quincy Adams. There is, perhaps, no figure more remarkable in the lengthening list of the Secretaries of State. Acidulous, combative, suspicious, Adams was none the less a great personality, great in his unswerving and intense patriotism, great in his powerful and logical intelligence, great in his immense industry, great in his high integrity. No man who ever directed American foreign policy came to his post with a wider background of experience, with a better education, academic, linguistic, legal, with a broader conception of his task. Adams was hard-headed and practical; but he also recognized the importance of ideas and general principles. And this fact he was to make clear in his working out the so-called noncolonization dogma. Long before 1823 the Secretary of State had begun to formulate his ideas with regard to the exclusion of European influence from the American continents. When he negotiated the Florida treaty in 1819, he took special satisfaction in the extension of American territory to the Pacific by Spain's renunciation of all rights north of 42 degrees. As early as November of 1819 he had declared in the cabinet that the world "must be familiarized with the idea of considering our proper dominion to be the *continent* of North America." In a heated dispute with Stratford Canning, the British Minister, in January of 1821, over the title to the Columbia River region, Adams stated, "We certainly did suppose that the British government had come to the conclusion that there would be neither policy nor profit in cavilling with us about territory on this North American continent." "And in this," asked Canning, "you include our northern provinces on this continent?" "No," said Adams, "there the boundary is marked and we have no disposition to encroach upon it. Keep what is yours, but leave the rest of this continent to us." These statements, compared with what followed, were remarkable only for their modesty. In July of 1822, in one of those Fourth of July addresses so dear to American national pride, the Secretary went on to attack the whole colonial principle, as applied to both North and South America. By November he was ready to confide to the British Minister that "the whole system of modern colonization was an abuse of government, and it was time that it should come to an end."

In part, the position so boldly taken was a matter of political theory. The United States was not yet half a century from the Declaration of Independence, from its own shaking off of the chains of colonial tutelage. But, in part, Adams' doctrine had an economic basis. Adams disliked colonialism not alone because it was a reminder of political subordination, but because it was connected in his mind with commercial monopoly, and the exclusion of the United States from the markets of the New World. A New Englander of New Englanders, the representative of the great mercantile section of the Union, and that at a time when the American shipping interests were more important in relation to other interests than at any time in our history, the Secretary was to do battle for the trade of the American people no less than for more abstract notions of political righteousness. It was, indeed, a commercial controversy that sharpened his pen for the famous declaration with regard to colonization that we have quoted at the beginning of this page.

This controversy was one with Russia. In 1823 Russia still had colonial claims on the northwest coast of America. For more than a decade, indeed, there had been a Russian establishment, Fort Ross, at Bodega Bay on the coast of California, whose existence, though it had occasioned no diplomatic discussion, had been noted with some mild apprehension. But more important, in September of 1821 the Tsar Alexander, acting at the instigation of a corporation known as the Russian American Company, had issued an imperial decree which conferred upon this concern exclusive trading rights down to the line of 51 degrees and forbade all foreign vessels to come within one hundred Italian miles of the shore on pain of confiscation.

This imperial decree was, from the outset, challenged by the American government. In connection with it John Quincy Adams, with a boldness that excelled that of his cabinet colleagues, wished to deny the right of Russia to any American territory. And though he was overruled in a measure, since the instructions to Middleton at St. Petersburg, sent in July of 1823, were based on possible recognition of Russian claims north of *fifty-five*, the Secretary nevertheless would not give up his viewpoint in principle. To Tuyll, the Russian Minister at Washington, he declared on July 17, 1823, that "we should contest the right of Russia to *any* territorial establishment on this continent, and that we should assume distinctly the principle that the American continents are no longer subjects for any new European colonial establishments." Five days later he set forth the same theory in a dispatch to Richard Rush, our minister at London, and set it forth in some detail. In December, when he came to draft for the President the customary sketch of foreign policy to be used in the preparation of the annual message, he used almost the identical words that had been used five months before in speaking to Tuyll, and Monroe took them over bodily and inserted them in his message of December 2.

This, in essentials, is the origin of the noncolonization clause, one of the two important elements in the enunciation of the Monroe Doctrine.

It cannot be said that this clause was particularly important or particularly influential in its immediate effects. It was not enthusiastically received by the general public. It was rarely commented upon in the newspapers. It occasioned no favorable word in Congress. The Tsar had already determined upon concession long before the message, as early as July, 1822, and in the discussions at St. Petersburg Monroe's language was politely thrust aside by Alexander's Foreign Minister, who declared "it would be best for us to waive all discussions upon abstract principles of *right*." The President's declaration was without effect upon the actual compromise which was worked out between the two governments, limiting Russian rights to the line of 54 degrees 40 minutes, and conceding American trading privileges north of this line for a period of ten years. It was not favorably received by official opinion in any European country. In France Chateaubriand, the Foreign Minister, asserted on first reading it that Monroe's declaration "ought to be resisted by all powers possessing either territory or commercial interests in that hemisphere." In Great Britain Canning flatly challenged the new doctrine in an interview with Rush, our minister at London, early in January of 1824. Monroe's thesis, said the British Foreign Secretary, "is laid down broadly, and generally, without qualification or distinction. We cannot acknowledge the right of any power to proclaim such a principle; much less to bind other countries to the observance of it." Six months later, when Richard Rush attempted to introduce the Adams theory into the negotiations over Oregon, he was met with an "utter denial" of its validity, and with the categorical statement that "the unoccupied parts of America" were "just as much open as heretofore to colonization by Great Britain ... and that the United States would have no right whatever to take umbrage at the establishment of new colonies from Europe in any such parts of the American continent." In the immediate sense, the assertion of the non-colonization principle accomplished nothing positive, and aroused resentment rather than respect. There is room to doubt its wisdom as a diplomatic move, and a harsh critic might even go so far as to describe it as a barren gesture. . . .

More important, however, than the noncolonization clause are those resounding paragraphs of the message of 1823 which focused the attention of every European chancellery on the American attitude toward the new republics of the South. . . .

The discussions that preceded the enunciation of the famous message of 1823 form one of the most interesting chapters in the history of the Monroe Doctrine. They involved, as we shall see, not only the drafting of the President's message, but also the drafting of a suitable reply to Canning's overtures, and an answer to the ideological pronunciamento of the Tsar. Fortunately we have a most remarkable record of them. For the Secretary of State of the United States kept a diary, rising often in the wee small hours to fill in the narrative of events of high significance to posterity. And that diary, despite its egocentric character, is a precious memorial of the discussions on the Latin-American question between the President and his advisers.

The story of these discussions begins with the seventh of November. Very early it becomes clear that the President and John C. Calhoun, the

Secretary of War, were seriously concerned lest the Holy Alliance should act in the New World to restore to Spain her ancient dominions. The President, Adams reported on the thirteenth, was "alarmed far beyond anything that I could have conceived possible," and "the news that Cadiz has surrendered to the French has so affected him that he appeared entirely to despair of the cause of South America." Calhoun, in the language so characteristic of the Secretary of State, was "perfectly moonstruck" at the danger. In later cabinet meetings the panic of the President, if panic it was, seems somewhat to have abated. But in these later meetings he seems still to have believed in the peril, and in this conviction he was, apparently, still supported not only by Calhoun, but by Wirt, the Attorney General.

John Quincy Adams, on the other hand, took a very different view. He was by no means averse to some ringing declaration of policy; he positively yearned to try epistolary conclusions with Baron Tuyll. But the peril he thought was much exaggerated. Again and again, in the course of the cabinet discussions, he expressed skepticism as to the danger of intervention. Canning's alarm, as indicated in his interviews with Rush, he believed to be affected; the real purpose of the British Minister, he suspected (and the suspicion, we have seen, was partly justified), was to obtain a self-denying pledge from the United States, and was only "ostensibly" directed against the forcible interference of the Holy Alliance against South America. Judging, and, as the upshot was to prove, correctly judging, that self-interest and not romantic attachment to principle would be the real mainspring of the action of the Continental powers, he found it difficult to imagine that these powers would act at all. They would have no reason to restore the old commercial monopolies. Why should they seek to maintain the power of the decrepit Spanish monarchy across thousands of miles of ocean? "Was it in human absurdity to imagine that they should waste their blood and treasure to prohibit their own subjects upon pain of death to set foot upon those territories?" No, if they took action at all, their object would be to partition the colonies among themselves. But how could they agree upon the spoils? And how could they induce Great Britain to acquiesce? "The only possible bait they could offer . . . was Cuba, which neither they nor Spain would consent to give her." "I no more believe that the Holy Allies will restore the Spanish dominion upon the American continent," he stated in the cabinet meeting of November 15, "than that Chimborazo will sink beneath the ocean." This view he reiterated on the eighteenth, and again on the twenty-first.

But if Adams was inclined to minimize the actual danger, he was not, as we have said, inclined to let the situation pass without action. Like the President himself, like all the other members of the cabinet, he believed that the time was ripe for a state paper which would, if it did nothing else, thrill American pride and—even an Adams may have thought of this—tickle the ears of the groundlings. As early as November 7 he stated this view in the cabinet. The communications received from Baron Tuyll in October would, he believed, afford "a very suitable and convenient opportunity for us to take our stand against the Holy Alliance, and at the same time to decline the overture from Great Britain. It would be more candid as well as more dignified to avow our principles explicitly to Russia and France, than to come in as a cock-boat in the wake of the British man-of-war."

In making this assertion, the Secretary of State was thinking in terms not of a Presidential message, but of diplomatic correspondence, correspondence which might, of course, be released for publication to the greater glory of the United States and of John Quincy Adams. It was the President and the President alone who decided that at least one of the methods of replying to the homilies of the Tsar and the overtures of Canning, and of making the American position clear, should be a straightforward declaration in the forthcoming message to Congress. In the message's sketch on foreign affairs, prepared by Adams for his chief, there is no mention of the Latin-American problem. In the famous diary there is no intimation of the Secretary's suggesting that the forthcoming communication to the national legislature deal with the matter of the former colonies. It was Monroe who, on his own initiative, brought into the cabinet meeting of November 21 the first draft of what was to become the very heart of the Monroe Doctrine. This draft was certainly not marked by timidity. It was, indeed, too strong for John Quincy Adams. It was, if our diarist is to be believed, a ringing pronouncement in favor of liberal principles in both the Old World and the New. It "alluded to the recent events in Spain and Portugal, speaking in terms of the most pointed reprobation of the late invasion of Spain by France, and of the principles upon which it was undertaken by the open avowal of the King of France. It also contained a broad acknowledgement of the Greeks as an independent nation, and a recommendation to Congress to make an appropriation for sending a minister to them." ...

That declaration ... proclaimed the superiority of American institutions, and the peril to the United States of any attempt on the part of European powers to extend their political system to the New World. It was, of course, the expression of a faith rather than a closely reasoned justification of American opposition to the reconquest of the colonies. Monroe assumed these propositions rather than debated them; and perhaps the strength of the message lies in the unwavering firmness of its tone, and the complete confidence of the President in the postulates which he put forward. Yet there is, I think, much more than this to be said for it. Monroe rested his opposition to European intermeddling in Spanish America on the danger to "the peace and safety" of the United States. In so doing he took a strong position from both a legal and a moral point of view. He was basing American policy on the right of self-preservation, a right that is and always has been recognized as fundamental in international law. If in very truth the interposition of the Holy Alliance in the New World imperiled the peace and safety of the United States, then the right to protest against it was obvious. And of this who should be the judge if not the chief magistrate of the republic? How, at any rate, could any European challenge him? Did he not stand secure on his own ground? ...

For at least half a century it has been persistently asserted that the President's action saved the New World from deadly peril, that it frustrated the wicked designs of the members of the Holy Alliance, and established the liberties of Latin America upon a basis secure and irrefragable. Unfortunately this notion is purely legend; and if we survey the facts candidly we must admit that the message of 1823 was directed against an imaginary menace. Not one of the Continental powers cherished any designs of reconquest in the New World in November or December of 1823. . . .

COMMITTEE REPORT FROM MESSRS.
ELBRIDGE GERRY, JACOB READ,
HUGH WILLIAMSON, JEREMIAH T. CHASE,
AND THOMAS JEFFERSON OF THE
CONTINENTAL CONGRESS, APRIL 22, 1784   *Document 1*

The situation of commerce at this time, claims the attention of the several States, and few objects of greater importance can present themselves to their notice. The fortune of every Citizen is interested in the fate of commerce: for it is the constant source of industry and wealth; and the value of our produce and our land must ever rise or fall in proportion to the prosperous or adverse state of trade.

Already has Great Britain attempted a monopoly which is destructive of our trade with her West India Islands. There was reason to expect that a measure so unequal, and so little calculated to promote mercantile intercourse, would not be persevered in by an enlightened nation: but the measure seems to be growing into a system, and if it should be attended with success, there is too much reason to apprehend other nations might follow the example, and the commerce of America become the victim of illiberal policy.

It would have been the duty of Congress, as it was their wish, at an earlier period, to have met the attempts of Great Britain with similar and adequate restrictions on her commerce, but their powers on this head were not explicit; and though they are not to suppose that a free people would be jealous of men whom they chose from year to year to consult and guard their interest, yet it is with reluctance that Congress now make a proposition which may be suspected to have originated in a desire of power, although the measures already adopted by the legislatures of the several States seem to render it their duty to take the general sense of the union on this subject.

It will certainly be admitted, that unless the United States can act as a nation and be regarded as such by foreign powers, and unless Congress for this purpose shall be vested with powers competent to the protection of commerce, they can never command reciprocal advantages in trade; and without such reciprocity, our foreign commerce must decline and eventually be annihilated.

That the United States may be enabled to secure such terms of equality in their commerce with foreign nations, is the object of this address; and it will appear by the papers herewith transmitted, that however desirous some of the states may be, that further powers should be vested in Congress for the external regulation of trade, much time and valuable opportunities might be lost before any thing effective could be done, considering the vague and different powers that are proposed to be given by different States. Hence it seems necessary that the States should be explicit, and fix on some particular mode by which foreign commerce not founded on principles of reciprocity, may be restrained. Imposts or duties have been the general instruments for effecting this purpose, but Congress has agreed to recommend another measure which is more simple, equally effective, and may be less exceptionable: For this purpose they have

Resolved, That it be recommended to the Legislatures of the several States, to vest the United States in Congress assembled, for the term of fifteen years, with power to prohibit any goods, wares or merchandise from being imported into or exported from any of the States in vessels belonging to or navigated by the subjects of any power with whom these States shall not have formed Treaties of Commerce.

Resolved, That it be recommended to the legislatures of the several States, to vest the United States in Congress assembled, for the term of fifteen years, with the power of prohibiting the subjects of any foreign state, kingdom or empire authorized by Treaty from importing into the United States, any good wares or merchandize which are not the produce or manufacture of the Dominions of the Sovereign or whose subjects they are.

Thomas Jefferson to John Jay, August 23, 1785.

I shall sometimes ask your permission to write you letters, not official but private. The present is of this kind, and is occasioned by the question proposed in yours of June 14 'Whether it would be useful to us to carry all our own productions, or none?' Were we perfectly free to decide this question, I should reason as follows: We have now lands enough to employ an infinite number of people in their cultivation. Cultivators of the earth are the most valuable citizens. They are the most vigorous, the most independent, the most virtuous, and they are tied to their country and wedded to its liberty and interests by the most lasting bands. As long therefore as they can find employment in this line, I would not convert them into mariners, artisans, or any thing else. But our citizens will find employment in this line till their numbers, and of course their productions, become too great for the demand both internal and foreign. This is not the case as yet, and probably will not be for a considerable time. As soon as it is, the surplus of hands must be turned to something else. I should then perhaps wish to turn them to the sea in preference to manufactures, because comparing the characters of the two classes I find the former the most valuable citizens. I consider the class of artificers as the panders of vice and the instruments by which the liberties of a country are generally overturned. However we are not free to decide this question on principles of theory only. Our people are decided in the opinion that it is necessary for us to take a share in the occupation of the ocean, and their established habits induce them to require that the sea be kept open to them, and that that line of policy be pursued which will render the use of that element as great as possible to them.... But what will be the consequence? Frequent wars without a doubt. Their property will be violated on the sea, and in foreign ports, their persons will be insulted, emprisoned &c. for pretended debts, contracts, crimes, contraband &c. &c. These insults must be resented, even if we had no feelings, yet to prevent their eternal repetition. Or in other words, our commerce on the ocean and in other countries must be paid for by frequent war. The justest dispositions possible in ourselves will not secure us against it. It would be necessary that all other nations were just also. Justice indeed on our part will save us from those wars which would have been produced by a contrary disposition. But how to prevent those produced by the wrongs of other nations? By putting ourselves in a condition to punish them. . . . If a war with England should take place it see[ms] to me that the first thing necessary would be a resolution to abandon the carrying trade because we cannot protect it. Foreign nations must in that case be invited to bring us what we want and to take our productions in their own bottoms. This alone could prevent the loss of those productions to us and the acquisition of them to our enemy. Our seamen might be employed in depredations on their trade. But how dreadfully we shall suffer on our coasts, if we have no force on the water, former experience has taught us. Indeed I look forward with horror to the very possible case of war with an European power, and think there is no protection against them but from the possession of some force on the sea. Our vicinity to their West India possessions and to the fisheries is a bridle which a small naval force on our part would hold in the mouths of the most powerful of these countries. I hope our land office will rid us of our debts, and that our first attention then will be to the beginning a naval force of some sort. This alone can countenance our people as carriers on the water, and I suppose them to be determined to continue such.

JAMES MADISON DISCUSSES
THE VIRTUE AND NECESSITY
OF A LARGE REPUBLIC   *Document 2*

Madison to Jefferson, October 24, 1787.

It appeared to be the sincere and unanimous wish of the Convention to cherish and preserve the Union of the States. No proposition was made, no suggestion was thrown out in favor of a partition of the Empire into two or more Confederacies.

* * *

It may be said that the new Constitution is founded on different principles, and will have a different operation. I admit the difference to be material. It presents the aspect rather of a feudal system of republics, if such a phrase may be used, than of a Confederacy of independent States. And what has been the progress and event of the feudal Constitutions? In all of them a continual struggle between the head and the inferior members, until a final victory has been gained in some instances by one, in others, by the other of them. . . .

It may be asked how private rights will be more secure under the Guardianship of the General Government than under the State Governments, since they are both founded on the republican principle which refers the ultimate decision to the will of the majority, and are distinguished rather by the extent within which they will operate, than by any material difference in their structure. A full discussion of this question would, if I mistake not, unfold the true principles of Republican Government, and prove in contradiction to the concurrent opinions of theoretical writers, that this form of Government, in order to effect its purposes must operate not within a small but an extensive sphere. I will state some of the ideas which have occurred to me on this subject. Those who contend for a simple Democracy, or a pure republic, actuated by the sense of the majority, and operating within narrow limits, assume or suppose a case which is altogether fictitious. They found their reasoning on the idea, that the people composing the Society enjoy not only an equality of political rights; but that they have all precisely the same interests and the same feelings in every respect. Were this in reality the case, their reasoning would be conclusive. The interest of the majority would be that of the minority also; the decisions could only turn on mere opinion concerning the good of the whole of which the major voice would be the safest criterion; and within a small sphere, this voice could be most easily collected and the public affairs most accurately managed. We know however that no Society ever did or can consist of so homogeneous a mass of Citizens. In the savage State indeed, an approach is made towards it; but in that state little or no Government is necessary. In all civilized Societies, distinctions are various and unavoidable. A distinction of property results from that very protection which a free Government gives to unequal faculties of acquiring it. There will be rich and poor; creditors and debtors; a landed interest, a monied interest, a mercantile interest, a manufacturing interest. These classes may again be subdivided according to the different productions of different situations and soils, and according to different branches of commerce and of manufactures. In addition to these natural distinctions, artificial ones will be founded on accidental differences in political, religious and other opinions, or an attachment to the persons of leading individuals. However erroneous or ridiculous these grounds of dissention and faction may appear to the enlightened Statesman, or the benevolent philosopher, the bulk of mankind who are neither Statesmen nor Philosophers, will continue to view them in a different light. . . .

. . . If then there must be different interests and parties in Society; and a majority when united by a common interest or passion can not be restrained from oppressing the minority, what remedy can be found in a republican Government, where the majority must ultimately decide, but that of giving such an extent to its sphere, that no common interest or passion will be likely to unite a majority of the whole number in an unjust pursuit. In a large Society, the people are broken into so many interests and parties, that a common sentiment is less likely to be felt, and the requisite concert less likely to be formed, by a majority of the whole. The same security seems requisite for the civil as for the religious rights of individuals. If the same sect form a majority and have the power, other sects will be sure to be depressed. Divide et impera, the reprobated axiom of tyranny, is under certain qualifications, the only policy, by which a republic can be administered on just principles. It must be observed however that this doctrine can only hold within a sphere of a mean extent. As in too small a sphere oppressive combinations may be too easily formed against the weaker party; so in too extensive a one a defensive concert may be rendered too difficult against the oppression of those entrusted with the administration. . . . In small republics, the sovereign will is controlled from such a sacrifice of the entire Society, but it is not sufficiently neutral towards the parts composing it. In the extended Republic of the United States, the General Government would hold a pretty even balance between the parties of particular States, and be at the same time sufficiently restrained by its dependence on the community, from betraying its general interests.

Federalist Paper No. 10.

Among the numerous advantages promised by a well constructed Union, none deserves to be more accurately developed than its tendency to break and control the violence of faction. The friend of popular governments, never finds himself so much alarmed for their character and fate, as when he contemplates their propensity to this dangerous vice. He will not fail, therefore, to set a due value on any plan which, without violating the principles to which he is attached, provides a proper cure for it. . . .

By a faction, I understand a number of citizens, whether amounting to a majority or minority of the whole, who are united and actuated by some common impulse of passion, or of interest, adverse to the rights of other citizens, or to the permanent and aggregate interests of the community.

There are two methods of curing the mischiefs of faction. The one, by removing its causes; the other, by controlling its effects.

There are again two methods of removing the causes of faction: The one, by destroying the liberty which is essential to its existence; the other, by giving to every citizen the same opinions, the same passions, and the same interests.

It could never be more truly said, that of the first remedy, that it was worse than the disease. Liberty is to faction what air is to fire, an aliment, without which it instantly expires. But it could not be a less folly to abolish liberty which is essential to political life because it nourishes faction, than it would be to wish the annihilation of air, which is essential to animal life, because it imparts to fire its destructive agency.

The second expedient is as impracticable, as the first would be unwise. As long as the reason of man continues fallible, and he is at liberty to exercise it, different opinions will be formed. As long as the connection subsists between his reason and his self-love, his opinions and his passions will have a reciprocal influence on each other; and the former will be objects to which the latter will attach themselves. The diversity in the faculties of men, from which the rights of property originate, is not less an insuperable obstacle to an uniformity of interest. The protection of those faculties is the first object of government. From the protection of different and unequal faculties of acquiring property, the possession of different degrees and kinds of property immediately results; and from the influence of these on the sentiments and views of the respective proprietors, ensues a division of the society into different interests and parties. . . .

The inference to which we are brought is, that the *causes* of faction cannot be removed; and that relief is only to be sought in the means of controlling its effects. . . .

The question resulting is, whether small or extensive republics are most favourable to the election of proper guardians of the public weal; and it is clearly decided in favour of the latter by two obvious considerations. . . .

The smaller the society, the fewer probably will be the distinct parties and interests composing it; the fewer the distinct parties and interests, the more frequently will a majority be found of the same party; and the smaller the number of individuals composing a majority, and the smaller the compass within which they are placed, the more easily will they concert and execute their plans of oppression. Extend the sphere, and you take in a greater variety of parties and interests; you make it less probable that a majority of the whole will have a common motive to invade the rights of other citizens; or if such a common motive exists, it will be more difficult for all who feel it to discover their own strength, and to act in unison with each other. Besides other impediments, it may be remarked, that where there is a consciousness of unjust or dishonourable purposes, communication is always checked by distrust, in proportion to the number whose concurrence is necessary.

Hence, it clearly appears, that the same advantage, which a republic has over a democracy, in controlling the effects of faction, is enjoyed by a large over a small republic—is enjoyed by the union over the states composing it. . . .

In the extent and proper structure of the union, therefore, we behold a republican remedy for the diseases most incident to republican government.

Federalist Paper No. 14.
. . . The error which limits republican government to a narrow district, has been unfolded and refuted in preceding papers. I remark here only, that it seems to owe its rise and prevalence chiefly to the confounding of a republic with a democracy and applying to the former, reasonings drawn from the nature of the latter. The true distinction between these forms, was also adverted to on a former occasion. It is, that in a democracy, the people meet and exercise the government in person: in a republic, they assemble and administer it by their representatives and agents. A democracy, consequently, must be confined to a small spot. A republic may be extended over a large region. . . .

If Europe has the merit of discovering this great mechanical power in government, by the simple agency of which, the will of the largest political body may be concentred, and its force directed to any object which the public good requires; America can claim the merit of making the discovery the basis of unmixed and extensive republics. It is only to be lamented, that

119

any of her citizens should wish to deprive her of the additional merit of displaying its full efficacy in the establishment of the comprehensive system now under her consideration.

As the natural limit of a democracy is that distance from the central point, which will just permit the most remote citizens to assemble as often as their public functions demand, and will include no greater number than can join in those functions, so the natural limit of a republic is that distance from the centre, which will barely allow the representatives of the people to meet as often as may be necessary for the administration of public affairs. Can it be said that the limits of the United States exceed this distance? It will not be said by those who recollect, that the Atlantic coast is the longest side of the union; that during the term of thirteen years, the representatives of the states have been almost continually assembled; and that the members, from the most distant states, are not chargeable with greater intermissions of attendance, than those from the states in the neighbourhood of Congress. . . .

Hearken not to the unnatural voice, which tells you that the people of America, knit together as they are by so many chords of affection, can no longer live together as members of the same family: can no longer continue the mutual guardians of their mutual happiness; can no longer be fellow-citizens of one great, respectable and flourishing empire. Hearken not to the voice, which petulantly tells you, that the form of government recommended for your adoption, is a novelty in the political world; that it has never yet had a place in the theories of the wildest projectors; that it rashly attempts what it is impossible to accomplish. No, my countrymen shut your ears against this unhallowed language. Shut your hearts against the poison which it conveys.

PRESIDENT JAMES MONROE DISCUSSES
THE RELATIONSHIP BETWEEN INTERNAL
IMPROVEMENTS AND THE THEORY OF AN
EXPANDING NATION, MAY 4, 1822   *Document 3*

It may be presumed that the proposition relating to internal improvements, by roads and canals, which has been several times before Congress, will be taken into consideration again. . . . It is of the highest importance that this question should be settled. If the right exist, it ought forthwith to be exercised; if it does not exist, surely those who are friends to the power ought to unite in recommending an amendment to the Constitution to obtain it. I propose to examine this question. . . .

Our first bond of union [provided by the Articles of Confederation] was soon found to be utterly incompetent to the purposes intended by it. It was defective in its powers; it was defective, also, in the means of executing the powers actually granted by it. . . .

The Constitution was adopted for the purpose of remedying all defects of the Confederation, and in this it has succeeded, beyond any calculation that could have been formed of any human institution. . . .

If we recur to the causes which produced the adoption of this Constitution, we shall find that injuries resulting from the regulation of trade, by the states, respectively, and the advantages anticipated from the transfer of the power to Congress, were among those which had the most weight. Instead of acting as a nation in regard to foreign powers, the States, individually, had commenced a system of restraint on each other, whereby the interests of foreign Powers were promoted at their expense. . . . From this deplorable dilemma, or rather certain ruin, we were happily rescued by the adoption of the Constitution. . . .

Good roads and canals will promote many very important national purposes. They will facilitate the operations of war, the movements of troops, the transportation of cannon, or provisions, and every warlike store, much to our advantage, and to the disadvantage of the enemy in time of war. Good roads will facilitate the transportation of the mail; and thereby promote the purposes of commerce and political intelligence among the people. They will, by being properly directed to these objects, enhance the value of our vacant lands, a treasure of vast resource to the nation. To the appropriation of the public money to improvements, having these objects in view, and carried to a certain extent, I do not see any well founded Constitutional objection. . . .

. . . In the preceding inquiry, little has been said of the advantages which would attend the exercise of such a power by the general government. I have made the inquiry under a deep conviction that they are almost incalculable, and that there was a general concurrence of opinion among our fellow-citizens to that effect. Still it may not be improper for me to state the grounds upon which my own impression is founded. . . .

The facility which would thereby be afforded to the transportation of the whole of the rich productions of our country to market, would alone more than amply compensate for all the labor and expense attending them. . . . Every power of the General Government and of the State governments, connected with the strength and resources of the country, would be made more efficient for the purposes intended by them. In war, they would facilitate the transportation of men, ordnance, and provisions, and munitions of war, of every kind, to every part of our extensive coast and interior. . . . In every other line their good effect would be most sensibly felt. Intelligence by means of the Post Office Department would be more easily, extensively, and rapidly diffused. Parts the most remote from each other would be brought more closely together. Distant lands would be made more valuable, and the industry of our fellow-citizens on every portion of our soil be better rewarded.

It is natural, in so great a variety of climate, that there should be a corresponding difference in the produce of the soil—that one part should raise what the other might want. It is equally natural that the pursuits of industry should vary in like manner; that labor should be cheaper, and manufactures succeed better, in one part than in another; that, were the climate the most severe and the soil less productive, navigation, the fisheries, and commerce, should be most relied on. Hence the motive for an exchange, for mutual accommodation and active intercourse between them. Each part would thus fund for the surplus of its labor, in whatever article it consisted, an extensive market at home, which would be the most profitable because free from duty.

There is another view in which these improvements are of still more vital importance. The effect which they would have on the bond of Union itself affords an inducement for them more powerful than any which have been urged, or than all of them united. The only danger to which our system is exposed arises from its expansion over a vast territory. . . . Ambitious men may hereafter grow up among us, who may promise to themselves advancement from a change, and by practicing upon the sectional interests, feelings, and prejudices, endeavor under various pretexts to promote it. The history of the world is replete with examples of this kind. . . . I have little fear of this danger. . . . But still it is proper to look at and to provide against it, and it is not within the compass of human wisdom to make a more effectual provision than would be made by the proposed improvements. With their aid, and the intercourse which would grow out of them, the parts would soon become so compacted and bound together that nothing could break it.

The expansion of our Union over a vast territory cannot operate unfavorably to the States individually. On the contrary, it is believed that the greater the expansion, within practicable limits, *and it is not easy to say what are not so*,[1] the greater the advantage which the States individually will derive from it. . . . Manifest it is, that to any extent to which the General Government can sustain and execute its functions with complete effect, will the States, that is, the people who compose them, be benefited. It is only when the expansion shall be carried beyond the faculties of the General Government, so as to enfeeble its operations, to the injury of the whole, that any of the parts can be injured. The tendency, in that stage, will be to dismemberment, and not to consolidation. This danger should, therefore, be looked at with profound attention, as one of a very serious character. I will remark here, that, as the operations of the National Government are of a general nature, the States having complete power for internal and local purposes, the expansion may be carried to very great extent, and with perfect safety. It must be obvious to all, that the further the expansion is carried, provided it be not beyond the just limit, the greater will be the freedom of action to both Governments, and the more perfect their security; and, in all other respects, the better the effect will be to the whole American people. Extent of territory, whether it be great or small, gives to a nation many of its characteristics. It marks the extent of its resources, of its population, of its physical force. It marks, in short, the difference between a great and a small power.

To what extent it may be proper to expand our system of Government, is a question which does not press for a decision at this time. . . . A range of States, on the western side of the Mississippi, which already is provided for, puts us essentially at ease. Whether it will be wise to go further, will turn on other considerations than those which have dictated the course heretofore

---

[1] Italics added.

pursued. At whatever point we may stop, whether it be at a single range of States beyond the Mississippi, or by taking a greater scope, the advantage of such improvements is deemed of the highest importance. It is so, on the present scale. The further we go, the greater will be the necessity for them. . . .

EXPANSIONIST PRESSURES FOR
WAR AGAINST GREAT BRITAIN

Document 4

Representative Richard M. Johnson of Kentucky, December 11, 1811.
  . . . The expulsion of the British from their North American possessions, and granting letters of marque and reprisal against Great Britain are contemplated. Look at the Message of the President. At a moment least to be expected, when France had ceased to violate our neutral rights, and the olive branch was tendered to Great Britain, her Orders in Council were put into a more rigorous execution. Not satisfied with refusing a redress for wrongs committed on our coasts and in the mouths of our harbors, our trade is annoyed, and our national rights invaded; and, to close the scene of insolence and injury, regardless of our moderation and our justice, she has brought home to the "threshold of our territory," measures of actual war. As the love of peace has so long produced forbearance on our part, while commercial cupidity has increased the disposition to plunder on the part of Great Britain, I feel rejoiced that the hour of resistance is at hand, and that the President, in whom the people have so much confidence, has warned us of the perils that await them, and has exhorted us to put on the armor of defence, to gird on the sword, and assume the manly and bold attitude of war. He recommends filling up the ranks of the present Military Establishment, and to lengthen the term of service; to raise an auxiliary force for a more limited time; to authorize the acceptance of volunteers, and provide for calling out detachments of militia as circumstances may require. For the first time since my entrance into this body, there now seems to be but one opinion with a great majority—that with Great Britain war is inevitable; that the hopes of the sanguine as to a returning sense of British justice have expired; that the prophecies of the discerning have failed; and, that her infernal system has driven us to the brink of a second revolution, as important as the first. Upon the Wabash, through the influence of British agents, and within our territorial sea by the British navy, the war has already commenced. Thus, the folly, the power, and the tyranny of Great Britain, have taken from us the last alternative of longer forbearance.
  Mr. J. said we must now oppose the farther encroachments of Great Britain by war, or formally annul the Declaration of our Independence, and acknowledge ourselves her devoted colonies. The people whom I represent will not hesitate which of the two courses to choose; and, if we are involved in war, to maintain our dearest rights, and to preserve our independence, I pledge myself to this House, and my constituents to this nation, that they

will not be wanting in valor, nor in their proportion of men and money to prosecute the war with effect. Before we relinquish the conflict, I wish to see Great Britain renounce the piratical system of paper blockade; to liberate our captured seamen on board her ships of war; relinquish the practice of impressment on board our merchant vessels; to repeal her Orders in Council; and cease, in every other respect, to violate our neutral rights; to treat us as an independent people. The gentleman from Virginia (Mr. Randolph) has objected to the destination of this auxiliary force—the occupation of the Canadas, and the other British possessions upon our borders where our laws are violated, the Indians stimulated to murder our citizens, and where there is a British monopoly of the peltry and fur trade. I should not wish to extend the boundary of the United States by war if Great Britain would leave us to the quiet enjoyment of independence; but, considering her deadly and implacable enmity, and her continued hostility, I shall never die contented until I see her expulsion from North America, and her territories incorporated with the United States. . . .

Representative Nathaniel Macon of North Carolina, January 4, 1812.
. . . Mr. M. said, every restrictive measure having been resorted to in vain, and all our attempts at negotiation having failed, the nation is preparing for the last resort of Kings, and of Republics too. But now we are told we cannot contend with Great Britain. But we must either contend with her, or surrender our right to export any of our surplus produce. But why not contend with her? Let the worst come to the worst, we know what to do. We once succeeded with paper money, and if we were driven to that necessity, we could succeed again with it. We have now manufactories of arms and munitions of war, and whether money could be raised or not, if ever this nation engages in war, she engages never to surrender her rights. Every war is an evil, and amongst the greatest of evils; but we are compelled to fight or give up what we have, except the return of the Hornet should alter the situation of things.

No man, said Mr. M., would have more pleasure to see our differences accommodated with Great Britain than I should; but if this cannot be effected, we must change our situation; and though he could not vote for this bill, for the reasons which he had stated, he should go on with measures for putting the nation in a state of defence.

It had been said, that standing armies are dangerous to liberty. He believed it; but war cannot be carried on without them. The war which the United States are about to enter into is not of the character which has been given to it. He meant a war for the sake of conquest. Its object is to obtain the privilege of carrying the produce of our lands to a market. It is properly a war of defence; but he believed no war, after it was entered into, continued long to be strictly of that character. . . .

Representative Henry Clay of Kentucky, December 31, 1811.
. . . What are we to gain by war, has been emphatically asked? In reply, he would ask, what are we not to lose by peace?—commerce, character, a nation's best treasure, honor! If pecuniary considerations alone are to gov-

ern, there is sufficient motive for the war. Our revenue is reduced, by the operation of the belligerent edicts, to about six million of dollars, according to the Secretary of the Treasury's report. The year preceding the embargo, it was sixteen. Take away the Orders in Council, it will again mount up to sixteen millions. By continuing, therefore, in peace, if the mongrel state in which we are deserve that denomination, we lose annually, in revenue only, ten millions of dollars. Gentlemen will say, repeal the law of nonimportation. He contended that, if the United States were capable of that perfidy, the revenue would not be restored to its former state, the Orders in Council continuing. Without an export trade, which those orders prevent, inevitable ruin would ensue, if we imported as freely as we did prior to the embargo. A nation that carries on an import trade without an export trade to support it, must, in the end, be as certainly bankrupt, as the individual would be, who incurred an annual expenditure, without an income.

He had no disposition to swell, or dwell upon the catalogue of injuries from England. He could not, however, overlook the impressment of our seamen; an aggression upon which he never reflected without feelings of indignation, which would not allow him appropriate language to describe its enormity. Not content with seizing upon all our property, which falls within her rapacious grasp, the personal rights of our countrymen—rights which forever ought to be sacred, are trampled upon and violated. The Orders in Council were pretended to have been reluctantly adopted as a measure of retaliation. The French decrees, their alleged basis, are revoked. England resorts to the expedient of denying the fact of the revocation, and Sir William Scott, in the celebrated case of the Fox and others, suspends judgment that proof may be adduced of it. And, at the moment when the British Ministry through that judge, is thus affecting to controvert that fact, and to place the release of our property upon its establishment, instructions are prepared for Mr. Foster to meet at Washington the very revocation which they were contesting. And how does he meet it? By fulfilling the engagement solemnly made to rescind the orders? No, sir, but by demanding that we shall secure the introduction into the Continent of British manufactures. England is said to be fighting for the world, and shall we, it is asked, attempt to weaken her exertions? If, indeed, the aim of the French Emperor be universal dominion (and he was willing to allow it to the argument,) what a noble cause it presented to British valor. But, how is her philanthropic purpose to be achieved? By scrupulous observance of the rights of others; by respecting that code of public law, which she professes to vindicate, and by abstaining from self-aggrandizement. Then would she command the sympathies of the world. What are we required to do by those who would engage our feelings and wishes in her behalf? To bear the actual cuffs of her arrogance, that we may escape a chimerical French subjugation! We are invited, conjured to drink the potion of British poison actually presented to our lips, that we may avoid the imperial dose prepared by perturbed imaginations. We are called upon to submit to debasement, dishonor, and disgrace—to bow the neck to royal insolence, as a course of preparation for manly resistance to Gallic invasion! What nation, what individual was ever taught, in the schools of ignominious submission, the patriotic lessons of freedom and independence? Let those who contend for this humiliating doctrine, read its refutation in the history of the very man against whose insatiable thirst of dominion we are warned. The experience of desolated Spain, for the last fifteen years, is worth volumes. Did she find her repose and safety in subserviency to the will of that man? Had she boldly stood forth and repelled the first attempt to dictate to her Councils, her Monarch would not now be a miserable captive at Marseilles. Let us come home to our own history. It was not by submission that our fathers achieved our independence. The patriotic wisdom that placed you, Mr. Chairman, said Mr. C., under that canopy, penetrated the designs of a corrupt Ministry, and nobly fronted encroachment on its first appearance. It saw beyond the petty taxes, with which it commenced, a long train of oppressive measures terminating in the total annihilation of liberty; and, contemptible as they were, did not hesitate to resist them. Take the experience of the last four or five years, and which, he was sorry to say, exhibited in appearance, at least, a different kind of spirit. He did not wish to view the past further than to guide us for the future. We were but yesterday contending for the indirect trade—the right to export to Europe the coffee and sugar of the West Indies. To-day we are asserting our claim to the direct trade—the right to export our cotton, tobacco, and other domestic produce to market. Yield this point, and to-morrow intercourse between New Orleans and New York—between the planters on James river and Richmond, will be interdicted. For, sir, the career of encroachment is never arrested by submission. It will advance while there remains a single privilege on which it can operate. Gentlemen say that this Government is unfit for any war, but a war of invasion. What, is it not equivalent to invasion, if the mouths of our harbors and outlets are blocked up, and we are denied egress from our own waters? Or, when the burglar is at our door, shall we bravely sally forth and repel his felonious entrance, or meanly skulk within the cells of the castle?

He contended that the real cause of British aggression was not to distress an enemy but to destroy a rival. A comparative view of our commerce with England and the continent would satisfy any one of the truth of this remark. Prior to the embargo, the balance of trade between this country and England was between eleven and fifteen millions of dollars in favor of England. Our consumption of her manufactures was annually increasing, and had risen to nearly $50,000,000. We exported to her what she most wanted, provisions and raw materials for her manufactures, and received in return what she was most desirous to sell. Our exports to France, Holland, Spain, and Italy, taking an average of the years 1802, 3, and 4, amounted to about $12,000,000 of domestic, and about $18,000,000 of foreign produce. Our imports from the same countries amounted to about $25,000,000. The foreign produce exported consisted chiefly of luxuries from the West Indies. It is apparent that this trade, the balance of which was in favor, not of France, but of the United States, was not of very vital consequence to the enemy of England. Would she, therefore, for the sole purpose of depriving her adversary of this commerce, relinquish her valuable trade with this country, exhibiting the essential balance in her favor—nay, more; hazard the peace of the country? No, sir, you must look for an explanation of her conduct in the jealousies of a rival. She sickens at your prosperity, and beholds in your growth—your sails spread on every ocean, and your numerous seamen—the foundations of a Power which, at no very distant day, is to make her tremble for naval superiority. He had omitted before to notice the loss of our seamen, if we continued in our present situation. What would become of the one hundred thousand (for he understood there was about that number) in the American service? Would they not leave us and seek employment abroad, perhaps in the very country that injures us?

President James Madison to the South Carolina Legislature, January 8, 1812.

Acquiescence in the practice and pretensions of the British Govt. is forbidden by every view that can be taken of the subject. It would be a voluntary surrender of the persons and property of our Citizens sailing under the neutral guaranty of an Independent flag. It would recolonize our commerce by subjecting it to a foreign Authority; with the sole difference that the regulations of it formerly were made by Acts of Parliament and now, by orders in Council. And whatever benefits might be reaped by particular portions of the community, whose products are favored by contingent demands, but whose patriotism will not the less make a common cause with every other portion, experience warns us of the fatal tendencies of a commerce unrestricted with G.B., and restricted by her pleasure and policy elsewhere. Whilst the limited Market would continue overcharged with our exports, the disproportionate imports from it would drain from us the precious metals, endanger our monied Institutions, arrest our internal improvements, and would strangle in the cradle, the manufactures which promise so vigorous a growth. Nor would the evil be confined to our commerce, our agriculture, or our manufactures. The Ship owners & Shipbuilders and mariners must be equally sufferers. Should the regulating power submitted to afford no new preferences to British Navigation, those derived from existing laws & orders would exclude American vessels from the carriage of the products of their own Country, from its own ports. Finally, an acquiescence in the regulation of our Commerce, by the Belligerent having the command of the sea, would be the surest method of perpetuating its destructive Edicts. In a state of things so favorable to its interests, and so flattering to its power, the motives to a change would cease, if a change were otherwise likely to take place.

REPORT AND RESOLUTIONS OF THE
HARTFORD CONVENTION, JANUARY, 1815   *Document 5*

REPORT: The convention is deeply impressed with a sense of the arduous nature of the commission which they were appointed to execute, of devising the means of defence against dangers, and of relief from oppressions proceeding from the acts of their own government, without violating constitutional principles, or disappointing the hopes of a suffering and injured people....

It is a truth, not to be concealed, that a sentiment prevails to no inconsiderable extent, that administration have given such constructions to [the Constitution], and practised so many abuses under colour of its authority, that the time for a change is at hand....

...A reformation of public opinion, resulting from dear-bought experience, in the southern Atlantic states, at least, is not to be despaired of. They will have felt that the eastern states cannot be made exclusively the victims of a capricious and impassioned policy. They will have seen that the great and essential interests of the people are common to the south and to the east....They may discard the influence of visionary theorists, and recognize the benefits of a practical policy....

Without pausing at present to comment upon the causes of the war, it may be assumed as a truth, officially announced, that to achieve the conquest of Canadian territory, and to hold it as a pledge for peace, is the deliberate purpose of administration....

In the prosecution of this favorite warfare, administration have left the exposed and vulnerable parts of the country destitute of all the efficient means of defence...the enemy scours the sea-coast, blockades our ports, ascends our bays and rivers, makes actual descents in various and distant places, holds some by force, and threatens all that are assailable with fire and sword. The sea-board of four of the New-England states, following its curvature, presents an extent of more than seven hundred miles...accessible by a naval force, exposing a mass of people and property to the devastation of the enemy, which bears a great proportion to the residue of the maritime frontier of the United States....

These states have thus been left to adopt measures for their own defence....

The administration, after a long perseverance in plans to baffle every effort of commercial enterprize, had fatally succeeded in their attempts at the epoch of the war. Commerce, the vital spring of New-England's prosperity, was annihilated....The fisheries have shared its fate. Manufactures, which government has professed an intention to favour and to cherish, as an indemnity for the failure of these branches of business, are doomed to struggle in their infancy with taxes and obstructions, which cannot fail most seriously to affect their growth....

To investigate and explain the means whereby this fatal reverse has been effected would require a voluminous discussion. Nothing more can be attempted in this report than a general allusion to the principal outlines of the policy which has produced this vicissitude. Among these may be enumerated—

First.—A deliberate and extensive system for effecting a combination among certain states, by exciting local jealousies and ambition, so as to secure to popular leaders in one section of the Union, the controul of public affairs in perpetual succession....

Sixthly.—The admission of new states into the Union formed at pleasure in the western region, has destroyed the balance of power which existed among the original States, and deeply affected their interest. . . .

Eighthly.—Hostility to Great Britain, and partiality to the late government of France, adopted as coincident with popular prejudice, and subservient to the main object, party power. . . .

Lastly and principally.—A visionary and superficial theory in regard to commerce, accompanied by a real hatred but a feigned regard to its interests, and a ruinous perseverance in efforts to render it an instrument of coercion and war. . . .

THEREFORE RESOLVED . . . That the following amendments of the constitution of the United States be recommended to the states represented as aforesaid, to be proposed by them for adoption by the state legislature, and in such cases as may be deemed expedient by a convention chosen by the people of each state. . . .

Second. No new state shall be admitted into the Union by Congress, in virtue of the power granted by the constitution, without the concurrence of two thirds of both houses.

Third. Congress shall not have power to lay any embargo on the ships or vessels of the citizens of the United States, in the ports or harbours thereof, for more than sixty days.

Fourth. Congress shall not have power, without the concurrence of two thirds of both houses, to interdict the commercial intercourse between the United States and any foreign nation, or the dependencies thereof.

Fifth. Congress shall not make or declare war, or authorize acts of hostility against any foreign nation, without the concurrence of two thirds of both houses, except such acts of hostility be in defence of the territories of the United States when actually invaded. . . .

Seventh. The same person shall not be elected president of the United States a second time; nor shall the president be elected from the same state two terms in succession. . . .

[Signed by the delegates from Massachusetts, Connecticut, Rhode Island, New Hampshire, and Vermont.]

EXECUTIVE AGREEMENT

WITH GREAT BRITAIN CONCERNING

NAVAL ARMAMENTS ON THE GREAT LAKES   *Document 6*

Secretary of State Richard Rush to His Majesty's Minister at Washington, Charles Bagot, April 29, 1817.

. . . The Undersigned has the honour to express to Mr. Bagot the satisfaction which the President feels at His Royal Highness the Prince Regent's having acceded to the proposition of this Government. . . . And in further answer to Mr. Bagot's note, the Undersigned, by direction of the President, has the honour to state, that this Government, cherishing the same sentiments . . . agrees, that the naval force to be maintained upon the lakes by the United

States and Great Britain shall, henceforth, be confined to the following vessels on each side, that is:

On Lake Ontario to one vessel not exceeding one hundred tons burden, and armed with one eighteen-pound cannon. On the Upper Lakes to two vessels not exceeding the like burden each, and armed with like force, and on the waters of Lake Champlain to one vessel not exceeding like burden and armed with like force.

And it agrees, that all other armed vessels on these lakes shall be forthwith dismantled, and that no other vessels of war shall be there built or armed. And it further agrees, that if either party should hereafter be desirous of annulling this stipulation and should give notice to that effect to the other party, it shall cease to be binding after the expiration of six months from the date of such notice. . . .

HENRY CLAY ON THE REVOLUTIONS
IN LATIN AMERICA

Document 7

Remarks in the House of Representatives, March 24 and 28, 1818.

. . . I beg, in the first place, to correct misconceptions, if any exist, in regard to my opinions. I am averse to war with Spain, or with any power. . . . I can not, however, approve, in all respects, of the manner in which our negotiations with Spain have been conducted. If ever a favorable time existed for the demand, on the part of an injured nation, of indemnity for past wrongs from the aggressor, such is the present time. Impoverished and exhausted at home, by the wars which have desolated the peninsula, with a foreign war, calling for infinitely more resources, in men and money, than she can possibly command, this is the auspicious period for insisting upon justice at her hands, in a firm and decided tone. . . . Yet . . . the Secretary of State . . . after ably vindicating all our rights, tells the Spanish minister, with a good deal of *sang froid*, that we had patiently waited thirteen years for a redress of our injuries, and that it required no great effort to wait longer! I would have abstained from thus exposing our intentions. Avoiding the use of the language of menace, I would have required, in temperate and decided terms, indemnity for all our wrongs. . . . Contemporaneous with that demand, without waiting for her final answer, and with a view to the favorable operation on her councils in regard to our own peculiar interests, as well as in justice to the cause itself, I would recognize any established government in Spanish America. I would have left Spain to draw her own inferences from these proceedings, as to the ultimate step which this country might adopt, if she longer withheld justice from us. And if she persevered in her iniquity, after we have conducted the negotiation in the manner I have endeavored to describe, I would then take up and decide the solemn question of peace or war. . . .

In contemplating the great struggle in which Spanish America is now engaged, our attention is first fixed by the immensity and character of the country which Spain seeks again to subjugate. . . . We behold there a spectacle still more interesting and sublime—the glorious spectacle of eighteen millions of people, struggling to burst their chains and to be free. . . .

I am no propagandist. I would not seek to force upon other nations our principles and our liberty, if they did not want them. I would not disturb the repose even of a detestable despotism. But, if an abused and oppressed people will their freedom; if they seek to establish it; if, in truth, they have established it; we have a right, as a sovereign power, to notice the fact, and to act as circumstances and our interest require. . . .

In the establishment of the independence of Spanish America, the United States have the deepest interest. I have no hesitation in asserting my firm belief, that there is no question in the foreign policy of this country which has ever arisen, or which I can conceive as ever occurring, in the decision of which we have had or can have so much at stake. This interest concerns our politics, our commerce, our navigation. There can not be a doubt that Spanish America, once independent, whatever may be the form of the governments established in its several parts, these governments will be animated by an American feeling, and guided by an American policy. They will obey the laws of the system of the New World, of which they will compose a part, in contradistinction to that of Europe. . . . We are their great example. Of us they constantly speak as of brothers, having a similar origin. They adopt our principles, copy our institutions, and, in many instances, employ the very language and sentiments of our revolutionary papers. . . .

No nation ever offered richer commodities in exchange. It is of no material consequence that we produce but little that Spanish America wants. Commerce, as it actually exists in the hands of maritime states, is no longer confined to a mere barter, between any two States, or their respective productions. It renders tributary to its interests the commodities of all quarters of the world; so that a rich American cargo, or the contents of an American commercial warehouse, present you with whatever is rare or valuable, in every part of the globe. . . . We may safely trust to the daring enterprise of our merchants. The precious metals are in South America, and they will command the articles wanted in South America, which will purchase them. Our navigation will be benefited by the transaction, and our country will realize the mercantile profits. Already the item in our exports of American manufactures is respectable. They go chiefly to the West Indies and to Spanish America. This item is constantly augmenting. And I would again . . . ask gentlemen . . . to reflect . . . that we are not legislating for the present day only; and to contemplate this country in its march to true greatness, when millions and millions will be added to our population, and when the increased productive industry will furnish an infinite variety of fabrics for foreign consumption, in order to supply our wants. . . .

I am aware that, in opposition to the interest, which I have been endeavoring to manifest, that this country has in the independence of Spanish America, it is contended that we shall find that country a great rival in agricultural productions. . . . But it is not true to any extent. Of the eighty odd millions of exports, only about one million and a half consist of an article which can come into competition with us, and that is cotton. . . .

Having shown that the cause of the patriots is just, and that we have a great interest in its successful issue, I will next inquire what course of policy it becomes us to adopt. I have already declared it to be one of strict and impartial neutrality. It is not necessary for their interests, it is not expedient for our own, that we should take part in the war. . . . Recognition alone, without aid, is no just cause of war. . . .

I will next proceed to inquire into the consequences of a recognition of the new republic. Will it involve us in war with Spain? I have shown, I trust successfully shown, that there is no just cause of war to Spain. Being no cause of war, we have no right to expect that war will ensue. If Spain, without cause, will make war, she may make it whether we do or do not acknowledge the republic. But she will not, because she can not, make war against us. . . .

But the House has been asked, and asked with a triumph worthy of a better cause, why recognize this republic? . . . The moral influence of such a recognition, on the patriot of the South, will be irresistible. He will derive assurance from it, of his not having fought in vain. . . . I appeal to the powerful effect of moral causes. . . .

JOHN QUINCY ADAMS ON THE
BRITISH PROPOSAL FOR JOINT ACTION
IN LATIN AMERICA   *Document 8*

Excerpts from Adams' Diary of 1823.

Washington, *November 7th.*—Cabinet meeting at the President's from half-past one till four. Mr. Calhoun, Secretary of War, and Mr. Southard, Secretary of the Navy, present. The subject for consideration was the confidential proposals of the British Secretary of State, George Canning, to R. Rush, and the correspondence between them relating to the projects of the Holy Alliance upon South America. There was much conversation, without coming to any definite point. The object of Canning appears to have been to obtain some public pledge from the Government of the United States, ostensibly against the forcible interference of the Holy Alliance between Spain and South America; but really or especially against the acquisition to the United States themselves of any part of the Spanish-American possessions.

Mr. Calhoun inclined to give a discretionary power to Mr. Rush to join in a declaration against the interference of the Holy Allies, if necessary, even if it should pledge us not to take Cuba or the province of Texas; because the power of Great Britain being greater than ours to *seize* upon them, we should get the advantage of obtaining from her the same declaration we should make ourselves.

I thought the cases not parallel. We have no intention of seizing either Texas or Cuba. But the inhabitants of either or both may exercise their primitive rights, and solicit a union with us. They will certainly do no such thing to Great Britain. By joining with her, therefore, in her proposed declaration, we give her a substantial and perhaps inconvenient pledge against ourselves, and really obtain nothing in return. Without entering now into the enquiry of the expediency of our annexing Texas or Cuba to our Union, we should at least keep ourselves free to act as emergencies may arise, and not tie ourselves down to any principle which might immediately afterwards be brought to bear against ourselves.

Mr. Southard inclined much to the same opinion.

The President was averse to any course which should have the appearance of taking a position subordinate to that of Great Britain, and suggested the idea of sending a special Minister to *protest* against the interposition of the Holy Alliance. . . .

I remarked that . . . it would be more candid, as well as more dignified, to avow our principles explicitly to Russia and France, than to come in as a cock-boat in the wake of the British man-of-war. . . .

PRESIDENT MONROE'S MESSAGE
TO CONGRESS, DECEMBER 2, 1823   *Document 9*

. . . At the proposal of the Russian Imperial Government, made through the minister of the Emperor residing here, a full power and instructions have been transmitted to the minister of the United States at St. Petersburg to arrange by amicable negotiation the respective rights and interests of the two nations on the northwest coast of this continent. A similar proposal had been made by His Imperial Majesty to the Government of Great Britain, which has likewise been acceded to. The Government of the United States has been desirous by this friendly proceeding of manifesting the great value which they have invariably attached to the friendship of the Emperor and their solicitude to cultivate the best understanding with his Government. In the discussions to which this interest has given rise and in the arrangements by which they may terminate, the occasion has been judged proper for asserting, as a principle in which the rights and interests of the United States are involved, that the American continents, by the free and independent condition which they have assumed and maintain, are henceforth not to be considered as subjects for future colonization by any European powers. . . .

A strong hope has been long entertained, founded on the heroic struggle of the Greeks, that they would succeed in their contest and resume their equal station among the nations of the earth. It is believed that the whole civilized world take a deep interest in their welfare. Although no power has declared in their favor, yet none, according to our information, has taken part against them. Their cause and their name have protected them from dangers which might, ere this, have overwhelmed any other people. The ordinary calculations of interest and of acquisition with a view to aggrandizement, which mingle so much in the transactions of nations, seem to have had no effect in regard to them. From the facts which have come to our knowledge there is good cause to believe that their enemy has lost forever all dominion over them; that Greece will become again an independent nation. That she may obtain that rank is the object of our most ardent wishes.

It was stated at the commencement of the last session that a great effort was then making in Spain and Portugal to improve the condition of the people of those countries, and that it appeared to be conducted with extraordinary moderation. It need scarcely be remarked that the result has been so far very different from what was then anticipated. Of events in that quarter of the globe, with which we have so much intercourse and from which we derive our origin, we have always been anxious and interested spectators. The citizens of the United States cherish sentiments the most friendly in favor of the liberty and happiness of their fellowmen on that side of the Atlantic. In the wars of the European powers in matters relating to themselves we have never taken any part, nor does it comport with our policy so to do. It is only when our rights are invaded or seriously menaced that we resent injuries or make preparation for our defense. With the movements in this hemisphere we are of necessity more immediately connected, and by causes which must be obvious to all enlightened and impartial observers. The political system of the allied powers is essentially different in this respect from that of America. This difference proceeds from that which exists in their respective Governments; and to the defense of our own, which has been achieved by the loss of so much blood and treasure, and matured by the wisdom of their most enlightened citizens, and under which we have enjoyed unexampled felicity, this whole nation is devoted. We owe it, therefore, to candor and to the amicable relations existing between the United States and those powers to declare that we should consider any attempt on their part to extend their system to any portion of this hemisphere as dangerous to our peace and safety. With the existing colonies or dependencies of any European power we have not interfered and shall not interfere. But with the Governments who have declared their independence and maintained it, and whose independence we have, on great consideration and on just principles, acknowledged, we could not view any interposition for the purpose of oppressing them, or controlling in any other manner their destiny, by any European power in any other light than as the manifestation of an unfriendly disposition toward the United States. . . .

The late events in Spain and Portugal shew that Europe is still unsettled. Of this important fact no stronger proof can be adduced than that the allied powers should have thought it proper, on any principle satisfactory to themselves, to have interposed by force in the internal concerns of Spain. To what extent such interposition may be carried, on the same principle, is a question in which all independent powers whose governments differ from theirs are interested, even those most remote, and surely none more so than the United States. Our policy in regard to Europe, which was adopted at an early stage of the wars which have so long agitated that quarter of the globe, nevertheless remains the same, which is, not to interfere in the internal concerns of any of its powers; to consider the government *de facto* as the legitimate government for us; to cultivate friendly relations with it, and to preserve those relations by a frank, firm, and manly policy, meeting in all instances the just claims of every power, submitting to injuries from none. But in regard to those continents circumstances are eminently and conspicuously different. It is impossible that the allied powers should extend their political system to any portion of either continent without endangering our peace and happiness; nor can anyone believe that our southern brethren, if left to themselves, would adopt it of their own accord. It is equally impossible, therefore, that we should behold such interposition in any form with indifference. If we look to the comparative strength and resources of Spain and those new Governments, and their distance from each other, it must be obvious that she can never subdue them. It is still the true policy of the United States to leave the parties to themselves, in the hope that other powers will pursue the same course. . . .

JOHN QUINCY ADAMS ON
THE ROLE OF THE UNITED STATES
IN THE WESTERN HEMISPHERE   *Document 10*

From his diary entry of November 16, 1819.

Great Britain, after vilifying us twenty years as a mean, low-minded, peddling nation, having no generous ambitions and no God but gold, had now changed her tone, and was endeavoring to alarm the world at the gigantic grasp of our ambition. Spain was doing the same; and Europe, who, even since the commencement of our Government under the present Constitution, had seen those nations intriguing with the Indians and negotiating to bound us by the Ohio, had first been startled by our acquisition of Louisiana, and now by our pretension to extend to the South Sea, and readily gave credit to the envious and jealous clamor of Spain and England against our ambition. Nothing that we could say or do would remove this impression until the world shall be familiarized with the idea of considering our proper dominion to be the continent of North America. From the time when we became an independent people it was as much a law of nature that this should become our pretention as that the Mississippi should flow to the sea. . . . Most of the Spanish territory which had been in our neighborhood had already become our own by the most unexceptionable of all acquisitions—fair purchase for a valuable consideration. This rendered it still more unavoidable that the remainder of the continent should ultimately be ours. But it is very lately that we have distinctly seen this ourselves; very lately that we have avowed the pretension of extending to the South Sea; and until Europe shall find it a settled geographical element that the United States and North America are identical, any effort on our part to reason the world out of a belief that we are ambitious will have no other effect than to convince them that we add to our ambition hypocrisy. . . .

From a despatch to Don José María Salazar, Representative to the United States from the Republic of Colombia, August 6, 1824.

With respect to the question "in what manner the Government of the United States intends to resist on its part any interference of the Holy Alliance for the purpose of subjugating the new Republic or interfering in their political forms" you understand that by the constitution of the United States, the ultimate decision of this question belongs to the Legislative Department of the Government. The probability of such interference of the Holy Alliance, having in a great measure disappeared, the occasion for recurring to the dispositions of the Legislature did not occur during the late Session of Congress.

The sentiments of the President remain as they were expressed in his last annual message to Congress—Should the crisis which appeared then to be approaching, and which gave rise to the remarks then made, hereafter recur, he will be ready to give them effect by recommending to the Legislature the adoption of measures exclusively of their resort and by which the principles asserted by him would with the concurrence if given be on the part of the United States efficaciously maintained.

As however the occasion for this resort could arise only by a deliberate and concerted system of the allied Powers to exercise force against the freedom and Independence of your Republic; so it is obvious that the United States could not undertake resistance to them by force of Arms, without a previous understanding with those European Powers, whose Interests and whose principles would secure from them an active and efficient cooperation in the cause—This there is no reason to doubt could be obtained but it could only be effected by a negotiation preliminary to that of any alliance between the United States and the Colombian Republic, or in any event coeval with it.

The employment of Spanish force in America, while Spain is occupied by a French army and its Government under the influence of France and her allies, does not constitute a case upon which the United States would feel themselves justified in departing from the neutrality which they have hitherto observed—The force itself being necessarily small; and in no wise changing the nature of the contest in the American Hemisphere. . . .

MANIFEST

DESTINY

CHAPTER 4

Expansion for the Farmer

*M*anifest Destiny is a term—and an attitude—that grew out of the experience enjoyed by the people of the United States in the years from 1820 to 1850. Revolutionary leaders like Samuel Adams and George Washington had emphasized the importance of determination and preparation in order to take advantage of the few opportunities that were available to the colonists. Nothing was certain in the days of 1776. By 1848, however, Americans had concluded that it was their "manifest destiny to overspread the continent allotted by Providence for the free development of our yearly multiplying millions." There was little cause for them to think otherwise, for any unhappy memories of the War of 1812 had evaporated over the open acres of the Mississippi Valley, the Oregon territory, California, and Texas. Cocksure to the point of self-righteousness, Americans seldom reflected upon the possibility that their harvest of a continent might have been a windfall as much as it was a product of their exertions or a reward for their superior virtue. What they considered divine destiny may have been good luck and nothing more.

More dramatically than in the Era of Good Feelings (the time of compromise between the Federalists and Jeffersonians), the opportunities and the spirit of confidence which existed in the years of Jacksonian Democracy gave rise to a foreign policy of expansion. Even with a continent to develop, there was no lack of antagonism and rivalry among Americans, for northerners and southerners maneuvered throughout the period to control the

West. If this struggle did not yet eventuate in Civil War, the continued domestic peace was due to the abundance of land—enough to satisfy everybody—as much as it was to any special genius in the nation's leaders. Multiply as they would, Americans for the time being could not crowd one another to the point of violence. There was always a new diversion when such disaster threatened. The business of entering, holding, and developing land was, for several generations of Americans, an adventure in escaping from more fundamental problems. Democracy came to be identified with a foreign policy of expansion rather than with a thoughtful, balanced adjustment of internal tensions.

Americans advanced many explanations and justifications for their conquest of the continent. John Quincy Adams referred to a law of political gravitation which would someday deposit Cuba in the lap of America much as physical gravitation had caused the apple to fall on the head of Sir Isaac Newton. Adams and others also referred to natural rights and claimed that the geographical character of the country made it impossible to draw a natural boundary line at any place between the Atlantic and the Pacific oceans. Another argument was that only Americans knew how to farm the land in a proper manner. This is discussed by Professor Weinberg in his article on "The Destined Use of the Soil." Reginald Horsman explores the way that attitude was related to the developing sense of superiority in his essay on "American Indian Policy and the Origins of Manifest Destiny."

Despite their invocation of higher authority and abstract laws to account for and justify their expansion, Americans subjected themselves to much suffering and hard labor in the process of exploring and settling the continent. Some of them devoted themselves to carrying the word of God into the wilderness, but the majority were concerned with the more secular pursuit of agricultural and commercial rewards. Whatever their professions, all shared the rigors of frontier life. Document 1 is drawn from the diary of one such American who made the trip from Missouri to Oregon in 1834. People of other nations have exhibited as much stamina, resourcefulness, and determination without being rewarded with such treasure. Americans had the advantage of room to expand with little organized opposition. The Indians could only harass, not hold back, the white man's advance. The Mexicans in the Southwest could inflict occasional heavy losses, as at the Alamo, but they could not check for long the progress of the "gringo." The Russians in the Northwest could not develop territory so far from home, busy as they were with their own domestic progress and their rivalry with Great Britain. The English, for their part, were reluctant to wage a third war against the United States, for they depended on this country as a market for their manufactures, a source of raw materials, and a place for the investment of much of their surplus capital. Besides, they had to watch for trouble in Europe.

The friction between London and St. Petersburg was one of the reasons why the United States did not go to war with Great Britain over the conflicting claims to the Oregon territory. England could not ignore the possibility, however improbable, that Russia and America would come together and squeeze her out of western Canada altogether. There were more impor-

tant reasons, though, for the Anglo-American compromise on Oregon. Sometimes referred to as the most peaceful frontier in history, the line between Canada and the United States actually was anything but quiet in the mid-1830's. Border incidents recalled earlier American desires for Canadian land, raised anew the dispute over the Maine boundary, and excited the imaginations of those who wanted to export the republican form of government. Secretary of State Daniel Webster, a gifted spokesman for the commercial and industrial interests, was mistrusted by many westerners and southerners. But after prolonged negotiations, during which Webster took advantage of the growing British concern over expansionist sentiment in America (and conducted an astute promotional campaign in behalf of the treaty among his own countrymen), the differences over Maine were settled in the Webster-Ashburton Treaty.

Oregon was far more valuable than the contested acres of Maine. Though the British were not eager for a war over Oregon, they did not want to create the impression that they would abandon any part of Canada. American expansionists, meanwhile, were extreme in their demands, as indicated by the speech reproduced in Document 2. A good example of the way in which such congressional oratory finds its way into diplomatic correspondence is provided by Document 3, a report on the Senate's attitude toward Oregon made by the British minister in the United States. President James K. Polk's attitude also annoyed the British. But they had their own internal political and economic difficulties and were also occupied with the task of building an "informal empire" in Argentina. Some of the American grain exporters in the West lost much of their expansionist ardor when they heard about the prospective repeal of the English Corn Laws. They realized that British adoption of free-trade principles would offer a great market for American farm surpluses—if the two countries remained at peace. Professor Richard W. Van Alstyne tells the story of the final settlement in his article on "The Oregon Question."

Freed from danger in the north by England's willingness to compromise, American expansionists were able to play a strong hand against Mexico in the conflict over Texas. The Texas crisis, like the Oregon crisis, grew out of the westward movement of Americans in search of land. Professor William C. Binkley shows how the settlement of a Mexican area by American citizens led to rebellion and the creation of an independent nation. A good many Americans, northerners as well as southerners, were afraid that Great Britain might ally itself with Texas and thus defy the Monroe Doctrine and limit further American expansion; and southerners were particularly concerned that such an alignment would enable the English to subvert the institution (and curtail the profits) of slavery (Documents 4 and 5).

The agricultural expansion into Texas and Oregon offered leaders of both major parties an obvious opportunity to consolidate their power for the election of 1844 by promising Texas to southern planters and farmers while dangling Oregon before the freehold farmers of the North. The concern manifested by commercial interests in acquiring Pacific ports, discussed by Professor Robert G. Cleland, increased the attractiveness of that strategy for victory, as exemplified in Document 6. But antislavery and abolitionist sentiment in the North made it difficult for either Henry Clay or Martin Van Buren to exploit that approach (Documents 7 and 8). Expansionists in the Democratic party seized the opportunity, however, and nominated James Knox Polk of Tennessee on just such an imperial platform (Document 9).

Once elected, President Polk moved promptly to compromise the claim to all of Oregon in order to concentrate on acquiring Texas and California, and invoked the Monroe Doctrine as justification for such imperial thrusts (Document 10). Polk's first effort, described by Professor Richard R. Stenberg, was unsuccessful. The President then decided upon war, but was saved from shouldering direct responsibility for the conflict when Mexican troops attacked American forces that he had moved into the disputed territory between the Nueces and the Rio Grande. Representative Abraham Lincoln of Illinois was one of many Americans who realized, however, that the President's action had done much to provoke the outbreak of violence (Document 11); and his sharp criticism was part of the antiwar movement that pointed toward an increasingly embittered conflict over the question of what groups (and principles) would control the great empire gained in Oregon and the southwest.

THE DESTINED USE OF THE SOIL[1]   *Albert K. Weinberg*

The acquisition of satisfactory boundaries in the Spanish treaty of 1819 was followed by a movement aiming not at the extension of national boundaries and yet, paradoxically, at the enlargement of domain. The movement was expansionist in the sense that its purpose was the extension of the domain of States. The Indian was still tenant an vast tracts and enjoyed a degree of political autonomy described by Chief Justice Marshall as that of "domestic dependent nations." Before the third decade of the nineteenth century, it had usually been possible to satisfy recurrent need or fancy for lands through curtailing the Indian holdings by treaties—if such a name can be given to agreements so frequently reeking with alcohol and bribery. But after 1821 certain large Indian tribes of the South, having decided that their concessions had already exceeded reason, announced that they would cede no more land. The resultant prospect of permanent *imperia in imperio* was so repugnant to Southern States that from 1820 to 1840 the acquisition of Indian lands overshadowed every question of national boundaries and was even viewed with the emotion and ideology of expansionism.

Jefferson had written in 1786 that "it may be taken for a certainty that not a foot of land will ever be taken from the Indians without their own consent." In spirit if not in letter, the action of Americans of the Jacksonian period belied this optimistic prediction. Three Southern States passed bills declaring Indian laws void and in effect making all organized Indian society

[1] Selected from *Manifest Destiny: A Study of Nationalist Expansionism in American History* (Baltimore: Johns Hopkins Press, 1935), pp. 72–73, 89–90. Reprinted with permission.

impracticable. Of these States, Georgia prepared for forcible dispossession—a course in which it received moral support from President Andrew Jackson, himself no lover of Indians. The climax of this course of imperialism was the passage by Congress of the Indian Removal Bill of 1830. Although providing nominally only the administrative machinery for Indian removal by treaties, it was actually designed, as everyone recognized, so facilitate the plans of the Southern States willing to exercise constraint. By the end of the next decade, virtually all Indian tribes east of the Mississippi had taken their virtually enforced departure as "the victims of our destiny." The episode was typical of a phase of American history which has been described even by an American Secretary of the Interior as "in great part a record of broken treaties, of unjust wars, and of cruel spoliation."

Many contemporaries condemned the coercive policy as violative of the Indian's plain legal rights. Condemnation of the so-called "Century of Dishonor" has become even more general now that the completion of expropriation leaves no further temptation. This moral condemnation has directed itself upon motive as well as deed with the effect of influencing the interpretation of the former. It is generally believed that the motives of Indian policy were, if not profoundly villainous, at least not illustrative of the role of moral ideology in politics.

But an expansionist society "never admits that it is doing violence to its moral instincts" and is least disposed to do so when this violence is condemned by others. Thus in a congressional debate of 1830 an advocate of Indian removal contended with apparent sincerity that he had "advanced no principle inconsistent with the most rigid morality." So little, indeed, had the principles advanced appeared immoral to their exponents that the ultimate authority for them was ascribed to God. The principles centered in a philosophy of the use of the soil. The white race seemed to Senator Benton to have a superior right to the land because they "used it according to the intentions of the CREATOR." The theory that a use of the soil was ordained by God or morality figured not only in the entire history of Indian relations but also in all issues in which Americans found themselves desiring soil occupied by an "inferior" race. . . .

The removal of all Indians in the thirties—under conditions of hardship described lugubriously in a recent work of Grant Foreman—removed the destiny of this race from the American's view. It was not so with the doctrine of territorial utilization itself. "Manifestly," writes J. G. Wise in his *The Red Man in the New World Drama*, "such a people could not have dealt with a subordinate race . . . without an enduring effect upon their moral point of view." The doctrine of territorial utilization was destined not only to figure in many later issues but to undergo an often curious development. Tending always to enlarge its pretensions, it may seem in its later history to confirm the observation of R. H. Tawney that the children of the mind are like the children of the body: "Once born they grow by a law of their own being."

The first stage in the natural growth of the doctrine was its extension to territorial issues other than those involving Indians. This stage quickly arrived with the Oregon issue of the 'forties involving a territorial dispute between the United States and Great Britain. It was argued by John Quincy Adams and other expansionists that the right of Americans to the territory was greater than that of Englishmen because the former alone could utilize the country in accordance with the scriptural injunction to till the earth. But the allegation that the British desired Oregon only for hunting furs was as gratuitous as the former generalization about the occupational limitations of Indians.

The next territorial issue was of a different character and brought the principle of utilization into a new phase of development. It concerned the land of the Mexicans, who were tillers of the soil but did not till it efficiently or in more than relatively small part. California was claimed on the ground of the capacity of Americans to develop it more fully; after the outbreak of the Mexican War the territorial claim was enlarged until it embraced all of Mexico. The report of the New York State Democratic Convention of January, 1848, advocated annexation on the ground of a familiar philosophy:

We would hold it, not for our use, but for the use of man...Labor was the consecrated means of man's subsistence when he was created. To replenish the earth and subdue it, was his ordained mission and destiny.

About the same time, Sam Houston observed with his delightful ingenuousness that Americans had always cheated Indians, and that since Mexicans are no better than Indians "I see no reason why we should not go on the same course, now, and take their land." In the following decade Caleb Cushing, affirming annexation of Mexico to be destiny, asked the rhetorical question: "Is not the occupation of any portion of the earth by those competent to hold and till it, a providential law of national life?" The answer was given by Representative Cox in a general "law of annexation": "That no nation has the right to hold soil, virgin and rich, yet unproducing..." According to the *United States Democratic Review* of 1858, "no race but our own can either cultivate or rule the western hemisphere." The principle of cultivation, at first applied only to Indians, had been developed by expansionists to a generality contesting the land tenure of all other peoples of the continent.

AMERICAN INDIAN POLICY AND THE

ORIGINS OF MANIFEST DESTINY[1]   *Reginald Horsman*

... It seems clear that American attitudes towards the Indian tell us a great deal about the American attitude to other peoples and about the development of an ideology of expansion. In dealing with the Indians the United States developed a rationale of expansion which was readily adaptable to the needs of an advance over other peoples. Certainly later American expansionists did not view the Indian as a separate concern. By the late nineteenth century the American Indians were viewed as merely one of a number of

---

[1] Selected from the *University of Birmingham Historical Journal*, XI, No. 2 (1968), 128–40. Reprinted with permission.

inferior or degenerate races that had been overwhelmed by the all-conquering Anglo-Saxon.

Even before the American Revolution there were those who had sensed the ultimate destiny of this richly endowed continent. Franklin had envisioned Americans spreading westwards across the Mississippi Valley and outnumbering the people of England, and the young poet Philip Freneau in 1772 had even spoken of the time when this new population would "spread Dominion to the north and south and west Far from th' Atlantic to Pacific shores." In the years after the Revolution these early dreams of physical expansion were given a new dimension. The original Puritan ideal of a religious "city upon a hill" developed into a vision of a bountiful society blessed by Providence, which as it expanded in numbers and territory would set an example of free, republican government for the rest of the world....

The initial reaction of the United States to the Indians in the post-1783 period was conditioned by the frontier violence of the Revolutionary years. The Indians had allied with the British in the Revolution, and the impoverished Confederation government at first demanded an eye for an eye; the attacks of the Revolution would be expiated by forced cessions of lands. The Indian resistance to this concept, and the inability of the United States to raise the military force to carry out a blatant policy of conquest, had forced the United States to revert to the colonial policy of purchase by the end of the 1780's. At the same time a new philosophy of Indian relations was coming into being, a philosophy which entwined morality and expansionism.

* * *

In the late 1780's, and particularly after the formation of the new government in 1789, American leaders began to show a great desire to justify their expansion westwards over the Indians. Their solution to the dilemma of advocating an enlarged area of liberty and the blessings of a free government, while at the same time exterminating the aboriginal inhabitants, was conditioned by the eighteenth-century view of natural man and his improvability. Whatever the attitudes of the frontiersmen, those who formulated American opinion and a national policy in the late eighteenth and the first quarter of the nineteenth century saw the solution to their dilemma in the bringing of civilization to the Indian inhabitants of North America. This attitude was essentially one of great optimism. It did not preach any innate Indian inferiority, but rather viewed the Indian as existing at a lower stage in the evolution of society and civilization. These aboriginal inhabitants were to give up their state of nature, but in exchange were to be given the inestimable blessing of American civilization; the highest and happiest state that man had yet attained.

* * *

... This civilization meant, of course, making the Indians into Americans. The ideal was that of an American agrarian society. Ignoring the extensive agricultural development among the Indian tribes with whom the United States was in contact, [Secretary of War Henry] Knox and the other nation-

143

al leaders of this period placed the whole confrontation in the simple context of a primitive hunting society, on a lower stage of human evolution, encountering an American agrarian society at the highest stage of human development. The Indians were to be civilized by the adoption of private property, by the men farming in the American manner, by the women learning to spin and weave, and by the introduction of the rudiments of education and Christianity. Knox asserted in 1792 that the United States wanted the opportunity to impart to the Indians "all the blessings of civilized life, of teaching you to cultivate the earth, and raise corn; to raise oxen, sheep, and other domestic animals; to build comfortable houses, and to educate your children, so as ever to dwell upon the land."

The full expression of this philosophy of expansion over the Indians came with the Presidency of Thomas Jefferson, who combined a sense of mission to the Indians with a clear vision of the expansionist destiny of the United States. Jefferson was too imbued with eighteenth-century ideas of the natural man to doubt the improvability of the Indian. "I believe the Indian then," he wrote in the 1780's, "to be in body and mind equal to the whiteman." Like Knox, Jefferson ignored the agricultural aspects of Indian society, and preached the adoption of agriculture and private property as the route to the blessings of civilization. "Let me entreat you therefore," he told a delegation of Indians in December 1808, "on the lands now given you to begin every man a farm, let him enclose it, cultivate it, build a warm house on it, and when he dies let it belong to his wife and children after him."

... After telling the Indians to adopt farming and private property, he then argued for the next logical step: "You will unite yourselves with us, and we shall all be Americans. You will mix with us by marriage. Your blood will run in our veins and will spread with us over this great island." In January 1809 Jefferson told another delegation of Indians that "I consider my red children as forming one family with the Whites." ...

Whatever Jefferson thought of the natural man, however, he was not giving the Indians a choice between their existing state of society and American civilization. Jefferson had no doubt that the United States was offering the Indians the chance of participating in the greatest state of society the world had ever known; a chance to leap over the intervening steps to the high plateau of American civilization. As late as 1824 Jefferson wrote that a traveller coming eastwards from the Rockies to the seaport towns would see the equivalent of a survey in time "of the progress of man from the infancy of creation to the present day." He wrote that living in the first range of mountains in the interior of the country, "I have observed this march of civilization advancing from the seacoast, passing over us like a cloud of light, increasing our knowledge and improving our condition, insomuch as that we are at this time more advanced in civilization here than the seaports were when I was a boy. And where this progress will stop no one can say. Barbarism has, in the meantime, been receding before the steady step of amelioration; and will in time, I trust, disappear from the earth." With this confidence in the ultimate good of what the United States was accomplishing, the Indians could not be allowed to stand in the way.

144

If they did not accept the inestimable benefits of American civilization, then they were doomed. In 1812 he commented of Indians who were resisting that "the backward will yield, and be thrown further back. These will relapse into barbarism and misery, lose numbers by war and want, and we shall be obliged to drive them, with the beasts of the forest into the Stony mountains."

The philosophy argued for so eloquently by Jefferson remained the official hope of the United States through to the mid-1820's, and for many individuals persisted even after that date. Madison argued in his inaugural in 1809 that he intended "to carry on the benevolent plans which have been so meritoriously applied to the conversion of our aboriginal neighbors from the degradation and wretchedness of savage life to a participation of the improvements of which the human mind and manners are susceptible in a civilized state." Those who formulated governmental policy continued to argue for assimilation in the following years. In 1816 Secretary of War William Harris Crawford reported to the Senate that it was the desire of the government "to draw its savage neighbors within the pale of civilization." A similar attitude was expressed in 1818 by the chairman of the committee of the House of Representatives on that part of the message of the President regarding Indian affairs. "In the present state of our country, one of two things seems to be necessary," wrote Henry Southard, "either that those sons of the forest should be moralized or exterminated. Humanity would rejoice at the former, but shrink with horror from the latter." Jefferson's ideals were not easily overthrown, for even in the late 1820's James Barbour, Secretary of War under John Quincy Adams, at first hoped that he would be able to incorporate the Indians fully within American society.

. . . Jefferson was not only the most earnest in desiring an amalgamation of Americans and Indians, he was also the most realistic in assessing what civilization would mean in terms of acquiring Indian lands. He argued in 1803 that the bringing of civilization to the Indians, with its private property and farming instead of hunting, "will enable them to live on much smaller portions of land." This, argued Jefferson, would produce "a coincidence of interests." While the Indians were learning to live better on less land, an expanding America would require more land. The interrelationship would be for the good of both. These founding fathers had a supreme confidence in the merits of what their government and society had to offer. Its expansion would be for the good of all. If any were so perverse as to refuse what was offered to them, then their disappearance in the name of progress was to be regretted but was unavoidable.

In the years between 1815 and 1830 American Indian policy was confronted with a major dilemma, a dilemma which inevitably affected the ideology of expansion. On the one hand confidence in the American mission and progress reached new heights. In the early days of independence there had always been a lingering fear that the experiment of a free, republican government would prove a failure, that those Europeans who prophesied chaos for the American "mobocracy" would prove correct. Yet, in the years after 1815, it was quite clear that the United States was advancing dramatically in total strength. Immigrants were entering American ports in increasing numbers, settlers were pouring west, new states were entering the Union; from one end of the country to the other the story was one of growth and prosperity. Confidence in America as the bastion of freedom and progress reached new heights. . . .

Yet, while the United States reached new heights of confidence, there seemed little doubt that the dream of Knox and Jefferson was collapsing. In most of the country the Indians were not accepting American civilization, except for its vices. Indian culture had often collapsed, but all too often no coherent pattern had taken its place. Only in the South, among the Cherokees, were American ways winning major victories, and there it was quickly becoming apparent that realities were overwhelming the ideal. At the last instant even privately owned plots of land were wanted by adjacent American settlers. As the United States grew in confidence, as her sense of mission increased, a new rationale had to be found as a basis for Indian relations and expansion. For Knox and Jefferson the Indians had been men in a natural state, capable of improvement, men of equal capabilities in a different stage of society. Yet, as the Indians apparently showed themselves unwilling or incapable of becoming American farmers, and as the United States more than ever became convinced that her expansion benefited the whole world, the feeling that the original inhabitants did not deserve to retain what they possessed became stronger. There had, of course, always been those in the United States who regarded the Indians as mere obstacles to progress, but this view became increasingly powerful in American thinking in the second quarter of the nineteenth century. It ultimately evolved into a philosophy which could justify the appropriation not only of the lands of the Indians but also of those of the Mexicans.

As might be expected, this belief in the ultimate inability of the Indians to be assimilated successfully became most powerful amongst those who had the most interest in acquiring Indian lands, whether held in common or in severalty. Governor George M. Troup of Georgia in 1824 attacked the concept of the amalgamation of the Indians within American society: "The utmost of rights and privileges which public opinion would concede to Indians," wrote Troup, "would fix them in a middle station, between the negro and the white man; and that, as long as they survived this degradation, without the possibility of attaining the elevation of the latter, they would gradually sink to the condition of the former—a point of degeneracy below which they could not fall; it is likely, before they reached this, their wretchedness would find relief in broken hearts." In the following year Senator Thomas Hart Benton, in supporting a road to connect the West with the possessions of Mexico, lamented any Indian interference with this object: "Shall a measure of such moment be defeated by a parcel of miserable barbarians, Arabs of the desert, incapable of appreciating our policy, and placing a higher value upon the gun of a murdered hunter, than upon the preservation of all the republics in the world!" This was a long way from Jefferson's concept of the noble savage.

Perhaps the most revealing insight into the new attitude came in a discussion in John Quincy Adams' cabinet in December 1825. This cabinet in many ways well represented the transformation that was occurring in

American thinking. Barbour, the Secretary of War, was still hoping for a solution in Jeffersonian terms, but Secretary of State Henry Clay, who in his public statements often attacked ruthlessness in American expansionism, argued that "it was impossible to civilize Indians; that there never was a full-blooded Indian who took to civilization. It was not in their nature. He believed they were destined to extinction, and, although he would never use or countenance inhumanity towards them, he did not think them, as a race, worth preserving. He considered them as essentially inferior to the Anglo-Saxon race, which were now taking their place on this continent. They were not an improvable breed, and their disappearance from the human family will be no great loss to the world. In point of fact they were rapidly disappearing, and he did not believe that in fifty years from this time there would be any of them left." Adams tells us a good deal about his own opinions as well as those of Barbour by the comment in his diary that "Governor Barbour was somewhat shocked at these opinions, for which I fear there is too much foundation."

The idea that the Indian represented not merely man at a different stage, who could readily be assimilated, but rather an inferior savage who blocked progress, gained considerable ground in the late 1820's and 1830's. It seems quite clear that Indian removal must be viewed against this background of disillusionment. Although many men of good will, including Barbour himself, ultimately reached the conclusion that for the good of the Indians, and even to civilize them, they should be removed west of the Mississippi, it is quite clear that many of the politicians who took up the policy of removal had no faith in ultimate civilization. Adams believed that the idea of civilizing the Indians by putting them together in one region west of the Mississippi was impractical, as did several of his cabinet; he was ready to approve the idea because there was nothing better to offer. Removal was a way out of an immediate difficulty; there are few signs that practical politicians really believed those who argued that this was a better way to civilize the Indians.

. . . There were, of course, still those who believed in the improvability of the Indian, and argued for eventual assimilation, but the prevailing mood and policy of the government had changed. Removal in reality acknowledged the failure of the post-Revolutionary policy of assimilation, and was known to be only a temporary expedient. By 1830 it was quite clear to many Americans that the American population was going to sweep forward to the Pacific.

In the 1830's and 1840's the American view of the Indian merged into a more elaborate ideology which built a basis of justification for American expansion over any lands. The Americans had no need to develop a whole new set of attitudes, for they had already been deeply involved in the problem of rationalizing an advance which ruined and dispossessed those with whom they came into contact. More and more the talk was of superior or inferior race rather than of different stages of human society. The idea of the Anglo-Saxons or related races as divinely appointed to civilize the world assumed an increasingly important share of the argument. The confidence in American institutions also reached new heights. "Foreign powers do not seem to appreciate the true character of our Government," Polk announced in his inaugural in 1845. "Our Union is a confederation of independent States, whose policy is peace with each other and all the world. To enlarge its limits is to extend the dominions of peace over additional territories and increasing millions."

Having convinced themselves in the 1820's and 1830's that the failure of the Indians to benefit from the American advance had stemmed from their inherent inferiority, and that Providence had ordained that the Americans would bring peace, freedom, and a better civilization to the world on a stepping-stone of less able races, the proponents of expansionism had no difficulty in extending their arguments to cover the Mexicans. One newspaper made a simple and direct connection: "The Mexicans are *aboriginal Indians*," it was maintained, "and they must share the destiny of their race." Most expansionists were merely content to use analogy. "The Mexican race now see, in the fate of the aborigines of the north, their own inevitable destiny," argued the *Democratic Review*. "They must amalgamate and be lost, in the superior vigor of the Anglo-Saxon race, or they must utterly perish."

* * *

In the years from the Revolution to the Mexican War the United States had begun with the presumption that the destruction of the Indians would be a major blot on the national character; a blot for which the United States would have to answer to other nations throughout the world, to future historians, and to God. It can easily be maintained that even in the early years the United States never translated this concern into a practical program, and that indeed, like Maria Theresa, the more she cried, the more she took. Yet, at least in the 1790's and the first decade of the nineteenth century, there was an optimism that all would be well, a belief, however misinformed, that the Indians would assume American civilization, and thus American expansion would directly benefit not only those expanding but also those who stood as a barrier. By the 1820's this concept of Indian improvability was under major attack, and in the 1830's and 1840's a more common assumption was that the Indians had succumbed because they were doomed by Providence, and that the sufferings of whoever stood in the way of expansion was nothing beside the benefit to humanity of extending the area of American civilization and freedom. This doctrine was so convenient that it could be used to extend a slave system over a Mexican area that had abandoned slavery.

To treat American Indian policy as a purely domestic concern is to ignore what it tells us of the American attitude towards alien peoples. It would seem fruitful to regard American Indian policy as part of the expansion of Western Europe, particularly the so-called Anglo-Saxons, over peoples throughout the world; an expansion which reached its height at the close of the nineteenth century. In this way American Indian policy can help explain not only the assumptions of what for convenience is called "Manifest Destiny" but also the underlying assumptions of imperialism.

THE OREGON QUESTION[1]   *Richard W. Van Alstyne*

. . . It was a tardy colonizing movement on the part of individualistic American families, albeit a great and a speedy one. In a half-dozen years it occupied the two great farming valleys of the Pacific Northwest, the Willamette and the Walla Walla, both of them *south* of the Columbia. As late as 1846 practically no Americans had penetrated north of the river. Why did the advantage held by the Hudson's Bay Company go unchallenged for well-nigh twenty years? The Company had the initial leadership and drive which until the 1840's were utterly lacking on the American side. No one comparable to the Texan *empresarios* appeared to lead American families into the Oregon wilderness. No one appreciated the latter's value until it began to be publicized by returning missionaries and trappers and by newspapermen. Oregon began to be "news" in the late 1830's, after which it became a popular theme among Western Congressmen and editors. The depression in Western land values and prices for farm products that followed in the wake of the panic of 1837 probably furnished the immediate background. It was in February 1838 that the first bill to organize Oregon into a territory was introduced into Congress. This would have meant military occupation and a civil authority established in advance of actual colonization. It was sponsored by a Missouri Senator, Lewis F. Linn. Senator Linn also led a movement to grant six hundred and forty acres of land free in Oregon to each settler. His proposed measures failed of passage at the hands of Eastern and Southern Congressmen, but the emigration to Oregon nevertheless may well have been based in part on hopes of their ultimate success. For the same reason the pioneers congregated naturally south of the Columbia, where they could be more certain of having their titles confirmed when the country should be officially divided with Great Britain.

From the standpoint of actual development of the country, the Columbia was the natural line of division, and until 1843 at least there was some indication that it would be such. In fact the American government, chiefly under the influence of Daniel Webster in 1842, was interested in a tripartite division of the West Coast among the United States, Great Britain, and Mexico. Great Britain was to take everything north of the Columbia and the United States everything to the south as far as the thirty-sixth parallel. Such a division would give the two English-speaking powers all the important harbors on the Coast, the United States getting San Francisco and Monterey as well as free use of the Columbia. This plan went as far as a confidential sounding of the British government in 1842 at the time Webster was carrying on an important negotiation in Washington with Lord Ashburton; and it was conditioned upon British help in getting Mexican consent. Apparently,

---

[1] Selected from *American Diplomacy in Action*, pp. 564–65, 567–72. Reprinted with permission of the author and Stanford University Press. Copyright 1947 by the Board of Trustees of Leland Stanford Junior University.

149

too, it implied a willingness to end the Texas question, including perhaps an American guaranty never to seek the annexation of Texas. Surely no bargain could have been entered into with either Mexico or Great Britain at that time unless that bugbear had been thoroughly disposed of. We know that Lord Ashburton expressed himself favorably at least to the United States' getting San Francisco, and that Tyler was ready to send Webster on a special mission to London for the purpose of arranging the matter. We know, moreover, that it was the country between the Columbia and San Francisco Bay in which Captain John C. Frémont, sent by President Tyler to explore in 1842, was chiefly interested. Webster was never favorable to Texas. Four years later, after both the Texas and the Oregon questions had been dealt with, but *before* California was acquired, he still saw San Francisco as the main goal. "You know my opinion to have been, and now is," he remarked to his son, "that the port of San Francisco would be twenty times more valuable to us than all Texas."

This interesting project for a tripartite division of the vast land west of the treaty lines of 1818–1819 experienced a sharp reversal in 1843. Tyler for reasons of his own took up the cause for the "re-annexation" of Texas, and his Secretary of State, Abel P. Upshur, a fellow Virginian, in October proposed to substitute the forty-ninth parallel for the Columbia River as the line of division in Oregon. . . .

Reduced to simple realities, any permanent agreement, lacking war, would have to be made on the basis of either the American or the British idea of a boundary, the forty-ninth or the Columbia.

Thirsting for re-election to office, however, and ignoring the simple amenities of truth, President John Tyler recklessly declared himself in favor of the whole of Oregon. The germ of this abandonment of sweet reasonableness can be seen as far back as 1838–1839 in the perhaps irresponsible efforts of Senator Linn of Missouri to excite opinion in favor of excluding the British from the whole of the country. The honorable Senator exclaimed in December 1839:

> I would not be surprised that this [Oregon] question continued with that of Maine should lead to war between us and Great Britain. She rarely lets go her grasp, and is proud, boastful and insolent. The people of England will never respect us as we merit until we give them a right down good flogging. War is always a sad alternative, but let it come when it will, we must never leave it *until we drive our old enemy from the continent*, not even leaving them a spot of ground upon which they leave a footprint.

This speech discloses an ideology often voiced throughout American history but never realizable—the idea that Britain must evacuate the whole of the continent if America is to be safe. *Total* expulsion of British dominion and British influence was to be the grand war aim of the United States, which would thus achieve permanent security. Those who held to it made no concealment of their expectation that sweeping annexations and establishment of an absolute hegemony over the continent by the United States would follow the desired British capitulation as surely as day follows night. Thus do concepts of security serve as springboards for programs of aggression.

The Oregon situation furnished an unusually fertile ground for rationalization of this kind. The question received its first great popular fillip in 1843. The important Webster-Ashburton Treaty, partitioning the disputed country in the Northeast, had recently been concluded, and rumors were already afloat regarding Webster's proposed tripartite division of the Pacific Coast. Determined to scotch such a plan, Western Senators set their caps for the whole of Oregon. Local meetings in the Western states, inspired by politicians on the lookout for a likely campaign issue, spread the movement. By the time the Democratic party convention foregathered at Baltimore in 1844 it was definitely identified with the Texas question, and thus the "re-occupation" of Oregon and the "re-annexation" of Texas became virtually the exclusive issues of the day. Party politicians and journalists built the bridge between the need for security and the need for the whole of Oregon. A Democratic assembly held in Cincinnati in July 1843 declared that "the rumored negotiation for a surrender of *any* part of Oregon for an equivalent in California was *dangerous to peace and a repudiation of Monroe's doctrine* 'that the American continents are closed to European colonization.' ..."

From this assertion it was an easy step to the breath-taking effusions of 1844–1846: the insistence by a committee of the Democratic convention "that our title to the *whole* Territory of Oregon is *clear and unquestionable*..."; the famous war whoop, "Fifty-four forty or fight," a slogan nothing short of a stroke of genius by Senator Allen of Ohio, the fire-eating chairman of the Senate Committee on Foreign Relations; the toast offered by Senator Hannegan of Indiana, "Oregon—Every foot or not an inch; 54 degrees and forty minutes or delenda est Britiania [*sic*]"; and, finally, the divine revelation of "manifest destiny" as the "right ... to overspread and to possess the whole of the continent which Providence has given us for the development of liberty and federated self-government entrusted to us. ..."

Such was the current generated by the fifty-four-forty men, as the radicals came to be called. It was chiefly a Western agitation, whipped up by Senators Allen of Ohio, Hannegan of Indiana, Cass of Michigan, and Atchison of Missouri, and Representative Stephen A. Douglas of Illinois. Naturally the Oregon pioneers were themselves infected with it. ...

... While the presidential campaign was in progress, every Democrat appeared to be a fifty-four-forty man. Polk took full advantage of the slogan, and even the wary Buchanan, while still a Senator, posed as a fifty-four-forty. Straightway the latter became Secretary of State he faced about and proved the most persistent worker in Polk's cabinet for compromise.

The situation was as follows in March 1845 when Polk entered office: the British government was officially committed to the line of the Columbia, but was secretly willing to retire to the forty-ninth, provided certain important details could be arranged—navigation rights at least for a term of years to the Columbia River, full indemnification of the Hudson's Bay Company, and some practicable arrangement for the use of the Straits of Juan de Fuca. The new American administration was deeply involved with the fifty-four-forty men, but was secretly anxious to compromise on the line of the forty-ninth. On July 12 Buchanan made the offer secretly to the British minister,

Richard Pakenham. The latter's inconsiderate refusal, without reference to London, threw the whole question into a deadlock once again. Pakenham's action is almost incomprehensible in view of the fact that he already knew of Lord Aberdeen's attitude in the matter. Even so, the deadlock need not have continued long if President Polk had had any desire to dissolve it. Apparently Polk feared the power of the fifty-four-forties. Having been rebuffed by the British minister in Washington, there was nothing to prevent him from obtaining a response from the British government through the American minister in London, Louis McLane. But instead of encouraging negotiation in this way (which was what Pakenham expected him to do), Polk withdrew his offer. Then followed months of diplomatic sparring, into the details of which it is unnecessary to plunge. *Before* withdrawing his offer, the President had received a report from McLane that the British government was prepared to compromise on the forty-ninth. Accordingly he felt fairly safe in keeping up appearances of *hauteur* himself. He told his cabinet he would submit any proposition made by the British government to the Senate, allowing that body to decide on acceptance or rejection.

But months passed by with neither party making a direct move. In spite of his personal convictions Aberdeen hesitated to propose the forty-ninth. The traditional British stand was on the Columbia as the essential boundary. Even though the Hudson's Bay Company had proved by its action that this was a fallacy, it was not easy to make the official readjustment at once. The whole American election campaign had been one of bluster, and it was out of the question to give up immediately a position maintained steadfastly for more than twenty years.

The corner was turned in January 1846. By that time Lord Aberdeen had secured a pledge of support in favor of the compromise from the leader of the opposition party, Lord John Russell. Moreover, he won the editor of the London *Times* to his point of view. The latter's editorials supporting the cause of compromise gave the cue to British opinion. Meanwhile the Senate and the House of Representatives in Washington debated the question of giving the year's notice required by the Treaty of 1827 to bring the period of "joint occupation" to an end. This protracted discussion pushed the fifty-four-forties more and more into the minority. For nearly five months the debate went on, accompanied by numerous consultations between the leading Senators on the one side and the British minister on the other. Buchanan also kept alert in the matter, and knew from McLane of the progress being made in England in favor of compromise.[2] Finally, on April 2, the Senate voted the joint resolution to give due notice. This broke the deadlock that all informed persons had known for at least two months would be broken. The British proposal for compromise on the line of the

---

[2] Author's note.—The British intended to stand firm on this compromise, however, and to accept eventualities if necessary. And since Polk had ignored the simple truth in his annual message to Congress in December 1845, they considered it possible he would launch a sudden attack. Early in February 1846 Aberdeen informed McLane that preparations would be made "not only for the defense and protection of the Canadas, but for offensive preparations. In the course of the conversation," McLane reported, "I understood that these would consist, independent of military armaments, of the immediate equipment of thirty sail of the line, besides steamers and other vessels of war." The warning seems to have had a sobering effect on Polk.

McLane's dispatch remained unpublished until 1937. See Miller, *Treaties*, V, 57–59, and also Julius W. Pratt, "James K. Polk and John Bull," *Canadian Historical Review*, XXIV (1943), 341–49.

forty-ninth reached Washington in the form of a draft treaty on June 6. Four days later Polk sent it to the Senate for advice, and the latter body after only two days advised acceptance by a vote of 38 to 12. The treaty was signed on June 15 in the precise form in which it had been received from London, was submitted to the Senate the next day, and the latter's advice and consent were secured by a vote of 41 to 14, a full vote except for one absence. On both occasions the Senate abandoned the customary practice of submitting questions of foreign affairs to its Committee on Foreign Relations and proceeded to a direct vote.

* * *

Oregon was thus partitioned along practical lines and greatly to the advantage of the United States, whose claims to the land north of the Columbia were very slender from every standpoint. From the time of Canning all parties were sensitive to the importance of the seacoast. British policy until 1845 was motivated largely by the belief that the Columbia was a navigable inland waterway and that it must at least be shared if Britain was to have a part in the transpacific trade. Lord John Russell, the leader of the Whig party, was not actually disabused of this belief until the end of that year. This seems to have been a material factor in alternating the British viewpoint. Actually, of course, the country was so divided as to leave the British with an almost equally good stake in the deep harbors of the coast. From the American viewpoint, moreover, the agreement of 1846 simply insured what had been sought for forty years, the window on the Pacific. Reference was made to this phase of the problem at the outset of this discussion. But there was another window on the Pacific—California, with its spacious bay of San Francisco—whose future was still in doubt. The same men who got the lion's share of the Oregon country were equally bent on forcing conclusions over the long stretch of coast to the south.

ON THE EVE OF

REVOLUTION IN TEXAS[1]   *William C. Binkley*

... The details of the general background need not concern us here, but certain salient points must be hastily reviewed. We know that in 1821 Anglo-American frontiersmen, pressed by the combination of the panic of 1819 and the termination of the credit system in the disposal of public lands in the United States, began to seek new economic opportunity in Texas, where the Spanish authorities were showing signs of a more liberal attitude toward foreigners. We know also that in that same year the Mexican subjects of Spain established their independence and began the arduous task of transforming the former Spanish viceroyalty into a federal republic. In a penetrating analysis of the train of events which stemmed from these two

---

[1] Selected from *The Texas Revolution* (Baton Rouge: Louisiana State University Press, 1952), pp. 2–7, 20–23, 25, 33–35. Reprinted with permission.

concurrent developments, Professor Eugene C. Barker has shown that the basic factor was the difference in the background of the two groups of people who thus came into contact with each other on Mexican soil. On the one side was the influence of the Anglo-American frontier experience, which had promoted a spirit of resourcefulness and self-reliance and had provided for a practical application of their democratic theories of government and individual liberty as the pioneers had moved westward on their own responsibility. On the other side was the effect of nearly three centuries of autocratic Spanish rule, which had left little room for the acquiring of political wisdom or the development of initiative and resourcefulness as the Mexican frontier had been advanced northward by official propulsion. "With the political ascendancy of the two elements reversed," says Barker, "the situation would have held no threatening aspects, but with the Mexicans in the political saddle conflict was certain."

In adopting the federal constitution of 1824 the Mexicans provided themselves with a complex system of government which was beyond their capacity to understand or administer, and in their stumbling efforts to follow its provisions they soon became involved in political confusion. Factional strife was so intense that only the first president was able to serve out the term for which he was elected, and in one four-year term the office changed hands four times. Because the official actions sometimes impinged upon rights or privileges which the Anglo-Americans considered to be guaranteed under a federal system, minor misunderstandings inevitably developed. In its enumeration of the states which it was bringing into existence to form a federal union, the constitution arbitrarily joined Texas with the neighboring province of Coahuila, and the national congress then instructed this artificial state to work out its own program of local government. With only one representative in the legislature, the Anglo-Americans were clearly at the mercy of the Mexican majority; but, in general, the authorities were so preoccupied with their own quarrels that they neglected either to provide for the needs or to enforce the regulations incident to the colonization of Texas. Under the guidance of Stephen F. Austin the settlers managed for a time to avoid becoming involved in the domestic upheavals, but their ability to remain aloof was compromised when the repeated efforts of the United States to purchase Texas led the Mexican authorities to suspect that the influx of colonists was part of an organized scheme to despoil Mexico of territory. By 1830, therefore, they were determined to take issue with their Anglo-American subjects.

Three problems which had already caused the colonists some concern were the requirement that all settlers in Texas must be Catholics, the recurring indications of Mexican opposition to slavery, and the failure to make adequate provision for the machinery of local government through which they might have a direct voice in the administering of their own affairs and the maintaining of order. Thus far, however, the authorities had shown little disposition to raise any question concerning the religious affiliation of the immigrants; and on the question of slavery, prohibitory measures which had been adopted by both the state and the national governments were virtually nullified when Mexican officials collaborated with the colonists in working out a system of contract labor which permitted its continuation in fact if not in name. But in both cases the continued existence of the restrictions constituted a potential danger that could not be ignored. The third problem, on the other hand, grew out of a need for positive action. In their efforts to obtain a more adequate system of local administration the Anglo-Americans were simply following the precedents of earlier frontier experience in the United States, but the suspicious Mexican mind construed their requests as evidence of a plot to undermine Mexican institutions, instigated no doubt by the aggressive neighbor to the north. The response was the passage of the famous law of April 6, 1830, which placed a ban on further immigration into Texas from the United States and provided for the garrisoning of the province with convict soldiers to ensure the enforcement of Mexican laws.

To the Texans the adoption of these provisions indicated that the period of easy indifference on the part of Mexican authorities was about to be superseded by regulation and enforcement. Although they strongly resented the sudden change from neglect to a policy of control, they accepted Austin's conservative counsel to refrain from demonstrations while he attempted to obtain the suspension of the most objectionable features of the law. As usual, however, the Mexican's enthusiasm for enunciating principles was tempered by his incapacity in trying to apply them, and in the end neither of the general aims of the law was carried out as planned. Efforts to put the military plan into operation were thwarted in large part by the particularistic attitudes of the state governments, and the few troops that got to Texas served to irritate rather than intimidate the colonists until the overthrow of the authorities who had sent them forced their withdrawal. Austin succeeded in obtaining an interpretation of the ban on immigration which left the door open for a diminished flow on an authorized basis, while in the absence of an effective military force many others continued to come without authorization. For the time being the plans for more rigid control obviously had failed, but the new legislation remained on the statute books. The net result was to increase the apprehension of the Texans concerning their status under Mexican rule and to strengthen their conviction that if the authorities would permit them to work out their own solutions for their problems, much of the cause for friction could be removed. . . .

Economically, the Anglo-American in Texas was advancing rapidly by 1834, and his increasing prosperity was due in large measure to his ability to take advantage of the agricultural possibilities of the country itself. Six years earlier Austin had said, with a sincerity of enthusiasm which would be an asset for the modern real-estate salesman: "Nature seems to have formed Texas for a great agricultural, grazing, manufacturing, and commercial country. . . . It combines in an eminent degree all the elements necessary for those different branches of industry." In 1833, however, he reported to the Mexican government that it was exclusively agricultural, the other "branches of industry" apparently remaining little more than potentialities. As a matter of fact his own early descriptions of the country, together with the character of the Mexican land policy, appealed primarily to the farmer rather than to the trader or manufacturer. Thus far the Anglo-Americans had been sufficiently resourceful to produce their own foodstuffs and at the same time to establish a reputation for producing the best quality of cotton that went to the New Orleans market. But they had also combined their agriculture with stock raising, and Almonte in 1834 estimated the number of livestock at about 75,000 head of cattle, something over 100,000 head of hogs, and nearly 10,000 head of sheep, practically all of them being found in the two departments occupied by the Anglo-Americans.

As a natural accompaniment to their successful agricultural and stock-raising enterprise, these people were becoming more and more conscious of the necessity for commercial expansion beyond the limits of their own province. The available information concerning their foreign commerce about 1834, while perhaps not always accurate as to totals, shows that the balance of trade was against them. They were exporting agricultural products and other raw materials amounting to about $500,000 annually, while their imports, consisting largely of manufactured articles such as clothing, shoes, implements, weapons, and other necessities, ran as high as $630,000 a year. It is not surprising, therefore, to find Almonte reporting that "money is very scarce in Texas, and one may say with certainty that out of every hundred transactions made not ten involve specie." The conviction was fast growing that without adequate market facilities for their surplus products economic progress would soon reach its limit; consequently no possibility was being overlooked. As articles of export they could offer cotton, corn, lumber, salted meats, hides, and even livestock, while the abundance of such wild animals as beavers, otters, bears, deer, and buffalo furnished an opportunity for the development of an important fur trade.

But the only market to which they had ready access was New Orleans, and since all these commodities were already available in the United States, they were forced to trade under unfavorable conditions. They were convinced that their produce could be sold at Vera Cruz or Matamoros for a higher price than at New Orleans, but the lack of shipping connections and the accompanying lack of a constructive commercial policy on the part of either the state or the national government in Mexico made this impossible. Perhaps the best evidence of the nature of the adjustment needed appeared in the fact that Austin, interested in obtaining separate statehood for Texas, and Almonte, desirous of ensuring closer relations between the Anglo-Americans and the Mexicans, described the same general economic conditions and suggested similar plans for carrying out their commercial programs. To both men it was evident that the best interests of Texas lay in the development of its trade with Mexico. . . .

Such was the vision of the commercial possibilities for Texas in 1834. The presence of such prospects was proof that the province had reached a turning point in its economic growth, and had the Mexican authorities been in a position to give their undivided and sympathetic attention to the accordant features in the report of their own inspector and that of the Texas agent, they could have removed almost at a single stroke the chief basis for discontent. The Texans admitted that they needed Mexican markets, and Almonte showed that trade with Texas would be an economic benefit to

Mexico. The solution seemed obvious, and the Texans could not comprehend the failure of the Mexican government to take favorable action. . . .

As if these fundamental questions of securing satisfactory arrangements in their general political, economic, and social conditions were not enough to keep the Texans fully occupied, certain special difficulties were gradually demanding more and more attention. For example, the facilities for adequate communication between the different parts of the province had not kept pace with increasing needs, and the Anglo-Americans were trying with little success to interest the state government in the development of a program of internal improvements which would provide good roads and improve the usability of the numerous streams. They were also concerned over the ever present danger of depredations from the Indian tribes along their frontier, but the only response that came to their requests for permission to organize their own militia force was a suggestion from the government that convict troops would be sent to handle the problem. More serious than either of these, however, was the adoption by the state legislature of 1834 of a new series of land laws by which the *empresario* system was abolished and the gates apparently opened to speculation on a wholesale plan. To the Texans this seemed to mean the concentration of land in the hands of a few at the expense of the people in general, and from their point of view the whole episode furnished a clearer illustration of the defectiveness of the state government.

So many questions of vital importance had been raised within this short period and so few had been settled, that it was becoming increasingly evident that from several points of view Texas had reached a turning point in its development. The importance of the period lay in the fact that it marked the cumulation of hitherto diversified frontier interests into one general problem of securing a satisfactory adjustment to the changing conditions which accentuated the difference between the Texans and the rest of the Mexican republic. While it was true that a certain sense of incompatibility had been present from the beginning of Anglo-American colonization, it was equally true that the pacifying influence of Stephen F. Austin had thus far made compromise a possibility. But through the fatuity of the Mexican government Austin was being detained in Mexico City while Texas was awakening to its real needs, with the result that both sides were deprived of the services of the one man who might have found an equitable solution for the problem. Certainly Texas had not yet developed a substitute who possessed his understanding of the situation and his power of inspiring men with confidence in his leadership; and it was during this period of leaderless and futile attempts at realization of economic possibilities, at stabilization of social developments, at adjustments in political organization, and at the solution of other problems of special significance that the seeds were sown which were eventually to germinate into an open revolt against the uncertainties and inefficiencies of Mexican rule.

ASIATIC TRADE AND THE AMERICAN
OCCUPATION OF THE PACIFIC COAST[1]   *Robert G. Cleland*

"On all great subjects," says Walter Bagehot, quoting from Mill, "much
remains to be said." Certainly this is true with regard to the westward
expansion of the American people, a movement which, forming the
characteristic feature of our national life, was the product of many complex
and diverse motives. In the present paper an attempt is made to show the
influence of one of these motives, namely, the desire to secure control of
Asiatic trade upon the acquisition of Oregon and California. Owing to
limitations of space the treatment of the subject is confessedly inadequate,
and should be regarded more as a general survey than as a finished treatise.

If we look first at the occupation of Oregon, we shall find that American
interest in that Territory owed its very beginning to commercial motives.[2]
Thomas Jefferson, whose far-sighted wisdom began the trans-Mississippi
westward movement, throughout his long life cherished a desire to secure a
share of Oriental trade for the United States. With this object in view he
encouraged the somewhat chimerical but none the less heroic scheme of
John Ledyard to journey eastward from Paris to the northwest coast and
from there to explore a way across the continent to the American settlements, thus opening an overland route for the transportation of the
merchandise of China.

Some 10 years later, when engaging the services of André Michaux on
behalf of the American Philosophical Society for the proposed explorations
of the regions west of the Mississippi, Jefferson showed that his interest in
the idea of Ledyard had not abated and that the primary purpose of the
Michaux enterprise was the discovery of the suggested route for eastern
commerce. Michaux was given permission to disregard all instructions
concerning the conduct of the expedition, "except, indeed, what is the first
of all objects," as Jefferson wrote, "that you seek for and pursue that route
which shall form the shortest and most convenient communication between
the higher parts of the Missouri and the Pacific Ocean."

The same purpose also constituted the principal motive for the explorations of Lewis and Clark. "The object of your mission," ran Jefferson's
instructions to Lewis, "is to explore the Missouri River and such principal
streams of it as by its course and communication with the waters of the
Pacific Ocean may offer the most direct and practical water communication
across the continent for the purpose of commerce." As Benton afterwards
said, "Jefferson thus was the first to propose the North American road to

[1] Selected from the *Report of the American Historical Association for 1911,* pp. 283–89. Reprinted
with permission.
[2] Author's note.—In this discussion no attempt whatever is made to describe the actual commerce
which American merchants carried on with the Orient. Their first acquaintance with the Pacific
Northwest and California was due to the fur trade from those regions to China. This continued to be
a most lucrative enterprise until well along in the nineteenth century, when other and more ordinary
forms of commerce took its place.

India and the introduction of Asiatic trade on that road." Benton might have added that Jefferson thus was the first to bring about the exploration of Oregon and prepare the way for the American advance to the Pacific.

The first settlement in Oregon, like its exploration, had its beginning in Oriental trade. In later years, giving his reason for the establishment of Astoria, Astor wrote that he desired it "to serve as a place of depot [deposit] and give further facilities for conducting a trade across this continent to that river [the Columbia], and from there . . . to Canton in China, and from thence to the United States."

In 1818 when the agitation for the occupation of the regions around the Columbia began to assume considerable proportions, the influence of Asiatic trade becomes even more important. The chief objection to the treaty of joint occupation with Great Britain was the strategic position of Oregon relative to the Orient. And when Floyd, as chairman of the House Committee on the Occupation of the Columbia River, brought in his report, he was careful to lay emphasis upon this point.

From every reflection [he said] which the committee have been able to bestow upon the facts connected with this subject, they are inclined to believe the Columbia, in a commercial point of view, a position of the utmost importance; the fishing on that coast, its open sea, and its position in regard to China, which offers the best market for the vast quantities of furs taken in those regions, and our increasing trade throughout that ocean, seems to demand immediate attention.

Elsewhere in the report, following Jefferson's idea, Floyd outlined a plan for a route from the Atlantic to the Pacific by making use of the waterways of the continent and constructing a road from the headwaters of the Missouri to those of the Columbia. This road he believed could be built by 20 men in 10 days. A final suggestion was offered that an immediate settlement of Chinese colonists be made in Oregon to hold the territory until the arrival of sufficient Americans to displace them.

When this report was politely but effectually killed by an incredulous Congress, the interests of Oregon passed into the hands of a small group of western Senators and Representatives one of whose leaders was Thomas H. Benton. The motives of Benton in advocating the occupation of Oregon were numerous. His chief purpose, however, is best expressed in the following extract from one of his public addresses near the close of his political career. After tracing the historical development of the idea of a transcontinental route for Asiatic commerce, going back indeed to the very early days of French and Spanish colonization, Benton continued:

About 30 years ago I myself began to turn my attention to this subject and conceived the plan of the establishment of a route extending up the Missouri River and down the Columbia. I followed the idea of Mr. Jefferson, La Salle, and others, and I endeavored to revive attention to their plans. . . . I believed that Asiatic commerce might be brought into the Mississippi Valley along that line and wrote essays to support that idea. The scope of these essays was to show that Asiatic commerce had been the pursuit of all western nations from the time of the Phoenicians down to the present day—a space of 3,000 years; that during all this time this commerce had been shifting its channel, and that wealth and power followed it and disappeared upon its loss; that one channel more was to be found—a last one, and our America its seat. . . . Occupied with this idea I sought to impress it upon others. Looking to a practical issue I sought information of the country and of the mountains from all that could give it...and the results were most satisfactory.

The final contest over the Oregon question from 1842 to 1846 brought out afresh the important part Asiatic trade had in quickening American interest in securing the territory. Frémont, having found that the mythical Buena Ventura River, supposed to flow from the Salt Lake to the Pacific, was nonexistent, laid new emphasis upon holding the Columbia as the only feasible continental route. Calhoun, while opposing the abrogation of the treaty of joint occupation, agreed with Benton's estimate of the importance of the territory.

A vast market in China and India will be created, and a mighty influence will be given to commerce [he declared]. No small portion of the share that will fall to us...is destined to pass through the ports of the Oregon Territory to the valley of the Mississippi....It is mainly because I place this high estimate on its prospective value that I am so concerned to preserve it.

The whole issue I have so far been trying to set before you was well summed up by C. J. Ingersoll in the course of an address before the House in February, 1845.

The Oregon question [said Mr. Ingersoll], by too many deemed a mere matter of land or territorial acquisition, is, in its larger and better estimate, a commercial question.... It embraces consequences to the Republic equal, if not superior, to any question of acquisition or annexation that has arisen.... The American Continent presents extraordinary advantages to its population for commercial intercourse. Its position is one of nature's monopolies. From its Atlantic ports it can grasp the commerce of Europe; from those on the Pacific it may seize the trade of the East Indies and China. Seat the United States firmly in Oregon and the commercial enterprise and the wealth of the world will centralize within our limits.... It [Asiatic commerce] would diffuse its stores throughout the Union—the long and dangerous passage around the Capes would be given up—and Europe would seek in our Atlantic ports the products of the tropical garden of southern Asia. No question has yet arisen in our history so closely connected with the extension of American power and greatness.

Asiatic trade as a motive for annexation was even more apparent in the case of California than of Oregon. It is significant that the first extended description of California to attract the attention of American readers was written by a sea captain engaged in the Chinese trade and bore the title, "Journal of a Voyage between China and the Northwestern Coast of America made in the Year 1804." The author, a New Englander named Robert Shaler, devoted especial attention to a description of the harbors of the California coast and to the latent commercial possibilities of the province, making no attempt to conceal his purpose of arousing interest in its acquisition.

In later years, also, when the sentiment for securing California had begun to crystallize throughout the United States, commercial motives continually intrude themselves into the foreground. In the several attempts that Jackson made to secure the province from Mexico, he emphasized chiefly the importance of acquiring the harbor of San Francisco because of the advantages it possessed for the trading interests of the nation. During the presidency of Tyler, when principally through the activities of Daniel Webster the California movement was given new impetus, San Francisco continued to appear the chief object of desire. Webster's interest in securing the Pacific port was for the most part of commercial concern. As part of the same program, he advocated sending a special diplomatic mission to China, largely for the purpose of fostering trade relations between the two countries, and of strengthening a commercial intercourse that, already of considerable proportions, was susceptible of enormous increase.

The natural interest of the administration in the commercial importance of California was still further increased by dispatches from Waddy Thompson, the American minister to Mexico, whose chief purpose during his diplomatic career was the purchase of California. A single extract from one of his communications to the home government will serve to illustrate the general tenor of the remainder. On April 29, 1842, he wrote Webster:

I believe that this Government would cede to us Texas and the Californias....As to Texas, I regard it as of but little value compared with California—the richest, the most beautiful, the healthiest country in the world. Our Atlantic border secures us a commercial ascendency there; with the acquisition of Upper California we should have the same ascendency on the Pacific. The harbor of St. Francisco is capacious enough to receive the navies of all the world, and the neighborhood furnishes live oak enough to build all the ships of those navies. Besides this there is the Bay of St. Iajo [San Diego], Monterey, and others....The possession of these harbors would...no doubt, by internal communication with the Arkansas and other western streams, secure the trade of India and the whole Pacific Ocean.

Although Thompson was mistaken in thinking that Mexico would sell California to the United States, Webster and Tyler still hoped to secure its cession by the so-called tripartite agreement. The sanction of Congress was sought for a special mission to England which Webster himself should head for the purpose of securing Upper California for the United States. Upon the defeat of this plan, Tyler proposed to Everett, minister to England, that he accept the position of minister to China and allow Webster to take his place at London and push forward the negotiations for California and the settlement of the Oregon dispute. Everett declined and Webster's active part in the acquisition of the province came to an end. His interest in it, however, remained unabated. Four years later he wrote Fletcher Webster: "You know my opinion to have been, and now is, that the port of San Francisco would be twenty times more valuable to us than all Texas." The President who succeeded Tyler was from the beginning an avowed expansionist and particularly an ardent advocate of the annexation of California. Commonly this policy is ascribed to a desire to extend the area of slavery; yet the dominant motive was not slavery but Oriental trade. A few citations from Polk's official correspondence and messages should make this clear.

In the instructions issued to guide Slidell in his negotiations for California, emphasis was placed entirely upon the purchase of the ports of Monterey and San Francisco. "The possession of the bay and harbor of San Francisco," ran Buchanan's note, "is all important to the United States. The advantages to us of its acquisition are so striking that it would be a waste of time to enumerate them here. If all these should be turned against us by the cession of California to Great Britain, our principal commercial rival, the consequences would be most disastrous." Instructions of similar character were sent to Larkin upon his appointment as confidential agent of the United States Government at Monterey. "The interests of our commerce and of our whale fisheries on the Pacific Ocean demand that you should exert the greatest vigilance in discovering and defeating any attempts which may be made by foreign governments to acquire control over that country."

On another occasion Polk told Benton that the "Fine Bay of San Francisco" was to be kept from the clutches of Great Britain at all hazards. And, indeed, from the beginning to the end of his dealings with California runs this note of the necessity of holding the commercial possibilities of the Pacific coast as a monopoly for the United States. It occurs, for example, in his third annual message of December 7, 1847, when Congress is urged to keep California as indemnity for the Mexican War, because otherwise European nations, long eager for commercial opportunities, will seize the province; and its ports, certain one day to become "the marts of an extensive and profitable commerce with China and the countries of the East," will be lost to the United States.

In two subsequent messages Polk similarly brought out the importance of Chinese trade to the commercial interest of the country; while in his last formal communication to Congress, justifying the policy of his administration in foreign affairs and predicting large benefit from the acquisition of California because of its great resources, he added:

From its position it [Upper California] must command the rich commerce of China, of Asia, of the islands of the Pacific, of western Mexico, of Central America, the South American States, and the Russian possessions on that ocean. A great emporium will doubtless speedily arise on the California coast which may be destined to rival in importance New Orleans itself. The depot of the immense commerce which must exist on the Pacific will probably be at some point on the Bay of San Francisco, and will occupy the same relation to the whole western coast of that ocean as New Orleans does to the Valley of the Mississippi and the Gulf of Mexico.

. . . If the view I have been endeavoring to set before you is correct, then the American occupation of the Pacific coast assumes a new and peculiar interest. It becomes a chapter in the oldest movement of our history—a movement that reaches back from this present day to the far voyages of Columbus, of Magellan, of Henry Hudson, of La Salle, of that adventurous host of Spanish explorers who sought through unknown seas the mysterious and fabled Straits of Anian; of that even larger host of English colonists on the Atlantic coast who "looked to find the South Sea up the nearest northwest branch of the spreading river at their feet." At the same time, it becomes a part of the great world-struggle for the control of the rich and varied Eastern trade—a trade which has been one of the powerful forces of the world's past, as it is of its present, and bids fair to be through the unknown years of the future. As a phase of this old rivalry for commercial supremacy through the control of Asiatic trade, especially in this day of Oriental awakening and canal construction, to those of us whose faces turn hopefully across the Pacific, the early American occupation of Oregon and

California takes on new meaning and becomes clothed with fresh significance. . . .

THE FAILURE OF POLK'S
MEXICAN WAR INTRIGUE OF 1845[1]   *Richard R. Stenberg*

History long accepted the contemporary view that Polk made war in 1846 very deliberately to seize the much-coveted Mexican borderlands from Texas to the Pacific, bringing up the private claims against Mexico merely as a justificatory pretext. . . . Although the outstanding incidents—*e.g.*, Slidell's mission and Taylor's march to the Rio Grande—are of such uncertain meaning as to give rise to conflicting interpretations, all recent writers have been at one in the manner of approach: in search for causal incidents, motives and maneuvers leading to the war, they have gone no further back than the Slidell mission in the latter half of 1845, neglecting Polk's diplomacy in the earlier half of the year. . . . This neglect of the early half of 1845 seems an oversight of some moment, without which it would have been impossible to view Polk as scrupulous and peaceable.

According to President Anson Jones, of the Texas Republic, President Polk tried secretly, before the annexation of Texas was consummated, to instigate the "Lone Star Republic" to conquer the "disputed" territory between the Nueces River and the Rio Grande and so precipitate a Mexican war, which war he could then *annex* along with Texas—he, the American President, wishing to escape the invidious, well-nigh insoluble Texas boundary question and to have opened, apparently by some other hand than his own, the forbidden door through which he could lead "manifest destiny," stimulated to new eagerness by the anticipated triumph in Texas. As Jones says, too, such a movement was well calculated to precipitate Texas into the Union by frustrating the efforts then making towards a Texo-Mexican conciliation. But President Jones turned a cold shoulder and defeated the intrigue, leaving Polk the task and responsibility of provoking war. The truth of Jones's statement of this abortive intrigue (which curiously foreshadows the means by which Polk actually brought on the war) there seems no reason to question and every reason to believe, as the present paper will indicate. The few historians who have even so much as noticed Jones's version have rejected it summarily, upon the mere ground that it is "inconsistent" with the "peaceable" Slidell mission—whereas, of course, they might just as logically, on the contrary, have seen in this apparent inconsistency reason for doubting the "peaceableness" of the Slidell mission.

Mexico severed relations with the United States in March, 1845, when Congress passed the Texas annexation measure; and uttered threats to reconquer the "lost department." But all this proved mere "sound and fury," for she acquiesced in the annexation, desiring only to save appearances and

---

[1] *The Pacific Historical Review*, IV, No. 1 (March, 1935), 39–68. Reprinted with permission.

protect her right to her territory west of the Nueces, to which Texas had no right either legally or by conquest. It suited Polk to declare after war began that hostilities were commenced by Mexico because of annexation—a convenient fiction hardly plausible then and long since exploded. Yet in a certain way the annexation did lead to the war: Polk gave pledges to Texas, when trying to induce her to accept annexation, that he would maintain her claim to the Rio Grande, and in his fulfillment of this (by military occupation, or conquest, instead of by peaceable negotiation, as Congress had intended) he provoked the War with Mexico.[2] Such an outcome had been apprehended by many who had opposed Texas annexation; they saw in it only one link in a chain of forthcoming expansions towards Mexico. Certain senators, notably, had opposed the House resolutions for annexation largely from fear that the "re-annexation" of Texas with her unsettled western boundary would pave the way to aggression upon Mexico and usher in war. President-elect Polk privately promised these senators, in late February, 1845, that he would proceed to annexation by new negotiations under Senator Benton's plan, which by amendment was then attached to the House resolutions as an alternative.[3] After his inauguration Polk similarly gave pledges to Texas to do many good things for her if she would accept annexation—pledges which likewise he made no effort afterwards to fulfill, save only that to uphold the Texas paper-claim to the Rio Grande. This last significant pledge placed him in an unpleasant dilemma. Texas claimed to the Rio Grande, though she had never extended west of the Nueces; and the advanced Democratic expansionists had seemingly endorsed the claim at the Baltimore Convention (May, 1844) by demanding the "reannexation" of Texas, a most irrelevant expression historically. But the Whigs and a strong section of the Democracy led by Benton and holding the balance of power in the Senate held that the Nueces, and not the Rio Grande, was the western boundary of Texas. If Polk should fail to uphold the Texas claim he would anger the Texans and many of his own countrymen; if he upheld it he would be forced to aggress against Mexico—unless (which was very doubtful) she could be bought off or brought peacefully to acquiesce—and thereby would in all probability incur war and be attacked by a Whig-Benton coalition. In this dilemma it is not strange that Polk should have sought some remedy to relieve himself of an invidious task! The setting of circumstances was just that in which such an intrigue by Polk in Texas as President Jones describes would have been logical, almost imperative—especially if Polk had ulterior aims against Mexico which only war could realize.

---

[2] Author's note.—Polk to Sam Houston, June 6, 1845, and Polk to A. J. Donelson, June 15, 1845, in Polk MSS. (in Library of Congress); Milo Milton Quaife, ed., *The Diary of James K. Polk* (Chicago, 1910), III, 196; Anson Jones, *Memoranda and Official Correspondence relating to the Republic of Texas* (New York, 1859), pp. 53, 54; Smith, *War with Mexico*, I, 139. Despite the fact that Congress had plainly left the disputed boundary to be settled by negotiation with Mexico, Polk blandly affected in public pronouncement to be unaware of any boundary question. Observe how he announces the annexation of Texas in his message of December, 1845: "The jurisdiction of the United States . . . has passed the Capes of Florida, and been peacefully extended to the Del Norte," or Rio Grande.
[3] Author's note.—The senators then voted for the measure; without their votes it would not have passed. Despite his pledge to negotiate, Polk offered the House resolutions to Texas. Later he denied having pledged himself in the matter; but his denial only serves to shed light on his character. For evidence as to Polk's pledges to senators and to Texas see Richard R. Stenberg, "President Polk and the Annexation of Texas," in *Southwestern Social Science Quarterly*, XIV (March, 1934), 333–56; *Texas National Register* (Washington), June 19, 1845.

A word, therefore, as to Polk's aims: these were such as war only could fulfill (for it was impossible to suppose that Mexico would willingly dismember herself). Polk on taking office in March, 1845, told Secretary Bancroft that the acquisition of California was one of the chief measures he would endeavor to accomplish. In this he could expect the approval of his countrymen: expansive talk of "manifest destiny"—a term coined in 1845—was rife, and predictions assigned the whole continent to the ambitious Americans, who were now moving in ever-increasing numbers into California and Oregon, and perfecting a title (which diplomacy by itself had failed in) to the southern half of the Oregon territory. There were fearsome reports in 1844–45 that "grasping" England was about to gain California peaceably from Mexico. At the time the Slidell mission was conceived Polk records in his *Diary* his determination to take New Mexico and California by war if Mexico should refuse to yield a minimum of territory—that east of the Rio Grande—to satisfy private American claims against Mexico.[4] Such evidence is eloquent of Polk's imperialistic desires. The coercive Slidell mission, in which the private claims were newly and so much in evidence, gives Polk's conduct a peaceful and somewhat scrupulous appearance which it seems, when viewed closely and in the light of Polk's earlier and subsequent maneuvers, not even remotely to deserve. One may perhaps best judge whether the claims were the real cause, or were made the pretext, for war after observing the character of Polk's intrigue early in 1845, only after the failure of which the claims were brought on the scene by Polk and urged against bankrupt Mexico in so useful a way. And this was at a time when the American states had repudiated bonded debts, held largely by exasperated but helpless European creditors, to a sum beside which the claims against Mexico were as a crumb to a loaf.

Polk on entering the White House had an abundance of counselors for a policy of covert aggression through Texas, using her as a cat's-paw. Duff Green, who had been sent to Mexico by Tyler in September, 1844, "to aid in conducting the negotiation for the acquisition of Texas, New Mexico and California," reported that Mexico would never sell willingly and must be chastised. Returning to Texas he intrigued with the war party, which desired both annexation to the United States and the conquest of northern Mexico. His project, broached to high officials, was to employ "the Indians of the United States and Texas in the invasion of Mexico and revolutionizing the country from the Rio Grande to the Pacific under the flag of Texas." With the Texas officials it seems to have found little favor. Green wrote later of his scheme that

an arrangement was made for a movement in Texas which would enable the United States to interpose and thus obtain the concessions wanted. I came to Texas, explained to the President and to Congress the measure which had been agreed on, and which would have been approved and adopted but for the intereference of Mr. Elliot, the British chargé to Texas, who induced the President, Mr. Jones, to believe that he could and would induce the Mexican Government to recognize the independence of Texas.

---

[4] Author's note.—It is the writer's opinion that Polk neither intended the Slidell mission to be successful nor supposed that it would be—and that the mission was but a maneuver calculated to place Mexico in the light of wrongdoer to justify a declaration of war against her.

The "arrangement" and whom it was arranged with is now uncertain. It is to be noted, however, that Green was back at Washington and was consulting with Polk in March, 1845. His advice was no doubt consonant with his late "project for the defense of the Western frontier and the invasion of Mexico."

The British consul at Galveston, Kennedy, reported on March 22, 1845, that a large force was preparing in the United States

with a view to invasion of the Mexican Provinces south of the Rio Grande. I have reason to believe that secret communications have for some time been carried on, between certain of the Federal leaders in those provinces, and parties resident in Texas, who, at present,—I am told—are in the United States, urging forward the military preparations reported to be in progress.

Kennedy added: "The force to be raised and the object for which it was to be organized, were lately announced in Galveston by Doctor Branch T. Archer." Still later he learned that "Archer, and the partner of his counsels, General Thos. J. Green, who formed one of the Texan expedition beyond the Rio Grande in 1842, have spent the greater part of their time in Washington, . . . where they appear to have been favourably noticed by the President, and the leading members of his cabinet." The example and advice of these gentlemen was for expansion by conquest. But ever since 1841 the spirit of war against Mexico for revenge and conquest had been running high in Texas, so that Polk and his expansionist advisers would have needed no special counsel from Texas to have conceived the convenient scheme of inciting Texas to war against Mexico on the eve of annexation, a war which the United States could annex and so wage without suffering the odium of apparent responsibility or "war guilt."

President Jones, who was suspected (and probably rightly) of being opposed to the annexation of Texas to the United States, temporarily withheld the American offer from the people and sought hastily to procure through the mediation of the British chargé, Charles Elliot, a Mexican offer of recognition of Texan independence in return for a guaranty by Texas to preserve her independence. What was known of Jones's dealings with Elliot alarmed the American agents and the annexation party in Texas. The more militant of this party, which included the popular Texas commander-in-chief, Major-General Sidney Sherman (formerly of Kentucky), were in a ready mood for hostilities with Mexico, both to ensure annexation and for possible conquest.

Such was the situation when Polk sent a number of special agents to Texas with secret, confidential instructions, to further his schemes and assist the regular minister, Donelson. The first, Archibald Yell (ex-Governor of Arkansas) left for Texas on March 10, 1845; after him went Charles A. Wickliffe (Postmaster General under Tyler) at the end of March. Finally, thus preceded by Yell and Wickliffe, Commodore Robert F. Stockton of the Navy was sent to Texas, where he arrived off the coast May 12–15, anxious to extend the "protection" of his fleet. The Commodore—like Wickliffe, whom Polk had designated "confidential agent to Texas to counteract the contemplated interference of Great Britain and France to prevent the annexation of Texas to the United States"—had secret unwritten instructions; and they were, as his secretary frankly told President Jones, to instigate Texas to seize the "disputed" territory west of the Nueces and start a war with Mexico, in which the United States would immediately join in "defense" of Texas.

Immediately, on reaching Texas, Stockton proceeded to interview General Sherman, who concurred enthusiastically with Stockton's proposal that Sherman gather and lead a force of Texans to occupy and eject the Mexican troops from the "disputed" territory. Stockton was to finance the scheme from his own wealth....

After the failure of the Stockton expansion scheme Polk turned to a new plan of coercion—the Slidell mission. Was he now really disposed to settle disputes with Mexico amicably, and renounce his designs on California if Mexico would yield merely the territory claimed by Texas, in satisfaction of the American claims? Or was the Slidell mission simply a hoax, its abortion foreseen and intended, its aim to make Mexico appear as an intransigent villain in order to justify a demand for a declaration of war by Congress? The writer believes (partly on the basis of evidence that has been overlooked) that the latter supposition is the more probable. The Slidell mission cannot be discussed here. Nor can we examine extensively its relation to American military movements in Texas after her acceptance of annexation (July, 1845). Immediately upon this Texan acceptance, Polk sent General Taylor with an army into the new state with instructions to occupy and protect its "frontier," which was confidently described to the General as the Rio Grande. All through the summer and autumn of 1845 Taylor was *subtly encouraged, but not explicitly ordered*, to march to the Rio Grande and occupy "the whole of Texas." The instructions sent him by Secretary of War Marcy were masterpieces of that cunning, deviousness and underhandedness which characterized Polk, whose policy it was never to assume responsibility for unscrupulous or invidious acts he wanted done if he could shift it to some cat's-paw. Consider Marcy's dispatch to Taylor of July 30, 1845:

The Rio Grande is claimed to be the boundary...and up to this you are to extend your position, only excepting any posts on the eastern side thereof, which are in the actual occupancy of Mexican forces, or Mexican settlements over which Texas did not exercise jurisdiction at the period of annexation, or shortly before that event. It is expected that...you will approach as near the boundary line—the Rio Grande—as prudence will dictate....The President desires that your position...should be near the river Nueces.

Taylor *appears* to be ordered to move to the Rio Grande to occupy the "Texas" (now "American") territory west of the Neuces—while at the end of the dispatch are inconspicuously inserted a few saving words, wholly inconsistent with what preceded: "The President desires that your position ...should be near the river Nueces"! This last clause saves the President and will enable him later, if Taylor advances, to make the General the scapegoat of the aggression upon Mexico! Quite conscious of Polk's wish that he should go to the Rio Grande, Taylor noted that his orders were so equivocally worded as to place on his shoulders too great a share and burden of responsibility—so he remained at Corpus Christi, advising the administration that he would advance when explicitly ordered to do so. Polk's apologists have been loath to perceive in Taylor's instructions this insidious character, which is nevertheless unmistakable. Only when Polk finally assumed full responsibility and expressly ordered Taylor to the Rio Grande on January 13, 1846, did the cautious General make the advance movement so long desired by his intriguing superiors. Was this order of Polk's peaceable in intent, as his apologists insist, or was it well calculated underhandedly to provoke the war which he now avowedly desired? (And he could scarcely have been so optimistic as to believe that, even after Slidell's failure in Mexico, he could produce war *constitutionally* by inducing Congress, on the mere basis of the claims, to declare it—a scheme that even President Jackson had tried in vain.) As to this, we will note only one fact which the late apologists of the war have failed to mention: namely, that some days before the issuance of his war message in May, 1846, Polk more than once remarks in his *Diary*, with evident anxiety and chagrin, that *he has not heard from* the "frontier," where he *anticipates*, using his own words, "a collision between the American and Mexican forces"—if he could only hear of which, he says, he would hesitate no longer, and send a war message to Congress! Polk knew from the very beginning of his administration that Mexico was disposed to defend her occupancy and ownership of the "disputed" territory, a fact which has been obscured and even denied by Polk's apologists but which has been made sufficiently clear in this paper; thus his anticipation that the seizure of this (rightly Mexican) territory would result in hostilities was by no means new to his mind when he made the above confession, so inadvertently, in his *Diary*. A few days after the first querulous entry his anticipation was justified, news arriving of the engagements at Palo Alto and Resaca de la Palma on the Rio Grande, the "frontier"; he was then able to subordinate the claims against Mexico and to demand war of Congress on the ground that it existed in fact by the Mexicans' having "invaded" and shed American blood "on American soil." Without these hostilities—without his act which provoked them—it is extremely improbable that Polk could have induced Congress to make a war on Mexico, upon the grounds ostensibly of claims. Contemporary observers reject the idea that he could have succeeded in doing so. The private claims were, during the war, thrust more and more by Polk into the public eye by way of justification, to offset criticism of his usurpation of the boundary; but this could little conceal his aggression and real motive for war—his desire to seize northern Mexico from the Nueces to the Pacific—which the general public, infected strongly by the spirit of "manifest destiny," approved.

The strength of Polk's policy of expansion by covert aggression lay in the popular support he could count upon in bringing on war if Mexico should plausibly be presented as the aggressor. Confining his secret plans of conquest to the discreet circle of his immediate agents and advisers, and leaving the public to learn them only through events, Polk, soon after the war began, hypocritically assured the New York Democratic leaders—and doubtless others—that he "had no schemes of conquest in view in respect to Mexico, no intention to take possession of any portion of her territory with a view to hold it"! If he openly avowed his intention of taking a large territorial indemnity (which he had determined upon long before the actual coming of the war), the world would perhaps be even less credulous of his inconsistent assertions that he was waging a war "commenced by Mexico" to "redress American grievances." Even by magnifying the private claims— which could not be taken seriously as *cause* for a large and costly war—the apologists have not been able to make a very plausible case for "peaceable Polk," for vain is their endeavor to ignore or read away Polk's aggressive view and belligerent handling of the Texas boundary question, a matter in which contemporaries perceived the most significant key to the Mexican War and its instrumental cause. In conclusion, it may be noted that the foregoing view of an intriguing, war-desiring Polk invites one to accept fully, with regard to the much-mooted question of Frémont's activities in California, his own asseverations that he had been instructed secretly by Polk, through the messenger Gillespie and his father-in-law, Senator Benton, to seize or revolutionize California "if necessary to anticipate England."

THE DIARY OF REVEREND JASON LEE, ON HIS TRIP FROM MISSOURI TO OREGON, 1834

Document 1

Sunday, April 20, 1834—arrived at Liberty, Mo., on my way to the Flat Head Indians.

Sunday evening—attempted to preach in the Court House, but when about half through, the wind frightened the people away and I dismissed by pronouncing the blessing, although I did not apprehend any danger....

22. —Went 9 miles to Independence and found Brother Shepard and slept very comfortably with him in the tent designed for our journey....

Saturday. —Purchased some cows and more horses and removed 4 miles from the river with the intention of camping with Captain [Nathaniel J.] Wyeth about 9 miles from the river, but was belated and accepted an invitation to turn in and lodge with a man by name Rickman,—pitched our tent....

Thurs. May 1.—A little before we encamped, saw a few families of Caw [Kaw] Indians, they are a band broken off from the Osage. No sooner had we encamped than they came from their village of bark huts and thronged around us to our annoyance.

They are a miserable looking set of beings—half-naked—the children [of] some of them entirely so. Bro. Shepard remarked that he never before felt half so much like trying to benefit the Indians....

Sat. 3. —Struck tent.... The company soon came up and immediately set about crossing the baggage in a flatboat [across the Kansas River].... Swam the horses all safe but the horned cattle were very troublesome and when drove in would swim back. Our beef cow swam far down the river and went ashore, below the men and ran into the woods a man followed her but lost her in the bushes. Four or five went in pursuit of her but could not find her. . . .

Sun. 11. —I have found very little time for reading, writing or meditation since reached Liberty for I was almost momentarily employed in making preparations previous to leaving the civilized world and we now find constant employment from daylight till it is time to decamp and then I am engaged in driving cows till we camp, to pitch our tent and make all necessary arrangements for the night fills up the residue of the day. . . .

Mon. 12. —While I was writing in my Journal the word came that two cows were gone one of them ours. Bro. Edwards and myself caught our horses to hunt them and started in haste on our back track judging that our cow had returned where we killed her calf yesterday distant I suppose about 10 m. all undulating or open Prairie except a few trees and shrubs on a little creek. . . . The different portions of the prairie so much resemble each other that it is impossible for those who [are] not acquainted with them not be deceived by them. . . .

Sat. May 17, 1834. —Started this morning at 7 o'clock. Made a severe march of 9 hours from the Blue [River] to the Platte [River]. Left the main Blue on the left hand, crossed a small branch or brook and having left the trail on the right we came by compass N. W. till we found the trail of Mr. Wm. Sublet after marching say 15m. We then took nearly a W. Course and soon found the old wagon trail. . . . We came to day 15 m. N.W. and 10 m. W. Total 25 m.

Sun. May 18. —This seems more like Sabbath than any we have passed since we left the settlements. The rain prevents the men from being out hallooing cursing and shooting. Can it be that such men believe that the day will come when the Omnipotent Jehova "will judge all men in righteousness? . . ." I have no doubt that many are complete Infidels who have taken but very little thought on the subject. . . . We packed in the rain and marched 5 hours. . . .

Mon. 19. —Started at ½ past 7 o'clock A. M. After marching a few miles saw two men horseback some miles distant approaching us. . . .

They were two Pawnees and made signs that their party was just behind us and would overtake us tomorrow but they will not if we can avoid it for the Capt. intends to make a forced march to keep ahead of them. . . .

Wednes. 21. —Traveled say 26 m. to day. The Indians have not overtaken us and we are confident they cannot. . . . Saw at least thousands of Buffaloe to day some were killed by the men they are very good if fat. I think perferable to beef. The bottom lands along the river are literally black with them for miles. . . .

Sat. 24. —This morning forded the south fork of the Platte without accident except one man lost his gun. We have marched six days on the Platte. . . .

Tues. 27. —For a warm dry day never did I travel in such a disagreeable one. The wind was so strong that it was with great difficulty that I could make headway when on foot, and it was of course very severe on the horses.

The bottom of the vessels which contained our dinner was covered with sand and those who eat most dinner eat most sand, and it was drived with such force that it made the face tingle, and in such quantities that it had the appearance of snow driven before the wind at a distance. We have no wood and are obliged to substitute buffaloe dung which makes a very good fire but does not last long and has a disagreeable smell. . . .

Mon. June 9. —Found good grass this evening which is a matter of rejoicing and thankfulness for our poor Horses were nearly starved. . . .

Wednes. 11. —Was constantly engaged in repairing halters fixing the horses shoes &c. until time to pack up. There is more to be done on such an expedition as this [than] any one could possibly think who has never tried it.

The provision is getting short in Camp and some have had very little to-day and we have eaten our last Buffaloe meat for dinner except some we have dried in case of emergency. . . .

Sat. J. 14, 1834. —One of our horses tired and though he had carried nothing but his saddle that day we could not get him along and were forced to leave in the Prairie. . . . The cattle nearly failed and fell some miles behind.

Night drew on fast and no water nor grass. . . . We cooked no supper for two reasons first because of the labour and time necessary to do it and secondly because we were in the most dangerous part of the Indian country and a light might attract them. . . .

Friday, June 20, 1834. —We call this Rendevous or the place where all the Companies in the Mountains or in this section of them have fixed upon to meet for the transaction of business.

Some of the companies have not come in, yet most of them are a mile above us on the same creek. They threatened that when we came they would give them Missionaries "hell" and Capt. W. informed us and advised us to be on our guard. . . .

I replied that I was much obliged to him. I *feared* no man and apprehended no danger from them when sober and when drunk we would endeavor to [keep] out of their way. . . .

Sun. July 6. —Made a very long severe march crossed the Bear River twice and came over some of the most mountainous country that we have crossed. . . .

Wednes. July 9, 1834. —Did not move camp was employed most of the day in repairing pack-saddles &c. . . .

Sun. 13. —Traveled only a short distance. Was glad to get a little rest on the Lord's day. The [men] are engaged playing cards drinking swearing wrestling &c. May God have mercy upon them. . . .

AN EXPANSIONIST DISCUSSES

MAINE AND OREGON   *Document 2*

Speech of Senator J. Semple of Illinois, January 25, 1844.

... I have not the most unlimited confidence in negotiations, as the best mode of securing our rights; we have frequently been outrageously cheated in negotiations. We have surrendered our territory by negotiations in the Southwest and in the West. ... We have surrendered territory in the Northeast, and in the North, to Great Britain; and, sir, I want to see no more surrendered. For this reason I am a little afraid of negotiations, and I am not willing to let any other go on to a final termination without first giving some opinion as to what should be done, or, in other words, *advising* the President what to do. ...

It is well known to every Senator present, that the occupation of the Oregon Territory has, for some time past, engaged the attention of the people of the United States generally, but more particularly the people of the Western States. ...

The people of the West have not contented themselves with expressing opinions—they have acted. For many years our citizens have gone into the country west of the Rocky Mountains for the purpose of hunting, trapping, and trading with the Indians. They have also more recently gone for the purpose of making permanent settlements. ...

The joint occupation of the country never ought to have been a subject of negotiation. Our Government committed a great error, in my opinion. ...

This thing of a joint occupation of a country; and of a joint jurisdiction by two independent Governments, is an anomaly in the history of the world. ...

I believe sir, that the recent surrender of a part of the State of Maine to the British Government is probably the only instance recorded in history where a great and powerful nation, with full and complete conviction of its right to the soil, has tamely surrendered a part of its domain from fear of war. That was a question of limits; this also is a question of limits. We have surrendered a part of the State of Maine; shall we also surrender a part of the Oregon?

It was after the treaty of 1842 that we of the West began to have doubts as to the propriety of treating on this subject. It was after this that we began to doubt the efficacy of negotiations to maintain our rights; and for this reason we have passed the strong resolutions which have been passed in the West, expressing a determination not to abide by any treaty that shall surrender any part of the Oregon. Our people will go there, and they will not submit to British domination. ...

Upon presenting the Resolutions, Mr. SEMPLE offered the following remarks:

... He said that he had been for the last four or five years placed in a situation where it became his duty as well as inclination to study the commercial interest of the United States. He had during that time made himself acquainted with the importance to us of the vast trade of the Pacific ocean, and of the immense wealth that would flow into our country by means of the occupation of the Oregon Territory....

He considered the right of the United States to the whole of Oregon, as far north as the Russian boundary, as clear as the noon-day sun.... He concluded by hoping that the West would never give up one acre of that country, though war, and repeated wars, might be the consequences of such refusal.

THE BRITISH AMBASSADOR REPORTS ON
AMERICAN EXPANSIONIST SENTIMENT   *Document 3*

Despatch to the British Foreign Office, March 29, 1846.

...But a fact which I must not omit to point out to Your Lordship's notice is that it seems to have become a received opinion among even the most moderate members of the Senate, that the claims of the United States extend fully to the parallel of 49, which they consider ought to be insisted on as the basis of any arrangement.

So certain is this, that the advocates of a peaceful settlement of the question are now universally designated as 49 men, in contradistinction to those who go for the whole of Oregon even at the risk of war, and are called 54.40 men.

In the course of this debate, a good deal of interest was excited by the speech of Mr. Haywood of North Carolina...who from the intimacy which has long subsisted between him and Mr. Polk was supposed to speak, in a certain degree, the President's opinions.

Mr. Haywood's language was entirely in favor of compromise upon the basis of 49, and he gave it to be understood that those who imagined that the President was inclined to persist in asserting at all risks a claim to the whole of Oregon, or that he felt bound by the resolution to that effect, passed at the Convention which nominated him to the Presidency, were mistakes.

This avowal was received with violent indignation by the advocates of extreme measures. I beg leave to request Your Lordship's attention to the extraordinary language made use of on the occasion by Mr. Hannegan of Indiana ... who did not hesitate to declare that if it was true that the President thus belied the pledge taken by the Baltimore Convention:—

"The story of his infamy would be circulated from one end of the land to the other, and his perfidious course would sink him in an infamy so profound, in a damnation so deep, that the hand of resurrection could never reach him,—a traitor to his country so superlatively base need hope for neither forgiveness from God nor mercy from man."

This is what the President has brought down upon himself by the imprudent lengths to which he allowed himself to go in his inaugural address, as well as in his Message of the 2nd December, and in the correspondence of his Secretary of State on the subject of Oregon.

Fortunately for the country, the party in the Senate who think with Mr. Hannegan, is so insignificant, not numbering as it has repeatedly been asserted in the course of the debate, above a fourth, or as some say, a fifth, of that body, that Mr. Polk need have no fear that he will not be supported amply, both in and out of the Senate, if he should wisely determine to adopt a moderate and pacific course of policy,—but what his real intention in this respect may be, he has given the public no opportunity of judging, since the scene in the Senate of which I have above spoken. . . .

JOHN C. CALHOUN

ON BRITISH POLICY IN TEXAS   *Document 4*

Letter to Duff Green, September 8, 1843.
. . . I have, in the present remarkable state of things, not been inattentive to the course of events in England, and have come to the conclusion, that it would take the turn you anticipate. England has but one alternative; to harmonize her interests with that of the other portions of the civilized world, or resort to force to maintain her pre-eminence. If she adopts the former, freedom of commerce and non-interference with the institutions of other nations must be the basis of her policy; but if the latter, she must prepare for universal conflict with the civilized world. . . .

Strange as it may seem, the discussion of the corn law question and the sugar duties, will go far to decide this great issue. In the advanced state of commerce and the arts, the great point of policy for the older and more advanced nations is to command the trade of the newer and less advanced; and that cannot be done, but by opening a free trade in provisions and raw materials with them. The effect of the contrary policy is not only to cripple their commerce and manufactures, by curtailing exchanges; but to force the newer and less advanced portion to become prematurely their competitors. This England now sees and feels, and that to remedy the evil, the corn laws and sugar duties in favor of her colonies, must be repealed, or that she must resort to force to maintain her commercial and manufacturing superiority. But, if force is resorted to, the blow will first be struck at the U. States, Brazil, and other slave holding countries. The reason is obvious. It is indispensable to give her a monopoly of the trade of the world. The abolition of slavery would transfer the production of cotton, rice, and sugar etc. to her colonial possessions, and would consummate the system of commercial monopoly, which she has been so long and systematically pursuing. Hence the movements in Texas and elsewhere on the abolition subject. . . .

BRITISH OVERTURES TO TEXAS   *Document 5*

The Texan Minister to Great Britain to the Secretary of State of Texas, June 24, 1844.

...Lord Aberdeen observed that Her British Majesty's Government and that of France had communicated with each other touching the "annexation";—that, entire harmony of opinion subsists and that they will act in concert in relation to it:—that, though the rejection of the Annexation Treaty by the American Senate was regarded as nearly quite certain, nothing would be done by these Governments until the American Congress shall have finally disposed of the subject for the present session. He stated that then the British and French Governments would be willing, if Texas desired to remain independent, to settle the whole matter by a "Diplomatic Act:"— this diplomatic act in which Texas would of course participate would ensure peace and settle boundaries between Texas and Mexico, guarantee the separate independence of Texas, etc., etc.;—the American Government would be invited to participate in the "Act" as one of the parties guaranteeing etc., equally with the European Governments;—that Mexico, as I think I clearly understood his Lordship, would be invited to become a party to the Diplomatic Act, and in case of her refusal, would be forced to submit to its decisions;—and lastly, in case of the infringement of the terms of settlement by either of the parties, to wit, Texas or Mexico, the other parties would be authorized under the Diplomatic Act, to compel the infringing party to a compliance with the terms....

Other parties could not be expected to make a treaty of this nature limited for such a period as would suit the convenience of Texas. Such act would too, as you will have already remarked, give to the European Governments, parties to it, a perfect right to forbid for all time to come the annexation of Texas to the United States, as also even the peaceful incorporation of any portion of Mexico beyond the boundary to be settled, which might hereafter wish to unite itself with Texas....

I have believed that the objections to a Diplomatic Act as mentioned above will be deemed by our Government greater perhaps than the inconveniences of our unsettled relations with Mexico....

ADDRESS BY SECRETARY OF WAR
WILLIAM WILKINS TO THE PEOPLE
OF PENNSYLVANIA, APRIL 13, 1844   *Document 6*

... The inhabitants of Allegheny county are a mining, manufactury, commercial, agricultural, and navigating people. Every interest of these several branches of industry will be vastly promoted by securing to us, under our present tariff, thus extended by annexation over all its territory, the entire markets of Texas. The navigation of Red river, one of the chief tributaries of the Mississippi, furnishing one thousand miles of navigation into the heart of a rich country, now a divided and common right, will then be exclusively our own; to that add the important rivers, the Trinity, Brazos, Dolorade, Rio Bravo del Norte, and many other smaller but navigable streams, and we behold the vast demand from that region, on the boat builders and mechanics of the Ohio valley, adding at least one hundred steamboats, large and small, yearly, to the many now built for the wants of western navigation.

Our boats, which will benefit by the great carrying trade between Texas and her sister states, will in return for our manufactures of iron, cotton, wool, hemp and glass and the products of the farms and forests carried there, receive and bring back her cotton and sugar, her rice and indigo, and probably, even her coffee and other tropical products.

The Santa Fe trade, which has already become so lucrative to many among you, would be cut off from us by a foreign and by no means, necessarily, friendly power, whose territories intervene between us and that region, if the treaty should fail to be ratified. Manchester wagons, and Hartley's strong harness will no longer serve to carry American domestics and Pittsburg wares across the prairies, to be converted at Santa Fe into bullion and Mexican dollars.

On the other hand, with our territories bordering on New Mexico this trade would soon be vastly increased; for a Pittsburg steamboat with a cargo on board, can ascend the Red river to a point less than three hundred miles remote from Santa Fe, and at a distance of 500 miles from Chihuahua, the first great interior city of the integral provinces of Mexico, which is but slightly further than that city is from Santa Fe, the present mart at which our traders meet those from the region of Chihuahua.

To the entire people of the United States this question is of vast and weighty moment. If the treaty for the annexation should now be rejected, the re-action of feeling in Texas must then inevitably render it a commercial dependency, in fact if not in name, of Great Britain. You may rest assured that even should a free trade treaty not be concluded between England and Texas, that the latter will so modify and relax her tariff by discriminating duties, augmenting the imposts upon flour, grain, beef, pork, lard, and such articles, whilst taking off those on iron and all its manufactures, glass, cotton bagging, and all cotton and woollen fabrics and similar articles, thereby excluding American products, and admitting England's free of duty. Such is the avowed policy of Texas, as a separate republic, and thus, even without a treaty with England, that country will monopolize her markets. But it will not end here; Texas like Gibraltar and Portugal to Spain, will be made the great entrepot and channel of British commerce, by means of which her active merchants will in defiance of all imports and tariffs, not only flood the interior of Mexico with British wares, but through the channels of the Trinity, Sabine, and Red rivers, our own country with a multiplicity of every kind of her extensive manufactures, breaking up our very best establishments, and carrying ruin and bankruptcy into every manufacturing district of the United States.

The imports, which we must receive from abroad, instead of being brought as they now are, chiefly in American vessels into our ports, will, to escape the duties, be carried to Texas, to be smuggled into the United States. This will impair, if not destroy, our great navigating interests on the high seas, which it has always been the policy of our government to foster....

But the evil does not cease with the injury to the shipping interest. Our revenues from imposts on foreign commerce, necessarily falling short of the wants of the government, we shall be forced to resort to direct taxation to support and maintain the government.

* * *

Should Texas be refused admission into the union, she must become a most dangerous theatre for foreign intrigue, from which the most deplorable consequences to our welfare may ensue. Indeed, at some future and not distant day, we may be compelled, for the safety and perpetuity of the union, to gain by conquest what is now so freely offered for our acceptance.

But with the coast of Texas added to ours, we should then have nearly the entire shore of our own great sea, the Gulf of Mexico, and would then not only be beyond the reach of smugglers, but would also set at defiance any attempt at invasion, directed against New Orleans or the great outlet of the Mississippi and Ohio rivers.

Now, my fellow citizens, having given you my views on this subject, let me recall your attention, without reference to Florida, to the acquisition of Louisiana, without which we should not at this moment be the united and happy people, which constitute this great nation. Yet that noble purchase was not without opposition of a decided and indeed most violent character. However, no patriot of that day lives to regret that addition to our territories.

OPPOSITION TO THE
ANNEXATION OF TEXAS   *Document 7*

March 3, 1843

... WE HESITATE not to say that *annexation*, effected by any act or proceeding of the federal government, or any of its departments, WOULD BE IDENTICAL WITH DISSOLUTION. It would be a violation of our national compact, its objects, designs, and the great elementary principles which entered into its formation, of a character so deep and fundamental, and would be an attempt to eternize an institution and a power of nature so unjust in themselves, so injurious to the interests and abhorrent to the feelings of the people of the free states, as, in our opinion, not only inevitably to result in a dissolution of the union, but fully to justify it; and we not only assert that the people of the free states "ought not to submit to it," but we say, with confidence, THEY WOULD NOT SUBMIT TO IT....

To prevent the success of this nefarious project—to preserve from such gross violation the constitution of our country, adopted expressly *"to secure the blessings of liberty"* and not the perpetuation of slavery—and to prevent the speedy and violent dissolution of the union, we invite you to unite, without distinction of party, in an immediate expression of your views on this subject, in such manner as you may deem best calculated to answer the end proposed.

John Quincy Adams,	*Joshua R. Giddings,*	*John Mattocks,*
Seth M. Gates,	*Sherlock J. Andrews,*	*Christopher Morgan,*
William Slade,	*Nathaniel B. Borden,*	*Joshua M. Howard,*
William B. Calhoun,	*Thos. C. Chittenden,*	*Victory Birdseye,*
		Hiland Hall.

HENRY CLAY'S "RALEIGH LETTER"
ON THE ANNEXATION OF TEXAS   *Document 8*
                                                  April 17, 1844

Subsequent to my departure from Ashland, in December last, I received various communications from popular assemblages and private individuals, requesting an expression of my opinion upon the question of the annexation of Texas to the United States.... The rejection of the overture of Texas, some years ago, to become annexed to the United States, had met with general acquiescence. Nothing had since occurred materially to vary the question. I had seen no evidence of a desire being entertained, on the part of any considerable portion of the American people, that Texas should become an integral part of the United States.... To the astonishment of the whole nation, we are now informed that a treaty of annexation has been actually concluded, and is to be submitted to the senate for its consideration. The motives for my silence, therefore, no longer remain, and I feel it to be my duty to present an exposition of my views and opinions upon the question. . . .

If, without the loss of national character, without the hazard of foreign war, with the general concurrence of the nation, without any danger to the integrity of the Union, and without giving an unreasonable price for Texas, the question of annexation were presented, it would appear in quite a different light from that in which, I apprehend, it is now to be regarded. . . .

Annexation and war with Mexico are identical. Now, for one, I certainly am not willing to involve this country in a foreign war for the object of acquiring Texas. I know there are those who regard such a war with indifference and as a trifling affair, on account of the weakness of Mexico, and her inability to inflict serious injury upon this country. But I do not look upon it thus lightly. . . . Honor and good faith and justice are equally due from this country towards the weak as towards the strong. . . .

Assuming that the annexation of Texas is war with Mexico, is it competent to the treaty-making power to plunge this country into war, not only without the concurrence of, but without deigning to consult congress, to which, by the constitution, belongs exclusively the power of declaring war?

I have hitherto considered the question upon the supposition that the annexation is attempted without the assent of Mexico. If she yields her consent, that would materially affect the foreign aspect of the question, if it did not remove all foreign difficulties. On the assumption of that assent, the question would be confined to the domestic considerations which belong to it. . . . I do not think that Texas ought to be received into the Union, as an integral part of it, in decided opposition to the wishes of a considerable and respectable portion of the confederacy. . . .

It is useless to disguise that there are those who espouse and those who oppose the annexation of Texas upon the ground of the influence which it would exert, in the balance of political power, between two great sections of the Union. I conceive that no motive for the acquisition of foreign territory would be more unfortunate, or pregnant with more fatal consequences, than that of obtaining it for the purpose of strengthening one part against another part of the common confederacy. Such a principle, put into practical operation, would menace the existence, if it did not certainly sow the seeds of a dissolution of the Union. It would be to proclaim to the world an insatiable and unquenchable thirst for foreign conquest or acquisition of territory. For if today Texas be acquired to strengthen one part of the confederacy, tomorrow Canada may be required to add strength to another. And, after that might have been obtained, still other and further acquisitions would become necessary to equalize and adjust the balance of political power. . . .

I consider the annexation of Texas, at this time, without the assent of Mexico, as a measure compromising the national character, involving us certainly in war with Mexico, probably with other foreign powers, dangerous to the integrity of the Union, inexpedient in the present financial condition of the country, and not called for by any general expression of public opinion. . . .

PORTIONS OF THE DEMOCRATIC
PARTY PLATFORM OF 1844
PERTAINING TO FOREIGN AFFAIRS   *Document 9*

. . . *4. Resolved,* That justice and sound policy forbid the federal government to foster one branch of industry to the detriment of another, or to cherish the interest of one portion to the injury of another portion of our common country; that every citizen and every section of the country has a right to demand and insist upon an equality of rights and privileges, and to complete and ample protection of person and property from domestic violence or foreign aggression. . . .

7. *Resolved,* That Congress has no power, under the Constitution, to interfere with or control the domestic institutions of the several States, and that such States are the sole and proper judges of everything appertaining to their own affairs not prohibited by the Constitution; that all efforts of the Abolitionists or others, made to induce Congress to interfere with questions of slavery, or to take incipient steps in relation thereto, are calculated to lead to the most alarming and dangerous consequences, and that all such efforts have an inevitable tendency to diminish the happiness of the people, and endanger the stability and permanency of the Union, and ought not to be countenanced by any friend to our political institutions. . . .

Resolved, That our title to the whole of the territory of Oregon is clear and unquestionable; that no portion of the same ought to be ceded to England or any other power; and that the re-occupation of Oregon and the re-annexation of Texas at the earliest practicable period are great American measures, which this convention recommends to the cordial support of the Democracy of the Union. . . .

PRESIDENT POLK ASSERTS
AMERICAN POWER   *Document 10*

Inaugural Address of March 4, 1845.
. . . The Republic of Texas has made known her desire to come into our Union, to form a part of our Confederacy and enjoy with us the blessings of liberty secured and guaranteed by our Constitution. Texas was once a part of our country—was unwisely ceded away to a foreign power—is now independent, and possesses an undoubted right to dispose of a part or the whole of her territory and to merge her sovereignty as a separate and inde-

pendent state in ours. I congratulate my country that by an act of the late Congress of the United States the assent of this Government has been given to the reunion, and it only remains for the two countries to agree upon the terms to consummate an object so important to both.

I regard the question of annexation as belonging exclusively to the United States and Texas. They are independent powers competent to contract, and foreign nations have no right to interfere with them or to take exceptions to their reunion.... Foreign powers should therefore look on the annexation of Texas to the United States not as the conquest of a nation seeking to extend her dominions by arms and violence, but as the peaceful acquisition of a territory once her own, by adding another member to our confederation, with the consent of that member, thereby diminishing the chances of war and opening to them new and ever-increasing markets for their products....

None can fail to see the danger to our safety and future peace if Texas remains an independent state or becomes an ally or dependency of some foreign nation more powerful than herself.... Whatever is good or evil in the local institutions of Texas will remain her own whether annexed to the United States or not.... Upon the same principle that they would refuse to form a perpetual union with Texas because of her local institutions our forefathers would have been prevented from forming our present Union. Perceiving no valid objection to the measure and many reasons for its adoption vitally affecting the peace, the safety, and the prosperity of both countries, I shall on the broad principle which formed the basis and produced the adoption of our Constitution, and not in any narrow spirit of sectional policy, endeavor by all constitutional, honorable, and appropriate means to consummate the expressed will of the people and Government of the United States by the reannexation of Texas to our Union at the earliest practicable period.

Nor will it become in a less degree my duty to assert and maintain by all constitutional means the right of the United States to that portion of our territory which lies beyond the Rocky Mountains. Our title to the country of the Oregon is "clear and unquestionable," and already are our people preparing to perfect that title by occupying it with their wives and children. ... To us belongs the duty of protecting them adequately wherever they may be upon our soil....

Message to Congress, December 2, 1845.
... The rapid extension of our settlements over territories heretofore unoccupied, the addition of new States to our Confederacy, the expansion of free principles, and our rising greatness as a nation are attracting the attention of the powers of Europe, and lately the doctrine has been broached in some of them of a "balance of power" on this continent to check our advancement. The United States, sincerely desirous of preserving relations of good understanding with all nations, can not in silence permit any European interference on the North American continent, and should any such interference be attempted will be ready to resist it at any and all hazards.

It is well known to the American people and to all nations that this Government has never interfered with the relations subsisting between other governments. . . . We may claim on this continent a like exemption from European interference. . . . The people of the United States can not, therefore, view with indifference attempts of European powers to interfere with the independent action of the nations on this continent. . . . We must ever maintain the principle that the people of this continent alone have the right to decide their own destiny. Should any portion of them, constituting an independent state, propose to unite themselves with our Confederacy, this will be a question for them and us to determine without any foreign interposition. We can never consent that European powers shall interfere to prevent such a union because it might disturb the "balance of power" which they may desire to maintain. Near a quarter of a century ago the principle was distinctly announced to the world, in the annual message of one of my predecessors, that—

The American continents, by the free and independent condition which they have assumed and maintained, are henceforth not to be considered as subjects for future colonization by any European powers.

This principle will apply with greatly increased force should any European power attempt to establish any new colony in North America. In the existing circumstances of the world the present is deemed a proper occasion to reiterate and reaffirm the principle avowed by Mr. Monroe and to state my cordial concurrence in its wisdom and sound policy. . . .

REPRESENTATIVE ABRAHAM LINCOLN
ATTACKS PRESIDENT POLK,
JANUARY 12, 1848   *Document 11*

. . . When the war began, it was my opinion that all those who because of knowing too little, or because of knowing too much, could not conscientiously oppose the conduct of the President in the beginning of it should nevertheless, as good citizens and patriots, remain silent on that point, at least till the war should be ended. Some leading Democrats, including ex-President Van Buren, have taken this same view, as I understand them; and I adhered to it and acted upon it, until since I took my seat here; and I think I should still adhere to it were it not that the President and his friends will not allow it to be so. Besides the continual effort of the President to argue every silent vote given for supplies into an indorsement of the justice and wisdom of his conduct; besides that singularly candid paragraph in his late message in which he tells us that Congress with great unanimity had declared that "by the act of the Republic of Mexico, a state of war exists between that Government and the United States," when the same journals that informed him of this also informed him that when that declaration stood disconnected from the question of supplies sixty-seven in the House, and not fourteen merely, voted against it; besides this open attempt to prove by telling the truth what he could not prove by telling the whole truth—demanding of all who will not submit to be misrepresented, in justice to themselves, to speak out,—besides all this, one of my colleagues [*Mr. Richardson*]at a very early day in the session brought in a set of resolutions expressly indorsing the original justice of the war on the part of the President. Upon these resolutions when they shall be put on their passage, I shall be compelled to vote; so that I cannot be silent if I would. Seeing this, I went about preparing myself to give the vote understandingly when it should come. I carefully examined the President's message, to ascertain what he himself had said and proved upon the point. The result of this examination was to make the impression that, taking for true all the President states as facts, he falls far short of proving his justification; and that the President would have gone farther with his proof if it had not been for the small matter that the truth would not permit him. Under the impression thus made I gave the vote before mentioned. I propose now to give concisely the process of the examination I made, and how I reached the conclusion I did. The President, in his first war message of May, 1846, declares that the soil was ours on which hostilities were commenced by Mexico, and he repeats that declaration almost in the same language in each successive annual message, thus showing that he deems that point a highly essential one. In the importance of that point I entirely agree with the President. To my judgment it is the very point upon which he should be justified, or condemned. In his message of December, 1846, it seems to have occurred to him, as is certainly true, that title—ownership—to soil or anything else is not a simple fact, but is a conclusion following on one or more simple facts; and that it was incumbent upon him to present the facts from which he concluded the soil was ours on which the first blood of the war was shed.

Accordingly, a little below the middle of page twelve in the message last referred to he enters upon that task; forming an issue and introducing testimony, extending the whole to a little below the middle of page fourteen. Now, I propose to try to show that the whole of this—issue and evidence—is from beginning to end the sheerest deception. The issue, as he presents it, is in these words: "But there are those who, conceding all this to be true, assume the ground that the true western boundary of Texas is the Nueces, instead of the Rio Grande; and that, therefore, in marching our army to the east bank of the latter river, we passed the Texas line and invaded the territory of Mexico." Now this issue is made up of two affirmatives and no negative. The main deception of it is that it assumes as true that one river or the other is necessarily the boundary; and cheats the superficial thinker entirely out of the idea that possibly the boundary is somewhere between the two, and not actually at either. A further deception is that it will let in evidence which a true issue would exclude. A true issue made by the President would be about as follows: "I say the soil was ours, on which the first blood was shed; there are those who say it was not."

I now proceed to examine the President's evidence as applicable to such an issue. When that evidence is analyzed, it is all included in the following propositions:

(1) That the Rio Grande was the western boundary of Louisiana as we purchased it of France in 1803.

(2) That the Republic of Texas always claimed the Rio Grande as her western boundary.

(3) That by various acts she had claimed it on paper.

(4) That Santa Anna in his treaty with Texas recognized the. Rio Grande as her boundary.

(5) That Texas before, and the United States after, annexation had exercised jurisdiction beyond the Nueces—between the two rivers.

(6) That our Congress understood the boundary of Texas to extend beyond the Nueces.

Now for each of these in its turn. His first item is that the Rio Grande was the western boundary of Louisiana, as we purchased it of France in 1803; and seeming to expect this to be disputed, he argues over the amount of nearly a page to prove it true; at the end of which he lets us know that by the treaty of 1819 we sold to Spain the whole country from the Rio Grande eastward to the Sabine. Now, admitting for the present that the Rio Grande was the boundary of Louisiana, what, under heaven, had that to do with the present boundary between us and Mexico? How, Mr. Chairman, the line that once divided your land from mine can still be the boundary between us after I have sold my land to you is to me beyond all comprehension. And how any man, with an honest purpose only by proving the truth, could ever have thought of introducing such a fact to prove such an issue is equally incomprehensible. His next piece of evidence is that "the Republic of Texas always claimed this river (Rio Grande) as her western boundary." That is not true, in fact. Texas has claimed it, but she has not always claimed it. There is at least one distinguished exception. Her State constitution—the republic's most solemn and well-considered act; that which may, without impropriety, be called her last will and testament, revoking all others—makes no such claim. But suppose she had always claimed it. Has not Mexico always claimed the contrary? So that there is but claim against claim, leaving nothing proved until we get back to the claims and find which has the better foundation. Though not in the order in which the President presents his evidence, I now consider that class of his statements which are in substance nothing' more than that Texas has, by various acts of her Convention and Congress, claimed the Rio Grande as her boundary, on paper. I mean here what he says about the fixing of the Rio Grande's as her boundary in her old constitution (not her State constitution), about forming congressional districts, counties, etc. Now all of this is but naked claim; and what I have already said about claim is strictly applicable to this. If I should claim your land by word of mouth, that certainly would not make it mine; and if I were to claim it by a deed which I had made myself, and with which you had had nothing to do, the claim would be quite the same in substance— or rather, in utter nothingness. I next consider the President's statement that Santa Anna in his treaty with Texas recognized the Rio Grande as the western boundary of Texas. Besides the position so often taken, that Santa Anna while a prisoner of war, a captive, could not bind Mexico by a treaty, which I deem conclusive—besides this, I wish to say something in relation to this treaty, so called by the President, with Santa Anna. If any man would like to be amused by a sight of that little thing which the President calls by that big name, he can have it by turning to "Niles's Register," Vol. L, p. 336. And if any one should suppose that "Niles's Register" is a curious repository of so mighty a document as a solemn treaty between nations, I can only say that I learned to a tolerable degree of certainty, by inquiry at the State Department, that the President himself never saw it anywhere else. By the way, I believe I should not err if I were to declare that during the first ten years of the existence of that document it was never by anybody called a treaty—that it was never so called till the President, in his extremity, attempted by so calling it to wring something from it in justification of himself in connection with the Mexican war. It has none of the distinguishing features of a treaty. It does not call itself a treaty. Santa Anna does not therein assume to bind Mexico; he assumes only to act as the President—Commander-in-Chief of the Mexican army and navy; stipulates that the then present hostilities should cease, and that he would not himself take up arms, nor influence the Mexican people to take up arms, against Texas during the existence of the war of independence. He did not recognize the independence of Texas; he did not assume to put an end to the war, but clearly indicated his expectation of its continuance; he did not say one word about boundary, and, most probably, never thought of it. It is stipulated therein that the Mexican forces should evacuate the territory of Texas, passing to the other side of the Rio Grande; and in another article it is stipulated that, to prevent collisions between the armies, the Texas army should not approach nearer than within five leagues—of what is not said, but clearly, from the object stated, it is of the Rio Grande. Now, if this is a treaty recognizing the Rio Grande as the boundary of Texas, it contains the singular features of stipulating that Texas shall not go within five leagues of her own boundary.

Next comes the evidence of Texas before annexation, and the United States afterward, exercising jurisdiction beyond the Nueces and between the two rivers. This actual exercise of jurisdiction is the very class or quality of evidence we want. It is excellent so far as it goes; but does it go far enough? He tells us it went beyond the Nueces, but he does not tell us it went to the Rio Grande. He tells us jurisdiction was exercised between the two rivers, but he does not tell us it was exercised over all the territory between them. Some simple-minded people think it is possible to cross one river and go beyond it without going all the way to the next, that jurisdiction may be exercised between two rivers without covering all the country between them. I know a man, not very unlike myself, who exercises jurisdiction over a piece of land between the Wabash and the Mississippi; and yet so far is this from being all there is between those rivers that it is just one hundred and fifty-two feet long by fifty feet wide, and not part of it much within a hundred miles of either. He has a neighbor between him and the Mississippi—that is, just across the street, in that direction—whom I am sure he could neither persuade nor force to give up his habitation; but which nevertheless he could certainly annex, if it were to be done by merely standing on his own side of the street and claiming it, or even sitting down and writing a deed for it.

But next the President tells us the Congress of the United States understood the State of Texas they admitted into the Union to extend beyond the Nueces. Well, I suppose they did. I certainly so understood it. But how far beyond? That Congress did not understand it to extend clear to the Rio Grande is quite certain, by the fact of their joint resolutions for admission expressly leaving all questions of boundary to future adjustment. And it may be added that Texas herself is proved to have had the same understanding of it that our Congress had, by the fact of the exact conformity of her new constitution to those resolutions.

I am now through the whole of the President's evidence; and it is a singular fact that if any one should declare the President sent the army into the midst of a settlement of Mexican people who had never submitted, by consent or by force, to the authority of Texas or of the United States, and that there and thereby the first blood of the war was shed, there is not one word in all the President has said which would either admit or deny the declaration. This strange omission it does seem to me could not have occurred but by design. My way of living leads me to be about the courts of justice; and there I have sometimes seen a good lawyer, struggling for his client's neck in a desperate case, employing every artifice to work round, befog, and cover up with many words some point arising in the case which he dared not admit and yet could not deny. Party bias may help to make it appear so, but with all the allowance I can make for such bias, it still does appear to me that just such, and from just such necessity, is the President's struggle in this case.

... Now, sir, for the purpose of obtaining the very best evidence as to whether Texas had actually carried her revolution to the place where the hostilities of the present war commenced, let the President answer the interrogatories I proposed, as before mentioned, or some other similar ones. Let him answer fully, fairly, and candidly. Let him answer with facts and not with arguments. Let him remember he sits where Washington sat, and so remembering, let him answer as Washington would answer. As a nation should not, and the Almighty will not, be evaded, so let him attempt no evasion—no equivocation. And, if, so answering, he can show that the soil was ours where the first blood of the war was shed,—that it was not within an inhabited country, or, if within such, that the inhabitants had submitted themselves to the civil authority of Texas or of the United States, and that the same is true of the site of Fort Brown,—then I am with him for his justification. In that case I shall be most happy to reverse the vote I gave the other day. I have a selfish motive for desiring that the President may do this —I expect to gain some votes, in connection with the war, which, without his so doing, will be of doubtful propriety in my own judgment, but which will be free from the doubt if he does so. But if he can not or will not do this,—if on any pretense or no pretense he shall refuse or omit it—then I shall be fully convinced of what I more than suspect already—that he is deeply conscious of being in the wrong; that he feels the blood of this war, like the blood of Abel, is crying to Heaven against him; that originally having some strong motive—what, I will not stop now to give my opinion concerning— to involve the two countries in a war, and trusting to escape scrutiny by fixing the public gaze upon the exceeding brightness of military glory—that attractive rainbow that rises in showers of blood—that serpent's eye that charms to destroy,—he plunged into it, and has swept on and on till, disappointed in his calculation of the ease with which Mexico might be subdued, he now finds himself he knows not where. How like the half-insane mumbling of a fever dream is the whole war part of his late message! . . .

CLIPPER SHIPS

AND

OPEN SEAS

CHAPTER 5

Commerce Holds Its Own

*T*he appeal of Manifest Destiny led some old-time Federalist merchants to give up their overseas activities and invest their profits in the development of America's continental empire. Some became land speculators or bankers, while others went into manufacturing or helped build canal systems, steamboat lines, and railroads. Most of them made the transition with little effort and many retained their earlier interest in trade. Others devoted themselves exclusively to the business of exporting America's growing agricultural and manufactured surpluses and with importing other goods from abroad.

While the landed expansionists elected presidents and fought a war for more territory, thus attracting a greater share of the attention, the commercial groups enjoyed a steady revival of strength after 1815, the low-water mark of their influence. John Quincy Adams kept a sharp eye on their interests, and he was followed by Daniel Webster, whose oratory could ennoble the most mundane business transaction. As time went on even the spokesmen of territorial expansion had to pay more attention to these overseas activities. Not only were the merchants and exporters worth cultivating as a source of political strength, but also the farmers themselves demanded government aid in finding, entering, and protecting markets for their produce.

This growth of trade is reviewed by George Rogers Taylor in the first article, giving particular attention to the expansion of domestic exports. Earlier patterns of exchange were revived and extended where possible, and *new openings were exploited as opportunities became available. Americans were very active in the Far East. New Englanders had begun to trade with Asia even as independence was being won. Stopping on the northwest coast of North America to load furs and in Hawaii to take on valuable hardwoods, they sailed on to China, where they obtained tea and other items to sell in Latin America and the United States. Though long and dangerous, these voyages returned high profits; a single ship could start a family fortune.*

The trade in opium, for example, was especially rewarding until it was taken over during the latter part of the 1830s by the British and the French. In Hawaii, on the other hand, where whalers, traders, and missionaries established a colony in residence at an early date, the Americans were the victors. The first missionaries concentrated on converting the islanders to Christianity. But many of their descendants gave up the life of the cloth to become men of affairs. Sugar and real estate operations took them into politics, and by the 1840's they and other less religious Americans were exercising a major influence in the islands. Retaining their original citizenship, as did those who settled in Oregon and Texas, these Americans looked back to the United States for aid and protection. Nor were they disappointed. Even before President Polk spoke of the Monroe Doctrine with reference to Texas, his predecessor, President John Tyler, had added a paragraph to that pronouncement concerning Hawaii (Document 1). Tyler's Secretary of the Navy, Abel Upshur, provided an illuminating discussion of the administration's general concern with commerce in his annual report for 1842 (Document 2).

The loss of the opium trade did not mean that Americans abandoned Asia. Some worked along with the British and French in China, taking the initiative wherever they could. One such figure was the Reverend Peter Parker, whose enthusiasm for the secular business of empire building led him to lobby for the occupation and annexation of Formosa (Document 3). While the State Department declined to embark upon that project, it was not so hesitant in pushing other proposals. Professor Foster Rhea Dulles reviews the opening of Japan and the penetration of China proper in his account of later "American Interest in China." Commercial interests played the main role in this activity. Missionaries like Peter Parker were sometimes more dramatic, perhaps, but even in the case of Formosa two traders had preceded him in raising the American flag. Secretary of State Webster worked closely with the merchants. His instructions to Caleb Cushing, for example, were written along the lines they desired (Document 4).

The traders likewise wanted to penetrate Japan (Document 5); but so did the Navy, which was beginning to have a voice in policy decisions. Commodore Matthew Calbraith Perry was given much latitude in planning his celebrated voyage to Tokyo, and even wrote a large part of the orders under which his task force sailed (Document 6).

In a similar fashion the Navy became involved in promoting American influence in Africa. The connection with Africa had begun, of course, with the importation of slaves, and the efforts to deal with the increasingly grave moral and social problem created by that action led on to greater involvement. The American Colonization Society (founded in 1817) hoped to solve

189

*the dilemma by resettling the blacks in Africa, and for that purpose estab-
lished the Republic of Liberia in 1821–1822. But commercial interests were
eager to exploit the opportunity, and the Navy likewise desired to strengthen
its influence by supporting the attempt to combine morality with business
enterprise (Document 7).*

*Such worldwide commercial activity increased the traditional interest in
improving travel between the Atlantic and Pacific oceans. William O.
Scroggs reviews the wild struggle for control of one route across Central
America in his selection on "Walker and Vanderbilt in Nicaragua." The
rising concern of many groups, including those who wanted to expand ter-
ritorially as well as merchants and naval officers, to win control of a canal
route produced two major results. It involved the government ever more
directly, and it led to a confrontation with Great Britain. Secretary of State
James Buchanan's instructions on the issue (Document 8) were followed by
a treaty with Colombia in 1848 and an understanding with the British in 1850
(Documents 9 and 10).*

*The disputes with England over affairs in Canada, Maine, Oregon, Texas,
and Central America never produced an open break between Great Britain
and the United States. One reason was the economic interdependence of the
two countries, as Thomas P. Martin shows in his discussion of "Cotton and
Wheat in Anglo-American Trade and Politics, 1846–1852." Rather than
causing an Anglo-American war, the politics of wheat and cotton actually
helped bring on the Civil War in the United States. By 1850 the rising
domestic antagonism over land and slavery was being injected into the foreign policy proposals of wheat growers and cotton growers, of northern
farmers and southern planters. Some politicians looked to new expansionist
schemes as a way to solve the internal crisis. Whether presenting their own
proposals or opposing the plans of others, the commercial groups enjoyed a
steadily increasing influence in these debates.*

THE EXPANSION OF FOREIGN TRADE[1]   *George Rogers Taylor*

The very great increase which took place in the foreign commerce of the
United States from 1815 to 1861 has been somewhat overshadowed by the
even more rapid strides which were at the same time being taken by internal
trade and industry. Probably foreign commerce was never again *relatively*
so important a part of the whole American economy as in the period preceding the War of 1812. But this consideration should not be permitted to obscure the picture of remarkably rapid growth after 1815.

... Although many year-to-year irregularities appear, the general trend
of American foreign trade development was strongly upward to the Civil
War. For the five years 1816–1820 the total foreign trade of the United
States averaged $186,000,000 a year. This was the highest five-year average

---

[1] Selected from *The Transportation Revolution, 1815–1860* (New York: Rinehart & Co., 1951),
pp. 176–77, 185–90. Reprinted with permission.

yet reached and may be compared with an average of $518,000,000 which was the annual value for the total foreign trade of the United Kingdom for the same period. By the five-year period ending in 1860, American foreign trade had more than trebled, to average $616,000,000 a year. This period from the close of the Napoleonic Wars to 1860 was one in which the United Kingdom, by virtue of its rapid industrialization, extensive foreign loans, and the dominant position of its merchant marine, was experiencing one of its great periods of foreign trade development. For the years 1856–1860 the annual value of its foreign commerce averaged $1,602,000,000. Yet it is significant that the United States, whose industrialization was still in its early stages and whose dependence on foreign loans was relatively small, nonetheless, in these forty-five years, increased its foreign trade at an even more rapid rate than did the United Kingdom. From 1816–1820 to 1856–1860 the total value of the foreign trade of the United States increased by 230 per cent; that of Great Britain by 205 per cent.

* * *

By far the major part of American purchasing power abroad arose from American commodity exports. But what commodities could America offer which would permit it to expand imports from $65,000,000 in 1816 to $316,000,000 in 1860? The great tropical staples—tea, coffee, and spices—which found such profitable markets in Europe, could not be advantageously produced in the American climate. Domestic sugar production was, throughout the period, insufficient for home needs, and, until the discovery of gold in California, the export of mineral products was unimportant.

Fortunately, the United States did have one great staple, cotton. The rapid expansion of the demand for this product to feed the factories created by the industrial revolution is one of the most striking phenomena of the nineteenth century. The southern states could produce cotton at a relatively low cost and in seemingly unlimited quantities. In 1815 the United States exported 83,000,000 pounds of cotton valued at $17,500,000; by 1860 the quantity had risen to 1,768,000,000 pounds, worth nearly $192,000,000. For the period 1815–1860 as a whole this single product made up more than one half of the total value of domestic exports, and cotton alone paid for three fifths of total imports for consumption in 1860.

No other product even approached the role played by cotton in the export trade. It is true that two commodities, wheat and tobacco, were strong contenders at the beginning of the period. For the years 1816–1820 wheat and wheat flour constituted 16 per cent of the value of domestic exports, unmanufactured tobacco 15 per cent, and cotton 39 per cent, but in terms of percentage of total exports this proved to be the high point for both wheat and tobacco.

The great staple of colonial times, tobacco, continued to be an important export, though of declining relative significance. Foreign demand was limited by competition from newly developed sources of supply as well as by highly restrictive taxes. In the United States, soil exhaustion in the old tobacco areas and the comparative advantage of cotton over tobacco contributed to its reduced importance. Exports of domestic tobacco were valued at $47,500,000 for the period 1816–1820, but this total was not reached again until 1851–1855. For the five years ending in 1860, tobacco exports were valued at $86,000,000, which was only 6 per cent of total domestic exports. As in the previous century, western Europe was the important market, and England the chief importer of unmanufactured tobacco.

Only intermittently did wheat play a major role in the exports of this period. In view of the fact that new farming lands in the West were being settled even more rapidly than the cotton areas of the new South, this may seem surprising. But the fact is that throughout the period, so far as the European market was concerned, the United States remained a marginal wheat-producing area. Only when European prices were unusually high, as for example in 1816–1818 and frequently after 1845, were large shipments of American wheat profitably disposed of in British markets. Not only did Great Britain remain largely self-sustaining, at least during the early part of the period, but flour from the Continent continued to have a competitive advantage over that from America. Even after the repeal of the British corn laws, when American flour exports greatly expanded, transportation costs (chiefly the cost of getting the wheat to the seaboard) were still so great that only in years of crop failures abroad or of special need when prices were unusually high did large quantities of American wheat or flour continue to reach the rapidly expanding British market. Thus domestic exports of wheat and flour totaled $50,500,000 for 1816–1820 and constituted 16 per cent of total domestic exports. This percentage was not again equaled for any five-year period before the Civil War. The value of wheat exports was greatest for the five years ending in 1860 ($158,000,000) but even then amounted to but 11 per cent of total domestic exports.

Had it not been for the demand for American flour in the West Indies and South America, especially Brazil, flour exports would have approached the vanishing point in much of the period between 1820 and 1845. Here was an area in which the United States could compete on favorable terms with other sources of supply. On the other hand, this was at best a limited market, for, while under the impetus of the industrial revolution European (especially British) markets were expanding marvelously, those to the south increased but slowly and at times actually declined.

In addition to flour and wheat, the United States was, of course, in a position to produce tremendous quantities of other food products of the Temperate Zone, but none of these was exported in relatively large quantities. . . . Only corn and rice were of appreciable importance among the grains, and the first of these, corn, amounted to more than 2 per cent of total domestic exports only in the five-year period which includes the Irish potato famine; and the second, rice, contributed 4 per cent to the value of domestic exports in 1816–1820 and only 1 per cent by the close of the period. Nor were meat and dairy products of great importance as exports. Pork and pork products, the most important of these, increased in value from $4,000,000 in 1816–1820 to nearly $54,000,000 in 1856–1860, when they represented about 4 per cent of the value of domestic exports. For all these food products the situation was similar to that for wheat and flour. Except for periods of exceptionally high prices, American provisions were still at a competitive disadvantage in western European markets, and the West Indian and South American markets failed to expand consistently. Finally, it may be noted that exports of fish, so important in colonial times, suffered both an absolute and a relative decline in this period.

By far the most significant of American nonagricultural exports were manufactured goods, which increased in value eightfold during the period, thus eclipsing even raw cotton in rate of growth. Manufactured products, which were 7 per cent of total value exports in 1816–1820, equaled 12 per cent of the total in the last five years of the period, when they were valued at $167,000,000. . . . The dominant position of cotton manufactures beginning in 1830 is noteworthy. Even in the previous decade cotton manufactures were, although not first, undoubtedly well up on the list, but they cannot be placed exactly at that time as they are not clearly separated in the original Treasury reports. In the early part of this period the chief foreign buyers of American cotton manufactures were Mexico and the West Indian Islands. In the 1840's Mexican imports of American manufactured goods declined in relative importance, and China, during much of the rest of the period, became the leading customer. Important shipments were made also to South America, to the West Indies, to Canada, and even to Africa and the East Indies.

Manufactures of cotton constitute the only important manufactured export which was to a large extent the product of relatively large-scale factory production. By the end of the period this was also beginning to be true of iron and steel products which, from eleventh place in 1820, moved steadily upward to second place in the final decade of the period. But before 1840, iron, and throughout the whole period practically all of the other manufactures, were largely the products of household or small-scale, neighborhood industries.

This is well illustrated by chemicals, which were the leading manufactured export in the 1820's and remained important throughout. About nine tenths of this category was made up of pot and pearl ashes, from which came potash, essential in the manufacture of such products as glass, soap, and explosives. The chief source of ashes was domestic fireplaces in the Middle and New England states. The process of leaching the ashes to produce pot and pearl ashes was always a neighborhood industry, carried on typically in a farmer's shed by not more than two or three workers. Soap, spirits, candles, leather, and "wood, other" (which included staves, shingles, boards, and so on) were largely the product of neighborhood or even household manufacture and were directly dependent upon cheap domestic materials. In fact, chemicals and soap, the two leading manufactured exports of the 1820's, might be looked upon as by-products of the agriculture of the period. Pot and pearl ashes, a product destined not for immediate consumption but for further use in manufacturing, was the only export of American manufacture which was sent chiefly to European markets. All the other important manufactured exports found their best markets in the West Indies (especially Cuba and Haiti), Mexico, South America, and, for the later decades, British North America.

. . . The leading position of Europe and especially the United Kingdom in American export trade serves again to illustrate the extent to which domestic exports were dominated by raw cotton. The place of southern North America and South America is a reflection of their demand for American foodstuffs and manufactured goods, a demand which was expanding throughout the period but not as rapidly as total exports. Taking the period as a whole, the absolute value of domestic exports increased to practically every part of the world. There was a tendency for the percentage of domestic exports sent to Europe and northern North America to increase moderately. Exports to Asia and South America declined slightly as a percentage of total domestic exports; for exports to the West Indies the percentage drop was very considerable, from 19 per cent in 1821–1825 to 7 per cent in 1856–1860.

* * *

AMERICAN INTEREST IN CHINA[1]   *Foster Rhea Dulles*

... As a consequence both of settlement on the western coast and the high drama of the clipper ship era, Americans looked toward Asia in the middle of the century as they would not again until its close. It was not only China that caught their imagination; but that great country remained the key to the period's expanding interest in the Pacific world. We came near to annexing the Hawaiian Islands as a way station on the road to China, and Commodore Perry's expedition to open up Japan was in part inspired by the need to obtain coaling depots for the new steam vessels on the long voyage to Chinese ports. Looking deep into the future, William H. Seward proclaimed in an often-quoted statement that the Pacific Ocean, its shores, its islands and the vast regions beyond would become the chief theater of events in the world's great hereafter. He even projected the idea that our commerce with Asia, having brought the ancient continent near to us, "created necessities for new position—perhaps connections or colonies there."

Commodore Perry shared these imperialistic views, and his epochal voyage to Japan first raised the question of possible overseas expansion. His all-important objectives, after bringing his "black ships" to anchor in the harbor of Yedo in 1853, were to secure adequate protection for American sailors shipwrecked on the Japanese coast, obtain for the United States the coaling privileges it desired, and to open up Japan for foreign trade. They were successfully achieved in the conclusion of Japan's first treaty with a foreign power. But in his dispatches to the State Department, Commodore Perry also urged American annexation of what were then called the Liuchiu Islands. In the middle of the last century these islands—the principal one now has world fame as Okinawa—were still under Chinese sovereignty. The suggestion that they be annexed was consequently rejected not only on the ground that the United States had no desire for "connections or colonies" off the Asiatic

---

[1] Selected from *China and America: the Story of their Relations since 1784* (Princeton: Princeton University Press, 1946), pp. 36–37, 41–43, 49–50, 57–62. Reprinted with permission.

coast, but because it was no part of our policy to infringe upon China's territorial rights. To calm whatever fears Commodore Perry's ambitious imperialism might possibly have aroused in Peking, our commissioner was instructed to assure the Imperial Government that the United States did not have any intention of interfering in Chinese affairs, attacking Chinese sovereignty, or trying to gain a foothold in Chinese territory. . . .

In the cultural influences which flowed from the United States to China, the role of missionaries was far more significant than that of the traders. The latter had few personal associations except with hong merchants and factory servants. They very seldom learned Chinese. The American Protestant missionaries, however, became the medium for the transmission of western culture in all its many manifestations. As early as 1834, one of them was instructed by his home board not only to employ his medical skill in relieving the afflictions of the people, but to be ready to give them "our arts and sciences."

The first American missionaries to China, David Abeel and Elijah C. Bridgeman, reached Canton in 1830. They had been given passage in one of the ships of D. W. C. Olyphant, whose zeal for missionary enterprise, as already noted, earned for his factory the name of Zion's Corner, and they began at once upon the heroic task of converting the Chinese to Christianity. Within a few years the American Board of Commissioners for Foreign Missions, the Presbyterians, the Baptists and the Episcopalians had sent additional men to this foreign field. In close cooperation with English missionaries, they were busily engaged in translating the Bible into Chinese, distributing tracts among the natives, establishing schools and preaching the gospel. Among these pioneers were such men as Samuel Wells Williams, whose book *The Middle Kingdom* became a classic account of Chinese civilization; W. A. P. Martin, another author as well as missionary; Peter Parker, the first medical missionary and later an American diplomatic representative; and Issachar J. Roberts, a Baptist evangelist whose principal convert was later to become the leader of the Taiping Rebellion.

After 1844, this slowly growing band of missionaries extended their activities to the new treaty ports, and under the protection assured through treaty provisions they began to expand their work. There was no disposition on their part to forego any privileges obtained from the Chinese government through force of arms. As time went on, indeed, the missionaries became fully as zealous as the foreign merchants in insisting on their rights, and they continually exercised strong pressure on their home governments to secure additional concessions. Their demand for protection both for themselves and for their Christian converts, after mid-century based upon the toleration clauses of a new American-Chinese treaty, led to what became known as the "gunboat policy" of supporting missionary enterprise. It was always a great source of friction with the Chinese officials. The bitterness roused in some quarters by aggressive missionary tactics was illustrated toward the close of the century by the outburst of Prince Kung, the Minister of Foreign Affairs. "Take away your opium and your missionaries," he exclaimed, "and you will be welcome."

Some eighty-eight American Protestant workers had arrived in China by

1860, and they had established stations in all of the treaty ports. They organized a Society for the Diffusion of Christian and General Knowledge; set up printing presses with the aid of the American Bible Society to publish Bibles, religious literature and tracts; and started not only schools but also a number of colleges. Even the education of girls fell within their province, the Methodist establishing in 1859 the Baltimore Female Seminary at Foochow.

Missionary influence either in this mid-century period or in later years is difficult to evaluate. Although some few of the Chinese persuaded to accept the new faith were eventually to play an important role in their country's life, the number of converts to Christianity among the great masses of the people was negligible. More significant was the part played by missionaries in spreading other western ideas and practices, and the subsequent impetus given to secular education and reform. As the principal channel through which China gradually learned more of the West, the missionaries were preparing the ground for the revolution that was to lead to the overthrow of the Manchu dynasty and establishment of a Chinese republic. Their activities were not by any means the sole cause for these later events. China finally began to adapt herself to the modern world as a consequence of the general impact of the West upon her national life in many different forms—military, political and economic as well as cultural. Nevertheless, the influence of American missionaries helped materially to shape the course of future events. . . .

It was in these mid-century years that China was swept by the bloody scourge of the Taiping Rebellion.

This great revolt, breaking out in the general vicinity of Canton in 1849, reflected the underlying discontent of the Chinese masses with Manchu rule. It was inspired in part by the failure of the imperial authorities to protect China from the western barbarians and foreshadowed later upsurges of nationalistic feeling directed against both the Manchus and other foreigners. Thousands of peasants were attracted to the banner of its visionary leader, Hung Hsui-chuan, and they had gradually swept northward in a victorious march to the Yangtze Valley. There they had set up, in 1853, a new government, in sharp defiance of the Son of Heaven. The movement had a pseudo-religious as well as political character. Hung Hsui-chuan had come under the influence of the Baptist missionary, Issachar J. Roberts. Interpreting as revelations from Heaven the visions that came to him during the epileptic fits to which he was periodically subject, Hung became convinced that he was himself a second Son of God, a divine younger brother of Jesus Christ. The rule which he established at his capital in Nanking, where twenty thousand Manchus were slaughtered in consolidating his authority, was to revive the ancient glories of China through establishment of the Taiping Tienkuo, or Heavenly Kingdom of Great Peace.

The Manchu bannermen and other imperial forces had been unable to halt the advance of these fanatical rebels who laid waste villages, massacred the peasants and cut down all forces sent against them. Dominating the Yangtze Valley, they menaced Shanghai and attempted to march farther north to Peking itself. "Any day may bring forth the fruits of successful revolution, in the utter overthrow of the existing dynasty," Commissioner Marshall reported home in April 1853. But the attitude of the foreigners was for a time one of hope rather than fear. Disregarding the excesses that had marked the rebels' northward march and the tyrannical nature of Hung Hsui-chuan's government, they believed that the Taipings had truly adopted Christianity and that their triumph might mean a new day for China and the breaking-down of her hostility to the West. These optimistic views, crossing the Pacific, were reflected in President Pierce's annual message to Congress. "The condition of China at this time," he declared, "renders it probable that some important changes will occur in that vast empire which will lead to a more unrestricted intercourse with it."

Missionary circles both in China and at home showed even more sympathy for the Taipings. The professions of religious faith made by Hung Hsui-chuan were taken very seriously. He had summoned Issachar J. Roberts to Nanking "to assist in establishing the truth." While his missionary mentor was not to reach the capital until several years later, when disillusionment had already set in as to the nature of the Taiping movement, this invitation was regarded as proof of the rebel chieftain's sincerity.

Among Americans whose interest was trade and commerce, the conversion of the Chinese to Christianity did not seem so important, but what appeared to be the impossibility of working with the Imperial Government made them welcome the prospect of any other regime replacing it. There was also the belief in some quarters that the Taipings might overthrow the Manchu dynasty, but would then prove incapable of maintaining their own nationwide control. And the expected result was the break-up of China, and new opportunities for the foreigner. "It will not be many years," a writer who held this point of view wrote in the *North American Review*, "ere we find European influence, hitherto so powerless in the high exclusive walls of Peking, operating with wonderful force at the courts of a score of kingdoms, petty in comparison with the great aggregate of which they once formed a part. . . ."

The State Department disapproved of all suggestions for forceful action or for seeking to gain a territorial stake in China. It might prove necessary to increase our naval forces in Chinese waters to assure greater respect for American rights, Secretary Marcy declared, but "the President will not do it for aggressive purposes." The desirability of treaty revision was fully recognized in Washington, but it was to be obtained, if at all, by peaceful persuasion rather than any threat of force. Moreover, overtures from England and France for joint action to present a united front against China were rejected. The United States, as we have seen, would take no part in the hostilities that had already broken out at this time between England and China in the so-called Arrow War, and it was determined at all costs to pursue a policy of friendly neutrality in all phases of its Chinese policy.

Nevertheless a highly anomalous situation was rapidly developing. England and France were resolved to force the Imperial Government to revise its treaties, and a highly unfortunate train of events was soon to lead to what is known as the Anglo-French war with China. President Buchanan, coming into office in 1857 in succession to President Pierce, at one and the same time declared his sympathy for Anglo-French aims and his refusal to give them any armed support. William B. Reed was sent out to China in the new capacity of envoy extraordinary and minister plenipotentiary, to place him on a level with the other foreign envoys, with instructions to cooperate with the British and French envoys, but under no circumstances to let such cooperation involve the United States in any hostilities.

In 1858 the curious spectacle was consequently presented of the American minister, together with the Russian minister who had somewhat comparable instructions, accompanying the British and French ministers to the mouth of the Peiho, and calmly standing aside while Anglo-French naval forces battered down the Taku forts which guarded the river's approaches. As the British and French ministers then proceeded triumphantly upstream in a vessel flying both their national flags, Reed and his Russian colleague followed more sedately in a steamer flying American and Russian ensigns. Negotiations were then held at Tientsin between the chastened plenipotentiaries of the Imperial Government and the envoys of both the belligerent and neutral nations, which resulted in a complete revision of China's treaty relations with the western world.

The major interest of the United States in these negotiations, as Humphrey Marshall had first declared, was to secure more binding guarantees for the protection of American lives and property, additional opportunities for trade through the opening of the Yangtze ports, full religious toleration for both missionaries and their converts and direct access to the Imperial Court at Peking. These objectives were obtained and through application of the most-favored-nation clause, such additional privileges as Great Britain and France secured were also shared by the Americans. Trade with the interior was largely opened up, and, most important, China was restricted to levying no more than a 5 per cent duty on imports, to be wholly collected by the foreign-controlled Inspectorate of Maritime Customs. Included in the new tariff schedules was a customs duty on opium, in effect legalizing a traffic which the Americans had formerly declared to be contraband.

It is true that in negotiating the Treaty of Tientsin the United States sought to demonstrate its continued friendship for China. It was expressly stipulated that "if any other nation should act unjustly or oppressively, the United States will exert their good offices . . . to bring about an amicable arrangement of the question. . . ." Yet we made little effort to safeguard what even several members of the American mission considered China's justified rights. We not only held ourselves aloof while England and France struck a disastrous blow at Chinese sovereignty by forcefully compelling treaty revision, but after the deed was done, we claimed our share of the plunder. Whatever may be said as to China's bringing of such treatment upon herself through her own supercilious and arrogant attitude, the role of the United States had very little to commend it.

The treaty was signed on June 18, 1858, and duly ratified by the United States and Chinese governments. Normally this would have meant an end to the matter, but the formal exchange of ratifications brought up once again the bitterly disputed issue of the reception of foreign envoys at the Imperial Court. When the United States minister especially deputed to exchange ratifications, John E. Ward, reached the mouth of the Peiho in company with the other foreign envoys charged with the same mission, it quickly became apparent that Peking was not prepared even yet to receive these emissaries on terms of equality. Barriers placed across the river's mouth barred the entrance of the foreign vessels.

The situation confronting Ward closely paralleled that with which Reed had been faced just a year earlier. For while the United States was not prepared to use force in breaking down this new show of Chinese resistance, both Great Britain and France were ready to do so. So once again the Americans stood aside while the Anglo-French allies attacked the Taku forts. On this occasion, however, an unexpected incident marred the otherwise perfect picture of our magnanimous neutrality. When the Allies were unexpectedly repulsed in their assault and the English admiral wounded, Commodore Tatnall of the U.S. Frigate *Powhatan*, the vessel which had brought Ward north, went to the rescue and American sailors briefly helped to serve the guns on a British ship. It was an occasion which gave birth to a famous phrase, Commodore Tatnall reputedly shouting "Blood is thicker than water" as his men went to the Englishmen's aid.

The risks of further hostilities caused the British and French envoys to return to Shanghai for reinforcements after this encounter, but when Ward was informed that he would be allowed to proceed to Peking by another route, he pursued his mission independently. The Chinese provided carts for his party and it reached the capital without further incident. Only then did our envoy learn, as still another ironical touch in this long battle over diplomatic usage, that these carts were the traditional conveyances for the emissaries of tribute-bearing nations.

Ward nevertheless stanchly upheld national dignity when the Emperor insisted that if he were to be received at court, he should comply with the custom of the kowtow. "I kneel only to God and woman," was his proud reply. As the Chinese refused even to accept his conciliatory undertaking "to bend the body and slightly crook the right knee," he thereupon left the capital. If the issue were so important as a matter of prestige to the Chinese, Ward felt he could make no further compromise. The treaty ratifications were exchanged, however, at the coast.

It was left to England and France, for the third time, to assume the responsibility of enforcing the demand for recognition of international equality. After another and successful attack on the Taku forts, Anglo-French troops marched overland to occupy Peking. Once in the capital they callously looted the city and, in stern retribution for alleged Chinese atrocities, burned down the Emperor's rich and splendid Summer Palace. The Imperial Government now had no alternative other than complete surrender and unreserved acknowledgment of the right of diplomatic residence in Peking.

It may well be asked what attitude was being taken toward the Taipings while this war was fought against the Imperial Government. In sharp contrast to their policy in the north, the western powers were in central China doing what they could to uphold the Manchu dynasty. Although they did not intervene officially in the civil war, which continued to rage bitterly for all the alarms and excursions on the international front, they lent their tacit support to Peking's campaign against the Taipings and allowed their nationals to enlist in the imperial armies. Once the Emperor had been forced to make the concessions they considered so essential to their own commercial interests, the powers were then all the more convinced that reestablishment of the Manchu dynasty's control over central China had become necessary for Asiatic peace.

An American played an important role in the aid given the imperial troops. Frederick Townsend Ward, soldier of fortune, was supported by both the American and British envoys in Shanghai in raising a heterogeneous force of westerners, Filipinos and Chinese to wage war against the Taipings on a contract basis. With the promise of substantial bounties for every city he recovered from the rebels, Ward led his little army to a series of spectacular victories that for the first time made serious inroads on Taiping power in the Yangtze Valley. A colorful, romantic figure, who went into battle carrying only a walking stick, as casually as if he were on an afternoon stroll, this adventurous Yankee won the devotion of his men for his unfailing courage as well as military skill. The Chinese showered him with honors. His successes, however, were not destined to continue for very long. In an attack against one of the rebel strongholds in 1862, he was fatally wounded. What had become known as the Ever Victorious Army lost its driving force and appeared about to break up.

Its work had proved so effective that the American and British envoys were not willing to let Ward's death bring this form of foreign aid to an end, and they persuaded the imperial authorities to name a new commander for the Ever Victorious Army. Eventually Major Charles G. Gordon, of the British forces in China, took over the post, and in the final suppression of the Taiping Rebellion, following a succession of imperial victories in 1864 and 1865, "Chinese" Gordon and his troops played a notable part.

Torn between the conflicting desires to maintain the friendship of the Chinese and to secure new trade privileges, the United States had followed a policy that was neither war nor peace in these complicated developments in North China. To some degree we had exercised a restraining influence upon the rapacity of the other powers. We had definitely taken the lead in supporting the Imperial Government against the Taipings. Yet we had also sought to attain the same objectives for which England and France went to war, stood aside while they brought the Chinese to terms, and then insisted upon the right to enjoy the new privileges which the Imperial Government had been compelled to concede.

"The English barbarians," the Imperial Commissioner wrote the Emperor about this time, "are . . . full of insidious schemes, uncontrollably fierce and imperious. The American nation does no more than follow in their direction."

WALKER AND VANDERBILT

IN NICARAGUA[1]   *William O. Scroggs*

. . . In spite of British intrigue and arrogance, American influence made itself felt in Nicaragua in no small degree. It was the enterprise of the American capitalist, however, and not of the American diplomat that achieved such a result. The importance of Nicaragua to the United States as a consequence of the Mexican War and the discovery of gold in California has already been indicated. With the first rush of adventurers to the gold fields the question of an interoceanic canal aroused great interest. A prime mover in the promotion of this canal was Cornelius Vanderbilt, the greatest captain of industry of his time. At this time the Pacific Mail Steamship Company had a monopoly of the transportation service via the isthmus, sending its vessels from New York to Aspinwall and from Panama to San Francisco. A company had been organized in 1850 to construct a railway across the isthmus of Panama, and after enormous expense and great loss of life the road was completed in 1855. While the Panama company was developing its business, Vanderbilt and his associates were busy with plans for a rival route through Nicaragua. In 1849 he with Joseph L. White and Nathaniel J. Wolfe organized the American Atlantic and Pacific Ship Canal Company and secured a charter from the republic of Nicaragua giving the company a right of way through the country and the exclusive right to construct the canal. In 1850 Vanderbilt visited England to secure the cooperation of British capitalists in financing the undertaking, and they agreed to assist in the project if fuller surveys should show that it was practicable. The new surveys were made and indicated that the waters in the lake were insufficient to make the construction feasible. The earlier surveys were shown to have been inaccurate. The scheme for a canal was then abandoned, but Vanderbilt and his associates obtained a new charter for another corporation, styled the Accessory Transit Company, which was "grafted on the body" of the American Atlantic and Pacific Ship Canal Company. This Accessory Transit Company received a right of way between the oceans and the monopoly of navigating the waters of the State by steam. Vanderbilt was president of the company, and he soon made it a formidable competitor of the Panama line. Shortly after returning from England he proceeded to Nicaragua, where for several weeks he directed soundings on the river and lake and satisfied himself that a steamship route from San Juan del Norte to the western shore of Lake Nicaragua was entirely practicable. He had planned at first to make Realejo the Pacific port, but found a new and unnamed harbour at a more convenient point, which became San Juan del Sur. From this point to the lake the distance was only twelve miles, and he planned to connect the lake and the ocean with a macadamized road. After his return home he sent down

[1] Selected from *Filibusters and Financiers: The Story of William Walker and His Associates* (New York: Macmillan, 1916), pp. 78–81, 133–38, 151–53, 155–58.

201

two small steamboats for the river and a larger boat for the lake. He also despatched three steamers to the Pacific, and was soon ready to carry passengers to and from California. Another steamer which he had constructed for the lake he was told by his engineers could never be conveyed up the river on account of the rapids. Vanderbilt thereupon went to Greytown with the boat and himself conveyed her over the rapids. New ocean steamers were built in 1852, and an additional line from New Orleans to Greytown was inaugurated.

Passengers at Greytown would proceed up the river in boats of light draft until they reached the lake. There, at a point called San Carlos, they would transfer to larger steamers provided with comfortable state-rooms and cross the lake to the town of Virgin Bay. Next there would be before them a twelve-mile ride by land to San Juan del Sur, where they would take the steamer for San Francisco. This ride at first was made on mules over a bridle path through a very rugged country, and the discomforts were serious, especially for women and children. In 1854, however, the macadamized road was completed, and comfortable carriages were placed upon it. Each of these was painted in the national colours of Nicaragua, white and blue, and was drawn by four mules. The vehicles would move in a line of twenty-five at a time, carrying the passengers of the latest ship to arrive, and being followed by many wagons conveying freight and baggage. This of itself was an impressive sight, and the scenery along the route was another feature.

The new interoceanic route was completed in the face of tremendous difficulties, with no governmental favours and in spite of the opposition of a powerful competitor. As a result of competition the fare between New York and San Francisco was reduced from six hundred to three hundred dollars, and travel by sea between East and West was further stimulated. By the Nicaraguan route the distance was reduced somewhat over five hundred miles, and the average time saved was about two days. When the company was at the height of its prosperity it would transport as many as two thousand Americans through Nicaragua in the course of a single month.

These facts in connection with the history of the Accessory Transit Company have necessarily been given in considerable detail because of the intimate relation of this corporation to the rise and fall of Walker in Nicaragua. The existence of the company drew the attention of the filibusters to Nicaragua; its favouritism is responsible for whatever success they achieved while there, and its hostility compassed their downfall. . . .

It has already been shown that the Transit Company had allowed Walker to use one of its steamers to capture Granada and shortly thereafter had advanced the new government the sum of twenty thousand dollars in gold. Having observed this manifestation of its good intentions, the commander-in-chief, whose situation was still extremely critical, wrote to Crittenden, urging him to make some arrangement with Garrison for sending five hundred Americans to Nicaragua as soon as possible on his company's steamers. In doing this, Walker naturally avoided consulting Rivas and his cabinet. Garrison received the proposal kindly, and every steamer to San Juan del Sur brought its quota of recruits, practically all of whom were carried at the company's expense. At length, in December, 1855, Garrison sent his son, accompanied by Edmund Randolph and C. J. McDonald, to Granada to make arrangements with Walker for securing some return for the assistance rendered; for it must not be supposed that such a practical, self-made business man as the San Francisco manager had been acting from altruistic motives. With young Garrison, as an earnest of his father's friendly attitude, came a hundred more recruits, who, as usual, received free passage. Randolph now revealed to Walker the agreement which Crittenden had made with Garrison, whereby the American forces were to be recruited. The Transit Company, he explained, had failed to fulfil its obligations to the State and had forfeited its right to corporate existence. It was proposed, therefore, that Walker should secure the annulment of its charter and obtain a new concession for the benefit of Garrison and the New York manager, Charles Morgan, whom Garrison proposed to associate with himself. In return for this favour Morgan and Garrison were to transport to Nicaragua free of charge any and every person who cared to go. The why and the wherefore of the visit of McDonald and of the loan of twenty thousand dollars in October now becomes readily apparent. Garrison was doing this at the expense of the company but for his own personal benefit.

It was generally known in the United States during the autumn of 1855 that the Transit Company was rendering Walker valuable services, and the prevailing opinion was that the expedition had been fitted out by the officials of this corporation in the hope of introducing a stable element into Nicaragua and thus putting an end to the revolutions that were so injurious to the company's interests. It has already been shown, however, that this idea was erroneous. The real explanation of the favours shown Walker involves a sketch of certain stock manipulations on Wall Street and of the previous relations of the company with the Nicaraguan government. For many months the stock of the Accessory Transit Company had served as a football on the New York exchange. Cornelius Vanderbilt, the first president, had retired from this position in 1853, on the eve of departing for his famous tour of Europe, and was succeeded by Charles Morgan. During Vanderbilt's absence Morgan and Garrison had manipulated the business so as to make large sums out of stock fluctuations and incidentally to occasion considerable financial losses to Vanderbilt, who was then abroad and unable to help himself. After Vanderbilt's return he is said to have sworn to get revenge. "I won't sue you," he is quoted as saying to his rivals, "for the law is too slow. I will ruin you." At once there began a struggle for control of the company, with the odds in favour of Vanderbilt. But there was another factor to be reckoned with, and that was the republic of Nicaragua. The corporation was a creature of that government, and in return for its right to exist as a legal person it owed certain duties to the State. When the company received its first charter in 1849, it agreed to pay annually the sum of ten thousand dollars until the canal had been completed; and for the exclusive right of navigating the interior waters and opening a line of transit it agreed to pay ten per cent of the profits accruing from its transisthmian traffic. From 1849 to 1855 inclusive the corporation had paid regularly the annual dues of ten thousand dollars, but it had never seen fit to pay any of the ten per cent quota of profits, for the stated reason that no profits had accrued. Against this assertion the Nicaraguan government had no recourse, as the company's methods of bookkeeping gave the State nothing on which to base a claim. The number of passengers and the shipments of freight and specie were known to be very large, but the officials were careful to keep no records in the country that would enable the government to prepare a balance sheet. Expenditures for permanent improvements, such as a pier at Virgin Bay, were said to have come out of current receipts. It was also alleged that the company had fixed a low rate for conveying passengers through Nicaragua with the distinct purpose of eliminating profits and had made its ocean rates high enough to secure an ample return on both its marine and trans-isthmian business. Just a week before Walker landed in Nicaragua the Legitimist government had appointed two agents to proceed to New York and attempt to settle the claim by negotiation or arbitration. The Nicaraguan agents, perhaps without any definite idea of what was due the State, claimed thirty-five thousand dollars. The company offered to settle for thirty thousand, thus admitting that it had avoided the payment of its just dues; but the offer was rejected. Both sides then agreed to refer the matter to special commissioners for arbitration. The company, however, did all it could to delay matters, and before the commissioners could begin their work the Nicaraguan government changed hands, Walker having taken possession of the capital. This caused further proceedings toward adjusting the controversy to be abandoned.

This was the situation when Morgan and Garrison began to court the favour of Walker. Seeing that they were about to be ousted from the control of the company, they proposed to use Walker and checkmate their powerful rival. Their plan was simple; the filibuster commander, by virtue of his authority, was to use the government's claim against the Transit Company as a ground for annulling its charter and confiscating its property, while Morgan and Garrison, in return for the aid they had given and were to give to Walker, were to receive the property of the defunct corporation and a charter constituting them a new company for doing a transportation business within the territory of Nicaragua. Such was the plot which had germinated in the brains of unscrupulous captains of industry seeking to thwart the designs of an equally unscrupulous rival. When the scheme was broached to Walker he had no alternative but to become a party to the transaction. To refuse meant no more recruits or supplies from the States; it meant defeat and probably death. To accept meant growing strength, victory, glory, the realization of his fondest ambitions. "We have the power and have helped you; you have the power, now help us," was virtually the ultimatum of the steamship managers. Walker consented with no qualms of conscience. His legal training enabled him to find justification in law for every step of the procedure. . . .

Walker in this way repaid the favours he had been receiving from the company's two managers. He had acted partly from a feeling of obligation and partly from a feeling of necessity. Without the opportune aid from this source his expedition would long ago have ended in failure. To Morgan and Garrison he owed most of his present success, and he had placed them in a position where they could aid him still more and enable him to reach .

the goal of his ambitions. But unfortunately for his cause, he had at the same time raised up a terrible enemy in the person of Vanderbilt. He could not foresee, of course, when he entered into the scheme suggested by Randolph, that Vanderbilt was soon to come to the head of the company and lend his assistance as Morgan had done. It would have paid him to cast his fortunes with the stronger party, and when the plans were made Walker probably thought that he was doing so, for Morgan and Garrison then represented the "ins," while Vanderbilt was an "out." Even as Walker and Randolph worked on the new charter the tables were turned in Wall Street, and they found, when it was too late, that they really had cast their fortunes with the "outs." Vanderbilt was able to influence the filibusters' fortunes, for good or ill, tenfold more effectively than his rivals, and from the day that he was tricked things were in a bad way for the Americans in Nicaragua.

When the news of the transaction reached Vanderbilt he was greatly enraged. On March 17, and again on March 26, he addressed long letters to Secretary Marcy, urging that the government intervene and protect the property of American citizens in Nicaragua. But it was now the government's turn to laugh. There was small comfort from the State Department for a corporation that a few weeks before had sneered at the neutrality laws and defied the government's officers. Vanderbilt could not shift the blame of aiding Walker on the shoulders of Charles Morgan, as his correspondence shows that he tried to do, for Marcy knew that both men were tarred with the same brush. The government had been told by White that it had nothing to do with this company, which took into consideration only the State of Nicaragua. Newspapers now hurled this back into the teeth of Vanderbilt and White, and jocularly referred them to Nicaragua for relief.

On Wall Street the news of Walker's action created amazement. Financiers at first refused to believe the report, but it was sufficient to cause a panic among the company's stockholders, who rushed to see who could get out first. The stocks had been slowly advancing ever since the new government in Nicaragua had appeared firmly established. On January 1, 1856, they were quoted at 18; on February 14 at 23¼; on March 13, the day before the news reached the Street, the closing price was 22½. On the next day five thousand shares were sold and the price fell to 19¼; on the 18th it fell to 13, and during the preceding four days fifteen thousand shares had changed hands. Men in the Street suspected the real reason for Walker's action, but knowing Vanderbilt's power they could hardly believe the filibuster leader foolhardy enough to match strength with him. The financial editor of the *Herald* declared that Wall Street regarded Walker as a fool and a knave. "The great mass of the American people sympathize deeply with the present government of Nicaragua and will regret to find that its gallant head has perilled its hitherto bright prospects. It will be seen that it is in Mr. Vanderbilt's power to kill off the new government by opening another route and thus cutting off Walker's communications with San Francisco and New York."

Vanderbilt immediately announced the withdrawal of the company's ocean steamers, and as Morgan was not yet ready with his new line the interests of Walker were at once put in jeopardy. For six weeks there were no steamers for Nicaraguan ports, and the filibusters received no reinforcements or supplies. Garrison did try to keep the steamers running from San Francisco to San Juan del Sur after Vanderbilt had withdrawn the vessels from the Atlantic. His scheme was thwarted, however, for Vanderbilt sent an agent from Panama with orders to intercept any of the company's steamers headed for the Nicaraguan port and order them to Panama, where they were to transfer their passengers to the Atlantic by rail. This was done in the case of two steamers, and the Transit for the time being was closed. . . .

COTTON AND WHEAT IN ANGLO-AMERICAN TRADE AND POLITICS, 1846–1852[1] *Thomas P. Martin*

By 1846 the cotton of the South and the wheat of the North and West had come to be symbolic of certain great interests in those sections which during the second and third quarters of the nineteenth century played important and at times decisive parts in Anglo-American relations. Cotton, for example, was to many people both at home and abroad chiefly the product of slave labor in the southern states; while wheat and agricultural produce in general in the North and West was the product of free labor. Slave grown cotton from the southern states had also a certain stigma attached to it, in the minds of many people, because it had long enjoyed comparatively free access to the British market, where it held a commanding position; while "free grown" agricultural produce, especially wheat, had been excluded from those markets to what was believed to be an injurious degree by the corn laws, which were not repealed until 1846 and not finally disposed of until 1849. Other interests might be mentioned. Therefore, it should be understood that the writer may not limit himself strictly to cotton and wheat in this discussion.

With respect to supplies of raw cotton for her great manufacturing districts, Great Britain was definitely and vitally dependent upon the United States, and had been so since about 1823 when John Gladstone, the father of William E. Gladstone, began to warn George Canning, the member of Parliament for Liverpool, that the situation was dangerous. . . .

How far southern politicians and statesmen acted after 1828 on the knowledge that Great Britain was seriously and even vitally dependent upon their constituents for supplies of raw cotton remains in large part to be shown. But it seems not unlikely that northerners, keenly aware of the potence of the weapon in the hands of the southerners and afraid of the possible consequences of its use, presumed too much and allowed their fears and suspicions to stand in the place of realities. Northern antislavery leaders soon alleged that southern slaveholders in control of the government were conducting the business of the state department, in commercial negotiations,

---

[1] *The Journal of Southern History*, I, No. 3 (August, 1935), 293–319. Reprinted with permission.

in their own interest and grossly neglecting the agricultural interests of the free labor sections of the North and West.

During the 1830's the British cotton industry, which was rapidly expanding and keeping pace with the extension of cotton culture in the South, suffered from high prices whenever the American cotton crop fell short of expectations; and in 1838–1839 the evil was greatly aggravated when Nicholas Biddle and some southern associates—planters, they were called—attempted with some success to corner the cotton market and to charge exorbitant prices. A great outburst of feeling arose in cotton trade and financial circles and disclosed a situation not unlike that of 1822, when the East Indian traders and their friends, the manufacturers, allied themselves with the antislavery movement. A British India Society was organized, June 1, 1839, with George Thompson as secretary but with substantial cotton interest support, to promote cotton growing by free labor in India. By the time James G. Birney and Henry B. Stanton arrived, a year later, to attend the first general antislavery convention, Thompson had covered the country; and a large section of British antislavery public opinion, at least, was prepared to accept Joshua Leavitt's suggestion, conveyed by Birney and Stanton and later argued at length by John Curtis of Ohio, that the repeal of the corn laws would strengthen antislavery in the north-central states.

In time the cotton crisis of 1839 passed while Great Britain weltered through various adverse conditions which prolonged the depression until 1841. Good seasons and the westward extension of cotton culture in the United States through the South into Texas restored abundant supplies at low prices and made possible another expansion of the British cotton industry through the erection of many new mills in the north of England. The trade promptly forgot Biddle's speculation and the precariousness of its position with reference to an adequate supply of raw cotton in the event of short crops in America and became indifferent to the work of the British India Society. Thompson's flaming speeches, in so far as they were noticed at all, were dismissed simply as so much antislavery twaddle.

By 1846 the day of reckoning was at hand. The cotton cloth markets, especially those in India, had become "saturated" with goods poured in at declining prices. Two consecutive short crops in the United States, those of 1845 and 1846, had produced first an exhaustion of surplus stocks of raw cotton on hand and next a sudden realization in the autumn of 1846 that the speculative rise in prices, evident in September, would continue to the point of stopping purchases for consumption by the mills. A corresponding rise in the price of cotton cloth was impossible. Orders would cease to come in and manufacturers would refuse to build up stocks of expensive goods. By late November, 1846, the situation was generally understood, and the question of the British raw cotton supply was thrown into politics along with antislavery, the latter being used by the cotton interest to promote its own selfish ends. . . .

An unusually large and productive cotton crop in the southern states in 1849 gave relief from the protracted dearth and high prices; consumers' markets presented a good demand; bread was again plentiful and cheap;

and the business depression was lifted as unemployed thousands of people went back to work. But the British cotton trade had learned a lesson; and many petitions were sent to Parliament in 1850 requesting that measures be taken to promote the cultivation of cotton in India. The British East India Company stood opposed to the movement, which was hardly less than an indictment of that company's policy over many years; and John Bright served notice at once that, when the company should come to seek a renewal of its charter, which would expire on April 30, 1854, there would be an accounting. What was wanted from India was cotton; and it was cotton that the East India Company had failed to supply in satisfactory qualities and quantities.

The grain crop failures of 1845 in Europe and in Great Britain were but the beginning of a series of calamities to the food crops of the Old World, the momentous effects of which can hardly be set forth satisfactorily in a single approach or within the limits of a single article. Cheap bread in particular as well as cheap food in general was a factor in British industrial and social life somewhat analogous to cheap raw cotton and rather more of social than industrial significance. In the United States, the matter of foreign markets for surplus agricultural produce, especially breadstuffs, assumed a new importance in the late thirties, because of the rapidly increasing production of the Northwest. . . .

The blow fell in 1845, when bad harvests prevailed over all western Europe as well as the British Isles; and a potato blight equally widespread combined with the bad harvest to create a situation which both Graham and Peel recognized as one calling for the total repeal of the corn laws. This is not the place to tell of the political struggle in Great Britain which eventuated in that repeal; but it should be noted that contemporaneously the new Democratic administration in the United States strove for a reduction of the Whig tariff of 1842 and eventually enacted (July 30) the Walker "revenue" tariff of 1846. Contemporaneously, also, the Oregon question, which had threatened war between the two countries, was settled.

The American farmers were therefore placed in a very favorable position. As soon as news of the food crisis in Great Britain arrived in American ports, prices of agricultural produce of all kinds began to rise; and in the end it was estimated that the produce of 1845 brought to those farmers an increase of income amounting to about $170,000,000. This "streak of luck," in addition to the better times arising from the moderate increase in the general price level of 1843 and 1844, served to cancel many of their most pressing obligations and to prepare them for future prosperity; or, for adversity, if the predictions of the Whigs, that foreign demand was temporary and deceptive, had come true.

Unhappily for themselves, the American Whigs were, especially in 1845 and 1846, arguing against fate. In reality a new era had dawned in the agricultural history of the western world. In the British Isles and in western Europe, the normal condition was coming to be scarcity instead of plenty in the supply of home grown food; while in the American West the reverse was the rule; and there rose, in spite of the food production of Baltic and Black Sea countries, a more or less constant foreign demand for American agricultural produce.

The food situation in Great Britain at the end of the harvest of 1846 was soon seen to be much worse than it had been twelve months earlier. The harvest was not only very bad, the potato rot was worse, in western Europe as well as the British Isles; and there were no reserves of food supplies left over from the last year. Again it seemed that relief must come chiefly from America—not that America was expected to supply all the food required, but enough to prevent a ruinous rise of prices. Apparently there was no general apprehension or fear of an approaching crisis, for farmers and country dealers and millers throughout both the British Isles and western Europe freely disposed of their stocks at the unusually good prices prevailing during the autumn and winter of 1846–1847, and the consumption of food in the great industrial centers and on public works and railroad construction went on as usual.

In the United States, the Democratic low-tariff press, to the great chagrin of the Whig high-tariff press, hailed the bad harvest abroad as a godsend, declaring that there probably never was a time when a combination of circumstances conspired to throw, to such an extent, into the lap of the western country the surplus wealth of England and Europe in exchange for its produce. At the same time, however, the American public was cautioned against the alarmist reports which had been given out by such papers as the London *Times*, with evil purpose later admitted; and American farmers characteristically marketed their produce on a limited scale during the fall and winter while prices continued to rise, doing exactly the reverse of what was meanwhile being done in Great Britain and on the Continent. Thus there was held in the interior, until after the close of navigation, great quantities of wheat which could not be shipped to the seaboard until spring.

Over all western Europe and the British Isles, the stage was set for catastrophe. In the spring, to the great astonishment of intelligent people everywhere, there began an influx of country buyers (instead of sellers) of foodstuffs; for country stocks had been exhausted by the overselling of the previous autumn, and the rural and country town populations were in some cases threatened with starvation. By the middle of April, 1847, prices were rising. Ships set out to all possible sources, reports from America were scanned for evidences of the expected spring shipments, and fresh inquiries were made. But spring was unusually late, the northern waterways were still locked with ice, and the Atlantic seaboard was bare. Indeed, the price of bread in New York had risen so much that charitable organizations and the poor were threatened likewise with starvation if relief did not soon arrive. When these conditions became known in Great Britain, a veritable panic, the "corn panic" of 1847, struck with great force and affected the Continent as well. Industry curtailed its activities, public works were suspended, the Government terminated the Irish relief, and unemployment and distress became general. The consumption of and demand for food were greatly reduced; and the prices of breadstuffs naturally fell from great speculative heights to more "reasonable" levels—to an average price comparable with that of 1846.

In the United States there was all the excitement imaginable at the extraordinary demand for agricultural produce. On the arrival of the *Hibernia* with British news to May 19, 1847, the price of flour soared to ten dollars a barrel, in spite of the large shipments which were at length coming from the interior; but dealers became alarmed and refused for the most part to engage in transactions for flour at more than nine dollars a barrel. In-cautious speculators lost heavily, of course, when the price slumped, as it did abroad, when the first paroxysm of demand had passed; but their losses were slight loss to the country. At the somewhat lower but still very high prices which soon prevailed, the remainder of the produce of the American harvest of 1846 changed hands, leaving in the pockets of farmers, brokers, dealers, merchants, shippers and others in the United States an immense amount of cash representing the excess value of exports over imports.

Good harvests returned to the British Isles and the Continent in 1847; and the prices of agricultural produce declined in proportion to the nar-rowing of the margin between supply and demand, but they remained well above the average price of 1843–1844 in the United States. They were only a little lower on the average in 1849—still well above the levels of 1843–1844. And the protectionists in the United States did not fail to make the most of their opportunity to repeat the old dire predictions that American foodstuffs could not compete abroad with those of the Black Sea and Baltic regions. But the American "wheat interest," invigorated by its recent experi-ence, since 1842, was not unduly discouraged, and it retained its faith in an early return of that foreign demand, which though it might be small would be a leaven in the current prices of American breadstuffs. In this it was not disappointed. Industrial recovery abroad gradually increased the consump-tion of foodstuffs by the people; and in the fall of 1849 there began a new upturn of prices of agricultural produce in the United States which con-tinued, with occasional interruptions (as in 1851), until a high peak was reached in 1855. A shary decline from this high point followed in 1856; but a still higher peak was attained in 1857, on the eve of the panic of that year.

The experiences of 1847 showed conclusively, if those of 1845 and 1846 did not, that cheap and rapid transportation overland during the winter as well as other seasons was the greatest and most pressing need, if the surplus agricultural produce of the West was to bring to the country the fullest returns obtainable, after the repeal of the British corn laws. Northern canals and rivers were useless during the stoppage of navigation by ice; and through them rapid transit was impossible under any conditions. . . .

It is unnecessary to repeat the familiar story of the rivalries of the eastern cities, southern seaboard as well as northern, for the trade of the West and of the development of the American railway net. It is here in-tended only to call attention to the underlying force—the attraction between complementary sections of the Old World and of the New, primarily the British food-consuming industrial section, on the one hand, with dry goods, hardware, railway iron, etc., to exchange for food and raw materials, and the American agricultural West, on the other, with a "ruinous" surplus of food (that which the "home markets" of the protectionists could not absorb at fair prices) which could be exchanged for much needed manufactured goods and railway material. This force, the foundations of which had been decried by interested protectionists on both sides of the Atlantic, was not so intermittent as those who are too much imbued with the protectionist propaganda of the time would tell us in their version of history. Thanks to the increasing industrialization of Europe and to the westward movement or extension of agricultural activities and populations in the United States, it had gathered such strength by the end of 1852 that the protectionists in both countries had to disband and await some national calamity, like the outbreak of the War for Southern Independence, to renew their efforts. . . .

Therefore, one may say that by 1852 the people of the Mississippi valley had established their wheat (and related) trade on a sound basis, not only with the East and the South but with Great Britain and the Continent, and were receiving in return foreign as well as domestic merchandise. Their freight was carried on railway lines built in response to the needs of that trade; while the telegraph brought instant communication with the seaboard and other parts of the Union. The laying of a trans-Atlantic cable became merely a question of time.

It seems impossible to overestimate the significance of this development of the West, after the repeal of the British corn laws; it is comparable in some ways to that of the South, after the invention of the cotton gin, fifty-three years earlier. The railroad building alone revolutionized life in the East, not to mention the West; for it made possible country dairying (putting an end to the feeding of cows on swill in the city), poultry raising, and truck farming on a large scale throughout the seaboard states having large urban populations to feed. Railroads permitted the continuance of important branches of business through the winter and, with the telegraph, helped to smooth out extreme seasonal variations and resultant violent speculation. In value and volume, the wheat (and related) trade of the Mississippi valley came to equal and rival the cotton trade of the South; and in such cities as Boston, New York, Philadelphia, and Baltimore there arose new sets of commission merchants, brokers, bankers, wholesalers, and others who catered especially to the needs of the West; while the interests of those whose business had hitherto been largely confined to the South were in numerous cases extended to the West. Capital investment, eastern as well as British and European, went into the railroads and lands of the West, some of it being shifted from the South where it had earlier taken the form of loans to planters for the purchase of slaves as well as land. Thus southern connections with other sections at home and abroad were not necessarily weakened; they rapidly became relatively less important than they had formerly been; and the western antislavery "wheat interest" of Joshua Leavitt's dream of less than a score of years before was now able to make itself felt in politics in such ways as to foreshadow the end of the dominance of the cotton and slaveholding interests in the affairs of the nation.

The developments and the changes in the relative positions of the cotton and wheat interests in the affairs of the United States, the changes in Great Britain and on the Continent which had in part induced developments and changes in America, and the shifting tides of world politics naturally had their direct and indirect effects on the course of Anglo-American diplomatic relations. . . .

During the strenuous times of bad harvest, potato famine, deficient supplies of raw cotton, and "corn panic" of 1847, Palmerston found no occasion for any violent diplomatic collisions with the United States. Instead, he exercised in hardly exceptionable manner good offices during the war between the United States and Mexico, refrained from interference in the Californias and Texas and disavowed interest in those regions when pointed inquiries came from America, assisted George Bancroft and Henry Labouchere in bringing the British navigation laws into accord with the navigation laws of the United States, and pressed the rights of free colored British citizens in the southern states only so far as to ascertain that it was in fact impossible for the United States government to control the people of the South in a matter which they considered vital. At his suggestion the masters of British vessels and others in British possessions in the West Indies and North America were warned of the consequences which free colored persons must expect to suffer on visiting the southern states; and he informed the protesting executive committee of the British and Foreign Anti-Slavery Society, though he had every reason to suppose they would not be satisfied, that nothing further could be done for the present to relieve the situation. Also, he seems to have recognized that it was important that cordial relations be maintained with the United States until it could be seen whether the Walker "Revenue" tariff, so greatly prized by the British free traders, was on a secure basis. Secretary Walker's friendly disposition toward British trade with Mexico during the American occupation was appreciated.

On the other hand, the British foreign office acted much in accordance with the old Castlereagh and Canning policy regarding the American littoral from the southernmost boundary of the United States to Cape Horn and the western coasts—to forestall as much as possible the penetration of Yankee influence and the development of Yankee control in those quarters. The aim was to do this as quietly as might be and without unnecessarily arousing American sensibilities. But Lord Aberdeen's recent co-operation with Guizot in proceedings distinctly reminiscent of the spirit of the old Holy Alliance had aroused them; and President Polk, in his first annual message to Congress not only reiterated and affirmed the Monroe Doctrine but declared "that no future European colony or dominion shall, with our consent, be planted or established on any part of the North American continent."

Polk's feeling and utterance were mild in comparison with what was felt and done in New Granada. Until the summer of 1846, when Palmerston returned to the foreign office, the New Granadans had made unyielding resistance to the efforts of the United States to secure a treaty of commercial advantage, though they had noted with much misgiving the extension of British encroachments from the Bay Islands and the Mosquito Shore southward toward the Isthmus of Panama. When this was followed on the other side by British and Spanish aid to Juan José Flores, who was seeking to re-establish himself in Ecuador, the New Granadans lost their courage. Turning to the United States as the lesser of two evils, they yielded on all points with respect to the commercial treaty and even added an article (Article XXXV) requiring the United States to guarantee "positively and

212

efficaciously ... the perfect neutrality" of the whole isthmian area from its southernmost limits to the Costa Rican border.

The mounting alarms and fears of the New Granadans, their sudden scamper to the rear of the Yankee camp, and the entire willingness of the United States to protect them in the sovereignty of their own territory naturally caused a concentration of British effort about the termini of the prospective route of a Nicaraguan canal—the mouth of the St. John river and the Gulf of Fonseca; and in those regions there were moves and counter-moves, in the course of which the British actually resorted to violence, particularly in the bombardment of Greytown and the seizure of Tigre Island. Diplomatic sparring and the exigencies of the presidential election campaign of 1848 deferred the final settlement of the issue until the new Whig administration felt obliged to undertake it in the latter part of 1849.

There could be no long delay. The gold rush to California had intensified American interest in the isthmian routes; and Secretary John M. Clayton and President Zachary Taylor had to take the initiative and if possible secure creditable results before the congressional elections of 1850 should come on. For (as the British foreign office well knew, through Crampton) the Democrats, now in opposition, were eager to seize upon any issue that would divert public attention from the "Wilmot Proviso." The slavery issue threatened to split not only the Democratic party but the nation. On the other hand, British North American wheat interests were pressing persistently and even belligerently (it was feared the annexationists would make trouble) for a favorable, reciprocal trade arrangement with the United States; while American Whig protectionists bitterly opposed them and attempted to draw the red herring of the New England fishery interest in privileges along the British northeastern coasts across the trail.

It is indeed difficult to say which side had the advantage in such a welter of conflicting interests as that described above. But it is worthy of note that during the years 1849–1850, when the crisis in Anglo-American relations over the Isthmian issue was reached and inconclusively adjusted, Great Britain was under no such pressing need for American raw cotton or agricultural produce (or both) as she had been during the years 1846–1847. It might be asked whether the result would have been different if she had been; but this is a question history cannot answer.

Perhaps the diplomatic was the least important phase of Anglo-American relations in the middle of the nineteenth century. Business recovery in 1848 and 1849 had been accompanied by large demands for articles which were the produce of slave labor—sugar and cotton; and these in turn had stimulated the African slave trade and had stirred antislavery interests to attempt as never before the abolition of slavery itself as the only way of putting an end to the slave trade; while the South, taking new courage from the fresh evidences of British dependence upon its plantations for supplies of raw cotton, had developed a sense of nationality which was destined to grow until cut short by the failure of the War for Southern Independence. It was a singular combination of sections and interests in Great Britain and the United States which was ultimately to defeat the aim of the South. As soon as the Fugitive Slave Law was passed, American abolitionists solicited funds of their British brethren who were supported, as has been shown, by the British cotton manufacturing interest which desired any way out of its vital dependence upon the United States for raw cotton supplies. An aggravation of the slave labor problem of the South, the limitation of slave territory, and the abolition of slavery itself—in short, an increase in the cost of cotton growing in the South to a point where large quantities of raw cotton could with profit be produced in other countries, particularly in British India, might deliver Great Britain from dangerous dependence. This was one aim. Another was to bring about the abolition of slavery for political and economic reasons peculiar to the United States. Still others might be mentioned, but further discussion falls outside the limits of this paper.

PRESIDENT TYLER'S VIEWS ON

HAWAII AND THE CHINA TRADE   *Document 1*

Message to Congress, December 30, 1842.

... The condition of those islands has excited a good deal of interest, which is increasing by every successive proof that their inhabitants are making progress in civilization and becoming more and more competent to maintain regular and orderly civil government....

Owing to their locality and to the course of the winds which prevail in this quarter of the world, the Sandwich Islands are the stopping place for almost all vessels passing from continent to continent across the Pacific Ocean. They are especially resorted to by the great number of vessels of the United States which are engaged in the whale fishery in those seas....

Just emerging from a state of barbarism, the Government of the islands is as yet feeble, but its dispositions appear to be just and pacific, and it seems anxious to improve the condition of its people by the introduction of knowledge, of religious and moral institutions, means of education, and the arts of civilized life.

It can not but be in conformity with the interest and wishes of the Government and the people of the United States that this community, thus existing in the midst of a vast expanse of ocean, should be respected and all its rights strictly and conscientiously regarded; and this must also be the true interest of all other commercial states. Far remote from the dominions of European powers, its growth and prosperity as an independent state may yet be in a high degree useful to all whose trade is extended to those regions; while its near approach to this continent and the intercourse which American vessels have with it, such vessels constituting five-sixths of all which annually visit it, could not but create dissatisfaction on the part of the United States at any attempt by another power, should such attempt be threatened or feared, to take possession of the islands, colonize them, and subvert the native Government. Considering, therefore, that the United States possesses so large a share of the intercourse with those islands, it is deemed not unfit to make the declaration that their Government seeks, nevertheless, no peculiar advantages, no exclusive control over the Hawaiian Government, but is content with its independent existence and anxiously wishes for its security and prosperity.... Under the circumstances I recommend to Congress to provide for a moderate allowance to be made out of the Treasury to the consul residing there, that in a Government so new and a country so remote American citizens may have respectable authority to which to apply for redress in case of injury to their persons and property, and to whom the Government of the country may also make known any acts committed by American citizens of which it may think it has a right to complain....

The importations into the United States from China are known to be large, having amounted in some years, as will be seen by the annexed tables, to $9,000,000. The exports, too, from the United States to China constitute an interesting and growing part of the commerce of the country. It appears that in the year 1841, in the direct trade between the two countries, the value of the exports from the United States amounted to $715,000 in domestic produce and $485,000 in foreign merchandise. But the whole amount of American produce which finally reaches China and is there consumed is not comprised in these tables, which show only the direct trade. Many vessels with American products on board sail with a primary destination to other countries, but ultimately dispose of more or less of their cargoes in the port of Canton....

Experience proves that the productions of western nations find a market to some extent among the Chinese; that that market, so far as respects the productions of the United States, although it has considerably varied in successive seasons, has on the whole more than doubled within the last ten years; and it can hardly be doubted that the opening of several new and important ports connected with parts of the Empire heretofore seldom visited by Europeans or Americans would exercise a favorable influence upon the demand for such productions....

Being of the opinion...that the commercial interests of the United States connected with China require at the present moment a degree of attention and vigilance such as there is no agent of this Government on the spot to bestow, I recommend to Congress to make appropriation for the compensation of a commissioner to reside in China to exercise a watchful care over the concerns of American citizens and for the protection of their persons and property....

SECRETARY OF THE NAVY UPSHUR
DISCUSSES COMMERCE AND THE NAVY,
DECEMBER 7, 1842   *Document 2*

... Nothing has occurred, since my last report, to interrupt the friendly relations of our country with the nations bordering on the Pacific coast of America. Our squadron has, at all times, ably and faithfully performed its duty; but it is much too small to render all the services expected of it, in that remote region. Every part of that vast ocean is traversed by our trading vessels, and in every part of it the protection of our naval flag is consequently required. The few ships allowed even to the largest squadron that we have ever sent to the Pacific, are not enough to guard our whaling interest alone. It can scarcely be expected that five or six vessels, most of which are of the smallest class, can properly protect our commerce and our people, along a coast of three thousand miles in extent, and throughout an ocean four thousand miles wide. I respectfully suggest that too little attention has heretofore been paid to the important interests of our country in the Pacific ocean. There is at this time, a stronger necessity than ever, for more strict vigilance and more active exertion on our part, to prevent other nations from subjecting our trade to injurious restrictions and embarrassments. The English settlers have, by their enterprise, nearly engrossed the trade from the Columbia river to the islands, so that our countrymen are as effectually cut off from it, as if they had no rights in that quarter. The people of various countries are rapidly forming settlements all along the shores of the Pacific, from Columbia river to the gulf of California; and this, too, with the countenance and support of their respective Governments. In the meantime, we are doing literally nothing for our own interests in that quarter. To those of our people who are inclined to settle there, we do not even hold out the encouragement of a reasonable expectation that we will protect them against the violence and injustice of other nations. A few small vessels, scarcely as many as we ought to keep constantly upon the coast of each of the South American nations on the Pacific—these, too, charged with duties which twice their number would not be able to perform, can offer but little aid or support to the infant settlements of our people, remote from each other, and demanding the constant presence of some protecting power. There are many considerations, connected with this subject, of deep importance in themselves, but which belong rather to other departments of the Government than to this. I advert to them only so far as to justify me in recommending a very large increase of the Pacific squadron.

In the East Indies we have only two ships, the frigate Constellation, Captain Kearny commanding the squadron, and the sloop-of-war Boston, Commander Long. It is owing more to our good fortune than to our strength, that our commerce has suffered no material interruption. That little squadron has done all that could have been expected of it, and it deserves much credit for its great vigilance and activity, and for the prudence and sound discretion with which Commodore Kearny has acquitted himself of the important trusts reposed in him.

On the coast of Africa we have *no* squadron. The small appropriation of the present year was believed to be scarcely sufficient to answer the pressing demands of more important stations; and hence no vessel has been equipped expressly for the African seas. The sloop-of-war Vandalia, Commander Ramsay, belonging to the Home Squadron, was assigned to that service in March last, and is still on the coast. The ratification of the treaty with England renders it necessary that a squadron of at least eighty guns should be assigned to that service.

216

I regret to say that, in consequence of the unprotected condition of our trade on that coast, several of our vessels have been captured by the natives, and their crews barbarously murdered. The last aggression of this sort was upon the schooner Mary Carver, Captain Farwell, in the district of Beribee, ninety miles south of Cape Palmas. Instructions have been given to Commander Ramsay to proceed to that point and demand such reparation as the circumstances of the case may require. This, however, will be at best but little satisfactory, since no chastisement which can be inflicted upon such savages can either do honor to our flag, or prevent other outrages of the like kind. Our commerce with Africa is rapidly increasing, and is well worthy of all the protection which it asks. This protection is to be derived, not from any terror which can be inspired by the destruction of a few miserable villages on the sea beach, but from the presence of armed vessels, able to *prevent*, as well as to punish, all violations of the rights and laws of fair trade.

* * *

When I had the honor to present to you the usual report from this department, at the commencement of the last session of Congress, I proceeded upon the idea that it was the settled policy of the Government gradually to increase the navy. Notwithstanding the favorable change which has since occurred in our foreign relations, and notwithstanding the present *unfavorable* condition of the public Treasury, I have seen no reason to believe that this policy is less approved now than heretofore, by the great body of our people. It is true that the circumstances in which we are now placed, render necessary very great modifications of the systems which would otherwise be proper; but the opinion is as general now as it ever has been, that a *suitable navy* is absolutely necessary to the protection of our trade, the security of our people, and the respectability of our Government. Fortunately, there is nothing in the circumstances of our country to render this in any degree a local question. Apart from the general proposition that what is best for the general interest should be regarded as best for the whole, there is a local and particular interest in nine tenths of our country which demands a respectable naval establishment.

The commercial towns on our seaboard, by which nearly all our foreign and coasting trade is conducted, have so immediate and direct an interest in the subject, as to render unnecessary any remarks upon that point. The various agricultural and manufacturing classes, scattered throughout the country, and connected with, and dependent upon, this trade, have an indirect interest, not less apparent. The great and increasing commerce of the lakes, although less exposed than that of the ocean, is yet far too important to be left undefended, even against the single power which may become its enemy. But the gulf of Mexico has peculiar claims. It is believed that there is not in the world, an equal amount of commercial and agricultural interest belonging to any one country, so much at the mercy of the most inconsiderable maritime force, as is that of the gulf of Mexico. Not only the States which lie immediately on that water, but all those whose streams enter into it, including the vast and fertile region of the Mississippi and its tributary waters, make this their chief channel of commerce. And we may properly add, also, no inconsiderable amount in the article of cotton, sent from Texas by means of the Red river, and paying tribute to our commercial agencies in its transit through our territory. . . .

It is to be borne in mind that nearly all this valuable trade is carried on through the gulf of Florida. I had the honor to present my views upon this subject, in a report which I made to the Senate, during the last session of Congress, but which was not acted on by that body. I respectfully refer to that document, as containing many suggestions connected with this inquiry, which I believe to be not wholly unworthy of public attention. I repeat here, only the well-known fact, that, in consequence of the strength of the gulf stream and trade-winds, there is virtually no passage for our trade eastward, on the south side of the Island of Cuba. It must, of necessity, pass through the Gulf of Florida—a narrow strait which can be effectually blockaded by two active steam-frigates, and probably by one. Even if a trading vessel should pass such a blockading force in the night, it would have but one path open to it for a great distance, and might, of course, be pursued with a certainty of being overtaken. It would not enjoy even the ordinary chances of a vessel escaping from a blockaded port, into a wide and open sea.

The facts to which I have thus adverted, show a striking peculiarity in our condition. The greatest portion of our commerce, confined to a single channel for some hundreds of miles, is exposed, in a peculiar manner, to any enemy having possession of the sea; and, what would render our condition still worse, if we be without a naval force, that commerce may be annihilated, at a cost which would not be felt by any tenth-rate maritime power!

If these views be correct, I am at a loss to perceive what portion of our country is not interested in them. To the States bordering on the gulf of Mexico, and to all those which use the Mississippi river as a channel of trade, the subject is of deep and daily increasing interest. So far as their prosperity depends on the outlet of the various productions of their country, they have but a single question to decide: Is, or is not, their commerce worth the cost of a naval power, adequate to protect it? . . .

. . . We must cherish our naval power, not as the institution of a day or of a year—not as a subject which we can lay aside, and take up again whenever we please, as the policy or the caprice of the moment may dictate, but as a great and permanent institution, worthy of a great people, and demanding the grave attention of Government—an institution resting upon a wise system, and worthy to be maintained in the spirit of a liberal, comprehensive, and stable policy.

These considerations forbid us to fall so far in the rear of other nations, and of the age in which we live, as to surrender our due share of the dominion of the seas. A commerce, such as ours, *demands* the protection of an adequate naval force. Our people, scattered all over the world, have a right to require the occasional presence of our flag, to give assurance to all nations that their country has both the will and the power to protect them. Our position among the nations is such as to leave us without excuse, if we voluntarily strip ourselves of a power which all other nations are anxious to grasp. Our forms of government and municipal institutions suggest that a naval force is our safest, and, perhaps, our only defence; and, as an additional recommendation, of no small weight, the expenditure which this defence requires, is to be made chiefly among our own people, encouraging their enterprise, invigorating their industry, and calling out the abundant and now almost hidden resources of our country.

DR. PETER PARKER PROPOSES
A PROTECTORATE OVER FORMOSA   *Document 3*

Dr. Parker to Secretary of State William B. Marcy, December 12, 1856.

... Were the three representatives of England, France and America, on presenting themselves at the Pei-ho, in case of their not being welcomed to Peking, to say [as a last resort], the French flag will be hoisted in Corea, the English again at Chusan, and the United States in Formosa, and there remain till satisfaction for the past and a right understanding for the future are granted; but, being granted, these possessions shall *instantly* be restored, negotiation would no longer be obstructed, and the most advantageous and desirable results to all concerned secured....

Dr. Parker to the State Department, February 12, 1857.

... The subject of Formosa is becoming one of great interest to a number of our enterprising fellow-citizens, and deserves more consideration from the great commercial nations of the West than it has yet received; and it is much to be hoped that the Government of the United States may not *shrink* from the *action* which the interests of humanity, civilization, navigation and commerce impose upon it in relation to Tai-Wan [Formosa], particularly the southeastern portion of it, at present inhabited by savages, to whose depraved cruelties we have every reason to believe many Europeans, and among them our own friends and countrymen, have fallen victims....

Dr. Parker to the State Department, March 10, 1857.

... In event of the establishment of a line of steamers between California, Japan and China, this source of supply of coal will be most advantageous. That the islands may not long remain a portion of the empire is possible; and in the event of its being severed from the empire politically, as it is geographically, that the United States should possess it is obvious, particularly as respects the great principle of the balance of power....

Great Britain has her St. Helena in the Atlantic, her Gibraltar and Malta in the Mediterranean, her Aden in the Red Sea, Mauritius, Ceylon, Penang and Singapore in the Indian Ocean, and Hongkong in the China Sea. If the United States is so disposed and can arrange for the possession of Formosa, England certainly cannot object....

If there ever was a State which has laid herself open to just reprisals it is China ... and in event of her persisting in this course, it seems clear that, by the acknowledged principles of international law, the United States have the right, if they have the inclination, to take Formosa by way of reprisal "until a satisfactory reparation should be made for injuries they have sustained." See Wheaton's *International Law*, p. 362. . . .

The State Department Replies.

. . . This country, you will constantly bear in mind, is not at war with the Government of China, nor does it seek to enter into that empire for any other purpose than those of lawful commerce, and for the protection of the lives and property of its citizens. . . .

SECRETARY OF STATE
DANIEL WEBSTER'S INSTRUCTIONS
TO CALEB CUSHING, MAY, 1843   *Document 4*

. . . Occurrences happening in China within the last two years have resulted in events which are likely to be of much importance, as well to the United States as to the rest of the civilized world. . . . The hostilities which have been carried on between that empire and England have resulted, among other consequences, in opening four important ports to English commerce, viz: Amoy, Ning-po, Shang-hai, and Fu-chow. . . .

A leading object of the mission in which you are now to be engaged is to secure the entry of American ships and cargoes into these ports in terms as favorable as those which are enjoyed by English merchants. . . .

As your mission has in view only friendly and commercial objects—objects, it is supposed, equally useful to both countries—the natural jealousy of the Chinese, and their repulsive feeling toward foreigners, it is hoped, may be in some degree removed or mitigated by prudence and address on your part. Your constant aim must be to produce a full conviction in the minds of the Government and the people, that your mission is entirely pacific; that you come with no purpose of hostility or annoyance; that you are a messenger of peace, sent from the greatest Power in America to the greatest Empire in Asia, to offer respect and good will, and to establish the means of friendly intercourse. . . .

You may expect to encounter, of course, if you get to Peking the old question of the Kotou.[1] In regard to the mode of managing this matter, much must be left to your discretion, as circumstances may occur. All pains should be taken to avoid the giving of offence, or the wounding of the national pride; but, at the same time, you will be careful to do nothing which may seem, even to the Chinese themselves, to imply any inferiority on the part of your Government, or anything less than perfect independence of all nations. . . .

It cannot be doubted that the immense power of England in India must

---

[1] The kowtow was a ceremony that involved, in part, the knocking of one's forehead on the ground before the Emperor.—Editor.

be regarded by the Chinese Government with dissatisfaction, if not with some degree of alarm. You will take care to show strongly how free the Chinese Government may well be from all jealousy arising from such causes toward the United States. Finally, you will signify, in decided terms and a positive manner, that the Government of the United States would find it impossible to remain on terms of friendship and regard with the Emperor, if greater privileges or commercial facilities should be allowed to the subject of any other Government than should be granted to the citizens of the United States. . . .

AARON H. PALMER, COUNSELLOR OF THE
SUPREME COURT AND DIRECTOR OF THE
AMERICAN AND FOREIGN AGENCY OF NEW YORK,
DISCUSSES THE PROBLEM OF TRADE
WITH JAPAN WITH SECRETARY OF STATE
JAMES BUCHANAN, NOVEMBER 28, 1846   *Document 5*

I have conducted during the last 15 years an agency in this city, under the above style, restricted to agency and commission transactions, and to making known in foreign countries the superior skill and ability of our mechanics, machinists, and manufacturers in some of the most prominent branches of American industry, particularly in the construction of steam-vessels, engines, and machinery generally. . . . This has been the means of eliciting a great variety of orders for many objects of our industry, including a large order from the Pasha of Egypt, and for several steamers that have been constructed here for foreign account. . . . This general distribution of those circulars, etc., has led me to an extensive correspondence with many remote countries of the East; and a desire has been manifested on different occasions, by several eastern princes, to open commercial relations and make treaties with the United States. . . . From such correspondence . . . I have been enabled to collect a mass of valuable geographical and commercial statistics, and much important information, relative to the movements and progress of civilization, trade, and commerce in the eastern hemisphere, which I am now desirous of placing at the disposal of our government, and render profitably available to the commerce, navigation, and industry of the country, by a special mission to the East. . . .

I now propose to offer some brief authentic information and details respecting the present state, productions, and commerce of each [of the countries of the East to which my missives have been sent], showing the importance and expediency of a special mission being sent by the government of the United States to open and extend our commercial relations with those countries. . . .

JAPAN. With regard to Japan, I have procured with great care and diligence, from official sources in Holland, personally, in 1839, from the journals and reports of the latest Dutch residents at Nangasaki and missions to Yedo, and from other reliable accounts and narratives, a variety of interesting facts and particulars, attesting the superior people above all the surrounding Asiatic nations. . . .

The Dutch have always found their trade with Japan to be very profitable; and in order to secure the exclusive monopoly thereof to their factory, it has been their uniform policy to oppose and frustrate all attempts of other nations to open intercourse with that country. The people evince an increasing desire for more enlarged intercourse with foreigners, and the government has gradually relaxed its arbitrary and rigid restrictions on their trade and intercourse with the Dutch and Chinese since the opium war with China. . . . The English and Russians have at various times attempted to open trade with Japan, but without success. . . .

In addition to the privileges of commercial intercourse with Yedo, Nangasaki, Kagósima, Ohosaka, and the other principal ports, it would be very desirable for our government to obtain permission for the numerous American whale ships employed in the lucrative fishery off the coast of Japan to enter any of the ports and harbors of the empire for repairs or refreshments only, and for hospitality and succor in cases of stress of weather or shipwreck. . . .

INSTRUCTIONS TO COMMODORE PERRY, NOVEMBER 5, 1852 *Document 6*

. . . I am directed by the President to explain the objects of the expedition, and to give some general directions as to the mode by which those objects are to be accomplished.

Since the islands of Japan were first visited by European nations, efforts have constantly been made by the various maritime powers to establish commercial intercourse with a country whose large population and reputed wealth hold out great temptations to mercantile enterprise. . . . All these attempts, however, have thus far been unsuccessful; the permission enjoyed for a short period by the Portuguese to trade with the islands, and that granted to Holland to send annually a single vessel to the port of Nagasaki, hardly deserving to be considered exceptions to this remark.

China is the only country which carries on any considerable trade with these islands.

So rigorously is this system of exclusion carried out, that foreign vessels are not permitted to enter their ports in distress, or even to do an act of kindness to their own people. . . .

When vessels are wrecked or driven ashore on the islands their crews are subjected to the most cruel treatment. . . .

Every nation has undoubtedly the right to determine for itself the extent to which it will hold intercourse with other nations. The same law of nations, however, which protects a nation in the exercise of this right imposes upon her certain duties which she cannot justly disregard. Among these duties none is more imperative than that which requires her to succor and relieve those persons who are cast by the perils of the ocean upon her shores. This duty is, it is true, among those that are denominated by writers on public law imperfect, and which confer no right on other nations to exact their performances; nevertheless, if a nation not only habitually and systematically disregards it, but treats such unfortunate persons as if they were the most atrocious criminals, such nations may justly be considered as the most common enemy of mankind. . . .

It can hardly be doubted that if Japan were situated as near the continent of Europe or of America as it is to that of Asia, its government would long since have been either treated as barbarians, or been compelled to respect those usages of civilized states of which it receives the protection. . . .

Recent events—the navigation of the ocean by steam, the acquisition and rapid settlement by this country of a vast territory on the Pacific, the discovery of gold in that region, the rapid communication established across the isthmus which separates the two oceans—have practically brought the countries of the east in closer proximity to our own; although the consequences of these events have scarcely begun to be felt, the intercourse between them has already greatly increased, and no limits can be assigned to its future extension. . . .

The objects sought by this government are—

1. To effect some permanent arrangement for the protection of American seamen and property wrecked off these islands, or driven into their ports by stress of weather.

2. The permission to American vessels to enter one or more of their ports in order to obtain supplies of provisions, water, fuel, &c., or, in case of disasters, to refit so as to enable them to prosecute their voyage.

3. The permission to our vessels to enter one or more of their ports for the purpose of disposing of their cargoes by sale or barter. . . .

You will, therefore, be pleased to direct the commander of the squadron to proceed, with his whole force, to such point on the coast of Japan as he may deem most advisable, and there endeavor to open a communication with the government, and, if possible, to see the emperor in person, and deliver to him the letter of introduction from the President. . . .

If, after having exhausted every argument and every means of persuasion, the commodore should fail to obtain from the government any relaxation of their system of exclusion, or even any assurance of humane treatment of our ship-wrecked seamen, he will then change his tone, and inform them in the most unequivocal terms that it is the determination of this government to insist, that hereafter all citizens or vessels of the United States that may be wrecked on their coasts, or driven by stress of weather into their harbors shall, so long as they are compelled to remain there, be treated with humanity; and that if any acts of cruelty should hereafter be practised upon citizens of this country, whether by the government or by the inhabitants of Japan, they will be severely chastised. . . .

223

AMERICAN INVOLVEMENT IN AFRICA   Document 7

*Address of John Latrobe of Maryland to the Eleventh Annual Meeting of
the American Colonization Society, January, 1828.*

. . . Cape Palmas is that part of Africa where the coast, after pursuing a
course due East and West from the Bight of Biafra, bends in nearly a North-
West direction, and passing by Liberia, continues in an almost uninterrupted
line to Cape Roxo. The Island of Bulama, in the mouth of the Rio Grande,
is near the other extremity of the South-West Coast, within a short run from
the Cape de Verds, and one of the points of the coast most easily made by
vessels sailing from this country.

By possessing Cape Palmas, we would hold the commercial key of all the
South Coast of Africa, and the countries immediately in the interior, down as
far East as the Bight of Biafra; and a Colony there, would in a few years become a great depot for all the articles of foreign produce and manufacture,
which would be required by inhabitants of the nations Eastward of the settlement. . . . Were a settlement made at Cape Palmas, it would, like Mon-
rovia, soon become the resort of the surrounding nations; and merchants
would prefer leaving their goods at such a market than running the risks of
proceeding further Eastward, even with the hopes of enhanced profits.
Paths would first be made, highways would take their place, until the uncivilized nations of the Ivory Coast and the Gold Coast, passing by the feeble
settlements of the Cape Coast and d'Elmina, would resort to meet civilization
at the nearest point of safe approach, the Americo-African City at Cape
Palmas. A great and prosperous trade would be the consequence; and the
facilities of gain would soon fill the new settlement with industrious inhabitants. Besides the commercial advantages of Cape Palmas, its road and an-
chorage are said to be the best between Montserado and the Voltu; and the
surrounding country is rolling and fertile, intersected with numerous small
streams, fit for the erection of mills. Being the Southern extremity of the
South-West Coast, it will form also a natural boundary to that Empire,
which we all hope will one day arise in Africa. . . .

*Address of William M. Blackford to the Auxiliary Colonization Society of
Fredericksburg, Virginia, May, 1828.*

The germ of an Americo-African empire has been planted; and though
our Society should be dissolved to-morrow, it will flourish and expand until
it overshadows a continent. Already has the miniature Commonwealth of
Liberia impressed the natives with respect for the strength, and admiration
for the beauty of the institutions of civilized life. By the justice which has
marked its intercourse with them, the Colony has already attained an almost
boundless influence over the neighbouring tribes. The ascendency will be
maintained, and must increase, until tribe after tribe, subdued by the bland
influence of civilization and the simple power of the gospel, shall melt into

and become incorporated with the community. No cruel process of extermination, such as marked with blood the settlement of this country, will there be necessary. The settlers and natives are of the same race, and amalgamation, so far from being there impracticable, will be natural, and indeed unavoidable. Let no one, then, refuse his aid, because years, generations, perhaps, must pass away, before the vast outline can be filled up. We may not live to enjoy the blessings which must result from the accomplishment of the plan; but with a firm faith in its ultimate success, it is our duty to bring heart, hand, and purse, to secure to our children and to our children's children the rich inheritance. The plan *will* succeed.—It is, I verily believe, from Heaven—and Heaven's blessing will attend it in every stage of its progress. A glorious era is yet in store for Africa, when we shall have rendered unto her the things which are her's—an era, more glorious than any she has known, awaits America, when, from the Atlantic to the Pacific, there shall be none other than one happy, united, homogeneous race of freemen. Then in the fulness of time shall two mighty continents rise up to call him blessed, who gave the first impulse to the cause of African colonization!!

Comments of Commander Andrew H. Foote, U.S.N., 1854.

    ... There has thus been presented a view of Africa and of its progress, as far as its condition and advancement have had any relation to our country and its flag. How far its growth in civilization has been dependent on the efforts of America has been illustrated; and how essentially the naval interference of the United States has contributed to this end, has been made evident. It cannot escape notice that this progress must in the future depend on the same means and the same efforts. Our own national interests, being those of a commercial people, require the presence of a squadron. Under its protection commerce is secure, and is daily increasing in extent and value.

    It is impossible to say how lucrative this commerce may ultimately become. That the whole African coast should assume the aspect of Liberia, is perhaps not an unreasonable expectation. That Liberia will continue to grow in wealth and influence, is not improbable. There is intelligence among its people, and wisdom and energy in its councils. There is no reason to believe that this will not continue. Its position makes it an agricultural community. Other lands must afford its manufactures and its traders. There will, therefore, ever be on its shores a fair field for American enterprise.

    The reduction, or annihilation of the slave-trade, is opening the whole of these vast regions to science and legal commerce. Let America take her right share in them. It is throwing wide the portals of the continent for the entrance of Christian civilization. Let our country exert its full proportion of this influence; and thus recompense to Africa the wrongs inflicted upon her people, in which hitherto all nations have participated. ...

SECRETARY OF STATE BUCHANAN
DISCUSSES AN INTER-OCEANIC CANAL,
JUNE 1845

Document 8

... The United States have strong motives for viewing with interest any project which may be designed to facilitate the intercourse between the Atlantic and Pacific oceans. Within a few years past the scheme of a railroad or a canal across the Isthmus of Panama, has been much agitated and it is understood that surveys have been made for the purpose of testing its practicability.... As it is important to us that no other nation should obtain either an exclusive privilege or an advantage in regard to such a communication between the two oceans, you will lose no time in transmitting to the department any information upon the subject which you may be able to collect. You will also use your influence, should this become necessary, with the government of New Granada, to prevent it from granting privileges to any other nation which might prove injurious to the United States.

Mr. Acosta addressed several communications to Mr. Blackford for the purpose of exposing the encroachments of the British authorities upon that part of the territory of New Granada [Colombia] commonly called the Mosquito Shore. The communications contained no application from that government to the United States, but you may avail yourself of a proper opportunity to assure its Minister for Foreign Affairs, orally, that the information was highly interesting to this government, which can never be indifferent to anything that concerns the interest and prosperity of New Granada.

TREATY BETWEEN THE UNITED STATES
AND NEW GRANADA

Document 9

Ratifications exchanged on June 10, 1848.

...*Article XXXV*.... For the better understanding of the preceding articles, it is, and has been stipulated, between the high contracting parties, that the citizens, vessels and merchandise of the United States shall enjoy in the ports of New Granada, including those of the part of the granadian territory generally denominated *Isthmus of Panamá* from its southernmost extremity until the boundary of Costa Rica, all the exemptions, privileges and immunities, concerning commerce and navigation, which are now, or may hereafter be enjoyed by Granadian citizens ... and that this equality of favours shall be made to extend to the passengers, correspondence and merchandise of the United States in their transit across the said territory, from one sea to the other. The Government of New Granada guarantees to the Government of the United States, that the right of way or transit across the *Isthmus of Panamá*, upon any modes of communication that now exist, or that may be, hereafter, constructed, shall be open and free to the Government of the citizens of the United States, and for the transportation of any articles of produce, manufactures or merchandise, of lawful commerce, belonging to the citizens of the United States; that no other tolls or charges shall be levied or collected upon the citizens of the United States, or their said merchandise thus passing over any road or canal that may be made by the Government of New Granada, or by the authority of the same, than is under like circumstances levied upon and collected from the granadian citizens... nor shall the citizens of the United States be liable to any duties, tolls, or charges of any kind to which native citizens are not subjected for thus passing the said Isthmus. And, in order to secure to themselves the tranquil and constant enjoyment of these advantages, and as an especial compensation for the said advantages and for the favours they have acquired ... the United States guarantee positively and efficaciously to New Granada, by the present stipulation, the perfect neutrality of the before mentioned Isthmus, with the view that the free transit from the one to the other sea, may not be interrupted or embarrassed in any future time while this treaty exists; and in consequence, the United States also guarantee, in the same manner, the rights of sovereignty and property which New Granada has and possesses over the said territory....

THE AMERICAN INTERPRETATION OF
THE CLAYTON–BULWER TREATY   *Document 10*

Views expressed by Minister to Great Britain James Buchanan, September 11, 1855.

The undersigned ... has been instructed by the President again to call the attention of the Earl of Clarendon, her majesty's principal secretary of state for foreign affairs, to the Central American questions pending between the two governments, under the convention of the 19th April, 1850....

It was, in his opinion, the manifest intention of the convention to exclude both the contracting parties from holding or occupying, as well as from acquiring territorial possessions in Central America; and that this intention is not clothed in ambiguous language, but is set forth in explicit terms. The United States have bound themselves not to acquire any such possessions, and Great Britain has stipulated not to "assume or exercise any dominion over any part of Central America." Indeed, without such a reciprocal engagement, no mutuality whatever would have existed between the covenants of the contracting parties. Whilst the United States are excluded from occupying, colonizing, or exercising dominion over any part of Central America, it cannot be admitted that the same restriction, imposed in the very same language, is not equally applicable to Great Britain.

The President, therefore, confidently believes that Great Britain is bound by the first article of the convention of 1850 to withdraw from the possession she now holds of Ruatan and the other Central American islands on the coast of the State of Honduras, as well as from the territory in Central America between the Sibun and the Sarstoon, which has been encroached upon by her majesty's subjects. He is also of opinion that the possession of the British government at the Belize should be restricted to the limits and objects specified in the treaties between Great Britain and Spain of 1783 and 1786.

In regard to the alleged protectorate over the so-called Mosquito kingdom, the President has instructed the undersigned to say it was his confident belief that this protectorate had been finally disposed of by the convention. It is therefore much to his regret that he finds it is still continued as the basis of British dominion over an extensive region in Central America. . . .

The declaration of the British government, that this protectorate is only employed for the security of the rights of the Mosquito Indians, and that it is ready to abstain from further interference in that country whenever these rights can, in a proper manner, be guaranteed to them, cannot be recognized by the United States as having any foundation in the convention. The President considers this to be a question between Nicaragua and the Indians within its territory, with which neither Great Britain nor the United States has any right to interfere, except in friendly conference with the authorities of that State. . . .

YOUNG AMERICANS AND ANXIOUS PLANTERS

CHAPTER 6

*The Sectional Conflict
at the Water's Edge*

A *foreign policy of expansion served as a means of maintaining a working balance of power between the North and the South from the Louisiana Purchase until the Mexican War. But the struggle over the empire gained in acquiring Oregon and defeating Mexico led on to the Civil War. Early distrust and enmity, which appeared even before the opening of hostilities with Mexico, are noted by Professor John Hope Franklin in the first article. The antagonism became ever more bitter after the introduction in the Congress of the Wilmot Proviso of 1846, which proposed to prohibit slavery in any territory claimed from Mexico (Document 1). For a short time, as Professor J. D. P. Fuller reveals, the idea of taking all of Mexico served to ease the tension; but the peace treaty negotiated by Nicholas P. Trist (against the orders of President Polk) ended the possibility of maintaining peace at home through conquest abroad (Document 2).*

The Compromise of 1850 was in effect no more than an uneasy truce between the North and the South. But the struggle between western farmers and southern planters (and their allies among the smaller farmers) was rapidly complicated by the demands of eastern commercial interests and the rising intensity of antislavery and abolitionist agitation. Such cross-currents made it difficult for leaders like Stephen A. Douglas of Illinois and Franklin Pierce of New Hampshire to use foreign policy as a basis for further compromise.

Landed expansionists, southern and northern, kept their eyes on Cuba and Canada respectively. Some of the rising manufacturing interests joined the old commercial group and pressed for a more vigorous policy of overseas economic expansion. Other manufacturers, concentrating on the domestic market, demanded a high tariff, which was also a foreign policy question. Abolitionists generally ignored foreign policy, but some antislavery men were interested in a vigorous foreign policy for the liberation of foreigners who were not enjoying the benefits of a republican form of government. Moderates on the slavery issue called for more expansion of all kinds as a way out of the domestic crisis.

As Professor Basil Rauch indicates in his article on "American Interest in Cuba," slaveholders who desired the island received some support from northern businessmen, who saw trade and investment possibilities there. Other northerners as well as some westerners supported this interest in Cuba as a concession to the South. In return, they hoped to get southern support for their own desire to expand elsewhere. The Ostend Manifesto (Document 3) represents the most direct proposal to get the island through the diplomacy of threat, which in this instance was only slightly less overt than the military expeditions against Cuba which the South also supported throughout the decade of the fifties.

Commercially minded Americans continued, meanwhile, to increase their influence in Hawaii (Document 4) and began to exploit Commodore Perry's opening of Japan (Document 5). During the same years, enthusiasm for the spread of American principles abroad led to agitation for a strong policy in Europe. Secretary of State Daniel Webster, a vigorous promoter of commercial expansion, sent a militant dispatch to the Austrian government concerning the repression of a rebellion in which the United States had been interested (Document 6). Webster's explanation of his motives for writing such a vigorous letter associate him with Senator Douglas, who also saw foreign policy as a means to avoid disunion. By the 1850's Douglas had come to think of America as a young giant on the march, an attitude which Professor Merle E. Curti analyzes in his article on "Young America."

One group of the Young Americans concentrated more and more on foreign policy. Some of these saw it as a good political issue. Others hoped expansion abroad might decrease tension at home. Douglas himself suggested in 1852 that Cuba would provide additional territory with which to maintain the balance between slave and free states. Supported by various railway and other business interests, Douglas saw the Mississippi Valley as the new center of a great world power (Document 7). President Franklin Pierce shared these ideas. He thought nationalism could avert a war within the Union and, as Professor Roy F. Nichols shows, worked hard to push expansion in many parts of the world. Many southerners supported this idea of aggressive foreign expansion more actively than did the northern commercial and business groups, who were more occupied and concerned with the development of the continent itself in these years. This hope of avoiding civil war by means of an aggressive foreign policy persisted right down to the eve of Secession. Frederic Bancroft reviews the extreme proposal of this type that expansionist Secretary of State William Seward advanced in April, 1861.

Many explanations have been advanced to account for the coming of the Civil War. Such factors as sectionalism, states' rights, and slavery undoubtedly did much to bring about the division within the country. But it is often forgotten that the foreign policy of expansion, which the United States followed from 1810 to 1850, made it easy to avoid dealing with these problems in a thoroughgoing way. When the country could expand further only by risking war with strong powers, or only in a direction that would satisfy but one side in the domestic conflict, the politicians proved incapable of making the principles of republicanism work successfully. Perhaps these leaders, sometimes called a "blundering generation," might be described more aptly as the men who reaped the whirlwind of Manifest Destiny.

The Confederacy counted on its control of cotton exports to bring England into the war on their side. Professor Henry Blumenthal discusses the reasons for the failure of this policy. President Abraham Lincoln and Secretary of State Seward concentrated their efforts on establishing a blockade which would be effective enough to hurt the nonindustrialized South yet not provoke Great Britain and other countries into open retaliation. The Union could not afford to risk a two-front war. This fact was emphasized even more when the French intervened in Mexico. Seward lacked the power to enforce the Monroe Doctrine until the Confederacy had been defeated.

Once internal resistance had been put down, the Union was far stronger than ever before, with the most powerful army and navy in its history. Of the two, the army was much the more potent, since naval warfare was changing as a consequence of the development of steam-driven iron ships. The presence of a battle-tested army deployed along the Gulf of Mexico, meanwhile, helped speed the French back to Europe (Document 8).

Seward and other expansionists were anxious to shift to the offensive and use American power to win new strongholds in the Gulf of Mexico and the Pacific. That proved very difficult, however, because most Americans gave more attention to domestic affairs during the decade after the Civil War, and because the economy was undergoing changes that called for a different kind of foreign policy. Seward understood those new developments, and was even a prophet of the new expansionism they produced, but he did not have the domestic support to act effectively on his vision of the United States as the world power.

SOUTHERN EXPANSIONISTS
OF 1846[1]   *John Hope Franklin*

The decade of the 1840's witnessed a remarkable growth in expansionist sentiment in the United States. . . .

Beneath the movement and giving it emotional and intellectual content was the agitation for expansion that came from many quarters, including the

---

[1] Franklin: Selected from *The Journal of Southern History*, XXV, No. 3 (August 1959), pp. 323–338. Reprinted with permission.

South. The expansionist views of many Southerners were represented by Richard Hawes, the Kentucky Whig, who told Calhoun in 1844 that it should be the policy of this country to own "all the cotton lands of North America if we can." In the House of Representatives an Alabama Democrat, James Belser, asserted that it was impossible to limit the area of freedom, "the area of the Anglo-Saxon race." In the Senate William Merrick of Maryland declared that the question of the annexation of Texas was "a subject which concerned the fate of empires, and which was to effect, for weal or for woe, through ages yet to come, millions of the Anglo-Saxon race." While visiting California in 1845 a Calhoun correspondent said, "We only want the Flag of the United States and a good lot of Yankees, and you would soon see the immense natural riches of the Country developed and her commerce in a flourishing condition. To see that Flag planted here would be most Acceptable to the Sons of Uncle Sam, and by no means repugnant to the native population." The editor of the Richmond *Enquirer* rejoiced that the Whig *American Review* had come out boldly for California in 1846. He had no fear of extending the area of freedom, he asserted, for he was satisfied that "a federative system of free republics like our own, is capable of almost indefinite expansion, without disadvantage."

The extent of the expansionist fever in 1846 can be seen in the resolution of Senator David Yulee of Florida proposing that the President open negotiations with Spain with a view to purchasing Cuba. In the first weeks of the Mexican War a Charleston friend described to Calhoun a fantastic scheme launched by Southerners for the acquisition of all Mexico. Some years earlier, he said, an undisclosed number of Southerners had taken an oath to enlist in the conquest of Mexico. Each person was to do everything possible to bring into the cause every man who would make a good soldier, to hold himself in readiness, and to report to any place he was summoned for the purpose of carrying out the scheme. Meanwhile, the sentiment for acquiring Oregon up to 54° 40' had gained currency during the first year of Polk's administration. Views supporting the occupation of Oregon ranged from the lusty expansionist aims of the venerable John Quincy Adams to the noisy demands of young Andrew Johnson.

There was, however, no unanimity regarding either the area into which the United States should expand or whether it should expand at all. Even in the South for instance, there was some sentiment against expansion. Meredith Gentry of Tennessee told the House of Representatives that he saw no reason for contaminating American institutions by expanding into new areas. "If England were to propose to cede Canada to this Government to-morrow in my humble judgment, it would be unwise to accept the cession," and if Mexico asked to be annexed, she, too, should be rebuffed. Men like Alexander Stephens and John Calhoun had such grave doubts about the validity of the American title to Oregon that they felt it would be extremely rash to press any claims above 49°. Meanwhile, they frowned on any involvement with Mexico, even though victory there would surely lead to the acquisition of new territory.

On the question of expansion, party considerations loomed important in 1846. The Democrats had won the Presidential election of 1844, and even if "Fifty-four Forty or Fight" was not their slogan, expansionist sentiment within the party was strong. But conservative Southern members of the party, gratified over the annexation of Texas, were not as enthusiastic about "reannexing" Oregon as they might have been, and their Northern colleagues chided them for it. This led Jefferson Davis, among other Southerners, to speak for the section. He defended the South's desire to get Texas by declaring that this was in the national interest. While he did not want to do anything to precipitate a war with Britain, he wished to preserve the whole of Oregon for the United States. As the Democrats argued among themselves about whether to demand all of Oregon, Southern Whigs showed little enthusiasm for the project. Many Northern Whigs, with their growing antislavery radicalism, hoped that Oregon would be acquired to offset the mounting strength of the slave power.

The lukewarm-to-indifferent attitude of many Southerners toward Oregon in 1846 was enough to raise suspicions regarding their lack of interest in territories into which slavery could not expand. . . .

Southern leaders in Congress who had little or no enthusiasm for Oregon were much too astute to oppose it on the obvious ground that eventually Oregon would enter the union as one or several free states. These men, to whom a duel was commonplace, who had fought Indians incessantly and bitterly, some of whom had agitated for war against England in 1812, suddenly became the leading peacemakers of the country. . . . Calhoun . . . insisted that he wanted Oregon as much as Texas, but the latter was being secured without endangering peace. The only possible way to obtain Oregon was through patient negotiation, which an "all or none" attitude would make impossible.

Calhoun received generous support in his position from Southerners on both sides of the aisle. Alexander Barrow, the Whig senator from Louisiana, said he was certain war would result if the United States adopted an uncompromising position on Oregon. He was equally certain that public sentiment was not prepared for war with England. He hoped that the government would not be ashamed to do what the people demanded, and would enter into negotiations leading to an amicable settlement. . . . Other Southerners followed Calhoun's lead, including men of great prestige like George McDuffie of South Carolina, Joseph Chalmers of Mississippi, and John Berrien of Georgia.

Some of the leading Democratic and Whig organs of the South were as opposed to a firm stand for all of Oregon as were Calhoun and his supporters. Even in Polk's own state there was considerable opposition to an uncompromising position on Oregon. . . .

A partially neglected consideration that influenced some Southern opposition to drastic action in Oregon was the South's interest in a relaxed trade and antislavery policy for England. As early as 1841 Duff Green went to England to promote a policy of free trade, arguing that the American West's interest in Oregon would cool if England would be willing to negotiate a treaty for the admission of American grain. If England dropped her campaign against slavery *and* repealed her Corn Laws, the West would be more kindly disposed to England; and the South, which purchased a good deal of

233

Western produce, would benefit from lower grain prices as well as from a softer British antislavery policy. In his endeavors Green undoubtedly spoke for Calhoun, McDuffie, and other Southerners who supported a compromise with England on the Oregon question.

Still, despite the great prestige and the eloquent arguments for peace of men like Calhoun and papers like the [Charleston] *Mercury*, they did not speak for the entire South.... After Polk declared that the title of the United States to Oregon was "clear and unquestionable," one of Howell Cobb's friends wrote him that the message had stimulated the mountain folk around Clarksville, Georgia, to thought and discussion. "Every one understands, or thinks he understands, all about the Oregon question," he said. "I heard a crowd on Christmas, not one of whom knew on which side of the Rocky Mountains Oregon was, swear they would support and fight for Polk *all over the world*, that he was right, and we would have Oregon and thrash the British into the bargain." Southerners like these, inured to the hard life, quick to defend themselves, and ever-willing to fight any nation large or small, would have rejected the olive branch that was being proffered so generously by their more conservative representatives in the Congress.

Southerners who favored unqualified expansion were not mere voices crying in the mountains and desolate countrysides of their section. They had an impressive group of able young men as their spokesmen in Congress—largely in the House. There were about twenty men in Congress who represented what may be termed the hard core of Southern expansionism. They came from every state of the South with the exception of South Carolina, where the Calhoun intransigence seemed pervasive. Twelve were serving their first terms in the Congress in 1846, and four had been elected for the second time. Thus only four can be regarded as veteran congressmen. Most of them were under forty years of age....

These Southern spokesmen for expansion seemed bound by neither the conservative traditions of Congress nor the vested interests of the section from which they came. Largely small-town lawyers and farmers, their only loyalties seemed to be to party and country. All of them except Henry Hilliard of Alabama were Democrats who took much more seriously than some of the older members the avowed expansionist commitments of the party.... No voices in the country spoke out more clearly or vigorously in behalf of the fulfillment of the American dream of empire than these young "War Hawks" of 1846.

The Southern expansionists thought that President Polk's description of the American title to Oregon as "clear and unquestionable" was modest and conciliatory. They spoke with great familiarity of the American claims, based on discovery, exploration, and settlement; and none of them entertained the slightest doubt as to the validity of the American title. "Oregon is *ours*," thirty-four-year-old Representative Henry Bedinger of Virginia cried. "Every acre, every poor rood of it—and we must and *will* have it.... This great territory is of such immense value and importance to this Union, that we would deserve to be regarded as idiots by the civilized world, if we should suffer any portion of it to be wrested from us by any power upon earth."

234

* * *

The sentiments of "Manifest Destiny" uttered by these Southern expansionists were as strong as those of any expansionists of any period in the nation's history. The Southerners deftly coupled the historic mission of the nation with the immense economic and military importance of the territory they sought, thus appealing to the realists as well as the idealists. It was Robert M. T. Hunter, one of the few veteran congressmen among the Southern expansionists, who was sufficiently practical and astute to develop this argument. "There is no man with an American heart in his bosom," he declared, "who could be insensible to the prospect of planting our flag and our settlements upon the shores of the Pacific. There is no such bosom which would not swell . . . at the prospect of the influence, commercial, political, and military, which we should derive from a position on the shores of Oregon and California. . . ." The possession of Oregon would place the Union in a position of "impregnable strength and stable greatness, with one arm on the Atlantic sea and the other on the Pacific shore, ready to strike in either direction with a rapidity and an efficiency not to be rivalled by any nation on the earth." . . .

Insinuations by Northerners that the people of the South were not really interested in acquiring Oregon deeply wounded the feelings of the Southern expansionists. Although they came from a section whose animosity toward the North was mounting steadily, they spoke for expansion as nationalists, not sectionalists. The Northern jibes were directed at the Southern pacificators, of course, but the expansionists also took offense and were quick to defend their constituency. . . .

The Southern expansionists tried to convince their opponents that the best way to avoid war was to take a firm stand against Britain. Seaborn Jones insisted that England would not dare go to war to defend Oregon. If she did, Ireland would rebel, Canada would strike for her liberty, and British commerce would be ruined. If British leaders were shortsighted enough to start a war, the United States would be victorious. Archibald Yell of Arkansas could not see why anyone feared England. "We have whipped her twice, and we can whip her again," he exclaimed inaccurately but confidently. Yell's colleague from Arkansas, Senator Ambrose Sevier, said that the people of Arkansas would go to war rather than lose any of Oregon. They were a warlike people, he asserted, who gave guns to their children for playthings!

It was Sam Houston who topped off the argument for the "War Hawks." Deprecating the compromise as a position that would merely make Britain more aggressive and unreasonable, Houston contended that the peacemakers had exaggerated the evils of war. War certainly had its virtues, such as "draining off the restless and dissatisfied portion of the population, who might be killed off with benefit to the remainder; and also the effect it had in disciplining the habits of men into subordination to the rules of order."

When the Oregon treaty was ratified in June 1846, settling the boundary at 49°, the score of Southern expansionists who led the drive to place the boundary at 54° 40′ could view with satisfaction their valiant struggle. There were some Southerners, such as Robert Toombs of Georgia and L. H. Sims of Missouri, who had spoken out for all of Oregon but who were finally won over to a policy of compromise. The "hard core" Southern expansionists stood their ground and seemed proud of what they had done. They had given about as much support for all of Oregon as any Southerners had given for Texas. Their consciences were clear, for they had acted as "Manifest Destiny" Americans, not as narrow-minded sectionalists. But they never seemed to realize that they had almost no chance for success. In the highest quarters there were always serious doubts about the validity of the American claim north of 49°, and the official contentions of the two governments never took serious cognizance of the American claim in that area. President Polk, moreover, doubtless took that into consideration when he offered in the spring of 1846 to settle at 49°.

* * *

In participating in the unsuccessful struggle to secure Oregon up to 54° 40′ the Southern expansionists of 1846 represented American "Manifest Destiny" at its best. Their Southern colleagues who had been enthusiastic for Texas revealed a strong sectional bias in dragging their feet so noticeably when the Oregon question arose. Some of them doubtless agreed with Robert Toombs who said that he did not care a "fig about *any* of Oregon. ... I don't want a foot of Oregon or an acre of any other country, especially without 'niggers.' These are some of my reasons for my course which don't appear in print." Many of the pro-Oregon Northerners indicated clearly that they regarded the Oregon question as a sectional matter when they castigated Southerners who did not support it and by declaring gleefully that it would be a new area of freedom. Only the Southern expansionists seemed to transcend sectional lines by contending for a territory whose acquisition they deemed to be in the national interest.

* * *

THE MOVEMENT FOR THE ACQUISITION
OF ALL MEXICO[1]   *J. D. P. Fuller*

... Until the fall of 1847 the demand for Mexican territory extended no further than the acquisition of Upper California and New Mexico. At the very beginning of the war, however, there appeared expressions of more extended ideas of expansion, very general in some cases, in others more specifically relating to Mexico. But not until the fall of 1847 did these ideas become widespread. Three fairly well-defined stages may be noticed in the development of the sentiment for all Mexico before October, 1847. There was at the outbreak of the war a sudden outburst of expansionist sentiment which looked toward all Mexico, but this soon died down, or at least ceased to receive vocal expression. There was general approval for the acqui-

---

[1] Selected from *The Movement for the Acquisition of All Mexico, 1846–1848* (Baltimore: Johns Hopkins Press, 1936), pp. 39–41, 47, 68–69, 78, 137–41, 159. Reprinted with permission.

sition of California, but the plans of the administration were not definitely known. For the first five or six months of the war, therefore, public interest was centered on the task of finding out just what territory the President would attempt to secure. By October, 1846, it was apparent to the public that California at least would become a part of the United States. But the war did not come to an end as quickly as was expected and Mexico rejected overtures for peace in the fall of 1846. Public opinion began to demand more drastic measures. There were frequent intimations that it would be in order to demand more territory from Mexico and if that country still refused to listen to reason it was declared that her existence as a separate nation would be endangered. Finally, beginning in the spring of 1847 after notable victories of the American forces in Mexico, there can be noticed an increasing tendency to believe that the war could end only in the absorption of all Mexico, not so much an avowed demand as a strong conviction which was in many cases, no doubt, created by an ardent desire to acquire Mexico. In the meantime, the issue as to whether or not slavery should exist in territory acquired from Mexico had assumed an ominous character. But by October, 1847, when developments in connection with the war seemed to point toward the absorption of Mexico, some of the explosive material in the slavery question had been removed. The way was thus prepared for the development of larger ideas of expansion.

Immediately after the outbreak of hostilities there were indications in widely scattered parts of the country of a spirit that could mean disaster to Mexico if the war continued a sufficient length of time for it to develop. Caleb Cushing, a Massachusetts Democrat, disclaimed any desire "to witness the extinction of Mexico," but asserted that by beginning the war she had "dared the worst; and the result may be . . . the complete dissolution and extinction of the Mexican Republic." The editor of the New York *Herald* thought that the war might be looked upon "as the commencement of a vast, a terrible, a magnificent future." It might "lay the foundation of a new Age, a new destiny, affecting both this continent and the old continent of Europe." The meaning of this oratory became more clear when the New York paper undertook to advise Polk as to the proper course of procedure in case he intended to annex Mexico. Shortly afterwards the *Herald* assured the public that even if the United States did acquire vast stretches of territory, republican institutions would not thereby be endangered. The *Democratic Review* asserted that the "task of the American people for the present century, is clearly to take and occupy the northern continent of America." Mexico had caused a war "which in itself must hasten the occupation of the whole continent by the people of the United States." There was apparently no clear expression of sentiment for the immediate absorption of Mexico in the Northeast. But the possibilities in the situation created by the war were distinctly recognized. Given time this recognition of a possibility might readily develop into a direct demand for all Mexico. . . .

The President's attempt to secure money from Congress to further his schemes of expansion was a notable event in connection with the movement for the absorption of Mexico. Then it was that the slavery issue appeared on the scene. Certain northern Whigs declared that the Mexican War had resulted from a desire to extend and maintain the institution of slavery. It was a northern Democrat, however, who actually introduced the issue into Congress. When White, a Whig of New York, intimated that the purpose of Polk's request for a special appropriation was to extend the area of slavery, the Democrat Wilmot, of Pennsylvania, partly in answer to White's challenge, offered an amendment to the appropriation bill which provided that slavery should not exist in any territory acquired from Mexico. Wilmot's Proviso failed along with the bill and as Congress adjourned on August 10, there had not been enough discussion on the subject to arouse the passions of the pro-slavery and anti-slavery forces. During 1847, however, the slavery question was destined to cause the expansionists much difficulty in mapping out their plans for the acquisition of Mexican territory....

The sentiment not only of the administration but also of the entire country would be powerfully affected by the receipt of unfavorable reports from Mexico. The belief was becoming widespread that the war could only be ended by the conquest of the whole country and long continued occupation by United States troops. Not many were as yet ready to recommend openly annexation in any form, but proposals for conquest and occupation, if carried out, could scarcely have had a different result. Moreover, one of the leading anti-slavery journals in the United States looked with approval on the annexation of all Mexico if it were accomplished with the consent of the Mexicans. In short, it might be said that increasing numbers of people in the United States were becoming familiar with the idea that the war might end in a permanent connection between Mexico and the United States. To many this would be a desirable consummation of events, and should Mexico continue to refuse an acceptable peace the expansionists could be expected to express themselves in more concrete terms.

The great obstruction which had hitherto prevented the expansionist forces from developing to their full strength was, of course, the sectional controversy over slavery. But by the fall of 1847 the way had been prepared for minimizing the effect of this issue on the expansionist movement. As we have seen, northern expansionists had been fighting the Wilmot Proviso on the grounds that it would prevent the acquisition of any Mexican territory. Was there not some means by which the slavery issue could be sidetracked until Mexico had made the desired cessions of territory? If the northern Democracy could be persuaded to waive the question, at least for the time, the threatened breach in the Democratic party might be closed. But how was such a feat accomplished? Could it not be shown that the Wilmot Proviso was not needed to prevent the introduction of slavery into territory taken from Mexico? This line of reasoning must have exerted considerable influence at the North, for from the first appearance of the question as a serious problem there appeared evidences of a sustained attempt to show the opponents of slavery that their fears of its extension were groundless....

It appears, then, that the slavery question which during the first year of the war acted in most instances as a deterrent to the forces of expansion, was by the fall of 1847 no longer such an obstacle to the acquisition of territory. Increasing numbers of people in the North were becoming convinced that the Wilmot Proviso was not an indispensable prerequisite for the addition of free territory to the Union. Such being the state of public opinion, would-be presidential candidates among northern Democrats, who had been forced to exercise caution at the beginning of the war, could now condemn the Wilmot Proviso and enlarge their schemes of conquest without fear of committing political suicide. On the other hand, at the South there were evidences that opposition to the acquisition of territory was increasing. In so far as slavery was a determining factor, northern approval and southern disapproval of expansion were based on a common belief that slave institutions could not be extended into the territory which the expansionists were proposing to annex. This belief had been gradually established by propaganda during 1847. It cannot be maintained that generalizations on this subject are any more valid than generalizations on any other subject. In the Southwest for instance, the Wilmot Proviso seems never to have caused any great amount of alarm. Moreover, many southerners were perfectly satisfied, provided the Wilmot Proviso were not adopted, to acquire all the territory it was possible to secure. On the whole it may be said that in the fall of 1847 conditions were more favorable for expansion than at any time since the beginning of the war. Just at this juncture events in Mexico seemed to play into the hands of the expansionists with the result that the movement for the absorption of all Mexico became a recognizable force in the United States. . . .

The demise of the sentiment for all Mexico occurred to all intents and purposes in the period from February 19 to March 10, 1848. It was the acceptance of the Treaty of Guadalupe Hidalgo by the United States which administered the death blow to the schemes of the expansionists. Of course there was a chance that Mexico would finally reject the treaty, and had that happened the annexationists might have carried the day sooner or later. But the treaty was not rejected by Mexico and as it actually happened the movement for absorption ceased to be a force in the United States after March, 1848. The story of the negotiations leading to the treaty which ended the war has been well and frequently told. The famous quarrel between Commissioner Trist and General Winfield Scott, their equally famous reconciliation and subsequent friendship, furnish a most interesting and unique chapter in American diplomatic history, but as such are of no particular importance in connection with this study. The possibility of the absorption of Mexico, however, was one of the chief factors which induced Trist to ignore his recall and continue negotiations. The treaty which resulted from these negotiations was of the utmost importance in preventing the absorption of Mexico. Hence the story of the Treaty of Guadalupe Hidalgo in its relations to the expansionist movement records the death of that movement.

The full significance of the negotiation of the treaty cannot be understood without a knowledge of conditions in Mexico after the capture of Mexico City on September 14, 1847. Two days after that event Santa Anna resigned the Presidency which then fell into the hands of Peña y Peña, one of the leaders of the *moderado* party. The *moderados* were desirous of peace, opposed to all dictators of Santa Anna's type, and supporters of existing institutions in Mexico. Scarcely less numerous than the *moderados* were the *puros*, a radical republican party which did not desire peace until the old Mexican army should have been virtually exterminated. A large number of *puros* favored annexation to the United States as the best safeguard for order and prosperity. The Santanistas and the monarchists were also opposed·to peace but for entirely different reasons from those advanced by the *puros*. The supporters of Santa Anna hoped that their leader would be restored to power and thus be able to bestow favors on his adherents. "Santa Anna's talents could be exercised only in troubled times, so that a program like Guizot's, offering only peace and bourgeois prosperity, promised nothing for faithful followers." The monarchists were opposed to peace because they were opposed to anything which seemed likely to strengthen the forces making for republicanism in Mexico. The *moderados*, however, held the reins of government for the time being, albeit on a rather precarious tenure of doubtful legality. President Peña and his party were determined to have peace if possible, but quick action was necessary as the government might at any time succumb to its foes. It seemed that now or never peace would be made.

Commissioner Trist, doubtless realizing the possibilities of the situation, undertook, on October 20, to reopen negotiations. On October 21, the Mexican foreign minister notified Trist that although there seemed to be little hope for an agreement commissioners would be appointed in a "few days" to continue the negotiations. This was the state of affairs when the American commissioner received notice of this recall on November 16. Poor communications between Vera Cruz and Mexico City resulted in Buchanan's dispatch of October 6, and a later one dated October 25, being placed in Trist's hands at the same time. When the latter dispatch was written the Washington government had official information concerning the negotiations which had broken down early in September. Trist was severely reprimanded for offering to refer the Nueces-Rio Grande question to Washington and was again directed to leave Mexico. The peace negotiations seemed destined to end in failure again. Given the conditions in Mexico the results might be disastrous in their effect on the peace party. The *moderado* government could scarcely survive the loss of prestige which would be occasioned by the collapse of its peace program. The fall of the *moderados* might mean the end of independent Mexico.

Until December 4, Trist fully intended to obey his instructions and leave Mexico at the first suitable opportunity. On this date, however, he suddenly decided to remain and continue his efforts to secure a treaty on the basis of the *sine qua non* provided in his instructions of April, 1847; that is, the Rio Grande boundary for Texas and the cession of Upper California and New Mexico to the United States for a money payment. To make a long story short, after much procrastination on the part of the Mexicans, the Treaty of Guadalupe Hidalgo was signed on February 2, and forwarded to Washington. Under the terms of the treaty Mexico surrendered Upper California and New Mexico and gave up all claims to the territory between the Nueces and the Rio Grande. In return the United States agreed to pay fifteen million dollars and assume all unpaid claims of its citizens against

Mexico. Mexico had finally agreed to give up the minimum amount of territory which had been demanded of her nine months before as the price of peace. She received, however, five million dollars less than Trist had been authorized to pay in the preceding April. The problem now was: would such a treaty be acceptable to the President and Senate of the United States? Before discussing the fate of the treaty in the United States we may turn our attention to the part played by the threatened absorption of Mexico in causing Trist to continue negotiations.

The belief that Mexico would be annexed by the United States if he left that country without a treaty, seems to have had considerable weight in determining Trist's conduct after his recall. The commissioner's correspondence shows that he reasoned somewhat as follows: the *puros* were anxious to secure a permanent connection with the United States and would do everything in their power to prevent the closing of the war; a breakdown in negotiations would strengthen the *puros* and weaken the *moderados*, whose prestige and continuance in power depended on the negotiation of a peace; the cession of New Mexico and Upper California was the greatest concession that the Mexican government could make; if the present opportunity were not seized at once all chance of making a treaty would be lost, perhaps for all time; the President of the United States was apparently determined to annex all Mexico; ultimate absorption might be desirable, but a dissolution of the Union would be better than immediate annexation. In other words, Trist thought that conditions in both Mexico and the United States pointed to an indefinite continuance of a state of war, with the absorption of Mexico as a probable result, if he obeyed his instructions. This consummation of events he desired to prevent. Hence his determination to negotiate a treaty if possible.

Whether Trist really desired to further the interests of his country as he saw them or whether he was interested in embarrassing the President is a moot question, and is not germane to this discussion. In any event the result was the same. The significant fact is that with the exception of his estimate as to Polk's intentions Trist, with Scott's and Thornton's help, had correctly interpreted the trend of events. It seems certain that had they not been faced with a *fait accompli* the Washington authorities would have demanded more territory from Mexico than was secured by the Treaty of Guadalupe Hidalgo. . . .

The expansionists were not able to overcome the obstacle presented by the Treaty of Guadalupe Hidalgo. Peace with Mexico on "just and honorable" terms was a contingency which they had not expected and for which they were not prepared. Consequently, when Mexico offered terms which a majority of the American people would undoubtedly consider as satisfactory, most of the expansionists yielded to necessity. Many senators, moreover, lent their support to a treaty which they did not like partly because they desired to frustrate the schemes of the expansionists. The negotiation of the treaty and its acceptance by the President was the beginning of the end; the consent to ratification by the senate furthered the dissolution; and the acceptance of the amended treaty by Mexico, delivered the final blow to the sentiment for the absorption of Mexico. . . .

AMERICAN INTEREST IN CUBA[1]   *Basil Rauch*

The climax of American interest in Cuba before the Civil War came in the first two years of the Pierce administration. Economic considerations deepened the current of that interest, and help to explain why the victorious Democrats, despite the glaring failures of Polk and López, renewed the former's attempt to purchase the island and even encouraged the use of force.

At the end of the Mexican War, the United States entered a period of great prosperity. The liquidation of wild-cat banks and the influx of new gold from California created strong foundations for the expansion of agriculture, commerce, transportation and manufactures. In 1850, according to the *Preliminary Report on the Eighth Census:*

The spirit of enterprise abroad was very strong, and the impression that prices were to rise by reason of the depreciation of gold was prevalent; hence the general desire to operate, in order to avail of the anticipated profits. Industry of all description was very active and productive, and there never was a period when national capital accumulated so fast. . . .

Increased investments and rising commodity prices stimulated production and enlarged purchasing power. A boom in American foreign trade resulted. The value of combined imports and exports more than doubled between 1846 and 1855 when it rose from 235 to 536 millions of dollars. Domestic exports increased from less than 133 millions of dollars in 1849 to more than 253 millions in 1854. Capital poured into the shipbuilding industry. The annual average tonnage built during the ten years before 1852 was 199,000 and it rose to 358,000 during the succeeding decade. The greatest part of the advance occurred between 1851, when 351,000 tons were built, and 1854, when the figure reached 583,000 tons.

The search for new markets and profitable employment of shipping met with considerable success as Great Britain led the way to free trade. Cuba became the most important American market where restrictions still hampered merchants and shippers. In November, 1850, in retaliation against the Cardenas Expedition, Spain raised still higher the Cuban tariffs on products imported chiefly from the United States and imposed onerous new rules on American shippers. Cuba continued third after Britain and France in the value of its combined American imports and exports, but the United States could not overcome its unfavorable balance of trade with Spain and her dependencies, which actually increased from 5 million dollars out of combined imports and exports of 25 million dollars in 1850 to 14 out of 37 millions in 1853. Cuban duties on American corn, ship bread, pork products, dried fish and similar items ranged from 50 to 175 percent.

[1] Selected from *American Interest in Cuba: 1848–1855* (New York: Columbia University Press, 1948), pp. 181–85, 191–93, 207–208. Reprinted with permission.

242

Most burdensome of all was the duty on American flour of $8.50 per barrel when imported in Spanish ships and $9.50 in American ships. In 1852, total duties of $73,000 were paid on $91,000 worth of American flour. This inhibited the sale in Cuba of its most "natural" import from the United States while the latter country lowered its duty on sugar in 1846 and bought the majority of the Cuban sugar crop, amounting to 77 percent of it in 1853. On the other hand, Cuban rates were favorable for the importation of American machinery. Richard H. Dana found that the railroad equipment in the island had been manufactured in Cambridgeport and Troy. Philadelphia, Boston and New York developed a thriving market in Cuba for steam engines to be used in the sugar mills.

The United States in 1848 made a gesture towards ending the tariff war with Spain by suspending all laws that exacted higher duties on Spanish steamships arriving in the United States than were imposed on American steamships arriving in Cuba. A month before he left office, Secretary of State Everett proposed to Spain that a commercial treaty be negotiated to put an end to the tariff war and other vexations that troubled American relations with Cuba. The proposal was renewed by Minister Pierre Soulé in 1854, but nothing came of these efforts because Spain was not interested. Nor would Congress act on the suggestion of Secretary of the Treasury Corwin in 1852 that American retaliations against Spain should all be repealed because they had injured American shipping and reduced exports to Cuba.

Commercial interest had been urged as a leading motive for Cuban annexation by the New York *Sun* when it initiated its campaign in 1847. *La Verdad* took up the argument, declaring as the Gold Rush began that industrial and mercantile speculations of Americans might better be directed to Cuba than to California's "remote and desert shores." The *Democratic Review* described the great commercial advantages from annexation of Cuba that would follow in the train of Manifest Destiny. Alexander Jones in his book, *Cuba in 1851*, published in New York, eloquently defended the filibusters and offered trade advantages as the chief reason why Americans should support annexation.

The North was less excited by such prospects than the South. *Hunt's Merchants' Magazine* of New York did not advocate annexation and only published objective news of Cuban trade developments. *Niles' National Register*, a Whig publication of Baltimore and Philadelphia, was more interested in annexation as a means of opening up an immense market for American wheat and flour. John S. Thrasher, former editor of *El Faro Industrial* in Havana, member of the Havana Club, and inmate of Spanish prisons, wrote a striking appeal to Americans to support annexation because they would find greatly increased markets in the island for products of every section of the Union. His attempt to stir up national interest in the commercial motive for annexation was made in 1856, after he had thoroughly identified himself with the South as an employee of the New Orleans *Picayune*, a propagandist of southern motives for annexation, and an associate of Quitman in filibuster enterprises. Nevertheless, his essay of 1856 was the best analysis written during the period of national motives, commercial and strategic, for Cuban annexation. The strength of the commercial motive for interest in Cuba is strikingly illustrated by the abolitionist *National Era* of Washington whose editor wrote longingly of the increased markets for New England manufacturers and western wheat and provisions that would follow annexation. Coffee and sugar prices in the United States would decline, he wrote, American commerce in the Gulf would be safe forever, and American influence would dominate the isthmus of Central America. He admitted that annexation would abolish the slave trade. If only the accession of power by the American slavery system could somehow be eliminated from the measure, the abolitionist editor would find much cause to rejoice in Cuban annexation.

Southern commercial interest in Cuba centered in New Orleans. That city's foreign trade advanced with astonishing rapidity as the cotton, grain and cattle of the Mississippi valley were sent to her wharves for export. The value of receipts of produce increased from 45 million dollars in 1842 to 134 million in 1853. The Crescent City ranked fourth in the Union in value of imports, but in exports it reached first place when they increased from 31 million dollars in 1846 to 67 million in 1853 and surpassed those of New York. James Dunwoody B. DeBow was the leading propagandist of the South's commercial interest in Cuban annexation. He was a native of Charleston, South Carolina, who migrated to New Orleans and there on the advice of Calhoun founded in 1846 *DeBow's Review*. After a severe struggle, his message of economic nationalism as a program for the South awakened interest and was itself stimulated by southern speculation on secession and separate nationality. The pages of the magazine presented a blueprint of economic policy for the South to strengthen it against the North. . . .

Shipowners rather than merchants were the chief northern supporters of Cuban annexation for whom economic considerations had personnel bearing. However, the distinction hardly exists, for example, in the case of the New York firm that operated the leading commercial house in Havana, Drake Brothers and Company. It led in the sugar trade, owned steamship lines between the United States and Cuba, and also owned Saratoga, one of the finest sugar plantations in the island. William Cullen Bryant visited this establishment and was much impressed by its "American efficiency." Drake Brothers was the Havana agent of the great, new United States Mail Steamship Company. Cuban slavery, trade and shipping all touched its interests and it was sufficiently sympathetic to annexation to serve as the secret communication agent between revolutionists in Cuba and their friends in the United States.

The Havana *Mercantile Report* stated in 1855 that American tonnage in the Cuban trade had increased more than 200 percent during the previous decade. Having had a fair lead in 1846 over the nearest competitor, Great Britain, the United States increased its tonnage until it was in 1855 more than seven times that of Britain and over four times that of Spain. The shipping of the latter country had benefited from discriminations sufficiently to surpass the tonnage of Britain but not that of the United States.

George Law, the President of the United States Mail Steamship Company, was the outstanding representative of shipping interests in the move-

ment to annex Cuba. Starting as a hod-carrier, he had risen to wealth and
political influence in the New York Democracy as a contractor who knew
how to exploit sound business schemes by combining the methods of the
promoter, political intriguer and lobbyist. A contemporary called Law as
unpopular a man as could be found in New York because of his ruthless
methods. His career set a pattern for the rising generation of "robber
barons." With Marshall O. Roberts, he gained control of a government
contract in 1847 that gave him mastery of a subsidized line of steamships
between New York and Panama by way of Havana and New Orleans. This
line and a connecting link between Panama and Oregon, later California,
was intended to serve manifold public purposes, all of them indicative of
the expansive national mood. The steamships were to be superior to any previous types and built under the supervision of the Navy Department according to designs readily convertible for war purposes. Naval officers served on
them as commanding and watch officers to gain experience in steam. As
the fastest route to Oregon and California, the lines carried the mails and
provided improved military communications. William H. Aspinwall took
the contract for the western line and with Law built the Panama Railroad
to improve the isthmian connection between their lines. Up to 1852, Law
failed to fulfill his contract, as he bought steamers instead of building them
and supplied fewer than the five specified, but, never lacking sympathetic
friends in Washington, his United States Mail Steamship Company was
nevertheless paid the full subsidy of $290,000 per year. This and the Gold
Rush, besides ruthless methods of competition, made Law's venture wonder-
fully profitable. He became the leader of the "steamboat crowd" and a
powerful figure in New York Democratic politics. Prosper M. Wetmore,
also influential in New York Democratic circles, was taken into Law's
company after being removed for defalcation as Navy Agent charged with
supervising construction of Law's ships. The political methods of Law
were notorious. He commanded an elaborate and efficient band of lobbyists
and the Congressmen who were loyal to his interests included representatives
of both parties and all sections. The New York *Evening Post* credited
him with controlling the Seward faction of the Whigs as well as the anti-
Marcy Democrats. . . .

This . . . suggests that economic motives played a part in the movement
to annex Cuba. They help to explain why New Orleans was the chief
center of annexation sentiment in the Union: it was the headquarters of
southern commercial, shipping and financial interests as well as the capital
of the cotton and sugar slave-plantation regions. Southern economic nationalism was irradiated from New Orleans by the indefatigable DeBow. The
filibusters gravitated to that city. And there the dream of a slave-commercial
empire flourished. . . .

Trade, shipping and financial interests also help to explain why New
York was the second center of the Cuban movement. The general tie between northern commerce, banking, and industry and the southern plantation system cemented the alliance in the Democratic Party of New York
business men and southern planters. Even the Whig business men of the
Northeast and their political leaders showed in the sectional struggle of

1850 that in the cause of profitable connection with the South they could rise above anti-slavery principles. The movement to annex Cuba expressed the economic community of interests between northern business and southern slavery. . . .

YOUNG AMERICA[1]

Merle E. Curti

When a slogan comes to be used commonly by politicians, editors, and diplomats it may be assumed that it expresses a set of ideals and emotions of some significance. "Young America" was such a slogan. Its adoption by an important group in the Democratic party during the election of 1852 was a political gesture that received serious attention at home as well as abroad. Since foreign powers are not always in a position to determine how deep the realities behind a gesture may be, it is the more important to evaluate the gesture and to determine its relation to the national psychology. The purpose of this paper is, first, to describe and evaluate the movement Young America, with special reference to its foreign policy and activities, and, secondly, to indicate the relation of the movement to national self-consciousness in the years following 1850.

The idea of a Young America seems first to have been formulated in a commencement address by Edwin de Leon at South Carolina College in 1845. He observed that as there was a Young Germany, a Young Italy, a Young Ireland, so there might well be a Young America. For "nations, like men, have their seasons of infancy, manly vigor, and decrepitude." The young giant of the West, America, was pictured as standing at the full flush of "exulting manhood," and the worn-out powers of the Old World could not hope either to restrain or to impede his progress. If there was to be a Young America, then the new generation, the young men of America, would have to express their faith in the glorious destiny of the country, by seizing political power to hasten the fulfillment of that destiny.

* * *

To Young America direct and immediate participation in the affairs of the world was the indisputable formula of procedure. The time, in their eyes, was thoroughly ripe for the realization of the American mission. Success in the Mexican War, easy and cheap, had acted like an intoxicant. It engendered a jingoism which demanded even more grand accomplishments! This urge for participation in world affairs found little expression because the country was absorbed in internal problems growing out of the war.

When, however, the European revolutions of 1848 had been crushed by reactionary governments, there was occasion for action. . . .

The year 1852 offered an admirable opportunity for a discontented group of young men within the Democratic party to adopt this phrase "Young America" as a slogan and a rallying cry. The enthusiasm Kossuth

---

[1] *The American Historical Review*, XXXII, No. 1 (October, 1926), 34–55. Reprinted with permission.

was arousing indicated that the country might be ready to assume an active role in championing the revolution which that Hungarian declared must shortly break out. The New York *Herald* declared that the cause of Hungary was a trump card which, skillfully played, might win the White House. Webster, Whig Secretary of State, attended the Congressional banquet given Kossuth on January 7, 1852, being led in part by a desire to repeat the popular success of his Hülsemann letter. It seemed to Hülsemann, Austrian chargé, that Webster's speech, candidly recognizing the justice of Hungarian independence and expressing a wish to see that independence accomplished, signified an intention to quit the Cabinet and to found his candidacy for the Whig nomination on an alliance with Kossuth. This was likewise the opinion of the Prusssian minister-resident, Baron von Gerolt.

As early as December, 1851, it had been plain that the Senate would be the stage for discussions regarding the expediency of assuming a more vigorous position in the interest of European republicanism. Senator I. P. Walker of Wisconsin (Democrat) announced on December 16 of that year that "the country must interpose both her moral and her physical power" against the interference of one nation in the affairs of another in violation of public law and morality. He maintained that the country ought to be ready, if necessary, to fight for Hungarian freedom. On January 20, 1852, Cass of Michigan introduced into the Senate a resolution to the effect that the United States had not seen nor could they again see, without deep concern, the intervention of European powers to crush national independence. Cass, although repudiated by the leader of Young America as an "Old Fogy," could not have represented that group more effectively than by his earnest plea for the adoption of the resolution. The country, urged Cass, must not remain a "political cipher." The world must know that there are "twenty-five millions of people looking across the ocean at Europe, strong in power, acquainted with their rights, and determined to enforce them."

* * *

The personnel of the group ... was not entirely definite, but it may be said that it represented, in general, frontier sections of the country. Stephen A. Douglas of Illinois was popularly reputed to be the soul of the movement. His colleagues in Congress, James Shields and William Richardson of Illinois, were also leading spirits in the group. Others were William Corry of Cincinnati, Robert J. Walker, formerly of Mississippi, William R. Smith of Alabama, William Polk of Tennessee, and E. C. Marshall of California. But regardless of whether the particular members of the group came from frontier regions or not, it is clear that the group as a whole represented frontier ideals. Among these was the typically frontier interest in the future development of capitalism. "Great, powerful and rich as are the United States," said Marshall, "they must become greater, more powerful, more rich." ... The general American conviction of a mission to extend free institutions, and thus to promote a better world order, was remembered and appealed to. It is significant that these idealistic sentiments, bombastically and pompously expressed, were as genuine elements of American self-consciousness as the materialistic ones linked with them.

247

This materialistic aspect of Young America was most ably expressed by Pierre Soulé during the Senate debates on Cass's resolution criticizing Russian intervention in Hungary. "What, speak of isolation!" exclaimed Soulé. "Have you not markets to secure for the surplus of your future wealth?" It was therefore in Soulé's eyes "our own interest, and if not our interest our duty, to keep alive . . . that reverence for the institutions of our country, that devout faith in their efficacy, which looks to their promulgation throughout the world as to the great millennium which is to close the long chapter of their wrongs." . . .

Still another factor in the force of Young America's appeal for intervention in behalf of European republicanism was the presence of large numbers of newly arrived immigrants in the United States, who, for the most part, were friends of republicanism at home. Tammany Hall, with its foreign complexion, ratified, as early as October, 1851, the Young American principle of "no more neutrality, active alliance with European republicanism throughout the world." William Corry, one of the most vehement partizans of Young America, addressed Tammany with a speech which might well be taken as the platform of Young America. The fact that large numbers of these newly arrived foreigners settled in the West was another reason why that section was the heart of Young America. The New York *Herald* professed to believe that the Young American crusade for intervention rested on a mere desire on the part of Western politicians to win votes. Although it is difficult to evaluate the degree of truth in this charge, there is evidence that such ambitions influenced in part the behavior of the group adopting the slogan "Young America" as a battle cry. But whatever part the desire to win German votes played in shaping the interventionist politics of the Westerners in Congress, there was unquestionably a close relationship between the expansive, missionary republicanism of the German exiles and the philosophy of Young America.

* * *

The Young Americans also asserted that the ritual of the Democratic party had come to be more important than its spirit. There was need of an evangelistic revival. Hollow complacency was not enough to maintain the party machine intact. Leadership in the party had long enough been in the hands of the Old Fogies. This was the keynote of the articles which Sanders began to print in the *Democratic Review*, an organ long representing the more progressive wing of the party, and of which he became editor in January, 1852. He insisted that the party must have a man for the presidency who realized that our national integrity had long enough been prostituted to foreign governments, that our flag and our armaments must no longer subserve the whims of foreign tyrants. The "Old Fogy" Democrats, J. C. Breckinridge and General W. O. Butler of Kentucky, and especially Marcy and Cass, were "superannuated wire-pullers," living in the shadows of great men, mimicking their gestures, words, bows. Without progressive ideas upon which to base its actions or to attract support, Old Fogyism had been forced to rely on subterfuges, corruptions, schemes in utter antagonism to democracy and the true national interests of the country. The programme of

Young America was drawn with rhetorical splendor. Sectional and party discord were to be healed through a progressive foreign policy, which included the principle of American intervention on the side of the struggling republics in Europe.

* * *

Although Young America had occasioned alarm among the Whigs as well as among the Democrats, the nomination of Pierce [rather than Douglas] had a quieting effect. The New York *Herald* considered Pierce a "discreet representative of Young America." The *Democratic Review* made the best of the situation by urging that since Pierce was a new man he was quite capable of becoming all that the *Review* had urged. During the summer Douglas, in campaigning for Pierce, appealed to the Young American sentiment. Edmund Burke succeeded in persuading Dr. Hebbe and a Mr. Flinchmann, both influential among the German population, to campaign for Pierce. "The grand ideas which are the most potent in the election," Burke wrote to Pierce, "are sympathy for the liberals of Europe, the expansion of the American republic southward and westward, and the grasping of the magnificent purse of the commerce of the Pacific, in short, the ideas for which the term *Young America* is the symbol." Kossuth wrote a circular to the German clubs and societies virtually urging them to support Pierce.

Although Young America had not nominated its candidate, the party platform incorporated many "Young American" ideas. This platform advocated "the full expansion of the energies of this great and progressive people," and the *Democratic Review* interpreted the meaning to its own satisfaction. The platform moreover resolved that "in view of the condition of popular institutions in the Old World, a high and sacred duty is devolved with increased responsibility upon the Democracy of this country." The New York *Herald* looked to the Pierce administration for the promotion of internal glory and prosperity and "the extension of our power and influence among the nations of the earth." At the same time it observed that appointment of Young Americans to cabinet positions would mean an unsettlement of the financial world, the electrical vibrations of which would be felt even on the London exchange.

The election of Pierce was regarded with concern by those Europeans who feared the growing influence of the United States and the prominence which that influence was lending to republican and democratic ideas. The Prussian minister resident in Washington, Baron von Gerolt, informed his government that the peace policy of Fillmore had ended, and that a new era designed to show the influence of the United States in Europe as well as the New World was about to begin. The Austrian minister of foreign affairs, Count Buol-Schauenstein, believed that the election would increase popular license in America, "so incompatible with the good faith of foreign relations." Apprehensive of the American movements against Cuba, he feared "a generally aggressive and annexing policy." Hülsemann, the Austrian chargé in Washington, expected that while the new government would be sympathetic with the revolutionary party in Europe, it would be deterred for the moment from offering any assistance. This was ascribed to the fact that the relations of the United States with Spain were bound to be precarious because of a determination to secure Cuba, and further, that difficulties with Great Britain and Mexico were not unlikely to develop. A victorious revolution abroad, no matter how momentary, would, nevertheless, in Hülsemann's opinion, change the probable pacific policy of the government. Yet Hülsemann clearly realized from the Kossuth excitement that the influence of the South would oppose measures which threatened their commercial and financial interests, as intervention in European affairs was bound to do. Yet the uncertainty in regard to the turn which the expansionist and interventionist sentiment in the United States might take caused Austria to modify her attitude towards this country.

* * *

The bitter fight between the "Old Fogies" and the representatives of Young America for spoils began almost immediately. George Sanders used every possible weapon to prevent the president-elect from offering to Marcy the chief office in the Cabinet. Almost every day and night during the early months of 1853 he was to be seen at the Astor House, with various Douglas men, seizing each opportunity to talk with influential citizens and travellers. A political enemy of Sanders, Thomas N. Carr, had reason to believe that in all these efforts he was financially supported by George Law. Despite everything, including interviews with Pierce, Sanders failed. Marcy was announced as the new Secretary of State. But the leader of Young America was not discouraged. Sanders publicly declared his determination to obtain an office in spite of Marcy's opposition. A letter to this effect was read at Tammany Hall. George Law, it seems, had committed Pierce to Sanders' appointment. It was also believed that Douglas was among the some hundred friends who were aiding Sanders. And so in the face of opposition by Marcy, Sanders was appointed in June (1853) consul at London.

* * *

Sanders had made many enemies before he assumed his position in London, and his open activities in behalf of the revolutionary cause did not diminish them. Hülsemann understood in January, 1854, that Sanders' letters to the New York *Herald* had so displeased the President that he hesitated to transmit the nomination to the Senate. In February, 1854, Sanders' nomination as consul in London was refused confirmation in the Senate by a vote of 29 against 10.

Sanders was outraged at the rejection. Blaming Douglas for deserting him, he even intimated that the Little Giant was one of the conspirators against his character. Douglas was surprised at the direction his wrath had taken. "I am not in the habit of suspecting my friends," Douglas wrote, "much less of condemning them. . . . When, in the prosecution of your cherished revenge, you shall ascertain the true state of the facts, and shall know who stood by you, and defended you to the last, you will feel more mortification and chagrin at having written your unkind letter to me than I did in reading it."

The exiles in London were thoroughly disappointed at the recall of

Sanders. On March 1, 1854, Kossuth, Ledru-Rollin, and Mazzini addressed a letter to him expressing "deep regret and mortification at this untoward occurrence." The rejection of his nomination by the Senate was "a hard and mischievous blow at the prospects" of democracy. Kossuth became furious when he thought of the way in which Sanders was treated by his government, and "sick at heart at considering what the cause of European democracy" lost by losing him. Louis Blanc took occasion to express his appreciation for the articles which had appeared in the *Democratic Review*. "My admiration rises to affection for you," wrote Victor Hugo. "When you write it is your soul that writes, a soul elevated and free." Campanella, the secretary of Mazzini, thanked Sanders for the favors he had received, and Garibaldi added to "a word of affection and gratitude" the comment that whatever it might be his fortune to accomplish for his country would be inaugurated "under the auspices of generous men (sympathizing in soul with my unhappy land) of whom you are the model."

Sanders' consular colleague in Liverpool, Nathaniel Hawthorne, "hoped to Heaven" that Pierce would do the right thing in Sanders' case, and felt certain that he would "if he follows his nature." Soulé wrote from Madrid that "there will not be a true Democrat throughout the land who will not deplore and bitterly condemn that you were not returned to a post which you filled with so much distinction."

Although Sanders' efforts in London were badly rewarded, slightly better success attended those of some other representatives of Young America. August Belmont, agent of the Rothschilds in New York, and sometime consul-general for Austria, was thoroughly sympathetic with the programme of American aid for European republicanism. Belmont owed his appointment as minister to the Hague very largely to Sanders' influence with Pierce. From the Hague, Belmont wrote Sanders that the Crimean War might very well make possible new and successful revolutions. "The day is not far distant, when self-preservation will dictate to the United States the necessity of throwing her moral and physical force into the scale of European republicanism. To prepare for such a day is the first sacred duty of our Government and Congress, and this can only be done effectively by reorganizing and increasing the navy. The sooner we prepare against the contingencies which our rapid growth and the jealousy of the European powers will bring about, the better it will be for us." But apart from forwarding Sanders' letter to the President of the Swiss Confederation, Belmont's activities in behalf of Young America were confined to the despatch of high-sounding demands to the Dutch government for the release of one Walter Gibson who had been imprisoned in Batavia on the charge of exciting native chiefs to overthrow Dutch royal authority.

* * *

We have seen that Young America had glorious ideals for the future of the country, and a very ambitious programme for realizing them. Yet the ideals were as vague as they were grand. Ways and means of applying the programme, of extending aid to the republican movements in Europe, were not definitely worked out, nor, apparently, were the serious practical problems that intervention would involve ever squarely faced. It would not be expected, then, that such a movement would meet with any great degree of practical success, partly because of its inherent weakness and partly because of sectional opposition and that of established economic interests.

Thus the movement itself was a failure. Yet the fact that it existed and flourished so strongly for a while is very significant. On the one hand it shows that Young America's grand ideals really expressed the feelings of many Americans. Idealists like Emerson and Whitman entertained the same essential ideals, though they expressed them less crudely. It was probably more true of the United States than of the European countries that its people tended, at that time, to have an exaggerated youthful faith in the glory of their institutions. Some wished to gain still further glory through territorial expansion and foreign trade. Others were especially interested in encouraging democracy abroad. How many of these latter were animated by commercial motives is a question. But such people, idealists and materialists alike, must have found their chief aspirations expressed in the programme of Young America. On the other hand, the fact that these already existing feelings found expression and some degree of organization and coherence in Young America could not but have helped to crystallize and still further develop them. Thus, this movement, though it failed of practical results, was significant, first, as a political gesture so vigorous as to arouse alarm in Europe, and, secondly, as a means of expressing and developing a certain type of national self-consciousness.

THE FOREIGN POLICY OF
PRESIDENT PIERCE[1]

Roy F. Nichols

When Pierce returned from Hillsborough Friday, November 5, to prepare for his new task he was deeply conscious of heavy responsibility. This responsibility was twofold, for he was both President-elect and titular chief of a powerful and victorious party. His position was likely to be difficult because of the bitterness of sectional rivalry. The disunion crisis of 1850 barely had been averted by the compromise of that year, and while the country was at the moment calm, Pierce was too fully alive to the dangers just escaped not to realize that skillful administration would be necessary to maintain equilibrium. Politically, his situation was difficult because of the factional organization of his party and the size of his victory; he had carried all states except four, Vermont, Massachusetts, Kentucky, and Tennessee. In 1848 the party had been badly split, in 1852 it had been wondrously united. Could this harmony be maintained? Too many would want rewards and there were not nearly enough positions to go around; the ideals and interests of the factions were so divergent that quarrels were bound to arise. . . .

---

[1] Selected from *Franklin Pierce: Young Hickory of the Granite Hills* (Philadelphia: University of Pennsylvania Press, 1931), pp. 216, 220, 259–69, 447–49, 533. Reprinted with permission.

By December, Pierce had reached some tentative conclusions. The fundamental proposition which he decided to adopt was harmony; by cabinet and inaugural he aimed to conciliate as many of the factions as possible....

His inaugural would stress a vigorous foreign policy of territorial and commercial expansion backed by an adequate army and navy; this would please "Young America" and the so-called progressive wing of the party, besides being generally popular....In a word, his inaugural was to provide expansion for the radicals and the preservation of the Union at all costs for the conservatives; unwittingly he had planned to carry out what proved to be a most dangerous and difficult combination of policies....

* * *

By far the most extensive and interesting were the problems which Marcy brought over from his department....

The President had spoken in his inaugural about territorial expansion and trade extension, but Marcy soon discovered that the United States must pursue a defensive as well as an aggressive foreign policy. Relations with Great Britain, Mexico, and Spain were not harmonious, and our interests in various parts of the Western Hemisphere seemed in danger. So to defense Marcy, with the active interest of his chief, first turned his attention.

There was friction with Great Britain in Central America and in Canada, friction of such a character that occasionally the hot-headed talked of war. The question of trans-isthmian communication had brought the United States into dispute with Great Britain several years before, and the Whigs had endeavored to resolve these difficulties by the Clayton-Bulwer treaty in which both sides agreed to extend their interests no further in Central America and to refrain from exercising exclusive control over any canal which might be built in that region....

An unexpected incident connected with the Central American difficulty brought British relations forcefully before the administration. American interests were established at the mouth of the San Juan river on the eastern coast of Nicaragua in the vicinity of a "free city," called Greytown, maintained by the British under grant from their protectorate, the Mosquito Indians. The Accessory Transit Company, in which Cornelius Vanderbilt was largely interested, had established the headquarters of its trans-isthmian route at a little settlement across the bay, called Punta Arenas. The officials of this company had continual difficulty with the citizens of the "free city" who were British in sympathy....

While considering the Central American problem Marcy had pushed his conversations with [British Minister John F.] Crampton in regard to Canadian matters. There seemed need for haste because American fishermen were arming to withstand the British fleet. Crampton went north to caution the British admiral; but nevertheless Pierce decided to send an American fleet to these troubled waters in July, under instructions: "If on any occasion you discover attempts maturing to deprive any of our citizens of their just rights, you will respectfully but firmly remonstrate, and if persisted in, you will take such steps as in your judgment will be best calculated to check and prevent such interference, never resorting to violence except as a matter of self defence and necessity." About August 1, Marcy and Cushing went to Berkeley Springs with Crampton, where they worked over the British *projet;* and after consulting Everett, Marcy submitted a *projet* of his own, which Crampton sent back to England for consideration. . . .

The next foreign controversy concerned the Mexican situation. Several phases of our relations with that republic were unsatisfactory; the provisions of the treaty of 1848, especially as regards the definitive boundary and the control of Indian depredations on the border, proved difficult to administer, and American capitalists were in trouble. Rival American companies, the Hargous and Sloo interests, each laid claim to a right of way over the isthmus of Tehuantepec and they wanted government support of their respective contentions. The Fillmore Administration had gone so far as to press the Sloo claim, and a treaty was in process of negotiation when Pierce was inaugurated. Also, many people felt that we had not acquired enough of Mexico, and if a southern Pacific railroad were to be built, a certain amount of additional Mexican territory was essential.

Pierce had been in office scarcely three weeks when first rumor, and then confirmed news despatches, brought word that Santa Anna, widely suspected of unfriendliness toward the United States, had been elected President of Mexico once more. Shortly thereafter news arrived that the treaty ratifying the Sloo grant had been signed March 21. When this treaty, known as the Conkling convention, arrived in Washington, it was found to bind the United States and Mexico to joint protection of the Sloo concession. Simultaneously came news that Governor Lane of the territory of New Mexico had brought the boundary question to a point of crisis by issuing a proclamation declaring that the Mesilla valley, an area in dispute, belonged to New Mexico and by this act taking possession of the region. To complicate matters further, a Frenchman, Count Raousset-Boulbon, in connivance with the French consul, Patrice Dillon, was using San Francisco as a base for plans looking toward the acquisition of Sonora, and an adventurer, William Walker, was becoming interested in a similar scheme.

To straighten out this confused situation, especially as Lane's proclamation brought protests from Santa Anna, Pierce and his advisers took up Mexican relations early in May. They decided to uphold Lane's contention that the Mesilla valley belonged to the United States, but to permit no steps toward taking forceful possession. Lane was recalled and David Meriwether of Kentucky was sent out as governor with instructions to refrain from seizing the valley and to avoid collision with Mexico, pending negotiations. James Gadsden, a South Carolina railroad promoter suggested by Davis, was then selected as minister to Mexico, and his instructions were pondered. The Conkling treaty was held to be unsatisfactory, because it abandoned the Garay-Hargous interest; but what attitude the Pierce administration was going to adopt toward that interest, they were not ready to decide. They concluded, however, to negotiate for sufficient territory south of New Mexico to provide a route for a possible southern Pacific railroad, and Gadsden accordingly was instructed to treat for the purchase of an additional area. He also was delegated to secure our release from the obligation to protect Mexicans from Indian incursions, and to provide for the settlement of claims and the improvement of commercial relations. Later in October when Gadsden reported that Santa Anna was in sore straits for money and probably ready to cede land, Pierce and Marcy sent down C. L. Ward of Pennsylvania, who was also interested in the Hargous grant. They despatched him secretly with verbal instructions to offer $50,000,000 for a large area to include much of northern Mexico and all of lower California. Pierce, like Jefferson, was not averse to adding large areas to the national domain. Expansion southward was about to begin, so Pierce hoped.

The third set of diplomatic problems which Marcy brought to the cabinet table were those connected with Spain and Cuba. The hint in Pierce's inaugural, that he was interested in acquiring further territory, was interpreted by many to mean Cuba. For this there was good precedent. Polk had offered $100,000,000 for the island, but without success, and the Taylor-Fillmore administration had witnessed foolhardy attempts on the part of American citizens to aid in freeing Cuba by filibustering. These private ventures had made negotiations very difficult, and the flag of the United States upon merchant vessels plying between Cuban and seaboard ports had been insulted. Controversies of this description were aggravated by the fact that our diplomatic officials could not treat, or make adjustments, with the Cuban authorities, but must take up all questions with the Spanish government at Madrid by way of Washington, a mode of procedure extremely slow and tantalizing. By no means the least of the complications was the evident willingness of Great Britain and France to interfere in order to prevent the increase of American influence in Cuba. These powers were suspected of blocking our attempts at purchase. In the last months of the Fillmore administration after Pierce's triumphant election Secretary Everett had rebuffed a proposal made by Great Britain and France, at Spain's instigation, that the three powers, Great Britain, France, and the United States join in disclaiming any intention of acquiring Cuba and agree to discountenance any such attempts by others in a letter that borrowed some Democratic fire. The Whigs indeed had stolen a march on the new administration and Pierce and Marcy decided, since Great Britain, France, and Spain were so evidently opposed, that it was not time to renew proposals for purchase. Marcy, in his first instructions issued to Soulé, merely endorsed Everett's doctrine, and for the time being ordered the new minister to bend his energies toward persuading Spain to make more flexible commercial and diplomatic arrangements to insure the security and development of American commerce in the West Indies. Our "security" was his principal interest.

Having mapped out a policy for protecting American interests, the Pierce administration sought to promote trade. Marcy wrote a series of instructions to our minister in Brazil and our chargés in Ecuador, Bolivia, Peru, New Granada and Venezuela, seeking to bring about a concert of action which would convince Brazil of the advisability of opening up the Amazon to our traders. Another subject of diplomatic instruction, especially to our chargé in Peru, was concessions in guano, a commodity much in demand for the manufacture of fertilizers; and the administration sought to follow up the commercial advantages recently obtained in the La Plata region by their predecessors. Even greater possibilities were visioned in the far east. There lay a tempting source of wealth, as none knew better than Cushing, who had negotiated the first treaty with China. Now there was rebellion in that ancient empire, and American interests might profit thereby. As Marcy wrote:

Immediately after the extension of our laws over Oregon and the acquisition of California, not only [Hawaii] but also the whole of Polynesia, assumed an increased importance [to the United States]. More recently this importance has been vastly augmented by the wonderful events in China, events which threaten the overthrow of the Tartar rule, and the establishment in its stead of a government more in accordance with the tenets of Christianity and by the probable abandonment, at a day not distant, of the non-intercourse system of Japan.

Pierce and Marcy soon learned that China was of the more immediate concern, as Great Britain was endeavoring to use the rebellion as a means of gaining more trade facilities and was asking the cooperation of the United States. Pierce favored such a policy and Marcy so instructed Humphrey Marshall, then commissioner to China, but these instructions left the form of cooperation to Marshall's judgment, as the President did "not enjoin upon him cooperation [with the British] but only cordial relations and free conference with them."

Pierce thereupon sought an enterprising Democrat to send to China in Marshall's place. He considered himself fortunate when he prevailed upon no less an individual than Robert J. Walker to accept the commissionership. Walker, however, was not destined to go to China. His wife, who was ill, became so much worse as the time for parting neared that it was feared his leaving might kill her, so he declined the appointment late in August after having drawn his expense allowance. It is interesting to note that this decision was made not long after the administration began to speak favorably of a Pacific railroad, a project in which Walker was deeply interested. Pierce finally appointed Robert McLane, who was instructed to seek reciprocal free trade from the celestial empire, and was empowered to call in Perry's fleet if necessary.

Hawaii, too, offered opportunities, so thought American interests who were working for annexation; the strength of the English and particularly the French, in this region, meant that the islands must be watched. Marcy sought to warn the other nations against too close a connection with Hawaii, and arrived at the conclusion that these islands must inevitably come under the control of the United States. As a preparatory measure he began to feel out English and French official attitude toward American annexation. News of Perry's trade negotiations with Japan also was awaited with interest. But for both Japan and Hawaii more information must be received before any action could be taken.

* * *

The Republicans in Congress and out began an intensive campaign to stir up resentment against the South and indefatigably to promote the free soil crusade. Kansas made admirable propaganda. The difficulties in that troubled territory were advertised and magnified so that all the world might see. Congress was in session and there was no easier source of publicity. . . . With untiring energy and shrewd knowledge of American political psychology the hopeful leaders of the new cause scrutinized every act of the Pierce administration and found them all wanting, and newspapers like the *Tribune* reported every occurrence in Kansas and found them all drenched in blood. Hale had led off in January in the Senate and with the President's Kansas message, his proclamation, the documents he sent to Congress, and Douglas's report came new opportunities which the Republicans were not going to miss. Wilson, Wade, Lewis D. Campbell, Grow, Sherman, and many others made innumerable speeches and devised well advertised parliamentary tactics to keep the issue going strong. They pilloried the President as a weakling who had sold out to the South in hope of renomination, the creature of a dangerous and callous oligarchy which demanded the spread of a cruel and barbarous institution. Seward even went so far as to arraign him as a tyrant, and likened his policies toward the oppressed Kansans to the despotism of George III. So heavy was the flood of criticism that history, swept along by its very mass, has generally accepted it as truth.

Pierce was in an unhappy position, for the "South Americans" were attacking him viciously on the other flank. As Senator Clay of Alabama put it:

> The Abolitionists charge that the President approved the Nebraska Kansas bill to open new fields for slavery; the South Americans, that he did so to enlarge the area of free soil. The Abolitionists say his Administration has been exerted to make Kansas a slave state, the South Americans, to make it a free state. The Abolitionists abuse the President for removing Reeder; the South Americans for appointing him. The Abolitionists say he was removed too soon; the South Americans, too late. The Abolitionists say he was removed for no official delinquency; the South Americans that he was retained after repeated delinquencies. The Abolitionists complain that squatter sovereignty is frowned upon and threatened with suppression; the South Americans that it is countenanced and encouraged. The Abolitionists complain that the proclamation is leveled at Free-Soilers; the South Americans, at pro-slavery men.

Clay even went so far in his speech as to express the hope that if ever the Republicans got into control, the South would take up the sword in self-defense. Clay in private also undertook to remonstrate with Hale for his agitation of the slavery question. No good, he felt, could come from it. To this Hale characteristically replied, "Mr. Clay, it sent me to the Senate and *I* think there is something in that."

In the meantime the Republicans were looking for a candidate who would command the support of the "North Americans" and conduct a campaign which would make out of the fusion movement a permanent party. . . .

The four years of Pierce's administration were but a fragment of a longer period marked by important social changes. The United States was shifting from a rural to an urban society; cities and towns, rather than farm and plantation communities, were becoming the centers of American life. . . . The progress of the great social change was not uniform throughout the country; the rise of cities and towns occurred largely in the North and West. The South, on the other hand, remained definitely rural because of the investment of its capital in cotton production and because a strong social system had developed, quite feudal in some of its aspects, which was stable, conservative, and not easily changed. Two definite societies had emerged, the slow-moving South and the rapidly expanding North.... Pierce was intensely alive to the menace of sectional animosity. This great future of the nation in which he so firmly believed was possible only if the Union survived; nothing was to be gained and everything lost by disunion. His most cherished hope was the achievement of a permanent nationalism based upon mutual good will and harmony of interests.... With this view of the problem he had certain clearly defined policies. He labored to strengthen and discipline his party, pledged to his ideals, and hoped by pursuing a vigorous foreign policy to divert public attention from sectional differences....

SEWARD'S PLAN TO AVOID
THE CIVIL WAR[1]
Frederic Bancroft

... Seward recognized that he was in dire straits. For months he had firmly believed he was the only man that could save his country from countless disasters. Now a course of action that was contrary to his previous plans, advice, and expectations was likely to begin. In fact, expeditions for the relief of the two critical points were already preparing. If the Sumter expedition should be ordered forward—and the current was very strong in that direction—the world would understand that Seward's counsel had been rejected and that he had lost his power. It would humiliate him by making it plain that either he himself had been deceived or that he had tried to deceive others, and perhaps both. If the Fort Pickens expedition—which was Seward's almost exclusively—should be despatched as designed, and be successful, it would save a part of his prestige. But if either expedition should be carried out, southern Unionism would swing into secession, and a civil war—which he confidently believed would end in complete disunion and the overthrow of his party—would soon break out. Was there no way to avert these calamities?

Evidently as a last, desperate effort he laid this novel, elaborate, and dashing programme before the President:

Some Thoughts for the President's Consideration,
April 1, 1861.

First. We are at the end of a month's administration, and yet without a policy either domestic or foreign.

Second. This, however, is not culpable, and it has even been unavoidable. The presence of the Senate, with the need to meet applications for patronage, have prevented attention to other and more grave matters.

Third. But further delay to adopt and prosecute our policies for both domestic and foreign affairs would not only bring scandal on the administration, but danger upon the country.

---

[1] Selected from *The Life of William Seward* (New York: Harper & Brothers, 1900), II, 131–37. Reprinted with permission.

Fourth. To do this we must dismiss the applicants for office. But how? I suggest that we make the local appointments forthwith, leaving foreign or general ones for ulterior and occasional action.

Fifth. The policy at home. I am aware that my views are singular, and perhaps not sufficiently explained. My system is built upon this idea as a ruling one, namely, that we must

CHANGE THE QUESTION BEFORE THE PUBLIC FROM ONE UPON SLAVERY, OR ABOUT SLAVERY, for a question upon UNION OR DISUNION:

In other words, from what would be regarded as a party question to one of patriotism or union.

The occupation or evacuation of Fort Sumter, although not in fact a slavery or a party question, is so regarded. Witness the temper manifested by the Republicans in the free states, and even by the Union men in the South.

I would therefore terminate it as a safe means for changing the issue. I deem it fortunate that the last administration created the necessity.

For the rest, I would simultaneously defend and reinforce all the forts in the Gulf, and have the navy recalled from foreign stations to be prepared for a blockade. Put the island of Key West under martial law.

This will raise distinctly the question of union or disunion. I would maintain every fort and possession in the South.

FOR FOREIGN NATIONS

I would demand explanations from Spain and France, categorically, at once.

I would seek explanations from Great Britain and Russia, and send agents into Canada, Mexico, and Central America to rouse a vigorous continental spirit of independence on this continent against European intervention.

And, if satisfactory explanations are not received from Spain and France,

Would convene Congress and declare war against them.

But whatever policy we adopt, there must be an energetic prosecution of it.

For this purpose it must be somebody's business to pursue and direct it incessantly.

Either the President must do it himself, and be all the while active in it, or

Devolve it on some member of his Cabinet. Once adopted, debates on it must end, and all agree and abide.

It is not in my especial province;
But I neither seek to evade nor assume responsibility.

Even if Seward had not supplemented these propositions by having certain naval officers transferred so that they came into his plans, we should have no doubts as to who expected to take command. Lincoln had as yet given few, if any, public indications of possessing greater abilities than such men as Bates, Smith, and Welles. His policy—or, rather, his lack of one— during March cannot be defended successfully; it can only be explained and excused. He had halted between two opinions and had acted on none.

It was Seward's foreign policy that was most startling. It resembled a reckless invention of a mind driven to desperate extremes, as the sole means of escape from ruin, rather than a serious outline for national and international action. Two or three days before the "Thoughts" were written, the newspapers reported that a revolution had overthrown the Dominican republic and had raised the flag and proclaimed the sovereignty of Spain. For some time, too, it was well known that France, Spain, and Great Britain were considering the question of intervening in Mexico in order to redress and stop the wrongs that their subjects had suffered from the anarchy and violence there. It was also rumored that a plan was developing to put a European prince upon a Mexican throne. Citizens of the United States had been subjected to so many outrages in Mexico that Buchanan had recommended to Congress that forcible intervention should be resorted to, but our domestic affairs had engrossed the attention of the statesmen at the Capitol. The three European powers had not yet reached any agreement; and it was wholly unwarrantable for the United States to assume that they intended to do more than enforce their just claims. As to Russia, the basis for demanding an explanation was to be found in the false reports in southern newspapers and in political circles in Washington that she was about to open diplomatic relations with the Confederacy.

How did it happen that such a gorgeous and dangerous scheme found lodgment even in a mind as imaginative and bold as Seward's? He had early observed how advantageously public men can appeal to popular passions in dealing with foreign relations, and on a few occasions he had shown that he could outstrip all rivals when he really cared to do so. Yet even when advocating a policy that pointed straight toward war, he had generally taken pains to show that he deprecated actual hostilities. In speaking on the Hungarian question, in 1852, he said he would "never counsel it [war] except on the ground of necessary defence." As has been noticed, he reproached Soulé, in 1853, for exciting the American people against some of the European powers. "I cannot sympathize with such a spirit," he declared. "A war between the two continents would be a war involving not merely a trial [as to] which was the strongest, but [it would involve] the integrity of our republic." As late as January 12, 1861, he plaintively asked in the Senate: "Have foreign nations combined, and are they coming in rage upon us? No. So far from being enemies, there is not a nation on the earth that is not an interested, admiring friend." He now ignored all these solemn opinions of the past. He was zealous to do what would be most certain to make enemies of great nations and justify their combining and "coming in rage upon us." He would let neither expedition depart until he had stirred up a foreign war as the main-spring of his policy, for it was the prerequisite of changing the issue. Why, in our critical condition, it would not have sufficed to pick a quarrel with one foreign nation at a time does not appear, unless it was that he was so bent on speedily having a conflict of that kind that he sought it in several quarters so as to avoid delay and disappointment.

Seward's theory of the unifying effect of a foreign war had long been revolved in his mind. At the dinner of the New England Society he had declared that if New York should be attacked by any foreign power "all the hills of South Carolina would pour forth their population to the rescue." During the war of 1812 Jefferson had maintained, Seward said in the speech of January 12th, "that states must be kept within their constitutional sphere by impulsion, if they could not be held there by attraction. Secession was then held to be inadmissible in the face of a public enemy." The news about Santo Domingo came just at the time when Seward was in the most distressing circumstances. So he resolved to test his theory. . . .

CONFEDERATE DIPLOMACY:

POPULAR NOTIONS AND

INTERNATIONAL REALITIES[1]   *Henry Blumenthal*

Citizens of the confederate states of America were fond of comparing their struggle for independence with that of the English colonies in America during the Revolution. Unlike their forefathers, however, they did not consider it necessary to seek an alliance with a major power. Blinded by their convictions of righteousness and invincibility, they misjudged their own needs as well as the realities of European politics, where no great power had an interest in assuming the role that France had deliberately chosen in the American Revolution.

Although the most skillful execution of the most realistic Confederate foreign policy might conceivably have failed to produce the desired results, the course actually pursued in response to popular notions and attitudes turned out to be as disastrous as it could possibly have been. Many secessionists were convinced that the North would let them depart in peace, and, when this expectation was shattered by the outbreak of the war, they continued to sustain their confidence by making a number of unduly optimistic assumptions. Encouraged by initial battle successes, which in their judgment demonstrated their superior fighting ability, they doubted that the war would last more than one year. In their opinion, the Yankees lacked the courage and motivation for fighting a long war; but, should it nevertheless develop, they anticipated that it would damage the North far more than the South.

Operating under these illusions, the people of the Confederacy did not properly appreciate the importance of foreign aid and recognition for the survival of their nation. . . .

In their eagerness, Confederate leaders seemed prone to accept second-hand statements of subordinate foreign officials as quite reliable indications of their governments' policies. Also the Southern people and press seized upon every little favorable indication to justify their original optimism. They interpreted Europe's recognition of the Confederacy's belligerency, following the proclamation of the blockade, as the first step toward formal recognition of their independence. . . .

Regardless of the particular school of thought they favored, Southerners looked upon recognition as an elementary act of justice. Many factors seemed to justify its early realization. Aside from the cotton question and the long-range implications of the North's high-tariff policy and commercial rivalry, Britain and France, many Southerners speculated, would welcome Southern independence. Had not English and French merchants tried

---

[1] Blumenthal: Selected from *The Journal of Southern History*, XXXII, No. 2 (May 1966), pp. 151–171. Reprinted with permission.

ever since the mid-1850's to establish commercial ties with the South that, in case of secession, would enable them to replace the businessmen of Boston and New York? And did not the agrarian South and the trading interests of Europe see eye to eye in regard to the desirability, perhaps even the necessity, of putting a halt to the all too rapidly growing commercial ascendancy of the North? An independent Confederacy, it was confidently argued, would finally enable Great Britain and the South to reap the benefits of their advocacy of liberal trade principles. It did not seem to matter that these general notions ran counter to the tested observation that trade travels along well-established channels.

Looking upon themselves as a separate nation with a mode of living quite distinct from that of the North, Southerners generally expected Napoleon III, the avowed defender of the principle of nationality, to support their national aspirations. The traditional closeness between the people of France and the Southland augured well for the future relationship of their two countries. British admiration of the social amenities of the Southern people and the kinship between the conservative plantation owners of the South and the aristocratic country gentlemen of England also held out the promise of far-reaching co-operation and understanding. Such influential publications as the London *Times* and the *Economist* reinforced this belief. Although the slavery issue constituted a disturbing problem, it was by no means certain that the British and French governments would be as troubled by it as many of their citizens. Southerners liked to persuade themselves therefore that these economic and cultural aspects would work in favor of their recognition.

The strongest ties between Europe and the South were provided by cotton. The phrase that "Cotton is King" was more than a boastful slogan to Southerners of the 1850's. Statistics confirmed that four million Englishmen and one million Frenchmen depended for their livelihood on Southern cotton. British textile manufacturers, politicians, and newspapers had encouraged the South to believe that their government would, if necessary, use its fleet to remove any obstacle in the way of the uninterrupted flow of cotton from America. Southerners accepted it as gospel truth that by shutting Britain off from the supply of cotton, they could "create a revolution in Great Britain." To prevent a social upheaval, they assumed, Britain would without delay recognize the independence of the Confederacy, a matter of vital importance to the newly proclaimed state and nation.

To win recognition, President Jefferson Davis tried different approaches, usually using cotton as an instrument of policy. At first he was so anxious to impress upon the world that a civilized and moderate administration had assumed the reins of the Confederate government that he opposed an all-out war. With the Confederacy asking for nothing more than independence, the President thought, Europe and the United States might perhaps come round and admit the legitimacy of this request. The original instructions to the commissioners the Confederate government sent to Europe did therefore not include requests for substantial foreign aid or alliances. All the Confederacy basically desired was the conclusion of the usual treaties of friendship and commerce with countries extending recognition to it. As the war dragged on, this policy was revised. But even then, though seeking loans and ships, pleading for the lifting of the crippling blockade, and demanding recognition as a right, the Davis administration continued to frown upon outright foreign intervention. As late as November 7, 1864, Davis told the Confederate Congress that all he desired was recognition. In spite of the Confederacy's precarious condition in 1864, he still thought that recognition would be a powerful factor in the restoration of peace. It would bolster the morale of the Confederate people and embolden those Northerners who favored peace.

In the absence of recognition, Confederate authorities placed high priority on the lifting of the blockade and on receiving access to ships, munitions, and other vitally needed supplies. To the surprise and chagrin of the Confederacy, the maritime powers found it expedient to ignore their frequent appeals not to respect the "ineffective" blockade. With an apparent genius for accomplishing the opposite of what it intended, the Davis administration's description of the blockade was extraordinarily inappropriate. For all practical purposes, an "ineffective" blockade justified intervention even less than an effective one, international law to the contrary notwithstanding. Instead of taking utmost advantage of the "ineffective" blockade, planters and local politicians prevailed upon the administration to make it more effective by creating an artificial cotton scarcity. They experimented with this course in the belief that the sooner Europe felt the impact of a calamitous cotton shortage, the sooner it would intervene in behalf of the Confederacy. Subsequent decisions to burn cotton and to reduce production were merely variations of the same vain attempt to bring pressure to bear on Europe.

When the Anglo-American crisis in the winter of 1861–1862 did not enlarge the scope of the war and the effects of the blockade began to be felt more severely, the Confederate Congress suggested that the President offer Britain, France, and Spain attractive commercial advantages in return for their support. In April 1862 Secretary of State Judah P. Benjamin was belatedly authorized to offer France not only generous trade privileges, but also 100,000 bales of cotton, provided it would send its ships to pick them up. When France declined this baited offer, and Britain and Russia subsequently refused to join France in what they regarded as a futile mediation attempt, the Confederate government felt let down. It also became clear that just as the Confederate cotton policy could not coerce the European powers into recognition, the repeated warnings that a Northern victory would be followed by Northern aggression against Canada and Mexico did not frighten them. This kind of argument once again lent itself to interpretations not intended by the Confederate Department of State. It evidently persuaded Britain even more than France not to provoke United States aggression. Moreover, if the United States was aggression-bound, as Southern spokesmen asserted, would it not have been reasonable for European powers to speculate that a Confederate victory might tempt the Union to compensate for the loss of the South by moving northward?

In spite of Europe's passive attitude, the Davis administration continued to interpret every hopeful indication, such as the Erlanger loan and the secret shipbuilding deals in France and Great Britain, as evidence of possibly more far-reaching aid in the future. As the war continued, Confederate leaders, including General Robert E. Lee, came reluctantly to the conclusion that their survival required much more foreign assistance than they had previously thought necessary. Their readiness to relax the virtual embargo of cotton came too late. But the duration of the war enhanced the attractiveness of European mediation as a means of ending it. Having originally underrated the importance of diplomacy, Confederates became increasingly interested in a diplomatic solution of the war. However, if such a solution had ever been possible, it became progressively remote with the passage of time and the vanishing prospects of victory.

Great Britain and France meanwhile made more determined efforts than ever to cultivate cotton in India and Algeria. During the war years Britain managed in this respect better than France. It succeeded in supplementing its considerable cotton reserves at the beginning of the war with cotton imported from India and Russia, and it maintained such a superior competitive position that it could continue to supply the Continent with cotton and cotton goods. The accelerated use of wool and linen during the war years also contributed to the collapse of the "King Cotton" theory.

A minority of self-reliant Confederates, among them Vice-President Alexander H. Stephens, contended from the beginning that it was a great illusion to count on Europe's co-operation. . . .

Alexander Stephens questioned the sincerity of Europe's intentions with respect to both the American belligerents. According to him, England and France would deliberately avoid intervention in any form in order to reap the benefits from a war that might exhaust the North and the South. Without any effort on the part of the French and British, America's dynamic republicanism and commercialism might thus be reduced to a less dangerous challenge. "To give such nations the power of settling our relations towards the United States," warned the Charleston *Mercury* on February 3, 1863, "would be fatal to our liberties." The Atlanta *Southern Confederacy* on July 23, 1862, doubted the disinterestedness of the European powers and cautioned its readers that European intervention "would most likely be accompanied with humiliating conditions." In any case, the value of European intervention depended on joint action of the major powers, since sole reliance on France might be canceled out by the co-operation between the United States and Great Britain.

During the crucial war years the traditional anti-British sentiments of the American people reached a climax in the South. At a time when the South needed Britain's political and economic co-operation very badly, many embittered Southerners developed a hostility against Britain that was incompatible with their own vital interests. Anti-British commentaries, however justified in substance, may have given some people at home a feeling of satisfaction, but they hardly helped the Confederate cause, the ultimate success of which depended on Britain more than on any other power.

* * *

The militants insisted therefore that the only realistic approach to victory and recognition was to mount offensive operations against such Northern cities as New York and Philadelphia. Naval officers suggested such daring projects as a surprise attack against the New York Navy Yard and a naval raid on the Great Lakes with the aim of establishing Confederate control of these strategically located waters. Only fear of complications with England and of provoking an intensified Northern war effort prompted Jefferson Davis to remain primarily on the defensive. . . .

Whether the militants' aggressive strategy would have been as successful as they imagined may be open to question. But whatever shades of opinion divided the Southern people, for a long time all overwhelmingly shared the notion of their superior military prowess. The belief in the invincibility of their army provided their most assuring promise of ultimate victory. And yet, some contemporaries contended that the boastful references to invincibility may have been one of the factors which deterred England and France from coming to the assistance of the Confederacy during the early stages of the war. Indeed, why should these powers assume great risks if the South could, as it claimed, take care of itself? The delusion of superior strength, prompted by understandable domestic considerations, may possibly have weakened the foreign political chances of the South. It is well known that many members of the British Parliament and quite a number of French officials doubted that the North would succeed in conquering the South.

Rumor and hope of divine intervention also affected Southern notions about foreign affairs. The gradual deterioration of the Confederacy's domestic and military situation after 1863 eliminated its last slim chances of foreign assistance. Nevertheless, left to their own fate and diminishing resources, Southerners continued to derive some benefit from the endless rumors of imminent European help. . . .

Until the bitter end rumors continued to float around to the effect that "the United States and England have already commenced hostilities," that "Napoleon has landed a large Army on the Texas coast," and that England, France, Spain, and Austria had extended recognition. For good measure, reports also circulated that the United States was at war with Emperor Maximilian. Even though experience had taught many people to be skeptical about these rumors, many Confederate patriots liked, at least for a moment, to believe they were true. They appeared to be answers to their prayers.

The more distant peace and victory seemed to be, the more ardently the people prayed for them. From President Davis down, Confederates found comfort in the belief so well summed up by a Southern lady: "Though all nations should be against us, yet will we trust in the Lord Jehovah, the God of Battles." And when foreign intervention did not materialize, the Southern editor and writer James D. B. De Bow contended that this misjudgment was beyond human explanation: "God knows why & God only." . . .

At a loss to understand why the European governments did not consider the fate of the Confederacy a vital issue, the Confederate government found it particularly humiliating that, in spite of earlier diplomatic pleasantries, France and Great Britain had never officially stated their reasons for nonrecognition or the conditions under which they would grant recognition. Disappointed that the maritime powers observed the "so-called blockade" in a way causing "the greatest injury to the Confederacy" and angered by their failure to honor their commitments regarding Confederate ships, the President and his secretary of state in the end accused them of duplicity and bad faith. France, once regarded as the most reliable friend, became the target of particularly scornful denunciation. Times and tones had changed indeed when John Slidell delivered in 1864 the curse, "A plague I say on both your houses."

Even a brief reference to the considerations that influenced European governments shows that the foreign policy of the Confederacy was narrowly self-centered and paid little attention to the Europeans' analysis of the American problem. Confederate leadership, for instance, gave little thought to the effect of America's permanent division on the world balance of power, a matter of major concern to European governments. Nor did it fully appreciate that, in addition to other considerations, the Emperor of the French had to be concerned with the likely reaction of the French masses to intervention in the affairs of the model republic. And Southern statesmen deluded themselves if they expected Europe to act in their behalf at the risk of war with the United States. Quite aside from the important conclusion that Europe's long-range interests lay with the United States, European statesmen wanted to avoid such a war in order not to lose their freedom of action in European affairs.

Each power had its own reasons for its official neutrality. Russia had been on friendly terms with the United States and favored its preservation as a counterbalance to British sea power. Under Bismarck's leadership, Prussia included the United States in its policy calculations with the view of enlisting America's naval resources in times of war and of expanding German-American trade, finance, and immigration in times of peace. Austria concluded that its national interests would be best served by the speedy restoration of the Union and that England's involvement in the American conflict would regrettably distract it from the European scene. Though concerned about the Confederacy's eventual policy with respect to Cuba, Spain, like most other European governments, was resigned to following the lead of Great Britain and France.

Although these two powers had in the spring of 1861 come to an understanding that they would co-ordinate their policies with respect to the war in America, their interests in that part of the world were in competition with each other. Basically, Great Britain had existing major territorial and trading interests in the Western Hemisphere to protect, whereas Napoleon III developed ambitious schemes to promote such interests. Napoleon's involvement in Mexico therefore frustrated rather than furthered the prospect of close co-operation between France and the Confederacy. The French foothold in Mexico not only constituted a challenge to the Monroe Doctrine, it also affected British interests in Canada and the West Indies. Indeed, while the French Emperor desired "to abate the pride of Americans," he also endeavored to halt and reverse the steady ascendancy of Anglo-Saxon influence in the world. It was therefore beyond the realm of serious discussion for Britain to steer any course that would enable Napoleon to assume a leading role in New World affairs. By the same token, the French Emperor heeded the counsel of Foreign Ministers Édouard-Antoine Thouvenel and

Édouard Drouyn de Lhuys to resist the temptation to side openly with the Confederacy, lest France be embarrassed by domestic and international complications resulting from such intervention.

Britain, without whose co-operation no other European power would intervene in the American conflict, took Northern threats more seriously than Southern assurances. No matter how much the Confederate secretary of state belittled its likelihood, Britain feared a Northern invasion of Canada if it abandoned its neutrality. Also, whatever economic advantages the Confederacy could offer Britain, Secretary of State William H. Seward's threat that any European intervention in the Civil War would in the future justify United States intervention in European wars could not be lightly dismissed. And it would have made little sense to risk losing Britain's best customer in exchange for one whose economic development and potential simply did not compare favorably with that of the United States. British investments in United States railroads, banks, and mining and land companies, moreover, exceeded those in the English cotton industry. Southern prophecies, particularly after 1863, of the North's impending bankruptcy therefore were most unlikely to rally British investors behind the Confederate flag.

Even without the benefit of hindsight, it would seem that the leaders of the Confederacy were limited to few choices in the determination of their foreign policy. Not anticipating that the international acknowledgement of their independence would create a problem, they treated foreign affairs so casually at first that their Department of State appeared to be virtually superfluous. The safest approach, of course, would have been just the opposite: namely, to attach extraordinary importance to the assistance foreign powers might be induced to give the Confederate cause in time of peace or in case of prolonged war....

The Confederacy paid dearly for simply ignoring the possibility of nonrecognition. Its leaders were of course responsible for this omission. Equally extraordinary and damaging was their repeatedly demonstrated lack of good timing. Or was it due to their overconfidence that they only belatedly became aware of the importance of diplomacy, of sending a Catholic emissary on a diplomatic mission to Europe, and of using cotton and abolition positively for purposes of international bargaining? In all these instances, their awareness came too late to exploit the maximum potential of their undertakings. In the atmosphere of self-deception in which the Confederacy had been created, it was perhaps natural that its leaders underestimated their foreign political difficulties to such a degree that they became in the end the tragic victims of their self-delusion.

PRESIDENT POLK'S REQUEST FOR MONEY
TO OBTAIN TERRITORY FROM MEXICO,
AND THE WILMOT PROVISO   *Document 1*

President Polk to Congress.

I invite your attention to the propriety of making an appropriation to provide for any expenditure which it may be necessary to make in advance for the purpose of settling all our difficulties with the Mexican republic. . . . It is probable that the chief obstacle to be surmounted in accomplishing this desirable object, will be the adjustment of a boundary. . . . In the adjustment of this boundary, we ought to pay a fair equivalent for any concession which may be made by Mexico. . . .

I would, therefore, recommend the passage of a law appropriating two millions of dollars, to be placed at the disposal of the Executive, for the purpose which I have indicated. . . .

Remarks of Representative Wilmot from the floor, August 8, 1846.

MR. WILMOT . . . would vote for this appropriation in case the amendment he intended to offer was adopted. . . . He believed it a necessary and proper war. . . . But he trusted it was not to be a war of conquest. . . .

But the President asked for two millions of dollars for concessions which Mexico was to make. . . .

Mr. Wilmot took it, therefore, that the President looked to the acquisition of territory. . . . To this he had no objection, provided it were done on proper conditions. On the contrary, he was most earnestly desirous that a portion of territory on the Pacific, including the bay of San Francisco, should come into our possession . . . by purchase or negotiation—not by conquest.

But whatever territory might be acquired, he declared himself opposed, now and forever, to the extension of this "peculiar institution" that belongs to the South. . . .

He concluded by offering the amendment. . . .

Provided, That, as an express and fundamental condition to the acquisition of any territory from the Republic of Mexico by the United States, by virtue of any treaty which may be negotiated between them, and to the use by the Executive of the moneys herein appropriated, neither slavery nor involuntary servitude shall ever exist in any part of said territory, except for crime, whereof the party shall first be duly convicted.

NICHOLAS P. TRIST EXPLAINS WHY
HE DISREGARDED HIS INSTRUCTIONS,
DECEMBER 1847   *Document 2*

...I place my determination on the ground of my conviction, "*first*, that peace is still the desire of my government; *secondly*, that if the opportunity be not seized *at once*, all chance for making a treaty *at all* will be lost for an indefinite period—probably forever; *thirdly*, that this (the boundary proposed by me) is the utmost point to which the Mexican government can, by any possibility, venture." I also state, that the determination of my government to withdraw the offer to negotiate, of which I was made the organ, has been "taken with reference to a supposed state of things in this country *entirely the reverse of that which actually exists*." These four points constitute the heads under which the development of the subject naturally arranges itself.

1. "*First*, that peace is still the desire of my government." Upon this point the words of the President, as I took leave of him, are still fresh in my memory: "Mr. Trist, if you succeed in making a treaty, you will render a great service to your country."...

I have carefully examined the despatches last received by me, (those by which I am recalled,)...with a view to discover whether any change has occurred in the President's mind, in other words the recognised mind of our government, on this particular subject. I have found there no intimation or indication of any such change; nothing whatever which would at all warrant the supposition that he has ceased to believe, or believes any the less strongly now than he did then, that the restoration of peace is highly desirable to the country whom he is charged with the grave responsibility of thinking for, and judging for, and determining for, at this fearful turning point of her destinies....It is...*because* of its supposed tendency *to prolong the war*, that the President apprehends that the continuance of this mission "*may do much harm*." Here, then, is a conclusive proof,..."*that peace is still the desire of my government*."...

2. *Secondly*, that if the present opportunity be not seized *at once*, all chance for making a treaty *at all* will be lost for an indefinite period—probably forever....

The efforts made by the friends of peace...have been crowned with success far exceeding their most sanguine expectations....And, finally, they have succeeded in bringing together at the seat of government the governors of the respective States; and, after full conference, in obtaining their concurrence (with one single exception—the governor of Potosi) in the peace policy, and the pledge of their support....

But this party cannot possibly stand, *unless the object for which alone it has formed itself be speedily accomplished*. Without this its destitution of pecuniary resources must become aggravated every day; and this cannot continue much longer without sealing its fate: a catastrophe which would involve a total dissolution of the federal government and of the Union. . . .

3. "*Thirdly*, that this (the boundary proposed by me) is the utmost point to which the Mexican government can, by any possibility venture."

Under this head, I can do but little else than state my perfect conviction, resulting from the best use I am capable of making of the opportunities, afforded by my position, that such is the fact. The nature of the subject scarcely admits of my doing more. I will, however, call attention to the fact, that, independently of Texas, this boundary takes from Mexico about *one half of her whole territory;* and upon this fact remark, that, however helpless a nation may feel, there is necessarily a point beyond which she cannot be expected to go, under any circumstances, in surrendering her territory as the price of peace. . . .

4. "That the determination of my government to withdraw the offer to negotiate, of which I was made the organ, has been taken with reference to a supposed state of things in this country *entirely the reverse of that which actually exists.*"

Under this head nothing more is requisite than a general reference to what has been stated under the three preceding. . . .

THE OSTEND MANIFESTO   *Document 3*

James Buchanan, John Y. Mason, and Pierre Soulé to Secretary of State Marcy, October 18, 1854.

The undersigned, in compliance with the wish expressed by the President . . . have met in conference, first at Ostend, Belgium, on the 9th, 10th, and 11th instant, and then at Aix la Chapelle, in Prussia, on the days next following, up to the date hereof.

There has been a full and unreserved interchange of views and sentiments between us, which we are most happy to inform you has resulted in a cordial coincidence of opinion on the grave and important subjects submitted to our consideration.

We have arrived at the conclusion, and are thoroughly convinced, that an immediate and earnest effort ought to be made by the government of the United States to purchase Cuba from Spain. . . .

We proceed to state some of the reasons which have brought us to this conclusion. . . .

It must be clear to every reflecting mind that, from the peculiarity of its geographical position, and the considerations attendant on it, Cuba is as necessary to the North American republic as any of its present members. . . .

The natural and main outlet to the products of this entire population, the highway of their direct intercourse with the Atlantic and the Pacific States, can never be secure, but must ever be endangered whilst Cuba is a dependency of a distant power in whose possession it has proved to be a source of constant annoyance and embarrassment to their interests. . . .

It can scarcely be apprehended that foreign powers, in violation of international law, would interpose their influence with Spain to prevent our acquisition of the island. . . .

Besides, the commercial nations of the world cannot fail to perceive and appreciate the great advantages which would result to their people from a dissolution of the forced and unnatural connexion between Spain and Cuba, and the annexation of the latter to the United States. The trade of England and France with Cuba would, in that event, assume at once an important and profitable character, and rapidly extend with the increasing population and prosperity of the island. . . .

Under no probable circumstances can Cuba ever yield to Spain one per cent on the large amount [$120,000,000] which the United States are willing to pay for its acquisition. But Spain is in imminent danger of losing Cuba, without remuneration. . . .

The sufferings which the corrupt, arbitrary, and unrelenting local administration necessarily entails upon the inhabitants of Cuba, cannot fail to stimulate and keep alive that spirit of resistance and revolution against Spain, which has, of late years, been so often manifested. In this condition of affairs it is vain to expect that the sympathies of the people of the United States will not be warmly enlisted in favor of their oppressed neighbors.

But if Spain, dead to the voice of her own interest, and actuated by stubborn pride and a false sense of honor, should refuse to sell Cuba to the United States, then the question will arise, What ought to be the course of the American government under such circumstances?

Self-preservation is the first law of nature. . . .

After we shall have offered Spain a price for Cuba far beyond its present value, and this shall have been refused, it will then be time to consider the question, Does Cuba, in the possession of Spain, seriously endanger our internal peace and the existence of our cherished Union?

Should this question be answered in the affirmative, then, by every law, human and divine, we shall be justified in wresting it from Spain if we possess the power. . . .

Under such circumstances we ought neither to count the cost nor regard the odds which Spain might enlist against us. We forbear to enter into the question, Whether the present condition of the island would justify such a measure? We should, however, be recreant to our duty, be unworthy of our gallant forefathers, and commit base treason against our posterity, should we permit Cuba to be Africanized and become a second St. Domingo, with all its attendant horrors to the white race, and suffer the flames to extend to our own neighboring shores, seriously to endanger or actually to consume the fair fabric of our Union. . . .

RELATIONS BETWEEN THE UNITED STATES
AND HAWAII, 1850–1870   *Document 4*

Treaty of Reciprocity, signed July 20, 1855, but not ratified by the Senate.

The United States of America and His Majesty the King of the Hawaiian Islands, equally animated by the desire to strengthen and perpetuate the friendly relations which have heretofore uniformly existed between them, and to consolidate their commercial intercourse, have resolved to enter into a convention for commercial reciprocity. . . .

Article I. For and in consideration of the rights and privileges granted by His Majesty the King of the Hawaiian Islands in the next succeeding article of this convention, and as an equivalent therefore, the United States of America hereby agree to admit all the articles named in the following schedule, the same being the growth or produce of the Hawaiian Islands, into all the ports of the United States of America free of duty:

Schedule.

Muscovado, brown, clayed, and all other unrefined sugars.
Sirups of sugar; molasses.
Coffee; arrowroot. . . .
Undried fruits not preserved. . . .

Article II. For and in consideration of the rights and privileges granted by the United States of America in the preceding article . . . His Majesty the King of the Hawaiian Islands hereby agrees to admit all the articles named in the following schedule, the same being the growth or produce of the United States of America, into all parts of the Hawaiian Islands free of duty:

Schedule.

Flour of wheat.
Fish of all kinds.
Coal.
Timber and lumber of all kinds, round, hewed, and sawed, unmanufactured, in whole or in part.
Staves and heading.
Cotton, unmanufactured. . . .
Pelts; wool, unmanufactured.
Rags.
Hides, furs, skins, undressed. . . .

Despatch from James McBride, United States Minister resident at Honolulu, to Secretary of State William H. Seward, December 10, 1863.

No. 16.

Sir: Doubtless you will remember that a proposal from the Hawaiian Government was made to the Government of the United States for a reciprocity treaty March 1, 1852, which was finally rejected by the United States. . . .

I avail myself of this opportunity to urge upon the Government the very great importance and propriety of now accepting the proposal....

2. It would stimulate commerce between the two countries, and give a more vigorous impulse to the production and manufacture of all the articles specified as articles of exchange free of duty. Whatever stimulates industry and enterprise, though in but a limited degree, should not be overlooked by American statesmen....

In my opinion, it would give fresh or vigorous impetus to industry and improvements in both countries, and would furnish useful and honorable employment for hundreds in the Pacific States who otherwise would be comparatively idle....

Such a treaty would place these islands, in their social and commercial relations with the United States, very much in the attitude of a State in the Union, which, I presume, would not be considered, in any sense of the word, injurious to us.

This treaty, if perfected, would not only give us the general commerce and trade of these islands, but would have a tendency to secure the friendship of this Government and people, and by that means thwart an inimical influence forever at work here against the Government and the people of the United States, and perchance crush it out silently.

Additional reasons which might be adduced may be found in the very significant fact that all the important sugar plantations on this entire group, with but two exceptions, belong to citizens of the United States; and hence, so far as it might favor the people of these islands, the chief benefit would fall to the share of American citizens owning said plantations....

Despatch of Secretary of State William H. Seward to Minister McBride, February 8, 1864.

No. 14.

Sir: I have given a careful perusal of your very interesting dispatch, No. 16, upon the subject of reviving negotiations with the Hawaiian Government in reference to a reciprocity treaty.

The peculiar circumstances in which this country finds itself at this time render it inexpedient to adopt a policy of such moment without a mature consideration of all the interests involved in the proposed negotiation. ...I have only now to assure you that the subject will receive earnest consideration.

TOWNSEND HARRIS NEGOTIATES

A COMMERCIAL TREATY WITH JAPAN   *Document 5*

Extracts from Harris' journal.

Saturday, December 12, 1857. Again visited the Minister for Foreign Affairs.... I have nothing to note except what relates to the conference I had with him....

It related to the changed condition of the world by the introduction of steam; that Japan would be forced to abandon her exclusive policy; that she might soon become a great and powerful nation by simply permitting her people to exercise their ingenuity and industry; that a moderate tax on commerce would soon give her a large revenue, by which she might support a respectable navy; that the resources of Japan, when developed by the action of free trade, would show a vast amount of exchangeable values; that this production would not in any respect interfere with the production of the necessary food for the people, but would arise from the employment given to the actual surplus labor of Japan, etc., etc.; that foreign nations would, one after another, send powerful fleets to Japan to demand the opening of the country; that Japan must either yield or suffer the miseries of war. . . .

I added that the three great points would be: first, the reception of foreign ministers to reside at Yedo; second, the freedom of trade with the Japanese, without the interference of government officers; and third, the opening of additional harbors. . . .

Friday, December 25, 1857. Merry Christmas! . . .

I ask every day when I may expect an answer to my great communications.

The invariable reply is, that a great many persons are to be consulted . . . and then the old story, "The Japanese do not decide important affairs until after long deliberation." . . .

Thursday, January 28, 1858. . . . The answer of the Minister of Foreign Affairs on harbors was final. No doubt more will be opened by and by, but not at present. *The merchants and common people are no doubt in favor of opening the country*, but the *daimiōs* and *military* oppose it.

The civilians at the head of the government understand these matters better. They have learned a great deal since you have been in the country; therefore they are in favor of a treaty which they see will make the country prosperous, and the government rich and powerful. . . .

Wednesday, February 3, 1858. This morning, at an early hour, the Prince of Shinano called to have some private conversation. He said there was an intense excitement among the old party at the Castle; that the concessions already made had greatly exasperated them, and he feared, if I persisted in insisting on Kioto being opened, and on the right of the Americans to travel in the country, I should run a great risk of losing the whole treaty. . . .

I gave him to understand that, if all the other parts of the treaty were arranged to my satisfaction, I should try to suit them on the two points. . . .

Wednesday [sic], *February 4, 1858.* Article 4 gives to the United States government [the right] to land, free of duty, stores for the use of its fleet at Kanagawa, Hakodate, and Nagasaki. By this I have secured the choice of three good harbors for our naval depot in the East, in a country that has the most salubrious climate in the world, where the men cannot desert, and with a power that is sufficiently civilized to respect our rights; and, above all, not a power with whom we might have a rupture, like England. I consider this clause of immense importance, as now the depot can be removed from that wretched place, Hong-Kong, and the stores out of the power of England. . . .

Monday, February 8, 1858. . . . We at last fix dates on which the various places shall be opened: —

Kanagawa, July 4, 1859.
Nagasaki, the same.
Niigata, January 1, 1860.
Yedo, January 1, 1862.
Sakai, January 1, 1863.
Osaka, January 1, 1863.

Adjourned at one P. M. for their dinner, and meet again at two P. M. The whole of this [afternoon] was spent in a vain attempt to fix the boundaries of the various places. They were so unreasonable and so inconsistent that I could not help suspecting the champagne which I sent to them had not operated favorably. . . .

Tuesday, February 9, 1858. . . . I now took up the tariff.

I began by stating the objections to all tonnage dues, and showed that they only served to check commerce, were unequal in their operation, and injurious to revenue.

I then stated the objections to export duties, saying that it was a burden on the industry of their own people, was vexatious to the merchant, led to great expense to prevent smuggling, and was not of much benefit to the revenue. . . .

I closed by saying that commerce could bear a certain burden and no more . . . and concluded this branch by urging the simplicity and economy of collecting their revenue from imports alone. . . .

Saturday, February 20, 1858. . . . I am told that large sums of money have already been distributed among the officers of the Mikado, and that still larger sums will be applied in the same manner. . . .

SECRETARY OF STATE WEBSTER

ON REPUBLICAN IDEOLOGY   *Document 6*

Reply to Chevalier J. G. Hülsemann, Austrian Chargé d'Affaires, December 21, 1850.

. . . The objects of Mr. Hülsemann's note are, first, to protest, by order of his government, against the steps taken by the late President of the United States to ascertain the progress and probable result of the revolutionary movements in Hungary. . . .

The principal ground of protest is founded on the idea, or in the allegation, that the government of the United States, by the mission of Mr. Mann and his instructions, has interfered in the domestic affairs of Austria in a manner unjust or disrespectful toward that power. . . .

And although the President does not see that any good purpose can be answered by reopening the inquiry into the propriety of the steps taken by President Taylor to ascertain the probable issue of the late civil war in Hungary, justice to his memory requires the undersigned briefly to restate the history of those steps, and to show their consistency with the neutral policy which has invariably guided the government of the United States in its foreign relations, as well as with the established and well-settled principles of national intercourse, and the doctrines of public law....

The undersigned ... freely admits that, in proportion as these extraordinary events appeared to have their origin in those great ideas of responsible and popular government, on which the American constitutions themselves are wholly founded, they could not but command the warm sympathy of this country. Well-known circumstances in their history, indeed their whole history, have made them the representatives of purely popular principles of government. In this light they now stand before the world. They could not, if they would, conceal their character, their condition, or their destiny....

The power of this republic, at the present moment, is spread over a region one of the richest and most fertile on the globe, and of an extent in comparison with which the possessions of the house of Hapsburg are but as a patch on the earth's surface. Its population, already twenty-five millions, will exceed that of the Austrian empire within the period during which it may be hoped that Mr. Hülsemann may yet remain in the honorable discharge of his duties to his government. Its navigation and commerce are hardly exceeded by the oldest and most commercial nations; its maritime means and its maritime power may be seen by Austria herself, in all seas where she has ports, as well as they may be seen, also, in all other quarters of the globe. Life, liberty, property, and all personal rights, are amply secured to all citizens, and protected by just and stable laws; and credit, public and private, is as well established as in any government of Continental Europe.... Nevertheless, the United States have abstained, at all times, from acts of interference with the political changes of Europe. They cannot, however, fail to cherish always a lively interest in the fortunes of nations struggling for institutions like their own....

In the course of the year 1848, and in the early part of 1849, a considerable number of Hungarians came to the United States. Among them were individuals representing themselves to be in the confidence of the revolutionary government, and by these persons the President was strongly urged to recognize the existence of that government. In these applications, and in the manner in which they were viewed by the President, there was nothing unusual; still less was there any thing unauthorized by the law of nations. It is the right of every independent state to enter into friendly relations with every other independent state. Of course, questions of prudence naturally arise in reference to new states, brought by successful revolutions into the family of nations; but it is not to be required of neutral powers that they should await the recognition of the new government by the parent state.... If, therefore, the United States had gone so far as formally to acknowledge the independence of Hungary, although, as the result has proved, it would have been a precipitate step, and one from which no benefit would have resulted to either party; it would not, nevertheless, have been an act against the law of nations, provided they took no part in her contest with Austria. But the United States did no such thing....

Toward the conclusion of his note Mr. Hülsemann remarks, that, "if the government of the United States were to think it proper to take an indirect part in the political movements of Europe, American policy would be exposed to acts of retaliation, and to certain inconveniences which would not fail to affect the commerce and industry of the two hemispheres." As to this possible fortune, this hypothetical retaliation, the government and people of the United States are quite willing to take their chances and abide their destiny. Taking neither a direct nor an indirect part in the domestic or intestine movements of Europe, they have no fear of events of the nature alluded to by Mr. Hülsemann. . . .

Letter to George Ticknor, January 16, 1851.
    If you say that my Hülsemann letter is boastful and rough, I shall own the soft impeachment. My excuse is two fold: 1. I thought it well enough to speak out, and tell the people of Europe who and what we are, and awaken them to a just sense of the unparalled growth of this country. 2. I wished to write a paper which should touch the national pride, and make a man feel *sheepish* and look *silly* who should speak of disunion. . . .

THE EXPANSIONISM OF

SENATOR STEPHEN A. DOUGLAS   *Document 7*

Senate Speech of February 14, 1853.
    . . . Now, sir, a few words with regard to the island of Cuba. . . . I have often said and now repeat, that, so long as the island of Cuba is content to remain loyal to the crown of Spain, be it so. I have no desire, no wish, to disturb that relation. I have always said, and now repeat, that, whenever the people of the island of Cuba shall show themselves worthy of freedom by asserting and maintaining their independence and establishing republican institutions, my heart, my sympathies, my prayers, are with them for the accomplishment of the object. I have often said, and now repeat, that, when that independence shall have been established, if it shall be necessary to their interest or safety to apply as Texas did for annexation, I shall be ready to do by them as we did by Texas, and receive them into the Union. I have said, and now repeat, that, whenever Spain shall come to the conclusion that she cannot much longer maintain her dominion over the island, and that it is better for her to transfer it to us upon fair and reasonable terms, I am one of those who would be ready to accept the transfer. I have said, and now repeat, that, whenever Spain shall refuse to make such transfer to us, and shall make it to England or any other European power, I would be among those who would be in favor of taking possession of the island, and resisting such transfer at all hazards. . . .

Senate Speech of March 10, 1853.
    I have a word or two to say in reply to the remarks of the senator from Delaware upon so much of my speech as related to the pledge in the Clayton

and Bulwer treaty never to annex any portion of [Central America]. I objected to that clause in the treaty upon the ground that I was unwilling to enter into a treaty stipulation with any European power in respect to this continent, that we would not do, in the future, whatever our duty, interest, honor, and safety might require in the course of events. The senator infers that I desire to annex Central America because I was unwilling to give a pledge that we never would do it. . . . I was unwilling to bind ourselves by treaty for all time to come never to annex any more territory. I am content for the present with the territory we have. I do not wish to annex any portion of Mexico now. I did not wish to annex any part of Central America then, nor do I at this time.

But I cannot close my eyes to the history of this country for the last half century. . . .

You may make as many treaties as you please to fetter the limbs of this giant republic, and she will burst them all from her, and her course will be onward to a limit which I will not venture to prescribe. Why the necessity of pledging your faith that you will never annex any more of Mexico? Do you not know that you will be compelled to do it; that you cannot help it; that your treaty will not prevent it, and that the only effect it will have will be to enable European powers to accuse us of bad faith when the act is done. . . . What is the use of your guarantee that you will never erect any fortifications in Central America; never annex, occupy, or colonize any portion of that country? . . . If you make the canal, I ask you if American citizens will not settle along its line. . . . And I ask you how many years you think will pass away before you will find the same necessity to extend your laws over your own kindred that you found in the case of Texas? . . .

Sir, I am not desirous of hastening the day. I am not impatient of the time when it shall be realized. I do not wish to give any additional impulse to our progress. We are going fast enough. But I wish our policy, our laws, our institutions, would keep up with the advance in science, in the mechanic arts, in agriculture, and in every thing that tends to make us a great and powerful nation. Let us look the future in the face, and let us prepare to meet that which cannot be avoided. . . .

I cannot go so far as the senator from South Carolina. I cannot recognize English as our mother. . . .

The proposition is not historically true. Our ancestry were not all of English origin. They were of Scotch, Irish, German, French, and of Norman descent as well as English. . . .

Gentlemen ask us to vote ships and money, and they talk to us about the necessity of a ship in China, and about outrages in Tampico, and disturbances in South America, and Indian difficulties in Puget's sound. . . . High-sounding resolutions, declaring in effect, if not in terms, that whereas Great Britain has perpetrated outrages on our flag and our shipping which are intolerable and insufferable, and must not be repeated, therefore, if she does so again, we will whip Mexico, or we will pounce down upon Nicaragua, or we will get up a fight with Costa Rica, or we will chastise New Granada, or we will punish the Chinese . . . but not a word about Great Britain. What I desire to know is whether we are to meet this issue with Great Britain? . . .

Sir, I tremble for the fame of America, for her honor, and for her character. . . .

We do not wish to bully England. . . . I would ask to have the United States act upon the defensive in all things—make no threat, indulge in no bullying, but simply assert our right; then maintain the assertion with whatever power be necessary. . . . I believe the moment England declares war against the United States, the prestige of her power is gone. It will unite our own people; it will give us the sympathy of the world; it will destroy her commerce and her manufactures, while it will extend our own. It will sink her to a second-rate power upon the face of the globe, and leave us without a rival who can dispute our supremacy. We shall, however, come to that point early through the paths of peace. . . .

Senate Speech of April 17, 1858.

Various objections have been raised to this bill [for the construction of a railroad to the Pacific], some referring to the route, involving sectional consideration; others to the form of the bill; others to the present time as inauspicious for the construction of such a railroad under any circumstances. . . .

What is the objection to these termini? San Francisco, upon the Pacific, is not only central, but it is the great commercial mart, the great concentrating point, the great *entrepôt* for the commerce of the Pacific, not only in the present, but in the future. . . .

I believe it is a great national measure. I believe it is the greatest practical measure now pending before the country. I believe that we have arrived at that period in our history when our great substantial interests require it. The interests of commerce, the great interests of travel and communication—those still greater interests that bind the Union together, and are to make and preserve the continent as one and indivisible—all demand that this road shall be commenced, prosecuted, and completed at the earliest practicable moment. . . .

It will extend our trade more than any other measure that you can devise, certainly more than any one that you now have in contemplation. The people are all anxious for the annexation of Cuba as soon as it can be obtained on fair and honorable terms—and why? In order to get the small, pitiful trade of that island. We all talk about the great importance of Central America in order to extend our commerce; it is valuable to the extent that it goes. But Cuba, Central America, and all the islands surrounding them put together, are not a thousandth part of the value of the great East India trade that would be drawn first to our western coast, and then across into the Valley of the Mississippi, if this railroad be constructed. Sir, if we intend to extend our commerce—if we intend to make the great ports of the world tributary to our wealth, we must prosecute our trade eastward or westward, as you please; we must penetrate the Pacific, its islands, and its continent, where the great mass of the human family reside—where the articles that have built up the powerful nations of the world have always come from. That is the direction in which we should look for the expansion of our commerce and of our trade. That is the direction our public policy should take. . . .

SECRETARY OF STATE SEWARD REQUESTS
FRENCH WITHDRAWAL FROM MEXICO,
FEBRUARY 1866   *Document 8*

... France is entitled, by every consideration of respect and friendship, to
interpret for herself the objects of the expedition, and of the whole of her
proceedings in Mexico.... Nevertheless, it is my duty to insist that, whatever were the intentions, purposes, and objects of France, the proceedings
which were adopted by a class of Mexicans for subverting the republican
government there, and for availing themselves of French intervention to
establish on its ruins an imperial monarchy, are regarded by the United
States as having been taken without the authority, and prosecuted against
the will and opinions, of the Mexican people.... The United States have
not seen any satisfactory evidence that the people of Mexico have spoken,
and have called into being or accepted the so-called empire which it is insisted has been set up in their capital. The United States, as I have remarked
on other occasions, are of opinion that such an acceptance could not have
been freely procured or lawfully taken at any time in the presence of the
French army of invasion. The withdrawal of the French forces is deemed
necessary to allow such a proceeding to be taken by Mexico....

While this question affects by its bearings, incidentally, every republican
state in the American hemisphere, every one of those states has adopted the
judgment which, on the behalf of the United States, is herein expressed.
Under the circumstances it has happened, either rightfully or wrongfully,
that the presence of European armies in Mexico, maintaining a European
prince with imperial attributes, without her consent and against her will, is
deemed a source of apprehension and danger, not alone to the United States,
but also to all the independent and sovereign republican States founded on
the American continent and its adjacent islands....

The United States have not claimed, and they do not claim, to know
what arrangements the Emperor may make for the adjustment of claims for
indemnity and redress in Mexico. It would be, on our part, an act of intervention to take cognizance of them. We adhere to our position that the war
in question has become a political war between France and the republic of
Mexico, injurious and dangerous to the United States and to the republican
cause, and we ask only that in that aspect and character it may be brought
to an end. It would be illiberal on the part of the United States to suppose
that, in desiring or pursuing preliminary arrangements, the Emperor contemplates the establishment in Mexico, before withdrawing his forces, of
the very institutions which constitute the material ground of the exceptions
taken against his intervention by the United States. It would be still more
illiberal to suppose for a moment that he expects the United States to bind
themselves indirectly to acquiesce in or support the obnoxious institutions.

On the contrary, we understand him as announcing to us his immediate purpose to bring to an end the service of his armies in Mexico, to withdraw them, and in good faith to fall back, without stipulation or condition on our part, upon the principle of non-intervention upon which he is henceforth agreed with the United States. . . .

With these explanations I proceed to say that, in the opinion of the President, France need not for a moment delay her promised withdrawal of military forces from Mexico, and her putting the principle of nonintervention into full and complete practice in regard to Mexico, through any apprehension that the United States will prove unfaithful to the principles and policy in that respect which, on their behalf, it has been my duty to maintain in this now very lengthened correspondence. The practice of this government, from its beginning, is a guarantee to all nations of the respect of the American people for the free sovereignty of the people in every other state. . . . Looking simply toward the point to which our attention has been steadily confined, the relief of the Mexican embarrassments without disturbing our relations with France, we shall be gratified when the Emperor shall give to us, either through the channel of your esteemed correspondence or otherwise, definitive information of the time when French military operations may be expected to cease in Mexico. . . .

THE TURN

TOWARD

IMPERIALISM

CHAPTER 7

Agricultural Businessmen Lead the
Metropolis into the World Marketplace

At first glance, American foreign policy between 1865 and
1897 appears to be a confusing combination of general indifference to world
affairs punctuated by periodic outbursts of militant activity in Asia and Latin
America. In truth, however, Americans moved steadily outward in an imperial thrust that came to a violent climax in the latter half of the 1890's. The
events of the period become far less contradictory and perplexing if several
points are understood and kept in mind.

First: many Americans, and particularly a significant number of leaders,
were preoccupied with the dilemmas of Reconstruction during the first
decade after the Confederacy was defeated. Men like Secretary of State
Seward (and even President Ulysses S. Grant) who wanted a more vigorous
foreign policy found it extremely difficult to muster active and sustained
support for their plans and proposals.

Second: the processes of industrialization, which accelerated rapidly after
1865, likewise engaged much interest and energy. And, for a time, that attention and concern were directed largely to the building of the domestic industrial system.

Third: despite such involvement with internal developments, most American businessmen were increasingly engaged in and with the world marketplace. This majority was composed of the commercial farmers of the North
and the South whose huge surpluses of food and fiber glutted the home market. They steadily influenced foreign policy in two principal ways. Their

282

overseas sales turned the trade balance in favor of the United States in 1876–1877, and that dramatic event served to educate an ever larger number of metropolitan leaders to the importance of overseas markets. At the same time, the agricultural businessmen failed to enjoy sustained prosperity, and their angry protests—and demands for relief through expanded markets—pushed the country ever closer to imperialism.

Fourth: that process was reinforced by the growing number of commercial and industrial businessmen who adopted and adapted the agricultural argument for overseas economic expansion for their own purposes. As with the farmers, for example, petroleum producers like the Rockefellers of necessity soon turned to foreign markets to maintain profitable operations.

Fifth: responding to those ideas and pressures from agricultural and metropolitan businessmen, a group of Republican leaders headed by President Benjamin Harrison, Secretary of State James Gillespie Blaine, and Secretary of Agriculture Jeremiah Rusk formulated a broad strategy of imperial operation and put it into operation between 1889 and 1893. With the advent of the great depression that began in 1893, therefore, the consensus on the need for foreign markets exercised a determining influence on the making of American foreign policy. That drive for markets was also powered by a strong ideological element, moreover, because the agricultural businessmen had always argued that their freedom at home was inherently tied to the expansion of freedom in the world marketplace. The result was a righteous crusade to extend the area of freedom while enlarging the American marketplace.

Secretary of State Seward developed a grand vision of such beneficent imperial expansion before the Civil War (Document 1), and very much wanted to act upon it after the Union victory. But, given the preoccupation with Reconstruction and the exploitation of the North's triumph, he was successful only in connection with the purchase of Alaska. Seward's large views appear very clearly in the remarks of President Andrew Johnson concerning Alaska, and are supplemented by those advanced by Senator Charles Sumner (Document 2). The central importance of Seward in the shift from territorial expansion to overseas market expansion is ably discussed by Professor Charles Vevier in his article on "American Continentalism," in which he also outlines the thinking of later imperialists like Brooks Adams and Theodore Roosevelt.

Often overlooked (or discounted) in discussions of American foreign policy, President Grant nevertheless enjoyed a basic understanding of the importance of foreign trade in a capitalist economy. His early years in the Middle West very probably account for his awareness that agricultural businessmen depended upon exports, and his persistent though unsuccessful effort to acquire Santo Domingo (Document 3) was a product of that concern, as well as of his desire to annex a strategically significant outpost in the Caribbean.

A great boom in agricultural exports (particularly of food from the North and West) played a vital role in pulling the American economy out of the terrible depression of the 1870's. That experience, which included the turn of the trade balance, impressed many Europeans with the power of the

American economy—and with the danger of being overwhelmed by such exports. They moved to protect themselves with tariffs and other barriers, and that in turn antagonized American farmers. Their anger was increased by the inability of the American economy to function in a way that sustained the short-lived prosperity of the boom. In response, the farmers not only generated great pressure on American leaders, but explained their troubles in a way that defined world markets as essential to their welfare and at the same time defined specific countries as major opponents or enemies. Professor David M. Pletcher reviews some of those consequences in his article on "The Controversy over American Pork Exports," and the continuing agitation by agricultural businessmen is typified in Document 4.

The international conference referred to by the Grange leaders in that item involved an assembly of American nations first proposed and scheduled by Blaine in 1881, when he served as Secretary of State under President James A. Garfield. Blaine was one of the first metropolitan leaders to recognize the need to respond to the agricultural demand for larger foreign markets, and to generalize the meaning of that agitation to include the growing industrial sector of the political economy. But the assassination of President Garfield removed Blaine from office for seven crucial years, and the men who led the country during that period lacked his insight and his sense of urgency.

The few who did recognize the importance of foreign markets thought largely in terms of commercial and industrial interests. They either concentrated on pushing into areas that offered little to the farmers (Document 5) or, like Secretary of State Frederick T. Frelinghuysen, moved very cautiously. The retrospective account of Frelinghuysen's approach provided by State Department bureaucrat Alvey A. Adee in Document 6 is also a classic example of how men of a later period turned to their predecessors for guidance in furthering American expansion.

The continuing economic difficulties of the mid-1880's gradually turned urban leaders toward the overseas economic expansion advocated by the agriculturalists. Documents 7 and 8 illustrate the various arguments advanced by those men, and Document 9 shows how such views created effective pressure for a larger navy. Professor Walter La Feber reviews the early stages of such new construction in his article "The Beginnings of the Modern Battleship Navy."

Though less dramatic, the rising support for reciprocity treaties that would open new markets for American agricultural and industrial surpluses led Republican leaders like Blaine, Harrison, and Rusk to commit their party to such a program of overseas economic expansion between 1887 and 1890. They capitalized on the agitation in their handling of the Pan-American Conference of 1889, and sought to win the allegiance of the farmers by embarking upon a vigorous effort to negotiate reciprocity treaties with Brazil, Cuba, and other Latin American countries. They also used the same principle to arrange for increased exports of meat to Germany. The expansionist spirit of Rusk is nicely revealed in the interview presented in Document 10. Other aspects of their diplomacy are reviewed in the article by Professor A. T. Volwiler, and the American role in the Hawaiian revolution that occurred just before Harrison left the White House in 1893 is indicated in Document 11.

Grover Cleveland had not been particularly responsive to expansionist pressures during his first term as President (1885–1889), and his initial action upon being inaugurated for the second time, after his victory in the election of 1892, suggested that he would continue to move very slowly in foreign policy. His decision of March 9, 1893, to withdraw the treaty for the annexation of Hawaii that had been negotiated by Harrison and Blaine served to intensify the campaign for expansion. It angered members of the agricultural protest movement, for example, because it seemed to mean that the islands would be allowed to retrogress from republicanism to monarchy, as well as because they wanted to control the islands as a steppingstone to the markets of Asia. Other expansionists were equally outraged, and Cleveland found himself on the defensive against a large number of Americans even before a grave depression was touched off by the stock-market panic of May–June, 1893.

The economic crisis operated in several ways to force Cleveland into more vigorous action in foreign affairs. He had never been flatly opposed to overseas economic expansion, arguing instead that it should develop naturally as the metropolitan, industrial sector of the economy developed its full strength, and insisting that overseas territories (such as Hawaii) should be taken only if absolutely necessary to gain control of foreign markets. In and of itself, however, the deep depression indicated the need for more positive measures. It also convinced many metropolitan spokesmen of the necessity for governmental assistance in market expansion, and Cleveland was primarily—even narrowly—a metropolitan politician. At the same time, moreover, he needed to make some response to the ever rising clamor from the angry agricultural businessmen who were on the verge of taking control of the Democratic party. Professor La Feber reviews the way in which all such factors affected the President's handling of the boundary dispute that developed between Venezuela and Great Britain.

In some ways, Cleveland was more expansionist in dealing with the Cuban revolution that erupted in February, 1895. His original approach involved trying to help Spain reassert its control over the island; but, faced with increasing agitation over the issue in the United States, he steadily increased his pressure on Spain to act in ways that would meet the demand for Cuban freedom and increased American penetration of the island's economy. His political intervention had become extensive by 1896, and Cleveland even considered setting a deadline for satisfaction before he left office. He backed away from issuing that kind of indirect ultimatum, however (Document 12), and left the decision concerning more forceful intervention for incoming President William McKinley.

AMERICAN CONTINENTALISM:
AN IDEA OF EXPANSION,
1845–1910[1]

Charles Vevier

Ideology is the means by which a nation bridges the gap between its domestic achievement and its international aspiration. American continentalism, as the term is used here, provided just such an order of ideology and national values. It consisted of two related ideas. First, it regarded the United States as possessing identical "national and imperial boundaries." These were located within the physical framework of a "remarkably coherent geographic unit of continental extent." Second, it viewed much of North America as a stage displaying the evolving drama of a unique political society, distinct from that of Europe and glowing in the white light of manifest destiny. This attitude sharpened the practice of American foreign policy. Encountering the opposition of Europe's powers, it asserted that the United States was engaged in a domestic and therefore inevitable policy of territorial extension across the continent. American diplomacy in the nineteenth century thus appeared to demonstrate national political and social worth rather than acknowledge its active involvement in international affairs. Relying on its separation from the Old World, the United States redefined the conventional terms of foreign relations by domesticating its foreign policy.

... In spite of its apparent territorial insularity, American continentalism was bound to an older doctrine that had been overshadowed by the record of land acquisition of the 1840's. In these years, and in the 1850's as well, there were some men who were affected by the outlook of American continentalism and who adapted for their own ends the great objective of European expansion that dated from the age of Columbus and the Elizabethans. They sought to deepen commercial contact with Asia, an ambition that added a maritime dimension to the era of territorial expansion preceding the Civil War.

Students of American Far Eastern policy have already pointed out the rough coincidence of the westward movement across the continent with the rising activity of American interest in the Pacific Ocean and trade in China. By the early 1840's, Hawaii had already shifted into the continental orbit. Exploration of the Pacific Ocean had been undertaken by the government beginning with the Wilkes expedition in 1838 and concluding with the Ringgold voyages to the northern Pacific in 1853–1859. The Cushing Treaty with China in 1844 and the opening of Japan by Perry a decade later reflected the attraction of Far Eastern trade markets to American merchants on the Atlantic seaboard. The gold strike of 1849 stimulated railroad passage across the Isthmus of Panama, encouraged shipping operations between New York and

---

[1] Selected from *American Historical Review*, LXV, No. 2 (January, 1960), 323–35. Reprinted with permission.

California, and suggested continuation of this traffic to the Orient. The wider commercial possibilities implied by these forces meshed with an older American interest in the Caribbean, particularly in Cuba and the picket line of West Indian islands that ran down to Latin America. . . .

Historians have been prone to examine American expansionism in terms of conflicting mercantile and agrarian interests. They have overlooked the presence of a unifying view of American world geographical centralism that was grounded in a "geopolitical" interpretation of American continentalism and its place in the history of Europe's expansion to Asia. What emerged was a combination of two deterministic patterns of thought reflected in the outlook of such men as William Gilpin, Asa Whitney, Matthew Fontaine Maury, and Perry McDonough Collins. These men shaped an expectation of commercial empire as an end in itself as well as a means of developing the internal continental empire. . . .

William Gilpin, "America's first Geopolitician," declared that the unifying geographical features of the North American continent, particularly the Mississippi Valley, contrasted favorably with Europe and Asia. A summary of his views in the period 1846–1849 reveals his belief that the physical environment of America promised the growth of an area equal in population and resources to that of the entire world. A Jeffersonian democrat and a devotee of the writings of Alexander von Humboldt, he believed in the inevitable westward march of an agrarian civilization to the Pacific Ocean. He also associated westward expansion with American commerce and whaling enterprise already established there. During the Oregon crisis in 1846, Gilpin advised congressmen, as he may have suggested to President James Polk, that settlers moving into Oregon from the Mississippi Valley, the geographically favored heart of the continent, would make the mouth of the Columbia River an outlet for the export of American farm produce to Asia. Since agriculture sought through commerce an "infinite market of consumption" in the Far East, Oregon became the "maritime wing of the Mississippi Valley upon the Pacific, as New England was on the Atlantic." A strong bid for Asian trade, therefore, depended on the construction of a transcontinental railroad from the Mississippi to the Columbia River that would link the agricultural heart of the North American continent with the Pacific Ocean. By developing the interior, thereby gaining access to the coast, the United States might become the center of a new world traffic pattern. America's "intermediate geographical position between Asia and Europe . . . invests her with the powers and duties of arbiter between them," he wrote in 1860. "Our continent is at once a barrier which separates the other two, yet fuses and harmonizes their intercourse in all relations from which force is absent."

The Pacific railroad, in fact, was closely identified with the career of Asa Whitney, who had returned from China after a successful career as a merchant and who had campaigned from 1845 onward for the construction of a railroad from the upper portion of the Mississippi Valley to Oregon. It was Whitney's project that dominated for five years the great American debate over this vital internal transportation scheme. Unless Oregon was bound to the rest of the country by a transcontinental railroad, Whitney warned, the nation would be forced to engage in a balance-of-power diplomacy in the European manner, an eventuality that he thought would destroy the continental homogeneity of America. In presenting his Pacific railway scheme, he proposed to connect Oregon with the rest of the country, open oriental trade marts to American commerce and agriculture, particularly if the railroad was tied to a Pacific Ocean shipping line, and provide an instrument for the internal development of the nation-continent that would serve as "the means, and only means, by which the vast wilderness between civilization and Oregon can be settled." Thus he exalted the continental potential of producing "the most necessary and important products of the earth—bread stuffs and meat," and stressed the value of an international "commerce of reciprocity—an exchange of commodities." The railroad, he insisted, would "revolutionize the entire commerce of the world; placing us directly in the centre of all . . . , all must be tributary to us, and, in a moral point of view, it will be the means of civilizing and Christianizing all mankind."

Matthew Fontaine Maury, hydrographer of the United States Navy and adviser on railroad and international commercial problems to southern businessmen and politicians, was also interested in the relationship of the Pacific railroad issue to the old dream of the "passage to India." But he formulated a wider geopolitical conception of the North American continent by linking it with Latin America as well as with Asia. He agreed that a Pacific railroad was needed to develop the continental interior as a means of raising land values, encouraging settlement of the western lands, and providing for the continental defense of the nation. He, too, shared the conviction of the importance of the Asian trade and, faithful to the interests of the South, he pressed for the construction of a transcontinental railroad from Memphis to Monterey.

Maury, however, was influenced by an old geographical-historical idea that river valley civilizations were the most enduring and fruitful forms of society. In his view, the basins of the Mississippi and the Amazon Rivers were united in a vast continental-maritime complex that depended upon American supremacy of the Gulf of Mexico and the Caribbean Sea, the "American Mediterranean" as he called it. . . . Cut a canal through the Isthmus of Panama that would link the Pacific Ocean with the "American Mediterranean" and the shortened route to Asia would force European commerce to use a passageway that Maury insisted should never be under the control of a foreign power since it violated traditional American policy to allow foreign interference in the Western Hemisphere. . . . The canal, taken in conjunction with the Pacific railroad, demonstrated his ambition for the United States to overcome the "barrier that separates us from the markets of six hundred millions of people—three-fourths of the population of the earth. Break it down . . . and this country is placed midway between Europe and Asia; this sea [Gulf of Mexico and the Caribbean] becomes the centre of the world and the focus of the world's commerce."

This doctrine of geopolitical centralism was reflected in the activity of Perry McDonough Collins, whose career had been shaped by the westward movement, experience with steamship operations on the Mississippi, and the California gold rush. Living on the West Coast in the 1850's, he not only absorbed the impact of the nation's new geographical position on the Pacific but also read about Russia's explorations of the northern Pacific Ocean and its expansion into eastern Siberia. Quickly he "fixed upon the river Amoor in Eastern Siberia as the destined channel by which American commercial enterprise was to penetrate the obscure depths of Northern Asia."

Supported by President Franklin Pierce and Secretary of State William Marcy, Collins traveled throughout Siberia in 1856 and saw there elements of the American West. He felt himself to be a "pioneer in these wilds in the shape of a live Yankee," encountering many of the "difficulties that all western men who have blazed the first trail in a new country know by experience." Russian expansion in this region he interpreted as similar in objective and spirit to that of American continental expansion. Russia, he predicted, would move into Manchuria just as the United States had gone into Louisiana. The Amur River in eastern Siberia he likened to the Mississippi in North America. In his mind the spirit of the American frontier had international and historical significance: the emergence of the United States in North America was the first vital step in linking Europe and Asia. "The problem of a North Western passage to India . . . , which has occupied the great minds of Europe for some centuries, has been solved by the continuous and onward march of American civilization to the West . . . the commerce of the world will find its path across this continent. . . ."

* * *

The outlook formulated by these various opinions suggests the existence of two related American worlds. The first was the nation-continent created through the interaction of foreign policy and territorial expansion that resulted in the acquisition of contiguous territory in North America. In turn, it projected the concept of the second American world, the continental domain that was fated to extend its influence over the entire world through the expansion of commerce and control of international communications. The relations of both worlds were reciprocal. All this, however, depended upon realizing the economic implications of the central position conferred upon the United States through its expansion in North America and the significance of this event in the general expansionist history of the European world.

. . . The fund of ideas that had projected American continentalism onto the world scene was restated and maintained by William Henry Seward, an expansionist, a worshipper of the continental tradition established and exemplified earlier by John Quincy Adams, and a man whose outlook matched the geopolitical determinism exhibited by Gilpin, Whitney, Maury, and Collins.

. . . "Even the discovery of this continent [North America] and its islands, and the organization of society and government upon them," Seward stated, "grand and important as these events have been were but conditional, preliminary, and ancillary" to the great goal of European expansion for four hundred years, the attainment of the seat of all civilization—Asia. The revolts of 1848 and the strain of maintaining the "crazy balance of power" forecast the destruction of Europe, and it fell to the United States to seize the torch and light the way. Because the United States was writ large on the sphere of

289

world geography and history, it had the obligation to extend by means of its institutions the "civilization of the world westward . . . across the continent of America," across the Pacific to Asia, on through Europe until it reached "the other side, the shores of the Atlantic Ocean."

This rhetoric was not separated from the realities that Seward encountered as Secretary of State. The continent under American dominion, he reported, "like every other structure of large proportions," required "outward buttresses" that were strategically favorable to the United States. Thus the policy of attempting to buy naval installations in the Caribbean after the Civil War reflected his conviction at the outbreak of the conflict that Spanish intrusion in the region partially justified the launching of a propaganda counterattack throughout Latin America as well as war against Spain. In 1864, he insisted that commerce and communication in North America were centralized in the United States and had to be extended as a means of uniting domestic and foreign commerce and encouraging the development of American " agricultural, forest, mineral, and marine resources." . . . And, it was Seward's system of roughhewn continental geopolitics and beliefs cut out of the American grain that gives depth to the vigor with which he pursued American interests in the Far East. Much of his ambitious program, however, was not fulfilled because, as he said, "no new national policy deliberately undertaken upon considerations of future advantages ever finds universal favor when first announced." But Alfred Thayer Mahan countered this argument when he remarked in 1902 that "all history is the aggressive advance of the future upon the past, the field of collision being the present."

Mahan might well have added, however, that it was his geopolitics as well as that of Brooks Adams that defined the "field of collision." For the serious domestic crisis in the United States occurring in the 1890's within the context of a global economy and an international transportation revolution forecast a pessimistic future. Each, in his own way, attempted to swamp it with a conception of the past that he carried with him. Both Mahan's quest for a new mercantilism and Adams' propaganda for a new empire illustrate a retreat into history for a model that might avert disaster. One theme emerged —the extension of the nation's economic power from the line of the West Indies, Panama, and Hawaii to Asia. Here, the expansionist projection of the American continental experience that was developed in the pre-Civil War period acquired some relevance in the outlook of Brooks Adams. Viewing the expansion of Europe and of the United States as complementary developments, he turned to geopolitics to explain the nature of the problem.

The Germans and the Russians appeared ready to march to the East. This move would reverse the historical westward trend of the exchanges that formed the basis of world power. Obsessed by the belief that control over Asia and its resources was the issue between the Russo-German bloc and what he believed to be a weakened England, Adams called for an Anglo-American rapprochement. This would allow the geographical center of the exchanges to "cross the Atlantic and aggrandize America." The result? "Probably," Adams suggested, "human society would then be absolutely dominated by a vast combination of peoples whose right wing would rest upon the British Isles, whose left would overhang the middle province of

China, whose centre would approach the Pacific, and who encompass the Indian Ocean as though it were a lake, much as the Romans encompassed the Mediterranean." Specifically, Adams, Mahan, and the imperial expansionists who clustered around Theodore Roosevelt urged upon the United States the "large policy of 1898," which revived the Caribbean-Panama-Pacific Ocean relationship that had been sketched out in the 1840's and 1850's and publicized by Seward. . . .

Contemporary students of the United States foreign policy that developed at the turn of the century are confronted with a problem of perspective. From the standpoint of the expansionist projection of American continentalism revealed in the pre-Civil War era, the imperialism of McKinley and Roosevelt was not a new departure in American history. It was not an "aberration" of national behavior which has been loosely defined as the emergence of the United States to world power. The geopolitical suggestions of Mahan and Brooks Adams helped American statesmen to install the United States as such a power. It was also a startling demonstration of the adjustment of the new ideological justifications of the 1890's to an older nationalistic expansionist base formulated by men of an earlier generation. Gilpin, Whitney, Maury, and Collins had sensed the meaning of the new technology, its effect upon geographical relationships, and the interrelations between aspects of the economic system at home, and these men were captured by a desire to assume the leadership of an entire Western civilization in order to make a lasting impression upon Asia.

* * *

THE CONTROVERSY OVER
AMERICAN PORK EXPORTS[1]
David M. Pletcher

In the early 1880's the accumulated European resentment toward American competition discharged itself in a series of lightning bolts against the American pork trade. Cheap pork imports furnished a valuable staple food to European cities, but they seemed to rob European producers of their rightful market. Furthermore, the occasional appearance of trichinae in American pork gave protectionist governments a providential opportunity to pose as guardians of the public health. At no time were experts agreed as to what caused trichinae in pork or whether American pork was actually worse infected than any other, but the economic nationalists never allowed this uncertainty to stand in their way. In 1878 a Viennese doctor published a letter warning that one-fifth of American hams might be infected with trichinae, and this letter started a "whispering campaign" all over western Europe. On June 25, 1880, the German government banned American pork sausage and chopped pork.

In Britain the publication of warnings from Her Majesty's consuls in the

---

[1] Selected from *The Awkward Years: American Foreign Relations under Garfield and Arthur* (Columbia: University of Missouri Press, 1962), pp. 161–67. Reprinted with permission.

United States began to attract attention. The climax of this series was a sensational report from Acting Consul Crump in Philadelphia, declaring that 700,000 pigs had died in Illinois that year from hog cholera, which he confused with trichinosis. Crump quoted a frightful description of a human victim: "Worms were in his flesh by the millions, being scraped and squeezed from the pores of his skin. They are felt creeping through his flesh, and are literally eating up his substance." When the Crump report appeared in an official Blue Book, the panic-stricken British readers felt their own flesh begin to creep. In answer to a question in Parliament the Government then tried to reassure the public. Minister Lowell, suspecting a speculators' plot, did what he could to counteract its effects, while the State Department challenged the accuracy of Crump's information. On Blaine's instructions Lowell delivered a formal protest to the Foreign Office, but inasmuch as the British government did not seem disposed to pass restrictive legislation, Blaine soon let the matter drop.

Across the Channel the pork question caused much more serious trouble in Franco-American relations, since it served to aggravate already existing grievances over the failure of Léon Chotteau's reciprocity project. Cheap American bacon and lard had practically driven French pork products off the market, and even before the appearance of the Crump report there was a strong movement in the French legislature for protective duties against American pork. In February, 1881, as a health measure the minister of agriculture and commerce forbade the importation of all American pork products. Interior farm towns rejoiced and urged the government to enforce the decrees rigidly, but there was consternation in the seaports, especially in Bordeaux, where several capitalists had just opened a steamship line to the United States and were even then awaiting the first eastbound steamer, loaded with pork and hams. Immediate protests brought a postponement of the prohibition, but the French government refused to withdraw its decrees altogether.

Blaine at once supplied Minister Edward F. Noyes with all possible information on sanitary conditions in American packing plants, but without effect. When Noyes hinted that the French desire for a reciprocity treaty might have been partly responsible for the decrees, Blaine replied sternly that the United States would not consider any sort of commercial negotiations until the restrictions were withdrawn. On November 25, in the midst of his hurried activity before leaving office, he sent a stiff note to the French Minister in Washington, defending wholesome corn-fed American pork and hinting at retaliation by Congress against French wines, which were not infrequently adulterated.

With Frelinghuysen's full aprproval, however, the new American minister, Levi P. Morton, abandoned Blaine's sternness and set out to ingratiate himself with the French government and upper classes, trusting that time would eventually soften their prejudices. In November, 1883, President Jules Grévy actually withdrew the decrees of 1881 and agreed to admit American salt pork, but the Chamber of Deputies set aside his action until a French system of inspection, completely unacceptable to American packers, could be established. The French government maintained this position for the rest of the Arthur administration, even though the French Academy of Medicine gave a clean bill of health to American pork by an overwhelming vote. On July 4, 1884, in the midst of the argument, however, the French government held a gala celebration and presented the colossal Bartholdi Statue of Liberty to Morton for the United States, as if to say that France appreciated America's ideals, if not her pork.

* * *

Before European fears had run their course, the governments of Italy, Austria-Hungary, Spain, Portugal, and even Turkey had shut out American pork products. It was in Germany, however, that the prejudice against American pork did the greatest damage to diplomatic relations. This was so, partly because the powerful German landowners regarded the United States with contempt and envy, and partly because many meat-packers in the United States were German-born and already hated Bismarck. During 1881 and 1882 the Chancellor contented himself with his earlier decree shutting out American sausage, but late in 1882 a new surge of protectionism began, disguised as fear of trichinosis. A member of the Reichstag introduced a bill to prohibit all importation of American pork, while German customs officials invoked every possible technicality against American meats.

Liberal opponents of Bismarck protested that the exclusion of American pork would raise its price, to the detriment of the poor; newspapers printed exhaustive defenses of American meat-packing; and German merchants urged the government to spare their flourishing import trade, which paid generous taxes and gave much business to German shipping. Hoping to forestall action at the last minute, President Arthur sent a telegram inviting the German government to appoint a special commission to inspect American packing plants. All in vain. On March 6 the Reichstag approved a decree prohibiting the importation of all American pork.

As in the case of France the German prohibition presented two alternative lines of action to the United States: retaliation against German products and the establishment of rigid inspection in American packing plants. The packing companies and many other commercial interests urged the government to shut out French and German wines and other imports. On the other hand, even before the European pork decrees, spokesmen for American stockraisers had argued that the foreign demand for adequate inspection was reasonable. In November, 1883, the National Livestock Convention drew up a formal petition to Congress along this line. Testimony about the packing plants varied widely. In 1879 and 1880 doctors employed by the Marine Hospital Service and the Bureau of Animal Industry reported filthy conditions and diseased hogs being marketed, but when Blaine sent the chief of the Bureau of Statistics to examine the stockyards, he found nothing censurable. In 1883 a special commission appointed by Arthur declared that existing methods of inspection were adequate. They reported, however, that it was possible for diseased meat to be exported, and that microscopic examinations could be performed if necessary. Naturally such contradictory findings did nothing to reassure the Europeans.

In Congress the debate on retaliation and inspection was soon broadened to tariff policy in general. When Senator H. B. Anthony of Rhode Island introduced a resolution looking toward retaliation, Senator Beck offered an amendment directing the Foreign Relations Committee to investigate discrimination of all kinds against American products by special trade agreements. Beck advocated what amounted to an economic Golden Rule: Do not object to other nations' protectionism while proclaiming it a good thing for the United States. After the Senate had passed Anthony's resolution with Beck's amendment, the problem was turned over to the Foreign Relations Committee, which worked closely with the State Department. Moving cautiously to avoid offending the nationalists in Congress, Frelinghuysen wrote confidentially to the chairman of the committee, Senator Miller of California, to discourage any sort of retaliation, indicating that he preferred to settle commercial questions by bilateral reciprocity treaties. The committee reported in favor of an inspection system, but the Senate refused to pass a bill for this purpose, although it took no further steps toward retaliation.

The failure of proposals for inspection or retaliation should have consigned the German-American pork dispute to the limbo of dormant controversies, like that with France. However, Bismarck's native dislike of republican America had been sharpened by resentment over the steady emigration of German men of military age to the United States. Also, by ill chance the State Department did not have a representative in Berlin as shrewd and persuasive as Levi P. Morton. The American minister to Germany, Aaron A. Sargent, was a former senator from California, not well trained in diplomatic subtleties but anxious to cut a proper figure before the voters at home. On his arrival at his new post, late in 1882, he had shown too little deference to suit Bismarck, and, disturbed at the agitation over pork, he had consulted the liberal opposition too freely. For these offenses he became the principal target of the Chancellor's wrath.

In Sargent's early dispatches he carried out his duty by reporting frankly that he believed agrarian pressure for protection to be largely responsible for the pork decrees. Unfortunately he overstepped both his instructions and diplomatic propriety by threatening the German government with retaliation, and when Bismarck's minister at Washington protested, Frelinghuysen had to disavow Sargent's statement and send him a mild reprimand. At about the same time the State Department committed an equally serious blunder by allowing one of Sargent's candid dispatches to slip into the *New York Tribune*, less than a month after he had written it. The government-subsidized press in Germany burst into denunciations, suggesting that the United States was trying to force its diseased pork on Germany, and newspapers in several European capitals criticized Sargent's actions. German liberals, favoring free trade, naturally defended him, and one of Bismarck's principal opponents in the Reichstag, Dr. Edward Lasker, chose this moment to make a lecture tour in the United States. His attacks on German tariffs and the applause which he received further grated on Bismarck's nerves.

* * *

THE BEGINNINGS OF THE
MODERN BATTLESHIP NAVY[1]   *Walter La Feber*

Commercial war could easily flash into a military conflict. This was the
lesson Alfred Thayer Mahan taught in his influential writings published after
1890. Between 1889 and 1892 other new empire expansionists arrived at the
same conclusion in a series of significant congressional debates. The result
was the creation of the United States battleship fleet.

Although the modern navy had its origins in the appropriation act of
1883, this and following measures authorized the building of small, unar-
mored cruisers in the range of 7,000 to 7,500 tons, vessels capable only of hit-
and-run destruction of commerce. The argument, later associated with
Mahan, for large armored battleships which could enjoy a wide cruising
range and hold their own in pitched major naval battles on the high seas
found inadequate support.

A congressional consensus on the battleship theory occurred after the
arrival of Benjamin F. Tracy as Harrison's Secretary of the Navy. The two
events were directly related. The President-elect had named Tracy in an effort to mollify competing Republican factions in New York, but Harrison
had done so only after receiving assurance from several close advisers that
Tracy could handle a post which the Chief Executive regarded "as one of
the most important in my Cabinet." As the Boston *Journal* reported, Congress was in a big-navy mood, and no cabinet post promised "more to statesmen who are ambitious to increase their reputations." A leading lawyer and
judge in New York during the 1870's and 1880's, Tracy fully lived up to
expectations. Besides initiating the battleship fleet, he organized the Bureau
of Construction and Repair to eliminate much of the red tape which had
restricted the designing and building of new ships. He also established the
Naval Reserve in 1891, issued a contract for the first American submarine in
1893, presided over the production of the first heavy rapid-fire guns, smoke-
less powder, torpedoes, and heavy armor, and reversed a former Navy Department decision in order to save the Naval War College, where Mahan's
The Influence of Sea Power upon History was gestating.

Tracy's first annual report in December, 1889, set the new battleship
navy on its course, but the Secretary received much help in properly arranging the stage for rapid congressional action. While writing the report,
he worked closely with Senator Eugene Hale, a powerful big-navy advocate from Maine. The confrontation of American and German naval units
at Samoa earlier in the year made some reticent Americans realize the power
implications of expansion into the closed frontiers of the South Pacific.
Finally, Tracy's report was followed by a message from the Naval Policy
Board, which made the Secretary's paper seem almost antiexpansionist.

[1] Selected from *The New Empire: An Interpretation of American Expansion, 1860–1898* (Ithaca, N.Y.: Cornell University Press, 1963), pp. 121–25. Reprinted with permission.

Reiterating the concepts of the new empire theory, the naval officers on the board noted that the United States wanted no colonies, but that the nation would have to protect its expanding foreign trade. The officers then asked for 200 ships, including a fleet of battleships with a cruising range of 15,000 miles. Extreme expansionists, including the leaders of the House Committee on Naval Affairs, found in this report much ammunition for their arguments; more moderate expansionists, such as Hale, disclaimed the paper and used it to illustrate to their conservative colleagues just how moderate Tracy's demands really were.

Although it was moderate relative to the board's report, the Secretary's 1889 message was nevertheless epochal. Tracy demanded a fleet not for "conquest, but defense." He defined a defensive fleet, however, quite differently from those who advocated fast cruisers for purposes of hit-and-run destroying of commerce. In words that could (and might) have been plagiarized from Mahan's manuscript, Tracy wrote: "We must have the force to raise blockades. . . . Finally, we must be able" to attack an enemy's own coast, "for a war, though defensive in principle, may be conducted most effectively by being offensive in its operations."

He then easily switched to the offensive: "The nation that is ready to strike the first blow will gain an advantage which its antagonist can never offset." Tracy evidently believed defense meant deterrent first-strike capability. He realized such a navy would be expensive, but "it is the premium paid by the United States for the insurance of its acquired wealth and its growing industries." The Secretary predicted that the theaters of future naval action would be the Gulf of Mexico and the Pacific, areas where American interests had grown so rapidly and were "too important to be left longer unprotected." He demanded two fleets of battleships, eight in the Pacific and twelve in the Atlantic, and asked for eight such capital ships immediately. He also requested five more first-class cruisers and "at least five" torpedo boats.

Tracy momentarily dropped his efforts to drive these measures through Congress when he lost his wife and younger daughter in a fire which swept their Washington home in February, 1890. But as Tracy grieved, big-navy advocates such as Hale and Representatives Charles A. Boutelle of Maine and Henry Cabot Lodge of Massachusetts rapidly took up the cudgels. In introducing the 1890 measure, which called for three armored battleships, Boutelle explained that the Naval Affairs Committee had had a choice of either larger, far-ranging armored vessels which could "go to any part of the world," or armored 8,500-ton ships which could capably protect the coasts of North and Central America. The committee chose the latter in the belief that there should be "evolution" toward greater battleships. This disarmed some opponents, as did Lodge's shrewd suggestion in committee that the ships be called "sea-going, *coastline* battleships." Opposition nevertheless appeared from several factions: those who rightly termed the bill a "new departure" and refused to strike out on a course which might have so many unpredictable conquences; those who believed that for defensive "coastline" purposes old-fashioned monitors would be more effective than battleships; those who stuck with the commerce-destroying thesis and so wanted only smaller, cheaper cruisers; those willing to vote only for land defenses in harbors; and those wanting as little as possible on grounds of economy.

But these arguments made few inroads on a Congress which had grown amazingly offensive-minded since 1888. Assuming extracontinental commercial expansion as a fact of life, the big-navy advocates proceeded to draw all the conclusions. They sketched horrible pictures of a possible war with the great commercial competitor, Great Britain. Hale pointed out several times that "we have got to be so that we can strike Bermuda, the West Indies, and Halifax . . . and the seas round about." Senator Joseph R. Hawley of Connecticut added that when in trouble with England "you can not negotiate without a gun." Hawley was also among those who based his argument for battleships on the necessity of safeguarding the future Isthmian commercial thoroughfare.

When some Populists arose to dispute the arguments for a powerful navy, they met quick challenges from other westerners who had a better grasp of the situation. "We have grown to first rank among commercial nations," proclaimed Jonathan Dolliver of Iowa. "We must have ships, not to make war on anybody, but to keep other people from disturbing either our prestige or our rights." The recalcitrant westerners also received a warning from William A. McAdoo of New Jersey (destined to be Assistant Secretary of the Navy under Cleveland, 1893–1897): "One month of blockade of our ports on the seacoast and you would burn more corn in Kansas than you now do. One month's blockade on the Pacific coast and you would find your trade with the Orient cut off." With obvious sectional and partisan divisions, Congress authorized the three first-class battleships and a 7,300-ton cruiser. The new empire expansionists had begun to acquire an adequate military arm.

* * *

HARRISON, BLAINE, AND
AMERICAN FOREIGN POLICY,
1889–1893[1]   *A. T. Volwiler*

The "Empire Days" of the United States did not dawn with McKinley's administration, as some writers have indicated, but rather with Harrison's. This drift toward imperialism was indicated in diplomatic notes, congressional debates, newspapers, books and lectures. In 1889, the year in which Benjamin Harrison entered the White House, Edward J. Phelps delivered the annual Phi Beta Kappa address at Harvard on the subject, "International Relations"; he declared that the halcyon days of isolationism were doomed forever.

Surveying the record of the Harrison administration after its close, anti-administration newspaper editors charged it with having followed "policies

[1] *Proceedings of the American Philosophical Society*, LXXIX, No. 4 (November, 1938), 637–48. Reprinted with permission, with later revision by the author.

of entangling alliances and intrigues," and "of departures of the gravest nature both from the old and fixed traditions of the Government and from the rules of international morality." "Are we ready," asked *Harper's Weekly* on March 18, 1893, "to alter the whole character of the government, with its beneficent traditional policies, to impose upon the people the burdens entailed by the building up and maintaining of immense armaments, and to expose this republic to all the political and economic consequences which such a policy would bring in its train . . . ?" These editors welcomed the second coming of Cleveland to Washington, for he was to meet in combat and put to rout the forces of expansion. The rout, however, was only temporary; for Harrison's foreign policy, and not Cleveland's, gave expression to the deeper currents of American life during the period from 1880 to 1920.

Among its departures from old and fixed traditions, was its "big navy" program, carried out by Benjamin F. Tracy, one of the ablest of all American secretaries of navy. He worked in close personal accord with President Harrison and was one of the two or three most trusted of Harrison's counselors. Under Tracy's direction, the process of replacing the old wooden ships with modern steel armored ships went on at a rapid pace. He saw the history-making battleship *Maine* launched in 1890, and in the next year, the great armored cruiser *New York*, with a speed of 20 knots and the ability to sail 13,000 miles without recoaling. The famous first class battleship *Oregon* followed in 1893, and, on November 5, 1892, the *Olympia*, flagship of Admiral Dewey at Manila Bay, was launched. These were the ships which, before the century closed, were to enable American imperialism to bear fruit. During the years from 1889 to 1893, cruisers flying the American flag were seen speeding here and there in all quarters of the globe.

Before Tracy took office, Cleveland's secretary of navy had ordered Captain Alfred T. Mahan to Puget Sound to select a site for a new navy yard, and had issued orders unfavorable to the Naval War College. When Tracy's own chief of navigation took the view that a captain in the navy should sail ships and not write books, Tracy, with Harrison's full approval, overruled him and provided for Mahan the leisure which enabled him to complete *The Influence of Sea Power upon the French Revolution and Empire*, the second of his epoch-making books on the influence of sea power on history. In four years, Harrison's secretary of navy had brought results, world-wide in their influence, and had elicited a spontaneous outburst of national pride in both Democratic and Republican newspapers.

In an interview in the New York *World* on November 26, 1891, Tracy declared: "the sea will be the future seat of empire. And we shall rule it as certainly as the sun doth rise! . . . To a pre-eminent rank among nations, colonies are of the greatest help." Tracy watched with an eagle eye all opportunities to secure new colonies for naval bases. In this he had the President's support. The latter wrote to his secretary of state, James G. Blaine on October 1, 1891: "You know I am not much of an annexationist; though I do feel that in some directions, as to naval stations and points of influence, we must look forward to a departure from the too conservative opinions which have been held heretofore." Among the acquisitions which Harrison, Tracy, and Blaine sought to secure were the Danish West Indies, a lease on Samana Bay in San Domingo, a concession of the Mole St. Nicholas in Haiti, a naval base at Chimbote, Peru, all of Canada—including sole jurisdiction over Bering Sea and sole property rights in its fur seal—and a naval base in Samoa. Located thousands of miles outside of the natural sphere of the traditional political influence of the United States, Samoa was to serve as a beacon to guide America to Guam and Manila.

While his chiefs in Washington were thus planning acquisitions in the western hemisphere and the Pacific, Whitelaw Reid, American minister in Paris, was conferring with an emissary from Portugal. The imperialistic, piratical 1890's were years of grave apprehension for Portugal. Awakening from centuries of lethargy, she began feverishly to forestall the British in their expansion northward from South Africa by trying to unite the Portuguese colony of Angola on the southwestern coast with Mozambique on the southeastern coast into a solid trans-African colony. In 1890, a British fleet appeared before Lisbon with an ultimatum, and, as a result, Portugal felt fortunate to retain Angola and Mozambique, though insecure even in these.

It was under these circumstances that the Portuguese minister of finance, Carvalho, came to Paris in 1891 to confer in deepest secrecy with Whitelaw Reid and unfold to him the most delicate and critical proposals. These included a far reaching reciprocity treaty and concessions for American-owned entrepots. One entrepot, on the Bay of Nakala in Mozambique, would give the United States its first station on the shores of the Indian Ocean; another, on the Bay of Tigres in Angola, would be located on one of the best harbors in this colony; a third was to be established in Lisbon itself. In addition, Carvalho proposed to grant concessions to the United States to establish naval bases at Tigres, Nakala, and on the Azores.

When Reid transmitted these secret, startling proposals to Harrison and Blaine, they refused to consider more than a reciprocal trade agreement. This came as a frustrating surprise to Reid, for both Harrison and Blaine elsewhere were laying strong foundations for the empire age of the United States. Reid was so far in advance of his two chiefs in Washington that while they were planning to secure naval bases in the West Indies and Peru, he was wistfully dreaming of bases on the other side of the globe on the Indian Ocean. "I had thought," he wrote Harrison on October 9, 1891, "that in view of the growing needs of our navy . . . we might . . . be able to evolve an offer of coaling stations in Africa. . . ."

It was with Chile, however, that the most strained diplomatic relations during Harrison's administration developed; war seemed almost inevitable at the close of 1891. Chilean animosity towards the United States was of long standing and grew out of unsettled claims of American citizens, the rivalry of English economic interests, and the unfriendly attitude of the United States during Chile's War of the Pacific with Peru and Bolivia. After revolution broke out in Chile early in 1891, relations were still further strained when the United States seized the *Itata*, a Chilean ship carrying munitions from California to the revolutionists, and when asylum in the American legation in Santiago was granted to political refugees hunted by the revolutionists. Many diplomatic notes were exchanged on the latter subject; because of Blaine's illness, most of the American notes were written by

Harrison with the aid of Tracy and the assistant secretaries, William F. Wharton, Alvey A. Adee, and John Bassett Moore—though such notes went out over Wharton's signature, and not Harrison's.

On the sixtenth of October, 1891, when a settlement of the refugee question had been almost effected, an incident occurred which threatened serious trouble; 117 members of the crew of the United States warship *Baltimore*, commanded by Captain Winfield S. Schley, had been granted shore leave in Valparaiso, Chile; towards evening, an infuriated Chilean mob murdered two and seriously wounded sixteen of the sailors. In answer to the Chilean accusation that the American sailors had been drinking in saloons, Commander Robley D. Evans later observed that Captain Schley's "men were probably drunk on shore, properly drunk; they went ashore, many of them, for the purpose of getting drunk, which they did on Chilean rum paid for with good United States money. When in this condition they were more entitled to protection than if they had been sober."

When the news of this incident reached Washington, Blaine was back at his post. There was disagreement as to the responsibility for the attack and also as to its gravity. Blaine, with his Pan-American and reciprocity policies at stake, was inclined to treat the incident as accidental and of minor importance. Harrison, who as a soldier had worn the military uniform of the United States, regarded the attack as of gravest importance. Rival newspapers charged Blaine with letting his unfriendly feeling towards Harrison dominate his views, and accused Harrison of generating war enthusiasm in order to get reelected. When Blaine presented his views in cabinet meeting, the President leaned forward, and, with an emphatic gesture, declared: "Mr. Secretary, that insult was to the uniform of the United States sailors."

It was under such circumstances that the President drafted the instructions of October 23, 1891, to the American minister, Patrick Egan, in Santiago. These gave Chile an opportunity to present its side of the incident: but, if the facts were as reported, then, concluded the note, the American government "can not doubt that the government of Chile will offer prompt and full reparation." When Egan presented this note, the Chilean foreign minister replied that the United States was formulating demands and advancing threats which, "without being cast back with acrimony, are not acceptable," and added, that a Chilean court would properly investigate the matter. The Anglo-Saxon sailors felt that their case was not being tried fairly in the strange Spanish courts using a legal system based on Roman law instead of Anglo-Saxon law.

While the case was pending, Harrison had an opportunity to explain his position, when, on November 14, the new Chilean minister, Montt, came to present his credentials. As usual in such cases, the department of state had prepared a draft of the President's speech. It expressed Blaine's spirit and policy, and may have been prepared by him. After Harrison read it, he wrote on it in clearcut letters "Rejected," and then made a careful revision which he read to Montt.

A few weeks later, on December 12, there appeared in American newspapers a "diplomatic atrocity" in the form of a letter from the Chilean foreign secretary, Matta, to the Chilean Minister, Montt, in Washington.

It had been read to the Chilean Congress before it was sent. In insulting words it charged that the President of the United States and his secretary of the navy had made official statements which were "erroneous or deliberately incorrect"; that there was "no exactness nor sincerity in what is said in Washington" with respect to the seamen of the *Baltimore*. It closed with asserting "the right, the dignity and the final success of Chile, notwithstanding the intrigues which proceed from so low a source, and the threats which come from so high a source." When Commander "Fighting Bob" Evans of the *Yorktown*, then anchored at Valparaiso, read this letter, he entered in his journal on December 12: "I don't see how Mr. Harrison can help sending a fleet down here to teach these people manners.... I certainly would like to hear what Mr. Blaine has to say in reply." Four days later, he wrote: "The papers here grow more and more insolent and I don't see how Mr. Harrison can avoid sending an ultimatum at a very early day."

American sailors and boats were now being stoned by Chileans. The Chilean naval commander held manoeuvers in the harbor during which torpedo boats apparently used the *Yorktown* for target practice, running by within six feet. "I then saw the officer in charge of the drills," wrote Evans, "and told him that he certainly had great confidence in the steering gear of his torpedo boats; that if anything should jam so that one of them struck me I would blow her bottom out. He replied that the water in the harbor belonged to his Government, and he proposed to use it for the purpose of drilling his boats. I answered that I was fully aware of the ownership he had stated, but that the Yorktown and the paint on her belonged to the United States, and that neither must be defaced by his torpedo boats. After this incident they did not run at us so much, though the newspapers encouraged them to do so." Evans spent sleepless nights in December. On the 28th he wrote in his journal: "the crew of the Yorktown will sleep at the loaded guns to-night, and every night until I get some better news."

Two weeks later, the Chileans finally permitted the refugees to leave the legation and to be carried to safety by the *Yorktown*. Evans now breathed a sigh of relief, but prematurely. What followed can best be told in his own words: "During the early part of the first night out, while running at very high speed, a suspicious noise was heard in the high-pressure cylinder of one of the engines. When the cylinder head was taken off I found two hardened steel wedges, which had been placed in the valve chest, no doubt, when we first arrived at Valparaiso by some evilly disposed person, with the intention of sending us all to the bottom.... It was simply a miracle that I escaped a serious disaster, for if the cylinder head had been knocked out with the pressure of steam I was carrying, the side of the ship would have gone with it. As I stood watching the group of machinists and firemen working about the engines I could see the blood come into their faces until the whites of their eyes were bloodshot. I knew pretty well what they were thinking...." Only excellent seamanship and sheer good fortune had averted a tragedy which might have been as fateful as the blowing up of the *Maine* in 1898.

Only two years before, Blaine had presided over his grand Pan-American Conference, which had advocated settling all disputes between its members by mediation or arbitration—not by war. Chileans proposed such a settlement now, but it was to prove an iridescent dream. Concerning this alternative Evans wrote in his journal on December 31: "When the United States is willing to submit the question of the murder of her sailors in uniform to arbitration, I must look for other employment—the Navy won't any longer suit me. They can arbitrate 'till the cows come home' about the people in the legation at Santiago, but if they ever hint at such a thing about the *Baltimore's* men, then I think the voice of the American people will be heard in no uncertain tones."

Meanwhile, in Washington, Harrison's private secretary, Elijah W. Halford, was writing in his diary on December 18, 1891, that the President feared there would be war with Chile. On January 1, 1892, he wrote: "The President stated that all the members of the Cabinet are for War." Evidently Blaine was vacillating. Elkins said to Halford on the 19th: "Blaine changes his mind every five minutes." Sir Cecil Spring Rice of the British legation wrote that Tracy wished for war to see his new ships fight, and to get votes for more, and that the naval officers were encouraged in their natural desire for distinction.

War preparations went on at a feverish pace in both countries during the winter. At Valparaiso, heavy Krupp guns were arriving from Germany, and Chile cabled for a Prussian major to supervise their mounting. Chileans were "working like beavers" to get their ships ready, while American navy yards were working day and night, including Sundays. At the request of Harrison, the navy department prepared an exact list of all warships showing the guns carried, and the number of days each would require to get to Valparaiso. Orders were also placed with Steyes in Austria for 3,000,000 cartridges. Blount, a leading Democratic member of the House committee on foreign affairs, called to assure the President that the Democrats would not embarrass him and that whenever he wanted to come to Congress with the Chilean question, it would be treated outside of partisan politics.

Blaine's department was especially active. Peru, an old enemy of Chile, seeing a chance for revenge, was friendly to the United States, and was seriously considering ceding to it a permanent naval base at Chimbote. Both Harrison and Blaine desired such a base. Brazil's new revolutionary and republican government had just sent an Admiral with a fleet to Washington to present Harrison with a medal in token of appreciation of the early and friendly recognition accorded by the United States; hence Brazil would be expected to follow a policy of benevolent neutrality. The American Minister to Brazil was instructed to ascertain secretly the quantity and kind of coal, and the speed and capacity of steamers available in Brazil. Argentina, like Peru, had a boundary quarrel with Chile and was already on the verge of war. It had ordered its navy to be in readiness, and informed the United States that it could easily furnish the United States army with beef cattle and other supplies by a short route over the Andes.

The war fever was rising rapidly. The body of one of the seamen with seventeen bayonet and knife wounds lay in state for a time in Independence Hall, Philadelphia—an honor previously accorded only to Henry Clay and Abraham Lincoln. Theodore Roosevelt, then civil service commissioner in Washington, was on fire to lead a cavalry charge against the Chileans. Young

Americans sang the song popular in the music halls of London at the time:

> We don't want to fight
> But by jingo if we do,
> We've got the men
> We've got the ships
> We've got the money too.

On the 18th James Findlay Harrison, cousin of the President, wrote him: "It looks to us outsiders that there may be war with Chili, and in that event I hope you will not class military appointments for your kinfolk, as you do civil. The right of a Harrison to military service cannot be abridged and I think from education and experience that I am able to render some service. ..." To this the President replied on January 26: "I think you make a good point on me. Certainly I ought not to be unwilling to sacrifice my relations—as Mark Twain would say—if there is war with Chili! I have always been hopeful that a sense of justice would lead the Government of Chili to do that which would avoid collision. I am, as you know, extremely full of urgent business and anxious thought and have only time to acknowledge your letter and to send you my affectionate greetings."

On January 19, Sir Cecil Spring Rice wrote: "We are on the verge of a war, here which is owing to inconceivable stupidity of our (that is, the American) side and trickery on the other ... [Blaine] has prevented war with Chile so far, and may do so still; but the President and the navy are bent on it." Events were widening the breach between Harrison and Blaine, and self-seeking politicians in both parties were trying through the newspapers to bring about an open break. Blaine was ill early in January and lost or disregarded a request for a conference with Harrison.

On January 2, 1892, Blaine forwarded some Chilean despatches which he regarded as conclusive and, in effect, an apology. This Harrison denied in a letter to Blaine on the 4th. "It still seems to me," he wrote, "to have been an assault upon our sailors as such, and to have grown out of the unreasonable irritation and animosity which the Junta had promoted among the Chilean people ... that it began by a Chilean sailor spitting in the face of one of our men, which was followed by a knockdown."

Harrison now asked Blaine to cable Egan for the complete records of the trial. These he studied carefully, together with all the diplomatic correspondence. On January 19, a grave Cabinet meeting was held. The President had prepared for discussion a two page memorandum on the crisis which suggested the form that the next note to Chile—virtually an ultimatum—should take. Before the Cabinet came to it, however, Blaine became ill and withdrew, and Harrison did not then present it. The memorandum called for apology and reparation for the attack on the *Baltimore* sailors, the withdrawal of the offensive Matta letter and a suitable apology for it; if these were refused, diplomatic relations were to be broken off and all correspondence submitted to Congress.

The very next day Chilean resentment reached its peak in a despatch which declared that Egan was no longer *persona grata* and asked for his recall. So breathlessly acute was the situation now, that when this note arrived at the Department of State the exact time of its arrival, 1:23 P.M., was marked on it, and within half an hour Adee had a deciphered copy on the way to the White House. In reply, Harrison dictated a note which, fortunately, was not sent. It would have resulted in handing passports to the Chilean minister in Washington, and in the recall of Egan.

On January 21, another draft, prepared at the department of state, probably by Blaine, was sent to the President for approval. It was an indecisive note declining to recall Egan. On the margin of this draft, still preserved among his *Papers*, Harrison wrote: "This prepared by State Department— but my note was substituted." Among his *Papers* is also preserved the clear copy of his note in his own hand with but few erasures. In sharp contrast to the department's draft, Harrison's note brushed aside the question of Egan's status, and in clear terse statements presented the substance of his Cabinet memorandum of the nineteenth as a virtual ultimatum. At the top of Harrison's draft—a document significant in the history of the United States— appears this note in his own hand: "After a talk with Mr. Blaine we agreed to put this in shape of a note to Egan and I made on the face of typed copy the necessary alterations. Mr. Blaine said it was just right, took high ground, and he approved every word of it."

The ultimatum, in Harrison's words, was sent on January 21 as instructions to Egan signed by Blaine, to whom historians have ascribed it. Ultimatums are usually answered within twenty-four hours. When no reply had come after four days, Harrison felt that the United States could delay no longer and still preserve its dignity and respect. Therefore, he labored all day on Sunday, January 24, on what might have become an historic "war" message. It was read on Monday in Congress and the members of the committees on foreign relations of the two Houses, Democrats as well as Republicans, came to the White House for a conference. A declaration of war was apparently near at hand.

During this critical week-end the President of Chile happened to be absent from Santiago, else a reply would have been received on Saturday. As it was, the reply came on Tuesday, January 26; Chile had bowed to the inevitable; apology and reparation followed. Blaine now drafted a note of acceptance and sent it to Harrison, who had also drawn up a draft. This he combined with Blaine's and returned it to him. "I liked your despatch better than mine," wrote Blaine on January 30, and ordered it put in cipher and sent. "The President feels a sense of relief, now that this Chilean affair is off his hands," wrote Halford in his diary on February 1. Doubtless Chile had counted on distance to nullify the greater power of the United States, but when Peru, Brazil, and Argentina gave support to the United States, Chilean resistance would have been foolhardy. Harrison's firm policy in dealing with the *Baltimore* and other incidents preserved the dignity and respect—and hence the influence—of the Unitd States. But it also left a rankling memory among Chileans. As late as 1948, when Professor Isaac J. Cox of Northwestern University and a specialist on Latin-American history, was listed to lecture at the University of Santiago, Chilean students posted a sign on the university's bulletin board reading, "Remember the *Baltimore!*"

Some years later, when Harrison, then ex-President, was discussing the

Baltimore incident with his intimate friend, Augustus L. Mason, he asked: "What in your opinion is the main function of government?" "The protection of the life, liberty, and property of its citizens," replied Mason. "Yes," added Harrison, "*wherever* they are."

The significance of American foreign policy as developed by Harrison, Blaine, and Tracy, was noted at the British legation, where Sir Cecil Spring Rice wrote: "the moral for us is: what will the U.S. be like when their fleet is more powerful, if the administration acts in a similar manner? I can't help thinking that serious difficulty may yet spring from the Bering Sea matter. . . . The danger is a real one, I think, but I can't say that it seems to be realized at home."

Two months after his ultimatum to Chile, Harrison was penning another terse, firm, diplomatic note, this time to England on the Alaska fur seal problem. Again the atmosphere in the Executive Mansion was electric. Everett F. Tibbott, a member of Harrison's staff, wrote in his diary on March 22, 1892: "The President today finished his reply to Lord Salisbury's note refusing to renew modus in Bering Sea matter and the outcome means a backdown on the part of G.[reat] B.[ritain], or war. Have been most of the day engaged in preparation of the reply and this evening took it in person to Mr. Wharton with instructions from the President that he deliver it to Sir Julian personally. This may be the beginning of a 'War' diary. . . ." England yielded, however, and events were set in motion which led to arbitration and the conservation of seal life.

When Harrison left the White House on March 4, 1893, Hawaii was casting "a sunset glow over his dying administration"; the American navy ranked seventh among the navies of the world, instead of only twelfth, as it had when he took office; and the rank of the highest American diplomats abroad had been raised on March 1, 1893, from "Envoy Extraordinary and Minister Plenipotentiary" to "Ambassador Extraordinary and Minister Plenipotentiary." As a result, at the Court of St. James's the representative of the United States marched eighth in line instead of thirteenth. America, in full confidence, was appearing upon the world stage with a note of joyful achievement, feeling that she would dominate the century about to dawn.

PRESIDENT CLEVELAND AND
THE VENEZUELAN CRISIS
OF 1895–1896[1]   *Walter La Feber*

The boundary difficulties had begun in 1841 when a British surveyor, Robert Schomburgk, mapped the western limits of British Guiana. He included Point Barima inside Guiana's boundaries. Venezuela immediately protested, for Point Barima controlled the mouth of the Orinoco River, and

---

[1] Selected from *The New Empire: An Interpretation of American Expansion, 1860–1898* (Ithaca, N.Y.: Cornell University Press, 1963), pp. 243–45, 258–68, 279–82. Reprinted with permission.

that river was the trade artery for the northern third of South America. In the 1840's and again in the 1880's, Great Britain offered to relinquish its claims to Point Barima if Venezuela would concede much of the remaining area within the Schomburgk line. Venezuela refused, asking that the entire disputed territory be settled by arbitration.

Venezuela had unsuccessfully attempted to bring the United States into the argument while Hamilton Fish was in the State Department. In the late 1880's, however, the Secretary of State, Thomas F. Bayard, became interested. The British Foreign Office increased its claim in the disputed area from 76,000 square miles to 108,000 square miles and capped its new demand by announcing that Point Barima was British territory. Venezuela broke off diplomatic relations with England. Bayard then sent America's first emphatic protest to Great Britain, but E. J. Phelps, the American Minister in London, thought the time inopportune and did not deliver the message.

The United States did little else until Venezuela began pleading its case with the newly installed Cleveland administration in 1893. By this time Venezuela was desperate. Her government was tottering and her economy was in shambles. She could not reopen diplomatic relations with England because of the fear that this would force the payment of huge debts to British citizens, debts which the bankrupt Venezuelan Treasury could not afford to honor. Finally, acute unrest permeated the eastern section of the country where the boundary dispute lay. If the government surrendered the boundary claim, open revolution would be sure to follow. These growing pressures forced Venezuela to step up its appeals to the State Department. Gresham responded with a message of July 13, 1894, to Bayard, now American Ambassador to England. The Secretary of State noted that British claims had "been silently increased by some 33,000 square miles" and now embraced "the rich mining district of the Yuruari," one of the wealthiest gold stores on the continent. The American Ambassador, who had grown to dislike the Venezuelan character as much as he loved the Anglo-Saxon cultural tradition, delayed taking the instruction to the Foreign Office and finally presented a weakened version of the note.

American interest markedly increased in December, 1894. Gresham again asked Bayard to protest England's new claim. Cleveland followed by declaring in his annual message that he would "renew the efforts heretofore made to bring about a restoration of diplomatic relations . . . and to induce a reference to arbitration." In January, 1895, Gresham sent several instructions to Bayard asking him to sound out Great Britain on the two points Cleveland had mentioned. These incidents in December and January marked the beginnings of full-fledged American participation in the boundary dispute. Events soon occurred in the United States and Latin America which picked up the momentum of American interest and speeded it first to Olney's epochal declaration of July, 1895, and finally to Cleveland's dramatic pronouncement in December.

Five general factors can be analyzed to indicate the background and immediate causes of these two messages: (1) new European encroachments in Latin America; (2) vigorous reaction by American public opinion to these encroachments; (3) the entry of commercial arguments into the American case, especially (4) the view that the Orinoco River was the vital pawn in the dispute; (5) the arrivals of Richard Olney into the United States State Department and Lord Salisbury into the dominating position in British politics.

* * *

... Olney [was not] in the colonialist camp. Like Gresham, he despised the thought of a colonial empire and strenuously opposed the acquisition of the Philippines. The attempt to ensure America's "free access to all markets" and the flexing of the fully developed muscles of one of the "powers of the earth" nevertheless envisioned a kind of vigorous foreign policy which even Lodge and Roosevelt could heartily endorse, as they did after Olney's July 20 note became public. Such a philosophy furthermore envisioned the extension of American responsibility abroad far beyond any previous limits.

Not the least of Olney's characteristics were his bluntness and stubbornness. As early as 1894 his vigorous statements and determination made him the most powerful member of Cleveland's cabinet. Shortly after he became Secretary of State, a man with similar characteristics rose to power in England. Lord Salisbury re-entered office in July, 1895, as both Prime Minister and Foreign Minister. Since the retirement of Bismarck, he was the dominant European statesman. Swept into office in July, 1895, with the largest majority any government had enjoyed in the House of Commons since 1832, Salisbury's vigor was abetted by the power both to carry out his decisions and to compel Parliament to abide by them. The clashing on the international diplomatic scene of two men such as Olney and Salisbury promised to be not only exciting, but explosive.

Olney's interesting personal traits and the blustering language of the July 20 note often make one lose sight of the fact that President Cleveland greatly influenced the formulation of the Venezuela policy. Some historians claim that Cleveland made the key decision of sending the July message and that he outlined the tone of the policy. It is definitely known that the President warmly endorsed Olney's first draft of the message, though he proposed "a little more softened verbiage here and there." In a letter to his Secretary of State, Cleveland called the message "the best thing of the kind I have ever read and it leads to a conclusion that one cannot escape if he tries—that is if there is anything of the Monroe Doctrine at all." The President declared in this letter that Olney had shown that there was "a great deal" in the Monroe Doctrine, and that the Secretary of State had placed "it I think on better and more defensible ground than any of your predecessors—*or mine.*" This letter indicates that Cleveland endorsed not only the language of the note, but also Olney's key point that the United States could intervene in the dispute because it was affected by events occurring elsewhere in the Western Hemisphere. Other than the President, the Secretary of the Navy, Hilary Herbert, the Secretary of the Treasury, John Carlisle, and the new Attorney General, Judson Harmon, read and endorsed the message before it was sent to Salisbury. Several weeks later the

Secretary of War, Daniel Lamont, added his blessings. No record has been found of any cabinet member who disagreed with the note.

The explosion.

Olney began the July 20 message by reviewing the respective claims. He concluded that neither party stood for a boundary line "predicated upon strict legal right." The Secretary of State then turned his fire directly on Great Britain for its attempt to move "the frontier of British Guiana farther and farther to the westward" of the Schomburgk line. Olney noted the vital point that these British moves included two recent advances: one by Salisbury in 1890 which "fixed the starting point of the line in the mouth of the Amacuro west of the Punta Barima on the Orinoco," and one by the Rosebery government in 1893. Venezuela had offered to arbitrate these claims, but Great Britain, so Olney claimed, had consistently refused. The Secretary closed this first section of the message by noting that to all this "the United States has not been, and indeed, in view of its traditional policy, could not be indifferent."

Olney then reached the transition to the next section, which concerned the Monroe Doctrine:

By the frequent interposition of its good offices at the instance of Venezuela...the Government of the United States has made it clear to Great Britain and to the world that the controversy is one in which its honor and its interests are involved and the continuance of which it can not regard with indifference.

This phrase provides the key to the remainder of the note, for Olney then tried to fit the Monroe Doctrine into the meaning of this sentence. The Secretary of State made a bad fitting, but this is irrelevant to the understanding of Olney's intention and to the aims of the administration's foreign policy. Olney advanced the argument that American interests as well as Venezuelan territory were at stake. In essence he was interpreting the Monroe Doctrine as the catchall slogan which justified protecting what the United States considered as its own interests. If the Monroe Doctrine had not existed, Olney's note would have been written anyway, only the term American Self-Interest would have been used instead of the Monroe Doctrine.

* * *

The note emphasized that the Monroe Doctrine was positive as well as negative. Monroe's declaration did "not content itself with formulating a correct rule for the regulation of the relations between Europe and America. It aimed at also securing the practical benefits to result from the application of the rule." Further, the Doctrine was a "distinctively American doctrine of great import to the safety and welfare of the United States." Olney advanced the thesis that the "safety and welfare of the United States" could be affected in two ways. One stemmed from the fact that the Latin-American nations were "friends and allies, commercially and politically, of the United States." Thus, "the subjugation of any of them by an European power...signifies the loss of all the advantages incident of their natural relations to us." Olney then moved beyond this in elaborating his second point: "But that is not all. The people of the United States have a vital interest in the cause of popular self-government." Using sentences which sound much like the phrases Woodrow Wilson used in 1917 when he proclaimed the ideal of extending the American form of democratic self-government to the world, Olney pronounced the extension of this form of government to Latin America as the most important factor to be protected if the self-interest of the United States was to remain unharmed. . . .

Olney coupled this closing reference to political ideals, however, with the more mundane matter of the Orinoco River. First, however, he wrote the famous phrase:

Today the United States is practically sovereign on this continent, and its fiat is law upon the subjects to which it confines its interposition. Why? It is not because of the pure friendship or good will felt for it. . . . It is because, in addition to all other grounds, its infinite resources combined with its isolated position render it master of the situation and practically invulnerable as against any or all other powers.

Olney did not include this declaration in the message as a debating technique. As his speeches prove, he earnestly believed that the United States possessed a commanding position among the powers of the world. From this double assumption that the United States had the right to intervene in Latin-American affairs whenever its rights were endangered, and further, that it had the power to protect its rights, Olney asked the crucial question whether American interests were involved in the Venezuelan boundary dispute to the extent that the United States could legitimately intervene. He answered with an emphatic affirmative: "The political control at stake . . . is of no mean importance, but concerns a domain of great extent . . . and if it also directly involves the command of the mouth of the Orinoco, is of immense consequence in connection with the whole river navigation of the interior of South America." After denying that Great Britain could qualify as an American state, Olney concluded the message by declaring that "peaceful arbitration" was the "one feasible mode" of determining the boundaries.

. . . Due partly to a misunderstanding of the time Cleveland's message was to be sent to Congress, partly to the fact that Salisbury was inundated by other matters, and partly to the Foreign Office's underestimation of the dispute's significance in American minds, the British reply did not arrive at the State Department until five days after the President's annual message had been delivered.

The State Department, meanwhile, endeavored to keep the note secret. Vigilant journalists nevertheless began reporting rumors of the message as early as September 2. The American public became especially aroused over these rumors when, in October, Great Britain sent an ultimatum to Venezuela. . . .

Two other events further disconcerted the State Department in the autumn of 1895. In October, the British Ambassador to the United States, Sir Julian Pauncefote, told a reporter that Great Britain would not think of submitting its "well-defined" territory in Venezuela to arbitration, especially that area which contained British settlements. Olney feared that this interview was a "foreshadowing" of the British reply from Salisbury on Venezuela.

Olney also became concerned over British actions in Nicaragua. Bayard reported in early November that the British had *"reserved their rights"* in the whole Nicaraguan affair. Later in November, the British-Nicaraguan indemnity treaty was made public. The pact expressly stipulated that no American could serve as the third commissioner on the arbitration board. England wanted to settle directly with Nicaragua. Adee believed that such an obviously anti-American provision was "an important indication of the drift of British policy."

Adee's fear was mirrored in the American press and political circles throughout the fall and early winter of 1895. During October and November journals freely expressed the opinion that Cleveland would present a vigorous interpretation of the Monroe Doctrine in his December address. Many of these papers fervently hoped for such a message. Politicians recognized that many constituents were intensely concerned with Latin-American affairs. Representative Thomas M. Paschal from Texas wrote Olney, "Turn this Venazuelan [*sic*] question up or down, North, South, East or West, and it is a 'winner.'" "Why, Mr. Secretary," Paschal exclaimed, "just think of how angry the anarchistic, socialistic, and populistic boil appears, on our political surface.... One cannon shot across the bow of a British boat in defense of this principle will knock more pus out of it than would suffice to inoculate and corrupt our people for the next two centuries." Other congressmen, as Representatives Joe Wheeler of Alabama and Charles H. Grosvenor of Ohio and Senator William E. Chandler of New Hampshire, published articles stressing the importance of the Orinoco River within the context of the necessity to expand the foreign commerce of the United States.

Salisbury's reply finally arrived at the State Department on December 7, five days too late for Cleveland's annual message....

In his consideration of the Monroe Doctrine, Salisbury simply disclaimed the relation of the hallowed dogma "to the state of things in which we live at the present day."...

Salisbury emphasized this vital point in another way. He challenged Olney and Cleveland to admit explicitly that the American economic and political system could not remain a viable system if it was forced to remain within the continental bounds of the United States....

Salisbury capped his argument by making a tactical concession. He admitted that, if American interests were involved or threatened, the United States had a right, "like any other nation, to interpose in any controversy" which endangered these rights. The Prime Minister granted that the United States was entitled to "judge whether those interests are touched, and in what measure they should be sustained." He merely wanted Olney and Cleveland to define these interests. Unless his allegations could be controverted, Salisbury denied that the United States had a right to demand arbitration in the dispute.

The second note, dealing with the boundary controversy proper, began by again declaring that the British government believed the boundary dispute "had no direct bearing on the material interests of any other country." Salisbury cited historical facts which ripped apart Olney's argument for the Venezuelan case. At one point Salisbury sarcastically commented, "It may reasonably be asked whether Mr. Olney would consent to refer to the arbitration of another Power pretensions raised by the Government of Mexico on such a foundation to large tracts of territory which had long been comprised in the Federation [of the United States]." . . .

. . . Cleveland was "mad clean through." He later wrote that it would have been "depressing" and "unpleasant" for the United States to learn that the great Monroe Doctrine was really "a mere plaything with which we might amuse ourselves."

Olney released his anger by drafting the President's message of December 17. Cleveland later asserted that Olney's draft "entirely satisfied my critical requirements"; in fact, "I have never been able to adequately express my pleasure and satisfaction over the assertion of our position." The draft was never submitted to the other members of the cabinet. This was unfortunate, for Carlisle and the Secretary of Agriculture, Sterling Morton, later expressed disagreement with the bluntness of the message. Olney and Cleveland thus unloaded their fury unmolested, and on December 17 the world heard of the American challenge to the British Empire.

The President's message was, in essence, a succinct summary of Olney's July 20 note. Cleveland's declaration is significant, however, because it emphasized and amplified Olney's crucial point that the United States was becoming involved in the controversy not for the sake of Venezuela, but for the welfare of the United States. . . .

. . . The Monroe Doctrine was "strong and sound," the President declared, "because its enforcement is important to our peace and safety as a nation and is essential to the integrity of our free institutions and the tranquil maintenance of our distinctive form of government." Such a principle could "not become obsolete while our Republic endures." This was an emphatic definition of the Monroe Doctrine as a doctrine of self-interest. Cleveland so defined the Doctrine explicitly: "The Monroe Doctrine finds its recognition in those principles of international law which are based upon the theory that every nation shall have its rights protected and its just claims enforced."

Cleveland and his Secretary of State did believe that American interests were greatly endangered. Nothing better illustrates their beliefs than Cleveland's statements in the closing part of his December 17 message: "The duty of the United States [is] to resist by every means in its power, *as a willful aggression upon its rights and interests*, the appropriation by Great Britain of any lands or the exercise of governmental jurisdiction over any territory which after investigation we have determined of right belongs to Venezuela." Cleveland emphasized the importance he placed on this sentence by then declaring, "In making these recommendations I am fully alive to the responsibility incurred and keenly realize all the consequences that may follow." He italicized the sentence, as it were, by saying that the United States would risk war in order to preserve the principle contained in the statement.

* * *

American historians have offered three interpretations to explain the Cleveland administration's policy in the boundary dispute. The most popular explanation states that Cleveland brought about the crisis in response to domestic political attacks on the general policies of his administration. A second thesis traces the policy's roots to Olney's bellicose, stubborn temper. A third interpretation declares that a "psychic crisis" struck influential segments of American opinion in the 1890's and that a new spirit of manifest destiny emerged from this "crisis."

There can be little doubt that Cleveland took domestic political pressures into account, but defining these pressures as major causative elements leaves key questions unanswered and raises many others. Cleveland's bellicose policy could not have permanently won political enemies to his side. The Republican jingoists and the Democratic silver bloc led the cheering for the December 17 message. Neither of these proups would have agreed with the President on national political objectives. Cleveland actually alienated many of his strongest suporters, especially the eastern bankers who had once saved the gold reserve and who, at Cleveland's request, repeated the rescue operation shortly after the December message. In other words, the administration's Venezuelan policy attracted groups which were irreconcilable in domestic politics and repelled some of the administration's staunchest supporters. Cleveland obviously realized that such maneuvers did not win national elections. War might have united the nation behind him, but the President certainly did not plan to turn the controversy into a war.

* * *

An interpretation which stresses Olney's bellicose character misses two important points. First, Gresham worked on a diplomatic note which concerned the Venezuelan situation several months before Olney assumed the top position. Judging from Gresham's letters in the late winter and early spring of 1895, this note was probably quite militant. Second, Cleveland initiated the dispatch of the Olney note, reworked the draft, and heartily endorsed his Secretary of State's language. The President played an extremely important part in the formulation of the policy, especially during the crucial incubation period of April-July, 1895.

A thesis which emphasizes that Cleveland bowed to the pressure of jingoism and a mass psychological need for vicarious excitement helps little in understanding the whole of the administration's foreign policy. After all, Cleveland defied these public pressures when they were exerted (often in even greater force) for Hawaiian annexation, the application of the Monroe Doctrine in the Corinto dispute, and compromises in the silver repeal act and the 1894 tariff. There is no reason to believe that he suddenly bent to the winds of jingoism in 1895, unless he had better reasons than pleasing irreconcilable political enemies. It should be further noted that it is impossible to put Cleveland and Olney in those social groups which supposedly were undergoing this psychological dilemma.

Olney and Cleveland acted because they feared that United States interests were in jeopardy. Both men emphasized this point at the time, and there is no reason to doubt their word. The Venezuelan dispute threatened American interests in three areas. As Lodge noted in his Senate speech of December 30, 1895, British military control of the Orinoco would make the Caribbean a "British lake." Second, if England controlled the entrance to this river, she could regulate the commercial traffic flowing into and out of the upper third of the South American continent. Third, if Great Britain either militarily or diplomatically coerced Venezuela into accepting the British position, not only would the Monroe Doctrine have become an empty shell, but the United States would have moved far in forfeiting its rights to, what Olney termed in his July note, "the practical benefits" which resulted from the "application" of the Monroe Doctrine.

Obviously, neither domestic political pressure nor mass psychological complexes could have endangered such interests. Rather, the danger would have had to come in the explicit form of European encroachments and threats to Latin America. These occurred in 1894 and 1895. In this short space of time, Great Britain and France made ominous moves in Venezuela, Nicaragua, Trinidad, Santo Domingo, and Brazil. Cleveland, Olney, and Adee carefully studied these moves. Even Bayard, the foremost apostle of Anglo-American friendship, admitted in January, 1896, that there were good reasons to "fear that there was an indefinite plan of British occupation in the heart of America."

The gravamen of the problem is, of course, that the Cleveland administration considered American interests to be endangered by such encroachments. Again, the time element is important. The United States had entered into the deepest trough of the depression in late 1894 and early 1895. Cleveland noted these factors in his annual message on December 2, 1895. The American commercial community believed that an expanding overseas commerce would revive the American economy. Cleveland and Secretary of the Treasury Carlisle expounded this commercial philosophy in its most detailed form throughout 1894. Secretary of State Gresham, who reopened the Venezuelan question in 1894, also emphasized the importance of foreign markets if the repressive weight of industrial glut was to be lifted from the American economy.

Richard Olney entered the State Department in June, 1895, with the two elements needed to touch off the explosion. He had realized in 1894 that the depression was no ordinary turn of the business cycle, but a "labor revolution" which marked a new era in American economic history. Second, he had a profound sense that the United States had matured to a point where it could exert its influence on the world stage. Olney naturally wanted to use this power to benefit American interests.

The two currents of economic overseas expansion and Olney's realization that the United States possessed the means to protect its interests converged into the Venezuelan controversy. A feeling of manifest destiny existed, but it was not a type of mob excitement which Cleveland and Olney would have disparaged. It was a rational opinion that American interests in Latin America would have to be expanded and protected....

SECRETARY OF STATE SEWARD'S VISION
OF AN AMERICAN EMPIRE   *Document 1*

Senate speech of March 11, 1850.

... We have thoroughly tried our novel system of Democratic Federal
Government ... and we know that it is a system equally cohesive in its parts,
and capable of all desirable expansion; and that it is a system, moreover,
perfectly adapted to secure domestic tranquillity, while it brings into
activity all the elements of national aggrandizement. The Atlantic states,
through their commercial, social, and political affinities and sympathies, are
steadily renovating the governments and the social constitutions of Europe
and Africa. The Pacific states must necessarily perform the same sublime and
benevolent function in Asia. If, then, the American people shall remain an
undivided nation, the ripening civilization of the West, after a separation
growing wider and wider for four thousand years, will, in its circuit of the
world, meet again and mingle with the declining civilization of the East on
our own free soil, and a new and more perfect civilization will arise to bless
the earth, under the sway of our own cherished and beneficent democratic
institutions.

We may then reasonably hope for greatness, felicity, and renown, excell-
ing any hitherto attained by any nation, if, standing firmly on the continent,
we lose not our grasp of the shore of either ocean. ...

St. Paul, Minnesota, speech of September 18, 1860.

... Standing here and looking far off into the northwest, I see the
Russian as he busily occupies himself in establishing seaports and towns and
fortifications on the verge of this continent, as the outposts of St. Petersburg,
and I can say, "Go on and build up your outposts all along the coast even
up to the Arctic ocean—they will yet become the outposts of my own
country—monuments of the civilization of the United States in the northwest." So I look off on St. Rupert's land and Canada, and see there an
ingenious, enterprising and ambitious people, occupied with bridging rivers
and constructing canals, railroads and telegraphs, to organize and preserve
great British provinces north of the great lakes, the St. Lawrence, and around
the shores of Hudson bay, and I am able to say, "It is very well, you are
building excellent states to be hereafter admitted into the American Union."
I can look to the southwest and see, amid all the convulsions that are
breaking the Spanish American republics, and in their rapid decay and
dissolution, the preparatory stage for their reorganization in free, equal and
self-governing members of the United States. ...

ARGUMENTS FOR THE PURCHASE

OF ALASKA   *Document 2*

President Andrew Johnson's Message of December 9, 1868.

... The acquisition of Alaska was made with the view of extending national jurisdiction and republican principles in the American hemisphere. ...

Comprehensive national policy would seem to sanction the acquisition and incorporation into our Federal Union of the several adjacent continental and insular communities as speedily as it can be done peacefully, lawfully, and without any violation of national justice, faith, or honor. Foreign possession or control of those communities has hitherto hindered the growth and impaired the influence of the United States. Chronic revolution and anarchy there would be equally injurious. Each one of them, when firmly established as an independent republic, or when incorporated into the United States, would be a new source of strength and power. ...

It can not be long before it will become necessary for this Government to lend some effective aid to the solution of the political and social problems which are continually kept before the world by the two republics of the island of St. Domingo, and which are now disclosing themselves more distinctly than heretofore in the island of Cuba. The subject is commended to your consideration with all the more earnestness because I am satisfied that the time has arrived when even so direct a proceeding as a proposition for an annexation of the two Republics of the island of St. Domingo would not only receive the consent of the people interested, but would also give satisfaction to all other foreign nations.

I am aware that upon the question of further extending our possessions it is apprehended by some that our political system cannot successfully be applied to an area more than our continent; but the conviction is rapidly gaining ground in the American mind that with the increased facilities for intercommunication between all portions of the earth the principles of free government, as embraced in our Constitution, if faithfully maintained and carried out, would prove of sufficient strength and breadth to comprehend within their sphere and influence the civilized nations of the world.

The attention of the Senate and of Congress is again respectfully invited to the treaty for the establishment of commercial reciprocity with the Hawaiian Kingdom entered into last year, and already ratified by that Government. The attitude of the United States toward these islands is not very different from that in which they stand toward the West Indies. ...

Senator Charles Sumner's speech of April 9, 1867.

... Foremost in order, if not in importance, I put the desires of our fellow-citizens on the Pacific coast, and the special advantages which they will derive from this enlargement of boundary. ...

But all are looking to the Orient as in the time of Columbus, although like him they sail to the West. To them China and Japan . . . are the Indies. To draw this commerce to the Pacific coast is no new idea. It haunted the early navigators. . . .

The advantages to the Pacific coast have two aspects, one domestic and the other foreign. Not only does the treaty extend the coasting trade of California, Oregon, and Washington territory northward, but it also extends the base of commerce with China and Japan.

To unite the east of Asia with the west of America is the aspiration of commerce now as when the English navigator recorded his voyage. Of course whatever helps this result is an advantage. The Pacific railroad is such an advantage. . . . This treaty is another advantage, for nothing can be clearer than that the western coast must exercise an attraction which will be felt in China and Japan just in proportion as it is occupied by a commercial people communicating readily with the Atlantic and with Europe. . . .

More important than the extension of dominion is the extension of Republican institutions, which is a traditional aspiration. . . .

The Republic is something more than a local policy; it is a general principle, not to be forgotten at any time, especially when the opportunity is presented of bringing an immense region within its influence. . . .

The present treaty is a visible step in the occupation of the whole North American continent. . . .

PRESIDENT GRANT REQUESTS THE ANNEXATION OF SANTO DOMINGO, DECEMBER 5, 1870

Document 3

. . . During the last session of Congress a treaty for the annexation of the Republic of San Domingo to the United States failed to receive the requisite two-thirds vote of the Senate. I was thoroughly convinced then that the best interests of this country, commercially and materially, demanded its ratification. Time has only confirmed me in this view. I now firmly believe that the moment it is known that the United States have entirely abandoned the project of accepting as a part of its territory the island of San Domingo a free port will be negotiated for by European nations in the Bay of Samana. A large commercial city will spring up, to which we will be tributary without receiving corresponding benefits, and then will be seen the folly of our rejecting so great a prize. The Government of San Domingo has voluntarily sought this annexation. . . . They yearn for the protection of our free institutions and laws, our progress and civilization. Shall we refuse them?

The acquisition of San Domingo is desirable because of its geographical position. It commands the entrance to the Caribbean Sea and the Isthmus transit of commerce. It possesses the richest soil, best and most capacious harbors, most salubrious climate, and the most valuable products of the forests, mine, and soil of any of the West India Islands. Its possession by us will in a few years build up a coastwise commerce of immense magnitude, which will go far toward restoring to us our lost merchant marine. It will give to us those articles which we consume so largely and do not produce, thus equalizing our exports and imports. In case of foreign war it will give us command of all the islands referred to, and thus prevent an enemy from ever again possessing himself of rendezvous upon our very coast. At present our coast trade between the States bordering on the Atlantic and those bordering on the Gulf of Mexico is cut into by the Bahamas and the Antilles. Twice we must, as it were, pass through foreign countries to get by sea from Georgia to the west coast of Florida.

San Domingo, with a stable government, under which her immense resources can be developed, will give remunerative wages to tens of thousands of laborers not now upon the island. . . .

San Domingo will become a large consumer of the products of Northern farms and manufacturers. The cheap rate at which her citizens can be furnished with food, tools, and machinery will make it necessary that contiguous islands should have the same advantages in order to compete in the production of sugar, coffee, tobacco, tropical fruits, etc. This will open to us a still wider market for our products. The production of our own supply of these articles will cut off more than one hundred millions of our annual imports, besides largely increasing our exports. With such a picture it is easy to see how our large debt abroad is ultimately to be extinguished. With a balance of trade against us (including interest on bonds held by foreigners and money spent by our citizens traveling in foreign lands) equal to the entire yield of the precious metals in this country, it is not so easy to see how this result is to be otherwise accomplished.

The acquisition of San Domingo is an adherence to the "Monroe doctrine"; it is a measure of national protection. . . . it is, in fine, a rapid stride toward that greatness which the intelligence, industry, and enterprise of the citizens of the United States entitle this country to assume among nations.

In view of the importance of this question, I earnestly urge upon Congress early action expressive of its views as to the best means of acquiring San Domingo. . . .

THE PATRONS OF HUSBANDRY

AGITATE FOR OVERSEAS

MARKET EXPANSION   *Document 4*

Resolutions of the National Grange, 1889.
Bro. Frederick Robie, Chairman of the Committee on Foreign Relations, read the following General Report of his Committee, and it was approved by the Grange:

* * *

The promotion of agriculture and the protection and elevation of the American husbandman should primarily constitute our highest aim, and is the field of duty for our best endeavors.

The Grange must however recognize this fact. In order that our country shall take the advance of all the nations of the earth, we should act and work together for each and every material interest which aims for a higher civilization, and a more powerful nation.

We rejoice with the representatives of the commercial and mercantile pursuits of a common country, that a wise statesmanship has inaugurated a policy, whereby a better understanding of the international relations, resources, and interests of all the North and South American Governments, may be obtained. We trust that a careful and wise investigation may bring about a reciprocity of trade, open new markets, new exchanges, and increased opportunities for the sale of the manufactured and agricultural products of this country.

In this new departure, we claim that nothing be done of that selfish character, which shall ignore the just claims of the American farmer.

We rejoice that the distinguished representatives of foreign nations, which have recently visited us, find so much in our material resources to admire, and are ready to extend the hand of business friendship to every section of the land.

The large increase of agricultural productions in this country, demand an equal opportunity for exportation of the same, with that of our manufactured articles, and we demand of Congress that every just facility shall be granted for the purpose.

This country furnishes the most profitable carrying trade of the world, but we have to depend largely for freights upon the ships of other nations.

The amount annually paid out to other countries for freight on exports and imports is said to be $150,000,000.

We recommend a judicious protective policy of government that will build up a commercial marine, that will give this nation the commercial supremacy that belongs to it; so that our country, while it is the first in agriculture, the first in manufactures, may also be the first in commerce.

These three great pillars of the nation's glory, stand together in a group. In the language of Daniel Webster, "the largest in the centre, and that is agriculture."

We claim that its interests should be equally protected, at home, abroad, and everywhere.

We respectfully ask the Secretary of Agriculture to continue his investigation in regard to a better and more profitable exportation of agricultural productions....

Bro. Ava E. Page, Chairman of the Committee on Agriculture, read the following General Report of the Committee, which was adopted:
...The number of farms [has] enormously increased. From 1870 to 1880 the number engaged in agriculture increased from 5,922,471 to 7,670,-493, while the number of improved acres increased nearly 100,000,000, or 50 per cent. The increase has gone forward rapidly since 1880. This vast in-

crease of farms and farm population barely maintained the total value of farms from 1870 to 1880. The next census will show little or no advance in the total valuation of farms. Rural population has not only fallen off in New England, where farms are being abandoned outright, but throughout the West, save in the recently populated sections. One State west of the Mississippi river lost last year population in sixty nine counties.

This decline of values and labor rates is not a decline pertaining to all industries, but is limited to agriculture alone, of all our important industries.

While the returns for men engaged in farming fell off from 1870 to 1880 68 per cent, the decline of the wages of those employed in manufacturing was but 9 per cent, and this disparity is widening. Your committee has not sought these figures from the dark shadows they cast; but finding them, could not in duty turn aside from them. They make a deep depression in our agriculture, gloomy and even dark in its significance, if the causes that have brought it about are permanent in this venture. It can ultimately end only in a poor and spiritless peasantry, if the future can be judged by the past.

Confidence in the intelligence, spirit and powers of our farmers, and the general interests of other industries in the "mother and nurse" of all other industries, leads us to expect other results. A due and clear recognition of this state of facts and of the causes that have led to them, are of fundamental necessity in determining the remedy. The low price of land, of free homes, has led to the erection of farm-houses faster than mills and factories; to the multiplication of producers faster than consumers. Our surplus products and those which determine home rates, are necessarily forced upon a foreign market. The inherent fertility of our farms from ages, enables us in its flush to sell in these markets and yet maintain the superior farm-homes of America. With the decline of this fertility has come an increasing pressure from competition for our old European markets, from new farms opened up to those markets by the penetration of the railroad into newly settled countries; into new fields in old countries, and by the cheapening to a radical degree of ocean transportation, so that more distant regions have been made tributary to Europe. Lower life and fresher fields are bidding against us. . . .

All the world is being brought into a commercial neighborhood in which our farm-life is the highest and justly the most costly. . . .

AMERICAN INFLUENCE IN ASIA   *Document 5*

Special Agent George H. Bates in Samoa to the Secretary of State, December 10, 1886.

. . . It is hardly extravagant to say that in the main all influence by private individuals in the government of these communities is prompted, to a greater or less degree, by selfish interests or designs. That it is so arises almost of necessity from the frailty of human nature. Philanthropists, pure and simple, are rare, even among the most enlightened peoples of the world. Self-interest is the mainspring of human action. . . .

The same considerations apply, to a large degree, to the interference in these groups by foreign powers, based solely upon what is termed protection of the interest of their own citizens or subjects. . . .

One of the most aggravating features of the present situation, which must undoubtedly be considered in connection with any plan for the future government of the country, is the necessity of an authoritative and final adjudication of the claims of foreigners to the ownership of lands in that country.

The methods of the acquisition of title to lands have, without doubt, been very loose, and it is impossible that the acreage claimed by foreigners has all been honestly or fairly acquired. . . .

Of course it was impossible for me to form any reliable opinion as to the validity of these respective claims, but the existence of claims to so large a proportion of land in this group of islands is sufficient of itself to indicate the necessity of some well-organized international land court which shall finally determine and settle all titles to land claimed by foreigners and between foreigners and natives.

Without a thorough investigation of these matters, enough has come to my knowledge respecting the general character of the dealings of white men with the natives in respect to land titles to convince me that even a moderate degree of justice to the latter requires an investigation into the circumstances under which they have parted with their lands. . . .

With respect to the relative interests of citizens and subjects of foreign powers it is quite impracticable to furnish any reliable statistics. . . . At the same time it is proper that you should be informed that citizens of the United States have acquired in Samoa substantial property interests, that a very large proportion of imports into that country consists of American goods, and that, with respect to exports, while they have until a recent period been principally by the German company, a very large proportion of the copra which is claimed by the Germans as having been exported by them from Samoa is in fact brought to Apia from other islands. . . .

The enunciation of the Monroe doctrine first qualified the general policy of non-intervention and prescribed the limits to which it was to be thereafter confined. This public notice to the world that we would not submit to an extension of the European system to this *hemisphere*, or to the establishment upon it of European colonies in addition to those then existing, was put upon the express ground that we should regard such action as dangerous to our peace and safety. . . .

It would be impossible, in view of the marvelous growth of the United States in population and its resources, and the extension of its territory, both by acquisition and settlement, that this limitation by President Monroe should at all periods of our history be geographically the same. . . .

As the extension of our commerce and the settlement of our Pacific coast made it apparent that the possession by a European power of the Sandwich Islands would be dangerous to our peace and safety—indeed, more so than would be true as to the South American republics—our Government has not hesitated to declare that their conquest or occupation by one of the great powers of Europe would be a result that we would not hesitate to prevent by force of arms if necessary.

Instructions to Lucius H. Foote, first American Minister to Korea, March 17, 1883.

.... You are the first Minister from the United States and so far as is known from any western Power accredited to Corea. You will of course impress the Government with the conviction that it is with no ulterior design that the United States seeks to cultivate friendly relations with it.

Your attention will be directed to the relations between Corea, China and Japan—a subject not without difficulty....

As far as we are concerned Corea is an independent sovereign power, with all the attendant rights,—privileges, duties and responsibilities; in her relations to China we have no desire to interfere unless action should be taken prejudicial to the rights of the United States.

In this connection it becomes important to examine certain so called trade regulations between China and Corea, recently promulgated, which may give rise to discussion. A copy of them is herewith enclosed and your attention is particularly directed thereto....

As to the relations between China and Corea we have, as I have already remarked, no immediate interest, but should the Chinese or Corean officials attempt by analogy to diminish the respect with which you are to be treated, and because the sovereign to whom you are accredited is treated as a subordinate, attempt to treat you as an agent sent to a subordinate, a different state of affairs will immediately be presented.... The Chinese commercial agents in Corea will be treated by you as subordinate officials appointed by a subordinate officer and not bearing the commission of the Emperor....

This question of trade and of the rights of the United States in relation thereto should receive your careful attention. By the Treaty between the United States and Corea our citizens may establish themselves at such Corean ports as are open to foreign trade. These ports are not specified in the Treaty but are understood to be those opened to the Japanese.... Chinese subjects are allowed to establish themselves and to follow their vocations at all these ports and also to reside in the two suburbs of Seoul and at two trading posts in the interior. Americans may not travel in the interior, while this privilege is allowed to Chinese. By virtue of a stipulation in the Japanese Convention operating through our Treaty with Corea, diplomatic and consular representatives of the United States may travel in the interior under passport. Chinese may transport merchandise to the four points in the interior and may at any place in the interior purchase and bring out native produce paying only an export duty. These privileges have not been granted to Americans....

Briefly the following privileges are denied to citizens of the United States and allowed to Chinese:

1. To reside and trade at four points in the interior.
2. To travel in the interior under passport.

3. To take foreign produce to four points in the interior and to proceed to the interior and bring out native produce.
4. To transport native produce from one open port to another.
5. A discrimination of ½ in one case and ⅝ in the other to our disadvantage and to the benefit of Chinese importers in the duties on all foreign merchandise imported *via* certain routes into Corea.

These concessions to China are extremely important. With the enormous advantage thus given them it is apparent that Chinese merchants will have a practical monopoly of Corean trade. To this the United States cannot consent and while the relations of China and Corea may not be of importance to us and while in the treatment of Coreans in China, or the rank of Chinese officials in Corea we are not interested, this practical abolishment of the rights secured to us by Treaty can not be assented to. For the present it may not be advisable to take any active steps in the matter as the participation of western nations in Corean trade is looked upon with jealousy by a large party, but your attention will be given to the matter as soon after your arrival as possible....

Briefly then your mission is

1st. To exchange the ratifications of the Treaty....
2d. To cultivate friendly relations with the Government and people of Corea....
3d. To report fully as to the relations of Corea, China and Japan that appropriate steps may be taken to secure for our citizens the privileges granted to the Chinese in the Commercial Regulations.
4th. To inform this Department fully as to all matters of political importance or of interest to those engaged in commerce....

SECRETARY OF STATE FRELINGHUYSEN'S

ANALYSIS OF EXPANSION

INTO LATIN AMERICA   *Document 6*

Alvey A. Adee to Secretary of State Elihu Root, November 24, 1906.

As Mr. Frelinghuysen used to say, in 1882–3,—to build up South American trade the buyer needs three facilities.

(a) for promptly ordering goods,
(b) for promptly and cheaply receiving the goods,
(c) for payment therefor at reasonable rate of exchange, and at reasonably steady rates. Violent fluctuations in the value of the currency in which the buyer deals handicap all speculative ventures on his part.

(a) requires direct and speedy postal service.
(b) requires direct lines of communication—with adequate subsidies. The carriers are little better than tramps.

(c) requires, besides stability of government, a sound system of banking, so correlated between the several states of the American hemisphere as to constitute in some degree a financial solidarity.

Mr. Frelinghuysen thought that, while all three are necessary together, the last was the most important. His idea was, a parent Intercontinental bank in New York, and associated banks in all South American Countries, each to be incorporated under the *lex loci* with capital to be supplied for the most part by American stock holders, the majority of the stock of each to be held by a holding company in the United States, whereby the whole system could be harmoniously controlled. The capital of each bank to be proportioned to the volume of trade of each country, giving the United States, say 10 millions, Argentina and Brazil, say 5 millions, and less to the others until $500,000 might be more than enough for Paraguay and Honduras.

Mr. Frelinghuysen used to talk to me by the hour about all this— He believed that some such comprehensive solution would have to come in the end, but that it was impossible so long as revolutions and financial irresponsibility continued to sap the energies and credit of the Spanish American states.

I tell you this as of probable interest, and as indicating Mr. Frelinghuysen's far-sightedness. He made very little impression on the men of his own time. They saw no future except indefinite continuance of the Spanish American regime of revolutions, repudiation, debased currency, and bankruptcy— They believed no good government or good faith was to be expected of 'half breeds' and 'niggers'—

But opportunities for better things 'are ripening fast, unfolding every hour.'

JOHN W. BOOKWALTER DISCUSSES
AMERICA'S POSITION IN THE
INTERNATIONAL MARKETPLACE,
DECEMBER 1885[1]   *Document 7*

It is the cherished belief of a large number of the American people that the United States is absolutely independent of foreign countries, and especially of those of the Eastern hemisphere; that we need not in any way concern ourselves with events which happen in the Old World, but may keep the even tenor of our course, reaping now and then a temporary advantage from war in Europe or famine in Asia, but secure in our destiny and undisturbed in our prospects, whatever aspect affairs may present on

---

[1] *Bradstreet's,* December 12, 1885.

that side of the globe. Taken in a purely political sense, this view is substantially correct. In a commercial and industrial sense it is unsupported by fact, and is vitally and perilously false. . . .

So far from being an exception to the interdependence of nations, the United States is a conspicuous example of that law. Its early settlers and their descendants have worthily maintained the character of the most vigorous and enterprising community in the world, but the means by which the country has become populous and rich have largely come to us from abroad. Our development has been in great measure from without. Both in numbers and wealth we have had constant and for a long time steadily increasing accessions from Europe. Since the year 1820, when the authentic record begins, 12,719,095 immigrants have landed on our shores, and prior to that time it is estimated that 250,000 had arrived since the organization of the Federal government. In all, therefore, about 13,000,000 souls have been added to the population of this country by foreign immigration. The amount of money which this vast number of people have brought with them cannot, of course, be accurately stated; but on the best attainable data it is placed at $68 per capita, or an aggregate sum of about $900,000,000. This, however, is but a fraction of the wealth which Europe has showered upon America. A far greater amount has come in the shape of foreign capital invested in the United States in the construction of its railways, in working its mines, in manufacturing enterprises, agriculture, and stock-raising, in the purchase of bonds and real estate, and in private loans. . . . It is by the purchase of our products that the European nations, and Great Britain more than any or all others, has helped in the upbuilding of our material interests. Upon no less comprehensive basis could their structure have been raised to the proportions which we now behold with a just and patriotic pride. To give a complete exhibit of the extent of our foreign trade in past years would involve a wearisome compilation of figures; but a glance at some of its salient features will enlighten us in some degree, and may possibly surprise a casual observer who has not paused to investigate the history of our commercial relations. In the last ten years, to go no farther back, the exports of the United States have amounted to more than $7,000,000,000. Of the single article of wheat, the value sent abroad from this country in the last twenty-four years was upwards of $1,600,000,-000, and of flour about $700,000,000. In the nineteen years which have passed since the close of the war, the shipment of cotton from our ports has been more than 55,000,000 bales, valued at more than $3,400,000,000. Our largest total exports in any single year were those of 1881, when the aggregate of domestic products sent abroad, not including specie, reached the colossal sum of $883,925,947. And it should further be borne in mind, as showing the dominant feature of our commerce, that by far the larger part of our exports has uniformly consisted of agricultural products. This class of commodities has seldom been less than three-fourths, and has frequently exceeded four-fifths of the total exports from this country. In 1880 the percentage of agricultural products in the total exports was 83.24. For the last five years the average percentage has been 78.42. It may be safely estimated, in general terms, that one-fourth of the product of agricultural labor in the United States for the last quarter of a century has been sent to a foreign market. Of the sustaining power of such a trade, or of its vital importance not only to the farming industry, but to every material interest of this country, it is not necessary here to speak in detail. It is a most valuable part of the aggregate trade of the country, but its chief importance is derived from the fact that 26,000,000 of the people of the United States are engaged in agriculture, and that only by this exportation of their surplus product can the price of that which is sold in the home market be fixed and maintained at a paying level. From the industry of this class the great railroad system of our country with its $7,000,000,000 of invested capital, largely draws its support. The carrying of their products to a foreign market has given in the last decade 80,000,000 tons of freight to be carried eastward by rail and water a distance of more than 1,000 miles, and a like amount to ocean transportation, representing altogether $800,000,000 worth of business to the carrying companies; and the domestic carrying trade in the same period has had from this source probably 500,000,000 tons of freight for internal distribution. The prosperity of this great class, comprising almost one-half our population, is indispensable to the national welfare. No part of the system can permanently thrive if this vital member languishes.

. . . We have reached, so to speak, the point of saturation, while China and other Asiatic communities, if the comparison may be permitted, are lying like a vast sponge, ready to absorb the energies, the products and the accumulating wealth of Europe. The exchange of commodities with a population of 400,000,000 is a commercial opportunity of which England, the greatest trading nation on the globe, will not fail to make profitable use. Nor will she find the gates of China shut against her in retaliation for the wholesale massacre of Chinamen within her borders. It is the policy of Great Britain to protect the races whose labor is, or may become, useful in building up her commerce; while it seems to have been reserved for our own country to set the example of a relentless persecution of an unoffending and industrious people.

The alarm with which China regards the advance of Russia on her northern and western frontier and of France on her southern border tends to draw her into friendly relations with England, by whom she is threatened with no such inroads. But the whole aspect of Eastern affairs justifies the belief that England and Russia will ultimately arrive at a peaceful, if not a cordial understanding, and that their solution of the problem will give to each what it chiefly desires, at the price of conceding what is but of nominal value. Above all things else, England seeks the security of its Indian empire and its Chinese trade, and the control of Egypt as incidental to these. For the sake of thus consolidating its empire and expanding its trade, it may well consent that Russia shall absorb the decaying remnant of the Ottoman power and extend its dominion to the Persian Gulf. With this ambition gratified, it is probable that Russia will not molest the fortifications of Herat, but will relinquish whatever designs she may have entertained upon Indian territory. The time seems not far distant when Asia will be wholly under the dominion of three races—the Muscovite, the Mongolian and the Anglo-Saxon—each possessing a vast portion of its area, and necessarily respectful of its powerful neighbors. Such an alliance, comprising nearly two-thirds of the population of the globe, would dwarf any political arrangement the world has yet seen. The partition of Asia would establish a balance of power whose huge proportions would impart a new significance to the term, and whose weight would be of itself a guarantee of permanence.

Of the fact that European capital and European statesmanship are both tending toward enlarged dominion in the Eastern hemisphere, Russia and England are the most prominent examples. But they are by no means alone in that regard. Other continental nations, according to their military resources or financial strength, are seeking to gain new footholds in Africa and Asia. France in Tonquin, Anam and Madagascar, Belgium on the Congo, Italy on the Red Sea, and even Spain in the islands of Oceanica, are each striving to plant the seeds of wider national expansion or tightening their grasp on acquisitions already made. Under the stimulus of this prevailing spirit of enterprise it may almost be said that another New World is rising within the boundaries of the Old. This formidable rival, if it does not take from us the title, bids fair to rob us of the benefits which of right should be ours. Hitherto they have flowed upon us in a copious stream, and would still be securely enjoyed if the laws of nature and the forces of trade were not perverted by erroneous legislation. It is a false, though a popular idea, that the East is a land of exhausted resources. On the contrary, it has vast and fertile regions waiting to be regenerated by the forces of civilization. The field has in many parts as yet been barely touched, while in others the results already attained show that no limit can be set to the possibilities of future growth. It is now nearly three years since the writer made the prediction, then regarded as a most incautious one, though based on personal observation, that India would speedily become a dangerous competitor with the United States in the production of wheat. How strikingly that prediction has been verified the statistics of the grain trade of 1885 abundantly prove. The wheat market of Chicago has testified to its accuracy by accumulated stocks and depressed quotations. The fact has been realized, and should always be borne in mind by those who examine this question, that to destroy the profits of the American wheat-grower it is not necessary that India should raise a crop which will meet the whole demand of Europe. It has but to furnish such a proportion of the amount as will prevent an advance in the price to a point which will repay the cost of production by our farmers. This it has now done, and will continue to do. And it can scarcely be doubted that the present and future capabilities of India as a wheat-growing country will be emulated by Egypt in the production of both wheat and cotton. . . .

Nor is it only in our wheat and cotton industries that we are threatened with loss by a rivalry to which our own folly has given rise. The foreign demand for American fresh meat has been for some years the source of a profitable trade; and here also competition has sprung up, and a British colony again stands in our path. Five years ago a commerce of this kind with Australasia was scarcely dreamed of; but so rapidly has it grown that great fleets of vessels are now employed in conveying the frozen beef and mutton of Australia to the English markets, and it is probable that little short of one million carcasses will be thus shipped during the present year. A trade in the same commodity has been established between England and the Argentine Republic, a country of vast extent and scarcely less favored than our own in variety of climate or fertility of soil. Hardly a decade since it was a purchaser of our agricultural products. No longer a customer, it has become under the stimulus of European capital an active competitor.

It may be a question whether American interests are most seriously menaced by the direct competition of the multiplying army of foreign producers, or by the diversion of European capital from investment here to more profitable, because free and untrammeled, use in Egypt, India and China. That it is finding such employment in constantly increasing volume is matter of daily observation....

The question of vital interest to America is this: By whom are the vast and growing wants of the European nations in future to be supplied? ...

This is America's great and imminent danger. The policy of exclusion, the doctrine that a foreign customer, the supplying of whose wants would be a source of incalculable wealth, should be repelled instead of invited, has already shown its blighting effect upon our commercial prospects. By our tariff laws we shut our gates against mankind. We lay an unequal burden on the American farmer by artificially increasing the cost of his clothing, his tools, his household utensils, of every article, in short, which his land does not produce; while that which he raises he is compelled to sell in competition with the low-priced labor of the Old World. In some important respects, it is to be feared, the mischief which has been accomplished no longer admits of repair. No revision of the laws by which American trade is bound can restore American supremacy in the grain markets of the world. The scepter of that dominion has passed from our hands. The American farmer no longer holds, as he once did, the position of dictator in the European market. It is rather the six-cent ryot of India who now takes precedence at that board, and who is able, if not to supply all the wheat which Europe requires, at least so to load the market with his cheap product as to depress the price below what to the American wheat-grower is a living figure. For the cotton industry of our country there may yet be hope, if wiser counsels than those of the past shall prevail. But a persistent denial of equitable trade relations will inevitably bring the same result in this as in our cereal exports, which have dropped to less than half their former volume. If our laws still make war upon our trade, the time is not far off when the cotton planter of our southern states will be thrust from his high place, and the despised Egyptian fellah will reign in his stead. Even the cattle-breeder of our western ranges may find a successful rival in the Australian bushman, whose cargoes of frozen meat are daily arriving in the ports of Liverpool and London. Thus the world's markets for food and textile products, which by right we ought well nigh to monopolize, are slipping from us one by one....

THE NEED OF LATIN AMERICAN MARKETS
TO AVOID STRIFE AT HOME   *Document 8*

Remarks of S. O. Thacher before the subcommittee of the Senate Foreign Relations Committee on the bill introduced by Senator Frye entitled "An Act to Promote the Political Progress and Commercial Prosperity of the American Nations," April, 1886.

... The question before the committee is one whose magnitude and far-reaching importance can not be too earnestly considered.

It brings into view questions affecting our own welfare as a nation, casting light upon the solution of a grave and ever-urgent problem. The industrial outlook of our land is not one of entire sunshine. There are more laborers than there is work for them to do. Where one man is discharged from almost any of the manual occupations there waits one to take his place.

The inflow of laborers from other lands to this is no more a great need. In every department of industrial life there is production beyond consumption. Labor is struggling to hold its position and is fearful of being displaced or of losing its present ground.... On the whole, as never before, our future growth, peace, and tranquillity depend on finding more consumers for what we have to sell. In this measure there is an effort to open to our producers of agricultural and manufactured wealth an adequate market.

In vain do we turn our eyes to any other part of the world for a people who at once need and are willing to take from our farms, looms, forges, and wells of mineral oils that we are able to produce and spare. The nations of Central and South America offer not alone the most alluring and most profitable markets whereby to relieve our excessive productions, but there is no other field.

The statesman who shall secure that great region so contiguous, so easily reached, and so prolific in wants, for the easy disposition of our merchandise will be entitled to the highest commendation.

Labor can be constantly employed at fair wages when what it produces can be sold at a fair profit....

It seems clear to me that the relations between employer and employee will readily adjust themselves when the venture to which each contributes is one of gain and not of loss....

The easy way and the only way out of the complications and disappointments that yearly are being intensified by the diminishing profitableness of all our industrial enterprises is to seek that market which so cordially invites us, and from which with strange fatuity we have for the last twenty-five years averted our thoughts....

Peace, progress, and the manifold blessings of contented producing classes wait on the footsteps of any measure that will insure to our laborers, our farmers, and our manufacturers a fair chance in the markets of Central and South America....

SENATOR JOHN F. MILLER OF CALIFORNIA
EXPLAINS HIS SUPPORT FOR A NEW AND
LARGER NAVY, FEBRUARY 28, 1884   *Document 9*

Mr. President, I am in favor of making liberal appropriations to be expended in the construction of a new navy or of a navy, for at this time we have no navy. It is not worthy of the name of a navy except the *personnel*. I am in favor of constructing American men-of-war from American material, by American workmen to be manned by American seamen, and to be used in the service of the Government of the United States, whatever that service may call for, and I am in favor of constructing just such ships as will be effective and useful and economical and will serve the purpose for which a navy is intended.

Here we are, a nation of 56,000,000 people, occupying the center of a mighty continent washed by the two great oceans, with a coast line greater in distance than the circumference of the globe, with its multifarious bays and inlets and sounds and deep river ways decorated by great cities and prosperous towns. Ours is a young nation, it may be, but growing with a marvelous growth and strengthening with a prodigious strength, a nation proud, it may be imperious, self-satisfied; and if this nation intends to take its place, as it should take its place, among the great nations of the earth and contend with the leading maritime powers for the commerce of the western hemisphere, it is time that she should be prepared to meet either the encroachments or the attacks of those powers which have become jealous of this great nation springing up here in the West and whose example of free government and free institutions is spreading the contagion of free thought and the freedom of individual action among all the peoples of the globe, and is engendering and exciting the hatred and malice and unfriendliness of imperialists and monarchists throughout the world. I say it is time that this nation should be prepared, because it can not expect to go forward in its career of prosperity without exciting the jealousy, and perhaps bringing upon itself the attacks, of great maritime powers.

*   *   *

I think that this Government is about to enter upon a new era. We have been busy in the development of our country, busy with ourselves. We have been not only engaged in the great work of the development of our natural resources, but we have been engaged in a great war between two sections of this Union; we have been, as I said, busy with ourselves, and for many years we have not looked out upon the world and seen those opportunities to extend our commerce and our trade which we might have seen had we not been thus occupied. The time has come now when the country is prosperous, when manufactures are springing up all over the land, *when new markets are necessary to be found in order to keep our factories running. Here lies to the south of us our India,* and if we have the nerve, and the foresight, and the sagacity to utilize it by proper methods we shall have new markets for our products and for our manufactures which will keep every loom, and every anvil, and every manufactory of this country in motion. If we reach out and attempt to secure this great prize of commerce we shall excite the jealousy of other peoples, and we shall be led, perhaps, into complications, which we shall extricate ourselves from if we are prepared to meet our enemies; but if we are not prepared we shall fall, for a time at least, an easy prey to the cupidity of those who will contend against us. . . .

SECRETARY OF AGRICULTURE JEREMIAH RUSK
DISCUSSES THE IMPORTANCE OF OVERSEAS
MARKETS FOR AGRICULTURE, 1892   *Document 10*

Referring to the section in the Act making appropriations for the Department of Agriculture for the current fiscal year which devotes $10,000 "to enable the Secretary of Agriculture to continue investigations concerning the feasibility of extending the demands of foreign markets for agricultural products of the United States," Secretary Rusk remarked that this wording was the same as used in two preceding acts for a small appropriation of $2,500 each year and which had been devoted exclusively to pushing the Indian corn interest in Europe. Being asked whether it was the intention to so limit in the future the appropriations under this clause, Secretary Rusk replied: "I have at present one very efficient corn agent in Europe whose work has so greatly increased that I have been obliged to give him clerical assistance, and in order to carry on our corn propaganda without delay in all the countries of Northern Europe, it will be necessary to increase our expenses considerably in the interest of Indian corn alone. However, my conviction is that my Department should make an exhaustive study of the market conditions of all crops, accessible to American agricultural producers, and what we have done so far as Indian corn is concerned, is, I think, the best testimony available as to the true policy of this country in opening up foreign markets for our agricultural surplus products. Our people should be thoroughly informed as to the requirements of all foreign countries in the way of food supplies, both as regards the extent and the character of the demand, and wherever a market exists for any product that can be grown upon the soil of the United States the department should know it and should be able to inform our farmers and merchants of its extent and character."

"You do not believe then, Mr. Secretary, that the time is not far distant when this country, as alleged by some, will not only have no surplus products to export, but will be obliged to import food stuffs for its own people?"

"You are right. I believe nothing of the kind. On the contrary I believe that there are very few States in the Union that, properly cultivated, will not support twice as many people as they now contain, and a great many of them many more than that. In the meantime, and probably for a considerable time, until great changes occur in the conditions of our agriculture, the bulk of our farmers will run to special crops of which we will consequently for many years to come raise a surplus. That surplus must be sold abroad, and we must know those markets where it will find the readiest sale, and, as we have recently shown in the case of Indian corn, we can very profitably devote some time and money to making foreigners acquainted with our resources in the way of food products.

"In all these things," concluded the Secretary, "we must look to the future—not working for to-day, but for what this great free country will be a quarter of a century hence. In course of time I expect to see a great trade established between this country and the Latin-American Republics, and not to be behindhand I have recently established a special section in our Statistical Division for the collection and diffusion of information on this subject, on which we have already issued one very interesting bulletin. The fact that the great portion of the countries to the south of us lies in semi-tropical and tropical regions, while our own vast country lies mainly in the temperate zone, would naturally suggest the possibility of a large reciprocal trade. You see, I believe in having a good market for all we can sell and buying nothing abroad which we can possibly raise in our own country."

AMERICAN INVOLVEMENT IN THE

HAWAIIAN REVOLUTION OF 1893   *Document 11*

Testimony of John L. Stevens, Minister Plenipotentiary from the United States to Hawaii, January 20, 1894.

THE CHAIRMAN. Was it your purpose in anything you did, from the time you left the *Boston* on Saturday up to the time of your making an official recognition in writing, to use the forces or the flag or the authority of the United States Government for the purpose of dethroning the Queen?

MR. STEVENS. Not the slightest—absolute noninterference was my purpose.

THE CHAIRMAN. Was it your policy in any of these things that you had done to aid any plan or purpose of the annexation of the Hawaiian Islands to the United States?

MR. STEVENS. Not at all. That was not the plan.

THE CHAIRMAN. Since your residence in Hawaii as minister have you personally—I do not speak of your ministerial character—favored the annexation of Hawaii to the United States? Have you been in favor of that movement?

MR. STEVENS. After I had been in Honolulu one year I came to the conclusion that the annexation of those islands was inevitable.... But in my calculations for annexation I never supposed, nor was it expected by the friends of annexation, that it would be by revolution, but through negotiation, legislative action, and the assent of the Queen on the lines of the treaty of '54. That was the only plan thought of.

In that time I kept my own counsel, and nobody except the United States Government knew what my real view was. In that time I may have chatted with individuals and given an opinion when talking of the situation of the islands.... But that was merely an academic opinion privately expressed.

THE CHAIRMAN. As a matter of interest to the people of Hawaii, and also the people of the United States and the Government of the United States, were your personal wishes or inclinations in favor of or against annexation?

MR. STEVENS. In the first twelve months I supposed something like a protectorate would be preferable.

THE CHAIRMAN. After that what?

MR. STEVENS. I came to the conclusion that while a protectorate would be possible, annexation was the only logical and practical solution.

THE CHAIRMAN. Did you favor it?

MR. STEVENS. Only as I reported to the Department.

THE CHAIRMAN. I do not mean whether you advocated it, but whether, in your own mind, you favored it.

MR. STEVENS. In my own mind I came to the conclusion that annexation was better than protectorate....

THE CHAIRMAN. During this period of time in Hawaii, did you believe that it would be advantageous to the Government of the United States, in a commercial sense, to acquire the ownership of the islands?

MR. STEVENS. Most emphatically. I came to that conclusion after a study of the future of the Pacific.

THE CHAIRMAN. You believed that the future of the islands lay in that direction?

MR. STEVENS. Exactly. I followed Mr. Seward for 25 years; I am a believer in his philosophy as to the future of America in the Pacific, and, of course, my investigations after I went to the islands confirmed me....

Testimony of Commander Nicoll Ludlow, United States Navy, February 7, 1894.

THE CHAIRMAN. At what time have you visited the Hawaiian Islands?

MR. LUDLOW. I have been there but once. I was commander of the *Mohican*. I arrived there on the 10th of February last and left there on the 1st of May.

THE CHAIRMAN. What American ship did you find in port?

MR. LUDLOW. I found the *Boston* there. Subsequently the *Alliance* came in and reported. The *Adams* was sent down to take the place of the *Mohican*, and on her arrival I went north. The *Mohican* was Admiral Skerrett's flagship; I was his chief of staff during the time I remained there....

SENATOR GRAY. Did you, with reference to the revolution of January 17, 1893, form any opinion from these sources of observation and information as to whether or not that revolution would have been accomplished when it was accomplished and as it was accomplished if it had not been for the presence on shore of the United States troops?

SENATOR FRYE. Do you consider that a legitimate question?

SENATOR GRAY. I do.

THE CHAIRMAN. I expect Mr. Ludlow had better answer that question....

MR. LUDLOW. My opinion is that the revolution would not have occurred in the way it did, and at the time it did, if the people who were the revolutionary party, had not been assured of the protection and assistance of the United States forces there.

Statement of William R. Castle, December 5, 1893.

My name is William R. Castle; I was born in Honolulu in March, 1849; my parents were American missionaries. My father arrived here in 1837 and still lives in Honolulu; he is the senior member of the mercantile house of Castle & Cooke.... I have been more or less connected with Island politics ... though always unwilling, as it has interfered with my business. Have been a member of the Legislature five sessions.

Until very recently I have constantly and consistently opposed annexation to the United States; I have a strong regard for the native people and have hoped that the native Government might continue, and it is only recently that I have felt compelled to change my views.... This conclusion has been reached very reluctantly, after closely watching political affairs since ... 1876....

I was intimately acquainted with Minister Stevens and Capt. Wiltse, with both of whom I often talked over the political situation. We all felt that trouble was impending, but I do not think that anything was more strongly impressed upon my mind by what either of these men said than the thought that if trouble came and our rights, our liberties, and property were threatened, we must help ourselves, for we could have no outside help, unless, indeed, such things should occur as might ensue from a state of anarchy, when, as I understood, Americans might expect assistance to the extent of personal protection and the protection of property against mob violence. Knowing what a Hawaiian mob meant from the illustration given in 1874, considerable uneasiness was felt in Honolulu when the [*U.S.S.*] *Boston*, with Minister Stevens, left Honolulu a week or ten days before the prorogation of the Legislature, and her return was observed with great relief upon the morning of the 14th....

It was felt that life, property, and liberty were seriously imperiled, and the meeting immediately elected a chairman and secretary, and a committee of public safety of thirteen members was at once appointed, of which I was a member. Subcommittees were at once appointed, which went about their business immediately, and the meeting adjourned to meet at my house....

The meeting was called for Monday, and its voice was so unmistakable that preparations were concluded as rapidly as possible to take possession of the Government by force, establish a Provisional Government, and ask for annexation to the United States, which was also the almost unanimous desire of the meeting.... There was no doubt as to the enthusiasm and determination of the respectable, conservative portion of the community to make an end of corrupt and misgovernment and get security and peace by good government....

PRESIDENT CLEVELAND'S VIEW OF THE CUBAN CRISIS, DECEMBER 1896   *Document 12*

The insurrection in Cuba still continues with all its perplexities. It is difficult to perceive that any progress has thus far been made toward the pacification of the island or that the situation of affairs as depicted in my last annual message has in the least improved.... Indeed, as the contest has gone on, the pretense that civil government exists on the island, except so far as Spain is able to maintain it, has been practically abandoned. Spain does keep on foot such a government, more or less imperfectly, in the large towns and their immediate suburbs. But, that exception being made, the entire country is either given over to anarchy or is subject to the military occupation of one or the other party....

The spectacle of the utter ruin of an adjoining country, by nature one of the most fertile and charming on the globe, would engage the serious attention of the Government and people of the United States in any circumstances. In point of fact, they have a concern with it which is by no means of a wholly sentimental or philanthropic character. It lies so near to us as to be hardly separated from our territory. Our actual pecuniary interest in it is second only to that of the people and Government of Spain. It is reasonably estimated that at least from $30,000,000 to $50,000,000 of American capital are invested in plantations and in railroad, mining, and other business enterprises on the island. The volume of trade between the United States and Cuba, which in 1889 amounted to about $64,000,000, rose in 1893 to about $103,000,000, and in 1894, the year before the present insurrection broke out, amounted to nearly $96,000,000. Besides this large pecuniary stake in the fortunes of Cuba, the United States finds itself inextricably involved in the present contest in other ways both vexatious and costly.

Many Cubans reside in this country and indirectly promote the insurrection through the press, by public meetings, by the purchase and shipment of arms, by the raising of funds, and by other means, which the spirit of our institutions and the tenor of our laws do not permit to be made the subject of criminal prosecutions. Some of them, though Cubans at heart and in all their feelings and interests, have taken out papers as naturalized citizens of the United States, a proceeding resorted to with a view to possible protection by this Government, and not unnaturally regarded with much indignation by the country of their origin.... The result is that this Government is constantly called upon to protect American citizens, to claim damages for injuries to persons and property, now estimated at many millions of dollars, and to ask explanations and apologies for the acts of Spanish officials whose zeal for the repression of rebellion sometimes blinds them to the immunities belonging to the unoffending citizens of a friendly power....

These inevitable entanglements of the United States with the rebellion in Cuba, the large American property interests affected, and considerations of philanthropy and humanity in general, have led to a vehement demand in various quarters for some sort of positive intervention on the part of the United States.... It is urged, finally, that, all other methods failing, the existing internecine strife in Cuba should be terminated by our intervention, even at the cost of a war between the United States and Spain—a war which its advocates confidently prophesy could be neither large in its proportions nor doubtful in its issue.

The correctness of this forecast need be neither affirmed nor denied. The United States has nevertheless a character to maintain as a nation, which plainly dictates that right and not might should be the rule of its conduct. Further, though the United States is not a nation to which peace is a necessity, it is in truth the most pacific of powers, and desires nothing so much as to live in amity with all the world....

It would seem that if Spain should offer to Cuba genuine autonomy—a measure of home rule which, while preserving the sovereignty of Spain, would satisfy all rational requirements of her Spanish subjects—there should be no just reason why the pacification of the island might not be effected on that basis....

It should be added that it can not be reasonably assumed that the hitherto expectant attitude of the United States will be indefinitely maintained....

When the inability of Spain to deal successfully with the insurrection has become manifest, and it is demonstrated that her sovereignty is extinct in Cuba for all purposes of its rightful existence, and when a hopeless struggle for its reestablishment has degenerated into a strife which means nothing more than the useless sacrifice of human life and the utter destruction of the very subject-matter of the conflict, a situation will be presented in which our obligations to the sovereignty of Spain will be superseded by higher obligations, which we can hardly hesitate to recognize and discharge.... Until we face the contingencies suggested, or the situation is by other incidents imperatively changed, we should continue in the line of conduct heretofore pursued, thus in all circumstances exhibiting our obedience to the requirements of public law and our regard for the duty enjoined upon us by the position we occupy in the family of nations....

ANTICOLONIAL

IMPERIALISM

AND THE

OPEN DOOR POLICY

CHAPTER 8

The Cuban Crisis of 1898–1900 and the
Crusade for a Free World Marketplace

*M*uch *of the embittered and exaggerated rhetoric of the*
presidential campaign of 1896 grew out of the feeling, shared by Republicans
and Democrats alike, that the other side was under the control of evil men
bent upon achieving personal or party gains at the cost of the national wel-
fare. William Jennings Bryan charged the Republicans with crucifying labor
(and small businessmen) upon a cross of gold. Republicans accused the
Democrats of surrendering their party to dangerous revolutionaries in
Nebraska and Chicago. These personalized explanations of the ills of the
country make it easy to exaggerate the radicalism of Bryan Democracy as
contrasted with the conservatism of McKinley Republicanism. Such an inter-
pretation of the election of 1896 creates much confusion about American
foreign policy from 1896 to 1900. For, in truth, Bryan and McKinley agreed
on the necessity and desirability of expanding the American marketplace, and
of extending American power and influence around the globe. Their dis-
agreements concerned the means, not the ends.

The agricultural businessmen of the South and West had by 1896 cap-
tured control of the Democratic party and were making a powerful bid to
improve their position in the domestic and international marketplaces
through a three-point program: regulate the giant industrial and financial
corporations, improve and lower the cost of transportation, and restore silver
to an equal footing with gold in the monetary system. The first of those ob-
jectives was largely domestic (though some Democrats did argue that such

reforms would enable American industrialists to win more foreign markets and thus enlarge the home market for food and fiber). The other two, how-ever, were fundamentally concerned with the agricultural drive for overseas markets.

The long campaign by the farmers to regulate the railroads was predi-cated upon an effort to improve their competitive position in the world mar-ketplace and at the same time keep more of the going price in their own pockets. Lowering the cost of shipping their cotton, grain, and meat would enable them to undersell foreign competitors and still show a greater profit. The demand to remonetize silver did involve the argument that the purely domestic inflationary consequences would help the farmer, but by 1896 the movement was stressing the point that silver would open the way for an American conquest of the markets of the world. Not only would remoneti-zation enable Americans to penetrate Latin America and Asia, but it would undercut Great Britain's economic empire, which was based on the gold standard. The agricultural anger at American gold bugs was intensified be-cause the farm businessmen saw them as allies of the British, who controlled the market for cotton and wheat.

McKinley countered the Democratic strategy for economic expansion with a sophisticated program likewise based on three proposals: he satisfied the metropolitan gold bugs with assurances that he would not abandon the gold standard unilaterally, appealed to the agricultural silverites with a prom-ise to work vigorously for an international agreement to remonetize silver, and argued that Blaine's program of reciprocity treaties offered the most ef-fective method of winning overseas markets. McKinley thus retained the backing of the metropolis while gaining crucial agricultural support in the upper Middle West with his emphasis on market expansion through reci-procity. Farmers of that region had always backed reciprocity, and had suf-fered direct economic losses when the Democrats had terminated (in 1894) Blaine's treaties with Cuba and other countries. Bryan was further weakened, moreover, by a late-summer rise in the world wheat market, which undercut his assertion that wheat prices could not improve until and unless silver was remonetized.

McKinley thus entered the White House committed to a program of vigorous overseas economic expansion, but he had no desire to go to war with Spain over Cuba. He hoped that a policy of firm pressure would force Madrid to devise a compromise that would end the revolution, create a quasi-autonomous government in Cuba, and open the economy of the island to American economic enterprise. Once that crisis was settled, he looked for-ward to a period of market expansion based upon a wide network of reci-procity treaties. The President embarked upon that strategy in July, 1897, by notifying Spain that he needed and expected a prompt settlement in Cuba (Document 1). He was fully aware that many Americans were beginning to exert increasing pressure for more militant action.

The activity (and influence) of such individuals and groups cannot be fully understood if they are approached simply in terms of whether or not they wanted war. A few of them, such as Assistant Secretary of the Navy Theodore Roosevelt, did advocate that solution to the problem from an early date (Document 2). And others, like Alfred Thayer Mahan, the Navy's most articulate and consequential expansionist, were fully prepared to accept war if it proved necessary (Document 3). But most Americans believed that the United States was strong enough to attain its objectives without war simply by asserting its desires in a vigorous and forthright manner. Indeed, some of them, as exemplified by the New York businessmen who petitioned McKinley (Document 4), couched their plea for more effective diplomacy in terms of securing peace. And, as with others who acted in a similar manner, there was no hypocrisy involved in their action. They simply were convinced that additional pressure of one kind or another would force Spain to accept American terms for settling the Cuban mess.

As Roosevelt notes in Document 2, McKinley also came under increasing attack by the members of the more militant wing of the agricultural protest movement. Their demands for intervention combined blunt references to the American economic stake in Cuba (as in Document 5) with appeals to America's duty to extend freedom to less fortunate peoples, as typified in the earlier comments of reformer Henry Demarest Lloyd in connection with the Venezuelan crisis (Document 6). But, as noted by Professor George Auxier in his study of midwestern newspapers, the same themes were stressed by more moderate spokesmen. As a result, many conservative metropolitan leaders (including big businessmen) who had opposed action that might lead to war came to fear that McKinley would lose control of the government to the agricultural militants unless he acted more forcefully. They ultimately concluded that war was a lesser risk than greater unrest at home.

McKinley was not as weak or indecisive as such men feared, but he was determined to make every possible effort to settle the crisis without war—and equally concerned to have the armed forces preparing for combat if that proved necessary. The latter consideration was particularly important because the administration had decided upon a two-front stategy if war was required. The battle plan called for action against Spain's Philippine colony in the Pacific as well as a campaign to free Cuba.

That far-reaching decision, which had its origins in the last year of Cleveland's term as president, grew out of the rising concern that America's economic expansion in China was being threatened by the activities of Germany, other European powers, and Japan. A typical warning from an American official in China is presented in Document 7, and Professor Thomas J. McCormick discusses the evolving pattern of McKinley's policy in his essay on the China market. The move into the Philippines provoked a heated argument between those who opposed traditional colonial expansion, and feared the occupation of the islands would lead to similar operations elsewhere, and others who defended the action as a special and limited operation required to ensure America's position in the China market.

The administration's analysis of the need for market expansion is provided in Document 8, and other arguments for expansion appear in Document 9. The debate between the anticolonialists and those who were willing to take the Philippines became confused and compounded—and embittered— by two factors: it probably never would have grown to such proportions if some Filipinos had not rebelled against the American occupation forces and *thus raised in dramatic and inescapable form the issue of violating the commitment to the principle of self-determination; and the administration appeared in a misleading light because, despite its action in the Philippines, it had neither the desire nor the intention to embark upon a general program of colonialism. The views of representative anticolonialists are presented in Document 13.*

For that matter, most of the anticolonialists favored market expansion as strongly as those who argued the necessity of taking the Philippines. The issue was resolved, though the debate did not run its course until after the election of 1900 (when Bryan failed to make an issue of the Philippines), by the administration's formulation and adoption of the Open Door Policy. Professor Charles S. Campbell, Jr., discusses some of the economic pressures for that policy in his article, and an official memorandum favoring it is presented in Document 10. The more general kind of agitation for economic expansion that generated wide approval of the policy is manifest in Document 11.

The Open Door Notes (Document 12) combined the economic and ideological themes of American expansion in classic form. On the one hand, the McKinley Administration committed American power to the principle of a free and open marketplace. Americans felt that would be enough to ensure their ultimate triumph in the worldwide struggle for economic supremacy. On the other hand, the Open Door Notes committed American power to the principle of self-determination in the forms of territorial and administrative integrity. That honored the tradition of expanding the area of freedom as part of America's expansion.

The Open Door Policy became the cornerstone of American foreign relations in the twentieth century. The diplomatic struggles to win acceptance of the policy, and the interventions and wars to uphold it, account for the political and military history of the modern era. And the outward thrust of American economic power created an empire that became both the marvel and the envy of the world. It also generated increasing opposition and antagonism.

MIDDLE WESTERN NEWSPAPERS AND
THE SPANISH-AMERICAN WAR,
1895–1898[1]   *George W. Auxier*

... Although it is difficult to make generalized statements regarding the exact influence of middle western newspapers in bringing about the Spanish-American War, their editorial comment would seem to indicate that they contributed to that end. Their chief influence, however, was not effected through sensational journalism—as the surveys previously made have assumed—but rather through continued emphasis on a number of basic factors which led

[1] *The Mississippi Valley Historical Review*, XXVI, No. 4 (March, 1940), 523–34. Reprinted with permission.

to war. These were: the fundamental interests of the United States in the Caribbean, Spanish violations of these interests, the propaganda activities of the Cuban *Junta*, and the implications of the Cuban question in the domestic politics of the United States.

The basic interests of the United States in the Caribbean were reflected in the editorial columns of middle western newspapers during the first year of the Cuban revolt. Embodied in the premises of the revived spirit of "manifest destiny," these interests were stated in terms of economic imperialism, military strategem, political idealism, and a large measure of humanitarianism. These were the fundamental considerations which determined editorial attitude on the Cuban question. These were the cornerstones upon which the future Cuban policy of the United States seems to have rested. Upon them the editors were stimulated by events and circumstances to prepare the way for their realization through the medium of national policy.

From the beginning of the Cuban revolt in February, 1895, the editors of middle western newspapers pointed out that Spain violated American interests in the Caribbean and that her presence in that area was inimical to the consummation of America's "manifest destiny." An interesting and effective repertoire of editorial arguments was accordingly evolved to prove these contentions. American economic interests were said to be jeopardized by the interruption of trade, the destruction of American property in the islands, and Spanish resistance to the natural expansion of industrial capitalism. American interests in military strategy and national security were said to be endangered because Spain's strategic possessions in the Caribbean might fall into the hands of a stronger European power. The interests of the United States in the extension of the American political system were said to be obstructed by the "political anachronism" of monarchical Spain in the democratic western hemisphere. Through editorial, cartoon, and indigenous verse, the editors also maintained that Spain violated the American conception of humanitarianism by her constant abuse of American nationals as well as her own downtrodden subjects. Couched in emotionalized terminology, these arguments contributed to the belief that Spain should be eliminated from the Caribbean, where the United States wanted to broaden her sphere of influence.

The development of a more aggressive Cuban policy was also stimulated by the activities of the Cuban *Junta*, whose headquarters were located in New York City, and its American counterpart, the Cuban *League*, whose branch units were situated in the larger cities throughout the Middle West and elsewhere. These two organizations, working in close cooperation with a sympathetic American press, had as their purpose the instigation of material and moral aid in promotion of Cuban independence. The practical program of these agencies was hypothecated on the premise that their own objectives could be achieved only through assistance from the United States. The *Junta*, therefore, devised a number of very tangible methods for achieving its purposes.

For the purpose of rendering material aid to the insurgents, the *Junta* organized and fitted out filibustering expeditions to Cuba. Illegal in character, these enterprises led to a number of exasperating incidents, the most notable of which were the "Allianca" case in 1895 and the "Competitor" affair in 1896. The Spanish government made frequent complaints to the American Department of State concerning the illegality of these expeditions, in response to which President Cleveland issued (June 12, 1895, and July 27, 1896) two proclamations of neutrality. The continuous propaganda of the *Junta*, nevertheless, moved federal officials and the editors of middle western newspapers to condone the practice of filibustering.

For the purpose of arousing moral support for the insurgent cause, the *Junta* adopted several methods which disclosed that its members possessed much more than an amateur knowledge of propaganda technique. Through "Sympathy Meetings," the stage, and the platform, the members of the *Junta* told the story of Cuba's wrongs and her heroic struggle for independence. Through the facilities of a friendly press, American humanitarianism was exploited to the fullest advantage; and through the same medium, the *Junta* very cleverly developed a belief in Cuban success by lauding the Cuban generals and exaggerating their exploits. The *Junta* likewise evolved a corresponding theory of Spanish failure by discrediting the Spanish captain-generals in their efforts to suppress the revolt in Cuba and by gloating over Spain's disintegration at home. It also fed the press with atrocity stories based on the alleged brutality of Spanish warfare. It sought further to promote its objectives through the publication of its own paper, *La Patria*, and through the systematic preparation and distribution of a deluge of propaganda pamphlets.

The activities of the *Junta* in thus promoting material and moral aid for the insurgent cause naturally involved the question of American neutrality and eventually led the editors of the Middle West to abandon a policy of non-interference in favor of intervention on behalf of the Cubans. The editorial comment of newspapers in the Middle West also indicated that the *Junta's* activities were instrumental in pointing out to the Republicans the political implications of the Cuban situation which the Democrats attempted to avoid. In seeking to discredit Cleveland's policy of neutrality the Republicans introduced the Cuban issue into American politics. The editorial columns of the area under consideration indicated that editorial attitude on the issue in question was influenced to a large extent by political considerations. The partisanship which resulted from editorial discussion was a reflection of a struggle between the waning dogma of Democratic isolationism and the rapidly emerging doctrine of Republican imperialism. In this struggle the Cuban question became the issue which determined the trend of American foreign policy. This fact was clearly evident during the administrations of both Cleveland and McKinley.

The partisanship of the Republican press toward Cleveland's policy of neutrality was apparent as early as midsummer, 1895, and became increasingly evident with the approach of the presidential canvass of 1896. The Democrats so successfully diverted the Cuban controversy that domestic reform and free silver became the leading issues of the campaign. The Republicans, nevertheless, emphasized the strong Cuban plank in their platform and during the election criticized the Democratic administration for its timidity on that point; but responsibilities of Republican victory in 1896 sobered the party's attitude toward the Cuban question. Immediately after the election in November, Republican editors reversed themselves and advised a Cuban policy equally as cautious as that which the Democrats had pursued under Cleveland. Yet, ostensibly for purposes of political consistency, the leaders of the Republican party in Congress urged immediate and positive action on the Cuban situation during Cleveland's last Congress, although surreptitiously they tried to thrust the onus of solving the problem upon the outgoing administration. The Republicans, however, were disappointed in their efforts and received much retributive denunciation from Democratic editors, who pointed out the inconsistencies of their political foes and sought to embarrass them precisely as they had been embarrassed by the Republicans during Cleveland's régime.

Editorial reaction to McKinley's Cuban policy was, therefore, similar in its political manifestations to that shown in response to the Cuban policy of Cleveland. McKinley's policy was subordinated, however, to a much more difficult task—that of preserving the integrity of the Republican party. The issues of reform and free silver had almost triumphed in 1896, and Bryan and the Democrats announced that these would remain the burning questions of the future. Mark Hanna had promised the Republicans continuation of political control by means of a return to prosperity. McKinley chose to accomplish this result through peaceful methods; although, in the end, he was encouraged by a series of immediate circumstances to forestall the loss of political power, which threatened in the elections of 1898 and 1900, by resorting to war with Spain. In the meantime he endeavored to facilitate the revival of business by preserving the peace and accordingly, in the fall of 1897, the President suggested that Spain attempt the solution of the Cuban question through the inauguration of a program of autonomous reforms for Cuba.

In addition to autonomy a wide variety of proposals for the solution of the Cuban question had been given editorial consideration between February, 1895, and October, 1897. These proposals included neutrality, purchase, arbitration, recognition of Cuban belligerency or independence, charitable intervention, and intervention for the protection of American life and property. For one reason or another, each of these proposals failed. Autonomy also failed, at first because it was rejected by Spain, and later because the United States refused to assist Spain in its effective operation. Neutrality was abandoned because it seemed inconsistent with the realization of American interests in the Caribbean. Purchase was cast aside because Spain gave no intimation that she would sell Cuba to the United States. Arbitration was discarded because the editors considered the Cuban question an American affair, while recognition of belligerency or independence, although given serious consideration, was not accorded because the insurgents were unable to prove that their *de facto* government was worthy of *de jure* status. Charitable intervention to assist the starving Cubans and intervention for the proection of American life and property proved nothing more than entering wedges for official intervention by force of arms.

Although there was no universal agreement on any one of the proposals discussed, the editors stood on common ground in consistently advocating

Cuban independence through "intervention" of some sort. Western newspaper opinion, between the autumn of 1897 and the spring of 1898, indicated that intervention did not necessarily mean intervention by force. Editorial comment on the events associated with the Cuban revolt, nevertheless, supports the thesis here presented—that the fundamental interests of the United States in the Caribbean, Spanish violations of these interests, propaganda activities of the Cuban *Junta*, and the political implications of the Cuban question in the domestic politics of the United States—were the real causes which led to war with Spain. These factors were particularly revealed in journalistic comment on the events immediately preceding the declaration of war. The political factor involved was especially reflected during this period; apparently, it was the force that determined McKinley's action.

A number of immediate considerations gave McKinley moral courage to pursue forceful intervention for reasons of political expediency. More specifically these were the De Lôme letter, the "Maine" tragedy, Senator Redfield Proctor's report on Cuban conditions, the report of the Naval Court of Inquiry on the causes for the "Maine" disaster, and the probability of European quiescence at American intervention in Cuba. But the tide of intervention did not set in until mid-March, 1898; and McKinley was largely responsible for shaping the events that finally culminated in war. The objective manner in which the editors of middle western newspapers suspended judgment on the insulting De Lôme letter and the "Maine" disaster showed that war, as far as they were concerned, was not a necessity on account of those incidents alone. Their progressive and continued emphasis on the basic interests of the United States in the Caribbean, their repeated laments that Spain violated these interests, the manner in which they served as a vehicle for the propaganda of the Cuban *Junta*, and the evident partisanship reflected in their discussions of the Cuban question, all suggest that the true causes which led to war were more fundamentally these factors than the influence of the press in demanding intervention in a sensational manner for reasons of increased circulation of the newspapers.

As further proof of this thesis one needs only to examine the editorial attempts of middle western newspaper editors to rationalize the war in April, 1898. Then the editors restated the fundamental interests of the United States as implied in the revived spirit of "manifest destiny." They reiterated these interests in the impelling tenets of American economic imperialism, military strategy, political idealism, and humanitarianism. They recapitulated Spanish violations of the foregoing American interests. They reflected the undoubted influence of the *Junta's* propaganda, which emphatically declared, through the medium of the press, that the insurgents would not accept any solution of the Cuban crisis short of complete independence. In this rationalization the political implications of the Cuban question in bringing about the Spanish-America War were most manifest. . . .

THE CHINA MARKET AND THE
RETENTION OF THE PHILIPPINES[1]

Thomas J. McCormick

... The incoming McKinley administration found sufficient reason to view Chinese affairs optimistically. Compared to the previous three years of chaos, most of 1897 proved relatively (albeit superficially) calm and stable—so much so that the *New York Times* could find no need between January and July to make a single editorial pronouncement about the eternal "Chinese question." To an administration that equated tranquility with prosperity (whether in Cuba or China), this must have been a welcome development indeed. In fact, evidence and analysis seemed to bear out the equation. Trade statistics, through their diplomatic interpreters, spoke forcefully of one key reality: the emergence of a favorable American trade balance with the Chinese Empire (the first in history), gained "chiefly in manufactured cotton, Indian yarn, kerosene, woolens and metals." Moreover, so Denby felt, even these statistics shed only a particle of light, for they ignored the immense amounts that China imported indirectly from the United States "*via* England, Hong Kong and other places." In support he unearthed one estimate that "60% of the goods exported and imported at Shanghai are of American origin or destination." Though he admitted the possibility of exaggeration, the American Minister did not "hesitate to predict an enormous development of our trade within the next few years."

In seeking to make good Denby's prophecy, the McKinley administration, in its first 250 days, engaged in a variety of unspectacular activities—but then the circumstances did not seem to demand heroics. Illustrative were the efforts to expand the right of foreign residence in the Chinese interior—on the assumption that so long as China restricted foreign merchants to the treaty ports, the expansion of the China market would proceed at a rather minimal pace. Accordingly, the American government did two things. First, it utilized the "most-favored-nation" clause to demand (and receive) the right of American citizens (including merchants) to reside throughout Hangchow province—a right secured by the Japanese two years earlier in the Treaty of Shiminoseki. Second, it sought to make better use of American missionaries who already held interior residence privileges; missionaries who, in their impact upon the existing social structure, created wants that only commerce could supply. Seeking to evaluate this impact and to exploit it more fully, the State Department ordered all its consuls in China to make a systematic survey of American missionary property and non-religious activities: for example, the operation of small, profit-making businesses, the practice of medicine for fees, or the local sale of goods produced in missionary-run industrial schools. As Denby noted, such a survey would be "of great usefulness" to his legation, the State Department, and American busi-

---

[1] Selected from *China Market: America's Quest for Informal Empire, 1893–1901* (Chicago: Quadrangle Books, 1967), pp. 84–90, 91–94, 98–101, 106–10, 116–17, 118–20. Reprinted with permission.

nessmen interested "in the trade and commerce with China." At the same time the government continued to encourage American missionaries to use their treaty rights to establish residence in new and untried areas of the interior. Thus, in late 1897, when an American missionary finally settled in Hunan province, Denby reported exultantly that "this is the first permanent lodgement made in Hunan by foreigners," and he waxed eloquent on the size, population, and natural resources of the province and their possible significance for American trade. Apparently he saw no religious importance in the event.

* * *

American efforts in behalf of trade expansion fared better than attempts to foster investments in China, particularly in railroads. Of course the two spheres were hardly distinct, for railroad investments would theoretically aid American commerce: immediately through the corollary sale of American steel rails, locomotives, and rolling stock; ultimately through the creation of a transportation system that would facilitate the distribution and sale of American products. Nevertheless, the initial concern of most would-be American investors was the potential profit to be gained from interest on concession loans. In this sense, American investors faced greater risks than their commercial brethren.

Chief example of the railroad-concession enterprise was still the famous American China Development Company. Having earlier bogged down and apparently failed in its efforts to secure the Peking-Hankow Railroad concession, the company suddenly resurrected the dead beast in early 1897, perhaps in the hope that the McKinley administration would be more helpful than its predecessor in a last-ditch effort to save the contract. But the new quest proved unavailing, and in mid-May 1897 the Chinese government awarded the contract to a Belgian syndicate. It did so for two reasons—or so the State Department believed. First was "the ominous suspicion that European politics" had subverted the influence of the pro-American Director of Railroads, Sheng Taotai, and intimidated the Chinese government. More specifically, it was widely assumed that old tandem of Russian diplomacy and French finance was responsible; that French bankers had gained internal control of the Belgian group and that Russia had then used its influence with China to "[aid] the Belgian Syndicate in securing the Railroad contract."

Second and equally important was the recurring realization that the American China Development Company, as before, either could not or would not meet the contractual terms insisted upon by the Chinese. Denby in fact admitted "that our fellow citizens failed solely because they were unwilling to accept the terms offered by China and which have been accepted by the Belgians." (Actually, the Belgian syndicate accepted terms even *more* stringent than those proffered the American, especially on the key issues of collateral and procurement procedures.) ...

Unfortunately for the open door, commercial or financial, the "quiet time" of 1897 was only ephemeral in the escalating spoilation of the Chinese Empire. Economically inviting but politically unstable, China simply proved too tempting a prey, particularly to those less-advantaged European nations

345

which could not afford an open-market situation on the Asian mainland. Thus, on November 18, 1897, Germany shattered the apparent calm by seizing Kiaochou, "an excellent port situated near the Shantung promontory." A participant in the *Dreibund* intervention of 1895, Germany had "received practically nothing" from China for her efforts, while profitable "favors . . . [had] been showered on Russia and France." Consequently, in 1896 and 1897 Germany "repeatedly demanded the cession of a port to be used as a naval depot." When such was not forthcoming, she acted aggressively and on her own. The transparent excuse offered for the Kiaochou takeover was the murder of two German missionaries, but the subsequent demands for exclusive railroad and mining rights in Shantung province, plus the insistence on a fifty-year occupation of Kiaochou, proved—if proof was needed—that the Kingdom of God weighed less in the balance than the mundane aspirations of Imperial Germany. China, too weak to resist alone and—ominously—unable to secure any Russian help, ultimately capitulated and in the first week of 1898 formally consented to the German demands.

The German action and the Shantung agreement forced agonizing reappraisals of China policy in almost all the great power chanceries. Nowhere were the results more dramatic than in Russia, where the response involved an internal power struggle which fulfilled the widespread fears that "if Germany retains possession of Kiaochou Russia will take [Port Arthur]." In fact, Russia decided quite early that it was in her interest to *permit* (even encourage) Germany to realize her aims in Shantung. Led by Count Mouraviev, the Foreign Minister, the territorial expansionists in the Russian government persuaded the Czar that "the occupation of Kiao-Chow . . . offered a favourable occasion . . . to seize one of the Chinese ports, notably Port Arthur or the adjacent Ta-lieng-wan"—ports of "enormous strategic importance." Count Witte predictably opposed such overt, territorial absorption and continued to advocate his past policy of peaceful penetration in the name of Chinese friendship. But Mouraviev carried the day with his insistence that England would take Port Arthur if Russia did not. Thus, on March 8, 1898, Denby confirmed that "Russia had demanded the cession of Port Arthur and Talienwan" on "the same terms which are accorded Germany." Fearful that this meant war or partition (with the open door as prime fatality), the American Minister urged "an energetic protest from our Government against the dismemberment of China" in an effort to strengthen "the hands of nations like Japan and Great Britain who are freer to act in this contingency than we are." In the meantime, China—with little choice—granted Russian demands for a twenty-five-year lease of a southern Manchurian zone (twenty-three by fifty-three miles), including the two desired ports.

These German and Russian moves threatened American commercial interests in several ways. Immediately they threatened existent American trade in northern China (including Manchuria), an area that absorbed two-thirds of all American exports to China. . . .

In its evolving response to the renewed Chinese crisis, the McKinley administration had to act within the framework of a number of internal forces. One of these was the pressure of special business groups with already existing vested interests in China—pressure which indisputably affected the timing and (perhaps) the substance of administration policy. The chief expression of these interests came from the Committee on American Interests in China (later broadened into the American Asiatic Association). Formed on the very day that China ratified the Shantung agreement, the committee numbered among its leaders the editor of the influential *Journal of Commerce*, the chief project engineer for the American China Development Company, a representative of Bethlehem Iron, the president of one of the largest export-import houses in Shanghai, and an executive in the textile-exporting firm of Deering, Milihen and Company. Overall the committee members were interested mainly in commerce and viewed financial concessioneering as neither profitable nor feasible. Even Clarence Cary, who only seven months earlier, as representative of the American China Development Company, had been trying to save the Peking-Hankow contract, concluded by January 1898 "that the undaunted concession-seeker" was "chasing rainbows"; that "it seem[ed] hardly worthwhile, under existing conditions, for foreigners to consider Chinese railway projects." Significantly, Cary remained more optimistic about trade expansion, despite his conviction that European powers would discriminate against it in their new spheres. Even in March 1898, at the height of the China crisis, he believed the situation could be stabilized if the American government would "abandon its policy of inaction and look to the care of our existing trade rights." Apparently his fellow committee members shared his views sufficiently to mobilize sixty-eight business firms in support of a general petition asking for protection of American trade against the threats of partitioning and discrimination.

Other business groups acted in similar fashion. The New York Chamber of Commerce, for example, under prodding from the *New York Times* and after much debate (weighing the potential profits of the China trade against the dangers of an alliance with England), sent a petition to the administration asking for "proper steps" for the "preservation and protection of . . . important commercial interest in [the Chinese] Empire." It, in turn, served as the model for petitions from the chambers of commerce in Boston and San Francisco. Those from Philadelphia, Baltimore, and Seattle differed in wording but conveyed the same sense. The first round of petitions during the Shantung crisis was fairly vague and cautious ("too colorless" said the *New York Times*), expressing only general concern while shying away from any specific policy recommendations. The second wave of petitions, occasioned by Russian actions in Manchuria, was somewhat stronger. For instance, the New York Chamber of Commerce not only reaffirmed its original memorial but seemingly endorsed a resolution passed by the cream of American merchants in Shanghai urging "immediate action necessary to protect American interests against aggression in Northern China." Throughout the crisis, leading commercial and financial journals gave fairly vigorous support. The *United States Investor* even talked of war to prevent "the door" from being "closed" on "equal trading rights." The *Commercial and Financial Chronicle* warned the administration that the possible "absorption of Manchuria in the Russian Customs area" required a "strong representation in favor of keeping open the trade on equal terms to all nations."

To emphasize only business pressures, however, would distort reality by ignoring the larger, quite receptive context in which these pressures took place and which helped to make them effective. For one thing, it would ignore the interesting fact that the conservative, non-jingoistic, big city newspapers—normally regarded as quite cautious on foreign affairs questions—often matched or even surpassed the clamor of business groups in demanding strong governmental support of the open door against the dangers implicit in partitioning. In New York the *Times* denounced the German attempt "at a monopoly" as "an act of hostility . . . to all mankind." It reminded its readers, when speaking of China, that "We need no more territory," but "we must have more markets, or suffer a terrible check to our growth and prosperity"; and it wailed that "We are in a fair way to lose all and get nothing." By mid-March 1898, with the Cuban confrontation visible on the horizon, the *Times* was denouncing "the headless State Department" for its "ignorance and apathy about our commercial interest abroad" (China) and pressuring for the removal of Secretary of State John Sherman. . . .

But practically the administration had neither the inclination nor the capacity to go beyond diplomatic dialogue in sustaining the open door against suspected subversion. There remained the lingering hope that Great Britain, perhaps aided by Japan, might use its power and influence in the Far East to halt or retard the apparent disintegration of China. But hope was one thing, certitude quite another. John Hay and his staff—good Anglophiles all—were totally convinced that the British were "clear and energetic on the China policy" and would support the "open door" by war if necessary. Denby, however, dismissed British "support for treaty rights" as little more than "grandiloquent declaration as to what she would do," and offered the contrary prediction that she would ultimately join the partitioning and convert the entire Yangtze Valley into her own sphere. McKinley, torn by such conflicting reports, rigorously followed daily press accounts of the China policy debates in the House of Commons—and waited.

In fact, British attitudes on the Chinese crisis were enormously ambivalent. The inclination of some "Home Office" officials to accept the inevitable and join partitioning was offset in part by the still vigorous support of the open door by those with special business interests throughout China. As a consequence, British policy vacillated wildly between these two approaches. Generally, the first steps reflected the division-of-spheres thinking. For one thing, England sought to protect and expand her own interests by pressuring China for the third indemnity loan award, a railroad concession from Burma to the Yangtze, the opening of three new treaty ports, the right of steam navigation on inland waters, and a non-alienation pledge for the Yangtze Valley. At the same time, she sought a general rapprochement with Russia on the basis of "a partition of preponderance" in all areas of Anglo-Russian competition—China and Turkey especially, but Persia and Africa as well. But Russia was apparently not interested. Her insistence that any agreement be limited to China made it clear that the British would give more than they received. Moreover, in China itself Russia worked hard and successfully to block a direct British government loan to China for the third indemnity payment. In the end the British got only an indirect and partial share as the Chinese gave the award to the same private, Anglo-German corporation that had financed the second loan. And worse, both Russia and France used even that as an excuse for additional concessions for themselves.

Rebuffed by the Russians, the British government, led by Colonial Secretary Joseph Chamberlain, reversed policies in midstream and returned to the traditional "open door" policy; but only (and there was the catch) if the United States or Germany, or both would "stand with us in our China policy." Forewarned of the move, Henry White, the American Chargé d'Affaires in London, informed the State Department to expect "overtures" for cooperative American support for equal trading rights—though he wrongly assumed the request would be limited to German encroachments in the Yangtze Valley. In fact, the "overture" (which arrived on March 8) went much further and asked "whether the United States would be prepared to join with Great Britain in opposing" either "preferential treatment" to foreign lessees or "the actual cessions of portions of the Chinese littoral."

The British inquiry was necessarily futile. For one thing, the American government was already committed to postponing action of any sort until faced with an overt effort at trade discrimination. Since, as the American reply noted, "there has been no occupation up to this time which proposes...to close the Chinese trade to the civilized world or to obtain exclusive commercial privileges," there seemed no pressing reason to give the British a blank check to be filled out and cashed at some future time and at their discretion. Moreover, even if the administration had been so inclined, it lacked the capacity to give the British any substantive help. Already on a collision course with Spain over the Cuban revolution, and totally without a power base of its own in the western Pacific, the United States could offer "Brother Jonathan" only the soothing words that "the President has not been unmindful of the situation in China" and "is in sympathy with the policy which shall maintain open trade" there. Finally, even had America had the capacity for dynamic action in Asia, it was unlikely (as it had been in 1895 and would be in 1900) to use it in conjunction with the British, save perhaps informally and for limited ends. For McKinley, as for Cleveland, the open door was a means of avoiding conflict, not creating it; a means of acquiring the economic fruits of empire without *extensive* political-military responsibilities and burdens. Accepting the British proposal would have cut across the whole grain of this orientation and involved America potentially in a dangerous polarization of power camps in the Far East. Better, thought McKinley, to maintain American freedom of action in the face of an uncertain future; better, so he told the British, to retain "traditional policy respecting foreign alliances and as far as practicable avoiding interference or connection with European complications."

Rejected by the Americans (and the Germans as well), England sought to put herself in a military-political position to defend the open door with force, if such seemed desirable, or effectively take part in partitioning, if such proved necessary. Thus she demanded and received a lease of the coast city of Wei-Hai-Wei—not for exclusive commercial privileges but as a military counterpoise to Russian power in the Gulf of Pechihli. Subsequently, and partly in response to French moves, Britain received an extension at Hong Kong (again for military rather than commercial purposes), a railroad concession from Nanking to Shanghai, and a non-alienation pledge for Yunnan and Kwangtung provinces. None of these moves, though, fully validated Denby's conclusion that England had been "driven by the logic of events to seize her share of the spoils of this empire." They made that course an easier one to fulfill in the future if Great Britain determined upon it, but for the moment she avoided the German and Russian mode of exercising potentially exclusive control over important treaty ports, such as Chefoo and Newchwang.

Whatever the intent of British moves, they did raise (as Denby lamented) the distinct possibility of "a complete partition of China"—certainly a death-dealing development to "[American] interests." . . .

* * *

. . . The McKinley era marked an important change in the tone and tactics of American expansionism—a change characterized by a more non-ideological, pragmatic approach; by more utilitarian, businesslike methods of doing a necessary job efficiently, but at the least possible cost. McKinley's policies were, in other words, essentially those of "pragmatic expansionism."

Specifically, the most obvious and vital difference centered on the question of insular imperialism. Among Democrats of the Cleveland ilk (as with Republicans of the Carl Schurz variety) anti-colonialism was an article of faith. Cleveland's rejection of Hawaiian annexation in 1893 and his later opposition to retention of the Philippines bore witness to that. But to Republicans like McKinley, weaned on the recent heritage of Seward, Grant, and Blaine, anti-colonialism was relative rather than absolute. One's right hand might affirm it in continental market areas, while one's left hand qualified it with a limited dose of "insular imperialism" in islands and enclaves that were potentially useful as strategic stepping-stones to those very same market areas. Such pragmatic niceties reflected the perceived realities that rapid communications necessitated oceanic cables and cable relay·points; that an enlarged Navy demanded operational bases; that market penetration could be facilitated by nearby possessions; that steam technology required coaling stations. (As the New York Tribune put it in March 1898, "COAL IS KING"—a fact that "The United States has begun to consider. . ." apparently in relationship to "Chinese waters.") In the Pacific, Seward's purchase of the Aleutians and the occupation of Midway Island, Harrison's attempt to annex Hawaii, and McKinley's revival of that project in 1897 and again in early 1898 all manifested a conscious, rational effort to foster and protect American trade in an "open" Asia through effective control of the Kiska-Honolulu axis (an early nineteenth-century geopolitical idea of Russian origin).

Analyzed against this backdrop, America's insular acquisitions of 1898 were not products of "large policy" imperialism. Hawaii, Wake, Guam, and the Philippines were not taken principally for their own economic worth, or for their fulfillment of Manifest Destiny, or for their venting of the "psychic crisis." They were obtained, instead, largely in an eclectic effort to construct a system of coaling, cable, and naval stations for an integrated trade route which could help realize America's overriding ambition in the Pacific—the penetration and ultimate domination of the fabled China market.

From the very beginning of the Spanish-American War, the McKinley administration intended to retain a foothold in the Philippines as an "American Hong Kong," a commercial entrepôt to the China market and a center of American military power. Formulation of this policy commitment began seven months before hostilities with Spain, when McKinley examined a Navy Department memorandum written by Assistant Secretary Theodore Roosevelt. This multipurpose paper made one especially bold suggestion: in the event of war with Spain, the Asiatic Squadron "should blockade, and if possible take Manila." Historical myth notwithstanding, it was a suggestion that fell on already prepared ground, for the influential Senator from Connecticut, Orville Platt, had earlier taken pains to impress upon the President "that Manila had become one of the most important ports of the Orient and that the importance of that station demanded most careful attention."

Temporarily put in abeyance by a short-lived détente with Spain in late 1897, the proposal was revived and made the basis of Roosevelt's famous February 25 orders instructing Commodore George Dewey to "start offensive operations in the Philippines" after eliminating the Spanish fleet. The view that this was simply a conspiratorial effort by "large policy" extremists misses two more significant facts: first, Roosevelt's superiors accepted his orders for the Philippine operations even though they unceremoniously countermanded nearly two-thirds of the other miscellaneous orders issued concurrently by the Assistant Secretary; second, the administration had already accepted the substance of Dewey's orders in principle and thereafter permitted the Naval War Board to incorporate the February 25 orders into overall strategy plans for the Pacific. Clearly, while Roosevelt's actions may have been precipitate, they fell within the main lines of the "large policies" of the administration. Of these, Roosevelt, as he privately admitted, was largely "ignorant."

With the outbreak of war the McKinley administration rushed (with almost unseemly haste) to implement its designs upon the likeliest entrepôt, Manila, by determining to send an army of occupation to the Philippine capital. It made this decision on May 2 *before* fully credible news of Dewey's victory at Manila Bay reached Washington and it formally issued the call for Philippine volunteers on May 4, three days *before* an anxious, jittery Secretary of the Navy received authoritative word that the Asiatic Squadron was safe—not immobilized by heavy damages, as he feared. The size of the Army force was to be "not less than twenty thousand men"—quadruple the number recommended by Dewey "to retain [Manila] and thus control the Philippine Islands." It was a move that confirmed Roosevelt in his belief that "the Administration is now fully committed to the large policy." It also persuaded the *San Francisco Chronicle,* on May 4, to splash across its front page the prophetic headline: "WE WILL HOLD THE PHILIPPINES."

On May 11, in one of the most important (and overlooked) decision-making sessions in American history, McKinley and his cabinet gave definite form to their war aims in the Pacific by approving a State Department memorandum calling for Spanish cession to the United States of a suitable "coaling station," presumably Manila. The islands as a whole, however, were to remain with Spain. Acting within the framework of this decision, McKinley on May 19 endowed the commander of the expeditionary force with sufficiently broad powers to effect "the severance of the former political relations of the inhabitants and the establishment of a new political power." Simultaneously, he instructed his Secretary of the Treasury to undertake a study of the islands with an eye "to substitut[ing] new rates and new taxes for those now levied in the Philippines." The stated purpose of both orders, as well as a similar one to Dewey (which he was to "interpret . . . liberally"), was to [give] to the islands, while in the possession of the United States, that order and security which they have long since ceased to enjoy. Shortly thereafter, on June 3, when it became apparent that the great distance between Manila and Honolulu demanded an intermediate coaling and cable station, the President broadened the American position to include "an island in the Ladrones" (Marianas). The choice made was Guam, and the United States Navy promptly seized it.

As of early June, then, the administration envisioned postwar control only of Manila and Guam as way stations to the orient. But dramatic events swiftly undercut this limited resolve and for a critical fortnight set American policy aimlessly adrift. First of all, as the State Department itself noted, the emergence of the Philippine "insurgents" as "an important factor" made it increasingly doubtful that the islands—minus Manila—could be returned to effective Spanish sovereignty. What then—bestow the largess of Philippine independence but with the stipulation of American control in Manila? Certainly it was within American power to impose such a solution upon the insurgents, by force if necessary. Moreover, the revolutionaries might even have accepted it peacefully, especially since they themselves had offered (as far back as November 1897) to turn over "two provinces and the Custom House at Manila" in exchange for an alliance against Spain (though theoretically these would not be permanent cessions but simply collateral pledges against eventual Filipino repayment for American aid). Nevertheless, relinquishing the rest of the islands ran counter to the administration belief that "if we evacuate, anarchy rules"; that (as Dewey later noted) "The natives appear unable to govern."

This presumption that an independent Philippines would be strife-ridden and unstable raised, in turn, the most frightening spectre of all: European intervention, especially by Germany, who considered herself heir-apparent to Spain's insular empire in the Pacific. . . .

The real and continuing danger was German intervention against a weak, fledgling republic that might well render the isolated American position in

Manila more vulnerable than useful. *This* was no chimera! By mid-June, Andrew White had already confirmed what the State Department feared: that Germany would use the expected "anarchy, confusion and insecurity under a 'Philippine Republic'" as an excuse "to secure a stronghold and centre of influence in that region." Less than a month later, Germany informed White (and Hay as well) that she expected "a few coaling stations" and "a naval base" in the Philippines (not to mention control of the Carolines and "predominant" influence in Samoa). Nor did the passage of time and the solidification of American intentions eliminate such German ambitions. Even after the armistice with Spain, rumors flowed freely that Germany still sought "the Sulu islands" in the southern Philippines—rumors given great credence by Assistant Secretary of State John Bassett Moore. And in late October the State Department continued to receive "trustworthy information" that if the United States failed to take all the Philippines, Germany has "every intention to establish a foothold there."

Rival intervention or nationalistic revolution: either could undermine American plans for Manila. Unable to decide on a course of action, American policy lay momentarily immobilized—at a time when the growing crisis in China itself least afforded the luxury of prolonged indecision. . . .

. . . Confronted with a nearly even, three-way split between departmental secretaries (Manila, Luzon, or the whole prize?), the President—in the calculating but affable manner that was his trademark—simply maneuvered his subordinates into accepting a position he had already predetermined. The policy glossed over internal differences; gave him the flexibility to move in whatever direction changing circumstances might dictate; and allowed him the time and opportunity both to test and educate public opinion. In the process he crushed a move headed by "Judge Day" (and backed by the Secretaries of the Treasury and the Navy) to limit American commitment to "a hitching-post," simply by declining to put the proposal to a vote. (". . . I was afraid it would carry," he said, only half-facetiously.) In sealing this extremity, he left open only the question of how far to journey toward the other—Luzon or the entire group? The beginning of the final peace negotiations in early October found this question still unresolved. While the American commissioners were instructed to demand only Luzon, they were also to "accumulate all possible information" on the possible necessity of controlling the whole archipelago. And since three of the five commissioners already favored the latter possibility publicly, it seemed likely that the information accumulated would lend itself to their interpretation. Whatever, less than a month later, on October 25, McKinley himself finally cut the knot by broadening his instructions to include all the Philippines.

In this evolution of Philippine policy, America's commercial stake in China played the primary role in the thinking of the business and government elite that chiefly shaped and supported McKinley's decisions. It also played a significant, though not paramount, part in the outlook of the military advisers who exercised a more limited but still crucial influence upon the President's policies.

Between June and October, economic and political leaders united vigorously in support of retaining all or a large part of the Philippines. But they de-emphasized the intrinsic worth of the islands and stressed instead their strategic relationship to China—both as a commercial stepping-stone and a political-military lever. Moreover, they increasingly affirmed that Manila alone would not suffice for these purposes, that the United States would have to take Luzon and perhaps the whole group. In part this support for enlarged control reflected the already pervasive fear that native revolution or European penetration might undermine the viability of American power in Manila. But it also indicated a growing belief, born of newly accumulated information, that the economic interdependence of the archipelago made efficient division most difficult....

...Led by the NAM and the American Asiatic Association, special business organizations urged retention of the islands "for the protection and furtherance of the commercial interests of our citizens in the Far East." In a survey of the trade journals of the country, the *Chicago Inter-Ocean* found it "remarkable with what unanimity they have advocated the retention of the Philippines." Even more remarkable was the unanimity of their reasoning: that (in the words of the *Insurance Advocate*) it would encourage "the teeming millions of the Middle Kingdom" to "buy largely from us"; that with "one-third of the human race within easy distance of us, coaling stations on the road, and Manila as the Hong Kong of Uncle Sam's alert and keen merchant trader," the result was preordained....

Most of McKinley's close associates in the federal government (many of whom were themselves products of the business community) pressed similar views upon their chief. There were exceptions, of course. Worthington C. Ford, head of the Bureau of Statistics, appeared to feel (like former Minister to China George F. Seward) that "*We do not want the Philippines at any price or under any circumstances.*" A few others like Judge Day held largely to the position (as Carl Schurz summarized it for the President) that "all desirable commercial facilities" and "all naval stations needed could be secured without the annexation of populous territories," without "dangerous political entanglements and responsibilities." But most thought and counseled otherwise. The redoubtable Mark Hanna, State Department economic expert Frederic Emory, Charles Denby and his successor Edwin Conger, Comptroller of the Currency Charles G. Dawes, Assistant Secretary of the Treasury Frank A. Vanderlip, to name a few, all shared in general the conviction (as Vanderlip stated) that an American-controlled Philippines would be "pickets of the Pacific, standing guard at the entrances to trade with the millions of China and Korea, French Indo-China, the Malay Peninsula, and the islands of Indonesia."...

Exerting a more narrow influence upon McKinley's Philippine policy was a third group, the military. In general the President's military advisers shared the widespread concern over the strategic relationship of the archipelago to the Asian mainland. Yet, attracted by the siren's call of *imperium* (in which they would play a prominent role), many military spokesmen also promoted retention of the Philippines as the first step toward an expansive territorial imperialism. These hopes were dashed as McKinley refused to heed their advice for a general American advance into Micronesia and the islands of the South China Sea. But military advice could claim one significant result: it resolved the President's ambivalence (shared by the business and government elite) between taking Luzon or the entire group by convincing him that the islands were an indivisible entity; that strategically and economically they were interdependent and inseparable. Especially persuasive were the lengthy and articulate reports of Commander R. B. Bradford and General Francis V. Greene. Coming in late September and early October, they were a decisive factor in broadening McKinley's instructions.

AMERICAN BUSINESS INTERESTS AND
THE OPEN DOOR IN CHINA[1]   *Charles S. Campbell, Jr.*

... The war with Spain, which began in April, 1898, brought with it a rising tide of imperialistic sentiment in the United States. Caught up in this tide and modified by it was the American attitude toward the complex situation in China. To be sure, there was no widespread thought of China as a possible colony, or even of a sphere-of-influence there, but, as Professor Pratt has shown, the foothold which the triumph at Manila Bay gave us in the Philippines was considered by many to be important chiefly because it might help us to hold open the door in the Far East. Then too the fact that America seemed to be suddenly growing up into a great power probably had the effect of making Americans more insistent that treaty rights, including those in China, be upheld.

During the war one of the most important developments in the history of the origins of the Open Door policy took place. The Committee on American Interests had come to the decision that a more permanent form of organization was needed, and to meet that need the committee was transformed in June, 1898, into the American Asiatic Association. The association had the same general aim as its predecessor. As stated in its constitution, this was "to secure the advantage of sustained watchfulness and readiness for action ... in respect of ... Asiatic trade, as well as in matters of legislation, or treaties affecting the same." All the members of the original committee became members of the Asiatic Association, and four of them became leading officials. Everett Frazer was the president; S. D. Brewster, the vice-president; John Foord, the secretary; and Clarence Cary, a member of the executive committee.

Both [Cary and Foord] were intimately associated with the campaign to influence the policy of the government. Consider the strategic position of each: Cary, counsel for the American-China Development Company and member of the executive committee of the American Asiatic Association; Foord, secretary of the Asiatic Association, editor of its magazine, *Asia*, and contributing editor of the *Journal of commerce*. Although these men

[1] *The Far Eastern Quarterly*, I, No. 1 (November, 1941), 43–58. Reprinted with permission.

were influential only in indirect ways, it is entirely possible that they had as much to do with the sending of the September notes as had such well-known figures as W. W. Rockhill and Alfred Hippisley.

Four days after its founding the Association had just under fifty members. Among them were the General Electric Company; the Guaranty Trust Company; the New York Central and Hudson River Railroad Company; Charles Denby; W. W. Rockhill; Calvin Brice and W. D. Washburn, both officials of the American-China Development Company; and a large number of men in the cotton business.

In order to reach as wide an audience as possible, the association undertook the publication of a periodical entitled *Asia: journal of the American Asiatic association*, the editor of which, as has been said, was John Foord. But propaganda by the association did not become particularly widespread at this time; for, like its predecessor, the association devoted its attention chiefly to the State Department.

The American Asiatic Association was the principal channel through which the special interests made their influence felt in Washington and in the country at large. It was strongly supported by the *Journal of commerce and commercial bulletin*, which devoted an extraordinary amount of editorial and news space to questions of the Chinese market and consistently advocated energetic action by the government to safeguard that market. Cooperation between the association and the journal was doubtless facilitated by the fact that John Foord occupied an important position in each of these guardians of American interests in the Far East.

The founding of the Asiatic Association was the chief event concerned with the origins of the Open Door policy which took place during the war with Spain. However, a few other developments of the same time, though of comparatively minor importance, may also be mentioned.

Perhaps the outstanding of these was a recommendation to Congress by Sherman's successor in the State Department, William R. Day, that a trade commission be sent to China to investigate possibilities for greater exports to that part of the world. Although Congress took no action at the time, the incident has some significance as marking a further step in the evolution of the government toward the point of view of the special interests.

Also of significance was the appointment of John Hay to the position of Secretary of State. In view of the memorials of the early part of the year and such a further indication of the opinion of influential businessmen as the establishment of the Asiatic Association, it is quite possible that Hay's well-known propensity for the Open Door in China was one of the reasons for his appointment. Hardly had he assumed office when the new Secretary showed that his Far Eastern policy was going to be stronger than that of his two predecessors. Perhaps as a result of a memorial from one of the American establishments in China, stating that there was a "probability of serious interference [by Russia] with America's important trade in cotton . . . unless immediate steps are taken in Pekin to insist that our treaty rights with China be maintained," Hay ordered two gunboats to proceed to North China. The New York Chamber of Commerce, incidentally, expressed its "high appreciation" of the act. For the time being, however, nothing further came of the Russian threat.

The last event we need mention which occurred during the war was the annual message to Congress of President McKinley. Repeating Day's recommendation of a trade commission, the President stated that the United States was not an "indifferent spectator" of what was going on in China but that it would preserve its "large interests in that quarter by all means appropriate to the constant policy of our Government." This strong declaration was naturally hailed with delight by those with business interests in China.

When the war with Spain formally came to an end early in 1899 with the ratification of the peace treaty by the Senate, the government was able to turn its attention from military matters to such peacetime considerations as trade with China. In January it received an important memorial. Coming from a large number of cotton manufacturers, the memorial stated that the Chinese market would be lost to American cotton exporters "unless a vigorous policy is pursued on the part of the ... Government"; it requested that the American diplomatic representatives at Peking and St. Petersburg "be instructed to give special attention to the subject." This memorial seems to have impressed Secretary Hay even more than the memorial of the preceding January had impressed Sherman. Referring to the "high character and standing of the signers," he ordered the envoys to give the "special attention" requested of them; and about a month later, apparently afraid he had not been sufficiently emphatic, he wrote a second time to the ambassador to Russia, asking him to continue "to act energetically in the sense desired by the numerous and influential signers of the petition."

Another episode of early 1899 worth mentioning was the Asiatic Association's strong support of a protest by the United States against an attempt by France to extend her concession in Shanghai. The association wrote to McKinley and Hay, urging that "all available means" be used "towards preserving for the world's commerce an 'open door' in the Far East." In sharp contrast with this was the association's viewpoint regarding an attempt to obtain an extension of the combined British and American concession. Negotiations with China has been going on for some time but without success. Angered and alarmed, the association informed Secretary Hay of "the necessity of ... vigorous action ... in order to obtain a definite solution." Sending a copy of this letter to the minister to China, Hay instructed him to devote his efforts to obtaining the extension. Two months later China gave way.

In March the campaign for the Open Door took a more decisive turn. It became known at that time that Italy was endeavoring to secure from the Chinese government a lease of Sanmen Bay, a bay located not far from Shanghai, the center of foreign business in China. Fears of partition once again rose quickly to the surface. There was widespread suspicion that Italy had the backing of Great Britain; if true, it would mean that the only remaining great power opposed to the partition of China was the United States.

The situation disturbed the American Asiatic Association to an extent which might seem surprising today. Today we know that the Sanmen Bay affair turned out to be a comparatively insignificant incident. But to those who lived at the time of the crisis itself this knowledge was lacking, and to them, fearful as they were that it would take very little indeed to start off the process of dismembering China, the spring of 1899 was a time of grave anxiety. So disturbing was the situation to the officials of the Asiatic Association that they held a series of meetings in order to discuss the possibility of a fundamental modification of the policy they had been pursuing.

As has been shown, this policy was to concentrate on the Department of State. True, there had been a certain amount of propaganda directed at the public in general through the periodical, *Asia: journal of the American Asiatic association*, and true it is also that this propaganda had been meeting with some success. As early as January the *Journal of commerce*, that close observer of anything pertaining to the Open Door, had pointed to the "new attitude of this country towards its commercial interests in China" and had stated that it was "partly the result of the American Asiatic Association." Nevertheless, greater success had been gained with the State Department. Secretary Sherman and Secretary Day had moved closer to the viewpoint of businessmen who were eager to see the Chinese market safeguarded. John Hay had not once failed to carry out any formal request regarding Far Eastern policy, and, indeed, the department under Hay had shown itself so willing to co-operate that there could be no doubt about its desire to maintain the Open Door in China.

Because of these facts the *Journal of commerce* and the Asiatic Association appear to have realized that pressure upon the State Department had become much less necessary than before. But this did not suggest to them that their usefulness was at an end. For although it was clear that many of the high officials in Washington were convinced that the Chinese market was of considerable value to the United States, it was equally clear that the general public was not convinced. Consequently, what had become desirable in place of so much attention to the State Department was, as the journal said, "education of the people, the press, and the politicians by those who see the vital necessity of the Chinese market"—in short, "active propaganda in the country at large." The Asiatic Association, as a faithful ally of the journal, came to the same conclusion. At the series of meetings which its officials were holding it was decided to embark upon "a campaign of public education in regard to the magnitude of the commercial interests of the United States in China." A committee to take charge of the campaign was appointed.

The writer has not been able to discover many details about the ensuing campaign. It is known that it was carried on in the press—the *Journal of commerce* presumably being the chief organ—and in publications of the association itself. It is also known that by the end of 1899 the association had at its disposal a fund for propaganda purposes amounting to several thousand dollars and that among the contributors to this fund were many of the exporters of cotton goods. Not much additional material, however, is available.

Did the campaign have any success in persuading the public of the importance of the market in China? No conclusive answer can be given to this question; for not only is it foolish to make too definite claims about the effects of any bit of propaganda, no matter how much one may know of its nature, but also we have here a propaganda campaign concerning which relatively little is known.

It is worth while, however, to point out that both the American Asiatic Association and the *Journal of commerce* were convinced that their propaganda did have very considerable success. The statement of the journal in January, 1899, regarding the influence of the Asiatic Association in moulding public opinion has been mentioned above. Ten months later, in November, the propaganda of the Association had had more time to make itself felt. At that time the *Journal of commerce* reported that "there has never been a more remarkable advance of public sentiment in this country than that which has taken place ... in regard to the responsibilities to be faced by our Government in the Far East." The journal boasted that "to the stage of public education which has been reached on this subject [the necessity of the Open Door to the United States] this journal may fairly claim to have largely contributed." The vice-president of the Asiatic Association said that the work of his organization would "take its place in history as part of one of the most memorable chapters in the annals of the American people. ... You have only to compare," he said, "the state of public sentiment which we found existing in regard to the responsibilities of our country in Eastern Asia with the feeling which exists on that subject to-day to appreciate what the influence of the Association has been."

Moreover, at least one contemporary observer supported their claims. James S. Fearon, one of the leading exporters of cotton to China and for years chairman of the Shanghai Municipal Council—presumably a man whose opinions regarding American relations with China are worthy of respect—stated that much of the credit for the changed attitude of the American people toward the Chinese market was due to the American Asiatic Association and to the *Journal of commerce*.

The propaganda campaign was the outstanding feature of the months just before the sending of the Open Door notes, but this period was also marked by further pressure brought to bear on the State Department by the special interests. Although they initiated no more memorials at this time, the officials of the Asiatic Association are known to have corresponded with Secretary Hay and to have called upon him frequently regarding the country's Far Eastern policy.

The activity of the special interests during these months of 1899 was of such a nature as to make it extremely difficult to evaluate its significance. It is, of course, quite understandable that no records exist stating explicitly whether or not the administration was influenced by the propaganda campaign, and it is equally understandable that Secretary Hay never wrote down anything which would enable us to judge whether or not his thinking was affected by the letters from the officials of the Asiatic Association and by the visits these men paid him. It is far easier to trace the effects of the memorials of 1898 than of the propaganda and informal contacts of 1899.

But it would be a great mistake to overlook the possibility that these later activities too were of considerable importance. It may well have been that the *Journal of commerce* and the Asiatic Association were quite correct in their belief that the propaganda campaign was successful. If it was successful, if it did in fact make the public more conscious of America's stake in the Far East, it doubtless made it easier for the administration to take action designed to preserve the Chinese market. As for the letters and visits from

the Asiatic Association to Hay, it is highly probable that such frequent re-
minders of the desires of certain businessmen had at least the effect of bolster-
ing up the Secretary's own inclinations with respect to China. At any rate,
it is clear that these activities of the special interests during the spring and
summer of 1899 must have, along with the memorials of 1898, a place in
any complete history of the origins of the Open Door policy.

On September 6, 1899, the first group of Open Door notes was dispatched. This was just the kind of step for which the special interests had
been hoping and for which they had been working. To the cotton exporters
the notes meant that their market appeared to be far more secure; and to the
American-China Development Company they meant that there was much to
be hoped for from a grateful China—and, indeed, a few months later the
company at last secured the contract which it had so long been seeking.

The sending of these notes resulted from a great many factors, one of
which was the organized attempt of certain business interests, particularly
the men connected with the American China Development Company and the
cotton exporters, to persuade the government to take just such a step. It has
been shown how these interests, fearful lest the turn of events in China
should result in financial loss to themselves, took measures designed to persuade the government to safeguard the Chinese market. First of all, they
established the Committee on American Interests in China; later on, when
this proved to be too weak an organization, they transformed it into the
American Asiatic Association. This association, consistently supported by
the *Journal of commerce and commercial bulletin*, was influential in persuading the administration (and very possibly the general public as well) that a
particular line of policy would be of benefit to the nation as a whole. In
these facts lies part of the explanation for the formulation of America's
Open Door policy.

PRESIDENT MCKINLEY NOTIFIES SPAIN
TO TERMINATE THE CUBAN CRISIS,
JULY 1897   *Document 1*

Instructions for the new U.S. Ambassador to Spain
  No. 4

Department of State
Washington, July 16, 1897

Sir: Before you go to your post it is proper to state to you the President's
views on the relation of your Government to the contest now being waged
in Cuba. . . .

It should by no means be forgotten that besides and beyond the question
of recognition of belligerency, with its usual proclamation of neutrality
and its concession of equal rights and impartial imposition of identical

disabilities in respect to the contending parties within our municipal juris-diction, there lies the larger ulterior problem of intervention, which the President does not now discuss. It is with no unfriendly intent that this subject has been mentioned, but simply to show that this Government does not and can not ignore the possibilities of duty hidden in the future, nor be unprepared to face an emergency which may at any time be born of the unhappy contest in Cuba. The extraordinary, because direct and not merely theoretical or sentimental, interest of the United States in the Cuban situation can not be ignored, and if forced the issue must be met honestly and fearlessly, in conformity with our national life and character. Not only are our citizens largely concerned in the ownership of property and in the industrial and commercial ventures which have been set on foot in Cuba through our enterprising initiative and sustained by their capital, but the chronic condition of trouble and violent derangement in that island constantly causes disturbance in the social and political condition of our own people. It keeps up a continuous irritation within our own borders, injuriously affects the normal functions of business, and tends to delay the condition of prosperity to which this country is entitled.

No exception can be taken to the general proposition that a neighboring nation, however deeply disturbed and injured by the existence of a dev-astating internal conflict at its doors, may be constrained, on grounds of international comity, to disregard its endangered interests and remain a passive spectator of the contest for a reasonable time while the titular authority is repressing the disorder. The essence of this moral obligation lies in the reasonableness of the delay invited by circumstances and by the effort of the territorial authority to assert its claimed rights. The onlooking nation need only wait "a reasonable time" before alleging and acting upon the rights which it, too, possesses. This proposition is not a legal subtlety, but a broad principle of international comity and law.

The question arises, then, whether Spain has not already had a reasonable time to restore peace and been unable to do so, even by a concentration of her resources and measures of unparalleled severity which have re-ceived very general condemnation. The methods which Spain has adopted to wage the fight give no prospect of immediate peace or of a stable return to the conditions of prosperity which are essential to Cuba in its intercourse with its neighbors. Spain's inability entails upon the United States a degree of injury and suffering which can not longer be ignored. Assuredly Spain can not expect the Government to sit idle, letting vast interests suffer, our political elements disturbed, and the country perpetually embroiled, while no progress is being made in the settlement of the Cuban problem. Such a policy of inaction would in reality prove of no benefit to Spain, while certain to do the United States incalculable harm. This Government, strong in its sense of right and duty, yet keenly sympathetic with the aspirations of any neighboring community in close touch with our own civilization, is naturally desirous to avoid, in all rational ways, the precipitation of a result which would be painfully abhorrent to the American people.

For all of the reasons before stated the President feels it his duty to make the strongest possible effort to help bring about a result which shall be in conformity alike with the feelings of our people, the inherent rights of civilized man, and be of advantage both to Cuba and to Spain. Difficult as the task may seem now, it is believed that frankness, earnestness, perseverance, and a fair regard for the rights of others will eventually solve the problem.

It should be borne in mind from the start that it is far removed from the feelings of the American people and the mind of the President to propose any solution to which the slightest idea of humiliation to Spain could in any way be attached. But no possible intention or occasion to wound the just susceptibilities of the Castilian nation can be discerned in the altogether friendly suggestion that the good offices of the United States may now be lent to the advantage of Spain.

You are hereby instructed to bring these considerations as promptly as possible, but with due allowance for favorable conditions, to the attention of the Government of Her Majesty the Queen Regent, with all the impressiveness which their importance demands, and with all the earnestness which the constantly imperiled national interests of the United States justifies. You will emphasize the self-restraint which this Government has hitherto observed until endurance has ceased to be tolerable or even possible for any longer indefinite term. You will lay especial stress on the unselfish friendliness of our desires, and upon the high purpose and sincere wish of the United States to give its aid only in order that a peaceful and enduring result may be reached, just and honorable alike to Spain and to the Cuban people, and only so far as such aid may accomplish the wished for ends. In so doing, you will not disguise the gravity of the situation, nor conceal the President's conviction that, should his present effort be fruitless, his duty to his countrymen will necessitate an early decision as to the course of action which the time and the transcendent emergency may demand.

THEODORE ROOSEVELT WRITES
OF HIS EFFORTS FOR WAR   *Document 2*

Assistant Secretary of the Navy Roosevelt to William Tudor, April 5, 1898.

Not only do I want to thank you for your letter to me, but especially for your letter to Lodge. For a week past he has been receiving twenty or thirty letters and telegrams a day from men who consider themselves to be the best and most representative citizens of Boston—its leading bankers, merchants and lawyers; and these letters and telegrams, almost without exception, are couched in terms of abject fear, and the abject anger that comes from that fear. Lodge stands firm, but his colleague has been turned over by these letters, and Lodge realizes that if the President and Hoar stand one way and he another, his own republican party will throw him out of the Senate next year. Nevertheless, as I say, he is playing, and will play, the part of a patriot; but I do think that all the men who feel as you and I do in

Boston should begin to send in telegrams entreating him to put the honor of the nation above the desire for that sordid peace which is begotten of fear and greed. During the last few days, however, I am happy to say that the pressure from the honest men of the country who are not careless of the nation's honor has been such that I believe the President will be forced to intervene. I have preached the doctrine to him in such plain language that he will no longer see me! If we will not fight for the blowing up of the *Maine* (and personally I believe we should have fought long ago because of the atrocities in Cuba) we are no longer fit to hold up our heads among the nations of the earth. It is one of the greatest crises in our history, and the men of means and the men of education in the northeast have behaved with lamentable lack of patriotism throughout it.

ALFRED T. MAHAN'S OUTLOOK

ON THE TWENTIETH CENTURY, 1895   *Document 3*

... The conditions which now constitute the political situation of the United States, relatively to the world at large, are fundamentally different from those that obtained at the beginning of the century. It is not a mere question of greater growth, of bigger size. It is not only that we are larger, stronger, have, as it were, reached our majority, and are able to go out into the world. That alone would be a difference of degree, not of kind. The great difference between the past and the present is that we then, as regards close contact with the power of the chief nations of the world, were really in a state of political isolation which no longer exists. ...

It is important to recognize this, for it will help clear away the error from a somewhat misleading statement frequently made,—that the United States needs a navy for defence only, adding often, explanatorily, for the defence of our own coasts. Now in a certain sense we all want a navy for defence only. It is to be hoped that the United States will never seek war except for the defence of her rights, her obligations, or her necessary interests. In that sense our policy may always be defensive only, although it may compel us at times to steps justified rather by expediency—the choice of the lesser evil—than by incontrovertible right. But if we have interests beyond sea which a navy may have to protect, it plainly follows that the navy has more to do, even in war, than to defend the coast; and it must be added as a received military axiom that war, however defensive in moral character, must be waged aggressively if it is to hope for success. ...

Like each man and woman, no state lives to itself alone, in a political seclusion resembling the physical isolation which so long was the ideal of China and Japan. All, whether they will or no, are members of a community, larger or smaller; and more and more those of the European family to which we racially belong are touching each other throughout the world, with consequent friction of varying degree. That the greater rapidity of communication afforded by steam has wrought, in the influence of sea power over the face of the globe, an extension that is multiplying the points of contact and emphasizing the importance of navies, is a fact, the intelligent appreciation of which is daily more and more manifest in the periodical literature of Europe, and is further shown by the growing stress laid upon that arm of military strength by foreign governments; while the mutual preparation of the armies on the European continent, and the fairly settled territorial conditions, make each state yearly more wary of initiating a contest, and thus entail a political quiescence there, except in the internal affairs of each country. The field of external action for the great European states is now the world, and it is hardly doubtful that their struggles, unaccompanied as yet by actual clash of arms, are even under that condition drawing nearer to ourselves. Coincidently with our own extension to the Pacific Ocean, which for so long had a good international claim to its name, that sea has become more and more the scene of political development, of commercial activities and rivalries, in which all the great powers, ourselves included, have a share. Through these causes Central and Caribbean America, now intrinsically unimportant, are brought in turn into great prominence, as constituting the gateway between the Atlantic and Pacific when the Isthmian canal shall have been made, and as guarding the approaches to it. The appearance of Japan as a strong ambitious state, resting on solid political and military foundations, but which scarcely has reached yet a condition of equilibrium in international standing, has fairly startled the world; and it is a striking illustration of the somewhat sudden nearness and unforeseen relations into which modern states are brought, that the Hawaiian Islands, so interesting from the international point of view to the countries of European civilization, are occupied largely by Japanese and Chinese.

In all these questions we have a stake, reluctantly it may be, but necessarily, for our evident interests are involved, in some instances directly, in others by very probable implication. Under existing conditions, the opinion that we can keep clear indefinitely of embarrassing problems is hardly tenable; while war between two foreign states, which in the uncertainties of the international situation throughout the world may break out at any time, will increase greatly the occasions of possible collision with the belligerent countries, and the consequent perplexities of our statesmen seeking to avoid entanglement and to maintain neutrality. . . .

It is because so much of the world still remains in the possession of the savage, or of states whose imperfect development, political or economical, does not enable them to realize for the general use nearly the result of which the territory is capable, while at the same time the redundant energies of civilized states, both government and peoples, are finding lack of openings and scantiness of livelihood at home, that there now obtains a condition of aggressive restlessness with which all have to reckon.

That the United States does not now share this tendency is entirely evident. Neither her government nor her people are affected by it to any great extent. But the force of circumstances has imposed upon her the necessity, recognized with practical unanimity by her people, of insuring to the weaker states of America, although of racial and political antecedents different from her own, freedom to develop politically along their own lines and according to their own capacities, without interference in that respect from governments foreign to these continents. The duty is self-assumed; and resting, as it does, not upon political philanthropy, but simply upon our own proximate interests as affected by such foreign interference, has towards others rather the nature of a right than a duty. But, from either point of view, the facility with which the claim has been allowed heretofore by the great powers has been due partly to the lack of pressing importance in the questions that have arisen, and partly to the great latent strength of our nation. ... But while our claim thus far has received a tacit acquiescence, it remains to be seen whether it will continue to command the same if the states whose political freedom of action we assert make no more decided advance towards political stability than several of them have done yet, and if our own organized naval force remains as slender, comparatively, as it once was, and even yet is. It is probably safe to say that an undertaking like that of Great Britain in Egypt, if attempted in this hemisphere by a non-American state, would not be tolerated by us if able to prevent it; but it is conceivable that the moral force of our contention might be weakened, in the view of an opponent, by attendant circumstances, in which case our physical power to support it should be open to no doubt.

That we shall seek to secure the peaceable solution of each difficulty as it arises is attested by our whole history, and by the disposition of our people; but to do so whatever the steps taken in any particular case, will bring us into new political relations and may entail serious disputes with other states. ... A navy, therefore, whose primary sphere of action is war, is, in the last analysis and from the least misleading point of view, a political factor of the utmost importance in international affairs, one more often deterrent than irritant. It is in that light, according to the conditions of the age and of the nation, that it asks and deserves the appreciation of the state, and that it should be developed in proportion to the reasonable possibilities of the political future.

PETITION FROM NEW YORK BUSINESSMEN
TO PRESIDENT MCKINLEY ASKING EFFECTIVE
ACTION TO RESTORE PEACE IN CUBA,
JANUARY 1898   *Document 4*

The undersigned, citizens of the United States, many of whom joined in sending to your Hon. Secretary of State in the month of May last,[1] a memorial reciting the great and increasing loss of trade and pecuniary damages to which they as Importers, Exporters, Bankers, Manufacturers, Steamship and Vessel Owners and Agents in the trade with Cuba, were subjected, by the long continuance of a ruinous armed conflict in that Island; feel impelled to lay before you the following additional facts:

---

[1] As indicated here, this is the second petition by the group.

The destructive war in Cuba has continued for three entire years, with an actual average loss of import and export trade between Cuba and this Country of $100,000,000. per year or a total loss of $300,000,000. import and export trade since the beginning of the war. To this may fairly be added heavy sums irretrievably lost by the destruction of American properties, or properties supported by American capital in the Island itself, such as sugar factories, railways, tobacco plantations, mines and other industrial enterprises; the loss of the United States in trade and capital by reason of this war being probably far greater and more serious than that of all the other parties concerned, not excepting Spain herself.

The steps thus far taken, in the hope of ameliorating existing unfortunate conditions, have not sufficed to save for the planters and factories the sugar crop of 1897–98, which with the exception of a small part, appears virtually lost like its two predecessors.

Only about 15% of the sugar factories of the Island were operated last year, and the same proportion are endeavoring to run their machinery this season, under circumstances constantly threatening their destruction.

Inasmuch as 80% of our entire trade with Cuba depends upon the sugar crop of the Island, it is readily seen that our commerce with the Island cannot be restored at present, nor until actual peace is established.

If peace be not established before May or June of this year, then it is certain that the 1898–99 sugar crop, and all the business depending upon it, will be lost, since the plantations, factories, railways and business houses in the different sugar districts of the Island, will require all the rainy season of summer and fall to prepare for next winter's crop, by repairing damaged fields, machinery, lines of railways, &c.

The close geographical juxtaposition of the Island to our own country, and the natural course of trade, have brought it about that in time of peace Cuba finds in this country a ready market for 90% of her exports, whilst the enterprise and manufacturing skill of our own people have found a profitable field in the ownership or management of Cuban sugar factories, railways and other enterprises.

Respectfully submitting these facts, we bespeak for them your most earnest consideration, and trust you may deem the magnitude of American interests jeopardized, besides the tremendous losses already inflicted upon American Commerce and industries in Cuba by this fierce and devastating conflict, of such importance as to warrant prompt and efficient measures by our Government, with the sole object of restoring peace.

Trusting firmly in your watchful care over the interests of all American citizens, your subscribers unite in praying for your aid and for this Government's aid, in bringing about actual peace, and with it restoring to us a most valuable commercial field.

THE EDITOR OF *THE PRAIRIE FARMER*
DISCUSSES AGRICULTURAL INTEREST
IN CUBA, APRIL 2, 1898   *Document 5*

Notwithstanding all that has been said and written about Cuba during the last two years, it is doubtful if a majority of people understand in what the real importance of the island to the United States consists. This, stripped of all questions of sentimentalism, is its trade, with its possible usefulness to us in case of a foreign war. And this trade, it should be said in passing, is of especial importance to the farmers of this country. With normal conditions prevailing, Cuba has been a large consumer of our agricultural products, and should be a much larger consumer of them than heretofore, with the establishment of peace and good government. This will be the more evident when it is remembered that Cuba is within a hundred miles of the Florida coast and is easily accessible for the transportation of the many products with which we can supply her 1,800,000 inhabitants, while the mode of transportation is the cheapest of any, namely, water. Flour can be shipped to Cuba from the mills at Minneapolis by the Mississippi river and the Gulf of Mexico, and she is readily accessible from all our Atlantic and gulf ports. In 1893 and 1894 Cuba was a considerable purchaser of American corn, flour, hams, bacon, lard, cars (sic), carriages, steam engines, agricultural implements, builders' hardware, miscellaneous machinery and manufactures of wood. In the fiscal year 1893 her purchases of flour were $2,821,557; hams, $761,082; and lard, $4,023,917, her purchases of these three products of the farm aggregating $7,606,556. Our aggregate exports to Cuba in 1893 were $24,157,698 and in 1894 $20,125,321. While the most of these exports, as the figures indicate, were of goods other than agricultural, in an indirect way even these were of benefit to agriculture, since their production and transportation employed many laborers, skilled and unskilled, a part of whose earnings were necessarily spent in purchases of the products of the farm. On account of the combined influence of the cessation of reciprocity arrangements and the breaking out of the insurrection in the island, our exports to Cuba have fallen off in a marked degree, so that in 1895 they were but $12,533,260, and in 1896 but $7,530,880. . . . This incomplete recital serves to show the promising nature of close commercial relations with Cuba, almost within sight of our shores. It is a market provided by nature for disposing of a part of our surplus agricultural products in exchange for her commodities, some of which we do not produce at all, and others only in inconsiderable quantities. The trade would be in almost every respect mutual, the products of one country conflicting but slightly with those of the other, and so far as the United States are concerned the larger market thus made for our products would amply compensate us for any small competition that might result. . . . The present obstacles to a large and profitable trade with Cuba, lie in the disordered state of the island and the heavy duties laid by the Spanish government on imports. If this government could see its way clear to bring peace to the island, it would doubtless be of lasting benefit to both countries, especially if it should succeed in gaining reforms for the Cubans which would relieve them of the onerous exactions of the Spanish government and secure some modification of the tariff imposed on our agricultural products. With peace restored to Cuba, commercial arrangements might be entered into by which our agricultural products should be allowed to enter the island free, or at a low rate of duty, in return for allowing some of her principal products to enter our ports on like terms. In view of the vast underdeveloped wealth of Cuba, some such arrangement could not but be of enduring benefit to the two countries. With the restoration of peace and the establishment of a stable government, capital and labor may reasonably be expected to enter Cuba to develop her resources, with the result of creating large and permanent demand for our agricultural and other products.

A REFORMER CONFRONTS THE ISSUE

OF WAR TO EXTEND FREEDOM   *Document 6*

Henry Demarest Lloyd to John C. Pirie, December 30, 1895.
    ... One who is dwelling upon visions of the Co-operative Commonwealth, and who wishes to proclaim the brotherhood of man as the supreme law of social life cannot but feel shocked and grieved when he finds that public duty as he conceives it compels him to contemplate the possibility of war. But precisely such has been the experience in the past of every party that advocated peace and brotherhood. The French Revolution, our War of Independence (with which possibly you do not, as an Englishman, sympathise), and the late Civil War were all directly brought about by the advocacy of the principles of the brotherhood of man. If war comes between the United States and Great Britain on this Venezuelan business, I must look upon it as an incident in the same sequence of events. The Great Britain of Lord Salisbury, of India, of Africa, of Ireland, of the House of Lords, and the English landed system, encroaching upon a neighbouring republic, refusing arbitration, represents to me, in this day, the same forces as those which in the past have stood against liberty and progress. The determination of the American people to use their power to protect the other republics on this continent seems to me the most respectable manifestation of public opinion this generation has seen. I see no difference in principle between this action, and that by which the American Colonies bound themselves together in 1774 by Committees of Correspondence to advise and help each other.
    I would extend the Monroe Doctrine to the defence of every Republic as far as Andorra and San Marino, and to the assistance of every people seeking to establish the republic. If anything could save America from her apparently impending Midas-like doom it would be such a mission. But it is too much to hope for.

THE DANGER TO AMERICAN

MARKETS IN CHINA   *Document 7*

Warning by American Minister to China Charles Denby, January 31, 1898.
... In the midst of these events it may not be improper to consider our own position regarding China. I am very thoroughly aware that since Washington's Farewell Address was uttered we have been, what may be called, innately conservative on the question of interfering in the affairs of foreign powers. He would be a bold man who in the United States would advocate political entanglement in the affairs of Europe, Asia, or Africa. That our abnegation tends to weaken our influence and to make us a quantité négligeable is undoubtedly true, but it has its compensations in the enforcement of the Monroe Doctrine.

Still, while preserving all the sanctity of the "Farewell Address," it is worth enquiring whether there is not some middle ground on which we may stand with advantage. We have fifteen hundred missionaries here. Should China be partitioned among the European powers it is quite certain that the work of these missionaries would be impeded. From any country under Russian control they would be excluded. In any country under French control they would be impeded and embarrassed. These missionaries are entitled to our protection just the same as mercantile people are.

Partition would tend to destroy our markets. The Pacific Ocean is destined to bear on its bosom a larger commerce than the Atlantic. As the countries in the Far East and Australia develop their resources the commerce of the United States with them will assume proportions greater in their directness and scope, than our commerce with Europe.

In these countries we are destined to find our best customers for manufactured, as well as natural, and agricultural products.

Here are diverse and varied sources of interest in the Far East which directly touch us.

Having such interests in China, it is our duty to remain mute should her autonomy be attacked? Is it exactly right to announce, as was lately done in Reuter's telegrams, that we take no interest in territorial questions? We have a certain moral interest in the affairs of the world, and, in my opinion, that influence should be exacted in all cases in which our interests demand its exercise. We should urge on China the reform of all evils in her government which touch American interests, and the adoption of vigorous measures in the line of material progress. This policy will to her be the surest pathway to independence and prosperity. I have persistently urged this policy. We should not hesitate, also, I think, to announce our disapproval of acts of brazen wrong, and spoliation, perpetrated by other nations towards China—should any such occur....

THE STATE DEPARTMENT DISCUSSES
THE IMPORTANCE OF AMERICAN EXPORTS,
APRIL 25, 1898   *Document 8*

... The United States is no longer the "granary of the world" merely. ... Its sales abroad of manufactured goods have continued to extend with a facility and promptitude of results which have excited the serious concern of countries that, for generations, had not only controlled their home markets, but had practically monopolized certain lines of trade in other lands. When we consider that this result has been reached with comparative ease, in spite of added impediments to United States exports in the form of discriminations of various kinds, and notwithstanding the fact that organized effort to reach foreign markets for our manufactures is as yet in its infancy, the ability of the United States to compete successfully with the most advanced industrial nations in any part of the world, as well as with those nations in their home markets, can no longer be seriously questioned. ...

The secret of the steady advance of United States goods in popular appreciation wherever they are introduced is to be found in their superior excellence at little, if any, difference of cost to the consumer. ... The American exporter is thus enabled to meet his foreign rival on more nearly equal terms, or even to undersell him. ...

It is frequently asserted of particular industries in the United States that the output of factories working at full capacity is much greater than the domestic market can possibly consume, and it seems to be conceded that every year we shall be confronted with an increasing surplus of manufactured goods for sale in foreign markets if American operatives and artisans are to be kept employed the year round. The enlargement of foreign consumption of the products of our mills and workshops has, therefore, become a serious problem of statesmanship as well as of commerce, and this fact is evidenced in the steps being taken to negotiate reciprocal agreements with various nations, as well as in the important efforts being made by such organized trade bodies as the chambers of commerce of great export centers, the National Association of Manufacturers ... the Philadelphia Commercial Museum, the export associations of New York, and other like organizations, to open new channels of trade as well as to improve the old ones. ... In all such enterprises, the zealous cooperation of the diplomatic representatives and consular officers of the United States is freely given, and substantial improvement, under special instructions from the Department of State, it is believed, has been effected in the character as well as in the volume of information which is constantly being obtained from these sources for the benefit of American industries and trade.

In view of what may be termed an American invasion of the markets of the world, the attitude of the leading commercial nations toward each other and the relation which their industrial activities and trade interests bear to the United States become matters of practical concern. The more important incidents of the past year in foreign diplomacy have, therefore, a significance for us which might not have attached to them in the absence of concerted efforts to extend the sale of our goods. It may be said that the chief business of European diplomacy at the present day is to secure new "spheres of influence" and wider opportunities for trade, as well as suitable territory for occupation by the overflow of population from the more densely inhabited countries. The world has watched the progress of the diplomatic drama in China with an interest which has been heightened by the knowledge that the practical outcome might be either the opening of new channels of trade to the commerce of the globe, or the appropriation of them by particular nations for their own special benefit. China has, for some years, been one of the most promising fields for American enterprise, industry, and capital, and the entrance of that vast empire upon the path of western development under conditions which would secure equality of opportunity to the United States, would doubtless result in immense gains to our manufacturers in the demand, sure to follow, for lines of supplies and goods of various descriptions that we are preeminently fitted to provide.

The solution of the problem of the future commercial conditions of the Chinese Empire has, therefore, an immediate and most important relation to the expansion of our export trade, especially that of the Pacific slope. The partition of Africa among the European powers offers considerations of an economic character of almost equal magnitude, while the plans of the more active commercial nations, for increasing their respective shares of the trade of the Latin-American markets, affect us even more seriously in the development of our commercial intercourse with the southern half of the Western Hemisphere. The "international isolation" of the United States, so far as industry and commerce are concerned, has, in fact, been made a thing of the past by the logic of the change in our economic requirements, and we can no longer afford to disregard international rivalries, now that we ourselves have become a competitor in the world-wide struggle for trade. . . .

IDEOLOGICAL ARGUMENTS FOR EXPANSION   *Document 9*

Editor Theodore Marburg argues the right of higher civilization, May 1898.
The past few months have witnessed a conflict of emotions in the breast of the people. A traditional policy and a wholesome horror of war have been drawing them in one direction, whilst indignation at inhuman acts impelled them in another. Those who felt the justice of America's position and at the same time valued the President's noble attempt to enforce that position without resort to war, realized that to give utterance to their thoughts could only serve to encourage the war spirit and further hamper the President. Now that war has begun, it is important to examine carefully the principles involved. . . .

If the unhappy island can realize in no other way the very reasonable wish for enlightened and humane government in this advanced age, is not our course proper? The world knows very well that it was not the desire to add Cuba to our territory which led to war, but if the Cuban question can be solved in no other way than by action which will ultimately bring the island to us, we should not hesitate to assume the full responsibility of such action. It is best to face such an issue squarely and frankly. If we are right, it matters not whether certain Powers approve of our course or not; the situation at home is too delicate for them to do more than enter a diplomatic protest. . . .

Another important consideration is that of the higher civilization supplanting the lower.

When the white man came to America there were about 500,000 Indians in what now constitutes the United States. To-day there still remain 225,000. We have then brushed aside 275,000 Indians, and in place of them have this population of 70,000,000 of what we regard as the highest type of modern man. The fact that the Indian, who was tolerably prolific, did not number more than 500,000 after all the centuries he must have lived here, indicates a formidable struggle against nature, a struggle against cold, famine, disease and loss of life through internecine war; in other words, a great sum of human misery which we have been quite justified in brushing aside and supplanting with the peace and comparative contentment and high pursuits which prevail over the continent.

The question presented by Cuba differs only in degree. The Spaniard and his American descendant are very much the same people they were several centuries ago. What are the Spanish countries of South America, what is Spain itself doing in all the walks of life which make for progress? In previous centuries Spain has done a splendid and useful work in the western world, but she has failed to keep abreast of the world in moral and intellectual progress, and must pay the penalty. The principle that the higher civilization is justified in supplanting the lower is a dangerous one to admit, because of every nation regarding its own type as the highest, but there are certain broad facts which must force the impartial observer to admit the superiority of our own race, the Anglo-Saxon, in the qualities that contribute to human advance. At any rate, we hold to the opinion that we have done more than any other race to conquer the world for civilization in the past few centuries, and we will probably go on holding to this opinion and go on with our conquests.

If we believe that there is a distinct purpose in all that is about us and in our own presence here, we cannot escape the conclusion that man's express duty is the uplifting of man. The duty to improve and elevate himself and his fellows thus becomes an end in itself and a justification of life. . . . Any nation which blocks the way of human progress must expect to be brushed aside by more powerful and vigorous blood.

Senator Albert J. Beveridge discusses the march of the flag, September 1898.

It is a noble land that God has given us; a land that can feed and clothe the world; a land whose coastlines would inclose half the countries of

Europe; a land set like a sentinel between the two imperial oceans of the globe, a greater England with a nobler destiny. . . .

Therefore, in this campaign, the question is larger than a party question. It is an American question. It is a world question. Shall the American people continue their march toward the commercial supremacy of the world? Shall free institutions broaden their blessed reign as the children of liberty wax in strength, until the empire of our principles is established over the hearts of all mankind?

Have we no mission to perform, no duty to discharge to our fellowman? Has God endowed us with gifts beyond our deserts and marked us as the people of His peculiar favor, merely to rot in our own selfishness, as men and nations must, who take cowardice for their companion and self for their deity—as China has, as India has, as Egypt has?

Shall we be as the man who had one talent and hid it, or as he who had ten talents and used them until they grew to riches? And shall we reap the reward that waits on our discharge of our high duty; shall we occupy new markets for what our farmers raise, our factories make, our merchants sell— aye, and, please God, new markets for what our ships shall carry?

Hawaii is ours; Porto Rico is to be ours; at the prayer of her people Cuba finally will be ours; in the islands of the East, even to the gates of Asia, coaling stations are to be ours at the very least; the flag of a liberal government is to float over the Philippines, and may it be the banner that Taylor unfurled in Texas and Fremont carried to the coast.

The Opposition tells us that we ought not to govern a people without their consent. I answer: The rule of liberty that all just government derives its authority from the consent of the governed, applies only to those who are capable of self-government. We govern the Indians without their consent, we govern our territories without their consent, we govern our children without their consent. How do they know that our government would be without their consent? . . .

The March of the Flag! . . .

Distance and oceans are no arguments. The fact that all the territory our fathers bought and seized is contiguous, is no argument. In 1819 Florida was farther from New York than Porto Rico is from Chicago to-day; Texas, farther from Washington in 1845 than Hawaii is from Boston in 1898; California more inaccessible in 1847 than the Philippines are now. Gibraltar is farther from London than Havana is from Washington; Melbourne is farther from Liverpool than Manila is from San Francisco.

The ocean does not separate us from lands of our duty and desire—the oceans join us, rivers never to be dredged, canals never to be repaired. Steam joins us; electricity joins us—the very elements are in league with our destiny. Cuba not contiguous! Porto Rico not contiguous! Hawaii and the Philippines not contiguous! The oceans make them contiguous. And our Navy will make them contiguous.

But the Opposition is right—there is a difference. We did not need the western Mississippi Valley when we acquired it, nor Florida, nor Texas, nor California, nor the royal provinces of the far northwest. We had no emigrants to people this imperial wilderness, no money to develop it, even no highways to cover it. No trade awaited us in its savage fastnesses. Our productions were not greater than our trade. There was not one reason for the land-lust of our statesmen from Jefferson to Grant, other than the prophet and the Saxon within them. But, to-day, we are raising more than we can consume, making more than we can use. Therefore we must find new markets for our produce. . . .

The commercial supremacy of the Republic means that this Nation is to be the sovereign factor in the peace of the world. For the conflicts of the future are to be conflicts of trade—struggles for markets—commercial wars for existence. And the golden rule of peace is impregnability of position and invincibility of preparedness. So, we see England, the greatest strategist of history, plant her flag and her cannon on Gibraltar, at Quebec, in the Bermudas, at Vancouver, everywhere.

So Hawaii furnishes us a naval base in the heart of the Pacific; the Ladrones another, a voyage further on; Manila another, at the gates of Asia —Asia, to the trade of whose hundreds of millions American merchants, manufacturers, farmers, have as good right as those of Germany or France or Russia or England; Asia, whose commerce with the United Kingdom alone amounts to hundreds of millions of dollars every year; Asia, to whom Germany looks to take her surplus products; Asia, whose doors must not be shut against American trade. Within five decades the bulk of Oriental commerce will be ours. . . .

We can not fly from our world duties; it is ours to execute the purpose of a fate that has driven us to be greater than our small intentions. We can not retreat from any soil where Providence has unfurled our banner; it is ours to save that soil for liberty and civilization.

W. W. ROCKHILL'S MEMORANDUM

ON COMMERCIAL POLICY IN CHINA   *Document 10*

August 28, 1899.

No one person has done more within the last few months to influence public opinion in the United States on the Chinese question than Lord Charles Beresford, by his book "The Break-Up of China," and by the speeches he has made in the United States. By these means he has sought to prove the identity of interests of our two countries and the necessity of an Anglo-American policy in China. . . .

British writers on Chinese questions, and especially Lord Beresford, have advocated in the strongest terms the "open door policy" or equality of treatment and opportunity for all comers, and denounce in the strongest terms the system of "Spheres of Influence" (or interest); but such spheres have now been recognized by Great Britain as well as by France, Germany and Russia, and *they must be accepted as existing facts.*

But while adopting the policy of spheres of interest, which, we will admit, political reasons may have forced it to do, Great Britain has tried to maintain also the "open door" policy, the only one which meets with the approval of its business classes, for by it alone can they be guaranteed equality of treatment in the trade of China. In this attempt to minimize the evils brought about by the necessities of her foreign policy, Great Britain has been, however, unable to secure to her people perfect equality of opportunity, for she has recognized special and exclusive rights first of Germany and then of Russia in their areas of activity, more particularly those relating to railways and mines. What these rights may eventually be claimed to include, no one can at present foretell, though it would not be surprising if the exercise of territorial jurisdiction and the imposition of discriminating taxation were demanded under them—at least by France. Should such rights be conceded, our trade interests would receive a blow, from which they could not possibly recover.

To sum up then, we find to-day in China that the policy of the "open door," the untrammeled exercise of the rights insured to Treaty Powers by the treaty of Tientsin, and other treaties copied on it or under the most favored nation clause, is claimed by the mercantile classes of the United States and other powers as essential to the healthy extension of trade in China. We see, on the other hand, that the political interests and the geographical relations of Great Britain, Russia and France to China have forced those countries to divide up China proper into areas or spheres of interest (or influence) in which they enjoy special rights and privileges, the ultimate scope of which is not yet determined, and that at the same time Great Britain, in its desire not to sacrifice entirely its mercantile interests, is also endeavoring to preserve some of the undoubted benefits of the "open door" policy, but "spheres of influence" *are an accomplished fact*, this cannot be too much insisted on. This policy is outlined by Mr. Balfour in his Manchester speech of January 10, 1898.

Such then being the condition of things, and in view of the probability of complications soon arising between the interested powers in China, whereby it will become difficult, if not impossible, for the United States to retain the rights guaranteed them by treaties with China, what should be our immediate policy? To this question there can, it seems, be but one answer, we should at once initiate negotiations to obtain from those Powers who have acquired zones of interest in China formal assurance that (1) they will in no way interfere within their so-called spheres of interest with any treaty port or with vested rights in it of any nature; (2) that all ports they may open in their respective spheres shall either be free ports, or that the Chinese treaty tariff at the time in force shall apply to all merchandise landed or shipped, no matter to what nationality belonging, and that the dues and duties provided for by treaty shall be collected by the Chinese Government; and (3) that they will levy no higher harbor dues on vessels of other nationalities frequenting their ports in such spheres than shall be levied on their national vessels, and that they will also levy no higher railroad charges on merchandise belonging to or destined for subjects of other powers transported through their spheres than shall be levied on similar merchandise belonging to its own nationality.

In other words, we should insist on absolute equality of treatment in the various zones, for equality of opportunity with the citizens of the favored powers we cannot hope to have ... though we should continually, by every proper means, seek to gain this also.

Such understandings with the various Powers, and it is confidently believed that they could be reached at present, would secure an open market throughout China for our trade on terms of equality with all other foreigners, and would further remove dangerous sources of irritation and possible conflict between the contending powers, greatly tend to re-establish confidence, and prepare the way for concerted action by the Powers to bring about the reforms in Chinese administration and the strengthening of the Imperial Government recognized on all sides as essential to the maintenance of peace....

It furthermore has the advantage of insuring to the United States the appreciation of Chinese Government, who would see in it a strong desire to arrest the disintegration of the Empire and would greatly add to our prestige and influence at Peking....

AGRICULTURAL SUPPORT FOR
ECONOMIC EXPANSION   *Document 11*

Remarks of Aaron Jones, Master of the National Grange, March 14, 1899.
    ... We also want a widening of the markets for the farmers. We feel that the great power of this Government and very large sums of money have been expended to widen the market for our manufacturing industries in foreign countries. We believe there should be no discrimination and that the same energies and efforts ought to be put forward by the Government for advancing the markets of agriculture in all foreign countries. Men in the consular service ought to be sent abroad with the view of ascertaining what the market requires in the various countries, the probable demand of this country for importation and the probable supplies it might have for export, so as to advise this country. Farmers are placed at a disadvantage, compared with the commercial interests of the country, because they are slower in learning the demand of the world for the products they have in hand than are the commercial interests. We believe it is within the legitimate province of the Government to protect all its citizens alike, and we believe that no man should be appointed in the consular service who is not imbued with the importance of agriculture and the sale of agricultural products equally with manufactured goods.... We believe it is within the province of this Government to see that when any discrimination in any of the laws of foreign countries is made against the interests of the agriculture of the United States, this Government should protect us by proper methods....

    Q. If we enlarge the foreign market for a given line of manufactured products, say 50 per cent, so that where 200 men have been employed in this country, 300 will be at work, would that additional 100 men create an enlarged market for the products of the farmer?

A. That would widen our home demand. Yes; we are decidedly in favor of that. We do not want to curtail our manufactures a particle; no, not that. In fact, if we could get all the men in our own country making goods, so as to eat up all we can produce, it would be still better....

Remarks of John Hanley, general business agent for the National Farmers' Alliance and Industrial Union, and the National Grain Growers' Association, August 12, 1899.

There is but one thing that will regulate and make farming profitable, and make it profitable for every crop raised and for every section of the country. I can sum the whole thing up in two words—oriental markets. Give us oriental markets or more and better markets for the products of the American farm, and the natural conditions of supply and demand will regulate and control every agency of producing and marketing such products, and pay a reasonable profit to everyone connected with the crop in its passage from producer to consumer....

England is our chief and practically our only customer on whom we must depend to take our crops off our hands. As a natural consequence, any agency that will create competition and give us another market for our surplus products will stimulate prices which competitors will establish in order to secure the products that they must have. Any advance on the prices of such products gained by this agency will go to the producer, and he at once becomes the direct beneficiary, because all the fixed charges, such as freight rates and handling charges, are always in effect and operation, whether the crop is light or heavy, whether prices are high or low. Thus it will be seen how important it is that we have a market and trade relations with the countries of the Orient, where we would dispose of that vast volume of grain on our western slope, which can be done in 4 to 6 weeks, and get this vast volume of grain out of the way, and not let it hang like a millstone around the neck of prices on our farm products at a time of year that farmers are marketing the bulk of their products. Why not then bend every energy of this great nation to establish new and friendly relations with Asiatic countries, whom we could induce to take a large share of our surplus products, and take it at a time of year that would help to stimulate prices and compel England, who is practically our only customer, to come to our Atlantic seaboard and compete for what is left of our surplus crop, which they must do if they wish to get it.

It has been computed that the increase in price to the American farmers by the establishment of this market would be 15 to 20 cents per bushel on the export crop of wheat, and as the export sets the price of the entire crop the gain to the American farmer would be between $75,000,000 to $100,000,000 annually on the item of wheat alone.

How can this be done? How can we get the Chinese to take our wheat flour when they are accustomed to rice and rice-made flour? In answering these questions it must be borne in mind that we are dealing with a big proposition. Only when we contemplate the figures can we get any intelligent idea of the immensity or significance of this matter. We should first consider the fact that the great bulk of the inhabitants of this earth lays within that country of whom we have such vague and erroneous ideas and impressions. The inhabitants with whom we would have a direct and easy contact from the sea would represent a population of about 400,000,000 people. If we could get them to take the 40,000,000 bushels of wheat on our western slope it would mean that all each inhabitant would receive would be less than half a peck, or not as much as would furnish pie crust for the wealthy inhabitants of that country. This will be better illustrated by the fact that our 70,000,000 people in the United States consume annually 40,000,000 bushels of wheat, or an average of 5¾ bushels per inhabitant.

In further answering this question it must be remembered that the Chinese are not all poor and ignorant, as is the popular notion with most people when speaking of the Chinese and Japanese and the people of the Orient. A large percentage of these people are wealthy or in moderate circumstances. The official, commercial, religious, and educational classes, comprise a large percentage of the people, besides the military. It would not be an insurmountable task to cater to the tastes of this large, intelligent, and wealthy middle class, and induce such people to accept a staple article of food that would be at once palatable, nutritious, and moderately cheap as compared with rice-made flour edibles. History has shown that wherever wheat flour came into competition with rice flour, the wheat flour displaced the rice flour permanently.

Commerce and trade, like water, flow along the route offering the least resistance, and it now becomes the mission our lawmakers to clear away every obstacle or impediment without regard to past policies or precedents, but with a determination to grasp the significance and importance of this question and leave no sentiment stand in the way of an early and successful solution of it....

... Our society has become firmly convinced that these matters are more of a national than a partisan political character. Thus, we can reasonably expect the active and earnest support of each national or state legislator when a measure is presented for his consideration as a great national movement, bereft of any partisan advantage....

Never was a nation situated so favorably as the United States to-day before the nations of the world. We are at peace with every nation on earth, except a few unfortunate people who mistake our intentions and have brought on a cruel war.

This is the opportunity of the United States; the conditions are so favorable that all it requires is a bold and determined stand on our part, and the battle is ours. Let us say to the nations of the world that, pursuing the policy of our nation since its foundation, we are the friend of the weak and struggling nation, and we will not permit might to rule against right. The 4 great powers to-day in China are seeking to carve that unhappy country up into provinces and spheres controlled by marauding nations, who are glaring and snarling at each other with jealous fears that one rival may secure an advantage over the other. The very condition of these great nations makes us strong and fortifies our policy and position on the Eastern question. We have but to say "Hands off," and these nations, with whom we have the most friendly relations, are willing to obey, rejoicing in the satisfaction that their hated rival must also retire from its sphere of influence. What would this mean for the United States? It would mean that we would earn the lasting gratitude of the Chinese nation and secure all the advantages of a favored nation in the shape of commerce and trade. This is what we want; that is what we must have if we expect to grow and expand as we have been. This is the question which will challenge the attention of our best statesmen, and provide the opportunity to take a tremendous stride in advance, and secure for this nation the good will of China and its vast population, and remove many of the obstacles that now lie in the way of securing this great multitude as customers for our vastly increasing products, which must find a market or we will become a pauper nation. The downfall of our country will date from the hour that we fail to make the occupation of the farmer and laborer profitable in this nation. We have everything to gain and nothing to lose by following this well-established policy of this nation, and by applying sagacity and enterprise to the successful operation of this great, profitable business. . . .

SECRETARY OF STATE HAY DECLARES
FOR THE OPEN DOOR IN CHINA   *Document 12*

Circular Letter of September 6, 1899.
. . . Earnestly desirous to remove any cause of irritation and to insure at the same time to the commerce of all nations in China the undoubted benefits which should accrue from a formal recognition by the various powers claiming "spheres of influence" that they shall enjoy perfect equality of treatment for their commerce and navigation within such "spheres," the Government of the United States would be pleased to see His German Majesty's Government give formal assurances and lend its cooperation in securing like assurances from the other interested powers that each within its respective sphere of whatever influence—

First. Will in no way interfere with any treaty port or any vested interest within any so-called "sphere of interest" or leased territory it may have in China.

Second. That the Chinese treaty tariff of the time being shall apply to all merchandise within said "sphere of interest" (unless they be "free ports"), no matter to what nationality it may belong, and that duties so leviable shall be collected by the Chinese Government.

Third. That it will levy no higher harbor dues on vessels of another nationality frequenting any port in such "sphere" than shall be levied on vessels of its own nationality, and no higher railroad charges over lines built, controlled, or operated within its "sphere" on merchandise belonging to citizens or subjects of other nationalities transported through such "sphere" than shall be levied on similar merchandise belonging to its own nationals transported over equal distances. . . .

Circular Letter of July 3, 1900.

In this critical posture of affairs in China it is deemed appropriate to define the attitude of the United States as far as present circumstances permit this to be done. We adhere to the policy initiated by us in 1857, of peace with the Chinese nation, of furtherance of lawful commerce, and of protection of lives and property of our citizens by all means guaranteed under extraterritorial treaty rights and by the law of nations. If wrong be done to our citizens we propose to hold the responsible authors to the uttermost accountability. We regard the condition at Pekin as one of virtual anarchy. . . . The purpose of the President is, as it has been heretofore, to act concurrently with the other powers, first, in opening up communication with Pekin and rescuing the American officials, missionaries, and other Americans who are in danger; secondly, in affording all possible protection everywhere in China to American life and property; thirdly, in guarding and protecting all legitimate American interests; and fourthly, in aiding to prevent a spread of the disorders to the other provinces of the Empire and a recurrence of such disasters. It is, of course, too early to forecast the means of attaining this last result; but the policy of the government of the United States is to seek a solution which may bring about permanent safety and peace to China, preserve Chinese territorial and administrative entity, protect all rights guaranteed to friendly powers by treaty and international law, and safeguard for the world the principle of equal and impartial trade with all parts of the Chinese Empire. . . .

Hay to the German Ambassador, October 29, 1900.

I have the honor to acknowledge the receipt of your note of the 20th October informing me of the agreement arrived at by the Imperial [German] Ambassador Count von Hatzfeldt and Lord Salisbury [of Great Britain] on the 16th of this month, and inviting the acceptance by the United States of the principles therein laid down. These principles are:

1. It is a matter of joint and permanent international interest that the ports on the rivers and littoral of China should remain free and open to trade and to every other legitimate form of economic activity for the nationals of all countries without distinction, and the two Governments agree on their part to uphold the same for all Chinese territory, so far as they can exercise influence. . . .

The United States have heretofore made known their adoption of . . . these principles. During the last year this Government invited the powers interested in China to join in an expression of views and purposes in the direction of impartial trade with that country and received satisfactory assurances to that effect from all of them. . . .

It is, therefore, with much satisfaction that the President directs me to inform you of the full sympathy of this Government with those of the German Emperor and Her Britannic Majesty in the principles set forth. . . .

VOICES OF ANTI-IMPERIALISM   *Document 13*

A. William Graham Sumner: "The Fallacy of Territorial Extension."[1]

The traditional belief is that a state aggrandizes itself by territorial extension, so that winning new land is gaining in wealth and prosperity, just as an individual would gain if he increased his land possessions. It is undoubtedly true that a state may be so small in territory and population that it cannot serve the true purposes of a state for its citizens, especially in international relations with neighboring states which control a large aggregate of men and capital. There is, therefore, under given circumstances, a size of territory and population which is at the maximum of advantage for the civil unit....

The notion that gain of territory is gain of wealth and strength for the state, after the expedient size has been won, is a delusion....

If the United States should admit Hawaii to the Union, the Fiscus of the former state would collect more taxes and incur more expenses. The circumstances are such that the latter would probably be the greater. The United States would not acquire a square foot of land, in property, unless it paid for it. Individual Americans would get no land to till, without paying for it, and would win no products from it except by wisely expending their labor and capital on it. All that, they can do now. So long as there is a government on the islands, native or other, which is competent to guarantee peace, order, and security, no more is necessary, and for any outside power to seize the jurisdiction is an unjustifiable aggression. That jurisdiction would be the best founded which was the most liberal and enlightened, and would give the best security to all persons who sought the islands upon their lawful occasions. The jurisdiction would, in any case, be a burden, and any state might be glad to see any other state assume the burden, provided that it was one which could be relied upon to execute the charge on enlightened principles for the good of all. The best case is, therefore, always that in which the resident population produce their own state by the institutions of self-government.

What private individuals want is free access, under order and security, to any part of the earth's surface, in order that they may avail themselves of its natural resources for their use, either by investment or commerce. If, therefore, we could have free trade with Hawaii while somebody else had the jurisdiction, we should gain all the advantages and escape all the burdens....

The case of Cuba is somewhat different. If we could go to the island and trade with the same freedom with which we can go to Louisiana, we could make all the gains, by investment and commerce, which the island offers to industry and enterprise, provided that either Spain or a local government would give the necessary security, and we should have no share in political

---
[1] Selected from *Forum*, Vol. 21 (June 1896), 414–419.

struggles there. It may be that the proviso is not satisfied, or soon will not be. Here is a case, then, which illustrates the fact that states are often forced to extend their jurisdiction whether they want to do so or not. Civilized states are forced to supersede the local jurisdiction of uncivilized or half-civilized states, in order to police the territory, and establish the necessary guarantees of industry and commerce. It is idle to set up absolute doctrines of national ownership in the soil which would justify a group of population in spoiling a part of the earth's surface for themselves and everybody else. The island of Cuba may fall into anarchy. If it does, the civilized world may look to the United States to take the jurisdiction and establish order and security there. We might be compelled to do it. It would, however, be a great burden, and possibly a fatal calamity to us. Probably any proposition that England should take it would call out a burst of jingo passion against which all reasoning would be powerless. We ought to pray that England would take it. She would govern it well, and everybody would have free access to it for the purposes of private interest, while our Government would be free from all complications with the policies of the island. If we take the jurisdiction of the island, we shall find ourselves in a political dilemma, each horn of which is as disastrous as the other; either we must govern it as a subject province, or we must admit it into the Union as a State or group of States. Our system is unfit for the government of subject provinces. They have no place in it. They would become seats of corruption, which would react on our own body politic. If we admitted the island as a State or group of States, we should have to let it help govern us. The prospect of adding to the present Senate a number of Cuban Senators, either native or carpet-bag, is one whose terrors it is not necessary to unfold. Nevertheless it appears that there is a large party which would not listen to free trade with the island while any other nation has the jurisdiction of it, but who are ready to grab it at any cost, and to take free trade with it, provided that they can get the political burdens too.

This confederated state of ours was never planned for indefinite expansion, or for an imperial policy. We boast of it a great deal, but we must know that its advantages are won at the cost of limitations, as is the case with most things in this world. The Fathers of the Republic planned a confederation of free and peaceful industrial commonwealths, shielded by their geographical position from the jealousies, rivalries, and traditional policies of the Old World, and bringing all the resources of civilization to bear for the domestic happiness of the population only....Any extension will not make us more secure where we are, but will force us to take new measures to secure our new acquisitions. The preservation of acquisitions will force us to reorganize our internal resources, so as to make it possible to prepare them in advance and to mobilize them with promptitude. This will lessen liberty and require discipline. It will increase taxation and all the pressure of government. It will divert the national energy from the provision of self-maintenance and comfort for the people, and will necessitate stronger and more elaborate governmental machinery. All this will be disastrous to republican institutions and to democracy. Moreover all extension puts a new strain on the internal cohesion of the pre-existing mass, threatening a new cleavage within....

B. William MacDonald: "The Dangers of Imperialism:"[1]

One of the prominent characteristics of American politics, which writers and speakers have frequently remarked, is the lack in recent years of any very fundamental differences in the tenets of the great political parties. Since, indeed, the question of slavery ceased to have other than historic interest, no political question at all comparable to that in intensity or divisive force has arisen. Neither the rehabilitation of the Southern States, nor the adjustment of tariff duties (though quite the first in importance of *post bellum* issues) ever made the same powerful appeal to the national thought that long characterized the earlier issue of slavery. And the reason is not far to seek. A question of public policy whose main interest is intellectual, which appeals primarily to men of education or fruitful experience, or concerns the choice of means to the attainment of some end generally regarded as desirable, can never become a ground of radical distinction between parties. A real issue, whatever its other elements, must take strong hold of the moral sense, must touch the feelings and emotions, and color, for better or worse, the views of the national mission and ideal entertained by the mass of the people. Something of this moral appeal, impossible in connection with any purely administrative question, has attached to the latest of our party issues, in the growing opinion that the maintenance of a sound currency is not alone a matter of scientific determination of standards, but a matter of national honesty and good faith as well.

There seems to be good reason for thinking that, as one result of our unhappy war with Spain, American politics has at last been provided with a real and living issue. Under the taking name of "imperialism," the people of the United States find themselves suddenly confronted with a question of national policy of profound significance and far-reaching relations. It is not a question of administrative detail, or of mere choice of means, or of observance of scientific law. It is not a question on which individual opinion must be guided wholly by extensive technical information. It is a question, rather, of our national hopes and desires, of our place and work in the world, of what we wish our America to become. In all our history no question has been presented to us whose answer may so radically change the face of our national life. How vital the issue is felt to be, how widely it is being discussed, is clear to any thoughtful observer. It bids fair to unite North and South, East and West, at the same time that it runs athwart existing party lines, and causes a man's foes to be those of his own political household. Such a situation as is presented in Massachusetts—where the two Republican Senators, each prominent in the councils of his party, occupy diametrically opposite positions on the question—is significant of the power of this new idea.

I understand by imperialism, in the best sense in which the term is used, a theory of national policy in accordance with which the United States is to add to its territorial possessions, for the purpose of extending American trade and American political influence. We are to change our traditional policy of independence and non-participation in the general politics of

---

[1] Selected from *Forum*, Vol. 26 (October 1898), 177–187.

the world, and to adopt a policy of territorial expansion, of wide contact and control. We are to have colonies and dependencies, coaling-stations and "keys." Incidentally, we are to get military and naval influence, and a reputation for physical prowess, not for purposes of wanton aggression, but to command wholesome respect. I do not understand that imperialism means political tyranny or meddlesomeness, or greedy scrambling for territory, or offensive and defensive alliances, but rather the extension, by reasonable and honorable means, of American influence and control beyond the North American continent. To use a hard-worked phrase, it is a policy of extensive, rather than intensive, growth. It is the cosmopolitan and international, as opposed to the provincial, idea.

Without discussing further the general nature of this new issue, or its theoretical bearings upon politics in a democracy, I propose to consider some of the dangers which seem to me to be inseparable from the pursuit of such a policy by the United States.

I. The right of the United States to acquire and govern territory is no longer open to discussion, nor is the particular method to be followed in either case a subject for other than academic debate. In the absence of any constitutional provision, the question of acquisition has been settled by precedent. . . .

While, however, Congress, in matters in which it is given discretion, is not bound to follow its own precedents, precedents nevertheless count for much in history and law. And one precedent in our dealings with Territories, of especial significance in connection with this new issue of imperialism, has been the general assumption, confirmed by long practice, of the merely temporary status of a territorial organization. . . .

One serious danger of imperialism, accordingly, is in the likelihood of pressure from our new acquisitions for admission to the Union as States. To admit them, sooner or later, is, as we have seen, to follow a long line of precedents; to debar them is to adopt a wholly new theory of national policy. The objections to the admission of Hawaii, for example (or of any other region we are likely to acquire), as a State, with Senators and Representatives in Congress, participation in presidential elections, and an equal voice in the conduct of national affairs, are many and cogent; and it is not surprising that some of the foremost advocates of an imperial America have hastened to declare in advance against such admission. . . .

II. Closely connected with this danger of forced admission of detached States is the danger of the abandonment, or, at least, the radical modification, of our belief in universal suffrage. The theory, that all adult male citizens of sound mind and independent status have a right to participate in the conduct of affairs, has been one of the most important and most distinctive bases of our political life. It was not the theory of our fathers, nor had it the sanction of any enlightened nation at the time our Constitution was framed; yet it has steadily and successfully made its way, and has long been regarded, in common thought, as one of the peculiar glories of our system. The emancipation of the negroes, thrusting upon the body politic a horde of human beings previously regarded, in law, alternately as chattels and as real estate, and to whom the status of "persons," within the meaning of the Constitution, had been denied by the Supreme Court, strained the doctrine to the utmost, and put the faith of its defenders to the severest test: but the argument from necessity overrode the argument from political philosophy; and the suffrage was extended to the blacks on the same terms as to the whites. Aside from the abolition of slavery, probably no single result of the Civil War has been more highly praised, or oftener cited as proof of far-seeing political wisdom, than this.

Yet it is not difficult to see that one of the strongest arguments against the admission, as a State, of such a dependency as Hawaii, involves a denial of universal suffrage as a measure of universal application. We shrink from entrusting political control to dark-skinned Hawaiians of uncertain pedigree and problematic civilization, for the same reason that we hesitate to entrust it to Cubans. The notion of equality, inseparable from the idea of universal suffrage, seems, in these mixed populations, to be hardly borne out by the facts. Here, again, the advocates of imperialism have already entered upon the new road. Their leaders are already telling us that "of course" the suffrage must be restricted, that "we cannot think" of putting the ballot into the hands of such people for other than local affairs, and that it is "out of the question" to consider giving to the Hawaiians and others a voice in national concerns.

I can but think that the Imperialists, however far removed from theoretical consistency, are at this point in close accord with common sense. At the same time, the logical application of the new doctrine is likely, I fear, to bring some unexpected and not wholly beneficent consequences. One need not admit all the extravagant claims of its extreme advocates, or ignore the objections of its extreme opponents, to realize that universal suffrage, as worked out in the United States, has served to stimulate profoundly the desire for individual betterment. It has not, as some predicted, saved American politics from corruption, nor freed us from the control of the spoilsman; but unquestionably it has deepened the sense of political responsibility, conduced to a higher average of citizenship, and extended to all the hand of hopefulness and cheer. Any attempt, accordingly, to deal with the people of our new possessions on terms less liberal than we have thus far accorded to the lowest elements in our own cosmopolitan population, can hardly be construed otherwise than as a withdrawal from our present advanced position, or operate otherwise than as an argument in favor of a restriction of the suffrage in certain States of the Union, particularly in the South, and as a check on democratic progress the world over. Universal suffrage for continental Americans, however ignorant and degraded, and restricted suffrage for Hawaiian Americans and others, would be a combination whose reactionary effect might well be feared.

III. In the third place, an imperial policy is a costly policy. Just as there are gifts which may impoverish the recipient, or compel a radical change in his accustomed mode of life, so there are opportunities of which even a wealthy nation may not avail itself without assuming a heavy financial burden. . . .

I suppose there can be little doubt but that the people of the United States are able to pay much higher taxes than they now pay. We do not commonly think of ourselves as overtaxed: certainly, in comparison with some other nations, the burden of governmental contributions cannot be said to rest very heavily upon us. The point to be attended to, however, in considering an imperialistic programme, lies in another direction. It has been more than once pointed out that, under a *régime* of vastly increased national expenditure, the sources of revenue provided by the Constitution have begun to show significant limitations. There are indications, political and economic, that tariff taxes have reached very nearly their maximum-point, and that we can no longer hope to meet increased appropriations by the simple device of "raising the tariff." We have at present a scale of duties at which our protectionist fathers would have looked aghast; nevertheless we have a deficit. Further, so long as the opinion of the Supreme Court remains unchanged, it seems impossible to frame a suitable income tax, while the Constitution in terms prevents the levying of any direct tax not susceptible of apportionment among the States in accordance with population. There are left, then, the two resources of indirect internal taxation and an increase of the national debt, upon both of which the war with Spain has forced us to draw heavily. In all probability, we have for the present seen an end to payment of the national debt, and a beginning of heavier internal taxation.

I regard the financial cost of imperialism, then, as a danger, not so much because of the increased burden it will lay upon the people, as because of its possible influence upon the national temper....

Unless the added weight of taxation can be offset by enlarged opportunities for capital and labor, and the tangible evidences of material prosperity still increase among us, the possession of islands in the Atlantic or Pacific, or coaling-stations in the Philippines or the Ladrones, may well come to seem too dearly bought.

IV. I have spoken of imperialism as the manifestation of a desire for intimate and influential relations with world affairs. Such relations are, indeed, a necessary result of territorial expansion. Yet it is open to question whether our habits have been such as to fit us for immediate success in such a sphere. Our long freedom from "entangling alliances," and our ability to conduct our affairs with little danger of collision with other Powers, while allowing remarkable liberty of action, have tended also to develop an easy-going habit of mind, and a comfortable willingness to make the best of unfavorable conditions. The particular illustration of this spirit is to be seen in the general indifference to purity and effectiveness in governmental administration. The idea of trained service, strict business methods, and absence of personal or party favoritism in the administration of government has grown but slowly in the United States. Public office has been too largely public plunder, and the spoils system has too effectually blunted the moral sense, to give to the obligations of government routine a very vivid appeal....

What sort of a civil service would a policy of imperialism demand? What sort of a civil service would probably be put in operation were that policy definitely entered upon to-day? We have not, nor has anyone in authority suggested, in this connection, that we ought to have, arrangements for the systematic training of candidates for the consular and diplomatic services; neither have we seriously contemplated the establishment of an administrative system such as has made English colonial management so signally successful. In the present condition of public spirit and political morality in this country, there is but too much reason to fear that new possessions, like the old, will fall under the control of the spoilsman, and be administered in the interest of the "machine." How great may be our latent capacity for dealing with new international relations, with their selfish rivalries and numberless points of hostile contact, no one, perhaps, would venture to say; but to turn over to a "boss" or a "leader" the political patronage of a distant dependency could hardly fail to insure, only on a larger scale, the same pernicious incapacity and lamentable maladministration which, but a short time ago, sent American troops to Cuba with antiquated rifles and inadequate supplies, and left sick and well alike to succumb like cattle to starvation and disease....

V. It may be pointed out that a policy of imperialism, consistently adhered to and logically developed, is not in harmony with the historic spirit of American government....

...If, as a people, we have never fully attained moral consistency, or freed ourselves wholly from those who would make our virtues a means to selfish aggrandizement, we have yet stood, in a peculiar sense and in a large way, for the best aspirations, the cleanest and healthiest political and social ambitions, of the human race. More than any other people, we have achieved political independence, abstained from international strife, spread education and enlightenment, cared for the poor and oppressed, and raised the standard of living for the mass of the people.

I cannot avoid the conclusion that some large measure of our success, in these several regards, has been due to the form of government under which we have lived, and to the national limitations which, from the beginning, we have set for ourselves. And I cannot think with indifference of the likelihood of change in these respects. We have no political ills to be remedied by foreign enlargement, and no political gains yet visible commensurate with the risks involved. We have no lack of territory, no pressure of population, no limited resources, and no want of respect from the world at large. If at any time we have been disliked abroad or accorded a consideration beneath our due, it has commonly been because of our own irritating acts. Imperial dominion and imperial influence, dissociated from the sordid elements attending them, are fascinating objects of national ambition; but they would be indeed dearly bought if their price were the sacrifice of any of the things which thus far have made us great.

C. J. A.: *"Our Imperial Destiny:"*[1]

...There is a pleasing delusion prevalent in America which has been relatively harmless in the past but promises to be dangerous in the future. This delusion is that the prosperity of our country is due to our peculiar capacity for dominating reluctant nature, for invention, for labor, and

---

[1] Selected from *The Sewanee Review,* Vol. 6 (1898), 472–479.

for self-government. We think it almost a truism that we are among the shrewdest of nations. In fact, we have been spendthrifts of an estate so rich by nature as to make us feel possessed of Fortunatus' purse, with the natural result that when the normal conditions of national economics began to assert themselves relentlessly among us as in the nations of Europe, we were disposed to look for our relief to the very sources of our ills. The history of our financial legislation during the past thirty years is the history of a series of blunders that would have brought bankruptcy to any country less favored by nature. The recent war was carried on with the same extravagance that characterized the civil one, and for the same disgraceful reasons, furthering the already perilous progress of a cancerous plutocracy. A few in this country will be much the richer for this war, as they have been made the richer by various financial acts in the past, while life for the majority has grown and will continue to grow harder, and a colonial policy will intensify the process.

Very large sums of money are obviously needed to conquer foreign possessions. We have already spent more than $100,000,000, and have secured undisputed control of—Porto Rico, rich in name alone. We shall probably spend a great many times that sum for the privilege of keeping a number of exposed colonial stations which must be fortified at additional expense, garrisoned and supported by a navy at least double the size of any that we have ever had, unless we wish to see them taken from us. To do this will increase materially the already heavy taxes of our people, none the less heavy because they are insidious and for the most part indirect. It will detract from the national prosperity, make it harder for us to maintain competition with Europe, and tend to assimilate our conditions of labor and wages to hers. And all that we may have places of refuge for a navy that we do not possess, in case of a war that we do not anticipate, to protect a canal that may never exist across Panama or Nicaragua, a canal with which we seem quite capable of dispensing, and which will certainly never be built without our consent and contributions. If the building of a Pacific canal involves what is claimed by Captain Mahan, it would be much cheaper to wage a war to prevent its construction than to pay for building what we need less than any and have reason to dread more than all.

It is said that trade follows the flag, that unless we have a navy we can have no merchant marine, and it is undeniable that one fosters the other; but surely we can forego some of the profits of the carrying trade if we are spared the cost of protecting it. A few months ago all territory controlled by the United States was in a compact mass, excepting of course Alaska. No navy was needed to maintain communication with any part of it. The nature of our country is such that we could endure the blockade of our entire coast and frontier with less annoyance than we should cause to our blockaders. The invasion of our territory tempts no foreign army. We therefore are not obliged to maintain the naval force that is necessary to the existence of the scattered British Empire or of France or even of Germany. Protection of commerce is only an incident to their unfortunate geographical position. We are sacrificing an economic advantage in creating a navy with all that it implies, to do for ourselves at greater expense what they will do for us at less, leaving precisely that amount of capital free for the needed development of domestic industry.

It would seem, therefore, that from the point of view of economic well-being there is no profit in sight from an imperial policy, however energetic or successful. Nor will the colonies themselves prove sources of revenue to us, unless our experience differs from that of other and more experienced nations. Individuals have squeezed great wealth from the Spanish colonies. The nation has been the poorer for them for a century. Even Java has in recent times barely sufficed to balance Sumatra in the Dutch budget. The English colonies at best pay for themselves, and hardly that if one takes into account their proportion of the maintenance of the naval establishment. The colonies of France are an annual drain of men and money. We shall be the weaker pecuniarily for every colony that we conquer. Our country is entering on this career with the ardor of Sancho Panza for the government of islands, the more distant the better. Experience is a dear school. Can it be that Americans are of that category of mankind that will learn in no other?

And politically? Why do we readily assume that we have a vocation, as it were from heaven, to govern others? Are we so eminently successful in governing ourselves that we should be eager to extend the blessings we enjoy to less fortunate races? ...

We believe Voltaire is the author of a homely exhortation to nations to wash their dirty linen at home. Where a nation has such a large laundry of this character it would seem well to attend to it as far as may be in the privacy of our back yards, and not to flaunt it in every quarter of the globe. Thomas à Kempis suggested centuries ago that he who would govern others should first learn to govern himself. The circumstances of Captain Mahan's life have perhaps tended to hide from him the necessity of this preliminary lesson in the United States. It would be impossible to teach it to the greater part of his abettors who, with motives as base as his are generous, seek to beguile the country into a debauch of colonial imperialism.

EXPORTERS, FINANCIERS,

AND IDEOLOGUES

CHAPTER 9

*The Struggle for Economic Empire
in Asia, 1900–1914*

A merican diplomacy in Asia between 1900 and 1915 was
designed to extend the power of the United States in the Far East. This did
not mean that the United States sought to conquer, occupy, or colonize
any large portion of the region. American policy makers were aware that
in an age of industrialism, economic penetration and control had replaced
the old-style colonialism as a more efficient form of influence and profit.
Brooks Adams, one of the major metropolitan theorists of American expansion, and Theodore Roosevelt, who became president when William
McKinley was assassinated in 1901, discuss several aspects of that strategy
in Document 1.

President Theodore Roosevelt's diplomacy is usually described in terms
of the balance-of-power principle. But balance-of-power politics is often
misunderstood, though the picture of a teeter-totter which is used to explain
the idea is sound enough in itself. The common assumption is that a
given country maintains the balance on the international teeter-totter by
shifting its power from one side to the other. Such action will, under ideal
circumstances, correct an imbalance. But, just as on the playground, this
method is crude and impractical in the world of nations. Unless the weight
added to one side is just right, it creates a new imbalance.

A much more subtle and effective method of trying to maintain such a
balance is to move toward but not to one end of the seesaw. But it is much
easier to use this technique to run the show on a playground than it is in

international politics. Even the extremely intelligent and absolute dictator of the most powerful nation who desired nothing but peace would find it next to impossible to shift back and forth in this fashion. Theodore Roosevelt lacked such absolute power, had to contend with changing weights at each end of the international seesaw, and (as with other American leaders) really wanted his side of the teeter-totter to control—rather than balance—the other. A good illustration of an unsuccessful effort to gain such an advantage, initiated largely by the Navy, is provided in Document 2.

Roosevelt's objective was to deploy American power to win a key position in Asia. Economic leaders at first went along with this program because it suited their own plans to win markets, resources, and investment opportunities in the area. They had already established, and continued to strengthen, their influence within the State Department and the Congress. Thus they felt confident that they could protect their own interests if Roosevelt tried to do anything that did not suit them. China, supposed to gain equal rewards through the Open Door, fared badly. Neither Roosevelt nor American economic interests paid much attention to suggestions from China unless Peking's requests coincided with their own aims. The Chinese found economic retaliation their most effective counterweapon against those parts of American policy that they disliked (Document 3).

American businessmen were successful, by 1905, in their efforts to establish a very strong position in the economic life of Manchuria. Professor Dana G. Munro's article, "American Commercial Interests in Manchuria," discusses this predominance in some detail, and states the problem created by the failure of President Roosevelt's diplomacy during the Russo-Japanese War (1905–1906). Roosevelt, in his efforts to push American power further into China, persistently treated Russia as the main opponent from 1901 to 1904. This action weakened the influence of those Russians who were working for a less aggressive policy and to reach some understanding with the United States. The Tsar listened instead to their opponents, who advocated vigorous expansion, and embarked on a policy that challenged Japan's increasing measure of control over Korea. Both Roosevelt and American financiers backed Japan in the resulting war, despite warnings that Japan was the power to be checked, not Russia. In his article, Professor Fred H. Harrington provides a dramatic account of that struggle over policy among American leaders.

Roosevelt's hope that Russia and Japan would wear themselves out to the advantage of the United States was not realized. Both powers were weakened by the war (it created the opportunity for the Revolution of 1905 in Russia), but not until Japan had entrenched itself in Korea and the southern half of Manchuria. Roosevelt could do little but protest when Japan slammed the Open Door and then, with the help of its occupation forces, took over the lion's share of the Manchurian trade. Indeed, he hastened to approve Japan's control of Korea in order to protect the Philippines (Document 4). Three years later he recognized Japan's gains from the war (Document 5).

The Tsar had other ideas about checking Japan's advance. Even before the war with Japan had ended he renewed Russia's earlier overtures for an understanding with the United States. Then, in 1907, he settled his differences with England. By doing this he hoped to decrease the chance that Japan would feel that the Anglo-Japanese Alliance provided an opportunity to attack Siberia. Neither President Roosevelt nor his successors, President William Howard Taft and Secretary of State Philander C. Knox, responded favorably to these Russian moves. Holding fast to the idea of American predominance, they thought they could still gain their objective without an ally on the Asian mainland.

The policy failed again, this time because American economic leaders vetoed the idea and because Russia could not stop Japan without assistance from the United States. American financiers split into two groups, but both opposed the plans of Taft and Knox. Railway magnate Edward H. Harriman, who received financial backing from Kuhn, Loeb and Company, first tried to do business with the Japanese. Blocked there, he turned to the Russians. But he died in September, 1909, just when it appeared that his economic alliance with the Russians might lay the foundation for political cooperation.

Instead of carrying through with Harriman's plans, Secretary Knox tried to use them for a different purpose. His suggestion to "neutralize" the Manchurian railroads (Document 6) was a thinly disguised maneuver to establish American financial control over that communication system. Nobody liked the idea. Neither the House of Morgan nor Kuhn, Loeb and Company was willing to antagonize the Japanese unless the American government stood firmly behind such a challenge. Knox could not promise to go to war. Unable to get such a guarantee, American financiers preferred to work with the Japanese in Manchuria and with the French and British in southern China. Russia saw its suspicions of the Knox proposal verified when the United States declined to talk seriously about cooperation against Japan. This left the Japanese in control. They encouraged American financiers and threatened the Russians. Both the bribe and the threat worked successfully. "Our policy in Manchuria," summarized one State Department official in 1910, "has won us the ill will of Russia, irritated Japan, and failed of support in France and Britain."

Even so, American policy did not change dramatically. But the consequences of Russian-American antagonism—reviewed by Professor Edward H. Zabriskie—continued to cause trouble. Japan was left free to continue its penetration into China. The implications of this development led Minister to Russia William Woodville Rockhill to reverse his earlier anti-Russian position. He warned his superiors in Washington that the only way to check Japan was to work with China and Russia (Document 7). His advice was ignored.

American policy did become more anti-Japanese in the years after the Russo-Japanese War. West Coast agitation against Japanese immigration, particularly in California, accounted for some of this shift. Those who opposed oriental immigration forced President Roosevelt to work out an arrangement which limited the number of Japanese immigrants (Document 8). This offended Japan and broadened its opposition to

American policy in Asia. American businessmen who had been forced out of Manchuria by Japan after 1905 also called for a more vigorous policy. And President Roosevelt had modified his own enthusiasm for the Japanese because of the way they ignored the principle of the Open Door in Korea and Manchuria. One of the reasons he sent the Great White Fleet around the world was to impress Japan with American power.

But the United States, working alone, had little chance to check Japan short of going to war. By antagonizing both Russia and Japan, American policy helped to drive them together in northeast Asia. Nor did America get much assistance from England. Great Britain wanted to continue its understanding with Japan (the Anglo-Japanese Alliance of 1902) in order to protect British interests in China. London also sought to reduce tensions with Russia because of the growing power of Germany. Thus British policy makers were more concerned about good relations between Japan and Russia than they were with supporting American expansion. All these factors help explain the difficulties encountered by Presidents Roosevelt and Taft.

President Woodrow Wilson at first seemed to abandon the vigorous policy of his predecessors. He supported and carried forward the plans for Philippine self-government and independence. This movement had been initiated by those who opposed colonialism on moral and political grounds, by others who argued that the cost and troubles of colonial rule brought no advantages that could not be obtained by economic control, and by those who doubted whether the United States could defend the islands in a showdown with Japan or Germany. Wilson also gave the impression, early in his first term, that he was unwilling to help the bankers in Asia (Document 9).

But the President was in reality a strong and sophisticated advocate of American expansion, and in his article Martin J. Sklar makes it clear that Wilson was fully prepared to make another and vigorous effort to push American interests in Asia. Secretary of State Bryan's commitment to that policy is apparent in Document 10, a speech that also indicates that Bryan's anticolonialism did not mean he was opposed to economic or ideological expansion. Both men acted on the same ideas and beliefs, moreover, in their handling of relations with Latin America.

AMERICAN COMMERCIAL INTERESTS IN MANCHURIA[1]

Dana G. Munro

The three Eastern Provinces of the Chinese Empire, collectively known as Manchuria, have a combined area of about 363,610 square miles, and a population variously estimated at from fifteen to twenty-five millions. They are remarkably rich, both in agricultural products and in minerals. The soil,

[1] *Annals of the American Academy,* XXXIX (January, 1912), 154–168. Reprinted with permission.

with the aid of an abundant and fairly uniform rainfall, produces heavy crops of beans and grain year after year, without showing signs of depletion; while underground there are immense deposits, as yet unexploited, of gold, silver, copper, lead, and coal. The population consists largely of immigrants, who are coming to Manchuria in great numbers from the less fertile provinces of the empire. These are more progressive and less opposed to foreigners than the people of many other parts of China; and because of this fact, and also because of the greater per capita wealth due to the richness of the land, Manchuria offers an unusually favorable market for foreign products. In the year 1910, although the provinces were just beginning to recover from the destructive war recently fought within their limits, the total volume of their trade amounted to $110,000,000.

This great commercial activity is partly due to the fact that there is no other part of the Chinese Empire so accessible to foreign enterprise. Most of the important cities have been opened to foreign trade, and an extensive railway system, combined with four large navigable rivers, has afforded transportation such as is unknown in other provinces. Until 1898, Newchwang, opened to trade in 1864, was the only port of entry for foreign commerce in Manchuria, although a certain amount of foreign goods came into the country over the Trans-Siberian Railroad in the North. From Newchwang, merchandise was sent into the interior by means of junks on the Liao River, or overland by cart. In 1898, Russia opened the port of Dalny, within her leased territory of Liaotung, but in spite of constant efforts to divert trade to the new port, Newchwang still retained its commercial leadership. In 1901, the Chinese Eastern Railway, built by Russia, was opened to traffic, connecting these two ports in the South with the Trans-Siberian system and with the cities of the interior. The Treaty of Portsmouth gave the southern section of this line, now called the Southern Manchurian Railway, to the Japanese, who rebuilt it and replaced the old Russian wide gauge by standard gauge, thus making it necessary to transship freight at Changchun, the point of division. Since the war, also, a great number of new ports have been opened, and Japan has built a railroad connecting Mukden, on the Southern Manchurian line, with Antung and the Korean Railway. China herself is building a railroad from Changchun to Kirin, which will draw traffic from a large section at present inaccessible.

In spite of these improvements in commercial facilities, trade in this section of China is by no means free from certain disadvantages which have hampered business elsewhere in the empire. The most serious of these is the appalling chaos of the currency system. This cannot be described here, but the state of affairs can be imagined from the statement that there are generally at least a dozen forms of money circulating at each port, and that these vary considerably from month to month in their rate of exchange, not only in regard to gold, but also in regard to each other. Such a condition adds a gambling element to the most conservative business. Recently, on account of pressure from the United States and other powers, steps have been taken towards the adoption of a uniform currency throughout the empire, and a substantial improvement is looked for in the next few years. Another hindrance to trade is the tariff system. Likin, or transportation, dues are levied on merchandise at every point where it is possible to establish a barrier, and the resulting expense and annoyance burden commerce considerably. The payment of a 2½ per cent ad valorem surtax at the maritime customs house is supposed legally to free foreign goods from these dues, but the transit passes secured in this way are often not respected in the interior.

Nevertheless, on account of the improvement of trade routes and the opening up of the country, there has in recent years been a great development both of the export and of the import trade of Manchuria. The principal exports are beans, bean-cake and bean-oil, produced mostly in the two southern provinces. Since the Chino-Japanese war of 1894–5, Japan has bought practically all of Manchuria's bean crop, and her control of the export trade has been an important factor in the competition for the import trade. Recently, small shipments of beans and bean-oil have been made to Europe, and European firms in the Orient hope to increase these to offset Japan's advantage. In the northern section much grain is produced, which is for the most part consumed locally. The neighboring Russian-Siberian provinces, however, are dependent on this section for flour, grain and wheat, and as they develop by colonization, Northern Manchuria is certain to become more and more prosperous. Other leading items in the export trade are lumber, wild silk, and minerals. The lumber is cut under Japanese direction from the forests on the Yalu River. The wild silk industry is chiefly in southeastern Shenking. The vast mineral resources of the country are as yet comparatively undeveloped, although there is an average annual output of about $10,000,000 in value from the gold, silver, copper, lead and iron mines, which are operated chiefly by the natives, and a large amount of coal is taken from the Japanese mines at Fushun, for use on the railroad and on steamers.

The import trade covers a wide range of articles, but there are certain great staples which have always formed the bulk of foreign shipments to this region. The most important of these are manufactures of cotton, which exceed in value all other foreign imports put together. Other items are kerosene, which is more and more widely used, lumber and tobacco. Flour, brought from the United States, once stood high in the list, but the great output of the mills in Northern Manchuria, which can grind the native wheat and sell it at a price which no foreign flour can touch, has driven out the American product. At present, there is a promising but as yet undeveloped market for machinery of all kinds, especially for modern agricultural implements, which could be used to good advantage on the rather large farms of the region. These goods must be sold by native dealers in native stores, and the primary consideration which determines the popularity of an article is its cheapness. The better grades of Western manufactures find a market only among the small European element, while inferior goods, produced by cheap Oriental labor, and sold at a low price, are readily accepted. The Chinese are, however, good judges of quality, and are ready to pay better prices for superior goods if they can afford to, so that as the country develops there will undoubtedly be an increasing demand for first-class products.

Before the Russo-Japanese war, Manchuria imported more goods from the United States than from any other foreign country, and American imports at Newchwang between 1900 and 1904 amounted to about five million dollars annually. By far the most important commodities in this trade were cotton piece goods. In 1901, out of a total of $24,813,692 native and foreign imports at Newchwang, $14,660,000 represented cotton products, and of this about one-third was native Chinese textiles, one-third American piece goods, and the rest chiefly imports of yarn from India, Great Britain, Japan, and China. In 1902, about thirty-five per cent of the total foreign imports at Newchwang came from the United States, and the greater part of this was cotton goods. In 1903, the total foreign imports were $13,314,012, and America's share was $5,562,255, of which $4,873,960 was cotton goods. These figures will suffice to show the position held by the United States in former years in regard to the most important import of Manchuria. The balance of the goods from America consisted chiefly of flour and kerosene, for each of which Manchuria offered a very important and continually expanding market.

Between 1901 and 1904, American commerce suffered considerably from the policy of Russia. This power had always exercised great influence in Manchuria, and she had, under various pretexts, finally established a measure of military control over the provinces. When she leased the Liao-tung Peninsula in 1898, and opened Dalny as a free port, she blocked the establishment of a Chinese customs house there until July, 1903. In 1901, as a result of the Boxer uprising, she occupied Newchwang. The same year, the Chinese Eastern Railway was opened to traffic, under her control. By discrimination in rates, and by preventing the collection of customs duties at Dalny, she attempted to divert to that port, where her own merchants were established, the trade formerly enjoyed by Newchwang, which was the base of the commerce carried on in Manchuria by other foreign countries. She also took measures to increase her own imports to the provinces. Fourteen steamers, subsidized to the amount of $309,000 annually, were put in operation between European Russia and Vladivostok, Port Arthur and Dalny; and the Russo-Chinese Bank advanced large sums to Chinese merchants for the purchase of Russian goods. The same bank established a commercial branch to sell Russian oil and sugar. While other foreigners were still excluded from the interior, Russian subjects were to be found everywhere, building flour mills, meat packing establishments, and factories, opening mines, and selling Russian goods. Harbin, founded by the railroad company in 1896, had a European population of 60,000 in 1904, and other Russian settlements increased rapidly in size.

This policy, however, was not entirely successful. Russian trade was stimulated, but it by no means drove out that of other nations. American cotton goods were imported in as great quantities as before, although the Russian government was exerting every effort to supplant them by the product of Russian mills, and the volume of American trade thus remained nearly the same. Nevertheless, because of the competition of Russian oil imported duty free at Dalny and carried at low rates on the railroad, the importation of American kerosene at Newchwang fell from 3,172,000 gallons in 1901, to 603,180 gallons in 1902; and American flour was almost driven from the market by the product of the Russian mills near Harbin.

But these articles made up only a small part of the total trade. Russia's control of the railroad was not so great an advantage as it seemed, since the cost of transporting bulky freight on it was prohibitive, and thus it was not nearly so effective a means of distribution in the interior as were the junks on the Liao River at Newchwang. It had already become evident that Russia could not hope to monopolize the commerce of Manchuria without a more serious disregard of the "open door" than she had yet shown, when the war with Japan drove her out of the southern province and confined her influence to the sparsely settled North.

After the restoration of peace, American trade in Manchuria seemed to have a clear field. The subsidized Russian lines to Port Arthur and Dalny had disappeared, and the disorganized condition of the country had caused the flour mills in the North to close, so that American flour was in greater demand than ever before. American kerosene was in full control of the market, and American cotton goods seemed to have no important competitor, for over $9,000,000 worth were imported into Manchuria in the year 1905. The year after the war was one of unprecedented commercial activity. There followed, however, a period of depression. Foreign imports at Newchwang decreased by one-half in 1906, and decreased further in 1907. This was due partly to the fact that Dalny was again without a customs house, but chiefly to the disastrous effects of the war on the interior. In 1908, a healthy revival set in, and the total imports increased steadily throughout Manchuria, especially with the opening of Antung, Mukden, and the important cities of the North. American trade, however, improved but little and soon began to fall off. In 1908 and 1909, American consuls reported serious decreases in the amount of goods coming from the United States. In 1910, our imports had fallen to a comparatively insignificant figure, and our trade in cotton goods, that is, the great bulk of all our trade, had largely passed into foreign hands. Our position of leadership in the Manchurian market was lost.

The nation which almost alone profited by this immense decline in American trade was Japan. In order to explain the great commercial advance of this power in Manchuria, it is necessary to sketch briefly the history of her systematic attempts to secure markets there for her products.

In the first place, Japan's geographical location gives her a decided advantage over Western nations competing with her for Manchurian trade. She is far nearer to China than any of her rivals, and is thus able to maintain regular, efficient, and cheap transportation with all of the ports in Shenking Province and with Vladivostok, where many goods are imported for use in the North. Her ownership of Korea makes it possible for her to send quick freight from Tokio to Harbin almost all the way by rail, over the Korean railroad and the Antung-Mukden line. She has a further advantage in her practical monopoly of the foreign export trade of the provinces, since a firm in China which does not do exporting as well as importing is exposed to serious financial difficulties from the variations in the rate of exchange.

Japan has not only made the most of her natural advantages in order to secure for herself the trade of Manchuria, but she has also taken extraordinary measures to assist her exporters. She had always enjoyed the greater part of the shipping and a fair share of the commerce of the provinces, but even before her war with Russia ended, it became evident that she intended to take advantage of her military occupation of the country to establish her trade still more firmly. Great quantities of goods were sent into the interior, and after the conclusion of peace, the transports which carried the army home made their return trips profitable by bringing thousands of immigrants, who established themselves everywhere as farmers and merchants. While these merchants were doing an excellent business, foreign traders were rigorously excluded from the interior on the ground that military secrets were involved. It was asserted that the Japanese, supported by their troops, refused to pay the likin dues to which the goods of other nationalities were subjected, and further that they seized all of the desirable land in the cities which, according to treaty provisions, were soon to be opened to foreign trade. All concessions obtained or claimed by the Russians were taken over by the Japanese as a matter of course. In the summer of 1906, a great industrial and commercial exposition was held at Mukden to promote interest in Japanese products, and similar expositions were subsequently organized in other cities. Great quantities of Japanese goods were brought in duty-free at Dalny and over the Korean boundary, while other foreign goods were going through the customs house at Newchwang. These conditions were ameliorated with the gradual opening of the interior in 1906 and 1907, and comparative equality of opportunity was again restored when customs houses at Dalny, Antung and Tatungkou, ports which had formerly been under Japanese control, were established on July 1, 1907.

Equality of opportunity, however, could not be said to exist. Japan still retained control of the railroad, and, to a certain extent, of the financial system. By means of the railroad, she attempted to divert the trade of Newchwang to Dalny, or Dairen, as it is now officially called, by discriminatory rates, much as Russia had done. This policy has undoubtedly increased the commercial importance of the latter, although the former is still the chief port of entry. Japan also retained a certain amount of control over the currency of the provinces, which gave her banks an opportunity practically to regulate the rate of exchange. During the war with Russia, Manchuria had been flooded with Japanese "war notes," which were called in after the conclusion of peace and exchanged for notes issued by the Yokohama Specie Bank. These made up a large part of the currency, especially in Shenking, and were naturally a great aid in establishing a strong Japanese banking system.

When Manchuria was finally re-opened to foreign trade, Japanese products had secured a firm footing in the interior. Foreign merchants believed that this would be lost with the removal of the extraordinary advantages conferred by military occupation, but it soon became evident that even with the "open door" Japan was now a very dangerous competitor. The imperial government and the great business interests of the country united in a systematic attempt to get control of the import as well as the export trade of Japan's new "sphere of influence," as a part of their general scheme for national economic and industrial development. The liberal and progressive element, which was in complete political control after leading the nation to victory over Russia, extended the time-honored system of economic paternalism and did every thing in its power to promote the national industrial prosperity. The railways were already owned by the government, and the steamship lines were controlled through large subsidies. Manufactures were encouraged, and where an industry was injured by competition a trust was formed and placed under government supervision. For the surplus manufacturing products, and especially for those of the cotton mills, Manchuria offered an excellent outlet, if the United States could only be ousted from its commercial leadership there. The government and the manufacturers accordingly turned their attention to this task.

On May 30, 1906, the *Jiji Shimpo* announced that several large Japanese spinning and weaving companies had united in the Manchurian Export Gild, to advance their common interests and to export their goods under a common trade-mark. The Mitsui Bussan Kaisha, the leading commercial house of Japan, was to act as the general agent of this gild in Manchuria, and the Yokohama Specie Bank and other institutions were to loan money at 4½ per cent to merchants doing business there to enable them to purchase Japanese goods. The government guaranteed these loans, and also secured favorable rates on the railroads and on the subsidized steamship lines. In Manchuria itself, permanent representatives were appointed at all important towns, and travelling salesmen, well equipped with samples of goods and speaking Chinese fluently, were sent throughout the country. The consuls in the Eastern Provinces offered every possible assistance, and the manufacturers at home carefully followed their suggestions. In addition, commercial students, paid by the government, and under the direction of the nearest consul, studied the trade conditions in each locality, and their reports enabled the export houses to work more intelligently than was possible for those of other nations. In Japan itself, the mills steadily endeavored to improve the quality of their output, which was at first of a very inferior grade, and finally succeeded in making it nearly as good as, while far cheaper than, similar Western products.

This policy has met with remarkable success. In spite of the ingrained respect of Chinese merchants for long established trade-marks, and in spite of the intense unpopularity of Japanese goods caused by the dispute over the seizure of the steamer Tatsu Maru in 1908, and by the resentment among the Chinese at the Japanese policy in Manchuria itself, the imports of cotton goods from the Island Empire have now taken the leading place in the Manchurian market.

The methods used to attain this position have been severely criticised. The counterfeiting of trade-marks, in particular, has caused much bitterness on the part of the Western merchants, and strenuous efforts have been made to secure adequate protection against this practice. In 1904, in accordance with her treaty obligations, China adopted a series of regulations for this purpose, which have proved entirely inadequate. In the following years, the United States made agreements with numerous powers for mutual protection by means of the consular courts in China, but Japan did not enter into such a compact. Trade-marks are of even more importance in China than in occidental countries, because the Chinese consumer always endeavors to secure the brand he has been accustomed to use, recognizing it by the trade-mark.

The decline of American trade in Manchuria is due primarily to Japanese competition, but the development of the native Chinese industries is a factor that should not be overlooked. The trade in native goods profited greatly from the steady decline in the value of silver which set in after the war, since this made the silver prices of foreign articles, which were manufactured by laborers paid in gold, much higher than those of goods made by laborers who still received their customary wages in silver. Chinese cotton goods, manufactured chiefly at Shanghai, have been gaining in popularity in Manchuria for at least ten years, since they are low-priced and are said to be of durable quality. The once large importations of American flour had already ceased before the war. After the war the mills in the North were unable to distribute their products in the South because of the destruction of part of the railroad, and great quantities of American flour were brought in. This importation practically ceased with the withdrawal of the army and the rebuilding of the railroad, and American flour is not now seen in Manchuria. . . .

YOU CAN'T TELL ROOSEVELT A THING[1] *Fred H. Harrington*

September 30, 1903, was a memorable date in the life of Horace Allen. On that day the doctor brought his diplomatic career to a climax by crossing swords with Theodore Roosevelt, president of the United States. The clash, a bitter one, took in the whole field of American Far Eastern policy, revealing a conflict that was fundamental then and continued so in the years to follow.

For a half decade before the interview Allen had been watching the Japanese gain strength in Seoul. In the Russian period he had considered Nippon "powerful enough to put a brake to the wheel." When Russia yielded power, in 1898, he saw "the Japanese . . . obtaining great influence." Soon there was an "amazing increase" in Japan's importance in Chosen, the native politicians being "chiefly controlled" from Tokyo. As early as 1899 Allen had reported, "gradually Japan has become aggressive here until they now seem to regard Korea as their own peculiar sphere of action and all others to be mere interlopers." Shortly thereafter he asserted that with Russia holding back, Japanese control of Chosen appeared to him "inevitable"; and down to 1903 there was no cause to change this view.

Japan had not advanced without resistance. Her every gain had been contested bitterly. Koreans had opposed her, Allen and his friends had put hurdles in her way, the Russians had tried to meet her challenge, all to no avail. Japan had come to stay.

Russia provided the severest competition. . . .

Yet, though the Russians took some tricks, Japan had the game in hand.

[1] Selected from *God, Mammon and the Japanese: Dr. Horace N. Allen and Korean-American Relations, 1884–1905* (Madison: University of Wisconsin Press, 1944), pp. 302–303, 305, 306, 309–10, 311–13, 314, 315–17. Reprinted with permission.

Her commerce far outran that of her rivals, her tonnage accounted for three fourths of all Korea's foreign trade. To balance the Russian artisans and French advisers she had thousands on thousands of colonists in all the major cities of Korea, and was pushing inland. While Russia talked of railroad possibilities, the Japanese had the Seoul-Chemulpo in operation and had started on the line to Fusan. So with the sea; Japan had forty thousand fishermen off the Chosen coast, and, with a later grant, outran the Russians in the whaling business. Fusan was all but ceded to Nippon after Russia had been denied the right to lease near-by Deer Island. Russian diplomats selecting land at Masampo found they had been anticipated, that the Japanese had bought the choicest property from native owners. And Baron Gunzburg's lumbermen, starting far behind their schedule, ran into island men who were ignoring Russian rights and felling Korean trees by arrangement with local dignitaries.

* * *

And as for Allen and the Americans? Theirs was the fate of the Koreans who favored neither the Mikado nor the Tsar—they were ground between two stones. Japan advancing. Russia in retreat....

In advising the [Korean] monarch and in laboring for his own countrymen, Allen ran head on into the clash between Japan and Russia. Time after time he had to choose between the two contestants, take sides in a quarrel not properly his own. Precedent would have allowed him either side. Years back, in the Manchu period, he had been pro-Japanese. Then, with Nippon on top, he had befriended Russia. Speyer had made him shift again, over to Japan; and in 1898 he was not sure just where he wished to go.

While still wavering, the doctor applied one of his oldest rules of thumb. He fought each move that meant monopoly and consequent loss of opportunity for the United States. Thus he joined forces with the Japanese and English representatives to block a projected Franco-Russian customs loan of 1901; (and perhaps, as one observer said, "his attitude went a long way towards helping the Emperor to make up his mind"). Again, he worked with other diplomats to force the opening of north Korean ports, giving trade to the Americans and helping to prevent the Russians from taking over there. Here, twice, the doctor had cooperated with the Japanese. As he also helped Japan in railroad matters, some came to feel that he favored the cause of Japan. Or, as one London journalist would have it, Allen "had no doubts whatsoever as to which side he should take in the long struggle between Russia on the one hand and Great Britain and Japan on the other."

This, though, was not the case. Allen had helped the islanders in what he thought to be the interests of America. He had no love for Japan....

Allen hesitated long before he took this stand. It was wise, he thought, to curb Japan; but it was far from easy to cooperate with the "treacherous" Russian agents in Seoul. Gunzburg and Matunin seemed reluctant to admit Americans like Hunt to their north Korean exploitation schemes. Pavloff's personality annoyed Allen (it was like the doctor's own) and Mrs. Pavloff, still in her teens, was far too gay a person for the straightlaced envoy from the United States. Worst of all was Ye Yong Ik, who positively refused to work with the Americans. "He has the idea that whatever is done to the

Americans will not be resented," commented Allen bitterly, "and his advice always opposes us so that even the most trivial matters of routine cannot be put through." But, be that as it might, it was advisable to throw a barrier in Japan's way. It was just possible that Korea might be saved; if not, there might at least be some hope for the Manchurian area beyond.

By 1903 the doctor was convinced that there was. And, being sure, he was prepared to do missionary work on his superiors, to preach his diplomatic gospel in true proselyting style. Not with dispatches, which headed straight for pigeon-hole obscurity. It must be done in person, while the Allens were on leave.

* * *

On the trip to Washington Allen's pro-Russian views were put to the test. For he and Fannie made the trip by way of Russia, travelling over the newly opened trans-Siberian railway. And they found much wrong with Russia. Siberian houses were "not nearly so good as the Korean peasant huts." The condition of the people was hopeless. They counted for nothing, were kept ignorant while the aristocracy was shamefully extravagant. There was inefficiency on every side, so many officials that none took any initiative; "the power house has a tile floor but the lights went out while we were at dinner." "Russia will have a severe awakening when she comes to a clash with Japan," was the traveller's first impression, "unless the red tape forms of the latter serve to counter-balance Russian tom foolery."

All true, but there was another aspect, which was to linger longest in the doctor's mind. This was the vastness of the Russian state, which seemed to guarantee a noble future. Moving along hour after hour one could not help feeling that this was a *"wonderful country* . . . an enormous country . . . It could almost accommodate the world. One cannot help feeling angry at the stupid blunder of England and Germany in preventing this vast country from getting an outlet on the Mediterranean. It simply bottled her up and made her phiz until she blew a vent hole for herself on the China sea, just as she will surely blow another on the Persian Gulf if she is kept in . . . on that side. There must be a great future for all this country."

Reaching the United States, Allen lost no time in expressing his views. He talked with Henry White the diplomat and the lawyer Joseph Choate, both of whom seemed to be impressed. Then he "went to Dep't and started things." On his way to Roosevelt he talked with his old friend, that "splendid fellow," W. W. Rockhill.

* * *

Rockhill, of course, was the man to see; but the interview gave Allen little satisfaction. The doctor was convinced that the United States should aid the Russians, in Manchuria at any rate; Rockhill was just as sure that the Japanese should be supported, should be allowed to swallow Chosen and should be helped to check the Tsarist drive to get Manchuria.

Disappointed, Allen went to Roosevelt "and told him he was making a mistake regarding Russia." Had the minister seen Rockhill, asked the chief executive. Yes, Allen had. Then all must get together, said the president, be at the White House at nine-thirty in the evening.

Toothaches are likely to come at inconvenient times. One came to Allen on that last day of September as he waited for the evening to arrive. Already uneasy at the thought of facing Roosevelt, he became extremely restless. Hour by hour his nervousness and irritation grew beyond the point of self-control.

The result was just what might have been expected. Roosevelt's "trip-hammer queries" rattled Allen, as did the chief executive's attempts to twist the doctor's words to form a Rooseveltian pattern. Whereupon the conversation took on a tone of violence, with the president insisting and Allen crying out, "I didn't say anything of the kind."

Before the fireworks started, Allen outlined his Russophile position, centering on the vital question of Manchuria. Roosevelt had erred, the doctor said, in opposing Russian occupation and acceptance of the Open Door. Because of trade, for one thing. Russia had opened up a "great commercial field" in pacifying Manchuria and constructing roads and railroads there; and "75% of this great and growing trade [was] coming to us." Would the president desire to sacrifice such gains?

Unwise commercially, the Rockhill-Roosevelt outlook was also pointless. Allen thought it foolish to suggest that Russia would yield hard-won supremacy; "there was no more likelihood of her voluntarily evacuating Manchuria than there was that we should evacuate Texas or to make the example better Hawaii."

Finally, Allen believed that the administration attitude made the United States the cats-paw of Britain and Japan. In fighting Russia, America appeared to be "getting the chestnuts out of the fire" for this imperial pair. If Roosevelt continued on this line, he "would undoubtedly lead Japan to count upon assistance from us which would lead her to adopt a too bellicose attitude towards Russia." After that, reluctantly or willingly, "we would simply be forced into more or less of an alliance with England & Japan."

Roosevelt took issue with the doctor on every point; and Rockhill backed up his chief in most impressive fashion. On trade affairs Rockhill accused Allen of "simply advocating a time serving policy in the interests of commerce." Such a policy was improper, all the more so since it was unnecessary. Anti-Russian action would not impair our chances in Manchuria, "the Russian Governm't had fully sanctioned all our attempts to secure the 'Open Door' and ... they favored our getting the open ports." With everything assured, a shift in policy would show inconsistency, "would simply 'stultify' ourselves and injure our standing."

Answering, Allen suggested that Russia might meet opposition from America with an attack upon the trade of the United States. No, snapped Roosevelt in his sharpest tone, the government had assurances on that point; and he had Rockhill say the same.

The chief executive also attacked Allen's claim that Japan would expect support. He had Rockhill "endorse him in saying that Japan had given the greatest assurance that she must under no consideration count on anything of the kind." Well, stated Allen, both Tokyo and St. Petersburg would know that moral aid was there; for a year G. Hayashi in Seoul had said "that the U.S. and England were friends and both were very strong friends of

Japan and that the United States was almost the same as in the Japan-English Alliance." A good blow, the doctor thought, but Roosevelt and Rockhill "had full swing" and the minister to Chosen could get nowhere.

Allen had called the Roosevelt position pointless. How so, the aggressive president seems to have asked; who would win if Russia and Japan should meet in war? Japan on the sea, asserted Allen, perhaps also on land. Well then, why back a loser? Simply because Russia "wanted us to have all her trade we could handle," insisted the envoy to Korea, while "Japan was just the opposite and would make us increasing trouble until we might have to cross swords with her."

But it was useless, absolutely useless, to try to convert Roosevelt. The president could not stand interference, saw only what he wanted to see, "like the Kaiser could not be crossed." Allen could do nothing but retire, expressing his regret that he had made so poor a showing, that he had reached his conclusions after a tour through the Russian empire and had stated them "as a duty."

So far, so good. Rockhill rightly censured Allen for excess of zeal, for being far too blunt with his country's chief of state. The matter might have ended there. But Allen smarted under what he took to be ill treatment, itched to appeal from Roosevelt to the people of America. Thus was he betrayed into insubordination. On his way back to Korea, the doctor gave a "careful interview" to Edward Rittenhouse, then editor of the *Daily Telegraph* of Colorado Springs. The Associated Press snapped up the statement and it was broadcast throughout the land, in sharp defiance of the State Department and the president of the United States.

AMERICAN-RUSSIAN RIVALRY

IN THE FAR EAST[1]   *Edward H. Zabriskie*

. . . Faced by Russia's persistence in staking off Manchuria as her own special preserve, Hay gradually retreated to his attitude in the first Open Door notes, apparently resigning himself to the fact that Manchuria was no longer an integral part of the Chinese Empire, but virtually a Russian protectorate, in which an Open Door for the United States was dependent upon the outcome of the diplomatic duel being waged between the two powers. On April 28, Hay wrote to Roosevelt:

I take it for granted that Russia knows as we do that we will not fight over Manchuria, for the simple reason that we cannot. . . . If our rights and interests in opposition to Russia in the Far East were as clear as noonday, we could never get a treaty through the Senate, the object of which was to check Russian aggression.

In a second letter to the President on the same day, Hay commented:

[1] Selected from *American-Russian Rivalry in the Far East: A Study in Diplomacy and Power Politics, 1895–1914* (Philadelphia: University of Pennsylvania Press, 1946), pp. 89–108. Reprinted with permission.

The only hopeful symptom is that they [the Russians] are really afraid of Japan. They know perfectly well that there is nothing in the situation which we would consider as justifying us in a resort to arms, but they know that, it would require the very least encouragement on the part of the United States or England to induce Japan to seek a violent solution of the question.

Meanwhile, the Russian Government was a house divided against itself. The Ministries of War and Finance, with their respective satellites, were powerful rivals. One, represented by the so-called palace clique and the military, were all for an aggressive policy and the building of strategic railroads; the other, with Witte as the dominant force, favored peaceful economic penetration of Manchuria. And the Tsar, while inclined toward the aggressive policy, occasionally acted as seemed best to His Imperial Majesty, without benefit of ministers. . . .

Meanwhile, the Japanese Government on July 28, 1903, proposed to Russia a general consideration of their mutual relations in the Far East. Russia accepted, and on August 12 received a draft of the Japanese demands, in which not only the interests of Japan but those of the other powers were upheld. Article I states that both powers agree to "respect the independence and territorial integrity of the Chinese and Korean Empires," as well as the principle of the Open Door. This is followed by the crux of the draft agreement which provides for

Reciprocal recognition of Japan's preponderating interests in Korea and Russia's special interest in railway enterprises in Manchuria, and of the right of Japan to take in Korea and of Russia to take in Manchuria such measures as may be necessary for the protection of their respective interests . . . subject to the provisions of Article I.

The Japanese draft collided sharply with the feudal-imperialist plans of the Bezobrazov clique, whose power to shape Russia's Far Eastern policy was rapidly increasing. In addition, on the same day that the Japanese note was presented to St. Petersburg, Admiral Alexeiev was appointed Viceroy of the Far East, by an Imperial decree which came "as a thunderbolt to disturb the East." By this appointment Alexeiev was released from the jurisdiction of the Tsar's ministers. Henceforward he received his orders directly from the Tsar. The organization of this Viceroyalty, comprising the Kwantung and Amur provinces (with Manchuria between) was interpreted by Japanese statesmen as signifying that Russia planned to incorporate Manchuria into the Russian Empire. Japan was additionally aggrieved over the fact that the creation of this new department in the Far East meant the passing of the control of Far Eastern affairs from the Russian Foreign Office into the hands of Viceroy Alexeiev and his friends Bezobrazov and Abasa. . . .

The outbreak of hostilities between Russia and Japan came as a surprise to Europe, which had been assured by the foreign offices of St. Petersburg, Berlin, and Paris that no danger of immediate war existed. The Tsar had also written to the Kaiser early in December 1903, guaranteeing that there would be no war because he, the Tsar, did not wish it. At the same time, the German Foreign Office gave assurance to the American ambassador, up to the actual break in Russo-Japanese negotiations, that war could be avoided.

Yet the United States had played an important part in the precipitation of hostilities. The vigorous policy this country had pursued in protection of her trade interests and ambitions in Manchuria revealed her attitude toward Russia, her determination to have a place of her own in the Manchurian sun. More direct, however, in its bearing upon the initiative taken by the Japanese at Port Arthur was the assurance given by the American Government to the Japanese Government on January 12, 1904, nearly a month before the outbreak of hostilities, that in case of war "the American policy would be benevolent toward Japan." This assurance, combined with the German affirmation of neutrality and the alliance between England and Japan, was the impetus that led the Japanese Government to take the reins into their own hands and declare war against Russia.

On February 11, the United States proclaimed neutrality. On the 12th China declared herself neutral. Meanwhile, acting upon the suggestion of the German Government, Secretary of State Hay had issued circulars to Great Britain, France, and Germany, calling upon them to urge the belligerents "to respect the neutrality of China and in all practicable ways her administrative entity." Although the initiative for the plea to the powers came from Germany, the Americanized version differed in one very vital point from the German model, which requested Russia and Japan "to respect the neutrality of China outside the sphere of military action." In other words, since the theater of the war was in Manchuria, that section was to be left free for Russian operations after the war.

Yes [wrote President Roosevelt], it was on the suggestion of "Bill the Kaiser" that we sent out the note on the neutrality of China. But the insertion of the word "entity" was ours. His suggestion originally was in untenable form; that is, he wanted us to guarantee the integrity of China south of the latitude of the Great Wall, which would have left Russia free to gobble up what she really wanted....

Russia, after consultation with Germany, refused to recognize the neutralization of Manchuria, and, turning to America, inquired, through Cassini, why the United States in her eagerness to deprive Russia of Manchuria had made no mention of the Japanese in Korea. American intentions, according to Cassini, were not clear.

Yet American intentions, in the light of documentary information, are clear. The United States, holding (together with England and Japan) a monopoly of foreign trade in Manchuria, knocking persistently upon doors that might close, demanding the integrity of China, had a vital interest in Manchuria and the outcome of the war. Kantorovich states that the Russo-Japanese War was not only an English but also an American war against Tsarist Russia and its policies of territorial conquests. Dennett agrees when he writes that no one can go through the records of 1898–1904 and not feel that Japan was fighting the battle of the United States in Manchuria. From surface appearances it was apparently to American interests that Japan, at that time considered weaker than Russia, should disturb the Russian over-balance in Manchuria. The United States considered that Japan, even if victor, would be more pliable than Russia backed by France. Hence, the bias of the American Government and also of its reflection, the American public, was unquestionably pro-Japanese at the beginning of the Russo-Japanese War.

President Roosevelt, influenced no doubt by the usual mixed motives of the human being, immediately threw his vigorous weight on the side of Japan. His sympathies were with this small, apparently under-dog of an island kingdom. But the commercial, industrial, and possibly political interests of the United States in Manchuria were also at stake. Her fate in the Far East might be sealed by the outcome of the war.

In a confidential letter to one of his sons, written two days after the Japanese attack upon the Russian fleet off Port Arthur, President Roosevelt wrote in part as follows:

It has certainly opened most disastrously for the Russians and their supine carelessness is well-nigh incredible. For several years Russia has behaved very badly in the Far East, her attitude toward all nations, including us, but especially toward Japan, being grossly overbearing. We had no sufficient cause for war with her. Yet I was apprehensive lest if she at the outset whipped Japan on the sea she might assume a position well-nigh intolerable toward us. I thought Japan would probably whip her on the sea, but I could not be certain; and between ourselves—for you must not breathe it to anybody— I was thoroughly well pleased with the Japanese victory, for Japan is playing our game.

Yet, however vigorous President Roosevelt was, especially in the early stages of hostilities, in expression of both his official and unofficial anti-Russian bias, he at no time favored Japanese predominance in Manchuria. His purpose, as shown at an early stage of the war, was to give Japan a free hand in Korea, to render her asistance, both morally and financially in her fight to loosen the clutch of Russia in Manchuria, with its menace to American commercial and industrial interests to prolong the war for a sufficient length of time to exhaust both Russia and Japan, and to leave a weakened Russia and a strengthened Japan facing each other at the end of the war, thereby equalizing the Manchurian balance of power. A war from which both powers would emerge financially, economically, and physically drained, with their appetites for territory temporarily appeased, would better serve the economic and commercial interests of the American republic....

THE EXPANSIONIST OUTLOOK OF
PRESIDENT WOODROW WILSON[1]

Martin J. Sklar

Perhaps the greatest source of historical misconception about Woodrow Wilson is the methodological compartmentalization of his mentality into two distinct components, the "moralistic" and the "realistic" or "commercialistic," as if they were discrete and mutually exclusive. From this point of departure, if one thinks or acts "moralistically," he can not be considered capable at the same time of thinking and acting "realistically," at least not consistently: if one is a "moralist," his political behavior can be considered as deriving only secondarily, if at all, from an understanding of, or a serious concern for, the affairs of political economy.

[1] Selected from "Woodrow Wilson and the Political Economy of Modern United States Liberalism," *Studies on the Left*, I, No. 3 (1960), 17–47. Reprinted with permission.

According to this approach, wherever Wilson is perceived to have spoken or acted for the "little man," "democracy," "liberty," "individual opportunity," and the like, he was "liberal" and moralistic; wherever he is perceived to have spoken or acted for corporate interests, economic expansion abroad, and the like, he was "conservative," "commercialistic," "expedient," or realistic. Where Wilson supported measures promoting large corporate interests at home or abroad, he is considered to have forsaken his moralism, to have been driven by political expediency, personal egoism, or implacable social and economic forces, or to have gathered the unintended consequences of a misdirected moralism. In this view, Wilson the moralist is generally considered the true type, and Wilson the realist, the deviant.

Aside from objections that may be raised against the naiveté and theoretical deficiencies of such an approach to social thought and ideology in general, certain specific objections may be raised against such an approach to Wilson, particularly should the main ideological components generally attributed to Wilson's mentality be granted at the outset, and their implications accorded a modicum of examination.

First, the "Puritan ethic," to which students of Wilson have attached fundamental importance as basic to his mentality, made no such mutually exclusive distinction between a transcendent morality and the world of political economy. Puritanism embraced a morality applicable not merely to the world beyond, but as well to the living individual and existing society; it sanctioned, indeed posited, capitalist social and economic relations. The affirmation of capitalist society was therefore implicit in Wilson's Protestant morality. From the straightest-laced New England Puritan of the seventeenth century to Poor Richard's Benjamin Franklin, to Gospel-of-Wealth Andrew Carnegie, to New Freedom Woodrow Wilson, religious conviction and "market-place materialism" were each practical, each the uplifting agent of civilization and Providence, each the necessary condition for personal salvation and general human improvement, each a function of the other, mutually interdependent and interwoven like the white and purple threads of the single holy cloth. To the extent, then, that Puritanism entered significantly into Wilson's world-view, the affirmation of the capitalist system in the United States (and throughout the world) was a function of his morality, not merely an auxiliary prepossession.

Second, Wilson's moral affirmation of capitalism sanctioned by Puritan conceptions found powerful confirmation in the economic writings of Adam Smith (himself a professor of moral philosophy), John Bright, and Richard Cobden; as student and professor he had become firmly grounded in their theories of political economy which he admired and enthusiastically espoused, and it is not difficult to perceive that such writings would strongly appeal to one reared on Puritanism. In Smith, Bright, and Cobden, Wilson found secular moral sanction for the bourgeois-democratic political economy as well as indefeasible economic principles. Private, competitive enterprise manifested natural law in the realm of political economy, and went hand in hand with republican institutions, comprising together the essential conditions of democracy, individual liberty, and increasing prosperity. To Wilson, much of whose economic thinking was based upon the assumption of the growing superiority of United States industry, the arguments of Smith, Cobden, and Bright were compelling: they, in their day, spoke for an industrially supreme Great Britain, and recognizing Britain's position, argued that the optimum condition for the nation's economic growth and expansion rested upon the "natural" flow of trade, a "natural" international division of labor, uninhibited by "artificial" hindrances.

Taken together, Puritanism and Smithian-Manchestrian economics instilled Wilson with the compulsion to serve the strengthening and extending of the politico-economic system he knew in the United States as a positively moralistic commitment, since that would strengthen and extend the sphere of liberty, democracy, prosperity, and Providence, and accorded with natural law. As William Diamond observes, such assumptions were to become "basic" to Wilson's "thought on foreign policy."

Third and finally, the organismic view of society that Wilson derived from Edmund Burke and Walter Bagehot provided him with the concept that whatever social phenomena or social system evolved "naturally" from the traditions and customs of the past, from the working of natural law through "irresistible" social forces, were not only inevitable as prescriptively ordained but morally indisputable. They represented both the evolution of the genius of human custom and institutions and the assertion of God's will in human affairs. To Burke, whom Wilson revered and assiduously studied, the market economy manifested the working of natural law, which in turn manifested divine law. In Burke, Wilson could find a reverence for the market economy akin to religious awe: "the laws of commerce ...are the laws of nature, and consequently the laws of God," Burke had said. American Puritan doctrine, as developed by Jonathan Edwards, had itself become firmly anchored in the natural law of Newton and Locke; it required the intensive study of society's concrete development and condition, in order to comprehend God's work in the universe. In this respect, Puritanism and Burke stood on common ground. Here both religious and secular morality converged upon the affirmation of things as they were and as they appeared to be evolving. That which was "natural" was moral. The part of wisdom, morality, and statesmanship was to comprehend, affirm, and work for the necessary institutional adjustments to, "natural" evolution and "the well-known laws of value and exchange." This evolutionary-positivist or conservative-historicist approach to society served to modify whatever predilections Wilson may have had for atomized economic relations; it provided him with philosophical ground for rejecting the doctrine of unrestricted competition, as did the institutional economists he encountered at Johns Hopkins in the 1880's, and for affirming, as an inevitable result of the laws of commerce and natural social evolution, the demise of the freely competing entrepreneur at the hands of the large corporation. As Wilson once remarked, explaining his approval of large-scale industrial corporations, "...No man indicts natural history. No man undertakes to say that the things that have happened by operation of irresistible forces are immoral things...."

That prior to 1912–1914 Wilson had been a firm advocate of United States economic expansion abroad is a matter of record upon which there is general agreement by historians. His views in this respect have been sufficiently observed and analyzed elsewhere. The main elements of his thought may be briefly summarized here. As an early adherent of Turner's frontier thesis Wilson defined the nation's natural political-economic development and its prosperity as a function of westward expansion. With the end of the continental frontier, expansion into world markets with the nation's surplus manufactured goods and capital was, in his view, indispensable to the stability and prosperity of the economy. It was also no more than a natural development in the life of any industrial nation, and, to him, in no way morally invidious since in his view, the nation's economic expansion was a civilizing force that carried with it principles of democracy and Christianity as well as bonds of international understanding and peace. Given the United States' superior industrial efficiency she would assume supremacy in the world's markets, provided artificial barriers to her economic expansion were eliminated. Accordingly, Wilson admired and championed Hay's open door policy and advocated vigorous government diplomacy and appropriate government measures to attain the ends in view.

Within this broad framework of thought, the application of the expanding-frontier image to economic expansion abroad, assumed a significance more fundamental than the invocation of a romantic metaphor: the West had been developed by the extension of railroads, the opening of mines, the development of agriculture—in short by the extension of the sphere of enterprise and investment that resulted in the widening of the internal market and fed the growth of large-scale industry. Markets for manufactured goods were in this way actively *developed, created,* in the West, by the metropolitan industrial and finance capitalists, and not without the significant aid of the federal government. Similarly with such markets abroad: foreign investments and industrial exports were seen by the corporate interests most heavily involved and by like-minded political leaders, such as Wilson, as going hand in hand, centered as their concern was on the needs of an industrial capitalist system in general and heavy industry in particular. Accordingly, the idea of "development" of agrarian areas in other parts of the world, and "release of energies," is prominent in Wilson's approach to economic expansion abroad.

Wilson's emphasis on exports of manufactures, his belief in their indispensability to the nation's prosperity, and his conception that the government should play a leading role in these matters, coincided in every essential respect with the views of the so-called Dollar Diplomatists, and of large corporate spokesmen within the U.S. Chamber of Commerce, the American Asiatic Association, the Pan-American Society, the American Manufacturers Export Association, and the National Foreign Trade Council. In like manner his advocacy of appropriate government measures to encourage an effective merchant marine and adequate international banking facilities flowed from this common concern for expanding the economic frontier; and his support of a low tariff was in large part informed by his belief that it was necessary to the nation's assumption of its proper role in world economic affairs.

But these were not merely the views of a supposedly "early" Wilson, later to be abandoned by the "New Freedom" Wilson; on the contrary, he carried them most emphatically, along with programmatic proposals, into his presidential campaign of 1912. Wilson's consistent theme, in this respect, during his bid for the presidency, is summarized in his address accepting the Democratic Party's presidential nomination: "... Our industries have expanded to such a point that they will burst their jackets if they cannot find a free outlet to the markets of the world ... Our domestic markets no longer suffice. We need foreign markets. ... " The alternative, as he had previously put it, was "a congestion that will operate calamitously upon the economic conditions of the country." The economic imperatives, therefore, required institutional adjustments on the governmental and private business levels to break an outmoded "chysalis," in order to "relieve the plethora," and "use the energy of the [nation's] capital." They also pointed to "America's economic supremacy" (a phrase which Wilson shared with Brooks Adams): "... if we are not going to stifle economically, we have got to find our way out into the great international exchanges of the world"; the nation's "irresistible energy ... has got to be released for the commercial conquest of the world," for "making ourselves supreme in the world from an economic point of view." He stressed three major reforms to meet the new necessities of the time—the downward revision of the tariff, the development of a strong merchant marine ("The nation that wants foreign commerce must have the arms of commerce"), and laws permitting foreign branch banking tied to a commercial-acceptance system ("... this absolutely essential function of international trade ... ").

Wilson's concern for the promotion of foreign trade and investment found expression in some of his key appointments upon assuming the presidency. To China, for example, he sent Paul S. Reinsch, long a prominent spokesman for economic expansion abroad. He appointed his intimate friend, Walter H. Page, as ambassador to Great Britain; as editor of *World's Work*, Page had published a series of articles on such topics as "the industrial conquest of the world," to which Reinsch contributed. Wilson's appointments of Edward N. Hurley and George L. Rublee to the newly formed Federal Trade Commission proved decisive, in its first few years, in making it a leading agency of foreign trade promotion, an aspect of its activities that was not then widely anticipated nor since been sufficiently appreciated.

Wilson appointed William C. Redfield to head the Department of Commerce, which, with its Bureau of Foreign and Domestic Commerce, shared with the State Department the central responsibility within the federal government for promoting foreign economic expansion. It is a mistake to dismiss Redfield, as Link does with the remark that "perhaps his chief claim to fame was the fact that he was the last man in American public life to wear side whiskers. ... " For Redfield was a prominent member of the corporate community, enjoying the respect and confidence of corporate leaders. As a New York manufacturer of iron and steel products he spent many years abroad developing markets and as a "business statesman" much of his time expounding the theme of expansion and downward revision of the tariff. Like Wilson he had been a gold-Democrat, and the views of the two men were strikingly similar in matters of trade expansion and the tariff. Indeed, Wilson, in January, 1912, acknowledged that "I primed myself on Mr. Redfield's [tariff] speeches." Of greater significance, indicating Redfield's prominence in the corporate community and the degree to which he represented corporate opinion, Redfield had been president of the American Manufacturers Export Association (organized in 1910), which, to use Robert A. Brady's terminology, was a peak association of large corporate interests. As Secretary of Commerce, with Wilson's support and approval, he immediately undertook to reorganize the Bureau of Foreign and Domestic Commerce for more efficient service in promoting foreign trade, and submitted a bill to Congress for the creation of a system of commercial attachés and agents, and trade commissioners, which Congress passed in 1914. Between the two of them, Redfield and Hurley, again with Wilson's approval, instituted many of the mechanisms of business-government cooperation in domestic and foreign trade, including the encouragement of trade associations, that are usually regarded as initially introduced by Herbert Hoover while Secretary of Commerce during the 1920's. Finally, it is important to note that while Wilson permitted Secretary of State William Jennings Bryan to make many ambassadorial appointments on the basis of patronage obligations, he refused to permit Bryan to disturb the consular service.

Against this background, the attitude of corporation leaders toward the three major pieces of "New Freedom" legislation of 1913–1914 (Underwood Tariff, Federal Reserve, and Federal Trade Commission acts), as well as the extent to which that legislation affected foreign trade expansion and to which, in turn, the nature of the legislation was determined by considerations relating to such expansion, may be more clearly understood.

Between 1910 and 1914, corporate leaders, particularly those connected with the large corporations and banking houses, were unusually active in organizing themselves for the promotion of their interests and programmatic objectives in domestic and foreign affairs. In 1910 industrial corporations organized the American Manufacturers Export Association (AMEA); in 1912, these corporations, along with other business organizations, such as the American Asiatic Association (AAA), established the United States Chamber of Commerce; and in 1914 the AMEA, the AAA, and the Pan-American Society joined together to form the National Foreign Trade Council (NFTC). These were all what might be called "peak associations" of large corporate interests; but the NFTC may be legitimately considered a peak association of peak associations. The officers and memberships of these associations interlocked as intricately as did the directors of the huge industrial corporations and finance houses of the time.

Of the more significant manifestations of the Wilson administration's concern for the promotion of foreign trade and of the community of agreement between large corporate interests and that administration, therefore, one was its endorsement of the purposes of the first National Foreign Trade Convention, convened in Wastington, D.C., May 27 and 28, 1914. The Convention, presided over by Alba B. Johnson, and the National Foreign Trade Council subsequently established, with James A. Farrell as its president, were led and dominated by men representing the nation's greatest industrial, mercantile, and financial corporations. As Johnson related,

"This Convention had its inception at a meeting in New York some time ago" with Secretary of Commerce Redfield. He gave the idea for such a convention "his most cordial approval, and, therefore, it is fair to say" that he "is in a sense the Father of this Convention...." Edward N. Hurley, the first vice-chairman and later chairman of the Federal Trade Commission, also played a leading role in the organization of the Convention and in the Council's subsequent affairs.

The Convention met in the afterglow of Secretary of State Bryan's appearance, in January, 1914, as guest of honor at the annual dinner of the American Asiatic Association, of which Willard Straight was then president. At that time, the Underwood Tariff and Federal Reserve acts, measures most closely associated with the "New Freedom," had been passed by Congress. The Association's expressed purpose for inviting Bryan to the dinner, which was attended by leaders of the corporate community, was to exchange views with him on, and have him clarify, the administration's foreign policy. Emphasizing that the "era upon which we are entering is not only that of the Pacific Ocean, it must be one of Pacific development as well," Straight cited the new tariff as a stimulant for "carrying the war into the enemies' camp and competing abroad with those who will now invade our own market...." And to the cheers of the diners, he observed that with the Panama Canal and the opportunity provided by the reserve act for the extension of foreign banking and investment, "... we are in a better position than at any time in our history aggressively to undertake the development of our export trade." In response, Bryan pointed out that his duties as Secretary of State kept him "in touch with the expansion of American Commerce and the extension of American interests throughout the world," with which both he and the President were in "deep sympathy," as he assured the business men that the administration "will see that no industrial highwayman robs you. This government stands committed to the doctrine that these United States are entitled to the greatest possible industrial and commercial development." In this respect, like Straight, he singled out the tariff and reserve acts as decisive instrumentalities for giving the doctrine practical effect.

The administration's endorsement of the National Foreign Trade Convention the following May assumed tangible forms. Secretary of Commerce Redfield delivered opening address of the Convention on the morning of May 27 and he served as toastmaster at its banquet that night; Secretary of State Bryan delivered the main after-dinner speech at the banquet; and Wilson the next day received the delegates at the White House for a short interview.

As the Council later announced, the national importance of the Convention was "attested by the fact that its purpose [to promote foreign trade and a coordinated national foreign trade policy based upon the cooperation of government and business] was cordially indorsed by the President of the United States, who received the delegates at the White House; by the Secretary of State, who delivered, at the banquet, an outline of the administration's policy toward American business abroad; and by the Secretary of Commerce, who opened the convention...."

In his address to the delegates in the East Room of the White House, after having been introduced to them by Edward N. Hurley, Wilson declared his "wish to express . . . the feeling of encouragement that is given by the gathering of a body like this for such a purpose." For, he said, "There is nothing in which I am more interested than the fullest development of the trade of this country and its righteous conquest of foreign markets." Referring to Secretary Redfield's address of the previous day, Wilson confided: "I think that you will realize . . . that it is one of the things that we hold nearest to our heart that the government and you should cooperate in the most intimate manner in accomplishing our common object." He expressed the hope that this would be "only the first of a series of conferences of this sort with you gentlemen." In reply, Alba B. Johnson assured the President that as business men they realized "the deep interest which this government takes in promoting legitimate foreign trade. . . . "

Bryan delivered two addresses at the banquet on the night of May 27, 1914, the first a short, prepared statement for release to the press, the second a lengthier extemporaneous speech. In the prepared speech Bryan declared the administration "earnestly desirous of increasing American foreign commerce and of widening the field of American enterprise. . . . " He reiterated its intention to cooperate with the business community to the end, and speaking for his own department he emphasized its "earnest purpose" to "obtain for Americans equality of opportunity in the development of the resources of foreign countries and in the markets of the world." Accordingly it was his "intention to employ every agency of the Department of State to extend and safeguard American commerce and legitimate American enterprises in foreign lands," consistent with the "sovereign rights of other governments."

In his extemporaneous remarks, Bryan explained to the men of capital that his department's policy was Wilson's policy—what it "does in foreign affairs is but what the President desires." This meant, he said, "policies which will promote our industry abroad as well as home"; already, in the short time of the administration's existence, it had taken measures that would "tend directly and necessarily to promote commerce," such as the tariff and reserve acts. But "more than that," Bryan continued, the administration's efforts to win friends for the United States, safeguard the peace, and conclude commercial treaties constituted a broad contribution to the stabilization and extension of foreign economic expansion. "One sentence from President Wilson's Mobile speech has done a great deal to encourage commerce." When he there renounced territorial conquest as an object of United States policy in Latin America, " . . . he opened the doors of all the weaker countries to an invasion of American capital and American enterprise. (Applause.)" As Bryan had put it at the Asiatic Association dinner, " . . . The doctrine of universal brotherhood is not sentimentalism—it is practical philosophy . . . The government could not create trade, but it was its "duty" to "create an environment in which it can develop." He looked forward with "great expectations" to the extension of United States trade and investment abroad; the Convention itself provided "evidence that we are going forward," and the statistics showing the increase in exports of manufactured goods left "no doubt" that the United States could compete successfully with the European industrial nations "in the newer countries that are awaiting complete development," and that the United States would thus become "an increasing factor in the development" of such countries.

Bryan's approach to economic expansion exemplifies a unified world view, embracing "moralism" and "commercialism" as interdependent and mutually consistent elements, that was so common to the expansionists of the time; the underlying assumptions of the "Good Neighbor" policy of later administrations were not basically different; and like the policy of Wilson or Straight it emphasized not merely trade but also "development" of agrarian countries, and the government's responsibility to foster those operations.

Promising the complete support of his Department for the extension of markets and investments abroad, and inviting close co-operation between the business men and the State Department, Bryan told the corporate leaders, "I promise you that the State Department—every agency of it— will be back of every honest business man in pushing legitimate enterprise in all parts of the world. (Applause.)" To emphasize the community of purpose between the Department and the corporate interests, he continued by extending a colorful analogy: "In Spanish-speaking countries hospitality is expressed by a phrase, 'My house is your house.' . . . I can say, not merely in courtesy—but as a fact—my Department is your department; the ambassadors, the ministers and the consuls are all yours. It is their business to look after your interests and to guard your rights." If any of them failed to fulfill his responsibility, advised Bryan, "we shall be pleased to have you report them." For his part, the Department would "endeavor to open all doors to you. We shall endeavor to make all people friendly to you . . ."

Given the general approach to expansion shared by men such as Wilson, Straight, Bryan, and corporate spokesmen, the question of "inner" motive is somewhat irrelevant. For example, what may be said of Straight's "inner" motive when he spoke of trade as the means to peace; or of the Steel Corporation's president, James A. Farrell, when he told the Convention: " . . . there is no factor which is so much involved in . . . [the nation's] material prosperity as the export trade," and then proceeded to say that "due to its significance with respect to the economic conditions of our financial relations with the markets of the world, the export trade is likewise a vital factor in international affairs . . . The contest today is for supremacy in the trade of the world's markets, because that country which is a commercial power is also a power in other respects." The important point is that they held in common the assumption that expansion of markets and investment abroad was indispensable to the stability and growth of the political economy. As Redfield had put it at the banquet while introducing Bryan as the next speaker, the mission of his fellow diners was "to make this land of ours one of continual increasing prosperity." For he continued:

...we have learned the lesson now, that our factories are so large that their output at full time is greater than America's market can continuously absorb. We know now that if we will run full time all the time, we must do it by reason of the orders we take from lands beyond the sea. To do less than that means homes in America in which the husbands are without work; to do that means factories that are shut down part of the time. And because the markets of the world are greater and steadier than the markets of any country can be, and because we are strong, we are going out, you and I, into the markets of the world to get our share. (Applause.)

The record leaves no reason to doubt that the knowledgeable corporate leaders understood and accepted as genuine the administration's policy statements. The difficulty, in their view, lay not with the administration, but with the people. In this respect, upon closer examination, it is apparent that many of the pronouncements by business men in this period that have been interpreted as directed against the Wilson administration, were more often directed against an "unenlightened" public and/or hostile senators or congressmen. As one business man put it, the public must realize "that governmental assistance to American shipping and the American export trade is not only a business but a patriotic policy, pertaining to national defense as well as to our industrial welfare." Or as Willard Straight phrased it, under current conditions of public opinion, "any administration may be attacked if it utilizes the power of the Government for the profit of private interests, no matter what indirect advantage might accrue to the country as a whole." The problem was to educate the people to accept government support of private foreign investments as action not on behalf of a special, but of the national, interest.

In the context of Wilson's approach to both foreign trade and the "trust" question, and of the community of views between large corporate interests and his administration in these areas, the significance for foreign trade of the Federal Trade Commission Act, as the legislative embodiment of the Rule of Reason, may be better comprehended.

It was generally recognized in business circles that the large industrial corporations were most suited to successful export trade, and that the rapid rise in exports of manufacturers from the late 1890's to 1914 had been due largely to the operations of these corporations. The large corporations enjoyed low unit costs necessary for competition in world markets, particularly in the capital and durable goods industries. Their superior reserves and intimate connections with the great financial institutions enabled them to carry the expense of foreign sales promotion, offer attractive foreign credit facilities, and reap the benefits of foreign loans and concessions, all indispensable to an expanding and stable export trade. It was these corporations that were most intimately involved in the "development" of agrarian nations. Since the export of manufactured goods was considered primary in maintaining the nation's international exchanges, in liquidating foreign debts, and in guaranteeing domestic prosperity, the success of any business or governmental policy looking to the promotion of export trade and the achievement of these related objectives appeared to stand or fall with the large corporation. A domestic policy, therefore, designed to atomize large corporations could only prove self-defeating.

These were the points emphasized by such prominent spokesmen for large corporate interests as John D. Ryan, president of the Amalgamated Copper Company, M. A. Oudin of General Electric, and Alba B. Johnson of the Baldwin Locomotive Works. As Johnson put it, "To attack our business interests because by reason of intelligent management they have grown strong is to cripple them in the struggle for the world's trade." But their views, in so far as they related to the maintenance of large business units, were in no essential respect different from those of Wilson, whose attitude, as already indicated, may be summed up by the declaration in his Acceptance Speech: "...I am not afraid of anything that is normal."

It is important to note, therefore, that the criticisms of "antitrust" bills pending in Congress by speakers at the 1914 National Foreign Trade Convention were leveled not against Wilson and his administration, but against "radicals" in Congress and what was considered misguided and dangerous public opinion. They particularly applied to the policy of the previous Taft administration, which in its last year and a half had "mined the Sherman Act for all it was worth." But Wilson's position on the "trust" question was clear to all who read or heard his speeches, at any rate by early 1914; indeed, in his special address on the "trusts" to Congress in January, 1914, he had specifically declared, "...no measures of sweeping or novel change are necessary.... our object is *not* to unsettle business or anywhere seriously to break its established courses athwart." Programmatically his position centered upon the legislative proposals advanced since the Hepburn amendments of 1908–1909, by large corporate interests through such organizations as the Chicago Association of Commerce, the National Civic Federation, and later the Chamber of Commerce. And by the end of 1914, large corporate interests found that they could look with satisfaction upon the status of the nation's "antitrust" laws.

The "New Freedom" legislation on "trusts" bore upon matters of foreign trade expansion in a more overt way. In February, 1914, the Chamber of Commerce devoted its principal session, in which Secretary Redfield participated, to a discussion of the administration's trust program. It was here that the Chamber appointed its special committee on trade commission legislation, of which William L. Saunders and Rublee were members. Other members included president of the Chamber R. G. Rhett, Professor Henry R. Seager of Columbia University, Charles R. Van Hise, president of the University of Wisconsin, and Guy E. Tripp, chairman of the board of directors of the Westinghouse Electric Manufacturing Company. One of the committee's recommendations, issued in the spring of 1914, urged that Congress "direct the Commission [when established] to investigate and report to Congress at the earliest practicable date on the advisability of amending the Sherman Act to allow a greater degree of cooperation" in the export trade. By a vote of 538 to 67 the Chamber's membership approved this specific recommendation (as did the National Foreign Trade Convention in May, 1914), along with the broader one supporting a trade commission act. Accordingly, in the drafting of the act, which Rublee wrote, it was this Chamber committee that inserted word for word section 6(h), which authorized the trade commission to investigate world trade conditions and submit approximate recommendations to Congress. With Rublee and Hurley appointed by Wilson as two of the agency's five commissioners, the FTC undertook and completed in its first year of operation four investigations, three of which dealt with foreign trade conditions. One of these resulted in the two volume *Report on Cooperation in American Export Trade*, which recommended that Congress pass what was to become the Export Trade (Webb-Pomerene) Act of 1918 permitting cartels in the export trade, a bill which Wilson strongly supported.

The requirements of foreign trade promotion also influenced, in a negative way, the nature of the Clayton Act. As Oudin reported to the Foreign Trade Convention of May, 1914, " . . . the Committee on the Judiciary of the House . . . has reported a bill containing strict prohibitions against discriminations in prices for exclusive agencies, but providing that such prohibitions shall apply only in respect to commodities sold within the jurisdiction of the United States. This emphatic recognition of the distinction between domestic and export commerce reflects the growing disposition of the Government to render sympathetic assistance to American exporters. . . . "

Just as the character of "New Freedom" legislation concerning the regulation of business related to the requirements of foreign trade promotion and reflected a community of views between the corporate community and the Wilson administration, the same was true, as already indicated, of the two most important "New Freedom" laws passed in 1913, the Underwood Tariff and the Federal Reserve Acts.

When Bryan, in his banquet address to the Foreign Trade Convention delegates, cited the tariff and reserve acts as measures taken by the administration for the promotion of foreign trade, he was not assuming the posture of protesting too much, nor was he merely waxing politically expedient to please his audience: the large corporate spokesmen among the delegates analyzed the two laws in precisely the same way. The two laws, it should be noted, were passed against the background of a trend among large industrial and financial interests, which had visibly emerged at least a decade before, toward tariff and banking structures oriented (*inter alia*) to their foreign trade and investment requirements. Bryan pointed to the elementary principle underlying the new tariff: "if we are to sell abroad, we must buy from people beyond our borders." The reserve act "will do more to promote trade in foreign lands than any other one thing that has been done in our history"; it had "set a nation free." From no less a figure in large corporate circles than John E. Gardin, vice-president of the National City Bank of New York, came a similar view. Complaining of the nation's immaturity in matters of international finance, Gardin found encouragement in the tariff and reserve acts. " . . . The administration . . . certainly has given us two things of which we might be proud: one, the reduction of the tariff . . . opening up the markets of the world,—if we want to sell we have got to buy; and the other is the Federal Reserve Law, which relieves us from the bondage" of an outmoded banking law, providing "relief just as important as the emancipation of the slaves. . . . " In view of these laws, Gardin looked forward to the projected program of the NFTC, as working "for the benefit of all those who wish to partake . . . of the new freedom."

Among those spokesmen of industrial and financial interests who praised the Underwood Tariff, representatives of smaller interests were conspicuously absent. It is a mistake to view the Underwood measure as part of a "New Freedom" crusade against large corporations. It *was* part of the "New Freedom" program; but the heathen were not necessarily the large corporations. It was part of an attack on "special privilege" conceived to be in conflict with the national interest understood in terms of the conditions of modern times; but it was the special privilege cherished by smaller and by non-industrial interests, no longer needed by the larger interests as export trade became increasingly more important to them.

Aside from its immediate intent to stimulate export trade, the tariff, consistent with Wilson's views, sought to enforce industrial efficiency by inviting world-wide competition, which would result in making United States industry and finance a more formidable competitor in world markets. The larger industrial interests could withstand, and expect to fatten on, such competition, but not the smaller. Those items placed on the free list by the tariff were, in the majority, articles of food, clothing, and raw materials, industries occupied by the "little man." Large corporations engaged in the capital and durable goods industries, and most heavily involved in the export trade so far as manufactures were concerned, could approve this provision, because should the tariff have the intended effect, it would operate to keep wage levels down, reduce costs of materials, and in the process enable more effective competition in world markets, aside from increasing the profit rate. The issue was analogous to the great Corn Law debates in England during the previous century, where the industrialists sought to abolish import duties at the expense of producers of food and raw stuffs. Wilson, after all, had learned well from Cobden and Bright, the apostles of what has been aptly termed the "imperialism of free trade."

At the same time, those items of heavy industry placed upon the free list, such as steel rails and agricultural machinery and implements, were already produced by the larger United States corporations with an efficiency and at a cost of production sufficient to permit not only successful competition in world markets in general, but within the national markets of the European industrial nations as well, a point Wilson frequently made. Of further aid to such competition, moreover, the Underwood Tariff granted drawbacks on exported items comprised in part or in whole of imported materials subject to import duties.

In effect, the Underwood tariff strengthened the position of the larger corporations as against the smaller, and as against producers of agricultural materials. In this case, legal reform served the interest of those seeking to buttress the socio-economic *status quo*, while adherence to established law and institutions rallied those whose interest lay in forestalling the onward rush of that *status quo*. Accordingly, the greatest danger to the Underwood bill's downward revisions while pending in Congress "came

from a horde of lobbyists," among whom the "owners and managers of industries that produced the great bulk of American industrial products were
unconcerned and took no part. . . . " As Link concludes, the Underwood
duties assumed their greatest significance "in so far as they reflected a
lessening of the pressure from the large industrial interests for a McKinley
type of protection." It is understandable, therefore, that among the Congressional critics of the Underwood tariff, as with the reserve law and the
trade commission and Clayton acts, were "radical" and insurgent Democrats
and Republicans claiming to represent the smaller and agrarian interests.
In so far as the tariff, perhaps more dramatically than other issues, brought
into unified focus the elements of efficiency, bigness in business, foreign
trade, and an expanding sphere of enterprise—the last holding out the
promise of more room for the "little man"—it may be accurately described
as one of the high points of Wilsonian reform.

It is not meant to imply that the corporate community had no criticisms
of the Underwood Tariff or Federal Reserve Act; but large corporate interests in particular viewed the new tariff either as a worthwhile experiment
or more positively as sound policy, and business opinion overwhelmingly
viewed the reserve law as basically sound, in need of perfecting amendments, rather than as a measure directed against their interests. The conflict over the reserve system bill during 1913 had not revolved so much
around the provisions of the bill as around the question of how and by
whom those provisions should be administered, except in so far as the "radical" and agrarian Republicans and Democrats insisted upon provisions that
Wilson rejected. Otherwise, with respect to the manner of administering
the system, the division lay not between Wilson and the "small" interests
on the one side and "big business" on the other: the large corporate interests
themselves were divided, particularly, the evidence indicates, along industrial and financial lines. As Link notes, the great mass of non-banking
business opinion approved the bill, and in October, 1913, for example, both
the Merchants Association of New York and the United States Chamber
of Commerce (the latter by a vote of 306–17) endorsed it.

The Federal Reserve Act may be interpreted, with respect to the issues
raised here, in terms of a movement of large finance and industrial corporate interests, extending back to and before the National Monetary Commission for branch banking, a commercial acceptance market for the
facilitation of foreign trade and investment, and a reserve system that
would protect the gold stock from foreign and domestic runs; a movement
that, by expanding the credit structure, would reduce industrial corporations' dependence upon the money markets for investment capital, and
insulate industrial operations from stock market fluctuations and speculators; a movement that Wilson approved and responded to favorably without himself being in any way responsible for its initiation, just as in the
case of the movement for the Federal Trade Commission Act.

* * *

If Wilson is properly understood in terms of the widely current
evolutionary-positivistic world view that he shared alike with leading indus-

trial and finance capitalists and with prominent politicians and intellectuals within the bi-partisan Progressive movement, and if the approaches taken by his administration to both foreign and domestic affairs are viewed as basically interrelated, rather than compartmentalized, as affecting each other, rather than operating in isolated spheres, then it is of greater analytical value to view the attitude assumed by Wilson and his administration toward "business" before and after November, 1914, as undergoing consistent development, rather than fundamental change. That attitude corresponded with a world view that affirmed large-scale corporate industrial capitalism as the natural and inevitable product of social evolution, and that regarded foreign investments and exports, defined in terms of the needs of industrial and finance capital, as indispensable to the nation's prosperity and social well-being. Beneficence at home and abroad, in this view, was a function of necessity. Large corporate production appeared as the vehicle of domestic material progress; foreign economic expansion, considered a decisive condition of such production, promised to carry "civilization," bourgeois-liberal ideas and institutions, and a better way of life, to the agrarian areas of the world, particularly as "development" of natural resources in those areas was considered essential to such expansion.

It no more occurred to such liberals as Wilson than it did to the so-called Dollar Diplomatists before him, or than it does today to the "internationalist" liberals, that investment in, and ownership of, other nations' resources, railroads, and industry, by United States capitalists, constituted imperialism or exploitation. Imperialism to them meant British- and European-style colonialism or exclusive spheres of interest; exploitation meant unscrupulous gouging, exorbitantly profitable concessions gained by undue influence with corrupt government officials, and the like, in short, "unfair practices" analogous to those characteristics that distinguished the "trust" from the large corporation in domestic affairs. Open door expansion, on the other hand, appeared to them as simply the implementation of the natural international division of labor between the industrialized and agrarian nations; it meant mutually beneficial (and beneficent) business relationships and trade; it meant the assumption by the United States of its natural place in the world economy *vis-á-vis* the other industrial nations, by the elimination of "artificial" impediments to the operation of the laws of competitive commerce; it meant "free trade."

BROOKS ADAMS AND THEODORE ROOSEVELT

DISCUSS THE AMERICAN EMPIRE   *Document 1*

"Reciprocity or the Alternative," by Brooks Adams, published in The Atlantic Monthly *of August, 1901.*

Each year society inclines to accept more unreservedly the theory that war is only an extreme phase of economic competition; and if this postulate be correct, it follows that international competition, if carried far enough, must end in war. An examination of history tends to confirm this view; and, thus stated, the doctrine concerns Americans, as the present policy of the United States is to force a struggle for subsistence, of singular intensity, upon Europe. . . .

International competition cannot be permanently carried on on a great scale by bounties; for bounties mean production at a loss. Bounties may be useful as a weapon of attack, but they cannot, in the long run, bring in money from abroad; for they simply transfer the property of one citizen to another by means of a tax. One nation can gain from another only by cheaper production. If a certain process costs more than another, the assumption of a portion of the cost by the state cannot make the transaction profitable to the community at large, though it may be to the recipient of the grant. . . .

Like any other corporation, a nation can run at a loss as long as its own savings last, or as long as it can borrow from others. . . .

Previous to 1890 America had remained chiefly agricultural, buying largely of European manufactures, and paying therefor, in part, in evidences of debt. Her own industries, like those of France under Louis XIV, were then organized on too costly a basis for international competition, and were mostly maintained by a system of bounties under the form of a tariff. . . .

If three quinquennial periods be taken, beginning with 1887, the first will fall substantially before the crisis of the Baring failure. From 1887 to 1891 the average annual excess of exports over imports amounted to about $44,400,000, a sum certainly not more than sufficient to pay interest due abroad and other like charges. After the failure of the Barings, creditors grew pressing, and the balance rose, between 1892 and 1896, to $185,400,000. In 1896 the United States reached the lowest point in her recent history. Her position then somewhat resembled that of France when Colbert adopted his policy of "selling without buying." The cost of production being too high, Americans could not export manufactures; agricultural supplies alone proved insufficient to yield the sum demanded of her; and the country, in that single year, had to part with $78,880,000 in gold. General insolvency seemed imminent. When confronted, in 1667, with stagnating commerce and failing industries, Colbert proclaimed his prohibitive tariff, and finding that this expedient did not correct exchanges, he invaded Holland; but he did not cut the evil he combated at the root, by reorganizing France. In 1897 the United States followed the precedent set by Colbert, so far as the tariff was concerned; but Americans, suppler than Frenchmen, did not go to war. They adopted a more effective method of routing the foe. They readjusted their entire system of industry and transportation, bringing the cost of production of the chief articles of modern commerce below the European level. No success has ever been more sudden or more startling. Between 1897 and 1901 the average excess of American exports over imports has risen to $510,000,000 yearly. The amount tends to increase, and it tends to increase for excellent reasons. . . . On the present basis, there seems no reason to doubt that, as time goes on, America will drive Europe more and more from neutral markets, and will, if she makes the effort, flood Europe herself with goods at prices with which Europeans cannot compete.

A moment's consideration will disclose the gravity of the situation. Whatever may have been, or may still be, the extent of America's foreign indebtedness, it is certain that, at the present rate of redemption, it must be soon extinguished. Then the time will come when the whole vast burden of payment for American exports will fall upon the annual earnings of foreign nations, at the moment when those earnings are cut down by the competition of the very goods for which they must pay. . . .

America's attack is based not only on her superior resources and her more perfect administration, but on her tariff. To make their gigantic industrial system lucrative, Americans have comprehended that it must be worked at the highest velocity and at its full capacity, and they have taken their measures accordingly. To guard against a check they rely on a practically prohibitive tariff. . . . No wonder the European regards America as a dangerous and relentless foe. . . . Lying like a colossus across the western continent, with her ports on either ocean, with China opposite and South America at her feet, the United States bars European expansion. South America and China are held to be the only accessible regions which certainly contain the iron, coal, and copper which Europe seeks; and the United States is determined that, if she can prevent it, South America and China shall not be used as bases for hostile competition. Regarding South America her declarations are explicit, and during the last twelve months her actions in Asia have spoken more emphatically than words. . . .

To make Asia pay, the country must be handled as a whole,—as America is handled, though not perhaps on so extensive a scale. . . .

Assuming, for the moment, for the sake of argument, that the United States is determined to yield nothing, but is resolved to push all her advantages to the uttermost, it is clear that an attack upon her would be profitable, if it could be made with reasonable hope of success. . . .

Combinations always have been made, under such conditions, and probably always will continue to be made. To be opulent, unarmed, and aggressive is to put a premium upon them. . . .

If a country would live in peace, experience has demonstrated that she must not be too grasping; for excessive greed makes her overthrow a benefit to all, and competitors act accordingly. On the other hand, certain races have felt themselves adapted to win victory in battle, and have prospered; if the American people, after due deliberation, feel aggression to be for their best interest, there is little to be urged by way of precedent against the logic of their decision. . . .

If Americans are determined to reject reciprocity in all its forms, to insist on their advantages, to concede nothing to the adversary; if, having driven in the knife, they mean to turn it in the wound, they should recognize that they are provoking reprisals in every form, and accept the situation with its limitations. To carry out an aggressive policy in some security, the United States needs 300,000 trained men whom she can put in the field in twenty days, with an ample reserve of officers and of material. She needs well-fortified coasts and colonies, and an effective transport service. More especially, she needs a navy. . . .

There is no middle course. Destruction has awaited the gambler who backs his luck; the braggart who would be at once rich, aggressive, and unarmed. Such a man or such a nation puts a premium on spoliation. It is only necessary to reflect upon the fate of France in 1870, to accept this inference as true. America enjoys no immunity from natural laws. She can pay for what she takes, or she can fight for it, but she cannot have the earth for nothing. . . .

Letter from President Theodore Roosevelt to Brooks Adams, September 27, 1901.

Dear Brooks:

Your letter of the 25th instant pleased me particularly.

Before I finish my message [to Congress] I would like to see you, for I intend (although in rather guarded phrase) to put in one or two ideas of your *Atlantic Monthly* article.

Faithfully yours,

Excerpts from President Theodore Roosevelt's Annual Message to Congress, December 3, 1901.

. . . The tremendous and highly complex industrial development which went on with ever accelerated rapidity during the latter half of the nineteenth century brings us face to face, at the beginning of the twentieth, with very serious social problems. . . .

The process has aroused much antagonism, a great part of which is wholly without warrant. It is not true that as the rich have grown richer the poor have grown poorer. On the contrary, never before has the average man, the wage-worker, the farmer, the small trader, been so well off as in this country and at the present time. . . .

The captains of industry who have driven the railway systems across this continent, who have built up our commerce, who have developed our manufactures, have on the whole done great good to our people. . . . Without them the material development of which we are so justly proud could never have taken place. . . .

An additional reason for caution in dealing with corporations is to be found in the international commercial conditions of to-day. The same business conditions which have produced the great aggregations of corporate and individual wealth have made them very potent factors in international commercial competition. . . . America has only just begun to assume that commanding position in the international business world which we believe will more and more be hers. It is of the utmost importance that this position be not jeoparded, especially at a time when the overflowing abundance of our own natural resources and the skill, business energy, and mechanical aptitude of our people make foreign markets essential. . . .

There is general acquiescence in our present tariff system as a national policy. The first requisite to our prosperity is the continuity and stability of this economic policy. Nothing could be more unwise than to disturb the business interests of the country by any general tariff change at this time. . . .

Reciprocity must be treated as the handmaiden of protection. Our first duty is to see that the protection granted by the tariff in every case where it is needed is maintained, and that reciprocity be sought for so far as it can safely be done without injury to our home industries.

Subject to this proviso of the proper protection necessary to our industrial well-being at home, the principle of reciprocity must command our hearty support. The phenomenal growth of our export trade emphasizes the urgency of the need for wider markets and for a liberal policy in dealing with foreign nations....

The condition of the American merchant marine is such as to call for immediate remedial action by Congress.... We should not longer submit to conditions under which only a trifling portion of our great commerce is carried in our own ships. To remedy this state of things would not merely serve to build up our shipping interests, but it would also result in benefit to all who are interested in the permanent establishment of a wider market for American products, and would provide an auxiliary force for the Navy....

The true end of every great and free people should be self-respecting peace; and this Nation most earnestly desires sincere and cordial friendship with all others.... Wars with barbarous or semi-barbarous peoples come in an entirely different category, being merely a most regrettable but necessary international police duty which must be performed for the sake of the welfare of mankind....

The work of upbuilding the Navy must be steadily continued. No one point of our policy, foreign or domestic, is more important than this to the honor and material welfare, and above all to the peace, of our Nation in the future. Whether we desire it or not, we must henceforth recognize that we have international duties no less than international rights....

Inasmuch, however, as the American people have no thought of abandoning the path upon which they have entered, and especially in view of the fact that the building of the Isthmian Canal is fast becoming one of the matters which the whole people are united in demanding, it is imperative that our Navy should be put and kept in the highest state of efficiency, and should be made to answer our growing needs....

Probably no other great nation in the world is so anxious for peace as we are. There is not a single civilized power which has anything whatever to fear from aggressiveness on our part. All we want is peace....

There should be no cessation in the work of completing our Navy. So far ingenuity has been wholly unable to devise a substitute for the great war craft whose hammering guns beat out the mastery of the high seas....

The American people must either build and maintain an adequate navy or else make up their minds definitely to accept a secondary position in international affairs, not merely in political, but in commercial, matters. It has been well said that there is no surer way of courting national disaster than to be "opulent, aggressive, and unarmed."...

Owing to the rapid growth of our power and our interests on the Pacific, whatever happens in China must be of the keenest national concern to us....

We advocate the "open door" with all that it implies; not merely the procurement of enlarged commercial opportunities on the coasts, but access to the interior by the waterways with which China has been so extraordinarily favored. Only by bringing the people of China into peaceful and friendly community of trade with all the peoples of the earth can the work now auspiciously begun be carried to fruition. In the attainment of this purpose we necessarily claim parity of treatment, under the conventions, throughout the Empire for our trade and our citizens with those of all other powers. . . .

AMERICAN EFFORTS TO SECURE
A NAVAL BASE ON THE CHINA COAST   *Document 2*

Secretary Hay to U.S. Minister to Japan, December 7, 1900.

The Navy greatly desires a coaling station at Samsah Inlet north of Fuchow. Ascertain informally and discreetly whether Japanese Government would see any objection to our negotiating for this with China.

U.S. Minister to Japan to Secretary Hay, December 10, 1900.

The Japanese Government declines to accede to the proposal for coaling station for the United States Navy at Samsah Inlet. Today Minister of Japan at Washington has been instructed by telegraph upon the subject fully. He will communicate particular reasons.

Japanese Minister to the U.S. to Secretary Hay, December 11, 1900.

. . . In the first place, in view of the fact that the Chinese Government have given to the Imperial Government a self-denying engagement on the nonalienation of any portion of Fuhkien Province, such an acquisition as is proposed by the United States Government would practically be an abrogation of that engagement, to which, for geographical and other reasons, the Imperial Government attach the highest importance; for should the door be once opened to enable one Power to secure territorial advantages in that Province, it would be impossible to prevent others from acquiring similar concessions. . . .

Ambassador to Japan Guthrie to Secretary of State William J. Bryan, March 21, 1915.

Yesterday I had a very full and frank interview with Japanese Minister for Foreign Affairs. . . . He dwelt especially on Fukien saying that Japan was very sensitive about it because of its proximity to Formosa, and that she had been made uneasy some years ago by Secretary Hay's suggestion that the United States desired to improve a harbor there for a naval coaling station, and that this uneasiness had been recently revived by published reports that the Bethlehem Steel Company was negotiating with China a contract for that harbor's improvement. . . .

THE CHINESE RETALIATE AGAINST

AMERICAN IMMIGRATION LAWS   *Document 3*

Minister Rockhill to the Secretary of State, Peking, July 6, 1905.

Sir: When I arrived in Shanghai on May 20, last, on my way to my post, I was informed by our consul-general that a few days previously the leading native merchant guilds of that place had held meetings for the purpose of declaring a general boycott against all American goods and persons residing in China for the purpose of forcing the Government of the United States to amend its laws concerning the exclusion of Chinese. The Chinese public was told that our government was attempting to force that of China to sign a treaty highly detrimental to Chinese interests and that the people of China ought by means of the proposed boycott to resist America's demands. Telegrams were sent by the meeting to some twenty cities in China, all interested in the American trade, urging them to take the proposed action, which was to be put in force on or about August 1 next....

On May 21, I met the committee of representative merchants and bankers of the local guilds and explained to them that they had been misled and were evidently not aware of the true state of the negotiations now pending between the two governments, otherwise they would have refrained from taking the hasty action they had, which could only tend to create bad feeling and embarrass trade without any object.... I asked them to make it known to their guilds. This they promised to do, and they left assuring me that they were perfectly satisfied with my explanation.

A couple of days later, the local native press continuing to print inflammatory articles against our country and encouraging the proposed boycott, I suggested to Mr. Davidson that he should see the taot'ai and ask him to put a stop to such foolish and lawless agitation. Mr. Davidson saw the taot'ai, but no action was taken by him....

Minister Rockhill to Prince Ch'ing, Peking, August 7, 1905.

Your Highness: I had the honor in interviews with you in the last two months of drawing your earnest attention to the very serious nature of the movement then being openly organized in Shanghai, Canton, and other large cities of China to interfere with, and, if possible, completely impede American trade as a means of intimidating the United States Government, which is seeking to meet with your wishes for a new treaty regulating the coming of Chinese into the United States and for forcing upon us a repeal of our laws concerning the exclusion of Chinese laborers....

In conversation with His Excellency Na-tung I have also on several occasions dwelt on the growing gravity of the situation in Shanghai, Canton, and Amoy, and urged on him, as I had on you, that the Imperial Government should take prompt and radical measures for putting an end to the

ever-increasing menace to our trade and the perfect cordiality and friendliness which characterized our relations so markedly.

I was answered by your note of July 1 that the high provincial authorities
had been urged by you to use their influence with the people to dissuade
them from the contemplated organized interference with our trade, but you
also stated therein, much to my astonishment:

My board finds upon investigation that this movement has not been inaugurated without
some reason, for the restrictions against the Chinese entering America are too strong,
and American exclusion laws are extremely inconvenient to the Chinese. The Coolies
immigration treaty has been abrogated, but, though the treaty is null and void, the
exclusion restrictions are still in force. The great inconvenience suffered by Chinese
merchants has thus led to this movement, but if the restrictions can be lightened by
your government and a treaty drawn up in a friendly manner then this agitation will
of its own accord die out.

I was constrained to conclude from this passage that the movement had
a certain amount of sympathy from your highness's government....

Your highness must be perfectly aware that the prime movers in the
agitation are men holding high official positions. I need only cite among
them Taot'ai Tseng, the president of the Chamber of Commerce of Shanghai,
who has given much time and money to strengthen and develop the movement and has done probably more than any other individual to intensify the
feeling of hostility toward my government and people by his false and
malicious statements in his eagerness to bring about the boycott. Other
officials could be named who, in Shanghai and elsewhere, have taken active
part in this campaign of slander and falsehood, but it seems needless at
this time to do so. I only refer to the active participation of officials in the
movement to show how easy it would have been for the central government
to have had stringent orders for the suppression of the movement carried
out, if it had been earnestly desirous of doing so.

The President of the United States, justly surprised at the extraordinary
supineness the Imperial Government has shown in this matter, which agrees
so little with the friendliness he thought he had reason to expect of it, directs
me to inform your highness that the Government of the United States will
hold it directly responsible for any loss our interests have sustained or may
hereafter have to bear through the manifest failure on the part of the
Imperial Government to stop the present organized movement against us,
which the President considers is allowed to continue in open violation of
the rights guaranteed to us by China in Article XV of our treaty of 1858.

THE TAFT-KATSURA MEMORANDUM, 1905   *Document 4*

... Count Katsura and Secretary Taft had a long and confidential conversation on the morning of July 27....

First, in speaking of some pro-Russians in America who would have the
public believe that the victory of Japan would be a certain prelude to her
aggression in the direction of the Philippine Islands, Secretary Taft observed

that Japan's only interest in the Philippines would be, in his opinion, to have these islands governed by a strong and friendly nation like the United States.... Count Katsura confirmed in the strongest terms the correctness of his views on the point and positively stated that Japan does not harbor any aggressive designs whatever on the Philippines....

Second, Count Katsura observed that the maintenance of general peace in the extreme East forms the fundamental principle of Japan's international policy. Such being the case, ... the best, and in fact the only, means for accomplishing the above object would be to form good understanding between the three governments of Japan, the United States and Great Britain....

Third, in regard to the Korean question Count Katsura observed that Korea being the direct cause of our war with Russia, it is a matter of absolute importance to Japan that a complete solution of the peninsula question should be made as the logical consequence of the war. If left to herself after the war, Korea will certainly draw back to her habit of improvidently entering into any agreements or treaties with other powers, thus resuscitating the same international complications as existed before the war. In view of the foregoing circumstances, Japan feels absolutely constrained to take some definite step with a view to precluding the possibility of Korea falling back into her former condition and of placing us again under the necessity of entering upon another foreign war. Secretary Taft fully admitted the justness of the Count's observations and remarked to the effect that, in his personal opinion, the establishment by Japanese troops of a suzerainty over Korea to the extent of requiring that Korea enter into no foreign treaties without the consent of Japan was the logical result of the present war and would directly contribute to permanent peace in the East. His judgment was that President Roosevelt would concur in his views in this regard, although he had no authority to give assurance of this....

THE ROOT-TAKAHIRA AGREEMENT, 1908   *Document 5*

K. Takahira to Elihu Root, November 30, 1908.

The exchange of views between us, which has taken place at the several interviews which I have recently had the honor of holding with you, has shown that Japan and the United States holding important outlying insular possessions in the region of the Pacific Ocean, the Governments of the two countries are animated by a common aim, policy, and intention in that region.

Believing that a frank avowal of that aim, policy, and intention would not only tend to strengthen the relations of friendship and good neighborhood, which have immemorially existed between Japan and the United States, but would materially contribute to the preservation of the general peace, the Imperial Government have authorized me to present to you an outline of their understanding of that common aim, policy and intention:

1. It is the wish of the two Governments to encourage the free and peaceful development of their commerce on the Pacific Ocean.

2. The policy of both Governments, uninfluenced by any aggressive tendencies, is directed to the maintenance of the existing status quo in the region above mentioned and to the defense of the principle of equal opportunity for commerce and industry in China.

3. They are accordingly firmly resolved reciprocally to respect the territorial possessions belonging to each other in said region.

4. They are also determined to preserve the common interest of all powers in China by supporting by all pacific means at their disposal the independence and integrity of China and the principle of equal opportunity for commerce and industry of all nations in that Empire.

5. Should any event occur threatening the status quo as above described or the principle of equal opportunity as above defined, it remains for the two Governments to communicate with each other in order to arrive at an understanding as to what measures they may consider it useful to take. . . .

SECRETARY OF STATE KNOX
PROPOSES CONTROL OF THE
MANCHURIAN RAILROADS, NOVEMBER 1909   *Document 6*

. . . Now that there has been signed and ratified by an unpublished imperial decree an agreement by which the American and British interests are to cooperate in the financing and construction of the Chinchow-Tsitsihar-Aigun Railroad, the Government of the United States is prepared cordially to cooperate with His Britannic Majesty's Government in diplomatically supporting and facilitating this enterprise, so important alike to the progress and to the commercial development of China. The Government of the United States would be disposed to favor ultimate participation to a proper extent on the part of other interested powers whose inclusion might be agreeable to China and which are known to support the principle of equality of commercial opportunity and the maintenance of the integrity of the Chinese Empire. However, before the further elaboration of the actual arrangement, the Government of the United States asks His Britannic Majesty's Government to give their consideration to the following alternative and more comprehensive projects: First, perhaps the most effective way to preserve the undisturbed enjoyment by China of all political rights in Manchuria and to promote the development of those Provinces under a practical application of the policy of the open door and equal commercial opportunity would be to bring the Manchurian highway, the railroads, under an economic, scientific, and impartial administration by some plan vesting in China the ownership of the railroads through funds furnished for that purpose by the interested powers willing to participate. Such loan should be for a period ample to make it reasonably certain that it could be met within the time fixed and should be upon such terms as would make it attractive to bankers and investors. The plan would provide that nationals of the participating powers should supervise the railroad system during the term of the loan and the governments concerned should enjoy for such period the usual preferences for their nationals and materials upon an equitable basis inter se. The execution of such a plan would naturally require the cooperation of China and of Japan and Russia, the reversionary and the concessionaries, respectively, of the existing Manchurian railroads, as well as that of Great Britain and the United States, whose special interests rest upon the existing contract relative to the Chinchow-Aigun Railroad. The advantages of such a plan to Japan and to Russia are obvious. Both those powers, desiring in good faith to protect the policy of the open door and equal opportunity in Manchuria and wishing to assure to China unimpaired sovereignty, might well be expected to welcome an opportunity to shift the separate duties, responsibilities, and expenses they have undertaken in the protection of their respective commercial and other interests, for impartial assumption by the combined powers, including themselves, in proportion to their interests. The Government of the United States has some reason to hope that such a plan might meet favorable consideration on the part of Russia and has reason to believe that American financial participation would be forthcoming. Second, should this suggestion not be found feasible in its entirety, then the desired end would be approximated, if not attained, by Great Britain and the United States diplomatically supporting the Chinchow-Aigun arrangement and inviting the interested powers friendly to complete commercial neutralization of Manchuria to participate in the financing and construction of that line and of such additional lines as future commercial development may demand, and at the same time to supply funds for the purchase by China of such of the existing lines as might be offered for inclusion in this system. The government of the United States hopes that the principle involved in the foregoing suggestions may commend itself to His Britannic Majesty's Government. That principle finds support in the additional reasons that the consummation of some such plan would avoid the irritations likely to be engendered by the uncontrolled direct negotiations of bankers with the Chinese Government, and also that it would create such a community of substantial interest in China as would facilitate a cooperation calculated to simplify the problems of fiscal and monetary reforms now receiving such earnest attention by the Imperial Chinese Government.

MINISTER TO RUSSIA ROCKHILL WARNS
AGAINST IGNORING RUSSIA'S OVERTURES
FOR HELP AGAINST JAPAN   *Document 7*

Minister Rockhill to Secretary of State Knox, January 21, 1911.
    ... Russian friendliness and cooperation in the Far East seem highly important and their value will increase steadily with Japanese expansion....

The Russian Government is disposed to give sympathetic consideration to our suggestions ... believing in our friendliness and in the identity of our political interests in regard to Japan. ...

Minister Rockhill to Secretary of State Knox, January 30, 1911.
... I cannot too emphatically reiterate my conclusion that the sympathetic cooperation of Russia is of supreme importance: for the realization of our policy of Chinese sovereignty and equality of opportunity in Manchuria and Mongolia, such cooperation is an essential condition. ... Russia can never withdraw from participation in Far Eastern Affairs or maintain an attitude of indifference towards them. ...

I am convinced that the present Russian policy in those regions is not aggressive but cautiously defensive, and that that will be its tendency for years to come. ... I have reason to believe that the Russian Government would at least be sympathetic with the purposes of the United States in these regions if it were confident of their sincerity, and convinced that the American Government would loyally and consistently respect Russia's established interests and make no unfriendly use of the resulting increase of its influence in Asiatic affairs. ...

At this critical juncture when Russia is reconsidering her relationship to Far Eastern Questions, and hesitating between a policy of coercion and one of cooperation with the United States ... I fear that the proposed Congressional Resolution to denounce the Treaty of 1832 ... might precipitate this Government's decision against the policies with which the United States is identified. ...

CORRESPONDENCE PERTAINING TO THE "GENTLEMAN'S AGREEMENT" OF 1907 BETWEEN THE UNITED STATES AND JAPAN *Document 8*

Memorandum of the Japanese Foreign Office to the Department of State, December 31, 1907.
The personal conference which took place at the Foreign Office on the 30th instant having placed His Excellency the American Ambassador in possession of the views of the Imperial Government upon the question of Japanese emigration to the United States, and having, it is hoped, demonstrated to His Excellency their earnest wish to arrive at a mutually satisfactory understanding, the moment seems opportune for more detailed comment ... as well as for a formal statement of the measures which the Imperial Government are prepared to adopt in order effectively to meet the situation. ...

By way of recapitulation and of additional explanation Count Hayashi now begs to present, for the information of the American Government, the following summary of the views of the Imperial Government and of the measures they are prepared to take.

1. The Imperial Government are determined to continue their announced policy of issuing no passports good for the American mainland to either skilled or unskilled Japanese laborers, except to those who have previously resided in the United States, or the parents, wives or children of Japanese residents.

2. They intend, however, to continue to grant passports to settled agriculturists. As was known to the predecessor of His Excellency the Ambassador on the 26th of May last the Japanese Government have exercised with reference to those persons very careful and rigorous supervision and restriction. The privilege has only been granted to bona fide agriculturists intending to settle in certain specified localities. In order to avoid all possible subterfuge, the central administration will continue rigidly to apply the precautionary measures set forth in the explanatory memorandum of May 26th.

3. The Imperial Government have formulated instructions to local Governors that in every case of application for a passport to the United States by a student, merchant, tourist or the like, thorough investigation must be made to determine whether the applicant is not likely to become a laborer after reaching the United States. A material and indispensable part of this investigation relates to the financial status of the applicant. If he is not rich enough in his own right to assure the permanence of his status as a student, merchant or tourist, surety will be required of his family or special patron in the case of a student, or of his firm or company in the case of a merchant or mercantile employee, guaranteeing the payment of expenses and a monthly allowance of say 40 yen; and, in the case of tourists, the payment of sufficient travelling expenses. The passport applied for will only be issued after this surety has been given. As a further precaution in the case of students no such passports will be issued except to students who have passed through the middle schools.

4. So far as concerns the Hawaiian Islands, which it is proposed to set aside from the scope of the questions under consideration, it is the present intention of the Imperial Government experimentally to stop all emigration to those islands for some time to come, except in isolated cases of returning emigrants and of the parents, wives and children, of those already resident in the Islands.

5. The Imperial Government intend to take measures regarding the emigration of Japanese laborers to foreign territory adjacent to the United States, which, in their opinion, will effectually remove all cause for complaint on that account.

Count Hayashi sincerely trusts that His Excellency the Ambassador and his Government will find in the foregoing recapitulation ample evidence of the desire and the intention of the Imperial Government to adopt administrative measures of regulation and control which will effectually meet the requirements of the situation.

The Department of State to the Japanese Foreign Office, January 23, 1908.
. . . In an *aide-memoire* after a conversation you may also lay before the Minister of Foreign Affairs the following points as requiring emphasis with reference to our suggestions.

1st. Passports should be exact and specific and issued with the greatest care to prevent forgery and false personation.

2nd. The issuance of passports to laborers who have formerly been in American territory or to the parents, wives, or children of laborers already there, should be carefully safeguarded and limited, otherwise abuses are, it is feared, certain.

3rd. With reference to settled agriculturists, the gist of the precautionary measures to be taken is noted and it is understood that a settled agriculturist is a small farmer capitalist and not merely a farm laborer paid under contract out of the produce of his agricultural work, and that with this criterion a reasonable number of passports only will be issued to persons of such economic status. It is to be observed that unless the alleged character of farmer is accompanied by actual title to land it is quite likely to be merely a cover for a violation of our contract labor laws and this should be specifically guarded against.

4th. It is quite important also that the Japanese Government's definition of laborer be conformable to our own.... For illustration, from December 27 to January 10 there arrived at Pacific ports 118 Japanese who were laborers according to our rules but who had obtained passports otherwise than as laborers. During that period only four arrived with passports as laborers.

We cannot believe that the Imperial Japanese Government will find serious difficulty in devising some quite unobjectionable system of registration or of certificates, or of renewed passports, or other evidence by which may be identified those engaged in manual labor in American territory lawfully and without violation of their passports.

Report of the Commissioner General of Immigration, 1908.

In order that the best results might follow from an enforcement of the regulations, an understanding was reached with Japan that the existing policy of discouraging emigration of its subjects of the laboring classes to continental United States should be continued, and should, by co-operation with the governments, be made as effective as possible. This understanding contemplates that the Japanese government shall issue passports to continental United States only to such of its subjects as are non-laborers or are laborers who, in coming to the continent, seek to resume a formerly acquired domicile, to join a parent, wife, or children residing there, or to assume active control of an already possessed interest in a farming enterprise in this country, so that the three classes of laborers entitled to receive passports have come to be designated "former residents," "parents, wives, or children of residents," and "settled agriculturists."

With respect to Hawaii, the Japanese government of its own volition stated that, experimentally at least, the issuance of passports to members of the laboring classes proceeding thence would be limited to "former residents" and "parents, wives, or children of residents." The said government has also been exercising a careful supervision over the subject of emigration of its laboring class to foreign contiguous territory.

PRESIDENT WILSON DISAGREES WITH
THE FINANCIERS ON THE TACTICS
OF DOLLAR DIPLOMACY, MARCH 1913   *Document 9*

... We are informed that at the request of the last administration a certain group of American bankers undertook to participate in the loan now desired by the Government of China (approximately $125,000,000). Our Government wished American bankers to participate along with the bankers of other nations, because it desired that the good will of the United States toward China should be exhibited in this practical way, that American capital should have access to that great country, and that the United States should be in a position to share with the other powers any political responsibilities that might be associated with the development of the foreign relations of China in connection with her industrial and commercial enterprises. The present administration has been asked by this group of bankers whether it would also request them to participate in the loan. The representatives of the bankers through whom the administration was approached declared that they would continue to seek their share of the loan under the proposed agreements only if expressly requested to do so by the Government. The administration has declined to make such a request, because it did not approve the conditions of the loan or the implications of responsibility on its own part which it was plainly told would be involved in the request.

The conditions of the loan seem to us to touch very nearly the administrative independence of China itself, and this administration does not feel that it ought, even by implication, to be a party to those conditions. The responsibility on its part which would be implied in requesting the bankers to undertake the loan might conceivably go the length in some unhappy contingency of forcible interference in the financial, and even the political, affairs of that great oriental State, just now awakening to a consciousness of its power and of its obligations to its people. The conditions include not only the pledging of particular taxes, some of them antiquated and burdensome, to secure the loan, but also the administration of those taxes by foreign agents. The responsibility of the part of our Government implied in the encouragement of a loan thus secured and administered is plain enough and is obnoxious to the principles upon which the government of our people rests.

The Government of the United States is not only willing, but earnestly desirous, of aiding the great Chinese people in every way that is consistent with their untrammeled development and its own immemorial principles. The awakening of the people of China to a consciousness of their responsibilities under free government is the most significant, if not the most momentous, event of our generation. With this movement and aspiration the American people are in profound sympathy. They certainly wish to participate, and participate very generously, in the opening to the Chinese and to the use of the world the almost untouched and perhaps unrivaled resources of China.

The Government of the United States is earnestly desirous of promoting the most extended and intimate trade relationship between this country and the Chinese Republic. The present administration will urge and support the legislative measures necessary to give American merchants, manufacturers, contractors, and engineers the banking and other financial facilities which they now lack and without which they are at a serious disadvantage as compared with their industrial and commercial rivals. This is its duty. This is the main material interest of its citizens in the development of China. Our interests are those of the open door—a door of friendship and mutual advantage. This is the only door we care to enter.

SECRETARY OF STATE BRYAN DISCUSSES
THE WILSON ADMINISTRATION'S COMMITMENT
TO OVERSEAS ECONOMIC EXPANSION   *Document 10*

Remarks at the Fifteenth Annual Dinner of the American Asiatic Association, January 26, 1914.

... The new administration in withdrawing approval from the Chinese loan did not question the good faith or good intent of those who had seen in it a means of increasing our influence, prestige and commercial power in China. The President believed that a different policy was more consistent with the American position, and that it would in the long run be more advantageous to our commerce. It would not be fair to attribute a falling off in trade, to which reference has been made, to the change in policy, because the new policy has not yet had time to bear fruit, even if political conditions had been entirely favorable (Applause.)

The interests of the American citizen will be amply protected wherever he goes; and in saying that I say only what the President himself has said, and it cannot be said any stronger. I may say that American interests will be protected everywhere; and when Americans are going abroad they could not do a better thing for the benefit of American trade than to carry with them the high ideals that obtain in that trade at home. But when an American expects this government to back a project, no matter how inconsistent that project may be with those high ideals, then I am afraid he will be disappointed not only in the lack of support from the President and this Government as a whole, but in failing to inspire any sympathy for himself among the honest and right-thinking people of this country. When the President insists that the American abroad must give a dollar for every dollar of value received, the President is the friend of the future.

Mr. Straight has called attention to one step already taken which means much for American trade, viz., the authorization of international banks. We have long needed such a law, and I am sure that our foreign trade will be stimulated not only in the Orient but also throughout South America by the new law which permits banks here to establish branches throughout the world. (Applause.)

Mention has also been made of the new tariff law in the promotion of foreign trade. This influence can hardly be appreciated at this time, because its operation has only just begun. In his last speech, delivered just before his tragic death, President McKinley called attention to the necessity for tariff reduction as a means of extending or increasing our exports. It was a prophetic utterance, to which the country has given a well-nigh universal response. We must show ourselves friendly if we would have friends. We must buy if we would sell. The new policy means a larger commerce between our nation and the world, and in this increase the Orient will have her share, and this advantage will be enjoyed not only in general by the public but especially by those merchants and manufacturers now turning their eyes to the Far East. (Applause.)

In addition to these specific instances, the President's policy contemplates the formation of an environment which will encourage the growth of all that is good. Man is not a creator in a fundamental sense. The farmer cannot put life into a grain of wheat, but he can give to the grain an environment which it can utilize. So the government, while it cannot create trade, can give to trade an environment in which it can develop, and that it is the duty of our government to do. If we can present to the world an example worthy of imitation, we shall be assisting ourselves while we assist others, for we shall reap a profit out of every nation's advance. If in any way we can stimulate education and bring it nearer to the ideal which contemplates the mental development of every human being, that larger intelligence will be of use to us as well as to the nations in which it is developed. (Applause.) If by our example we can assist any other nations in the improvement of their forms and methods of government, we shall share in the prosperity this better government brings. This government will see that no industrial highwayman robs you. This government stands committed to the doctrine that these United States are entitled to the greatest possible industrial and commercial development. (Applause.)

DOLLARS AND DIPLOMATS

IN LATIN AMERICA,

AFRICA, AND

THE MIDDLE EAST

CHAPTER 10

The Open Door Policy
from Panama to Persia

*A*merican policy in Latin America from 1900 to 1914 was in some respects more successful than it was in Asia. And though less spectacular than the diplomacy of the Open Door in China, intervention by the United States in the affairs of Africa and Europe was the prelude to American entry into the First World War. In its relations with these areas the United States began to develop policies which carried over into the postwar era. Geographic, military, and economic predominance in the western hemisphere gave the United States a particularly favorable opportunity to guide and help the development of the nonindustrialized Latin American nations.

This power carried with it more extensive responsibilities in the region and exposed the United States to criticism from friends and opponents alike. Here, and in other economically underdeveloped countries such as Liberia and Persia, America faced its old European rivals. Economic and political relations with these European nations complicated the situation and sometimes worked at cross-purposes with American policy in the underdeveloped areas. And finally, in the case of Mexico, the United States had another experience (as in China and the Philippines) in coping directly with revolutions that challenged American ideas and influence.

The central feature of American relations with all these areas was the adoption by policy makers of economic intervention as an end, as well as a means, of diplomacy. This coming together of economic means and ends did not solve all the problems of building and consolidating an economic empire.

Government officials disagreed among themselves and with economic leaders, for example, over the best tactics to be used in a given situation. One discussion centered on the problem of the role of the government. Some wanted the government to take the lead in finding and opening up new opportunities, and exercise some control over the way in which businessmen developed these operations. Others said the government should help, but only at the request of the private operators. The other principal argument was over the use of military force to open the way and protect American enterprises. One group maintained that force was necessary all along the line. Others drew back from such militancy, holding that force should be used only in emergencies, and then with great restraint. In general, President Roosevelt favored the more vigorous methods of expansion, while President Taft relied more on economic penetration. But despite these differences there was general agreement on the broad pattern of America's future expansion: American economic power would be used to secure and maintain both political influence and access to resources and markets.

This consolidation of economic ends and means was often lost sight of as the phrase "strategic considerations" became popular in discussions of American policy. But in its precise meaning strategy *refers to underlying problems of military security. Using it to cover the establishment of American economic and political predominance in other countries—something entirely different from trade or specific alliances—falsely makes every issue a problem of military security. This use of the term* strategic, *which has become more and more common, began in the course of America's expansion in Latin America between 1900 and 1914.*

President Theodore Roosevelt employed this argument in his drive for the Panama Canal (Document 1). Sometimes it appeared in the guise of the inherent rights of a higher civilization. But however stated, it was always behind Roosevelt's determination that the United States would own and run the canal without any restrictions from any quarter. Certain problems of the military defense of the Mississippi Valley and the Southwest did require exercising some authority in the Caribbean area. It was necessary to deny that area, as it was Canada, to an attacking enemy. But it was not necessary, in order to achieve military security, to dominate the economic and political life of the region.

Roosevelt ran roughshod over these facts in the same fashion that he bowled over his congressional critics and ignored the protests of Colombia. Howard C. Hill tells the story in his article "The Taking of Panama." Latin Americans and others who criticized Roosevelt's canal diplomacy did not question the usefulness of the canal. Rather did they ask, as others had asked of President Polk's Mexican policy, whether Roosevelt's lack of patience, his overblown arguments about security, and his arbitrary military intervention did not create a legacy of antagonism that ultimately might weaken America more than it was strengthened by the canal.

Roosevelt's canal policy was part of his effort to apply in Latin America his idea that the United States was the agent carrying civilization to—or forcing it upon—various peoples he considered to be barbarians. Vigorous action gave meaning to his assertions. But European nations also had dealings with these countries. They raised an embarrassing but practical point in reply to Roosevelt's policy. American policy in the area, they argued, could not be all one way. If the United States was to set limits on European participation in the development of the area, and enjoy the benefits of such control, then it also would have to take the responsibility for maintaining certain minimum standards of international conduct. Property rights, in particular, would have to be upheld by the United States if Europeans were to be denied the right to supply their own police force. Roosevelt accepted the obligation, in part because it furthered American economic penetration. His statement of the proposition is given in Document 2, and in his article Professor Howard K. Beale reviews how Roosevelt applied it in "The Confrontation over Venezuela."

President William Howard Taft talked less about higher civilization, but like Roosevelt he continued to push American expansion in the area. He had pushed trade with Latin America while serving in Roosevelt's cabinet (Document 3), and at the end of his own term in the White House he provided one of the most comprehensive statements of dollar diplomacy of the entire period (Document 4). As President, he gave full support to Secretary of State Knox's vigorous efforts to extend American financial penetration of the region (Document 5). Senator Henry Cabot Lodge, another expansionist from the 1890's, gave blunt expression to the general feeling that made foreign powers unwelcome in the western hemisphere (Document 6). The Wilson administration coupled intervention to further economic expansion with efforts to establish the rudiments of American-style representative government (Document 7).

Busy as it was in Asia and Latin America during these years, the United States did not neglect Europe. Dealings with European countries over affairs in China and Central America increased America's direct diplomacy with England, France, Germany, and Russia. England's favorable attitude during the Spanish-American War and its acceptance of Washington's leadership in the western hemisphere led to discussions pointing toward the arbitration of other differences. But the United States was not eager to lay its case on the judge's bench unless it felt confident of a favorable verdict. It was disinclined to arbitrate any issue which it chose to define as a matter of domestic policy or of national interest, a point of view which was shared by many other nations. America's attitude at the Hague Conference of 1907 reflected both of these reservations (Document 8).

Americans were more interested in overseas expansion than in international stabilization. Retreating temporarily from the Far East, they turned to Persia for new opportunities (Document 9); and, as noted by Professor L. J. Gordon in his article on "The Chester Project," they were equally active in Turkey. One aspect of their activity in Africa is described in Document 10. Another revolved around President Roosevelt's intervention in the dispute over colonies among Germany, France, and Great Britain. Professor Alfred L. P. Dennis outlines the President's performance as a balance-of-power politician in that episode, and the objectives of his diplomacy emerge in Document 11.

Other Americans, like the House of Morgan, were strengthening ties with

440

England and France in less dramatic fashion. Morgan's branch banks and co-operating agreements with financiers in London and Paris did much to link the United States with those capitals, rather than with Berlin, in the years before the First World War. American attention abruptly returned to Latin America, however, when the Mexican Revolution erupted in 1910. Not only did the revolution challenge American property rights, political authority, and ideas, but those influences in turn complicated and intensified the purely Mexican conflicts behind the revolution. The more it developed and permeated the fabric of Mexican life, the more the revolution took on the character of a direct assault on American predominance and leadership in Latin America. President Wilson rallied to the battle for American civilization with new vigor (Document 12). His personal interpretation of American society became the standard which Mexicans were told they would have to accept. Howard F. Cline outlines the results of such diplomacy. Theodore Roosevelt's "Big Stick" for the extension of civilization became Woodrow Wilson's "moral imperialism" in behalf of the same cause. The extension of America's economic power was in both instances a means and an end of the policy.

THE TAKING OF PANAMA[1]

Howard C. Hill

Roosevelt's interest in a canal which would join the Atlantic and Pacific oceans dates from before the Spanish-American War. In a letter to Senator Lodge (October 27, 1894) Roosevelt says: "I do wish our Republicans would go in avowedly to annex Hawaii and build an oceanic canal." Keenly interested in the Navy from early manhood, he was deeply concerned as assistant secretary of the navy during the months that preceded the struggle with Spain in the efficiency of that arm of the national defense. The long, doubtful voyage of the "Oregon" around the Horn on the eve of the war impressed him, as it did other thoughtful Americans, with the need of an interoceanic canal which would be not only of notable value to commerce but which would also virtually double the strength of American naval forces. Convinced of the nation's duty to expand, he believed that it was a natural corollary of the annexation of Hawaii and the Philippines to open the way for the Navy to operate with equal facility in either of the oceans which washed our eastern and our western shores. . . .

Of the numerous routes which had been suggested for the building of the canal, both expert and popular opinion in the United States favored either Nicaragua or Panama. For a number of years the United States had investigated the cost of constructing an interoceanic canal. In its report dated November 16, 1901, the Walker Commission, which had been appointed in 1899, estimated the cost of constructing a Nicaragua Canal at $189,864,062, and the cost of building a Panama Canal at $144,233,358. To

---

[1] Selected from *Roosevelt and the Caribbean* (Chicago: University of Chicago Press, 1927), pp. 31–67. Reprinted with permission.

the cost of the latter, however, the Commission reported, must be added $109,141,500 to pay for the rights and property of the New Panama Canal Company, a French corporation which years before had secured concessions on the isthmus, making the total cost by the Panama route $253,374,858. Since the value of the interests of the French company did not exceed $40,000,000, according to the Commission, it declared that "the most practicable and feasible route for an isthmian canal, to be under the control, management, and ownership of the United States, was that known as the Nicaragua route."

The recommendation caused a crisis in the affairs of the French company, changes took place in the management, and on January 4, 1902, an offer to sell at $40,000,000 was cabled to the Commission. By this time Roosevelt, who at first had favored the Nicaragua Canal, seems to have become thoroughly convinced of the superiority of the Panama route. Calling the Commission together, he induced the members to reverse their decision and recommend Panama. Nine days before the reversal (January 9, 1902) the House had passed a bill providing for a canal through Nicaragua. When the bill came before the Senate, Senator Spooner offered as an amendment what was in reality a substitute measure. His proposal was adopted by a vote of 42 to 34, was finally accepted by the House, and on June 25, 1902, received the signature of the President.

The Spooner Act, as the law is commonly known, authorized the President to purchase the concessions and property of the New Panama Canal Company at a cost not to exceed $40,000,000 and to acquire from Colombia, upon such terms as he might deem reasonable, perpetual control of, and jurisdiction over, a strip of land, not less than six miles in width, across the Isthmus of Panama; should he be unable to obtain a satisfactory title to the property of the French company and the control of the necessary strip of land from Colombia within a reasonable time and upon reasonable terms, the act directed him to secure control of the necessary territory from Costa Rica and Nicaragua and to proceed to construct a canal by the Nicaragua route. . . .

Negotiations for the Panama route were begun on March 31, 1902, with Dr. Concha, the Colombian minister at Washington, while the debate in Congress upon the relative merits of the Nicaragua and Panama routes was still in progress. The demands of the United States were so repugnant to the Colombian representative that he finally left Washington unceremoniously rather than put his name to the treaty. Negotiations continued, however, with the Colombian *chargé d'affaires*, Thomas Herran, and were brought to a conclusion on January 22, 1903, with the signing of the Hay-Herran Convention. This arrangement authorized the New Panama Canal Company to sell its properties to the United States and granted the United States full control over a strip of land six miles wide across the isthmus for the construction of a ship canal. The arrangement was to continue for ninety-nine years, and was to be renewable for similar periods at the option of the United States. In return the United States promised to pay in cash to Colombia $10,000,000 in gold and an annuity of $250,000 in gold beginning nine years after the exchange of ratifications. The convention was ratified by the American Senate on March 17, 1903. . . .

The spirit of the Roosevelt diplomacy, in so far as it concerns the more backward nations, is revealed clearly in the communications between Washington and Bogotá. The American dispatches show, in the first place, utter disregard of the attitude of the Colombian people or their representatives. The correspondence displays, in the second place, a fixed determination to secure the ratification of the treaty—to quote the American Minister—"exactly in its present form, without any modifications whatever." Indeed, the Colombian government was informed that the United States would be fully warranted "in considering any modification whatever of the terms of the treaty as practically a breach of faith on the part of the Government of Colombia." The contrast between this attitude of inflexibility and the action only two years before of the United States Senate in drastically amending the first Hay-Pauncefote Treaty needs no comment.

Imputations of ill faith form a third theme running through the American communications. Ill faith is charged if changes, no matter how minute, are incorporated in the convention by the Colombian Congress. Ill faith is charged if Colombia persists in its efforts to negotiate with the companies for the cancellation of contracts. Ill faith is charged if Colombia fails to ratify the convention. The correspondence contains, in the fourth place, veiled threats of retaliation in case the treaty is rejected. . . .

The relation of Roosevelt to the revolution in Panama now calls for consideration. The subject involves two important matters: first, Roosevelt's connection, if any, with the uprising; second, his employment of American forces on the isthmus. . . .

In the latter part of October, Amador returned to Panama. Doubt being expressed by his associates concerning the intentions of the United States, Amador cabled Bunau-Varilla that it would be necessary to provide reassurance by having an American naval vessel sent to Colon. Concluding from a remark of Loomis that the Navy would act at once, and calculating the time necessary for the "Nashville," then at Kingston, to reach Panama, Bunau-Varilla sent a dispatch to Amador stating that an American warship would arrive at the isthmus within two days and a half.

In this dispatch Bunau-Varilla may have expressed as a certainty what he felt as a hope. If so he had grounds for his expectation. Although he does not seem to have received direct assurance from the administration that American naval vessels would be sent to the isthmus if disturbances occurred, he would have been "a very dull man," as Roosevelt says, had he been unable to make "a very accurate guess" concerning what "our Government would do."

As early as October 16, from which date Roosevelt seems to have taken complete charge of the situation, the President had ordered the Navy Department to hold warships within striking distance of the Isthmus of Panama on both the Atlantic and Pacific sides. On October 30, the gunboat "Nashville" was ordered to Colon. On November 2, the following instructions were sent to the commanders of the "Marblehead" and the "Boston":

Proceed with all possible dispatch to Panama. Telegraph in cipher your departure. Maintain free and uninterrupted transit. If interruption is threatened by armed force, occupy the line of railroad. Prevent landing of any armed force, either Government or insurgent, with hostile intent at any point within fifty miles of Panama. If doubtful as to the intention of any armed force, occupy Ancon Hill strongly with artillery.... Government force reported approaching isthmus in vessels. Prevent their landing if in your judgment landing would precipitate a conflict.

Instructions of a similar character were sent to the commanders of the "Nashville" and the "Dixie."

The "Nashville" arrived at Colon on the afternoon of November 2. On the following morning Commander Hubbard learned that the Colombian gunboat "Cartagena" had come in during the night, having on board some four or five hundred soldiers. He immediately boarded the boat and was informed that the troops were on their way to join the garrison at Panama. Not having received the Washington dispatch of November 2 quoted above, Hubbard took no steps to prevent their disembarkment. Two hours later (10:30 A.M.) he received the cablegram and immediately went ashore. Meanwhile, the commanding officers of the Colombian troops had left by train for Panama accompanied by members of their staff. At this time Hubbard reported to Washington: "No revolution has been declared on the isthmus and no disturbances have occurred."

The intentions of the conspirators may have been known to the authorities at Washington. The plans may even have received their approval, although this seems improbable. Whatever the truth in the foregoing respect may be, the Department of State, aroused at the delay of the Panama leaders or stirred by a report published in the press, sent at 3:40 P.M., on November 3, the following dispatch to the American consuls at Colon and Panama: "Uprising on isthmus reported. Keep department promptly and fully informed.—LOOMIS, *Acting*." At 8:15 P.M., a reply came from the American Consul at Panama: "No uprising yet. Reported will be in the night. Situation is critical.—EHRMAN." An hour and a half later (9:50 P.M.) a second cablegram was received from Ehrman: "Uprising occurred tonight, six; no bloodshed. Army and navy officials taken prisoners. Government will be organized tonight.... Soldiers changed. Supposed same movement will be effected in Colon. Order prevails so far...."

Meanwhile, Hubbard had learned that a revolution had occurred in Panama; that the Colombian officers who had crossed the isthmus were prisoners; that a provisional government had been established and a military force organized; and that the provisional government desired that the Colombian troops at Colon be sent to Panama. On the following morning, November 4, Hubbard refused to allow troops to be transported in either direction.

Although a critical situation obtained during the next twenty-four hours, no shots were fired by either side and no blood was shed. On the afternoon of November 5 representatives of the provisional government succeeded, by bribery it is said, in persuading Colonel Torres to embark his troops on the "Orinoco," a Royal Mail steamer, and return to the city of Cartagena. The gunboat on which the Colombian troops had come had sailed away the preceding day. On November 6 the United States recognized the *de facto* government of Panama, and within a week seven American war vessels had arrived at Colon and at Panama.

On November 7 the American Minister at Bogota telegraphed Secretary Hay that the Colombian government had inquired whether it would be permitted "to land troops at those ports [Colon and Panama] to fight there and on the line of railway." On November 11 Hay replied that it was "not thought desirable to permit landing of Colombian troops on isthmus, as such a course would precipitate civil war and disturb for an indefinite period the free transit which we are pledged to protect." From November 2, when orders were sent to the commanders of the "Marblehead" and the "Boston" instructing them to "prevent the landing of any armed force . . . with hostile intent at any point within fifty miles of Panama," and throughout the entire insurrection the United States prevented every attempt of Colombia to reduce the uprising by military operations. . . .

The argument that national interests and safety required the action taken at Panama rests on the theory that "necessity knows no law." It is even doubtful that delay would have endangered such interests. Among its stipulations the Hay-Herran Convention provided for possible delays in the completion of the work totaling thirty-six years, an arrangement which suggests that a delay of a few years for further negotiations with Colombia would not have been a matter of major consequence. At all events the point was not made or the issue raised when Great Britain refused to accept the amended form of the first Hay-Pauncefote Treaty.

The truth is that Colombia's rejection of the treaty necessitated no delay whatever in the building of an interoceanic canal. If the need for speed were as urgent as Roosevelt maintains, steps could have been taken at once to provide a canal by way of Nicaragua in accordance with the Spooner Act. Indeed, under the provisions of this Act, it is at least open to question whether the President was not legally obligated, upon the rejection of the Hay-Herran Convention, to go to Nicaragua.

Furthermore, the construction of a canal through Nicaragua would have amply protected "the interests of collective civilization." Whether the United States could claim to have received a mandate from civilization for the construction of a canal may indeed be questioned; the method of determining the accuracy of the claim would in itself be a most difficult problem. But in any case, the obligations of the United States, if such existed, would have been met as fully by the Nicaragua route as by the Panama route.

But for almost a year Roosevelt's mind had apparently been made up: The Canal must be built across the isthmus. To accomplish the end in view, it is asserted, he brought pressure upon the members of the Walker Commission in order to secure a reversal of the recommendation in their first report. Little in his correspondence, either before or after the rejection of the Hay-Herran Convention (August 12), indicates serious consideration of the Nicaragua route. With the regular session of Congress only a few weeks off, when demands for construction by way of Nicaragua were certain to be made, Roosevelt seems to have seized upon the Panama revolution as a way out of the dilemma. Acting with a haste unparalleled in American history and unwarranted in international law, he immediately recognized the new republic and promptly concluded a treaty with it on terms most favorable to the United States.

Roosevelt may not have incited the insurrection, but he greeted it with delight; for it relieved him of all necessity of dealing with the "cut-throats of Bogotá" and enabled him to face Congress with an accomplished fact. . . .

THE CONFRONTATION OVER VENEZUELA[1]   *Howard K. Beale*

. . . In 1902 Germany, Britain, and Italy joined in the use of naval power to force Venezuela to pay debts and claims accumulated during local civil war in 1898–1900. Rumors that Germany had designs on territory in Latin America had periodically troubled the United States. On his return from Germany to his Washington post in November, 1901, for instance, Ambassador von Holleben denied rumors that the Kaiser had ambitions in America. Such reports were mere inventions of the enemies of German-American friendship, the Ambassador insisted. Concerning the Venezuelan dispute, Germany, eager not to offend the United States, notified her in December, 1901, that Germany might have to use coërcive measures to collect money due her citizens, but she gave assurance that she had "no purpose or intention to make even the smallest acquisition of territory." Hay drafted a reply in the President's name that disclaimed any objection to forceful collection of claims provided no territory was acquired. This response quoted what the President had already said in his annual message of December 3, 1901: "We do no guarantee any State against punishment, . . . provided that punishment does not take the form of the acquisition of territory by any non-American power." Joint intervention was probably first proposed by Britain rather than Germany. Britain was taking strong measures on her own initiative, and was more uncompromising than Germany. It is certain that she was not led into the venture by Germany, as Roosevelt later believed. In any case, by November, 1902, the two nations had agreed to act jointly. They sent several ultimata, the last on December 7. After some debate as to the best measures, they seized or sank Venezuelan gunboats on December 9, landed troops at La Guayra on the tenth, and bombarded Puerto Cabello on the thirteenth. On the sixteenth they were joined by Italy. Then, through the United States, Venezuela urged arbitration, and Germany and Britain agreed to it in principle, but with reservations. They invited Roosevelt to act as arbiter. Roosevelt was tempted, hesitated, was urged by Hay and others not to accept, and finally declined. He refused partly in order to resuscitate the dying Hague Tribunal by trying to send it an important dispute to settle. He urged the powers to take their arbitration to the Hague. Roosevelt's unwillingness to become arbiter led to several weeks of further argument over who should arbitrate, over the precedence of classes of claims, and over rules. Meantime, on December 20 Britain and Germany established a formal blockade pending detailed agreements. During this later phase Germany again twice bombarded Venezuelan territory. Finally on February 19 the

---

[1] Selected from *Theodore Roosevelt and the Rise of America to World Power* (Baltimore: Johns Hopkins University Press, 1956), pp. 396–99, 412–21. Reprinted with permission.

446

blockade was lifted and by May a series of protocols had been signed agreeing upon mixed claims commissions and ultimate Hague arbitration of certain disputed points. This is the simple outline of events.

The presence of foreign ships blockading and then bombarding the ports of a Caribbean country caused great excitement. In spite of Roosevelt's and Hay's formal approval of the action, and notwithstanding the fact that Dictator Castro of Venezuela had obviously misbehaved and had clearly shown himself irresponsible, the American press and American political leaders cried out in alarm. So, too, did the British press and British leaders over a partnership with Germany that was none too popular in Britain and that was now arousing hostility in America where Britain wished friendship. Because of the firm entente that was developing with Great Britain, she was on the whole exonerated from evil intent and the onus of American opinion fell on Germany, increasingly so after she alone bombarded again in January. Roosevelt later explained, "I had not the least fear of England and knew that there was no danger from England. . . . I also knew that English public opinion was already very hostile to the action of the English Government."

That Germany had any designs on Venezuelan territory seems doubtful. In the light of events from 1914 to 1945, many American historians have, however, persuaded themselves of the evil intent of Germany in her earlier relations with America. . . .

Even more controversial has been the rôle Roosevelt himself played in bringing the nations to arbitrate. At the time, the secret of whatever he did was kept so well that no one suspected he was doing more than to encourage arbitration, to refuse to act as arbiter himself, and to help persuade the disputants to use the Hague Tribunal instead. Then in 1916 as an appendix to a new printing of his *John Hay*, William R. Thayer published a long letter from Roosevelt written August 21, 1916, that told a startling story. The ex-President recounted how he threatened to make war on Germany, prepared his fleet for action, and sent a personal ultimatum to the Kaiser that forced him to submit his claims to arbitration, and to abandon his plans to acquire territory.

* * *

. . . On August 14, 1906, [Roosevelt also] recalled to Henry White: "On one occasion (that of Venezuela) [I] have had to make a display of force and to convince . . . [the Kaiser] definitely that I would use the force if necessary." This story, told to an intimate friend four years after the event, has the ring of authenticity. "I saw the German Ambassador privately myself," the President confided to White; "told him to tell the Kaiser that I had put Dewey in charge of our fleet to maneuver in West Indian waters; that the world at large should know this merely as a maneuver, and we should strive in every way to appear simply as cooperating with the Germans; but that I regretted to say that the popular feeling was such that I should be obliged to interfere, by force if necessary, if the Germans took any action which looked like the acquisition of territory." "This was not in any way intended as a threat," Roosevelt had assured the Kaiser, "but as the position . . . which the American people would demand." He wanted the Kaiser to understand the American position "before the two nations drifted into such a position that trouble might come." To White Roosevelt commented, "I do not know whether it was a case of post hoc or propter hoc." "But," he concluded, "immediately afterwards the Kaiser made to me the proposition that I should arbitrate myself, which I finally got him to modify so that it was sent to the Hague." Then Roosevelt admonished White that he must not tell anybody but George Meyer what the President had just revealed to him about the Kaiser, for, he quoted Carlyle, "the Kaiser . . . is 'gey ill' to live with, on occasions." . . .

. . . What, then, were the series of actions that can be established?

The use of force in Venezuela aroused criticism in both Britain and the United States. . . .

By December 15 criticism of the venture was troubling the British Government. On that day White reported the "whole Venezuelan matter, especially British acting with Germans, unpopular" in England. The same day Metternich described Lansdowne as deeply concerned not to offend America. King Edward, he said, was unhappy over the whole Venezuelan engagement. On December 15, too, the Government's Venezuelan venture was sharply criticized in a House of Commons debate and Germany and Britain were both vigorously attacked in the United States Senate. . . .

December 16 saw the climax of the first phase of the dispute. On that date Hay repeated Venezuela's proposal for arbitration and this time urged its acceptance. On the same day von Holleben from New York again cabled to describe the hostility of American papers and the alarm in German-American and English-American financial circles. He transmitted the views of Latin American merchants that German trade would be injured and passed on the rumor that Britain might desert Germany and join the United States. Finally, he recommended considering the acceptance of the principle of arbitration for the sake of the impression this would make on America. In London that day Lord Lansdowne spoke to German Ambassador Metternich of the British Cabinet's concern to withdraw from Venezuela by accepting arbitration if a good opportunity offered. Lansdowne was alarmed about Parliament and about "signs that in the United States a storm of public opinion was rising against which the Government there would be helpless." Lord Lansdowne wished Germany and Britain therefore to agree on replies whose substance would be similar. Metternich warned that the British Government was too weak to stand up against protests at home and in America and hence he advised his government to join with Britain in getting out of Venezuela with honor if that could be done. On the fateful December 16, finally, the British Cabinet agreed to an arbitration or joint commission for limited purposes at least and Lansdowne assured the Commons that Britain would not take territory or land more troops.

On December 17 Hay's urgent proposal of arbitration was delivered in both London and Berlin, and Lansdowne received that morning a cable from Sir Michael Herbert describing growing irritation in the American Congress and regret on the part of Britain's American friends that Britain was acting with Germany. The same day Prime Minister Balfour announced in the House of Commons that the British "never had any intention of landing troops in Venezuela or of occupying territory, even though that occupation might only be of a temporary character." That day, too, Henry White was notified informally of Britain's agreement to arbitrate. And in Berlin von Bülow sent instructions to Metternich to promise Lansdowne full coöperation in dispelling criticism of their joint action. Bülow urged Lansdowne to join him in seizing the initiative from Washington and making a proposal of arbitration before America abandoned its rôle as messenger for an active diplomatic rôle. Bülow proposed joint action before America should insist upon a program that would have strong support. Germany, indeed, hoped Roosevelt would act as arbiter. . . .

What was Roosevelt himself doing? First, he was holding the fleet in readiness for action. From the days when he was Assistant Secretary of the Navy, Roosevelt and the Navy had been interested in defense of the Caribbean. It was with this in mind that he tried in January, 1902, to buy the Virgin Islands. Only three days after the German Government informed him that to collect debts it might have to occupy Venezuelan territory temporarily, Roosevelt issued an executive order on December 17, 1901, transferring Culebra, off the coast of Puerto Rico, to the Navy Department so that a base could be established there "in case of sudden war." The Navy in January, 1902, sent Commander John E. Pillsbury to investigate German naval activities off Venezuela. In January, too, Congress was asked for money to finance a fleet mobilization at Culebra. In February the State Department sought information through its consuls about landing places and roads in Venezuela. In May the Navy became alarmed again over the activities of another German vessel. In the early summer a naval board inspected places where the Germans might land. Landing possibilities for Americans, too, were secretly explored, and plans drawn for the defense of the Venezuelan coast. In June a great mobilization of the fleet in the Caribbean was announced. In June, too, Roosevelt wrote Dewey and in July Secretary Moody informed the fleet that the President was deeply interested in the success of the manoeuvers. In November the fleet gathered at Culebra. Dewey consented to command during the mobilization and on November 18 received his orders. He was instructed to hold the fleet ready to move at a moment's notice. His fleet comprised "fifty ships including every battleship and every torpedo boat that we had." On December 8, the day after the final Anglo-German ultimata, Dewey took command. At the same time a naval attaché was stationed in Caracas, capital of Venezuela, to explore roads and to consult about defense of the country. Because of the crisis, Admiral Henry C. Taylor cabled December 14 for confirmation of his instructions to scatter the fleet during the holidays. On December 18, the day after fright over American opinion had brought both Germany and Britain separately to decide to conciliate America by agreeing to arbitrate, Taylor received instructions to divide the squadron as planned.

Several bits of contemporary evidence indicate that the fleet was being used to back up foreign policy concerning Germany and that by the end of December the objective had been won. Just before Christmas Captain William S. Cowles, then acting chief of the Office of Naval Intelligence, guardedly wrote Rear Admiral Taylor in the Caribbean that "the presence of the fleet" in the Caribbean, "concentrated and organized for work, was probably a convenience to the administration in discussing the Venezuelan situation." Cowles was the President's brother-in-law and always in close touch with him. On January 3, Dewey entered in his journal the comment, "The work laid out so long ago and with such care . . . is now ended and successfully accomplished. . . . When one considers the technical success . . . and the effect on foreign powers, particularly at the present moment of the demonstration against Venezuela, of so powerful and mobile a fleet in the Caribbean, it can only be considered as a work redounding immensely to our naval and national prestige." Some months later Secretary Moody declared in a speech, "This country was never upon the borders of a greater peril than at the time of the Venezuela difficulty. . . . We had a battle fleet within reaching distance." In March, 1903, Admiral Dewey had to be called to the White House and reprimanded because he had told newspaper men he saw in the manoeuvers "an object lesson to the Kaiser, more than to any other person." When four years later Roosevelt wrote him the ultimatum story, Henry White replied, "What you write of your action in respect to the Emperor . . . is especially interesting to me as I was in charge at London during the whole of that episode and always suspected that you had given that Potentate a warning which no doubt saved the situation as other similar warnings given privately have settled other incidents known to me without wounding any national susceptibilities or causing any friction."

Besides manoeuvering the fleet for foreign policy purposes, Roosevelt had been making periodic pronouncements insisting that no European power could be allowed to acquire American territory. Certainly his warnings in conversation with Consul-General Bünz in June and in letters to Speck von Sternburg in July and October were transmitted to the German Government. In October, 1901, and November, 1902, Speck came briefly to America and stayed with Roosevelt, and on his return to Germany was questioned both times about Roosevelt's views on South America. He was known to be one of the President's most trusted friends, and it is now known that he was on occasion used by the President as a confidential agent.

As the crisis approached, Roosevelt and Hay used every possible means to settle the controversy peacefully without actually officially intervening. On December 5, four days before the attack on Venezuelan ships, Hay cabled Chargé H. Percival Dodge in Berlin and Henry White in London that the President would be glad if an arrangement could be made that "might obviate the necessity of any exhibition of force on the part of Germany and Great Britain." On December 8, the day on which German and British representatives withdrew from Venezuela and the day before the naval engagement, White had a long confidential talk with Prime Minister Balfour, in which he expressed anxiety over the Venezuelan situation and pleaded with Balfour "not [to] allow his government to be led by Germany into doing anything to exacerbate our public opinion." White saw Balfour again later in the week, again on December 15, and then every day, occasionally twice a day, during the weeks preceding and following Christmas. White believed that it was partly because of these talks that Balfour persuaded the Cabinet to let him announce publicly on December 11 what they had intended to keep secret, namely, their decision not to land troops on Venezuelan soil.

Dates of talks of von Holleben and his chargé von Quadt with Roosevelt and Hay are important but difficult to ascertain. Von Holleben did have an interview at the White House December 8. This was the day after Britain and Germany had delivered their ultimata to Venezuela. It was the very day on which White sounded warning to the British Government and on which Dewey took command of the fleet Roosevelt had concentrated in the Caribbean to meet possible trouble. An "ultimatum" could well have been delivered that day. On December 13, the day after Hay sent his informal proposal of arbitration, von Holleben cabled the first of his two known warnings about public opinion. On December 16, the day before Hay's more urgent appeal, von Holleben's second warning was sent and this time he recommended considering the acceptance of arbitration, which already had been decided upon unbeknown to von Holleben and not publicly announced for another three days. On December 18, 20, and 29 von Quadt had talks with Hay and reported them to his government. Hay was friendly and assured von Quadt of his friendliness toward Germany, but on December 18, the day following Hay's urgent appeal and the day before the agreement to arbitrate was announced, Hay warned him and he warned his government that if Germany did not soon agree to arbitrate Congress might adopt a resolution instructing the President to enforce the Monroe Doctrine against her. On December 29, on the same day when von Quadt was reporting that Hay had no distrust of Germany, Sir Michael Herbert cabled his government that "the outburst in this country against Germany has been truly remarkable, and suspicion of the German Emperor's designs in the Caribbean Sea is shared by the Administration, the press, and the public alike." Sir Michael ventured the guess that the irritation was in part spontaneous but was in part stimulated by the Navy. "It will continue to be fostered," he predicted, "by the naval authorities . . . who wish to increase the navy, and by the powerful shipbuilding firms of Cramp in the East and Scott in the West, who want more orders for ships."

A fact whose importance has been overlooked by everyone, defenders and depreciators of Roosevelt alike, was a conversation that took place in Berlin two days after Roosevelt probably made whatever threat he did make to von Holleben. On December 10, the day after the sinking of the ships, when the newspapers of various countries were full of criticism of Germany's action, Speck von Sternburg, home on leave from India, was summoned to give the German Government his impressions of his recent visit to Roosevelt. "Nothing could have pleased me more," Speck wrote Roosevelt, "because it gave me a chance to tell them the truth. I've told them every bit of it and have used rather plain talk. When I left here a month ago found them comfortably basking in the illusions of the great visit [of Prince Henry to the United States]." "Fear I've knocked them down rather roughly," he confided to his friend the American President, "but should consider myself a cowardly weakling if I had let things stand as they were."

One other factor seems important. Through these years Germany was trying desperately to go "hand in hand" with America, to win and keep her friendship. She was aware of American sensitiveness over the Monroe Doctrine. She did everything she could to avoid trouble about it. She was more conciliatory toward Venezuela before the intervention than Britain had been. She sought and thought she had American approval for each step she took. Had she foreseen what the American reaction was going to be, she would almost certainly have refrained from the venture entirely. Ambassador von Holleben, however, and Chargé von Quadt had given the Kaiser and his Chancellor no hint of unfavorable reaction. On the contrary they had transmitted repeated assurances of American friendliness. Then on December 10 came the burst of hostility toward Germany in America, and on that same day Roosevelt's friend Speck, direct from long talks with the President, administered to the German Government the shock of a true picture of American sentiment and the failure of German diplomacy. . . .

THE CHESTER PROJECT[1]   *L. J. Gordon*

The roots of American imperialism ripened into a definite policy through the medium of the much maligned but little understood Chester concession which had its inception in 1907. In that year Mr. Arthur Moore and Mr. Homer Davenport journeyed to Arabia to buy horses. In the course of their trip they became enthusiastic over the prospect of a railway connecting Aleppo with the port of Alexandretta. Upon their return to the United States they discussed the plan with a group of financiers whose interest was aroused. . . . A short time later Commander Arthur Chester, a son of the admiral, arrived in Constantinople to lay out the plan for the proposed railroad. In March, 1908, formal application was made for a concession. The response again proving favorable, the younger Chester proceeded to Aleppo to decide on the exact route for the line. . . .

In spite of the difficulties, Commander Chester succeeded in obtaining favorable action on a nine-hundred-mile concession late in 1909 by an Ottoman Parliamentary Committee. Thus encouraged, he returned to the United States and in November organized the original Ottoman-American Development Company, chartered under the laws of New Jersey and capitalized at $600,000. Among those interested in the project were MacArthur Brothers, Laidlaw and Company, E. C. Converse and Company, and Charles A. Moore, all of New York.

At first European imperialists with vested interests in Turkey had paid scant attention to the possibility of real competition from amateur American imperialists, but when the threat began to assume serious proportions they girded themselves for battle. English, French, and particularly German concessionaires and governments took active steps to close the door to American capital investment in Turkey.

Responding to appeals from the Ottoman-American promoters, the De-

[1] Selected from *American Relations with Turkey, 1830–1930: An Economic Interpretation* (Philadelphia: University of Pennsylvania Press, 1932), pp. 257–64. Reprinted with permission.

partment of State rendered all possible assistance. Acting on instructions from the Department, Minister Straus actively supported Commander Chester in his negotiations with Ottoman authorities. The latter, however, quickly grasped the opportunity to bargain. They demanded American consent either to the abrogation or to the restriction of the capitulations and approval of the proposal to increase customs duties from 11 to 15 per cent *ad valorem.*

[In reply, American leaders agreed] that upon being officially notified of the final granting of the concession the Government of the United States would "take pleasure in immediately announcing its formal acquiescence in the proposed 4 per cent increase in Turkish customs duties upon the consent of the other interested Powers...."

With reference to the general question of capitulations the Ottoman official was informed that when his Government could give assurances of sufficient judicial reforms the Government of the United States would be found ready "to give the matter sympathetic attention."

Secretary Knox's note paved the way to favorable consideration of the American project by Ottoman authorities. But formidable opposition was encountered in the form of German determination to block the concession. Consequently, the next step required the removal of that obstacle. Upon being informed by Minister Straus that removal of German opposition would result in prompt approval of the concession, the Department caused "very discreet but strong oral representations" to be made to the German Government, referring to American-German cooperation in China and Liberia, alluding to Germany's open door policy in Persia, and intimating that "failing German cooperation and the removal of German opposition in this instance it might be necessary for this Government to cooperate in Turkey with other powers." The German reply expressed surprise and denied active opposition. It was added that there would be no objection to American cooperation in Turkey if the Chester group would modify its plans so as not to conflict with German interests already acquired.

Actually, however, German opposition became more intense, and a threat was made to Ottoman authorities that German consent to the proposed increase of customs duties would be withheld if the American project were approved. Threats alone were not used, however. The German promise to support Turkish sovereignty in Crete produced marvelous results. The project was referred to a Board of Jurists instead of to Parliament and the latter body closed its 1910 session without considering the project.

The German Ambassador then arranged for a meeting of certain of his diplomatic colleagues to persuade them to refuse to consent to the proposed customs increase if the Turks should grant the concession to the Americans. In retaliation the American Ambassadors at London, Paris, Rome, and St. Petersburg (Leningrad) were instructed by the Department "discreetly to sound the governments to which they were accredited, with a view to affecting favorably their attitude toward the American enterprise." The foreign offices in Paris and London responded favorably, while Rome was noncommittal. St. Petersburg objected on the basis of an agreement involving its interests in the Black Sea Region, but favored the project for political reasons provided a satisfactory agreement could be reached. Although the British Government had no objection to the proposal, upon being asked for active support by Ambassador Reid the Foreign Office stated that it was preoccupied with the task of pressing British interests at the southern terminus of the Bagdad railway and could not view with favor any oil grants at Mosul or Kerkuk.

Following the first defeat of the project in 1910, an official of the Ottoman-American Development Company was advised

to call at the Department at an early date, for the purpose of conferring and mapping out a line of action in order that we may exert every pressure as soon as Parliament convenes looking to the early granting of the concession.

At that point Ambassador Straus took a leave of absence from his post, leaving Mr. Hoffman Philip in charge. The Department, thinking that an official of higher rank should be in Constantinople at that crucial time, assigned Mr. John Ridgey Carter, who was then Minister to Bucharest, to Turkey. His instructions stated that among the many important matters then pending, the Chester Concession was paramount and one in which "the President takes a keen interest." Ambassador Carter was further instructed to study the history of the project carefully so as to be able to render intelligent advice and support.

In addition to the appointment of Ambassador Carter, Mr. Huntington Wilson, Assistant Secretary of State, was designated Ambassador Extraordinary on September 30, 1910, on a Special Mission to the Ottoman Empire. His ostensible duty was to return a visit of courtesy paid the previous year by Ziya Pasa who had traveled to Washington to announce the accession of Sultan Mehmed V. The real purpose, however, was "to create an atmosphere favorable to the Chester claim."

... The interpretation of Article IV [in the Treaty of 1830] proved to be the chief obstacle. In a Parliamentary speech in November the Grand Vizier stated that the American interpretation of that article was the chief obstacle to the granting of the concession. That being the case, Ambassador Carter immediately secured the Department's permission to propose a solution. A draft treaty was drawn up by the Department, but at the request of the Grand Vizier that procedure was discarded in favor of an exchange of notes which met the Turkish objection.

The Turkish law on mines required special research permits for each project, but that difficulty was avoided by granting a blanket permit for each province.

Finally the Americans yielded to the Germans in the dispute over the terminal, and all objections having been met the Grand Vizier, the Committee on Public Works, and the Council of Ministers approved the project and sent the papers to Parliament in May, 1911. Following a debate of two days the American proposal was defeated for the second time when it was voted to postpone final action to the autumn session.

In preparation for the final struggle in the fall of 1911 Ambassador Carter was relieved and Mr. W. W. Rockhill, who had been at St. Petersburg and was "one of the most distinguished officers in the service of the Department," was appointed Ambassador to Constantinople. He also was instructed to study the Chester Concession carefully "with a view to the prompt consummation of the concession upon the reopening of the Ottoman Parliament."

At that crucial point in the struggle the Ottoman-American Development Company began to waver. When Parliament convened in October the Company had no representative in Constantinople, and five days after the session had begun, the caution money amounting to $88,000 was withdrawn. When it became known in Washington that officials of the Company were considering the withdrawal of the deposit the Chief of Near Eastern Affairs rushed to New York to dissuade them, "but without avail." In spite of those developments the bill was presented for debate in Parliament on November 20 and was considered several times by that body. Finally on December 11 Ambassador Rockhill informed the Grand Vizier that the Company had withdrawn its caution money as well as its application for the concession. Consequently the bill was never put to a vote in Parliament.

After its determined efforts and near success the Department was greatly provoked with officials of the Ottoman-American Development Company. Secretary Knox addressed a final note to the Company which literally washed the Department's hands of any further responsibility on its behalf, and the first attempt at American imperialism in Turkey was unsuccessfully concluded.

THE ALGECIRAS CONFERENCE[1]   *Alfred L. P. Dennis*

... The negotiations which led to the Algeciras Conference took place at the same time that the preliminaries of the Portsmouth meeting were occupying a prominent place. Furthermore, though the attention of the statesmen of three continents was centered on the Portsmouth negotiations, the diplomacy of Europe was also concerned in trying to find a way to peace through the international maze of the Moroccan question. We may well ask why such a topic as the Algeciras Conference, which temporarily adjusted affairs in Morocco, should find a place in American foreign policy. What new diplomatic adventure placed the United States in a position of strategic importance as regards a problem which was of significance chiefly to European affairs?

The answer will become clearer if we recall the situation which was responsible for the Moroccan problem as it presented itself to the world in 1905. Briefly the fact of the establishment of the *entente cordiale* between Great Britain and France in 1904 was the inciting element. The situation of Morocco had been unsatisfactory in time past, but it was the agreement of Great Britain and France to wipe the slate clean of their previous and varied disputes that brought Morocco to the front as a major question of worldwide importance. France now recognized the predominant interest of En-

---

gland in Egypt, and Great Britain in turn recognized French interests in Morocco. Thus at a stroke through the Anglo-French accord so established German policy suffered a shock.

Since the time of the British occupation of Egypt in 1882 German diplomacy had used Anglo-French rivalry as to Egypt as a tool to forward German interests. German support had been necessary to the development of British policies in Egypt, consequently German approval had to be secured by Great Britain at a price. Now with the ending of Anglo-French differences German support was no longer to be of such value to England. There had been a new deal and the trump had changed. British foreign policy, which had been directed to an exaggerated degree by anxieties as to Egypt, was now to a great extent free from German influence. France in turn had taken a long preliminary step to the development of her African interests. Germany's "place in the sun" seemed to be shadowed by passing clouds and consequently the Kaiser and von Bülow looked about for support and naturally turned to the United States to try to use her in the Moroccan situation and if possible to drag her into the solution of a problem which was essentially of European origin. . . .

As the time approached for the conference, which was now definitely fixed for Algeciras, the anxiety and uncertainties of France came out more clearly. Both she and Great Britain were apprehensive of a German policy which might be too aggressive. Some of these anxieties were shown to Sir Edward Grey as he took office as British Foreign Secretary on Dec. 11, 1905, at the resignation of Lord Lansdowne. The French on January 10, 1905, put a critical question to Great Britain. The French Ambassador, M. Paul Cambon, asked "whether, in the event of aggression against France by Germany Great Britain would be prepared to render to France armed assistance?" This very question serves once more to demonstrate the mistake which the Germans made six months earlier in asserting that Great Britain had offered to France an offensive and defensive alliance against Germany. If that had been true why should such a question be asked at this late day? Sir Edward Grey had no objection to military and naval conversations taking place between the two nations but he refused to pledge England to more than a benevolent neutrality in the event of war.

After the general election of January, 1906, the question was repeated on January 31. In the meantime Sir Edward Grey had said to Count Metternich, the German Ambassador, that "in the event of an attack upon France by Germany arising out of our Morocco agreement, public feeling in England would be so strong that no British Government could remain neutral." It appears that British policy at this stage may be criticized, for in permitting the military and naval conversations to continue Great Britain came close to "an honorable understanding." In view of the situation would it not have been wiser either to give the undertaking asked for by France or to have refused permission to continue these unofficial yet direct conversations?

The atmosphere of suspicion and of dread that filled the minds of European statesmen was not cleared. Indeed it increased. . . .

President Roosevelt soon became convinced that "Germany was aiming in effect at the partition of Morocco, which was the very reverse of what she was claiming to desire." This was perhaps suggested by a memorandum submitted by the German Embassy on January 23, 1906. It dealt with the organization of police, protested against a mandate for France, and, for the policing of Morocco, favored the use of minor states such as Holland, Switzerland, Denmark, Norway or Sweden as the ones least likely to arouse jealousy. In each case, however, German influence at home was to be predicated.

On January 28, as France began to give way in her original demand that all police should be under her direction, Germany became bolder and proposed that the Sultan of Morocco should select such officers as he saw fit, under international control as to funds, etc. This Germany wished the United States to advocate. Mr. White, in reply to inquiries, pointed out the connection between police control and financial questions and advised delay. On February 1 these financial matters came to the front and occupied the attention of the delegates for some time especially as the organization of the state bank was involved. The sessions on the bank were at times rather bitter; but neither France nor Germany wished to have the conference go on the rocks entirely on this financial issue so compromises were made and plans for the bank were accepted. American interests were not involved though American bankers were invited to subscribe. Furthermore there was the minor point as to the protection of Jews in Morocco on which President Roosevelt had instructed Mr. White to take steps. Quite early it became apparent that any active intervention on behalf of the Jews by the United States would be misunderstood. So at the end of the conference Mr. White contented himself with the expression of the hope that all subjects of the Sultan of Morocco, including Jews, would be treated with justice and equity without distinction of creed.

We now come to the major question of the police with respect to which President Roosevelt directed that American influence should be cast to prevent a break-up of the conference and he himself interfered to persuade the Kaiser to give way. The police question, as had been foreseen by publicists of the day, involved the real control over the chief ports of Morocco and, therefore, implied the regulation of foreign commerce and the maintenance of the open door. . . .

The French position was that the police should be turned over to her and to Spain. To this, Germany had objected, favoring either some of the smaller disinterested European states or desiring that the whole matter should be left to the Sultan of Morocco, who of course had come to look on the Kaiser as his one friend in Europe. . . .

It was at this stage that the President interfered. He instructed Secretary Root to propose to the German Ambassador a possible compromise. This was (1) that the organization of the police force should be left to the Sultan, (2) that the funds for its support should be supplied by the proposed international state bank, (3) that French and Spanish officers and non-commissioned men should be in charge reporting annually to the Sultan and to Italy as a third Mediterranean power, and that in the fourth place:

full assurances be given by France and Spain, and made obligatory upon all their officers who shall be appointed by the Sultan, for the open door, both as to trade, equal treatment and opportunity in competing for public works and concessions.

On February 22, Germany replied accepting all points except the third. She expressed the most lively gratitude to the President for his mediation and proposed an alternative to point 3. This alternative would have left the Sultan free to choose the officers from among the states of Europe. Already all over Europe there were anxiety and alarm at the turn affairs were taking at Algeciras. From Austrian, British, Russian, French, Italian, and neutral sources there came but one plea, namely that some solution should be found. At first the notion had been that the Kaiser was not properly informed; now the cry was that his *amour propre* had been offended and that he was taking too great a personal interest in the matter.

So on March 7 a further letter was sent to von Sternburg by Secretary Root in which the President said to the Kaiser that he could not ask France to make any further concessions. He then reminded the Kaiser of what he had already done in the interests of peace and recalled the letter of the previous June, from the Kaiser, which stated that in case differences should threaten the proposed conference the Kaiser declared that "he, in every case, will be ready to back up the decision which you [Roosevelt] should consider to be the most fair and the most practicable." The President continued, saying that if Germany rejected the plan, proposed (by America), then:

the general opinion of Europe and America would be unfavorable, and Germany would lose that increase of credit and moral power that the making of this arrangement would secure to her, and might be held responsible, probably far beyond the limits of reason, for all the evils that may come in the train of a disturbed condition of affairs in Europe.

This was fairly plain speaking, or rather writing; but the Kaiser still hung on—this time to another alternative, which was proposed by Austria at the instigation of Germany. At first this proposal seemed to be acceptable to the delegates at Algeciras. The British representative, though nominally supporting the French, privately said he did not think France could continue to object to this German-Austrian plan. It was, as described by Mr. White:

French officers to organize police under Sultan in Tangiers, Safi, Rabat, Tetuan, the Spanish in Mogador, Larache, Mazagan, and Swiss or Dutch the officer of superior rank in Casablanca, the latter to be also inspector general of police in all other ports and report results to diplomatic body at Tangiers. General opinion favorable to Austrian proposals even Russian and British Ambassadors thinking it might, with modifications of detail, be accepted by France and that she could not afford to break up Conference by rejecting it. Casablanca is port in which German interests predominate.

At this point the President stepped in with vigor; and a telegram was despatched by von Sternburg retailing his views. There is of course no mention of this in Bishop. The telegram to Berlin reporting Roosevelt's views was as follows:

This Austrian proposal in my [Roosevelt's] mind is absurd because it favors the very ideas the conference has been trying to eliminate namely partition and spheres of influence. Placing Spanish and French officers in the same ports gives according to my view a safer guarantee than placing them separately in single ports. This has distinctly the flavor of a French, a Spanish and a Dutch or Swiss sphere of influence. I also do not see how the duties of the police inspector can be made compatible with military discipline. Austria wants an officer, who performs the same duties in the port of Casablanca as his French and Spanish comrades do, to act in all ports as their superior and inspector. That would bring friction at the start. The proposal I suggested is the better and safer and the only one I can support.

The same day, March 14, Secretary Root had a talk with von Sternburg and stated that the American delegates would not vote for the Austrian plan. This was followed three days later by a note to von Sternburg recapitulating the whole matter from the American point of view. However, on the same day, March 17, the President had a long talk with von Sternburg in which he pointed out the great difficulties of the United States with respect to the Algeciras Conference, the complaints and criticisms which were pouring in and the undoubted fact that the American people were rapidly taking sides against Germany. To this the Ambassador also bore witness. The result was a prompt reply in which von Bülow and the Kaiser gave way completely....

This change of front on the part of Germany is probably due to three things: (1) a real desire on the part of the Kaiser and von Bülow to avoid a European war, (2) the threat of President Roosevelt to publish all the correspondence, (3) an appreciation of the fact that public opinion in the world and particularly in America was against German contentions. At all events the President promptly expressed himself as greatly pleased at the result; and on March 20 he suggested to von Sternburg that, at a meeting of German-American veterans, praise should be given the Kaiser for this triumph of German diplomacy at Algeciras. This was done on April 12 in a speech by the President which previously had been carefully gone over by von Sternburg and also by Jusserand....

Perhaps the background of Anglo-American relations during these months and weeks of anxiety may be better seen in a letter which Ambassador Reid wrote to the President on June 19. In the course of this letter it is delicately suggested that perhaps the President's relations with von Sternburg had been such as to give pause to some Englishmen. Mr. Reid added:

The truth is that the Emperor's assiduous efforts to cultivate the most intimate relations with you have attracted the attention of all the chancellories in Europe, and a common comment upon it is that the Emperor overdoes his love-making as he does his diplomacy, with a certain German confidence in the value of brute vigor in either pursuit! What I have sometimes feared was that this might affect the feeling here which might not be beneficial in Mr. Root's coming negotiations on the questions still unsettled between us. The truth seems to me that our relations with England are of far greater importance to us than those with Germany—there being more points at issue, more chances of friction and greater difficulty in almost every question that arises.... I cannot personally see anything to be gained from unusually good relations with Germany which would compensate us for the least jar in our relations with Great Britain, since I know of no serious questions we have to settle with Germany, while there are certainly a good many with Great Britain still unsettled. Aside from that, Germany isn't planted all along our frontier, and our negotiations with her will ordinarily therefore be on subjects less acute and ticklish.

This was good advice; the future was to prove its value. Yet the President never did a more adroit thing in international affairs than in his intervention as to the Moroccan question in June, 1905, and in February and March, 1906. That most people supposed he was hand in glove with the Kaiser was perhaps not surprising. Yet his final stand was unquestionably in support of France. It was only natural that until that became very clear there should be some suspicion of his activities. As we turn to France there is prompt and unquestioned appreciation of his services. Mr. McCormick reported from Paris that the French government was eager to recognize "the signal aid rendered by President Roosevelt in arriving at a just solution of the differences between France and Germany with reference to Morocco—*Ni vainqueur ni vaincu.*" Such a view was "as profound as it is general in Europe, springing from President Roosevelt's successful intervention in the Russo-Japanese war, and now, strengthened and confirmed, it singles him out as the arbitrator to whom all can turn when dissensions threaten to bring on war in any part of the globe." There is furthermore a truly fine letter from the President to Ambassador Jusserand of April 25 in which credit for the happy solution is given whole-heartedly to Jusserand. This is especially significant as the lack of the physical and moral weight of Russia had been so evident during 1905–1906. The Russo-Japanese war had drawn Russia away from western Europe and her troubles both domestic and external had been a severe blow to her partner in the Dual Alliance. There can be no question, however, of the cordial relations between the United States and France as the result of the Algeciras Conference.

As regards Germany it was to be expected that following the tactical defeat of von Bülow's plans there should be a certain cooling off. The President, however, had aided Germany's strategical victory in securing the meeting of the Algeciras Conference. That was the clear fact. Germany neither by bluff nor by diplomatic persistence could have won such a victory without the aid of the United States. . . .

THE UNITED STATES AND MEXICO[1]   *Howard F. Cline*

Some of the most crucial decisions that determined the ultimate fate of Mexico and its Revolution were not made within the area at all, but in Washington, London, Berlin, and Paris. Perhaps the single most critical constant element of the whole era was the varying attitudes and actions taken by Woodrow Wilson, President of the United States from 1913 to 1921. The position of the United States vis à vis Mexico and the European crises that led to the first World War affected all parties, and formed the context in which relations with Mexico were carried on for nearly a generation.

Through a split in Republican ranks, Woodrow Wilson was elected Democratic President of the United States in 1912 and was inaugurated March 4, 1913. In most respects he was the opposite of his predecessor, Taft. Wilson felt that the President should be a strong leader. As the only member

---

[1] Selected from *The United States and Mexico*, pp. 130–50. Reprinted by permission of Harvard University Press. Copyright 1953 by the President and Fellows of Harvard College.

of the government who did not represent a special or partial interest, the President should personally represent the whole people.

Neither avowedly a pacifist nor an imperialist, Wilson was an idealistic nationalist. His political creed drew heavily on the stern Christian morality his Presbyterian father had inculcated in him as a youth. He sought the truth, and once he believed he had found it, rarely did he change his mind. He seemed intolerant of criticism, and often considered opposition to his views the result of insufficient study by his opponents. If they persisted in criticism he immediately suspected personal, materialistic interests. Like Carranza, Wilson made many friends but eventually lost most of them; his political opponents inevitably became personal enemies. Wilson thoroughly enjoyed political fighting, perhaps feeling that he alone was overcoming the forces of evil that would otherwise undermine the world, the United States, and the Democratic Party.

More than most Presidents, Wilson was his own Secretary of State. The first nominal incumbent of that important office was William Jennings Bryan, too great a party power to be kept out of the cabinet. Bryan was a pacifist and was notoriously indiscreet. Distrustful both of Bryan and the Republican-riddled Department of State, Wilson by-passed the orthodox handling of Mexico by using his own special agents and by keeping the tangled threads of negotiations in his own supple but unskilled hands. He personally wrote, often on his famous portable typewriter, every major diplomatic dispatch; copies of some of the principal ones are not even on file in the Department of State.[2]

From the inauguration until Bryan resigned when European affairs grew too hot in June 1915, Mexico was the chief international problem of the United States; Woodrow Wilson was almost the only policy-maker. In this field even the influential Colonel E. M. House stayed aloof. The President was unprepared by experience or inclination to handle delicate international matters. His tendency was to project his domestic policy—where he could control the situation—into international affairs and try to control those elements in the same manner that he could force tariff bills through Congress.

For many months before and after March 1913 Woodrow Wilson believed that Mexicans were fully prepared for democracy in the American style. He assumed that the Mexican nation, though at a less advanced stage, was basically the same as the Anglo-Saxon ones; by some quirk of circumstance Mexicans spoke Spanish instead of English and lived outside the United States rather than in it, but their problems and outlook were parallel to the ones with which he was familiar through study or experience. Wilson acted as though the differences were superficial rather than fundamental. His early policies were predicated on the belief that if Mexicans would hold a free election and follow constitutional practices their troubles would evaporate. He learned that such was not the case.

---

[2] Author's note.—I am indebted to Dr. Philip H. Lowry for permission to use materials from his excellent but unpublished "The Mexican Policy of Woodrow Wilson" (Ph.D. dissertation, Yale, 1949), which is based on a wide range of private and archival materials in the United States, hitherto unutilized. In addition, I have drawn on data furnished me by Professor Arthur S. Link, whose researches into Wilsonia are only partially published. Interpretations are mine.

In a program of moral imperialism President Wilson placed the weight of the United States behind a continuous, sometimes devious, effort to force the Mexican nation to meet his ill-conceived specifications. Though he oozed sympathy, good will, and idealism, his basic misunderstanding of the main elements of life in the southern republic brought disaster in its train. Unfortunately Woodrow Wilson in 1913 was a man with a single view of Mexico and that one was wrong. He learned from experiences in Mexico and these lessons stood him in good stead later on the world stage. A difficult man to appraise, Wilson was a great one. These first efforts in Mexico are a minor part of a significant career. The Mexican episodes here bulk large because of the restricted frames of time and space. In the larger perspective of Wilson's total national activity, they shrink to more modest proportions and are counterbalanced by qualities and achievements not evident in his first brushes with the ruder facts of international life.

Wilson was slow to voice a Latin-American, much less a Mexican, policy. He early issued a prepared statement, March 11, 1913, which assured the world that in Latin America the United States had no sympathy with those who "seek to seize the power of government to advance their own personal interests or ambition." The windy and unclear sentiments puzzled everyone. The pronouncement was widely interpreted to serve notice on Central American revolutionists that Wilson would not favor their attempts to overthrow existing governments and that he was displeased with Huerta. That was true.

The larger significance of the initial statement was that it heralded a new and deviant policy of recognition when changes in form and personnel broke continuity. When a government succeeds by overturn, recognition is required; since that has happened often, the United States had by mid-nineteenth century established a policy to guide its actions. Writing in 1848, Secretary of State Buchanan had summed up the historic policy by saying that the United States always recognized *de facto* governments—ones that really had come into control. "We do not go behind the existing Government to involve ourselves in the question of legitimacy. It is sufficient for us to know that a government exists, capable of maintaining itself; and then its recognition on our part inevitably follows." To this time-tested formula had been added the ability of governments formed by revolution to comply with international obligations, especially the protection of foreign interests. If it existed and was stable, recognition merely registered that fact; it carried no cachet of approval or of disapproval. It was almost a routine diplomatic operation. Wilson proposed to change that.

For the mere fact of existence—*de facto*—and occasionally a pledge that it would protect third parties, Wilson substituted a new doctrine to decide whether a new government should be recognized by the United States. He thus reversed the settled policy. His was the test of "constitutional legitimacy." It implied the right of the United States to inquire fully into whether the new government was complying with its own national constitution and even to go behind its existence to scrutinize whether it had come to power because its leaders were motivated by personal interests and ambition, or whether they were really trying to pry off despotism by the historic right of revolution. Scrutiny and inquiry seemed to most Latin-American nations the same as meddling in their internal affairs.

Thus there were "good" revolutions and "bad" revolutions in the Wilsonian view. The latter brought only venal, unidealistic people to power, while the former put the particular nation back on the constitutional track by overthrowing an unconstitutional tyrant. As events in Mexico and elsewhere ultimately showed, the test of "constitutional legitimacy" was unworkable, especially in Latin America. The United States once renounced it as a national policy in 1921, though its shades rise constantly to plague international affairs since Wilson's time. In the case of Mexico, Wilson had to decide whether Huerta's was a "good" revolution, worthy of recognition, or a "bad" one, unworthy. If the latter, some "good" revolution had to overthrow Huerta to win the coveted accolade which Wilson now had made of recognition.

Europeans followed the old rules; Wilson made up his own. That was a core issue in the subsequent Wilsonian conflicts with Huerta, with Huerta's domestic opponents, and with Europe. When Wilson formally announced the new departure on March 11, 1913 he did not foresee the snarls and entanglements that might ensue. He was against bad men and for constitutionalism, worthy attitudes but hard to fit to specific international situations. . . .

The Lind Mission. Wilson determined to "mediate," but in such a way that Huerta would be eliminated and so that the Constitutionalists, by default, would be favored. Wilson showed himself the veriest tyro in diplomacy by not first taking the elementary precaution of finding out whether the Constitutionalists were willing to have such "mediation." Wilson named John Lind as his special presidential agent to dicker directly only with Huerta.

Lind knew nothing of Mexico, Spanish, or diplomacy. He was a tall, gaunt Swede who was a Democratic party power in Minnesota, where as governor he had battled the trusts. His arrival in Mexico created confusion; in addition to the Embassy staff (under a Chargé d'Affaires), Hale was also voicing the President's presumed views. Now a third plenary United States representative was added. The Lind Mission was well-meaning, but doomed almost from the outset when newspapers in the United States and Mexico headlined a story that he was going to get Huerta's resignation.

His instructions were not quite that drastic. He was directed to tell Huerta that the United States was "acting on the behalf of the rest of the world" (whom Wilson had not let in on the secret) and to demand as the price of mediation, four things: an armistice between the government and the Constitutionalists, an early election, Huerta's promise not to be a candidate, and his assurance that he would accept the results.

Lind's orders closed with a novel plea, "Can Mexico give the civilized world a satisfactory reason for rejecting our good offices? If Mexico can suggest any better way in which to show our friendship, serve the people of Mexico, and meet our international obligations, we are more than willing to consider the suggestion." Huerta made such a suggestion: friendship and all these other matters could be unmistakably shown by recognizing his government, the traditional symbol of amity. Otherwise he refused to consider this unwarranted series of proposals to bring peace to the land. He viewed the Constitutionalists as troublesome bandits.

Lind wrote Wilson that Huerta needed money and suggested a loan. Wilson approved, and on his second attempt, Lind offered American presidential help in arranging such a New York loan if the General would call an armistice and hold early elections.[3] Huerta refused this bare-faced bribe. Lind, with permission, threatened that President Wilson would recognize the Constitutionalists or intervene directly in Mexico, but Huerta knew it was a bluff. The Constitutionalists had not even formed a provisional government, and in the United States Senate a resolution fathered by Republicans asking for armed intervention in Mexico had been snowed under by presidential orders to the Democratic faithful.

But in answering Lind's notes, Huerta's Secretary of Foreign Affairs wrote that the Mexican Constitution prevented the provisional president from standing for reëlection. Lind took this back-handed comment as agreement that Wilson's terms for mediation had been accepted, and wired the President on August 27, 1913 that the mission was a success. It was not. Huerta had agreed to nothing, let alone resignation or mediation. . . .

Wilson began in late October to sound out the United States Congress on the possibility of armed intervention in Mexico. At the same time he tried to isolate Huerta from Europe and to aid his domestic foes, the Constitutionalists.

Wilson and Europe. Huerta was being supplied with money and munitions from European sources, nations that had followed Britain's lead in recognizing his *de facto* regime in March. They were, Wilson found, following Britain's Mexican policy, so the diplomatic problem for Wilson boiled down to persuading the English Foreign Office to withdraw its recognition from the provisional government and join the United States in boycotting the obnoxious Mexican. A note to the British and other nations suggested this course; it drew noncommittal replies. Wilson wanted Great Britain, France, and Germany to follow his plans; when they proved recalcitrant it raised Wilson's temper and hardened his determination to bring them to heel, so that Huerta would disappear.

Especially irritating to Wilson were the British. On the very day after Huerta had imprisoned the Mexican deputies, the new British Ambassador, Sir Lionel Carden, had ostentatiously handed his credentials to the provisional president—reiterating unmistakable recognition of his regime. Huerta naturally publicized the ceremony as approval, which it may have been. Thus even before the Mexican elections Wilson was enraged at "perfidious Albion" and cynical Europe. He decided to bend them to the Wilsonian will.

On October 25 or 26, Wilson tapped out on his little typewriter a blister-

---

[3] Author's note.—Outlines of a scheme whereby Huerta would be recognized if he would hold early elections had been proposed by spokesmen for the Southern Pacific Railway (Mexico), Phelps Dodge, Green Cannanea Copper Co., and Doheny oil interests; Bryan thought it "seemed to offer a way out" and Wilson approved at this stage. Bryan and Wilson encouraged Huerta to send a confidential agent to Washington to work out details. (Arthur S. Link information, from manuscript sources.)

ing memorandum. He turned the draft over to John Bassett Moore, Counselor of the State Department, to put into shape for circulation to all the major powers. Wilson expected to dispatch the finished note after results of the Mexican voting—which Wilson now knew would be fraudulent—were made public. The proposed circular note was timed by the fact that when Britain had provisionally recognized Huerta in March, it had announced that the matter would be reconsidered after the October 26 elections. Wilson expected to sway the British, and Europe, at this critical point.

He was convinced that British policy was being dominated by English commercial interests, especially oil companies. The Foreign Office was now going to have to choose between supporting Huerta or the United States. The Memorandum is an extraordinary production, significant in its revelation of Wilson's ignorance of the rudiments of normal international intercourse. Never published, it contains a number of flat statements for Moore to put into "as strong and direct language as the courtesies and proprieties of pacific diplomacy permit."[4]

The note Moore was to write for Wilson was based on six propositions. The United States, as the nation of paramount influence in the Western Hemisphere, has the greatest responsibility toward Mexico. The political fortunes of all Central America are involved. The government of Huerta, based on usurpation and force, would long ago have broken down but for the financial aid derived from its recognition by other nations without regard to the wishes and purposes of the United States. The continuance of Huerta's rule is impossible without the consent of the United States. No joint intervention will be considered. Will other, that is, European, governments cooperate with the United States, or is it their policy "to antagonize and thwart us and make our task one of domination and force"? A good question, but irrelevant.

The Mobile Address. Wilson delayed dispatching his proposed note, but instead gave the gist of it in a famous public speech at Mobile, Alabama, on October 27, 1913. This was a day after the Mexican "elections," and though the speech purported to cover Wilson's general Latin-American policy, it was aimed specifically at Great Britain and Huerta. Its theme was that businessmen (meaning British) had handicapped the development of Latin America (Mexico); foreign policies of nations (Great Britain) there had been based on material ("sordid") interests that had retarded growth of political liberty. The United States was going to stop all that. Wilson foreswore any annexationist designs on Latin America (Mexico).

The President's self-denial of territorial aims was clever and purposeful. If Europe failed to cooperate, the only alternative to throwing Huerta out might be armed intervention. In advance the Mexicans were thus assured that such invasion would be for "idealistic" not "imperialistic" ends; the statement also anticipated and denied beforehand the growing Republican demands for annexation of all or part of Mexico if such armed intervention

---

[4] Author's note.—Dr. Lowry found this draft in the National Archives, State, 812.00/9625a, as did Dr. Link. I have followed their independent syntheses and gloss, but have reversed Propositions 5 and 6.

actually got under way. Wilson had decided Huerta must go, no matter how, short of declared war.

When Wilson returned from Alabama, Moore read him an unforgettable lesson on international manners, especially those concerning recognition, and impugning the motives of friends. No European power need ask permission of the United States to recognize governments, Latin-American or not. Moore pointed out that the "sordid motives" attributed to the British foreign policy operated similarly in the United States: the Congress had exempted American vessels from paying tolls at the Panama Canal, in violation of the 1901 treaty with Britain. Moore mentioned other cases where fundamental economic or strategic concerns were justified as mainsprings of United States foreign policy. Economic and strategic stakes are often as vital as idealistic ones, and in some cases are more so. Policy may compound them all. Never again did Wilson speak publicly or diplomatically about the commercial exploitation of Latin America by the British. Nor did he send his projected note asking if Europe was trying to "antagonize and thwart us" by following the standard international usages sanctioned by experience and time.

The month of November 1913 was a tense one in Mexico City. After all Wilson's threats, bombast, scurryings, and alarms, a rupture of relations and war between Mexico and the United States seemed imminent. Mexicans rallied behind Huerta, who now became (to his own surprise) a symbol of political independence in the face of Wilsonian pressures. Probably he was never so strong. He seemed impregnable.

Wilson had so far violated every rule of good diplomacy. He had opened negotiations without first obtaining support from groups and countries who might be affected. His first notes were strong and ominous, then they dribbled toward weakness. Time after time he said all patience was exhausted, but he always reopened negotiations. He had threatened, then failed to carry out his threats: Lind and others had told Huerta that if he stood as a candidate in October, Wilson would recognize the Constitutionalists or intervene. Neither had happened.

Huerta correctly saw through all this as a colossal bluff. He could count on the fact that two members of Wilson's cabinet (Bryan and Josephus Daniels, Secretary of Navy) were well-known pacifists. Republicans were demanding intervention, and it was doubtful if Wilson would let them direct his foreign policy. Congress was not fully behind Wilson. Further, parallel negotiations with Carranza to line him up with Wilson's Mexican policy were going as badly as those aimed at ousting Huerta....

THEODORE ROOSEVELT DISCUSSES
THE NECESSITY OF UNILATERAL
CONTROL OF THE CANAL   *Document 1*

Theodore Roosevelt to Secretary of State John Hay, February 18, 1900.

... When the Hay-Pauncefote treaty is adopted, as I suppose it will be, I shall put the best face possible on it, and shall back the Administration as heartily as ever; but, oh, how I wish you and the President would drop the treaty and push through a bill to build *and fortify* our own canal.

My objections are twofold. First, as to naval policy. If the proposed canal had been in existence in '98, the *Oregon* could have come more quickly through to the Atlantic; but this fact would have been far outweighed by the fact that Cervea's fleet would have had open to it the chance of itself going through the canal, and thence sailing to attack Dewey or to menace our stripped Pacific Coast. If that canal is open to the warships of an enemy, it is a menace to us in time of war; it is an added burden, an additional strategic point to be guarded by our fleet. If fortified by us, it becomes one of the most potent sources of our possible sea strength. Unless so fortified it strengthens against us every nation whose fleet is larger than ours. One prime reason for fortifying our great seaports is to unfetter our fleet, to release it for offensive purposes; and the proposed canal would fetter it again, for our fleet would have to watch it, and therefore do the work which a fort should do; and what it could do much better.

Secondly, as to the Monroe Doctrine. If we invite foreign powers to a joint ownership, a joint guarantee, of what so vitally concerns us but a little way from our borders, how can we possibly object to similar joint action say in Southern Brazil or Argentina, where our interests are so much less evident? If Germany has the same right that we have in the canal across Central America, why not in the partition of any part of Southern America? To my mind, we should consistently refuse to all European powers the right to control, in any shape, any territory in the Western Hemisphere which they do not already hold.

As for existing treaties—I do not admit the "dead hand" of the treaty-making power in the past. A treaty can always be honorably abrogated—though it must never be abrogated in dishonest fashion.

THE ROOSEVELT COROLLARY   *Document 2*

Annual Message from President Roosevelt to the United States Congress, December 6, 1904.

It is not true that the United States feels any land hunger or entertains any projects as regards the other nations of the Western Hemisphere save such as are for their welfare. All that this country desires is to see the neighboring countries stable, orderly, and prosperous. Any country whose people conduct themselves well can count upon our hearty friendship. If a nation shows that it knows how to act with reasonable efficiency and decency in social and political matters, if it keeps order and pays its obligations, it need fear no interference from the United States. Chronic wrongdoing, or an impotence which results in a general loosening of the ties of civilized society, may in America, as elsewhere, ultimately require intervention by some civilized nation, and in the Western Hemisphere the adherence of the United States to the Monroe Doctrine may force the United States, however reluctantly, in flagrant cases of such wrongdoing or impotence, to the exercise of an international police power. If every country washed by the Caribbean Sea would show the progress in stable and just civilization which with the aid of the Platt amendment Cuba has shown since our troops left the island, and which so many of the republics in both Americas are constantly and brilliantly showing, all question of interference by this Nation with their affairs would be at an end. Our interests and those of our southern neighbors are in reality identical. They have great natural riches, and if within their borders the reign of law and justice obtains, prosperity is sure to come to them. While they thus obey the primary laws of civilized society they may rest assured that they will be treated by us in a spirit of cordial and helpful sympathy. We would interfere with them only in the last resort, and then only if it became evident that their inability or unwillingness to do justice at home and abroad had violated the rights of the United States or had invited foreign aggression to the detriment of the entire body of American nations. It is a mere truism to say that every nation, whether in America or anywhere else, which desires to maintain its freedom, its independence, must ultimately realize that the right of such independence can not be separated from the responsibility of making good use of it.

In asserting the Monroe Doctrine, in taking such steps as we have taken in regard to Cuba, Venezuela, and Panama, and in endeavoring to circumscribe the theater of war in the Far East, and to secure the open door in China, we have acted in our own interest as well as in the interest of humanity at large.

Annual Message from President Theodore Roosevelt to the United States Congress, December 5, 1905.

... There are certain essential points which must never be forgotten as regards the Monroe Doctrine. In the first place we must as a nation make it evident that we do not intend to treat it in any shape or way as an excuse for aggrandizement on our part at the expense of the republics to the south. We must recognize the fact that in some South American countries there has been much suspicion lest we should interpret the Monroe Doctrine as in some way inimical to their interests, and we must try to convince all the other nations of this continent once and for all that no just and orderly government has anything to fear from us. There are certain republics to the south of us which have already reached such a point of stability, order, and prosperity that they themselves, though as yet hardly consciously, are among the guarantors of this Doctrine. These republics we now meet not only on a basis of entire equality, but in a spirit of frank and respectful friendship, which we hope is mutual. If all of the republics to the south of us will only grow as those to which I allude have already grown, all need for us to be the especial champions of the Doctrine will disappear, for no stable and growing American Republic wishes to see some great non-American military power acquire territory in its neighborhood. All that this country desires is that the other republics on this Continent shall be happy and prosperous; and they can not be happy and prosperous unless they maintain order within their boundaries and behave with a just regard for their obligations toward outsiders. . . .

Moreover, we must make it evident that we do not intend to permit the Monroe Doctrine to be used by any nation on this Continent as a shield to protect it from the consequences of its own misdeeds against foreign nations. If a republic to the south of us commits a tort against a foreign nation, such as an outrage against a citizen of that nation, then the Monroe Doctrine does not force us to interfere to prevent punishment of the tort, save to see that the punishment does not assume the form of territorial occupation in any shape. The case is more difficult when it refers to a contractual obligation. Our own Government has always refused to enforce such contractual obligations on behalf of its citizens by an appeal to arms. It is much to be wished that all foreign governments would take the same view. But they do not; and in consequence we are liable at any time to be brought face to face with disagreeable alternatives. On the one hand, this country would certainly decline to go to war to prevent a foreign government from collecting a just debt; on the other hand, it is very inadvisable to permit any foreign power to take possession, even temporarily, of the customhouses of an American Republic in order to enforce the payment of its obligations; for such temporary occupation might turn into a permanent occupation. The only escape from these alternatives may at any time be that we must ourselves undertake to bring about some arrangement by which so much as possible of a just obligation shall be paid. It is far better that this country should put through such an arrangement, rather than allow any foreign country to undertake it. To do so insures the defaulting republic from having to pay debts of an improper character under duress, while it also insures honest creditors of the republic from being passed by in the interest of dishonest or grasping creditors. Moreover, for the United States to take such a position offers the only possible way of insuring us against a clash with some foreign power. The position is, therefore, in the interest of peace as well as in the interest of justice. It is of benefit to our people; it is of benefit to foreign peoples; and most of all it is really of benefit to the people of the country concerned. . . .

WILLIAM HOWARD TAFT ON

COMMERCE WITH LATIN AMERICA   *Document 3*

November 20, 1906.

A little less than three centuries of colonial and national life have brought the people inhabiting the United States, by a process of evolution, natural and, with the existing forces inevitable, to a point of distinct and radical change in their economic relations to the rest of mankind.

During the period now past, the energy of our people, directed by the formative power created in our early population by heredity, by environment, by the struggle for existence, by individual independence, and by free institutions, has been devoted to the internal development of our own country. The surplus wealth produced by our labors has been applied immediately to reproduction in our own land....

Since the first election of President McKinley, the people of the United States have for the first time accumulated a surplus of capital beyond the requirements of internal development. That surplus is increasing with extraordinary rapidity. We have paid our debts to Europe and have become a creditor instead of a debtor nation; we have faced about; we have left the ranks of the borrowing nations and have entered the ranks of the investing nations. Our surplus energy is beginning to look beyond our own borders, throughout the world, to find opportunity for the profitable use of our surplus capital, foreign markets for our manufactures, foreign mines to be developed, foreign bridges and railroads and public works to be built, foreign rivers to be turned into electric power and light....

Coincident with this change in the United States, the progress of political development has been carrying the neighboring continent of South America out of the stage of militarism into the stage of industrialism. Throughout the greater part of that vast continent, revolutions have ceased to be looked upon with favor or submitted to with indifference; the revolutionary general and the dictator are no longer the objects of admiration and imitation; civic virtues command the highest respect; the people point with satisfaction and pride to the stability of their governments, to the safety of property and the certainty of justice; nearly everywhere the people are eager for foreign capital to develop their natural resources and for foreign immigration to occupy their vacant lands.

Immediately before us, at exactly the right time, just as we are ready for it, great opportunities for peaceful commercial and industrial expansion to the south are presented. Other investing nations are already in the field— England, France, Germany, Italy, Spain; but the field is so vast, the new demands are so great, the progress so rapid, that what other nations have done up to this time is but a slight advance in the race for the grand total.

The opportunities are so large that figures fail to convey them. The area of this newly awakened continent is 7,502,848 square miles—more than two and one half times as large as the United States without Alaska, and more than double the United States including Alaska. . . .

With the increase of population in such a field, under free institutions, with the fruits of labor and the rewards of enterprise secure, the production of wealth and the increase of purchasing power will afford a market for the commerce of the world worthy to rank even with the markets of the Orient, as the goal of business enterprise. The material resources of South America are in some important respects complementary to our own; that continent is weakest where North America is strongest as a field for manufactures; it has comparatively little coal and iron. In many respects the people of the two continents are complementary to each other; the South American is polite, refined, cultivated, fond of literature and of expression and of the graces and charms of life, while the North American is strenuous, intense, utilitarian. Where we accumulate, they spend. . . .

To utilize this opportunity certain practical things must be done. For the most part these things must be done by a multitude of individual efforts; they cannot be done by government. Government may help to furnish facilities for the doing of them, but the facilities will be useless unless used by individuals. This cannot be done by resolutions of this or any other commercial body; resolutions are useless unless they stir individual business men to action in their own business affairs. . . .

1. He should learn what the South Americans want and conform his product to their wants. . . .

2. Both for the purpose of learning what the South American people want and of securing their attention to your goods, you must have agents who speak the Spanish or Portuguese language. . . .

3. The American producer should arrange to conform his credit system to that prevailing in the country where he wishes to sell goods. . . .

4. The establishment of banks should be brought about. . . .

5. The investment of American capital in South America under the direction of American experts should be promoted, not merely upon simple investment grounds, but as a means of creating and enlarging trade. . . .

What action ought our Government to take for the accomplishment of this just purpose? . . .

To neutralize the artificial disadvantages imposed upon American shipping through the action of our own government and foreign governments by an equivalent advantage in the form of a subsidy or subvention. In my opinion this is what should be done; it is the sensible and fair thing to do. It is what must be done if we would have a revival of our shipping and the desired development of our foreign trade. We cannot repeal the protective tariff; no political party dreams of repealing it; we do not wish to lower the standard of American living or American wages. We should give back to the shipowner what we take away from him for the purpose of maintaining that standard; and unless we do give it back we shall continue to go without ships. . . .

PRESIDENT TAFT DEFINES

DOLLAR DIPLOMACY, DECEMBER 1912   *Document 4*

... The diplomacy of the present administration has sought to respond to modern ideas of commercial intercourse. This policy has been characterized as substituting dollars for bullets. It is one that appeals alike to idealistic humanitarian sentiments, to the dictates of sound policy and strategy, and to legitimate commercial aims. It is an effort frankly directed to the increase of American trade upon the axiomatic principle that the Government of the United States shall extend all proper support to every legitimate and beneficial American enterprise abroad. How great have been the results of this diplomacy, coupled with the maximum and minimum provision of the traffic law, will be seen by some consideration of the wonderful increase in the export trade of the United States. Because modern diplomacy is commercial, there has been a disposition in some quarters to attribute to it none but materialistic aims. How strikingly erroneous is such an impression may be seen from a study of the results by which the diplomacy of the United States can be judged. ...

It is not possible to make to the Congress a communication upon the present foreign relations of the United States so detailed as to convey an adequate impression of the enormous increase in the importance and activities of these relations. If this Government is really to preserve to the American people that free opportunity in foreign markets which will soon be indispensable to our prosperity, even greater efforts must be made. Otherwise the American merchant, manufacturer, and exporter will find many a field in which American trade should logically predominate preempted through the more energetic efforts of other governments and other commercial nations.

There are many ways in which through hearty cooperation the legislative and executive branches of this Government can do much. The absolute essential is the spirit of united effort and singleness of purpose. I will allude only to a very few specific examples of action which ought then to result. America can not take its proper place in the most important fields for its commercial activity and enterprise unless we have a merchant marine. American commerce and enterprise can not be effectively fostered in those fields unless we have good American banks in the countries referred to. We need American newspapers in those countries and proper means for public information about them. We need to assure the permanency of a trained foreign service. We need legislation enabling the members of the foreign service to be systematically brought into direct contact with the industrial, manufacturing, and exporting interests of this country in order that American business men may enter the foreign field with a clear perception of the exact conditions to be dealt with and the officers themselves may prosecute their work with a clear idea of what American industrial and manufacturing interests require. ...

THE KNOX-CASTRILLO CONVENTION   *Document 5*

Submitted to the Congress, June 7, 1911.

The Republic of Nicaragua, being now established on a firm political and constitutional basis, after eleven months of civil war and after seventeen years of administrative abuses resulting in the illegal diversion of public property and revenue, the accumulation of debts and claims in the hands of both natives and foreigners, and the existence of ruinous and disputed concessions in many of which foreigners are beneficiaries, finds the financial and economic situation of the country in urgent need of radical reconstruction;

And believing that this needed reconstruction on account of the circumstances above set forth will be difficult and complicated, especially as it involves the necessity of obtaining a loan adequate in amount yet in terms commensurate with the national resources—

The Republic of Nicaragua has dictated its desire for cooperation on the part of the United States for the refunding of its debt and the placing of its finances and administration upon a sound and stable basis with a view to meeting its foreign obligations, and to securing the tranquility, prosperity and progress of the country.

And the Government of the United States, animated by a desire to promote the peace and prosperous development of all the Central American countries, and appreciating the wish of Nicaragua to contribute to such development by establishing on a firm footing its own material strength;

And it being recognized as necessary, in view of the present conditions of Nicaraguan finances and resources, that, to afford efficient and legitimate security and to obtain the special benefits sought, the Governments concerned should assume a special relation thereto;

And the two Governments being convinced that some contract should be negotiated and concluded between the Government of Nicaragua and some competent and reliable American banking group, said contract to afford a beneficial, just and equitable accomplishment of the purposes in question, have, with these objects in view, named as their plenipotentiaries;

The President of the United States of America, Philander C. Knox, Secretary of State of the United States; and

The President of Nicaragua, Dr. Salvador Castrillo, junior, Envoy Extraordinary and Minister Plenipotentiary of the Republic of Nicaragua to the Government of the United States;

Who, having communicated to each other their respective full powers, found in good and due form, have agreed upon the following:

ARTICLE I

The Government of Nicaragua undertakes to make and negotiate a contract providing for the refunding of its present internal and external debt and the adjustment and settlement of claims, liquidated and unliquidated; for the placing of its finances upon a sound and stable basis; and for the future development of the natural and economic resources of that country. The Governments of the United States and Nicaragua will take due note of all the provisions of the said contract when made, and will consult, in case of any difficulties, with a view to the faithful execution of the provisions of said contract, in order that all the benefits to Nicaragua and the security of the loan may at the same time be assured.

ARTICLE II
The loan which shall be made by the Government of Nicaragua pursuant to the above undertaking shall be secured upon the customs of Nicaragua, and the Government of Nicaragua agrees not to alter the import or export customs duties, or other charges affecting the entry, exit, or transit of goods, during the existence of the loan under the said contract, without consultation and agreement with the Government of the United States.

ARTICLE III
A full and detailed statement of the operations under this contract shall be submitted by the Fiscal Agent of the loan to the Department of State of the United States and to the Minister of Finance of Nicaragua at the expiration of each twelve months, and at such other times as may be requested by either of the two Governments.

ARTICLE IV
The Government of Nicaragua, so long as the loan exists, will appoint from a list of names to be presented to it by the fiscal agent of the loan and approved by the President of the United States of America a collector general of customs, who need not be a Nicaraguan and who shall administer the customs in accordance with the contract securing said loan, and will give this official full protection in the exercise of his functions. The Government of the United States, should the circumstances require, will in turn afford such protection as it may find requisite.

ARTICLE V
This Convention shall be ratified and the ratifications hereof shall be exchanged at Managua as soon as possible.
In faith whereof, the respective plenipotentiaries have signed the present Convention in the English and Spanish languages and have hereunto affixed their seals.
Done in duplicate, at Washington, this sixth day of June, one thousand nine hundred and eleven.

Philander C. Knox
Salvador Castrillo

THE LODGE COROLLARY, AUGUST 1912   *Document 6*

Resolved, That when any harbor or other place in the American continents is so situated that the occupation thereof for naval or military purposes
might threaten the communications or the safety of the United States, the
Government of the United States could not see without grave concern the
actual or potential possession of such harbor or other place by any Government, not American, as to give that Government practical power of control
for naval or military purposes.

SECRETARY OF STATE BRYAN

INTERVENES IN LATIN AMERICA   *Document 7*

*Secretary Bryan to the American Minister to the Dominican Republic, May
28, 1914.*

You are instructed to immediately send a copy of the following to Commander of U.S.S. *Washington* . . . , requesting Commander *Washington* to
first present his proposition verbally to President Bordas and if he acceded
to it to then present it verbally to leaders of all factions:

The Government of the United States finds itself in the position that it
can not remain passive any longer in the face of the unsettled state of affairs
which is devastating the Republic of Santo Domingo and impeding the fulfillment of the Convention of 1907 and it will be obliged to take the most
effective steps to restore order in those sections of the Republic where the
operations of the customs houses are being affected and where the lives and
property of foreigners are in danger.

But the United States being desirous to avoid the necessity of taking
these steps appeals to the patriotism of the contending leaders in order that
they may through their own highminded motives put an end to this state
of unrest which now prevails.

United States suggests as a means to effect this end that any candidate
who has announced his candidacy and any leader of any political faction
who intends to announce his candidacy for the presidency shall publicly
withdraw his name and give his support to an honest and upright citizen of
Santo Domingo who has no connection with politics or with the present
situation and one who should be able to give to the country civil and
legislative reforms which are necessary.

The United States will use all means in its power to aid in the holding of
free and fair elections and will support the constitutionally elected president.

Secretary of State Bryan to Charles M. Johnston, June 1, 1914.

In accordance with the suggestion of His Excellency, the Provisional
President of the Dominican Republic, General José Bordas Valdés, trans-

mitted to the Department of State by the Dominican Chargé d'Affaires at this capital, under date of May 26, 1914, you are informed that you have been designated by the President of the United States, under Article I of the Convention of February 8, 1907, to assume the duties of Financial Expert to the Dominican Republic. You are specifically charged with the following duties:

(1) To render effective the clauses of the Convention of 1907, by aiding the proper officials of the Dominican Government in the adjudication and settlement of all its outstanding indebtedness;

(2) To devise and inaugurate an adequate system of public accountability;

(3) To investigate proper means of increasing the public revenues and of so adjusting the public disbursements thereto that deficits may be avoided;

(4) To inquire into the validity of any and all claims which may be presented against the Dominican Government;

(5) To countersign all checks, drafts, warrants or orders for the payment of Dominican funds;

(6) To enlighten both Governments with reference to any eventual debt and to determine if such debt is or is not in conformity with the Convention of 1907;

(7) To exercise all the powers of a Comptroller over the Receivership, the Department of Public Works and all other departments or bureaus of public accounts;

(8) To compose whatever differences may arise between the Receivership and the Department of Treasury and Commerce, in which matters not requiring the intervention of both Governments are involved;

(9) To assist the proper officials of the Dominican Government in the preparation of the annual budget and to aid them in correlating the governmental expenditures thereto.

It is understood that while your designation is made under Article I of the Convention, relating to the appointment of the Receiver General of Customs and other employees of the Receivership, you will not be under the jurisdiction of the aforesaid Receivership or subservient thereto.

Your compensation as agreed upon between the Presidents of the United States and the Dominican Republic will be eight thousand dollars ($8,000) per annum in United States currency, payable monthly in New York exchange. The Dominican Government will also allow you all necessary traveling expenses while in the discharge of your official functions, including also necessary clerical, office and miscellaneous expenses incurred in the orderly prosecution of your duties. The aforesaid compensation and expenses shall be defrayed by the Receivership from five per cent (5%) allotted under the Convention of 1907....

Secretary of State Bryan to the American Minister to the Dominican Republic, January 12, 1915.

You may say to President Jiménes that this Government will support him to the fullest extent in the suppression of any insurrection against his Government. The election having been held and a Government chosen by the people having been established, no more revolutions will be permitted. You may notify both Horacio Vásquez and Arias that they will be held personally responsible if they attempt to embarrass the Government. The people of Santo Domingo will be given an opportunity to develop the resources of their country in peace. Their revenues will no longer be absorbed by graft or wasted in insurrections. This Government meant what it said when it sent a commission there with a proposal looking to permanent peace and it will live up to the promises it has made. Reasonable delay in carrying out the proposed reforms is not objectionable but the changes advised are the reforms necessary for the honest and efficient administration of the Government and the early and proper development of the country. There should be no unnecessary delay therefore in putting them into operation. Keep us advised. A naval force will be sent whenever necessary.

AMERICAN POLICY AT

THE HAGUE PEACE CONFERENCE, 1907 *Document 8*

Secretary of State Elihu Root's instructions to the American delegates to the Hague Conference, May 31, 1907.

Gentlemen: ... It is not expedient that you should be limited by too rigid instructions upon the various questions which are to be discussed, for such a course, if pursued generally with all the delegates, would make the discussion useless and the conference a mere formality. You will, however, keep in mind the following observations regarding the general policy of the United States upon these questions: ...

5. In the general field of arbitration two lines of advance are clearly indicated. The first is to provide for obligatory arbitration as broad in scope as now appears to be practicable, and the second is to increase the effectiveness of the system so that nations may more readily have recourse to it voluntarily.

You are familiar with the numerous expressions in favor of the settlement of international disputes by arbitration on the part of the Congress and of the Executive of the United States.

So many separate treaties of arbitration have been made between individual countries that there is little cause to doubt that the time is now ripe for a decided advance in this direction. This condition, which brings the subject of a general treaty for obligatory arbitration into the field of practical discussion, is undoubtedly largely due to the fact that the powers generally in the First Hague Conference committed themselves to the principle of the pacific settlement of international questions in the admirable convention for voluntary arbitration then adopted.

The Rio Conference of last summer provided for the arbitration of all pecuniary claims among the American States. This convention has been ratified by the President, with the advice and consent of the Senate.

In December, 1904, and January, 1905, my predecessor, Mr. Hay, concluded separate arbitration treaties between the United States and Great

Britain, France, Germany, Spain, Portugal, Italy, Switzerland, Austria-Hungary, Sweden and Norway, and Mexico. On the 11th of February, 1905, the Senate advised and consented to the ratification of these treaties, with an amendment which has had the effect of preventing the exchange of ratifications. The amendment, however, did not relate to the scope or character of the arbitration to which the President had agreed and the Senate consented. You will be justified, therefore, in assuming that a general treaty of arbitration in the terms, or substantially in the terms, of the series of treaties which I have mentioned will meet the approval of the Government of the United States. The first article of each of these treaties was as follows:

Differences which may arise of a legal nature, or relating to the interpretation of treaties existing between the two contracting parties, and which it may not have been possible to settle by diplomacy, shall be referred to the permanent court of arbitration established at The Hague by the convention of the 29th July, 1899, provided, nevertheless, that they do not affect the vital interests, the independence, or the honor of the two contracting States, and do not concern the interests of third parties.

To this extent you may go in agreeing to a general treaty of arbitration, and to secure such a treaty you should use your best and most earnest efforts.

Such a general treaty of arbitration necessarily leaves to be determined in each particular case what the questions at issue between the two Governments are, and whether those questions come within the scope of the treaty or within the exceptions, and what shall be the scope of the powers of the arbitrators. . . .

AMERICAN PENETRATION OF PERSIA   *Document 9*

Persian Minister for Foreign Affairs to Persian Minister to the United States, December 25, 1910.

Request immediately Secretary of State put you in communication with impartial American financial people and arrange preliminary employment for three years subject to ratification by Parliament of disinterested American experts as treasurer general to organize and conduct collection and disbursement revenues, assisted by one expert accountant and one inspector to superintend actual collection in provinces; secondly, one director to organize and conduct direct taxation assisted by one expert inspector similar to above. American minister informs us Secretary of State ready and willing. Avoid other methods of proceeding and irresponsible persons who may offer advice and services. Give exact copy to Secretary of State and do whatever he may suggest.

Secretary of State Knox to the Persian Chargé d'Affaires in Washington, February 24, 1911.

I have the honor to acknowledge the receipt of your note of the 17th instant, in further reference to the matter of employment by your Government of five American financial assistants, stating that arrangements have now been practically concluded with Mr. W. Morgan Shuster, Mr. F. S. Cairns, Mr. R. S. McCaskey, Mr. R. W. Hills, and Mr. Bruce G. Dickey, for service with the ministry of finance.

It is a source of gratification to this Department that it has been able, as you so kindly intimate in your note, to be of assistance to your Government in this matter; and it is my earnest hope that the services rendered by the American advisers will be of material assistance in the development of satisfactory financial and economic conditions in the Persian Empire.

American Minister Charles W. Russell to Secretary of State, June 13, 1911.

I inclose a translation of an act of the Medjles passed to-day, giving full powers in financial matters or Treasury business to Mr. Shuster. This was passed by an almost unanimous vote. Little overt opposition.

Acting Secretary of State to Minister Russell, July 31, 1911.

In view of alarmist press telegrams, report concisely by telegraph concerning the political situation, with particular reference to the return of the deposed Shah and the attitude of the British and Russian Governments toward the internal situation and toward the American financial advisers.

Persian Minister for Foreign Affairs to the Persian Minister to the United States, November 25, 1911.

...the Russians...consider Mr. Shuster's activities such as the "opposition to the Belgians, the engaging of Major Stokes, and the appointing of Englishmen for the north, and especially the publication of communications and correspondence against Russia in the English papers"—as opposed to their policy and interest....Some days ago Mr. Shuster sent a long letter, either against Russia and England, and especially against Russia to the London *Times*, and he afterwards published and spread that letter in Teheran. Yesterday...the Russian minister brought up the subject of the letter, claiming it to be a "great insult to the Russian Government," and wishing to use it as a pretext against withdrawing the troops. I am certain that the proposal which they will make to us would be the dismissal of Mr. Shuster, and on this matter the affair of Persia and Russia will reach the point of extreme difficulty, in such a manner that we might either consent to Mr. Shuster's removal or to the actual, immediate destruction of the country....

The Department of State to the Persian government, November 27, 1911.

On November 26 the Department of State received from the Imperial Legation of Persia a copy of a telegram to the general effect that various activities of Mr. W. Morgan Shuster, treasurer general of Persia, including press propaganda critical of the attitude of certain foreign powers, are complained of by the Imperial Russian Government and have thus involved the Government of Persia in difficulties....

In view of the circumstances under which the Persian Government selected and engaged Mr. Shuster, an American citizen, to fill an important post as an official of Persia...the Secretary of State does not find it appropriate to offer any suggestion.

AMERICAN INTEREST IN LIBERIA   *Document 10*

Message from the President of Liberia to the Liberian Congress, December 13, 1910.
... The report of the American commission to Liberia was submitted by President Taft to Congress, March 25, 1910. A copy was received by the Government in August. Your honorable body will remember the points of the memorial which you caused to be submitted to the commissioners. They are briefly enumerated:

A guaranty of independence and integrity.

Advice and counsel with regard to international affairs.

Advice and counsel with regard to liquidation of foreign and domestic debt, control being assumed by American experts for the purpose of systematization and organization of the customs and financial administration.

Experts to be furnished to initiate and carry through reforms deemed necessary.

Establishment of an American bank with American capital, to assist the Government and to further public improvements.

Assistance in the settlement of boundary questions at issue between Liberia and her neighbors.

Establishment of a research station.

Aid in the establishment of industrial schools.

Aid in establishing civilized centers on the frontiers.

Supervision of organization of the police and frontier force under American officers.

And that warships of the United States should visit Liberia annually or oftener.

The commission made a very fair, well-digested, and exhaustive report. Its recommendations were:

1. That the United States aid Liberia in the prompt settlement of pending boundary disputes.

2. That the United States enable Liberia to refund its debt by assuming, as a guaranty for the payment of obligations under such arrangements, the control and collection of the Liberian customs.

3. That the United States lend its assistance to the Liberian Government in the reform of its internal finances.

4. That the United States should lend its aid to Liberia in organizing and drilling an adequate constabulary or frontier force.

5. That the United States should establish and maintain a research station in Liberia.

6. That the United States reopen the question of reestablishing a coaling station in Liberia.

I think the report of this commission should be carefully perused and studied, and it has been ordered to be printed.

The Government of the United States in the month of June of the present year informed our administration that the President had decided to lend Liberia assistance in the financial, military, and agricultural departments; and, further, that the said Government will affirmatively at the proper time enter upon negotiations to secure respect for the ascertained boundaries of Liberia.

It was suggested that financial assistance take the form of a loan to be raised by an American banking firm which would have British, French, and German partners, for the payment of the foreign and domestic indebtedness, to be secured on the customs and head moneys. The security for this loan would be a receivership of customs, to be held by an American official, who would be also the financial adviser of the Government of Liberia, assisted by three officers of British, French, and German nationalities. The revenue from customs and head moneys would primarily be received by these officers and, after meeting the obligations agreed upon by the two States, the balance to be paid into the treasury of the Republic for administrative purposes other than those coming under the supervision of the American receiver.

At the suggestion of the Secretary of State, Washington, Mr. R. P. Falkner, former chairman of the American commission sent to Liberia, was appointed financial representative of Liberia in the United States and Europe, to make arrangements for the proposed loan, subject to the approval of the Liberian Legislature. The Government of Liberia became responsible for the sum of $4,000 for his expenses, which amount the legislature is now requested to approve and place in the budget of 1911. Mr. Falkner has not yet submitted any scheme or reported the final results of his efforts. He has met with great difficulties.

Other matters mentioned in the note of the American Government have not as yet taken shape. . . .

Secretary of State Knox to the American Minister to Liberia, June 18, 1910.
. . . Financial arrangements have reached stage that makes it necessary for Liberia to appoint financial representative to negotiate ad referendum with bankers. Department suggests appointment of Dr. Falkner, chairman of the American commission to Liberia, who has been intimately associated with the negotiations. Kuhn, Loeb & Co., William and Pine Street, New York, the American bankers interested, are willing to advance Falkner's expenses up to $4,000, and charge same as part of expense of loan. If this plan agreeable to Liberia, Department suggests that Liberia first cable Falkner, care Department, notification of his appointment; secondly, cable bankers to place funds at Falkner's disposal on above understanding; thirdly, mail credentials in due form to Falkner, care American consul general, Hamburg. Credentials might read: "Know all men by these presents, that Roland P. Falkner, of the United States of America, is hereby appointed special financial representative of the Republic of Liberia with full power and authority for and in the name of the Republic of Liberia to negotiate, conclude, and sign an agreement with a banking firm or firms for the purpose

of raising a loan to pay off or refund the foreign and domestic debts of the Republic, the said agreement to be subject to the ratification of the President of Liberia by and with the advice and consent of the legislature thereof. In testimony whereof," etc. Foreign nations pressing for reorganization of Liberian finances and Department should have reply as soon as possible.

State Department memorandum on the Liberian loan, 1910.

After the most exhaustive and deliberate study, the Department of State reached the conclusion that it could support the bankers' agreement with Liberia as now drafted. In deference to the interests of Great Britain and France and to the commercial interests of Germany, the Department was glad to have the American group admit associates of those three nationalities, as well as of the Netherlands. The Department of State informed the German ambassador that it would probably be possible to have a German subject employed in some capacity under the receivership. It was afterwards thought appropriate that one person of each of the nationalities supplying most of the remainder of the loan should also be so employed. The inclusion of non-American capital and of a French, a German, and a British assistant is known to be the maximum non-American participation which would be acceptable to Liberia. Any plan more complicated or more costly than that embodied in the draft agreement would be quite out of proportion to the transaction and unnecessarily burdensome on Liberia and would seem unlikely to work well.

These and other considerations make it impossible for the Department of State to favor any material departure from the agreement as now drafted.

SECRETARY OF STATE ELIHU ROOT EXPOUNDS
ON THE NATURE OF THE OPEN DOOR POLICY
IN ITS APPLICATION TO MOROCCO, 1905   *Document 11*

Department of State,
Washington, November 28, 1905.

Gentlemen: The President having selected you to represent the United States at the forthcoming Moroccan conference, the following brief instructions are communicated to you for your guidance:

The United States is a participant in the discussions of the conference solely by reason of being a treaty power, having conventional engagements with Morocco dating back to 1836, by which this country not only enjoys special privileges, but is entitled to the most-favored-nation treatment for the time being. This government also shares in the right of protection of certain native Moors as defined in the multipartite convention of July 3, 1880. Our interests and right comprise and are limited to an equal share in whatever privileges of residence, trade, and protection are enjoyed by, or may be hereafter conceded by, the Shereefian Government to aliens and their local agencies, and it follows that we have a like concern in the enlargement of those privileges in all appropriate ways. With the special political problems of influence and association affecting the relations of the Moroccan Empire, as a Mediterranean state, to the powers having interests in that great sea and whose concern lies naturally in the conservation and extension of its commerce for the common benefit of all, the United States have little to do beyond expression of its wish that equality and stability be secured.

The French and German Governments have agreed upon a programme of the general subjects to be submitted to the conference. A copy thereof is attached hereto. It is not understood to exclude suggestions by other powers.

The first subject comprises two distinct features, as to one of which the United States shares the concern of the powers in a direct and large measure, while our interest in the other is indirect.

The organization, by means of an international agreement, of the Moroccan police outside of the border region is a measure whereby far-reaching reform may be accomplished to the benefit of all the powers having relations with Morocco. Intercourse with that country demands the existence of internal conditions favorable thereto. Security of life and property; equality of opportunities for trade with all natives; amelioration of those domestic conditions of religion and class which now weigh upon non-Mussulmans, and which impair the freedom of salutary foreign intercourse with the native population; improvement of the condition of the people that will enable them to profit by the opportunities of foreign traffic; orderly and certain administration of impartial justice; rigorous punishment of crimes against persons and property; exemption from erratic taxes and burdens; removal of class restrictions, and the power to repress subversive disorder and preserve the public peace—all these enter as important factors into the problems of effectively policing the interior and of removing the barriers which have heretofore opposed the foreigner at the threshhold and the non-Mussulman in the interior. In short, while it is to the advantage of the powers to secure the "open door" it is equally vital to their interests and no less so to the advantage of Morocco that the door, being open, shall lead to something; that the outside world shall benefit by assured opportunities, and that the Moroccan people shall be made in a measure fit and able to profit by the advantages of the proposed reform.

The second division of the first subject—suppression of the smuggling of arms in the border region between Morocco and Algeria—is qualified in the programme by restricting the enforcement of regulations to that end to the exclusive concern of France and Morocco. As a cognate subject, however, regulations for the repression of all contraband traffic, whether on the inland frontiers or on the coast, would inure to the benefit of all, and in that conception might well be considered by the conference.

The second subject—financial reform—as formulated in the programme, appears not to contemplate any discrimination in regard to the influence of foreign states. Here, again, the "open door" seems to be the sound policy to advocate, and in the absence of any suggestion that especial control or predominant influence of a foreign power or of any powers in concert in the financial administration of Morocco is contemplated it does not appear needful to give you particular instructions.

The third subject—to wit, the more economical collection of revenues and the establishment of new taxes or dues—would concern this country only in the event of such duties or other charges being levied as would in practice discriminate against the commerce of the United States or weigh more heavily upon American commercial, professional, or corporate enterprises in Morocco than upon the like ventures of other foreigners. Equality of treatment in all matters of trade, commerce, navigation, and individual pursuits being established, it would only remain to so adjust the revenues as to distribute the advantages of trade evenly among all the treaty nations and at the same time encourage the productive and assimilative capacity of the Moorish people.

The fourth subject, which aims at the prevention of private monopoly of the public services by farming them out or otherwise alienating them, is allied to the foregoing in the sense of averting discriminatory treatment and has a potential bearing upon the question of internal police and the maintenance of order in that it makes the Moroccan Government the responsible factor for the regular collection and economic application of its own revenues. The interests of the tax farmer and of the government are quite antipodal. This proposition may be cordially supported by you.

It is expected that your attitude in the proceedings of the conference will display the impartial benevolence which the United States feels toward Morocco and the cordial and unbiased friendship we have for all the treaty powers. Fair play is what the United States asks—for Morocco and for all the interested nations—and it confidently expects that outcome.

PRESIDENT WILSON

INTERVENES IN MEXICO   *Document 12*

Message from President Wilson to the Congress, August 27, 1913.

It is clearly my duty to lay before you, very full and without reservation, the facts concerning our present relations with the Republic of Mexico. The deplorable posture of affairs in Mexico I need not describe, but I deem it my duty to speak very frankly of what this Government has done and should seek to do in fulfillment of its obligation to Mexico herself, as a friend and neighbor, and to American citizens whose lives and vital interests are daily affected by the distressing conditions which now obtain beyond our southern border.

Those conditions touch us very nearly. Not merely because they lie at our very doors. That of course makes us more vividly and more constantly conscious of them, and every instinct of neighborly interest and sympathy is aroused and quickened by them; but that is only one element in the determination of our duty. We are glad to call ourselves the friends of Mexico, and we shall, I hope, have many an occasion, in happier times as well as in these days of trouble and confusion, to show that our friendship is genuine and disinterested, capable of sacrifice and every generous manifestation. The peace, prosperity and contentment of Mexico mean more, much more, to us than merely an enlarged field for our commerce and enterprise. They mean an enlargement of the field of self-government and the realization of the hopes and rights of a nation with whose best aspirations, so long suppressed and disappointed, we deeply sympathize. We shall yet prove to the Mexican people that we know how to serve them without first thinking how we shall serve ourselves.

But we are not the only friends of Mexico. The whole world desires her peace and progress; and the whole world is interested as never before. Mexico lies at last where all the world looks on. Central America is about to be touched by the great routes of the world's trade and intercourse running free from ocean to ocean at the Isthmus. The future has much in store for Mexico, as for all the States of Central America; but the best gifts can come to her only if she be ready and free to receive them and to enjoy them honorably. America in particular—America north and south and upon both continents—waits upon the development of Mexico; and that development can be sound and lasting only if it be the product of a genuine freedom, a just and ordered government founded upon law. Only so can it be peaceful or fruitful of the benefits of peace. Mexico has a great and enviable future before her, if only she choose and attain the paths of honest constitutional government.

The present circumstances of the Republic, I deeply regret to say, do not seem to promise even the foundations of such a peace. . . . As friends we could wait no longer for a solution which every week seemed further away. It was our duty at least to volunteer our good offices—to offer to assist, if we might, in effecting some arrangement which would bring relief and peace and set up a universally acknowledged political authority there.

Accordingly, I took the liberty of sending the Honorable John Lind, formerly Governor of Minnesota, as my personal spokesman and representative, to the City of Mexico, with the following instructions:

"Press very earnestly upon the attention of those who are now exercising authority or wielding influence in Mexico the following considerations and advice:

"The Government of the United States does not feel at liberty any longer to stand inactively by while it becomes daily more and more evident that no real progress is being made towards the establishment of a government at the City of Mexico which the country will obey and respect.

"The Government of the United States does not stand in the same case with the other great Governments of the world in respect of what is happening or what is likely to happen in Mexico. We offer our good offices, not only because of our genuine desire to play the part of a friend, but also because we are expected by the powers of the world to act as Mexico's nearest friend.

"We wish to act in these circumstances in the spirit of the most earnest and disinterested friendship. It is our purpose in whatever we do or propose in this perplexing and distressing situation not only to pay the most scrupulous regard to the sovereignty and independence of Mexico—that we take as a matter of course to which we are bound by every obligation of right and honor—but also to give every possible evidence that we act in the interest of Mexico alone, and not in the interest of any person or body of persons who may have personal or property claims in Mexico which they may feel that they have the right to press. We are seeking to counsel Mexico for her own good and in the interest of her own peace, and not for any other purpose whatever. The Government of the United States would deem itself discredited if it had any selfish or ulterior purpose in transactions where the peace, happiness and prosperity of a whole people are involved. It is acting as its friendship for Mexico, not as any selfish interest, dictates.

"The present situation in Mexico is incompatible with the fulfillment of international obligations on the part of Mexico, with the civilized development of Mexico herself, and with the maintenance of tolerable political and economic conditions in Central America. It is upon no common occasion, therefore, that the United States offers her counsel and assistance. All America cries out for a settlement.

"A satisfactory settlement seems to us to be conditioned on—

"(a) An immediate cessation of fighting throughout Mexico, a definite armistice solemnly entered into and scrupulously observed;

"(b) Security given for an early and free election in which all will agree to take part;

"(c) The consent of General Huerta to bind himself not to be a candidate for election as President of the Republic at this election; and

"(d) The agreement of all parties to abide by the results of the election and cooperate in the most loyal way in organizing and supporting the new administration.

"The Government of the United States will be glad to play any part in this settlement or in its carrying out which it can play honorably and consistently with international right. It pledges itself to recognize and in every way possible and proper to assist the administration chosen and set up in Mexico in the way and on the conditions suggested.

"Taking all the existing conditions into consideration, the Government of the United States can conceive of no reasons sufficient to justify those who are now attempting to shape the policy or exercise the authority of Mexico in declining the offices of friendship thus offered. Can Mexico give the civilized world a satisfactory reason for rejecting our good offices? If Mexico can suggest any better way in which to show our friendship, serve the people of Mexico, and meet our international obligations, we are more than willing to consider the suggestion."

Mr. Lind executed his delicate and difficult mission with singular tact, firmness and good judgment, and made clear to the authorities at the City of Mexico not only the purpose of his visit but also the spirit in which it had been undertaken. But the proposals he submitted were rejected. . . .

Meanwhile, what is it our duty to do? Clearly, everything that we do must be rooted in patience and done with calm and disinterested deliberation. Impatience on our part would be childish, and would be fraught with every risk of wrong and folly. We can afford to exercise the self-restraint of a really great nation which realizes its own strength and scorns to misuse it. It was our duty to offer our active assistance. It is now our duty to show what true neutrality will do to enable the people of Mexico to set their affairs in order again and wait for a further opportunity to offer our friendly counsels. . . .

All the world expects us in such circumstances to act as Mexico's nearest friend and intimate adviser. This is our immemorial relation towards her. There is nowhere any serious question that we have the moral right in the case or that we are acting in the interest of a fair settlement and of good government, not for the promotion of some selfish interest of our own. If further motive were necessary than our own good will towards a sister Republic and our own deep concern to see peace and order prevail in Central America, this consent of mankind to what we are attempting, this attitude of the great nations of the world towards what we may attempt in dealing with this distressed people at our doors, should make us feel the more solemnly bound to go to the utmost length of patience and forbearance in this painful and anxious business. The steady pressure of moral force will before many days break the barriers of pride and prejudice down, and we shall triumph as Mexico's friends sooner than we could triumph as her enemies—and how much more handsomely, with how much higher and finer satisfactions of conscience and of honor!

INDEX

Printed in U.S.A.